South France Pilot
GOLFE DU LION
Franco – Spanish Frontier to Cap Sicié

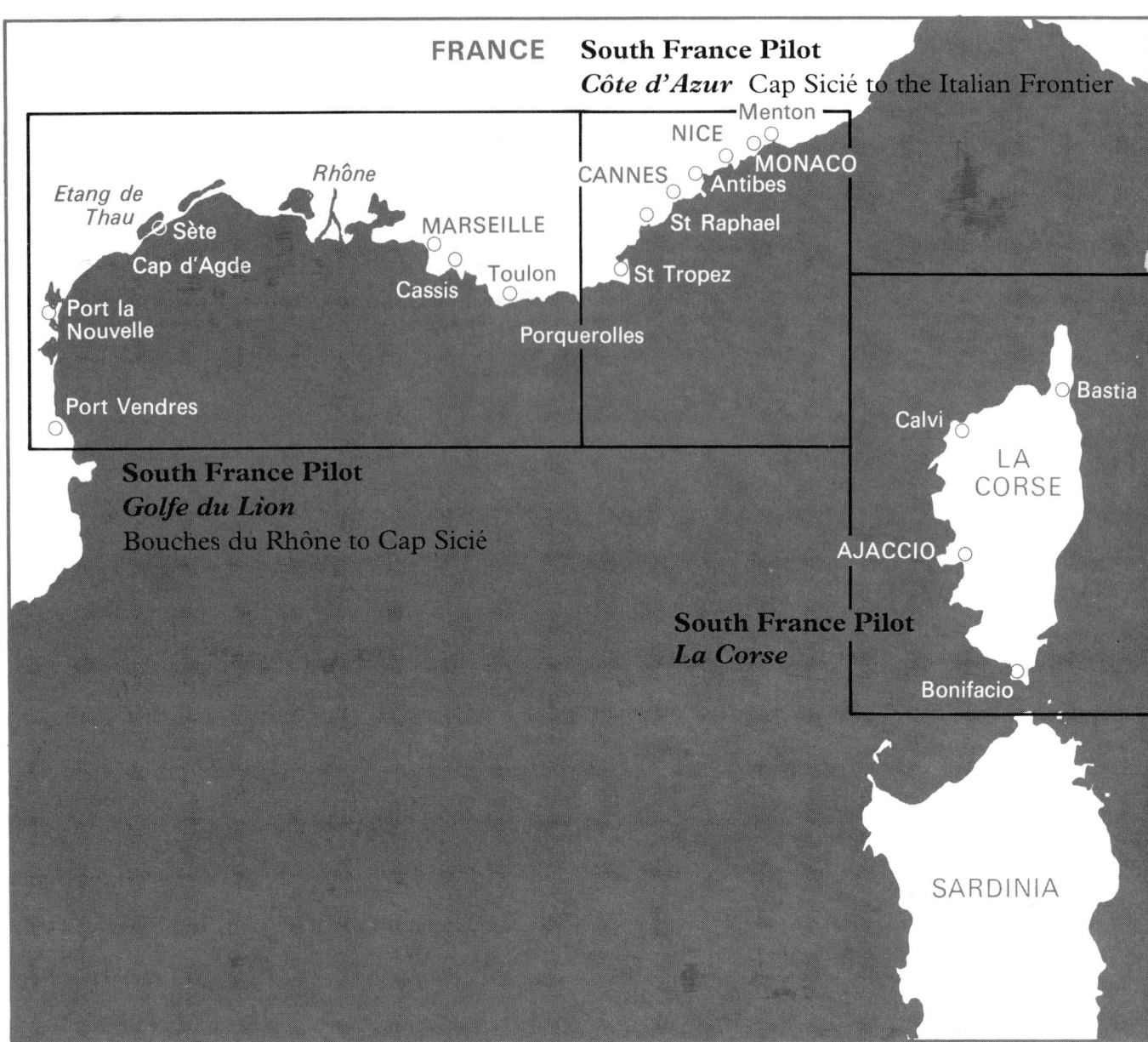

FRANCE **South France Pilot**

Côte d'Azur Cap Sicié to the Italian Frontier

Menton

NICE

MONACO

CANNES

Antibes

St Raphael

St Tropez

Porquerolles

Etang de Thau

Sète

Cap d'Agde

Rhône

MARSEILLE

Toulon

Cassis

Port la Nouvelle

Port Vendres

South France Pilot
Golfe du Lion
Bouches du Rhône to Cap Sicié

Bastia

Calvi

LA CORSE

AJACCIO

South France Pilot
La Corse

Bonifacio

SARDINIA

South France Pilot

South France Pilot
GOLFE DU LION
Franco – Spanish Frontier to Cap Sicié

Robin Brandon

Imray Laurie Norie & Wilson Ltd
St Ives Cambridgeshire England

Published by
Imray, Laurie, Norie & Wilson Ltd
Wych House St Ives Huntingdon
Cambridgeshire PE17 4BT England
☎ (0480) 462114 *Fax* (0480) 496109
1993

Robin Brandon 1993

ISBN 0 85288 163 0

Part I
First published as *South France Pilot I* 1974
2nd edition 1984
3rd edition 1989

Part II Languedoc-Roussillon
First published as *South France Pilot II* 1974
2nd edition 1984

Part III West Côte d'Azur
First published as *South France Pilot III* 1974
2nd edition 1987

British Library Cataloguing in Publication Data
A catalogue record for this book is available from the British Library.

This work has been corrected to June 1993 and amendments will be issued periodically after that date. A subscription form is enclosed at the end of the book.

IMPORTANT
While every effort has been made to check and cross-check the data and information given in this book, the Author and Publishers cannot accept responsibility for any accidents, injury or damage occasioned by the use of this information or data.

Readers should use this book with prudence and in a seamanlike manner. Their attention is directed to the many changes both manmade and natural that are certain to occur subsequent to publication. Furthermore reference should always be made to any amendments issued by the Publishers as well as the latest Admiralty *Notices to Mariners, Lists of Lights Volume E NP 78* and *Lists of Radio Signals*.

Furthermore, users of this guide themselves are asked to report any changes, omissions or corrections to the Publishers or Author. A correction reported immediately when noted, briefly on a postcard or by rough sketch, may prevent avoid another yachtsman from getting into difficulties. Your cooperation in this matter, therefore, is gratefully requested.

Printed in Great Britain at the Bath Press, Avon.

Contents

Preface

The original reconnaissance of the French coast from the Spanish frontier to Cap Sicié was undertaken in 1973 and the first edition was published in 1974. The second edition was published in 1984 and a third and fourth in 1987 after further visits to bring it up to date. During the intervening twenty years there have been many changes to the harbours and coast but in general they have been neither so large nor so widespread as those which have taken place on the mainland coast further east. The great change has been the vast increase in the number of yachts visiting the area, its harbours and anchorages. This factor has encouraged us to replan the layout of the book to include more anchorages, and harbours for small yachts also to undertake a virtual rewrite of its contents.

The original *South France Pilot Chapter I Introduction*, suitably amended, has been added to the rewritten *Chapters II* and *III* so that all the necessary data is in this one volume – *Golfe du Lion*. The planning guide has been expanded to include the anchorages which are described in this book. The details given for the harbours have been increased considerably and, above all, a large number of new photographs, many taken from the air, have been included. The welcome improvements in the quality of the printing and reproduction of the photographs, thanks to modern printing equipment, will also be noted.

It is hoped to keep up the production of an annual list of corrections and in this context I would once again appeal to anyone finding an error, change, or correction necessary to let me or the publisher know as soon as possible.

In conclusion may I wish all readers pleasant voyages and visits to this delightful area.

ACKNOWLEDGEMENTS

It is difficult for an author to know how to acknowledge those who helped with the earlier editions when drafting the acknowledgements for the third. My thanks to them are still given but life has moved on so I will concentrate on the present, due to lack of space!

The harbourmasters and their staff have continued to be most helpful and I am indebted to them for many corrections and details of future changes. I have continued the close two-way cooperation with the Royal Cruising Club which has been very helpful to both of us.

Help has been greatly appreciated from individuals who, in a seamanlike way, have sent in reports on errors and changes which have been invaluable and

have been a sound basis for the annual corrections sheets. I would like to thank them for their efforts. I would also like to thank Robert Quintaña who piloted a light aircraft so that I could take the photographs. He deserves a special mention for his skills.

Without a small crew it would have been very difficult to carry out an efficient reconnaissance. My thanks go to Robert and Faith Cox, my friends and crew for many years, not forgetting my wife, Jan, who crewed, cooked, cleaned and finally put all the new information onto a PC disk for the publishers.

Willie Wilson, Ettie Wilson and their excellent staff should also be mentioned with thanks, for without them there would be no end product. Their work has been detailed and difficult, and they have carried it out with considerable skill.

R. J. Brandon
Grimaud, France
April 1993

PART I
Introduction and general information

About this pilot book

Aim

This pilot book has been written with the intention of providing a simple and safe guide for the skipper who has not had a vast amount of pilotage experience, so that by following the series of instructions given he can visit the many pleasant harbours on this coast with the greatest ease and least risk. Those who are very experienced may find that the obvious has been stated too frequently for their need, but nevertheless they will find a large amount of useful and sometimes vital information for their use.

Amendments

It is important that readers finding any errors, omissions, additions or amendments necessary should notify the publishers. A postcard will be sufficient, just give the title, page and line numbers and details of the amendment, but for large corrections a sketch and/or photograph would be of assistance. Your help in doing this will be much appreciated.

This book can be kept up to date to an extent by extracting the relevant corrections from the weekly *Notices to Mariners* which are issued by the Admiralty. The French equivalent, the *Avis aux Navigateurs* published by the Service Hydrographique de la Marine can be obtained but it is expensive to have them sent to the UK. A better alternative is to obtain the annual list of corrections which is issued each May by the same office (address page 6) entitled *Corrections apportées aux Cartes Marines des Côtes de France et des Côtes Voisines.*

Layout

The layout of this book has been specially planned in a natural order of progression. *Part I* is concerned with the general background information necessary to equip the skipper and his crew with the knowledge and material items which will be needed for the voyage out and on arrival in France.

Under the heading *Preparation* are listed and discussed the major items of equipment, clothing, documents, medical supplies, etc., which may have to be provided or obtained before leaving Britain.

Under the heading *Technical information*, outline details of the French coast are given for planning purposes together with details of weather, radio signals, buoyage, special hazards to be found, etc.

The heading *France* covers a very brief introduction to the country and important facts that a visiting yachtsman should know. Finally there is an outline guide covering the various routes to the area, and a list of reference books.

Part II Languedoc-Roussillon has its own introduction for detailed planning and includes special information such as details of radiobeacons, weather forecasts, harbours of refuge, health services, etc. There is a valuable planning guide which lists harbours, anchorages, headlands and passages, showing the distances between important places and including the direction of the winds which can enter the anchorages.

Next comes the important *Pilotage* section which is dealt with in geographical order and includes the ports, harbours, headlands, passages and anchorages. The section dealing with the ports and harbours is laid out as follows. The first few lines answer the questions: Can I take my yacht into the harbour? How easy is it to enter? How big is it and how big is its nearest town? Is it a nice place? What facilities does it have? There follows a short description of the harbour to confirm these points.

Next is a list of technical data necessary for the approach and entrance, and a paragraph about possible problems. The approach by day and night from various directions is then discussed, followed by instructions on how to enter, again by both day and night. Advice is then given about berthing once in the harbour, and on where to report to complete formalities.

A list of facilities, both in the harbour and area, is given with a note about future developments. Finally where possible a short extract on local history is added.

The whole of the pilotage section is backed up by plans and photographs. The skipper/navigator will find that the information required to approach and enter a harbour is collected together onto one or two pages for ease of reference, and that the type and headings have been selected for easy reading under poor conditions.

Part III West Côte d'Azur is dealt with in the same way as *Part II Languedoc-Roussillon*.

Types of yacht

The pilotage and sailing directions have been written for yachtsmen with either power or sailing yachts drawing up to 2m (6·6ft) and of normal design. Mention is made of many smaller harbours that can be used by yachts drawing about 1m (3·3ft) and anchorages outside harbours have been described where larger yachts drawing more than 2m can lie.

Some very small private or commercial harbours have also been included for use only in case of emergency such as storms, medical problems, damage to yacht etc. Occasionally these small harbours may be enlarged into a full-sized public harbour.

Types of harbour

A port in this book is considered to be of large size and primarily concerned with commerce. A harbour, on the other hand, is small, often with a commercial and fishing quay. A yacht harbour (normally misnamed a marina in Britain) is a harbour mainly devoted to yachts, but may have a small fishing section. A marina is a complex of yacht harbour, shops, habitations and facilities especially designed for yachtsmen. In France the term *port* can cover the largest commercial port down through a normal harbour to a small cove or bay without any facilities.

Harbourmaster's office

On the French coast the harbourmaster's office used to be called *le bureau du port* but in recent years and often with new harbours there is a tendency to call it *le capitainerie*; both terms have been used in this book. Notices are usually posted near the office indicating where a yacht should secure on arrival. The following are some examples: *Accueil, Visiteurs, Plaisance* or *Passagers*.

Pontoons

Most yacht harbours are equipped with long narrow pontoons, jetties, catwalks, landing stages and piers to which yachts secure. There are many different types of design but for the purposes of this pilot book they have all been referred to as pontoons.

Plans

The plans that are provided for every harbour are of a simplified nature for the express use of yachtsmen. All irrelevant data such as depths over 5m have been excluded in most cases and extra data such as yacht clubs have been added. These have been produced from detailed surveys but in view of the great changes that are taking place and are planned they should be used with care and prudence. Plans labelled 'Sketch plan. Not to scale' should only be used as a guide and not for navigation.

Soundings

Soundings shown on the plans and mentioned in the text are in metres (m) and are based on the local datum which is the lowest astronomical tide (LAT). The water levels will only fall below this under extreme meteorological conditions.

Bearings

All bearings in this pilot book are given in 360° notation, true, and are from seaward. Cardinal points are used for approximate bearings.

Magnetic variation

The local magnetic variation for each harbour is given, together with the amount by which it decreases each year.

Times

Normal winter time in France is UT + 0100 and summer time is UT + 0200. These times are referred to as *l'heure locale* (local time). UT is sometimes referred to as *temps universel* (universal time) or TU and is the same as UT (formerly GMT).

Where times are used in this book they are given for UT. A note is made if local time is to be used.

Photographs

The majority of photographs were taken in difficult circumstances, for instance when the yacht was being navigated short-handed into a strange harbour. Others were taken under conditions of poor light and visibility, therefore the quality of the results is not always as good as would have been preferred. Many photographs inside the harbours were taken with wide-angle lenses and may show some distortion.

Classification of harbours

Each harbour has been classified by a three-digit code and this number is given in the planning section of each chapter and also at the top of the first section on the harbour concerned. The three numbers refer to *attractiveness, ease of approach and entrance*, and *facilities available*, the key being given below.

In selecting a code number every effort has been made to keep a constant standard throughout, but it will be appreciated that the code number selected for a particular harbour naturally represents a personal opinion and may have been influenced by weather conditions, the reception encountered and, the numbers and behaviour of tourists and other yachtsmen in the area, just to mention a few factors. Comparisons have not been made between large and small ports; like has been compared with like. A preference for a large port with all its facilities or for a small harbour with its simpler arrangements must remain the decision of the reader.

Attractiveness – First number
1 Very attractive, make every effort to visit
2 Attractive, go a little out of your way to visit
3 Normal, visit if convenient
4 Not attractive, expect to be disappointed
5 Most unattractive, only visit if really necessary

Ease of approach and entrance – Second number
1 Possible to enter under almost any condition
2 Possible to enter under almost any condition except with strong winds from one direction
3 Possible to enter in strong winds except those from several directions
4 Possible to enter in medium winds only
5 Possible to enter in light winds only

Facilities – Third number
1 All possible facilities for yachtsmen
2 Many facilities but no major repairs possible, a large number of shops
3 Limited facilities, only simple repairs of a minor nature possible, many shops
4 Very limited facilities, a few shops and no repairs
5 Virtually nothing except perhaps a water supply point

Key to symbols

Where practical, symbols are used on the plans. French terms are used where there is space. Users are referred to the comprehensive glossary of symbols on page 333.

	English	*French*
⚓	harbourmaster/ port office	*capitaine de port/ bureau du port*
	water	*eau*
	fuel	*gas-oil/carburant*
A	yacht chandler	*chandler*
	crane	*grue*
	telephone	*telephone*
	travel-lift	
	visitors' berths	*visiteurs*
	yacht club (initials)	*club nautique*
i	information	*Syndicat d'Initiative*
✉	post office	*la poste*
	mechanic	*mécanique*
	shipyacht yard	*chantier naval*
	customs	*douanes*
	ice	*glace*
	swimming pool	*piscine*
	slipway	*slipway*
	slip	*cale*
⚓	anchorage	*mouillage*
	anchoring prohibited	*mouillage interdit*
	yachts prohibited	*yachts interdit*
	yachts	*yachts*
	showers	*douche*
WC	water closet (WC)	*toilettes*
	laundrette	*laverie*

Spelling of place names

Due to the many changes of inhabitants, various places have several different names and/or the names are spelt differently. The current name has been used in this pilot book with the alternatives in brackets.

Preparation

Preferred design of yacht

It is beyond the scope of a pilot book to discuss in detail the type of craft most suited to the area and in any case the reader may already possess a yacht. However, for those about to purchase one and for those who can have their yacht adapted, the following may be of use.

Hull

The choice of material should be carefully considered. Steel is strong and can be repaired almost anywhere, but even if insulated it tends to make it hot below decks, and needs constant attention against rust. Aluminium has an electrolysis problem in addition to those experienced with steel. Wood has many advantages provided that it is looked after continually by a crew on board. GRP has fewer problems than other materials, but fibreglass repairs of any significance can only be undertaken in major harbours.

Engine power

A good reliable engine is essential because, due to calms, the engine will be used more frequently than in British waters. On occasions it may have to be used to drive the yacht against a Force 8+ *tramontane* or *mistral* wind into a harbour, so it should be powerful enough to make to windward in adverse conditions.

Space and ventilation

In the very hot conditions that prevail in the area during the summer months, adequate space and ventilation are essential for comfort. The 'well corked bottle' type of yacht which is ideal for the English Channel soon becomes uncomfortably stuffy. Deck insulation, extra cabin skylights and hatchways are of value.

Cockpit

Most of the time on board will be passed in the cockpit, therefore adequate space and comfortable seats are essential.

Decks

Good deck space where the crew can relax or sunbathe is also advisable.

Shower

A shower on board is well worth having if there is space, but it may require extra water tanks, a pressurised hot and cold water system and pump-assisted drainage. An alternative is to have a special plastic container, preferably dark-coloured, that can be pressurised by hand and has a pipe and rose. This water-filled can placed in the sun will soon give hot water for showering.

Mast steps

Permanent mast steps, or a special ladder which can be hoisted, are well worth having in order to be able to deal with mast problems when at sea. They also enable a crew member to climb aloft easily to 'con' the yacht into a shallow anchorage. When 'conning' a yacht, Polaroid glasses are of great value in spotting underwater dangers.

Ice box

An ice box or refrigerator is almost essential, and the larger the better. Large blocks of ice one metre long are obtainable at some harbours and if there is space for several of these blocks they last much longer. The most effective yacht refrigerators are those with engine-driven compressors. Small lumps of ice are usually available from bars etc at all harbours but are expensive.

Equipment for yacht

A yacht fully equipped for extensive cruising around the shores of the British Isles should require very little extra for a cruise in the Mediterranean, but the following items are useful to have on board.

Awnings

The sun in summer can be very hot around midday and awnings make life much more pleasant. If they are so designed that they throw a shadow onto the whole deck then the cabins will remain much cooler. Side curtains are also of value as they will keep the side decks cool and keep out the low evening sun. Awnings should be made of heavy canvas-type material; light nylon or *Terylene*-type materials flap in a light breeze and make a considerable noise.

The actual design is naturally dependent on the type of yacht concerned, but using strong points such as standing rigging, booms, wheelhouse roofs, etc., coupled with battens in pockets in the awnings and suitable lashings, an effective shelter can be made. Due to expense and the time factor it is best to have this awning made in England, though there are many places in the Mediterranean where it could be made. A large cowl made of canvas which can be suspended over the forward hatch to direct air below is well worth having.

Mosquito nets

Mosquitoes are prevalent in most areas of the western Mediterranean and house flies can at times be most annoying. It is well worth constructing mosquito nets to fit all hatchways and other openings. The alternative is to rely on the various chemicals, available from supermarkets and chemists, which can be sprayed around the cabin or rubbed on the skin.

Gangplanks

Most yachts that are kept in the Mediterranean have stern gangplanks (*passerelles*) which vary from an old bit of rough timber to the most complicated and elaborate affairs in stainless steel and beautifully varnished mahogany with stanchions and rope rails.

For the visiting yacht all these are quite unnecessary provided that the skipper and crew are agile enough to jump a metre-wide gap to the pontoon; they are also very awkward and difficult to stow on small and medium-sized yachts when not in use. For yachts that are going to spend weeks, months or even years in port without going to sea they have obvious advantages. Gangplanks may be essential to some modern yachts with sloping sterns which project a long way aft.

Cockpit tables

Most meals will be taken on deck and in the cockpit during spring, summer and autumn and a folding table is well worth having. A simple camping table will suffice.

Gas cylinders

If the yacht is equipped with a gas system for cooking etc., and uses *Calor Gas*-type bottles it will be necessary to make alterations because refills for *Calor Gas* are not obtainable in France. On the other hand *Camping Gaz* refills are obtainable in the very smallest harbours and are comparatively cheap.

There exists an adaptor which fits *Camping Gaz* cylinders and will take the reverse thread union of the *Calor Gas* equipment. This can be bought in Britain along with *Camping Gaz* cylinders, and a refund can be obtained when the cylinders are returned after the cruise.

Water hose

A length of hose some 25m long is of great value for refilling water tanks from the standpipes that are to be found on most pontoons and quays. There are several types and sizes of taps in use at the various harbours and suitable connectors can usually be bought at a local shop or the *bureau du port*.

Water filters and chemicals

Water from the public supply is usually safe to drink, but should the tanks be filled with contaminated water the 'bugs' will breed well in the warm environment and affect anyone drinking the water unboiled. The installation of modern water filters is one practical solution. The frequent use of various chemicals, specially prepared to sterilise the water, is another. The foolproof alternative is always to drink bottled water, which can be bought everywhere and is guaranteed to be pure.

Due to the excessive demand for water during the summer, many wells become contaminated with salty (brackish) water which is unpleasant to drink and to wash in.

Electric cable

Virtually every harbour provides electrical outlet sockets on the pontoons and quays, usually 220v AC. Some of the large harbours also have 385v AC 3-phase sockets for use by the bigger yachts. About 20m of 3-core heavy duty outdoor electric cable to bring a supply to the yacht will be invaluable. It can then be used with a trickle charger to keep the yacht's batteries charged up, or it can be used with a separate mains voltage system for lights etc.

Unfortunately there are many different types of electrical sockets to be found in the various harbours and it will be necessary to buy several types of plug. To save continually having to change the plug on the long cable fit a normal male plug to it and have a series of female plugs of the same type, each with a very short length of cable, one for each type of male harbour plugs.

Radios and tape recorders

France has several authorities which produce daily weather forecasts (*Météo*). These forecasts are broadcast on the long, medium, short (HF) (SSB) and VHF (FM) bands at various times. To receive these forecasts the installation of a VHF transmitter/ and receiver is advised if cruising within 20M of the coast is planned. A tape recorder is also advised because the forecasts are read very quickly in French. If sailing more than 20M from the coast is planned a shortwave (HF) (SSB) receiver or transmitter/ and receiver should be installed. For the long and medium VHF (FM) bands a normal house or car radio should suffice. See also *Radio weather forecasts*, page 16.

Charging engines

If an electric refrigerator or other extra electrical apparatus has been installed it may be considered essential to have a small petrol or diesel-driven battery charger aboard. These engines can be very noisy when running so do not run them in anchorages and yacht harbours where and when it will annoy your neighbours.

Flags

The courtesy flags of the various countries through whose waters it is planned to pass must be carried and it is worth remembering that there is a Monégasque flag which should be flown when visiting Monaco. The Corsican flag is the Moor's head and it is considered polite to fly it below the French courtesy flag. A full set of international code flags will be needed if it is intended to dress the yacht overall in company with most other yachts on days of celebration. On these days a number of yachts go to the trouble of dressing overall with lights at night usually powered with the supply from the quay. Spare ensigns and burgees should be taken, as due to the sun, salt and strong winds, they wear out much more quickly than in British waters.

Varnishes and paints

Though a good selection of paints and varnishes is available in the shops, they are more expensive than those in Britain, so a supply should be taken. Repainting and varnishing are important because in the hot sun with very salty spray, brightwork and paint deteriorate rapidly. However, in the Mediterranean the excellent painting conditions give a good chance to bring shabby yachts up to the high standard of most of the other yachts to be found in the harbours there.

Spares and expendables

If only to save time and money a comprehensive supply of spares and expendables should be carried. Spares for internationally known engines and equipment may be available at the larger ports. Equivalent replacement yacht parts of a non-specialist nature and normal yacht chandlery are usually available at the large yachting harbours, but in general are more expensive than they would be in Britain. The problem is to find the correct shop or agent that has the part required and this search can take some time. Large and heavy replacement parts sent from Britain may take several weeks to arrive, and they have to be cleared with customs. Good reserves of special batteries, oils, etc. for British equipment should be carried. See also under *Customs*, page 25.

Tool kit and manuals

A comprehensive tool kit which includes tools to fit the engine is a must, to which should be added the relevant manuals for all equipment on board. A large filing book with transparent pockets is ideal for keeping the manuals separate and immediately available.

Anchors

Much of the seabed near the coast in the Mediterranean where anchoring is possible is of hard-packed sand, covered with a thick layer of fine grass-type weed. Even anchors of the CQR and Danforth types which are so good elsewhere sometimes have difficulty in penetrating the weed and getting into the sand because as they drag they collect a mass of weed and then cannot dig in at all.

The best anchor for this type of bottom is the old fisherman-type or four-pronged Mediterranean anchor (a folding version can now be obtained), of a good size and weight, which will cut through the weed and get into the sand. Although awkward to stow, they are worth having should the yacht be caught in a blow. Anchors without sharp points are hopeless.

Two anchors are essential and a third advisable. The largest anchor should have 60m (197ft) of heavy chain. The others can have 10m (33ft) chain and 50m (164ft) nylon line. Anchors with sharp points, e.g. CQR, Danforth, etc., are strongly advised; again a four-pronged Mediterranean type is ideal but very difficult to stow. Some popular harbours and anchorages now have a bottom of loose sand due to the thousands of anchors which have been dropped and weighed; a pointed anchor is vital in this situation.

Anchor weight

A heavy anchor weight and chain saddle, sometimes called a 'chum', should be carried and used if the yacht is caught by a *mistral* when at anchor. It will take away most of the jerk when snubbing at the chain.

Berthing lines

Yachts that are kept in the Mediterranean for a long period and especially over the winter months need a pair of very strong stern lines for use when securing stern-to pontoons. Each of these lines should have a loop of chain at the outer end of similar weight to that used for the anchor. These loops are used to connect to the ring or bollard on the pontoon; they often incorporate large metal springs or rubber snubbers to smooth out any jerks. A similar line is sometimes used at the bow.

Materials for the construction of these lines can be taken on board and made up when a more accurate assessment of the length of each line can be made after practical experience in the Mediterranean. Extra-strong berthing lines should be taken for everyday use because, during gales, very heavy surges will be encountered in some harbours and lines normally used at home will not be strong enough unless doubled. See diagram on page 23.

Cleats

Strong cleats and large fairleads are required and they must be securely bolted through the deck. Extra cleats and fairleads may have to be fitted amidships to take holding-off and spring lines.

Charts

Admiralty charts of the area can be obtained from Imray, Laurie, Norie & Wilson Ltd, Wych House, St Ives, Huntingdon, Cambs PE17 4BT England ☎ 0480 462114 *Fax 0480 496109*.

In France, Admiralty charts are available from Lt Commander M. Healy, 10 rue Jean Brucco, 0631 Beaulieu sur Mer ☎ 93 01 30 00 *Fax 93 01 30 01*, and official chart agents.

At least three months' notice should be given to enable these agents to obtain foreign charts.

French charts can be bought at the major ports from large ships' chandlers and bookshops. They are also obtainable from Imrays, as above, or from the Etablissement Principal du Service Hydrographique et Océanographique de la Marine (EPSHOM), Section Délivrances, BP426, 29275 Brest Cedex. ☎ 98 02 09 17. Telex 940568 HYDRO. Minitel 36 15 SHOM.

The Navicarte series of charts for yachtsmen are available from French chandlers and bookshops or direct from Grafocarte, 64 Rue des Meuniers, 92220 Bagneaux, France ☎ 46 65 43 21.

It should not be necessary to purchase large-scale harbour charts as they are replaced by the plans in this pilot; the medium-scale coastal charts are useful to have for navigating between harbours.

The old French and Spanish charts do not have compass roses, so the use of a Douglas protractor or similar instrument is necessary in order to obtain or use bearings. The new edition charts have compass roses.

The French charts, most of which are available on waterproof material, are probably the best for this section of coast, though those who are more familiar with the Admiralty issues may find these easier to use. The obsolete charts are best for anchorages because they show detail which is not on new editions. They are now very difficult to find.

The figure following the title of each chart or plan denotes its natural scale.

British Admiralty charts

Chart	Title	Scale
South coast France		
149	Rade de Toulon	12,500
	Rade de Villefranche –	
	Monaco and Port of Nice	15,000
150	Marseille	20,000
1506	Plans on the South Coast of France	
	Port Vendres	5,000
	Port La Nouvelle	15,000
	Approaches to Port Vendres	50,000
1705	Cape St Sebastien to Iles d'Hyères	300,000
1780	Barcelona to Naples	1,000,000
1974	Toulon to San Remo including	
	Northern Corse	300,000
2164	La Rhône to Cap Sicié	75,000
	Port de la Ciotat	20,000
2165	Cap Sicié to Cap Camarat	75,000
2166	Cap Camarat to Cannes	60,000
	Saint Raphaël	20,000
2167	Cannes to Menton	60,000
	Cannes: Antibes	15,000
2606	Approaches to Sète	50,000
	Port de Sète	10,000
2607	Marseille to Agay Road	145,600
2609	Rade d'Agay to San Remo	145,500
3498	Golfe de Fos	25,000
Corsica		
1213	Bonifacio Strait	50,000
1424	Ports on the south and west coasts of Corsica	
	Bonifacio	7,500
	Ajaccio: Propriano	10,000
	Golfe d'Ajaccio and Golfo de Valinco	60,000
1425	Ports on the north and east coasts of Corsica	
	Macinaggio	10,000
	Bastia	15,000
	Calvi	17,500
	Porto Vecchio	25,000
	Approaches to Calvi	50,000
1985	Ajaccio to Oristano including	
	Bonifacio Strait	300,000
1992	Eastern Approaches to Bonifacio Strait	300,000
1999	Livorno to Civitavecchia including	
	Northern Corse	300,000

French SHOM charts
General area charts

1248	Du cap Creux aux îles des Mèdes	50,800
4827	De Tarragone au cap de Creux	231,000
5151	Rade d'Hyères	25,000
5255	Golfe de St Tropez	14,400
5266	Baies de Briande, de Bon-Porte et de Pampelonne	25,000
5325	Du Bec l'Aigle à la presqu'île de Giens	50,100
5329	De la presqu'île de Giens au cap Camarat	50,100
5477	Du Cap Sicié au Cap Bénat, rades de Toulon et d'Hyères	50,200
6610	De Bandol au Cap Sicié Rade de Brusc	20,000
6612	De Cassis à Bandol, baie de la Ciotat	20,000
6615	Iles de Port Cros et du Levant (Iles d'Hyères)	25,000
6616	Du Cap Bénat au Cap Lardier, rade de Bormes, baie de Cavalaire	25,000
6632	De Marseille à Menton, côte Nord-Ouest de Corse	285,000
6684	Golfe et Port de Fos	25,000
6693	Des Saintes-Maries-de-la-Mer à Port-Saint-Louis du Rhône	49,900
6739	Golfe de Marseille	17,000
6767	De Fos sur Mer à Marseille	49,900
6838	Abords de Saint-Raphaël. De la pointe des Issambres à la pointe d'Anthéor	20,000
6839	Etang de Thau	30,000
6843	Du Cabo Creus à Port-Bacarès	50,000
6844	De Port-Bacarès à l'embouchure de l'Aude	50,000
6863	Du Cap Ferrat au Cap Martin	20,000
6873	Du phare du Titan au Cap Roux	50,000
6881	Abords de Monaco. Ports de la Condamine, de Fontvieille et de Cap d'Ail	7,500
6882	De l'île de Planier à la Ciotat	50,000
6907	Etang de Berre	25,000
6951	De Fos-sur-Mer à Capo Mele	250,000
6952	D'Antibes à Menton	49,600
6953	De Monaco à San Remo	49,600
6954	Du Cap de Drammont au Cap d'Antibes	50,000
7002	Ports de Banyuls-sur-Mer, Port Vendres, Collioure, Saint-Cyprien	10,000
7003	Le Cap d'Agde – Embouchure de l'Hérault	15,000
7004	Golf d'Aigues-Mortes – Ports de Palavas-les-Flots, Carnon-Plage et des Saintes-Maries-de-la-Mer	15,000
7008	Du Cabo de San Sébastian à Fos-sur-Mer	250,000
7017	Du Cap Ferrat à Capo Mele	100,000
7053	De Sète à la pointe de l'Espiguette	50,000
7054	De l'embouchure de l'Aude à Sète	50,000
7072	Port de Sète	15,000
7091	Abords de Toulon	25,000
7093	Rade de Toulon	10,000
7200	Du Cap d'Antibes au Cap Ferrat, Baie des Anges – Rade de Villefranche	7,500, 10,000

Spanish charts

49	Golfo de León. De punta del Llobregat a cabo d'Antibes	400,000
121	Golfo de Génova. De las islas d'Hyères a la isla Elba y costa N de Córcega	400,000

Cartes-Guides Navicartes
Published by Grafocarte. General scale 1:50,000 with enlarged insets.

South coast France

500	Nice – San Remo
501	St-Raphael – Nice
503	Cavalaire – St-Raphaël
502	Toulon – Cavalaire – Iles d'Hyères
504	Marseille – Toulon
505	Port-Saint-Louis – Marseille
507	Port de Bouc – Port Camargue
508	Port-Camargue – Sète
509	Sète – Valras
510	Valras – Port Leucate
511	Port Leucate – Banyuls

Corsica

1006	Calvi – Bastia
1007	Porto – Ajaccio
1008	Propriano – Bonifacio – Maddalena

Routiers (1:250,000)

R1	Marseille – San Remo
R2	Golfe de Gênes (Hyères – Calvi – l'Elbe)
R3	Corse

Charts

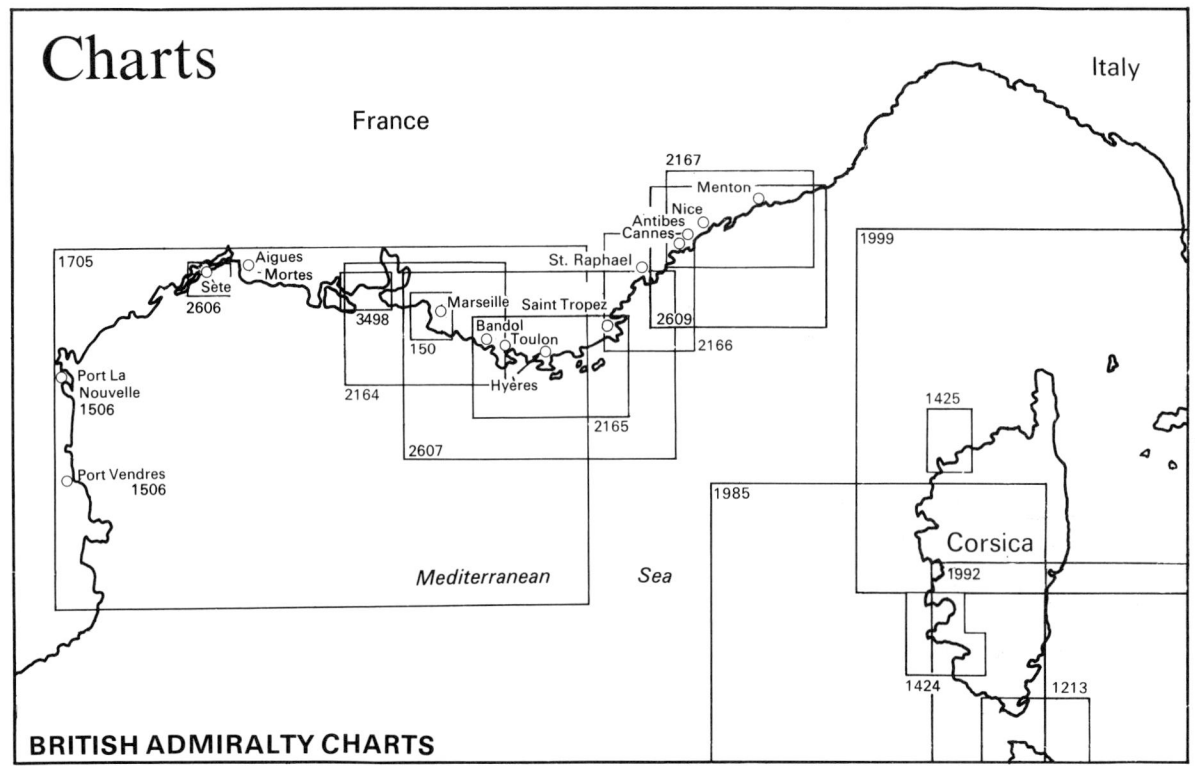

BRITISH ADMIRALTY CHARTS

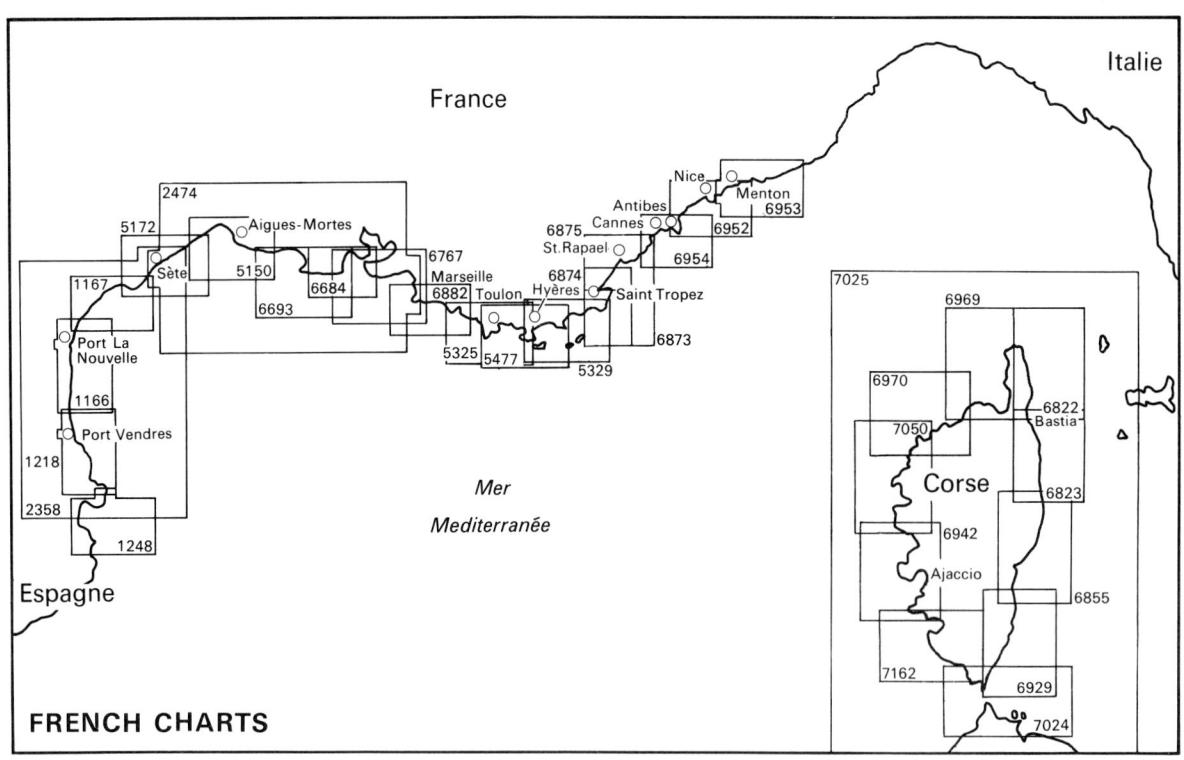

FRENCH CHARTS

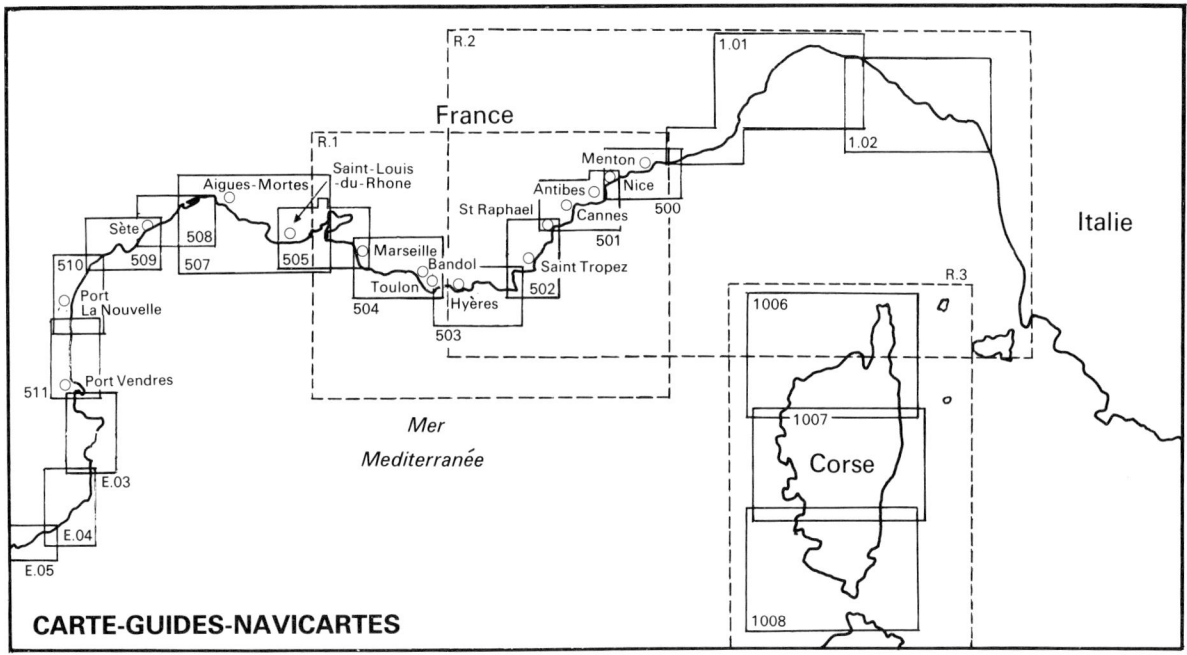

CARTE-GUIDES-NAVICARTES

Provisions

In addition to the normal stock of food required to cover the voyage out to the Mediterranean, it is advisable to carry stocks of the following, which are usually available but more expensive in France and La Corse: instant coffee, tea or preferably tea bags, tins of meat, breakfast cereals and any special types of British food required by skipper or crew. Visit the manager of the local cash and carry warehouse in England and explain what you want and what you plan to do; he may allow you to stock up at wholesale prices as you will be buying in commercial quantities. Most French *supermarchés* now carry stocks of foreign foods for visitors, but the prices are high.

Drink

Visit the local customs officer several weeks before you set sail and explain your plan for the voyage; he may allow you to take duty-free drink in bond. Make sure that he explains the necessary procedure to be followed and the requisite forms to be completed. In the Mediterranean duty-free goods can be bought at some major ports and harbours; you need only to find out which shop sells duty-free goods and place your order. The manager of the shop will contact the customs for you and arrange for a customs officer to be present when the goods are delivered on board. Stores in bond must naturally be consumed on board and never taken ashore, nor should they be taken out of bond through the inland waterways. When deciding the amounts of the various types of drink to buy, bear in mind that if you expect to have foreign visitors on board, they will almost invariably drink whisky. The new EC agreements which come into effect on 1 January 1993 will produce a new set of regulations.

Medicines

Specially prescribed or branded drugs should be bought in Britain in sufficient quantity to cover the length of the cruise. Medicines are very expensive in France and often have different brand names from those used in Britain. Your doctor will probably be able to advise you of the continental name for any particular drug.

Inoculations

It is advisable, though not essential, to have a series of two typhoid injections well in advance of the date of departure, and some doctors advise cholera and tetanus inoculations as well.

Urgent medical treatment

Medical treatment in France is very good but very expensive and has to be paid for directly the treatment has been concluded. You are strongly advised to obtain and *E111* certificate from post offices or local offices of the DSS before leaving Britain. This certificate enables overseas medical expenses to be reclaimed under international agreement. If insurance for private medical treatment in the UK is held it may be possible to extend its cover overseas.

Documents

Ship Under the current French regulations for visiting yachts the original certificate of registration, radio licence, insurance documents etc. must be on board at all times; photocopies are not accepted. These documents may be inspected on arrival in any harbour and are sometimes inspected at sea.

Crew Passports are essential and are frequently checked. These are also required as a means of identification when cashing cheques, etc. at a bank.

Changes in these rules are expected after 1 January 1993.

Insurance

It is unlikely that any yacht insurance policies held extend cover beyond the normal British cruising areas, and extra cover will have to be arranged for the Mediterranean with the insurance company concerned. At the same time separate cover for the voyage out can be negotiated. Check that personal insurances are valid outside Britain.

Clothing

Normal hot-weather yachting clothing, including bathing wear, is needed, and should include a good supply of items that can be washed easily and dried without ironing. Bathing costumes and bikinis (which can be topless) can be worn on most beaches without restrictions but are not permitted on the streets or in shops and cafés. In smaller places which are less frequented by tourists, abbreviated shorts may also cause offence if worn on the village street. Normal common sense should prevail in the choice of clothes to wear at official functions, in restaurants and away from the coast. On many secluded beaches it is now quite usual not to wear any clothes.

For those not used to the very hot sun in summer, some form of light head gear is required, preferably with a good brim to shield the eyes and the neck. If the cruise is planned to extend through the winter then warm sweaters, shirts, trousers, socks, etc. are required because it can become quite cold at night, and also during the day out of the sun especially if there is a strong wind blowing. Oilskins, which might not be used in the summer, will be essential in winter.

Banking and money

There are no exchange controls between France and Britain so it should be easy and quick to transfer money from one country to the other but it is not! The quickest method is called Express International Money Transfer (EIMT) and is the most expensive, but the transfer is sent by telex to agents in Paris, who take a long time to carry out the transfer to the receiving bank, which in turn takes still more time to transfer the money on to its local branch. The entire transfer may take anything between 3 days and 3 weeks. One way around this is to transfer the money to a branch of the same group as the dispatching bank, in which case there is a direct transfer inside the group concerned, without the use of an agent, so that the transfer only takes a few hours. Before leaving the UK obtain a list of overseas branches of your bank and arrange for the transfer of money to be made on receipt of a telephone call from you. It might be advisable to take a fair amount of cash with you, and some Travellers or Eurocheques. Visa and Access cards are sometimes accepted, but not always. The French Carte Bleu is nearly always accepted. One thing is certain: banks on both sides of the channel will take their share in some way or other for arranging the transfer.

British banks have no branches in La Corse, but they are represented by the French bank Société Général which has branches at Ajaccio, Bastia, Bonifacio, Calvi, Propriano and Saint Florent. On the mainland branches of British banks will be found in the large towns and ports.

It is worth noting that most items and services in France are more expensive than those in the UK; if the exchange rate is more than 10 francs to £1.00, the converse holds true. Areas where there are a lot of visitors and tourists are more expensive than country areas.

Technical information

Outline description of the French Mediterranean coast

The coast of Mediterranean France stretches from her boundaries with Spain at the east end of the Pyrénées chain of mountains along a varied coastline to the Italian border some 330 miles to the northwest. It also includes the island of La Corse, lying 100 miles offshore, which has a coastline of some 200 miles, and a number of other large islands near the mainland.

The first 10 miles of coast from the Spanish frontier is rugged and indented where the high mountains come down to the sea. It is very similar to the Spanish Costa Brava which adjoins it, and is called *la Côte Vermeille* (the Vermilion Coast) after the reddish colour of the rocks. Quite suddenly just beyond Collioure the coast becomes flat with miles of straight sandy beaches and a few very low rounded hills near La Nouvelle and Sète; this type of coast stretches as far as the Golfe de Fos on the east side of the mouth of the River Rhône, some 70 miles in all. There are no off-lying dangers with the exception of the delta of the River Rhône which should be given a good berth because of extending shoals. There exists just inland from this coast a series of very large lagoons, most of which are connected to the sea and are navigable.

From Cap Couronne on the E side of the Golfe de Fos, the coast becomes high and rugged with very bare white rock cliffs; this stretch is called *la Côte Bleue* (the Blue Coast) because of the colour of the sea over these rocks. This high spectacular rocky coast extends to Cap Sicié some 40 miles eastwards; there is a series of bare rocky islands offshore of similar nature to the mainland, some of which are quite large.

From Cap Sicié to Cap Ferrat, 80 miles further along lies *la Côte d'Azur* (the Azure Coast). Mountains which are some miles inland march with the coast, which is only reached by an occasional spur and headland. Between the headlands are large open bays with sandy beaches and some smaller inlets; off-lying dangers consist of the Iles d'Hyères, a group of large islands, and the Iles de Lérins, a smaller group, together with a number of tiny islands close inshore.

From Cap Ferrat the high mountain ranges of the Alps now come down to the sea and stretch along the Riviera as far as the border with Italy 15 miles distant, producing a coast of spectacular beauty.

Some 100 miles off the mainland lies the island of La Corse, which is mountainous with a number of very high peaks, the coast being in general rock-cliffed and steep-to. La Corse has some 200 miles of coastline, the west being more indented than the east, and the north of the island is the most spectacular part.

Meteorology

General
The weather pattern in the western Mediterranean is affected by the interaction of many differing systems around the basin which it forms and is largely unpredictable, being quick to change and often very different at places only a short distance apart. Due to the high surrounding land masses and the latitude, the climate can at times be extreme, but on average it is very pleasant, especially in the summer months.

Winds
The prevailing winds in this area of the Mediterranean are from a NW and SE direction, as will be seen from the diagram. The directions of these winds are altered to some extent by the local topography (see diagram), and the winds have special names in different areas. See also page 12.

NW mistral – tramontane
This wind is the most frequent, especially in winter, when it blows for over 50% of the time in some areas, for over 10% of the time at Force 8 or more. It is extremely dangerous because it can arrive out of a clear blue sky on a calm day and in a matter of minutes can blow a full gale. The warning signs are very clear visibility, very dry air, virtually no clouds (any that do appear are cigar-shaped) and a stationary or slightly rising barometer; away from the coast a swell from a northwesterly direction and a line of white on the horizon may provide a few minutes' warning. If a warning of a deep depression crossing France is received it is advisable to proceed directly to a safe harbour. This steady powerful wind can blow for up to a week without slackening, although it normally only lasts two to three days, raising a very nasty sea. Its domain extends from the French coast as far as the Balearics and Sardinia and it is advisable to keep a listening watch H+01 and H+33 on Marseille, Grasse radio or other stations (see page 16), for gale warnings when far from a safe harbour or anchorage.

Only a really bad *mistral* affects the coast from Cannes eastwards, and on many occasions a *mistral* blowing in the Golfe du Lion only reaches as far east as Toulon.

The *mistral* is caused by a strong NW wind of Force 4 to 6 creating a secondary depression in the Golfe de Gênes; about 4 to 6 hours after such a wind commences to blow, a true *mistral* may suddenly develop.

In winter a strong NW wind with high stratus cloud is sometimes referred to as a white *mistral* and a similar wind with lower and thicker layer cloud is referred to as a black *mistral*.

E-levant and SE-ceruse
Strong winds accompanied by dull wet weather and bad visibility. Low clouds forming on top of hills and the air becoming damp are warning signs. These winds cause heavy seas on E and SE-facing coasts.

S-marin
This is a wind which can blow from SE–S–SW, raising a heavy sea on coasts facing these directions. It is a warm and wet wind and though strong does not rival the *mistral*. It sometimes deposits reddish or yellow dust from the dust storms in the Sahara.

Vent du midi, vent solaire
This is the normal sea breeze caused by the convection currents rising over the land on a hot day and drawing air from over the cooler sea; it is more noticeable in calm conditions and usually blows towards the land following the sun by about 15°. It can add to or subtract from the strength of another wind already blowing, depending on this wind's own direction and strength. In summer it commences at around 1000 hours, increasing in strength until about 1500 hours, when it can sometimes reach almost gale force. It then starts to fall away and by 1800 hours it has ceased altogether.

Other winds
There are other winds which blow from different directions on occasion, and some which blow only on certain parts of the coast. They all have special names, but there is no agreement among the various sources of information as to what these names are, when the winds blow, how frequently they blow and how they can be predicted. It can only be advised that very occasionally winds can blow from other directions but that they are normally weak and short lived.

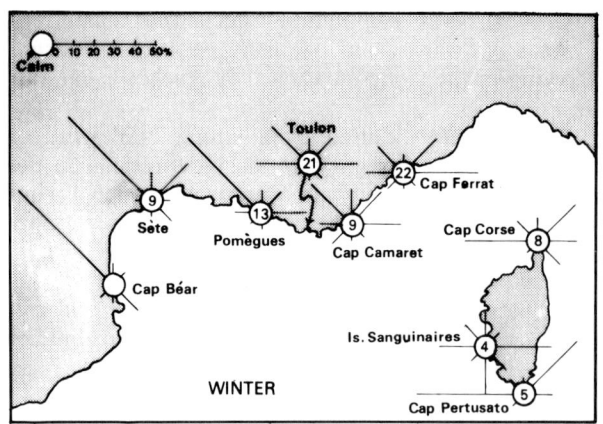

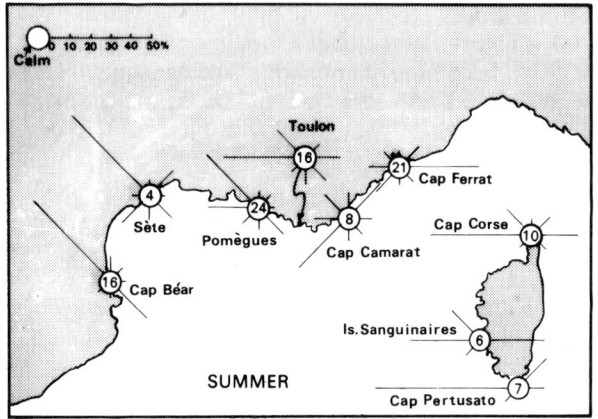

Percentage wind diagrams. Winds blow towards the centre of the rose

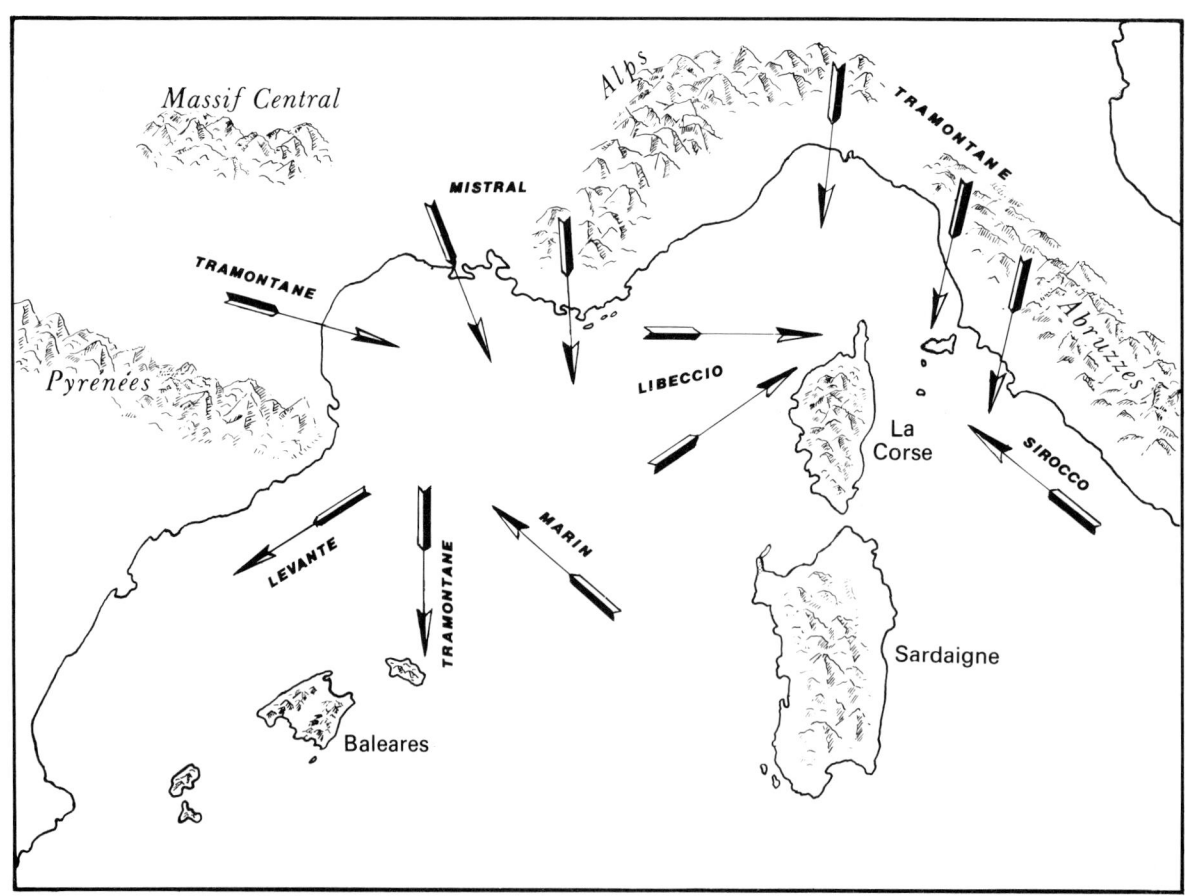

Local winds

French–English *Météo* **terms**

accalmie – lull
agité – moderate
amélioration – improvement
anticyclone – anticyclone
augmentation – increase
aujourd'hui – today
averse – shower
avis – warning
avis de coup de vent – gale warning
basse pression – low pressure
beau clair – fine, fair
Beaufort – Beaufort
belle (mer) – smooth
brise – breeze
brise de mer – sea breeze
brise de terre – land breeze
brouillard – fog
bruine – drizzle
brume – mist
bulletin – bulletin
calme – calm
carte – chart
côtier – coastal
coup de vent – gale
courant – current
couvert – overcast
demain – tomorrow
dépression (bas) – depression (low)
direction – direction
dorsale – ridge
échelle de Beaufort – Beaufort scale
éclaircie – bright interval
en cours – in force
en formation – forming
en baisse – falling
en hausse – rising
état de la mer – sea state
évolution – forecast
force du vent – wind force
frais – fresh
fréquent – frequent
front – front
front chaud – warm front
front froid – cold front
grain – rain squall
grand frais – near gale
grand large – far offshore
grêle – hail
haute pression – high pressure
heure – hour
houle – swell
instable – unstable
jour – day
large – offshore
léger – light
mauvais temps – foul weather
menaçant – menacing
mer – sea
météorologique – meteorological
moderé – moderate
moyen – medium
néant – none
neige et pluie – sleet
noeuds – knots
nuage – cloud
nuageux – cloudy
orage – thunderstorm
ouragan – hurricane

perturbation – disturbance
pluie – rain
précipitation – precipitation
pression – pressure
prévision – forecast
prévu – expected
probabilité – probability
profond – deep
rafale – gust
région – area
sans nuages – cloudless
semaine – week
situation générale – general situation
stationnaire – stationary
tempête – storm
temps (heure) – time
temps qu'il fait – weather
type de temps – type of weather
variable – variable
vent de – wind from
vent frais – strong breeze
visibilité – visibility
vitesse en noeuds – speed in knots
zone – area
zone de haute pression – high pressure zone

Numbers in French
Numbers French
1 – *un*
2 – *deux*
3 – *trois*
4 – *quatre*
5 – *cinq*
6 – *six*
7 – *sept*
8 – *huit*
9 – *neuf*
10 – *dix*
11 – *onze*
12 – *douze*
13 – *treize*
14 – *quatorze*
15 – *quinze*
16 – *seize*
17 – *dix-sept*
18 – *dix-huit*
19 – *dix-neuf*
20 – *vingt*
30 – *trente*
40 – *quarante*
50 – *cinquante*
60 – *soixante*
70 – *soixante-dix*
80 – *quatre-vingts*
90 – *quatre-vingt-dix*
100 – *cent*
1000 – *mille*

Clouds

This area is remarkably free of clouds; in winter the average cloud cover is only 4/8 and in summer 2/8 (English Channel 6/8 and 5/8).

Precipitation

The rainfall on average varies from between 450mm to 1300mm (18 to 52 inches) a year (English Channel 540mm to 835mm), which is surprising considering the lack of cloud cover, but when it does rain it usually does so very heavily and visibility is seriously reduced. October, November and March are the wettest months. Thunderstorms occur most often in summer and autumn but have a frequency of only 15 to 20 days a year (English Channel 24). Snow is very rare, appearing only two or three times a year (English Channel 8 to 12).

Visibility

Fog rarely exceeds a day a month (English Channel 24 to 28 days a year) and is more common in winter and around dawn, clearing by mid-morning. Smoke haze often causes poor visibility near large towns, of which Marseille is an example. Winds from the sea also tend to reduce visibility. Mirages form on calm days, particularly near the shore in the morning.

Temperature

January and February are the coldest months, but the mean temperature of 1°C to 11°C (34°F to 54°F) is relatively mild (English Channel -2°C to 12°C). July and August are the hottest months with a mean temperature of 17°C to 29°C (63°F to 84°F) (English Channel 11°C to 27°C).

Humidity

The humidity is moderate, around 75%. It is highest at dawn and in the winter (80%) and lowest at midday and in the summer (53%). Winds from the land reduce these values and winds from the sea increase them (English Channel 88%, 75%).

Ocean

Sea temperature

The mean sea temperature varies from 12°C (54°F) in February to 23°C (73°F) in August (English Channel 8°C (46°F), 16°C (61°F)).

Swell

Due to the shortness of the fetch the swell can never reach the proportions it reaches on the Atlantic coast. Nevertheless when strong winds have been blowing from the E–SE–SW for some time a large swell develops which can be dangerous in shallow water.

Water spouts

Water spouts occur occasionally off the Riviera coast, and sometimes in the Golfe du Lion and off La Corse.

Currents

There is a basic one-knot circulatory current that runs in a NE to SW direction along this coast, sometimes with a weaker current in the opposite direction close inshore. NW winds may reduce and sometimes reverse this flow; onshore winds will increase the flow in the W–SW direction and this increased rate often appears in advance of the wind

and may reach 4 knots. Details of local variations are given in the introduction to each chapter.

Tides

Tidal range

The tidal range in the area covered by this pilot reaches a maximum of 0·15m (0·5ft) at springs and is hardly detectable at neaps.

Tidal streams

The tidal streams caused by these tides can for all practical purposes be ignored.

Sea levels

The sea level can rise as much as 1m (3ft) during strong winds from the SE and fall 0·5m (1·5ft) in winds from the NW. The mean sea levels can be 0·5m (1·5ft) lower in winter than in summer.

Radio

Marine radiobeacons

The following radiobeacons operate in the area singly:

South France
Cap Béar BR (—···/·—·) 313·5kHz 50M
Sète SÉ (···/··—··) 287·5kHz 50M

East Corsica
Ile de la Giraglia GL (——·/·—··) 305kHz 100M

West Corsica
Pointe Revellata RV (·—·/···—) 295kHz 100M

Other stations
Cap Couronne CR (—·—·/·—·) 295·5kHz 50M

West Mediterranean
Cap Bon (Tunisia) BN (—···/—·) 296·5kHz 200M
Ras Caxine CX (—·—·/—··—) 287kHz 200M
Porquerolles PQ (·——·/——·—) 314kHz 200M

Air radiobeacons

The following air radiobeacons operate in the area but may not transmit continuously:
Nice, Mont Leuza LEZ (·—··/·/—··) 399kHz 75M 43°43'·52N 7°19'·63E
Ajaccio, Pointe de la Parata IS (··/···) 341kHz 50M 41°54'N 8°36'·9E
Pointe de Senetosa SNE (···/—·/·) 394·5kHz 15M 47°33'·50N 8°47'·90E
Solenzara SZA (···/———··/·—) 349·5kHz 80M 41°55'·9N 9°23'·7E. Bearings may be unreliable 080° to 120°.
Bastia, Poretta BP (—···/·——·) 369kHz 50M 42°25'·7N 9°32'·2E

VHF direction-finding service

This service is for Emergency use only. Each VHF direction-finding station is remotely controlled either by a Regional Operational Centre for Surveillance and Rescue (CROSS)[1], Signal Station or Naval Lookout Station.
[1]For operational details of CROSS stations see *Admiralty List of Radio Signals Vol 3* and *Vol 6(1)*.

CAPITAINERIE

Here is the weather forecast
for sea areas

BULLETIN POUR LE LARGE

SEA WEATHER FORECAST

| VOICI LE BULLETIN MÉTÉOROLOGIQUE POUR LES ZONES DU LARGE | still in force | expected |

1 - AVIS DE Warning of .... N° .... néant .. None .. , en cours .... , prévu ....

T.U.

Jour de la semaine Day   Date   Heure Time

Zones : .... Zones affected ....
Zones menacées

Vent de : .... Wind from .... Force .... Speed in knots ....
Direction   Beaufort   Vitesse en nœuds

2 - SITUATION GÉNÉRALE LE .... General situation .... A .... **HEURES   ET EVOLUTION**
.... Time and forecast ....

.... Forecast ....

2 - PRÉVISION   pour la journée   du ...... for the day of ....
pour la nuit   du .... for the night of .... au ....

ZONES	CARACTÈRE GÉNÉRAL DU TEMPS — Type of weather —	VENT — Wind —	ÉTAT DE LA MER Houle (facultatif) — Sea/swell state —	VISIBILITÉ — Visibility —

4 - PROBABILITÉS pour la nuit du ... Further forecast for the
night of .... au ....
pour la journée du for the day of ....

5 - TENDANCE GÉNÉRALE ULTÉRIEURE DU TEMPS Future tendency

6 - A .... **HEURES 6 ON OBSERVAIT** : Hours station reports were

A	à	à	à	à
un temps	: weather			
un vent de	: wind			
une visibilité de	: visibility			
une mer	: sea state			

French weather forecast format

CROSS Stations watch on Ch 16, 11; 67, (when a maritime rescue operation is already underway on Ch 11).

Signal stations and lookout stations keep a priority watch on Ch 16. Also available are 7 additional frequencies retained in memory (scanner sweeping) from amongst the following channels:

1-29 156·050MHz –157·450MHz
36 162·400MHz
39 162·550MHz
48 121·500MHz
50 155·525MHz
52 155·625MHz
55 155·775MHz
56 155·825MHz
60-88 156·025MHz – 157·425MHz

Ship transmits on Ch 16 (distress only) or Ch 11 in order that the station can determine its bearing.

Ship's bearing from the station is transmitted on Ch 16 (distress only) or Ch 11.

Hours of watch continuous. Controlled by Sig Stn unless otherwise stated.

La Garde RG Controlled by CROSS 43°06.3N 5°59.5E
Cap Bèar RG 42°30'·8N 3°08'E
Cap Leucate RG 42°55'·1N 3°03'·7E
Sète RG 43°23'·8N 3°41'·5E
L'Espiguette RG 43°29'·3N 4°08'·5E
Cap Couronne RG 43°20'·1N 5°03'·3E
Pomègues RG 43°16'N 5°17'·7E
Bec de l'Aigle RG 43°10'·5N 5°34'·6E
Cap Cépet RG Controlled by Lookout Stn 43°04'·8N 5°56'·5E
Porquerolles RG 43°00'N 6°13'·7E
Cap Camarat RG 43°12'·.1N 60°40'·5E
Cap du Dramont RG 43°24'·8N 6°51'·2E
La Garoupe RG 43°34'N 78°08'·2E
Cap Ferrat RG 43°41'·2N 7°19'·5E
Cap Corse RG 43°00'·3N 9°21'·6E
Ile Rousse RG 43°37'·9N 8°55'·4N
La Parata RG 41°54'·1N 8°36'·8E
Pertusato RG 41°22'·4N 9°10'·7E
La Chiappa RG 41°35'·6N 9°21'·9E
Alistro RG 42°15'·6N 9°32'·5E
Sagro RG 42°47'·8N 9°29'·4E

Coast radio stations

St Lys (FFL-FFS-FFT)
R/T watch on 4366, 8806, 13152, 17323, 22771kHz Continuous. The above coast radio station operates on this coast but it is normally only used for commercial purposes. Traffic lists on 4366, 8806, 13152, 17323, 22771kHz every H+03 and H+30 (0700–2230) so far as possible. See *Admiralty List of Radio Signals Vol. 1 Part I* for full details also WT(MF) service of stations listed below.

Perpignan
VHF Ch 02, 16 Continuous. Call *Marseille Radio.*

Marseille (FFM)
R/T 1671, 1906, 1936, 1939, 2625, 2628, 3792, 3795, 2182kHz 1kW. Traffic lists on 1906kHz at every odd H+10.
VHF Ch 16, 24, 26 Continuous. Call *Marseille Radio.*

Martigues
VHF Ch 16, 27, 28 Continuous. Call *Marseille Radio.*

Sète
VHF Ch 16, 19. Continuous. Call *Marseille Radio.*

Toulon
VHF Ch 16, 25, 62. Continuous. Call *Marseille Radio.*

Grasse (TKM)
R/T Transmits 1746, 2649, 3719, 3722, 2182kHz. Receives 2045, 2048kHz (for foreign registered vessels), 2051, 2054, 2057, 3168, 2182. 2090 working frequency for French registered vessels. Continuous. Traffic lists on 2649kHz every even H+33. VHF Transmits Ch 02,18 (0630–2100) Ch 16 continuous.

Cavalaire VHF Ch 04, 05 (0600–2100) and Ch 16 continuous, remotely controlled from Grasse.

Monaco (3AC, 3AF)
R/T Transmits 4363, 6504, 8728, 13146, 17260, 22750kHz. Receives 4071, 6203, 8204, 12299, 16378, 22054kHz. Traffic lists on all frequencies every H+03 (0503–2203). VHF Ch 16, 20, 22, 86. Continuous. Traffic lists Ch 16 every H+03 (0700–2300) UT.

Ajaccio Transmits and Receives Ch 16 continuous, Ch 24 (0600–2100). Remotely controlled from *Marseille*

Bastia Transmits and Receives Ch 16 continuous, Ch 65 (0600–2100). Remotely controlled from *Grasse*

Porto-Vecchio Transmits and Receives Ch 16 continuous, Ch 05 (0600–2100). Remotely controlled from *Grasse*

Details for automatic calls see *Admiralty List of Radio Signals Vol. 1.*

Port radio stations

All of the large ports and many of the yacht harbours have port radios and details are given in the section dealing with the port concerned. These radios all operate on low power in the VHF band, normally Ch 9 and 16.

Radio and other sources of weather forecasts

Details of local radio weather forecasts for a particular area are also given in the introductory sections of *Parts II* and *III* which deal with that particular length of coast.

The Mediterranean coast of France has probably more sources from which weather forecasts and warnings can be obtained than any other coast in the world. Original forecasts and warnings are drawn up and issued by several sources and the source is usually identified before the bulletin is read. The many systems of distribution listed below allow a yachtsman to keep up to date with what the meteorologist thinks is going to happen. However, the French Mediterranean basin is a microclimate, and it does not always follow that the forecasted weather will occur where the yachtsman is actually located; it may occur further along the coast, out to sea, on the other side of a headland or not at all. It must also be noted that at times any two sources may produce forecasts which differ in content and/or detail.

Weather forecasts and warnings by radio This is probably the best way to get a forecast and/or warning. Keep a watch on VHF Ch 16 and/or on HF (SSB) 2182kHz for *All ships*, *Sécurité*, *Météo*, call repeated several times giving Channel or frequency which will be used. A good source if in harbour is the harbourmaster's office, *capitainerie* or *bureau du port*. The harbourmaster's staff in virtually every harbour post weather forecasts several times each day, often with an English translation attached. The data from which these are compiled may come from any one of the means detailed above and below.

Telephone recorded forecasts Every area of the coast has a centre where weather forecasts are recorded on magnetic tape; the forecast is in French which is easier to understand when heard repeated several times. The telephone numbers are listed in the *Data* section of every harbour featured in this book. Some of these are the numbers of the meteorological office of a nearby airfield, and where this is the case French speakers can discuss the forecast with the meteorological officer on duty.

Try ☎ 36 65 02 83 Toulon for forecasts covering various departments or ☎ 36 65 08 08 Fréjus covering the coast and offshore.

Minitel The owners of telephones in France are entitled to a free *minitel* apparatus which, amongst many thousands of other functions, will produce comprehensive weather forecasts. These are often available for use in cafés and bars etc. Some *minitels* are equipped with printers, which is a bonus because the forecast can then be carefully studied. The code to use is 3615.METEO, then MER, follow the menu instructions. A forecast in English can also be obtained.

Antiope A diagrammatic display of the weather situation on a TV screen can be found in some *capitaineries*.

Daily newspapers Details of the weather situation and forecasts are available in all daily papers. *Le Monde* and *Figaro* give much greater detail than others and are recommended.

Television The various TV channels have short weather forecasts which are of value. Cafés and bars etc. often have a TV set in action. Obtain current times of broadcast from the daily paper. Note – UK TV sets will not receive any French transmissions.

Radio, fax and telex Weather forecasts, charts and warnings are available to those yachts with the necessary receiving and decoding equipment.

Translation The translation of the French transmission, often read very fast, is the major problem facing a foreign skipper but with the use of a tape recorder, along with the form on page 16 and the special glossary of words used by forecasters on page 13, and with practice, the translation will

Radio – Morse code A number of forecasts are transmitted from St Lys and coast radio stations in Morse code at professional speed. If an experienced radio operator is available it would be worth having an HF (SSB) radio and the relevant *Admiralty List of Radio Signals Volume* on board.

Radio France–France Inter In fast French. Times of broadcast sometimes vary by a few minutes, but the forecasts cover a very large area, and this is useful for personal forecasting of the future developments of the weather system.

France Inter 162kHz 0545 and 1905[1]

Radio France

Roussillon 92·1Mhz 0600[1]

Hérault-Montpellier 95·2, 103·8Mhz 0510, weekends 0725 and 1755 (every day)[1]

Marseille 96·7 and 103·1 Mhz 0615 and 0945[1]

Côte d'Azur 103·8, 101·4 and 92·6 Mhz 0630, 0730, 900, 1000, 1230, 14000, 1430, 1715 and 1630[1]

Coast radio stations

Radio weather services

Perpignan In French VHF Ch 02 (0633, 1133)[1]

Agde (CROSS) In French VHF Ch 09 (0735, 1720)[1]

Sète In French VHF Ch 19 (0633, 1133)[1]

Martigues VHF Ch 28 at 0633 and 1133 CROSS, see also page 214

Marseille (FFM) In French on 1906kHz (SSB) at 0103, 0705, 1220, 1615[1]. VHF Ch 24, 26

Toulon In French VHF Ch 25, 62 (0633, 1133)[1]

La Garde (CROSS) In French VHF Ch 09 at 0810

Grasse (TKM) In French on 2649kHz (SSB) at 0733, 1233, 1645[1]. VHF Ch 02 at 0633, 1133[1]

Monaco (3AC, 3AF) 4363, 8728kHz at 0803, 1303, 1715 and 0715, 1715. VHF Ch 03, 23 continuous. Ch 22 at 0803, 1303, 1715 in French and English.

Radio Monte Carlo In French on 218, 1466kHz at 0800, 1900[1]

Corse (CROSS) In French VHF Ch 09 at 0745, 1745[1]

Ajaccio In French VHF Ch 24 0633, 1133[1]

Bastia In French VHF Ch 65 0633, 1133[1]

Porto Vecchio In French VHF Ch 05 at 0633, 1133[1]

Radio Riviera 104·1, 106·5MHz at 0730, 1930 in English.[1] Coastal waters between St Tropez and Italian frontier.

Storm warnings are transmitted on receipt and at the end of the next two silence periods. Keep watch on Ch 16 for announcements.

France Inter (Allouis) in French on 164kHz at 0555 and 1905.

Radio France in French

Marseille 675kHz at 0555, 1905[1] 150 miles

Nice 1350kHz at 0555, 1905[1] 300 miles

[1] 1 hour earlier when daylight savings time (DST) is in force. (See also page 191.)

Lights

Details of major lights are given in subsequent sections. The bearings given are towards the light (from sea) in 360° true notation. The range is the nominal range at which a light can be seen under normal conditions of 10M visibility. Lights are illuminated from 15 minutes after sunset until 15 minutes before sunrise.

Minor lights are listed under each port. These minor, low-power lights are at times difficult to see against a background of lights emanating from the shore establishments nearby. The characteristics of lights are sometimes changed and others added. It is therefore advisable to check the data given against an up-to-date official light list before leaving Britain.

Lights occasionally fail or become faulty in that the period is not correct, and attention should be paid to the navigational warnings that are broadcast each day by the coast radio stations.

Buoyage

The area covered by this pilot book was changed to IALA System A (red to port) in 1980. In addition there are special coastal buoys; see diagram page 19.

Beacons

Use is made of beacon towers on isolated dangers and headlands. These often carry topmarks, and are coloured in accordance with IALA System A. The paintwork of some beacons and the topmarks of others have been washed away; this is noted in the text but may have been rectified since publication.

Signal stations (semaphores)

Signal stations and telephone numbers

Béar	68 82 01 02[1]	Dramont	94 82 00 08
Sète	67 74 60 81[1]	La Garoupe	93 61 32 77
L'Espiguette	66 53 05 44	Cap Ferrat	93 76 04 06
Couronne	42 80 70 67[1]	Cap Corse	95 35 61 06
Pomègues	91 59 00 20	Ile Rousse	95 60 07 45
Bec de			
L'Aigle	42 08 42 08	La Parata	95 52 02 03
Cepet	94 63 97 22[1]	Pertusato	95 73 00 32[1]
Porquerolles	94 58 30 15[1]	La Chiappa	95 70 03 58
Camarat	94 79 80 28	Alistro	95 38 80 76
Sagro	95 35 20 21		

The signal stations listed above are manned from sunrise to sunset. The stations marked [1] are manned day and night. Call on VHF Ch 16 or by telephone. Some stations can receive Morse code and/or flag signals. A station at Cap Leucate is due to open soon.

Storm and weather signals

Storm signals are flown from the signal stations listed above and from the *bureau du port* in some harbours. See diagram.

Many of the smaller yacht harbours may fly their own special signals and in certain cases verbal announcements are made by public address system or by a runner. These variations are detailed in the section dealing with the harbour concerned.

Traffic signals

The current and new traffic control systems are given with their meanings in the diagram. These signals are usually shown near the entrances of major ports and must be obeyed by yachts.

Any local variations from these general rules are given in the section dealing with the harbours concerned. The new international port traffic signals are being adopted.

Lifeboats

Lifeboats are stationed at all the major ports and many of the smaller harbours on this coast. These are listed below. Lifeboats are grouped in three classes depending on their size, the class 1 being the largest.

Inshore rescue craft are either all-weather (AW) pneumatic boats, pneumatic dinghies or runabouts (RA).

Charges may be made if the lifeboat is called out to assist unnecessarily.

Port	Type	Département	☎
Cerbère	RA	Pyr. Orient	68 38 41 60
Port Vendres	AW	Pyr. Orient	68 82 11 46
			68 82 02 54
St-Cyprien	2	Pyr. Orient	68 21 07 98
Canet en Roussillon	3	Pyr. Orient	68 80 20 66
Le Barcarès	2	Pyr. Orient	68 86 07 35
Leucate	2	Aude	
Port La Nouvelle	1	Aude	64 48 01 81
Gruissan	1	Aude	68 45 04 42
Valras Plage	2	Hérault	67 93 00 23
Agde	RA	Hérault	67 94 53
Mèze	2	Hérault	67 43 80 13
Sète	AW	Hérault	67 74 40 00
Palavas les Flots	2	Hérault	67 68 03 45
La Grande Motte	2	Hérault	67 56 03 01
Port Camargue	1	Gard	66 51 43 09
Stes Maries	2	Bouches du Rhône	90 97 83 07
Carro	RA	Bouches du Rhône	42 80 71 53
			42 80 74 04
Port St Louis de Rhône	RA	Bouches du Rhône	
Martigues	2	Bouches du Rhône	42 42 14 35
Marseille	1	Bouches du Rhône	42 95 91 70
La Ciotat	AW	Bouches du Rhône	42 08 47 63
Bandol	3	Var	
Toulon	1	Var	94 65 58 59
Hyères	2	Var	94 65 05 46
Porquerolles	1	Var	94 58 30 57
Le Lavandou	3	Var	94 71 13 09
Saint Tropez	AW		94 97 02 72
Ste Maxime	RA	Var	94 96 00 35
Théoule sur Mer	3	Alpes Maritimes	93 90 31 00
Cannes	3	Alpes Maritimes	93 39 28 39
Antibes	1	Alpes Maritimes	93 33 65 00
Cros de Cagnes	3	Alpes Maritimes	93 31 72 28
Nice	3	Alpes Maritimes	93 89 50 85
Menton	1	Alpes Maritimes	93 35 75 06
Ajaccio	1	Corse	95 22 39 18
			95 21 44 45
St Florent	2	Corse	95 30 00 51
			95 37 00 68
Bastia	AW	Corse	95 31 50 95
			95 31 62 24
Macinaggio	AW	Corse	95 35 43 20
Bonifacio	AW	Corse	95 73 00 33
Propriano	2	Corse	95 76 06 11

In addition to the lifeboats listed above, the following services and organisations have their own seagoing craft and helicopter which are sometimes employed in a back-up role: *Affaires Maritimes, Gendarmerie National, Douanes, CROSS* and *Protection Civile*.

Coastal security

The Centres Régionaux Opérationnels de Surveillance et de Sauvetage (CROSS) assist in the coordination of maritime rescue on the French coasts. They have eight stations, of which the following are located on the Mediterranean coast:

- CROSS MED Fort Ste Marguerite, 83130 La Garde (☎ 94 27 27 11) near Toulon
- CROSS MED AGDE Mont Saint-Loup, 34300 Agde (☎ 67 94 12 02)

New international signals

AIN SIGNALS	MAIN MESSAGES	REMARKS
(R)(R)(R) Flashing	SERIOUS EMERGENCY — ALL VESSELS TO STOP OR DIVERT ACCORDING TO INSTRUCTIONS	Some ports may use an Exemption Signal with Signal 2: see 2a.
(R)(R)(R)	VESSELS SHALL NOT PROCEED	Some ports may not use the full range of main signals, e.g. they may use only Signals 2 and 4, or only Signal 1.
(G)(G)(G) Occulting	VESSELS MAY PROCEED. ONE-WAY TRAFFIC	
(G)(G)(W) Slow or	VESSELS MAY PROCEED. TWO-WAY TRAFFIC	The uncoloured circle in Signals 4, 5 and 5a represents a white light.
(G)(W)(G) Fixed	A VESSEL MAY PROCEED ONLY WHEN IT HAS RECEIVED SPECIFIC ORDERS TO DO SO	Used when a vessel or special group of vessels must receive specific instructions in order to proceed. All other vessels must not proceed. Specific instructions may be given by Auxiliary Signal or by other means such as radio, signal lamp or patrol boat. Some ports may use an Exemption Signal with Signal 5: see 5a.

EXEMPTION SIGNALS	EXEMPTION MESSAGES	REMARKS
a (Y)(R)(R)(R) Fixed or Slow-Occulting	Vessels shall not proceed, except that vessels which navigate outside the main channel need not comply with the main message.	Some ports may use the additional yellow light (always displayed to the left of the top main light) to allow smaller vessels to disregard Messages 2 and 5.
a (Y)(G)(W)(G)	A vessel may proceed only when it has received specific orders to do so; except that vessels which navigate outside the main channel need not comply with the main message.	

AUXILIARY SIGNALS	AUXILIARY MESSAGES	REMARKS
Normally white and/or yellow lights, displayed to the right of the main lights.	Local meanings: e.g. added to Signal 5 to instruct a vessel to proceed; to give information about the situation of traffic in the opposite direction; or to warn of a dredger operating in the channel.	Special messages may apply at some ports with a complex layout, or complicated traffic situation. Nautical documents should be consulted for the details.

New international signals

MEANING	DAY	NIGHT
PORT CLOSED ABSOLUTELY FORBIDDEN TO ENTER	● ● ●	(R)(R)(R)
FORBIDDEN TO ENTER (EXIT PERMITTED)	● ▲ ● or ⎸R	(R)(W)(R) or (R)(R)
FORBIDDEN TO LEAVE (ENTRANCE PERMITTED)	▼ ▲ ▼ or ⎸G	(G)(W)(G) or (G)(G)
FORBIDDEN TO ENTER OR LEAVE	▼ ▲ ● or ⎸R ⎸G	(G)(W)(R) or (R)(G)
PORT OPEN NAVIGATE WITH CAUTION THERE MAY BE OBSTRUCTIONS OR NO RESTRICTION	APPROPRIATE INTERNATIONAL CODE FLAGS	(G)(G)(G)
	NO SIGNALS	NO SIGNALS

Current French signals

Buoyage

CARDINAL MARKS

Used to indicate the direction from the mark in which the best navigable water lies, or to draw attention to a bend, junction or fork in a channel, or to mark the end of a shoal.

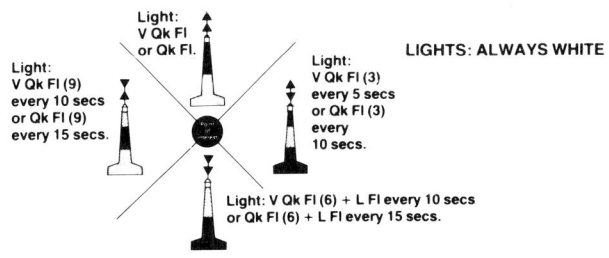

LIGHTS: ALWAYS WHITE

Light: V Qk Fl or Qk Fl.

Light: V Qk Fl (3) every 5 secs or Qk Fl (3) every 10 secs.

Light: V Qk Fl (9) every 10 secs or Qk Fl (9) every 15 secs.

Light: V Qk Fl (6) + L Fl every 10 secs or Qk Fl (6) + L Fl every 15 secs.

LATERAL MARKS

Used generally to mark the sides of well defined navigable channels

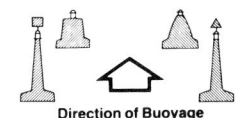

PORT HAND MARKS
Light: Colour — red
Rhythm — any

Direction of Buoyage

STARBOARD HAND MARKS
Light: Colour — Green
Rhythm — any

OTHER MARKS

ISOLATED DANGER MARKS
Use: to mark a small isolated danger with navigable water all around
Light: Colour — white
Rhythm — group flashing (2)

SAFE WATER MARKS
Use: Mid-channel or landfall
Light: Colour — white
Rhythm — isophase, occulting or 1 long flash every 10 secs.

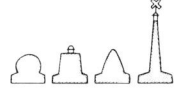

SPECIAL MARKS Any shape permissible
Use: of no navigational significance
Light: Colour — yellow
Rhythm — different from any white lights used on buoys

IALA buoyage system A

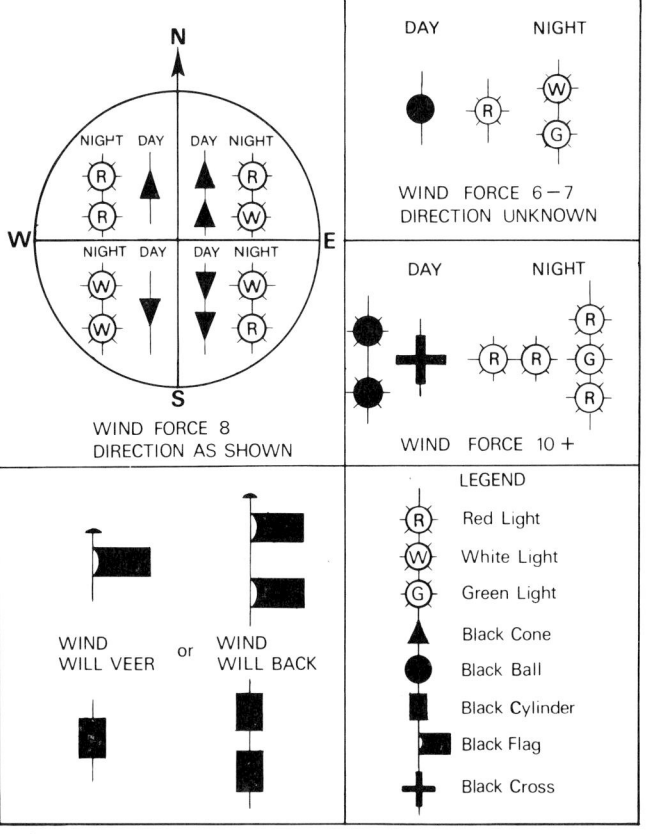

WIND FORCE 8 DIRECTION AS SHOWN

WIND FORCE 6–7 DIRECTION UNKNOWN

WIND FORCE 10 +

WIND WILL VEER   or   WIND WILL BACK

LEGEND

(R) Red Light
(W) White Light
(G) Green Light
▲ Black Cone
● Black Ball
■ Black Cylinder
▬ Black Flag
✚ Black Cross

Storm signals

- CROSS MED CORSE 20184 Ajaccio (☎ 95 20 13 63) Call VHF Ch 16 work Ch 9, or telephone for assistance etc.

These centres also transmit weather forecasts and storm and navigational warnings. They make a call on VHF Ch 19 and transfer to Ch 9 at 0845 and 1845 local time.

The French Police

France is policed by three separate bodies, and foreigners often find this confusing. They are:

Police Nationale Currently numbers around 130,000 officers. Divided into several directorates. Most familiar are the *Police Urbaine* (general police duties from traffic control to investigating minor crime) and the *Police Judiciaire* (investigation of major crime). The *Compagnie Républicaine de Sécurité* (CRS) is best known as 'the riot police' but has a wide range of duties from policing the *autoroutes* to lifeguard duties on summer beaches. Officers wear a flat cap and a *Police Nationale* shoulder-flash.

Gendarmerie National Integral part of the armed forces although almost entirely devoted to policing the civilian population. Currently numbers around 92,000 men. Its responsibility is for rural areas. In the Alpes-Maritimes it polices 80% of the territory containing 30% of the population. Special branches oversee ports and the runway zones of airports. Gendarmes wear blue uniforms in winter, khaki in summer, with a *képi* (pill-box cap).

Police Municipale Many towns in France have a municipal police force. In Nice the force numbers 200 officers, soon to rise to 220. Such forces have limited powers – basically related to traffic control and the enforcement of bye-laws – the powers of the *Police Municipale* seem likely to be extended. Officers wear a *képi* with an identifying shoulder-flash.

Fishing

Commercial fishing boats

The number of commercial fishing boats on this coast is not great nor are the boats large, but they should be given a wide berth when encountered as they may be:

- Trawling either singly or in pairs with a net between the boats.
- Laying a long net, the top of which is supported by floats.
- Picking up or laying pots either singly or in groups or lines.
- Trolling with one or more lines out astern.
- Drifting trailing nets up wind.

Tunny nets

Tunny nets are laid at places along the coast from the summer to autumn. These nets can be up to 1 mile long and are laid as far out as 20 miles from the coast, but are normally laid inshore in depths of 15–40m. It is usual for the outer end to be indicated by a red flag by day and a white light by night. If the net does not reach the coast a similar light or flag is shown at the other end. These nets are made with very strong rope and therefore care must be taken to avoid them. The lights and flags are also used on smaller and shorter nets.

Small fishing boats

The shallow waters of this coast have been heavily fished in the past and average catches are very small compared with those obtained on the Atlantic coasts, nevertheless many thousands of small fishing craft put to sea daily. They should be avoided as far as possible as they too can be using nets or trolling with lines astern. At night many put to sea and use very powerful electric or gas lights to attract fish to the surface, and when seen from a distance these lights appear to flash as the boat moves up and down in the waves, giving the appearance of a lighthouse.

It is not advisable to follow any fishing boat which appears to be taking a short cut because the skipper probably knows the area in great detail and may be following a narrow and twisting channel between rocks and sandbanks which are not shown on the chart.

Charter

In recent years some 50 charter fleets or agencies have been established offering yachts for hire. Most of the fleets are small with 3 or 4 yachts, others have a large number which are used for flotilla sailing. Many charter yachts will be encountered in harbours and popular anchorages. Suitable precautions should be taken because many charter skippers are lacking in the skills and knowledge necessary.

Hazards

Motor and ski-boats, etc.

One of the hazards encountered in the summer on this coast is the many small motor-craft and water scooters which are driven at high speed by unskilled and thoughtless drivers. These frequently approach far too close to yachts for safety and often cause annoyance by their noise and wash. They are not allowed to exceed a 5-knot speed limit within 300m of the coast. In recent years the use of large, very fast power-craft by inexperienced helmsmen has become an additional hazard and there have been many accidents. The problem is not confined to the open sea; it has spread to enclosed waters, canals, harbours etc. where actual damage is caused by the wash. Local fishing craft are also at fault for creating excess wash inside harbours.

Subaqua swimmers

A good lookout must be kept at all times for the many amateur subaqua and snorkelling swimmers who may stray well away from the coast and into the entrance channels to harbours, thereby offering another hazard to yachtsmen. Many professional and teaching groups of subaqua swimmers will be seen

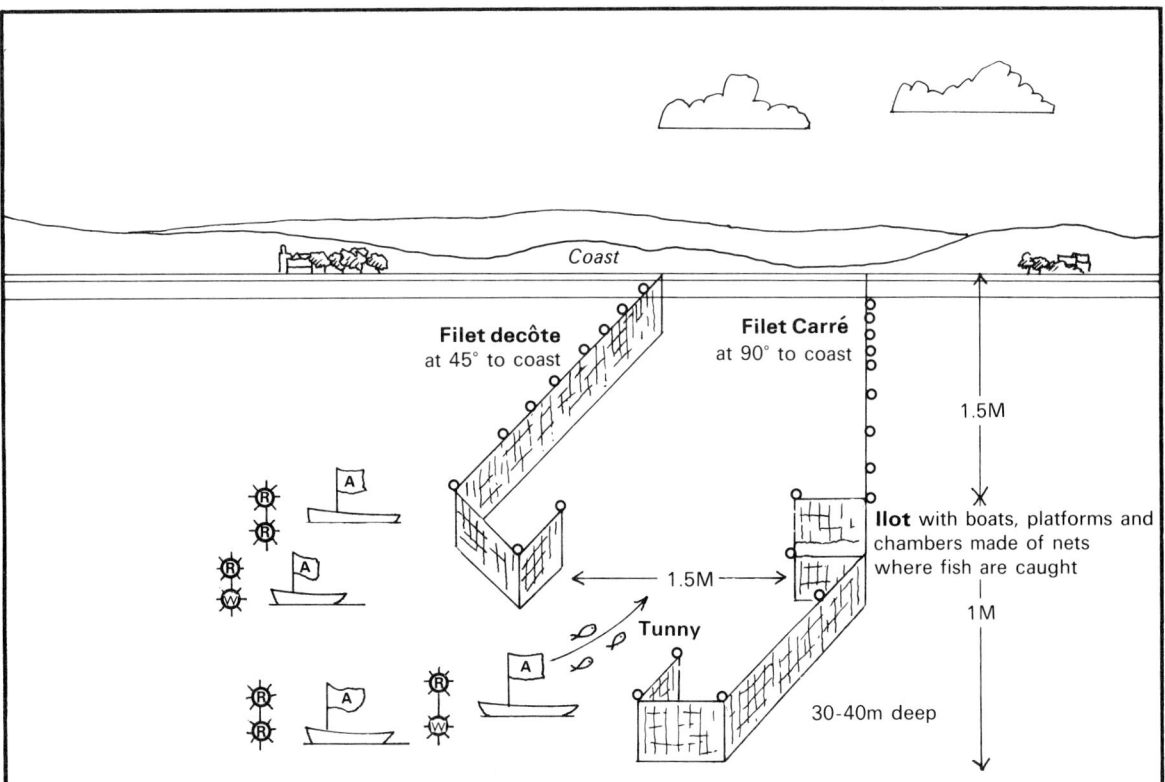

Arrangement of tunny fishing nets

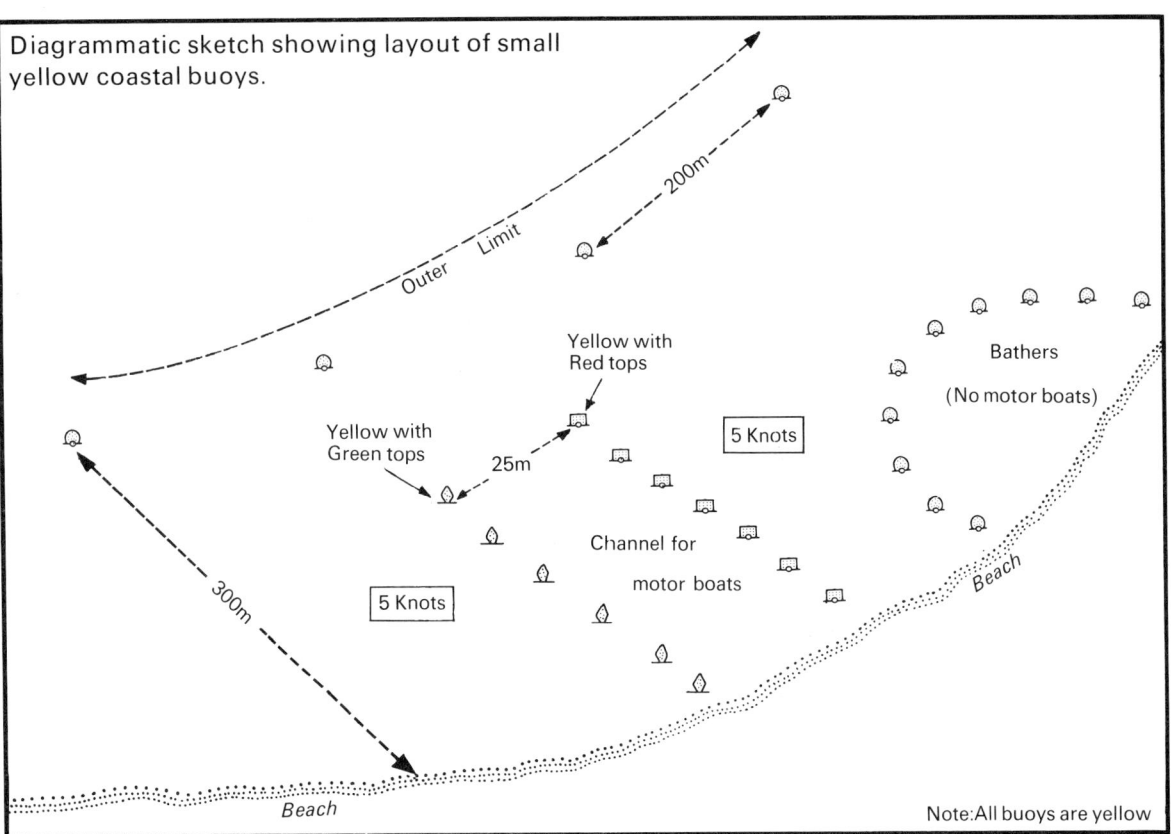

Layout of buoys off beaches

but these usually have an attendant boat with the special diving flag displayed: flag A (white with blue swallow tail) and/or a red flag with white St Andrew's cross.

Speed limits

All harbours have speed limits, usually 3 knots or less, and there is a blanket limit along the whole coast of 5 knots within 300m of the shore. Most harbourmasters and their staff enforce these speed limits especially against any yacht which, by virtue of its design and speed creates a heavy wash.

Coastal buoys

Small buoys are placed in series off many beaches where in summer there are numerous swimmers, as follows:

- Yellow spherical buoys, 0·96m diameter, are placed along the coast every 200m at a distance of 300m offshore. Speed limit inside them is 5 knots.
- Small yellow conical or can buoys, 0·64m high, mark the sides of a channel 25m wide from the beach out to sea, for use by water-skiing boats, etc.
- Large can buoys painted yellow and conical buoys, yellow, 1·28m high, mark the outer ends of this channel for water-skiing boats, etc.
- Small yellow spherical buoys, 0·64m high near the coast and close together, mark an area for swimmers only, nothing else is allowed inside.
- See diagram on page 21.

Dolphins and whales

Happily there are still a fair number of both in the western Mediterranean and it is usual to see a school of whales or dolphins on any deep-water voyage. Neither of these mammals is dangerous, but both can create some surprises by their sudden appearance by day or night. Whales will tend to keep to a steady course, while dolphins like to play around a yacht and appear to be trying to get it to join their school and sail in the direction in which they are travelling.

Anchorages

Harbour anchorages

Anchorage is forbidden inside almost every harbour, except in an emergency or for a very short period while selecting a berth or mooring. However, in a few harbours anchors have to be used to hold the yacht away from the quay or pontoon. Always use a sinking type of anchor tripline without a buoy attached when anchoring in a harbour or near moorings.

Coastal anchorages

The quality of the bottom in shallow water varies considerably on this section of the coast, and in many cases on the Côte d'Azur, Riviera, La Corse and Côte Vermeille it is steep-to and rocky. In the bays and creeks it is usually sandy, and on the coast of Languedoc-Roussillon it is sand and mud covered with a thick layer of fine grass-like seaweed, but there are often large areas of bare sand where the current and swell are strong enough to prevent the growth of this weed.

Suitable places to anchor off each harbour have been given in the harbour section concerned but the actual selection of the place to drop an anchor should be made at the time. Due to the clarity of the water it is usually possible to see the bottom and to select a suitable patch of bare sand. It should be remembered that light CQR and Danforth-type anchors tend to drag and fail to dig into hard-packed sand when it is covered with heavy weed, and that anchors without points are hopeless. Fisherman and Mediterranean-type anchors are better for this type of bottom. If possible try to snorkel over the anchor to check that it is holding.

If anchoring in rocky areas, an anchor trip-line is advisable as the flukes can easily become caught in the jagged broken rocks. When anchored off the coast, maintain a watch on the radio for storm warnings, and make contingency plans in advance in case a gale should blow up.

Calanque anchorages

There are many delightful anchorages to be found in the *calanques* (narrow creeks) and little bays on this coast, some of which are detailed in *Part II* and *Part III*.

Approach these anchorages with care and with a lookout forward, who should be stationed as high as possible, preferably up the mast whence the bottom can be seen and any obstruction will be very evident. The use of Polarised spectacles is advised.

Anchor in an area of bare sand and if necessary take a line ashore but make sure that its position will not obstruct the fairway.

When entering or leaving under sail remember that the wind may be very fluky if the sides of the *calanque* are high. This type of anchorage should only be used in good weather. If there is a warning of bad weather or if the wind or swell rises, the anchorage should be left at once as this may later become impossible due to the wind funnelling through the narrow entrance. These winds can even become dangerous when they blow down the river valley or creek from the shore.

It is unwise to leave a yacht unattended in such an anchorage and advance plans for a hurried exit should be made. In recent years the sandy bottoms of popular anchorages and harbour berths where anchors have to be used have been so dug up that the sand is now loose. CQR/Danforth-type anchors hold fairly well if used with a long chain, but Fisherman and Mediterranean four-pronged types are better. Sometimes, after heavy thunderstorms in the hinterland, dry riverbeds can become raging torrents in a few minutes carrying large chunks of wood. This should be kept in mind when choosing a place to anchor.

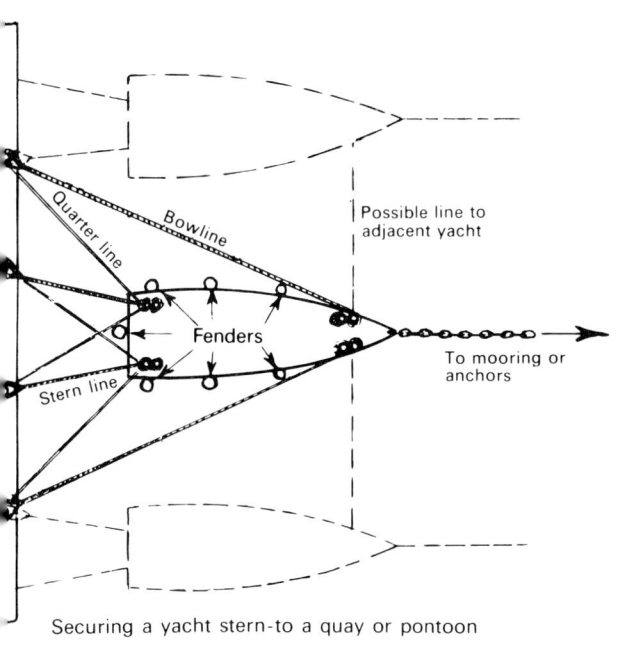

Securing a yacht stern-to a quay or pontoon

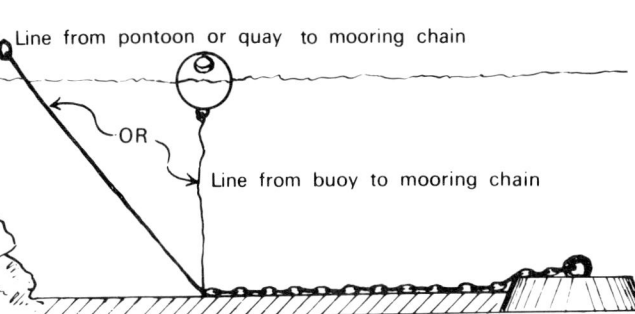

Two methods of securing a bow mooring line

Berthing

Berthing

Due to vast numbers of yachts and limited space, berthing stern-to the quays and pontoons is the method normally used in the Mediterranean. For greater privacy or because the design of the yacht prevents berthing stern-to, it may be desirable to berth bow-to the quay or pontoon.

Manoeuvring a yacht stern first into a narrow berth between two other yachts, sometimes with a cross wind blowing, is a skill which has to be acquired and it is most advisable that some practise at manoeuvring astern should be undertaken in advance. The only advice offered is:

- Have plenty of fenders out, especially near the stern.
- Approach the berth slowly from some distance off.
- If not fully satisfied with the approach draw off and try again.
- Warping the yacht or pulling her in by hand when close in is better than using the engine.

It is better to make several attempts in slow time and to berth quietly in a seamanlike manner than to go rushing around with engines roaring and endangering nearby yachts.

The yacht is usually secured to the quay or pontoon by two stern lines leading from the quarters. In order to hold the yacht away from the quay or pontoon, a bow mooring of some kind will have to be picked up. These take several different forms as follows:

- A small buoy with line or light chain attached to it which leads to a heavier chain which must be pulled in, brought aboard and secured.
- A line or light chain that has one end attached to the quay or pontoon and the other to the heavy mooring chain. This light chain has to be picked up from near the quay or pontoon and followed along to the heavy chain which has to be pulled in, taken on board and secured.
- Finally there are the mooring posts or piles located on either side of the berth which sometimes have chains running out to them from the quay or pontoon. In this case it is necessary to secure the bow lines to the posts (see diagram). In recent years many harbours, have replaced buoys, lines and chains with strong metal piles or posts because they are easier to use and cheaper to maintain.

In many cases the chains are heavy and dirty and gloves are advisable when handling them because they are often covered with small sharp barnacles. Where no mooring chains are provided yachts have to use their own anchors, which should be dropped at least 50m from the berth and should have an unbuoyed sinking type of anchor trip line attached to facilitate recovery should they become foul.

In winter and stormy weather these securing lines will have to be doubled and extra lines such as quarter lines, cross-stern lines and bow lines laid out. Extra fenders may be necessary, especially where the stern (or bow) could ride up to and touch the quay or pontoon (see diagram for details).

Winds of gale force can arise with great speed and if the yacht has to be left unattended even for a short period it is wise to lay out extra lines. In the few places where it is possible to lie alongside, holding-off lines are usually employed, especially by fishing boats, and can present an unexpected obstruction approaching a berth. Harbours in the Mediterranean are subject, during gales, to exceptionally strong surges of water much more powerful than those encountered in British harbours, and berthing lines should be stronger than those usually used at home.

It is advisable to shackle the anchor chain to the harbour's bow chain below the buoy (if any) if leaving the yacht through the winter. Wind the chain in tight so that it forms a 45° angle with the surface of the water.

Moorings

Virtually all moorings are privately owned, and if one is used it will have to be vacated should the owner return. There are often no markings to give any indication of the weight and strength of the moorings, so they should be used with caution.

Harbour facilities

Slipways
Because there is very little tide in the Mediterranean, it is impossible to dry out to scrub, or to carry out underwater repairs or painting, as is normal on other coasts. Yachts therefore have to be hauled out. Slipways and travel-lifts are to be found at most harbours. Outline details of these have been given in the sections dealing with the harbours concerned. The cost of hauling out and relaunching varies considerably, and quotations should be obtained from several places.

Repairs
Several of the large harbours and ports have good repair facilities and many self-employed artisans are to be found at all the harbours. These artisans can carry out repairs, although the quality of their work and their charges vary enormously. It is recommended that local advice be taken in the selection of a yard or craftsman to undertake any repairs, and that a clear and firm quotation should be obtained first, making sure that all extras such as travelling time and taxes have been taken into account. During the high season the demand on all repair services is considerable and a visitor will have to wait his turn.

Cranes
All harbours have small cranes and some have travel lifts and large cranes capable of lifting small and medium-sized yachts out of the water. Mobile cranes are also used in some harbours. Details are given for the harbour concerned.

Laying up

Many owners may wish to lay up their yachts for the winter in the Mediterranean so that they can use the boat the following year without the long outward passage.

Arrangements can be made with the yards or yacht harbours at many places for yachts to be looked after afloat or hauled out. The facilities and services provided vary considerably, as does the cost; it is therefore advisable to get several quotations and to find out exactly what will be provided. Local advice is also worth taking as to the quality of the services provided.

Employing another yachtsman, often living on his own yacht in the same harbour, to look after a yacht is fraught with risk as there is no guarantee that he will not be called away for some personal matter or just sail away for reasons of his own. Again local advice and the recommendation of others is essential.

The NW *mistral-tramontane* can be frequent and severe in winter and early spring and this should be borne in mind when selecting the area and site in which to lay up. The power of the sun which shines

on most days and the dryness of the air must also be considered by those with yachts that have wood decks and superstructure, and arrangements must be made for these to be watered daily and if possible covered by awnings. Varnish work will also deteriorate quickly if exposed without protection to these conditions.

Special rules and regulations for foreign yachts

On arrival in France
Take the yacht's papers and a photocopy of the owner's passport to the nearest customs office. A *titre de séjour* (visa) will be issued and the yacht's papers returned to the owner.

There are large numbers of foreign yachts kept either permanently or temporarily in the harbours on the south coast of France. In the past, many of the owners of these yachts have failed to comply with the existing rules and this has resulted in the regulations being strengthened and more severely enforced. The customs officers who are responsible for seeing that these laws are complied with have considerable power to investigate and take action as necessary.

Owners of visiting yachts are warned to make certain that these rules and regulations are meticulously observed. It is expected that these rules will be changed after 1 January 1993, but they are still under discussion. It would appear that all boats will have to have a document showing that *TVA* (VAT) has been paid or that they are excused.

Group A
Yachts registered in EC countries or in countries which have special financial arrangements with France, such as:

Gabon, Germany, Greece, Hungary, Iran, Ireland, Italy, Ivory Coast, Lebanon, Luxembourg, Madagascar, Malawi, Mali, Mauritania, Monaco, Morocco, Netherlands, Niger, Norway, Pakistan, Poland, Portugal, Romania, Singapore, Spain, Sweden, Switzerland, Thailand, Togo, Tunisia, United Kingdom of Great Britain, United States of America, Zambia.

Yachts must have the original certificate of registration on board at all times unless it is being taken to the customs office (see below). Photocopies are not valid.

Skipper/owner
The yacht can only be used or lived on when the skipper/owner is on board. His passport must agree with the name etc. of the skipper/owner as shown in the yacht's certificate of registration. A yacht can never be let or loaned to anyone with the exception of the owner's immediate family, i.e. spouses, sons and daughters, fathers and mothers.

Company yachts
An official document is required from the company specifying the directors with photocopies of their

passports, a list showing the allocation of shares, copies of the Articles and Memoranda of Association and a photocopy of the yacht's certificate of registration. With these documents the director with the majority shareholding must visit the customs office and fill in the appropriate form. Approval comes from Paris and takes several months.

Maximum period of use in French waters

Having obtained a *titre de séjour* (visa) from the customs office, a foreign yacht may be used in French waters for six months in any twelve without paying import duties and *TVA* (VAT). This document will have no value when the *TVA* (VAT) has been paid and will be withdrawn. At the end of the six months either the yacht must be laid up or it must leave French waters. The six months need not be continuous provided that the yacht is only in use for a total of six months in any consecutive twelve months. When the yacht is laid up, no one may live on board.

Renewal of Titre de Séjour

At the end of the twelve-month period the documents and the visa must be taken to the customs office for renewal.

Group B

Yachts registered in countries that do not have a special financial arrangement with France have to pay the customs a charge per registered tonne per day while in French harbours, in addition to the normal charges. They can remain in French waters for six months only.

Information – France

General

It is beyond the scope of this pilot to go into any detail about the characteristics of the area and its occupants but there are some important points of note which are detailed below and which will be of value to visiting yachtsmen.

Behaviour

The French have been subject to an annual avalanche of international tourism for many years and are not strangers to the outrageous behaviour of a small number of foreigners on holiday. However, if the visiting yachtsman wants to obtain the friendly cooperation and help of the local inhabitants and officials all he has to do is approach them in a pleasant manner and make every possible use of what little knowledge he has of their language no matter how bad his accent. Any rude or boorish behaviour will immediately result in an atmosphere of non-cooperation which will be difficult to overcome.

Tourists

The annual influx of tourists of all nations and from all walks of life is an event that has been taking place for generations. The older resorts of the Côte d'Azur and the Riviera are well adjusted to receive this invasion and although the area becomes jam-packed in July and August it is usually possible to obtain goods and services without waiting too long. The new resorts of Languedoc-Roussillon and places where packaged tourism is being developed present a different picture because the facilities have not yet caught up with the tremendous expansion of the tourist industry.

You are strongly advised to try to avoid this coast in July and August and to visit the area in May and June or September and October, or during the winter months.

Formalities

The officials on this part of the French coast carry out their duties with more care than those on the other coasts, but will normally adapt their rules with Gallic common sense to meet a particular situation. If on the other hand they feel that they are being imposed upon they will enforce the rules with severity.

On arrival in any harbour the skipper is expected to report as soon as possible to the *bureau du port* (harbour office, sometimes called *la capitainerie*), or occasionally to the yacht club, where he must complete a form giving particulars of his yacht and crew and his intentions regarding the proposed length of stay.

Instructions for large yachts

Many of the harbours described in this pilot are too small for a large yacht, which must anchor outside whilst its crew visits the harbour by tender. It is essential that the skipper of a large yacht who wishes to enter a harbour telephones or radios the *bureau du port* well in advance, to reserve a berth if practicable and receive necessary instructions.

Customs

The first port of call in France from a foreign port should be a major one, and on arrival the skipper must visit the customs with the ship's papers and his crew's passports as soon as possible. The customs office will then complete a *titre de séjour* (visa), a copy of which must be kept on board. There is normally no restriction on going ashore before clearance, provided that someone is left on board with the papers. The various officials may on occasion make a visit to the yacht, and they have been known to carry out searches on board; sometimes a yacht may be stopped at sea by customs officers and searched. See also page 24.

Harbour dues

Harbour dues are now charged in every harbour on the south French coast, and these charges can vary from the very modest to the exorbitant. They are levied in many ways and to many different scales which are constantly changing. It is impossible to list dues for any particular harbour because by the time this pilot is printed many will be out of date.

In some harbours the first day or two days are free, but beware, because if a yacht stays beyond the free period it is possible that payment will have to be made for all the back dues with no free period. In some harbours there is a sliding scale and the rate becomes greater as the days pass, in others a large sum of money has to be paid on arrival to cover a stay of several weeks with no reduction for a shorter period. Some rates are calculated on the overall length of the yacht, some on length multiplied by breadth and others on net or gross tonnage registered. In almost every case there is a sliding scale that varies with the time of year, the charges in July and August are much greater than those made during the winter. The procedure for paying these charges also varies from harbour to harbour; sometimes payment must be made on arrival, sometimes before leaving and sometimes even from day to day. The time of day from which these dues are calculated is also different and can be midday, midnight or any other hour. The only recommendation, therefore, is to visit the *bureau du port* on arrival and find out exactly how much it costs and when and where the dues have to be paid.

There are unfortunately a number of yachtsmen in the Mediterranean who, after using all the facilities of a harbour, take pleasure in trying to cheat their way out of paying their dues by leaving in a hurry, thereby getting the harbour staff into trouble with their employers. Visitors should therefore appreciate the reason for rather peremptory demands for harbour dues that they may occasionally experience.

Yacht clubs

A yacht club will be found in nearly every harbour. Their clubhouse can be large modern buildings with every facility, old or adapted buildings with only a bar, lounge and shower, or, at the other extreme, small wooden hut which serve as offices. Yacht clubs in general cater for practising yachtsmen and the vast majority do not have large social memberships as do the *club náuticos* in Spain. Visiting yachtsmen are welcome within reason to make use of the facilities available and should make themselves known to the secretary and fill in the visitors' book where one is provided. Many yacht clubs have a sailing school incorporated with the club and in some places it is difficult to find out where one ends and the other begins.

The Touring Club de France (TCF) has a number of clubhouses and other facilities for yachtsmen along the coast and some foreigners join this organisation in order to be able to use these facilities. Information can be obtained from the head office at 65 avenue de la Grande Armée, 75 Paris 16e or from the French Government Office in London at 178 Piccadilly, W1V 0AL (☎ 071 493 3171).

Fuel

Diesel

This is available at most harbours, usually from pumps on the quayside, as follows:

- Diesel (*gasoil or mazout*) is taxed and may be used in yachts and vehicles. It is normally available at most harbours, usually near the entrance.
- Diesel (*gasoil*), untaxed, from special pumps in fishing harbours may only be used in fishing boats.
- *Fuel-oil domestique (FOD)* is heating oil and also a form of diesel oil that carries only a small tax and cannot be supplied to yachts.

For those yachts that require large amounts of fuel, bunkering arrangements exist at the major ports. Details of these and of the credit card system should be obtained from the fuel company in Britain.

Petrol

Low-grade petrol is supplied in almost every harbour from a pump labelled *Essence* or *Normal*. Pumps with high-grade petrol labelled *Super* are only available in the major yachting harbours. Petrol/oil mixture may be obtained from many harbours from a pump labelled *mélange* or *2 temps*.

Oil

Many grades of oil are available at most harbours or from garages nearby, never dump oil in the water.

Used oil disposal

Most harbours have special tanks for the disposal of used oil.

Paraffin

This is available under the name *pétrole*. A better-quality product, *pétrole raffiné*, often called *kerdane*, is more suitable for use on a yacht and is available from *drogueries*, *épiceries* and ships' chandlers at most harbours. Methylated spirits, called *alcool à brûler*, may also be bought from *drogueries* and *épiceries*.

Water

Water is available almost everywhere and in most harbours water taps are established along the quays and pontoons. With a few exceptions the water from these taps is clean and can be drunk, but the careful may prefer to boil their drinking-water or buy bottled mineral water instead. The latter option is advised because the water tank of a yacht can become foul in a warm environment.

Due to the very salty water and the hot dry air and sun, any object subjected to sea spray rapidly becomes impregnated with salt crystals; rope and sails become heavy and stiff, difficult to use and harsh to handle. These salt crystals do in time weaken and damage the materials and should be removed as soon as possible. On arrival in harbour it is quite normal to hose down all sails and cordage that have been exposed to salt water and to hang them up in the rigging where they will dry in a surprisingly short time.

Water is expensive and in short supply along the south coast of France and should not be wasted. No-one will object to tanks being filled, decks and sails being washed to get the salt out of them, or wooden decks being swilled down to keep them leak-proof, but taps should be turned off directly these tasks are finished and should never be left running unnecessarily. In recent years, due to the huge increase in the number of people visiting and living on the coasts of the Mediterranean, the demand for water has exceeded the supply and wells have run dry or only supply brackish water. Always test water before using and before filling tanks.

Ice

Ice for ice boxes is available in the summer season at some harbours and can be bought in blocks of about one metre long by 20 centimetres cross section. The best way to carry these heavy slippery blocks is in a towel until they can be broken into smaller portions by using a sharp instrument such as a pointed marlin-spike. This ice should not be used in drinks, as it is sometimes made from impure water. It is also possible to buy special small ice, in most harbours from the bars, that is clean and has been prepared for drinking purposes but it is expensive.

Food

At first, food may be found to be somewhat expensive in France, but the quality is usually excellent. Much cheaper food is to be obtained in the larger ports, especially in the markets and the back-street shops. Cuts of meat will when encountered first seem to be very expensive, but the type of cut is different and the weight does not normally include fat and bone as in England. Fruit or vegetables which are in season are usually very cheap.

By careful shopping and choosing local foods it is possible to keep down the cost of feeding to British levels. Imported and special foods will be found to be very expensive.

Drink

Milk (*lait*) is obtainable at most harbours in glass bottles or paper or plastic cartons. Unless remaining in the area for some time, do not buy milk supplied in glass bottles, as these bottles will not be exchanged at another harbour. It is advisable to buy *lait stérilisé* as it is safer and keeps better.

Local wines (*vin du pays* or *vin ordinaire*) of excellent quality can be obtained by shopping around, but spirits and château wines will be found to be relatively expensive. By buying duty-free stores, however, this expense can be kept down. The cheaper wines are usually supplied in glass bottles with a ring of small stars around the base of the neck which are returnable for a refund, although today many wines are being supplied in non-returnable plastic bottles.

Shopping

The price of goods in the shops varies considerably from street to street and from town to town, and the difference in price between an item bought in the main street of a smart resort and exactly the same item bought from a back-street shop or supermarket in a large commercial port is considerable in winter and even greater in the summer season.

Most shops open by 0900 hours, but some food shops open as early as 0700; all with very few exceptions close at 1200 hours and do not reopen until 1400 or later. Some shops close for the day at around 1730, while others stay open until as late as 2100. Many food shops open on Sunday mornings.

Restaurants

Restaurants, cafés and bars will be found around every harbour; the quality of food and drink is in almost every case of a high order, and the price is reasonably low considering the cost of the food in the shops. The charges made in a high-class restaurant are considerable, as befits the standard of cuisine.

The French as a rule eat out more frequently than the English and have their main meal at midday, so that by twelve-thirty it will be difficult to find a table. Despite the earliness of this meal, their evening meal is usually taken later than the English equivalent, and the restaurants will not start to fill up until after eight. Menus are always displayed outside the establishments and a tour to study these is recommended. It is unwise to choose a restaurant by its location, décor or state of repair; the best quality and often the best value is to be found in an unpretentious restaurant in the back streets. Try to find out or see where the local people feed; this is bound to be one of the best places to visit. Some idea of the numbers of restaurants has been given for every harbour, but details have not been included because they change so quickly.

Hotels

Hotels have been listed by numbers and by classes under each harbour. This classification by the local Syndicat d'Initiative is similar to that used in Britain by the AA and RAC and gives some idea of what is available.

Holidays

There are a number of official holidays in France in addition to the normal weekends and these are listed below. Many places have local holidays on special feast days, but when these fall in the season many shops including food shops remain open, especially in the morning.

1st January	New Year's Day
Easter Monday	
Labour Day	1st May
Ascension Day	1st May
Liberation Day	
Whit Monday	8th May
Fête Nationale	14th July
Feast of the Assumption	15th August
All Saints' Day	1st November
Armistice Day	11th November
Christmas Day	25th December

Good Friday and Boxing Day are not holidays in France.

Laundrettes

Laundrettes (*laveries*) will be found near most harbours and ports and are usually situated in the back streets. In certain cases these establishments are not of the 'do-it-yourself' type common to Britain as the actual placing of the clothing in the machines and its removal is carried out by staff.

Garbage and pollution

The extent of the pollution of what was one of the fairest and cleanest seas in the world is frightening to behold. It is impossible when coasting on a calm day to find a stretch of sea free of floating rubbish, usually plastic, and the beaches and coves that are not cleaned daily are covered with flotsam consisting of every conceivable kind of man-made material. The French authorities have become aware of this menace and are taking steps to improve the situation, but the deplorable behaviour of many of the tourists, the local fishermen, the crews of commercial vessels and the occasional yachtsman in disposing of their rubbish into the sea nullifies much of their effort. Many bags and containers for rubbish are to be found on all quays and pontoons. Collect your rubbish when at sea and on return to port put it in one of the containers provided; never put it in the sea.

Sewage

The yacht's WC should not be used in harbour; there are usually WCs available not far from the yacht's berth.

Information offices

The information offices provided by the local Syndicat d'Initiative near every harbour should always be visited on arrival and free brochures and maps of the area obtained. These will make the visit more interesting as they usually contain a detailed history of the area with a list of places to visit, hotels, restaurants, entertainments, fiestas, sports shops and many other items.

Before leaving Britain much information of a background nature can be obtained from the French Government Tourist Office, 178 Piccadilly, London W1V 0AL (☎ 071 493 3171) in the form of brochures, maps, etc.

British Consul

The address and telephone number of the British consul on the mainland coast are:
24 avenue du Prado, 13006 Marseille. ☎ 91 53 43 32.
There is no consul in La Corse; contact Marseille.

Post offices

The *bureau de poste*, usually labelled *PTT* (*or la poste*), has been marked as such on the various plans. The hours of opening, which vary from place, to place are displayed outside the building. In addition to the normal telegraphic facilities they often have telephone cabins which work because they have not been vandalised as have the coin boxes outside.

There are now many call boxes using cards bought from the PTT; the old coin boxes are being phased out. The *poste restante* service works well and it is possible to have correspondence redirected to another town as you sail along the coast, but careful planning is necessary as this service will only hold mail for two weeks and after this time it will be returned to the sender. The postal service to and from Britain varies from amazingly fast to very slow for reasons that are not apparent.

Health

The three main health hazards encountered in the Mediterranean are sunburn, heat stroke (or heat exhaustion) and stomach upsets, all of which can be guarded against. The sun, which is more powerful than it is at higher altitudes, can produce sunburn after a very short exposure especially if coupled with the effects of wind and salt spray. In addition the reflection of the sun off the water will increase the rate of burning. Despite the heat, clothing should be worn and the skin should only be exposed for very limited periods at first until a tan has been acquired.

Heat exhaustion, and in more severe cases heat stroke, is caused by the loss of salt from the system through perspiration, and in a hot climate such as this it is essential to increase the daily intake of salt by adding more to dishes when cooking than is usual so that all members of the crew remain fit; alternatively, salt tablets should be taken. Stomach and bowel disorders can be occasioned by consuming contaminated food or water, or food that has gone bad, and this can only be guarded against by normal commonsense hygiene. Another cause of this trouble is the highly spiced foods, liberally cooked and served with olive oil, which if taken in quantity may be too much for systems used to more simple fare. Excessive consumption of cheap wine may also upset the digestion.

Medical

Excellent medical services exist along this stretch of the French coast but the services of doctors, hospitals, etc. have to be paid for directly after consultation or treatment and their fees are very high. It is therefore advisable to take out an insurance policy to cover medical and associated expenses or get National Health certificate *E111* from your local post office, or from the DSS, Overseas Branch, Newcastle upon Tyne, NE98 1YX, before leaving.

Bathing

As might be expected, bathing in the Mediterranean is excellent; the water warms up in May and remains warm well into the autumn. When bathing from rocks great care must be exercised in keeping a lookout for sea urchins, the spines of which if touched penetrate the skin and break off below the surface, being very difficult to remove and very painful. There are several different types of jellyfish to be found, some of which can sting if touched.

Other sports

Good facilities exist along the greater part of the coast for those who want to fish, shoot, ride, ski, fly, play games etc., and details can usually be obtained from the nearest information bureau of the *Syndicat d'Initiative*.

Communications

The communications to the south of France are excellent by both air and rail and it is very easy to change trains. There are frequent regular air services to Marseille and Nice from England and capital cities, and the charter airlines run services to Perpignan, Montpellier, Nîmes, Toulon, Hyères, Cannes, Calvi, Ajaccio, Solenzara, and Bastia, and sometimes to other minor airfields. There are direct rail connections between Paris and all the major ports along the coast, and some services from London go direct to Marseille and major coastal towns as far away as Italy. Comprehensive bus services run from the major towns to the smallest harbours along the coast.

There are both sea and ferry and air services from mainland Corsica.

Emergency messages

In a great emergency a close relative can have a message broadcast in France. The relative must phone the BBC News Room on ☎ 071 580 4468 Extension 4136. The BBC will contact Paris and the message will be broadcast in French on France Inter on 164 kHz (1829m) at 0200, 0445 (0345 Sundays), 0550, 0755 (0845 Sundays), 1157 and 1950.

History

Dates of historic events from 6000BC to 1944 AD which affected the W Mediterranean.

BC

6000	Neolithic pottery found near Martigues.
5000	Start of commerce at Byblos.
3800-800	Bronze Age, Ligurian occupation.
3000	Start of Egyptian history.
3500	First villages with stock raising, farming.
*2000-1500	Stonehenge constructed.
1500	Sidon becomes prosperous.
1400	Epoch of the Mycenaean.
1100	Prosperity of Tyr.
800	Foundation of Carthage.
800-400	Celts from Rhineland arrive in Provence.
753	Foundation of Rome.
700	Iron age. Iron weapons appear in Europe.
600	Foundation of Marseille by the Greeks and Phocaeans.
500-400	Greeks expand along the coast founding Hyères, St Tropez, Antibes, Nice and Monaco, and introducing olives, vines, figs, nuts, cherries, etc.
475	End of the Roman Kings and Empire.
381	Rome taken by the Gauls.
264-241	1st Punic war.
219-201	2nd Punic war.
218	Hannibal passes through Provence and crosses the Alps.

154	Roman legions take Nice and Antibes.
149-14	63rd Punic war; Cathage destroyed.
120	Occupation of S Gaul by Romans; Narbonne founded.
102	Marius (Roman) destroys the Teutons at Aix.
58-59	Romans take over Gaul.
*55	Julius Caesar lands in Britain.
46	Arles founded.
44	Julius Caesar assassinated.
27	End of the Roman Republic, start of the Empire.
AD	Birth of Jesus Christ.
79	Destruction of Pompei.
476	End of the Roman Empire.
IV to V century	Waves of invasions by Vandals, Visigoths, Burgundians, Ostrogoths and Franks. Christianity takes root in Provençal coastal towns.
536	Provence ceded to the Franks.
570	Birth of Mohammed.
843	Provence reverts to Louis the Debonair's sons.
884	The Saracens capture the Maures.
X century	The Saracens, Vikings and Magyars make many raids on Provence.
*1066	William the Bastard of Normandy invades England.
1090-1290	The Crusades.
*1215	Magna Carta established in England.
1486	Reunion of Provence with France.
*1492	End of the Middle Ages. Columbus discovers America.
*1337-1453	Hundred years' war with England.
*1558-1603	Reign of Elizabeth I.
*1588	Defeat of the Spanish Armada.
1562-1598	Wars of Religion.
*1600	Foundation of the East India Company.
*1620	Pilgrim Fathers land in America.
1687	Huguenots flee France.
1691	Nice taken by the French.
1643-1715	Reign of Louis XIV.
1720	Great plague reaches Provence via Marseille; population decimated.
1785	First steam-driven ship.
1789	French Revolution begins.
1790	The Assembly of the Revolution divides Provence into three departments: Basse-Alps, Bouches du Rhône and the Var.
1792	500 Marseille volunteers parade in Paris singing the song of the Rhine Army which became *La Marseillaise* and the national anthem of France.
1814	Napoleon exiled to Elba.
*1805	Battle of Trafalgar.
1812	Napoleon's army driven from Russia.
*1815	Battle of Waterloo and the fall of Napoleon, who was imprisoned on the island of St Helena.
1859	Frédéric Mistral writes his Provençal poem *Mireio*
1861-65	American Civil War.
1914-18	First World War.
1939	Second World War.
1942	German forces invade Provence.
1944	Allied troops land on the Côte d'Azur.

Notes

1. Different sources do not always give exactly the same dates for some of the various events listed above.

2. Events marked ★ are included to give those who know their English history a relative time scale.
3. The many changes in the ownership of areas of Provence have not been included for the sake of simplicity.

History of the port names

The history of the area is very complex and covers a very long period, from 6000BC and even before.

Short extracts of interesting events and an outline of the local history of each port (where data is available) have been given throughout this pilot book for further study, and on page 29 will be found a chronological list of events to act as a framework for any reading or study. Below is a list of names of ports through the ages, showing how they have changed.

Western Mediterranean port names through the ages

Greek Epoch	Roman Epoch	XIth century	XIIIth century	XVth century	XVIIIth century	Modern
	Arelate	Arelate	Arles	Arles		Arles
	Fossae Marianae	Fossas	Fos	Fos		Fos
	Maritima	Maritima	Martigues		Martigues	Martigues
				Bouc	Port de Bouc	Port de Bouc
	Dilis					Carro
	Incarus					Carry le Rouet
Massalia	Massilia	Marsilia	Marseille	Marseille	Marseille	Marseille
	Aemines					Port Miou
	Carcisis				Cassis	Cassis
Citharista	Citharista			La Ciotat	La Ciotat	La Ciotat
						La Madrague
					St-Nazaire	Sanary
Tauroentium						Le Brusc
Telo	Telo Martius	Tolonum	Toulon	Toulon	Toulon	Toulon
					St-Georges	St-Mandrier
Olbia	Olbia		Hyères	Hyères		Hyères
	Pomponiana					Giens
Pergantion						Brégançon
	Bormani					Bormes
Heraclia	Heraclea				Le Lavandou	Le Lavandou
Caccaboria	Caccoboria				Cavalaire	Cavalaire
Athenopolis				St-Tropez	St-Tropez	St-Tropez
	Forum Jullii	Forum Jullii	Fréjus	Fréjus		Fréjus
					St-Raphaël	St-Raphaël
	Lero		Lerins			Iles de Lerins
		Canua	Cannes	Cannes	Cannes	Cannes
Antipolis	Antipolis	Antipolis	Antibes	Antibes	Antibes	Antibes
Nikaia	Nicaea	Nicia	Nice	Nice	Nice	Nice
	Cemelenum	Cemelenum				
	Olivula			Villefranche	Villefranche	Villefranche
Monoikos	Portus Herculis Monoeci			Monaco	Monaco	Monaco

Routes to the Mediterranean

United Kingdom to the Mediterranean

General

There are three main routes to the Mediterranean from the UK.

- The sea route around Spain and Portugal and through the Strait of Gibraltar. This route is obligatory to the larger yachts which draw too much water for the canals, but has an advantage, as it is possible to visit very pleasant harbours on the way out and to see some interesting countries, although it entails a major sea voyage.
- The canal route via Paris and Lyon, by one or more of the many different canal systems from several English Channel to several Mediterranean harbours. This route has the shortest sea crossing and passes through some beautiful scenery, but it is in total a lengthy journey as the canals are not direct. The dangerous lower reaches of the River Rhône are now canalised and present no difficulty.
- By sea to the Gironde estuary and by the Canal du Midi to several Mediterranean ports. The shortest route and certainly the most beautiful, though it entails a longish sea voyage down the Biscay coast; however, there are many attractive harbours to visit on this route.

It is quite impossible to describe in detail the above routes in a book of this nature but the following notes may assist.

Selection of the route

The selection of the actual route to be used should be made after careful consideration of the following factors:

- Time available, bearing in mind the speed of the vessel, speed limits and the fact that canals are

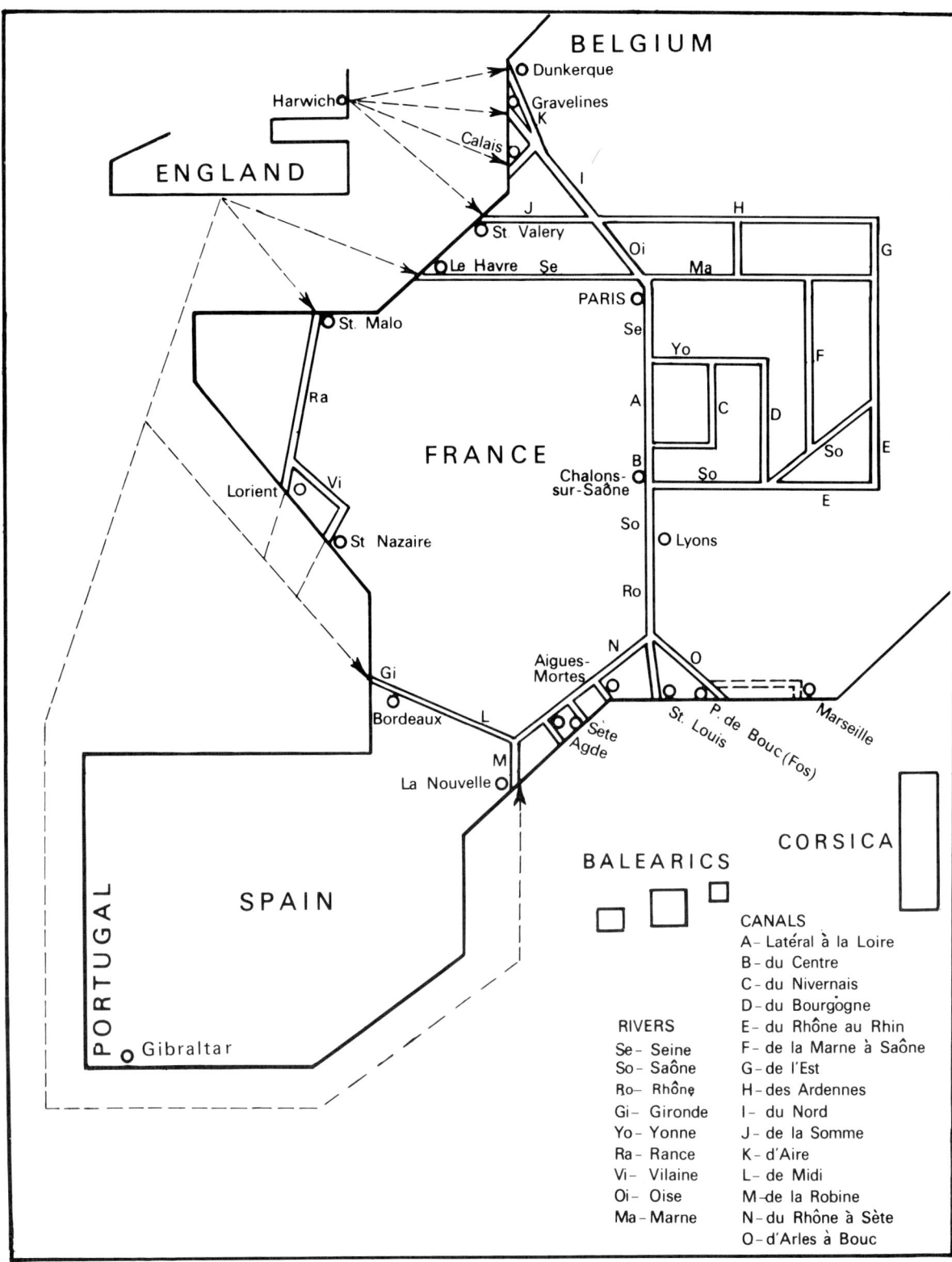

Routes to the Mediterranean

only open by day; allow 30 minutes per lock.
- Draught, height, beam and length of vessel – will it be small enough for the canal?
- Strength and capabilities of the crew. A strong crew is desirable for a sea voyage, and is also required in the canals if you are in a hurry.
- The wish to see other harbours and countries on the way out.
- If it is practical or desirable to remove and stow the mast on deck and to restep it on arrival in the Mediterranean.
- The comparative number of locks and the comparative distances.
- Is the canal open during the period concerned?

Sources of information

For those who may wish to make use of the canals detailed information may be obtained from:
- The French Government Tourist Office, 178 Piccadilly, London WIV 0AL, which provides several useful brochures and maps free of charge. It also has for sale guides and maps produced by the Touring Club de France which are worth having.
- *Inland Waterways of France* by D. Edwards-May (Imray, Laurie, Norie & Wilson). A comprehensive guide to all of the canals of France, fully illustrated with maps, available from most yachting bookshops. Also a separate map of the same title.
- *Notes on French Inland Waterways.* Cruising Association.
- *Afloat in France.* French Government Tourist Office.
- *Cruising French Waterways.* Hugh McKnight. Published by Stanford Maritime.
- *Cartes et Guide Vagnon de Navigation Fluviale.* A set of 9 atlases covering the through routes. Published in France with English translations. (Obtainable from Imray, Laurie, Norie & Wilson.)
- *Navicarte. Guide Fluviaux.* A set of atlases covering the navigable waterways. (Obtainable from Imray, Laurie, Norie & Wilson Ltd.)
- The Michelin series of maps and guides makes a useful adjunct to the above books; the series can be obtained from most large bookshops.
- There are a number of books of varying quality providing background information on the canals and France which can be studied at large bookshops. Prospective purchasers should realise that there are on the market a number of catchpenny books which are in fact almost useless. Imray, Laurie, Norie & Wilson Ltd will provide assistance in obtaining publications.

Bibliography

Navigational
Admiralty publications. Published by the Hydrographer of the Navy
Sailing Directions No. 46, Mediterranean Pilot Vol. II and supplement, South Coast of France, Corsica and Southwest Coast of Italy. Inclined to be out of date and caters for large warships and commercial vessels of over 1000 tons. (*NP 46*)
List of Lights, Vol. E Mediterranean, Black and Red Seas. (*NP 78*)
List of Radio Signals
Vol. 1 Part I Coast Radio Stations. (*NP 281 (1)*)
Vol. 2 Radio Direction Finding Stations, Radiobeacons, Coast Radar Stations and Radar Beacons. (*NP 282*)
Vol. 3 Radio Weather Messages Services and Navigational warnings. (*NP 283*)
Vol. 4 Meteorological Observation Stations. (*NP 284*)
Vol. 6 Part I Port Operations, Pilot Services and Traffic Management. (*NP 286 (1)*)

French Navy Publications. Published by Service Hydrographique de la Marine
Instructions Nautiques Series 'D' Vol.II, Mer Méditerranée, Côtes de France *Fascicule No. 2 des Corrections.* Covers the same area as this book and is the same as the Admiralty pilot but includes information for yachtsmen. It has a separate volume with harbour plans and photographs of the coast.

Other publications

Foreign Port Information Folio. Mediterranean France by the Royal Cruising Club, available only to members of the RCC and the Cruising Club of America. The Cruising Association also holds a copy.

Votre Livre de Bord Méditerranée. Bloc Marin. Distributed in Britain by Imray, Laurie, Norie & Wilson Ltd. A kind of Reed's *Almanac* with excellent plans and many advertisements, published yearly.

Guides Pratiques des Ports. Jacques Anglès (Editions du Pen Duick). Similar to but not as complete as *Votre Livre de Bord.*

Annuaire de Nautisme (Les Editions de Chabassol). A yearly publication which provides the names, addresses and phone numbers of all firms and persons connected with yachting for every French port.

Portulans – Nos 507/8 de Port de Bouc à Cap d'Agde and *503 de Toulon à Cavalaire.* Detailed guides with excellent photographs and charts covering small sections of the French coast.

Pilot Côtier No. 3 Fenwick Alain Rondeau (Praxys Diffusion). A series of small guides in French with many photographs. Nos. 1, 2 and 3 cover the South of France and La Corse.

Mediterranean France and Corsica – A sea guide. Rod Heikell. Imray, Laurie, Norie & Wilson Ltd.

Background

The South of France by Archibald Lyall (Collins). Interesting details of the area.

Sea of Seas by H. Scott (Van Nostrand). A half-guide, half-story covering the West Mediterranean, very out of date and now out of print, but a delightful book to read.

By Way of the Golden Isles by Anthony Rushworth Lund (Chapman and Hall). A pleasing description of a voyage.

Les Guides Michelin, Provence and Côte d'Azur – excellent background information.

Yachtsman's Eight Language Dictionary by Barbara Webb (Adlard Coles). Technical dictionary.

West of the Rhône by Freda White (Faber). A readable guide to Languedoc-Roussillon and the Massif Central.

Languedoc Roussillon by Neil Lands, published by Spurbooks Ltd, also *The French Pyrenees*, by the same author and publisher. Both are excellent and interesting works.

PART II
Languedoc-Roussillon

Introduction

General description

The 140-mile section of coast which starts at Cabo Falco on the Franco-Spanish frontier and stretches as far as the mouth of the rivière la Rhône consists of two completely different types of coast. The first eight miles commencing from Cabo Falco have a rocky coast with cliffs broken by inlets and headlands and high mountains close inland. This area, called *la Côte Vermeille* (the Vermilion Coast), is the NE end of the Pyrénées chain of mountains, and is similar to the Spanish Costa Brava (the Wild Coast) which adjoins it to the S. The dark red appearance of the rocks gives the name to this stretch of coast.

Cap Béar, a very prominent headland, divides this first section of coast into two almost equal parts. To the S of Cap Béar and facing E are two minor harbours while to the N of it are one major and one minor port facing N. This distribution of harbours allows the yachtsman to select the one most suited to the wind direction, which is of great value on a part of the coast where winds can be severe.

The remaining 132 miles of coast are monotonous, consisting as they do of an almost straight coastline that gently curves round to the E with long low flat sandy stretches of beach backed by very low sand dunes and *étangs*. Where there are hills of any consequence they are ten miles or more inland. This coast is broken every so often by the mouths of rivers and *graus* (natural canals) leading to one of the many *étangs* (inland salt or brackish water lagoons) that lie behind the sand dunes. The only small hills on the coast are at Leucate, Agde and Sète and by virtue of the miles of flat surroundings they can be seen from afar. This section of coast is called the *la Côte d'Or* (the Golden Coast).

The whole coast was virtually deserted with the exception of the old harbours of La Nouvelle, Agde and Sète and a few small holiday resorts until the last decade when the French government decided to develop the area as a holiday and yachting complex on a scale never before attempted.

There are now constructed, in the process of construction or being planned, a whole series of artificial yacht harbours, marinas and holiday centres complete with all the necessary ancillary buildings and equipment.

It is unfortunate that despite the fact that a number of architects have produced different designs for these yacht harbours, not one blends in with the area. Every dozen or so miles along the coast a monstrous mass of concrete is found around a yacht harbour which once entered seems very similar to the last one visited. As development proceeds, shrubs and trees are planted and more people occupy these complexes, their harsh angular outlines will blend better into the surroundings. There is no doubt that these harbours are efficient in that they provide all the requirements for yachtsmen and holidaymakers, and many will like to sail or motor the few miles from one harbour to the next, leaving and arriving at a berth which has all the necessary facilities available a few yards away.

The older ports, on the other hand, although they do not have all the convenient facilities of the new harbours, are at least attractive, interesting and full of life and colour. This area has a large number of interesting and historic places to visit inland. It has many well-known vineyards located not far from the coast. Wine can usually be bought direct from the château.

WARNINGS
Winds and seas

NW tramontane/mistral This section of coast being flat and lying between the Pyrénées, a wall-like chain of mountains, and the area covered by the Massif Central, form a natural corridor down which blows the NW *tramontane/mistral* with undiminished fury and little warning. This wind, which is the most frequent and strongest, blows on an average 103 days at force 6 (21 to 27 knots), 64 days at force 7 (28 to 32 knots), 30 days at force 8 (33 to 40 knots) and 11 days at force 9 (40 knots) and above, making a total 208 days of wind from this direction in the year. The worst time is early spring. Winds from other directions are nothing like as frequent, the SE and NE winds are the most usual. See windroses, page 37.

It is almost certain that a yacht cruising on this coast will encounter a *tramontane/mistral* and therefore contingency plans should always be made

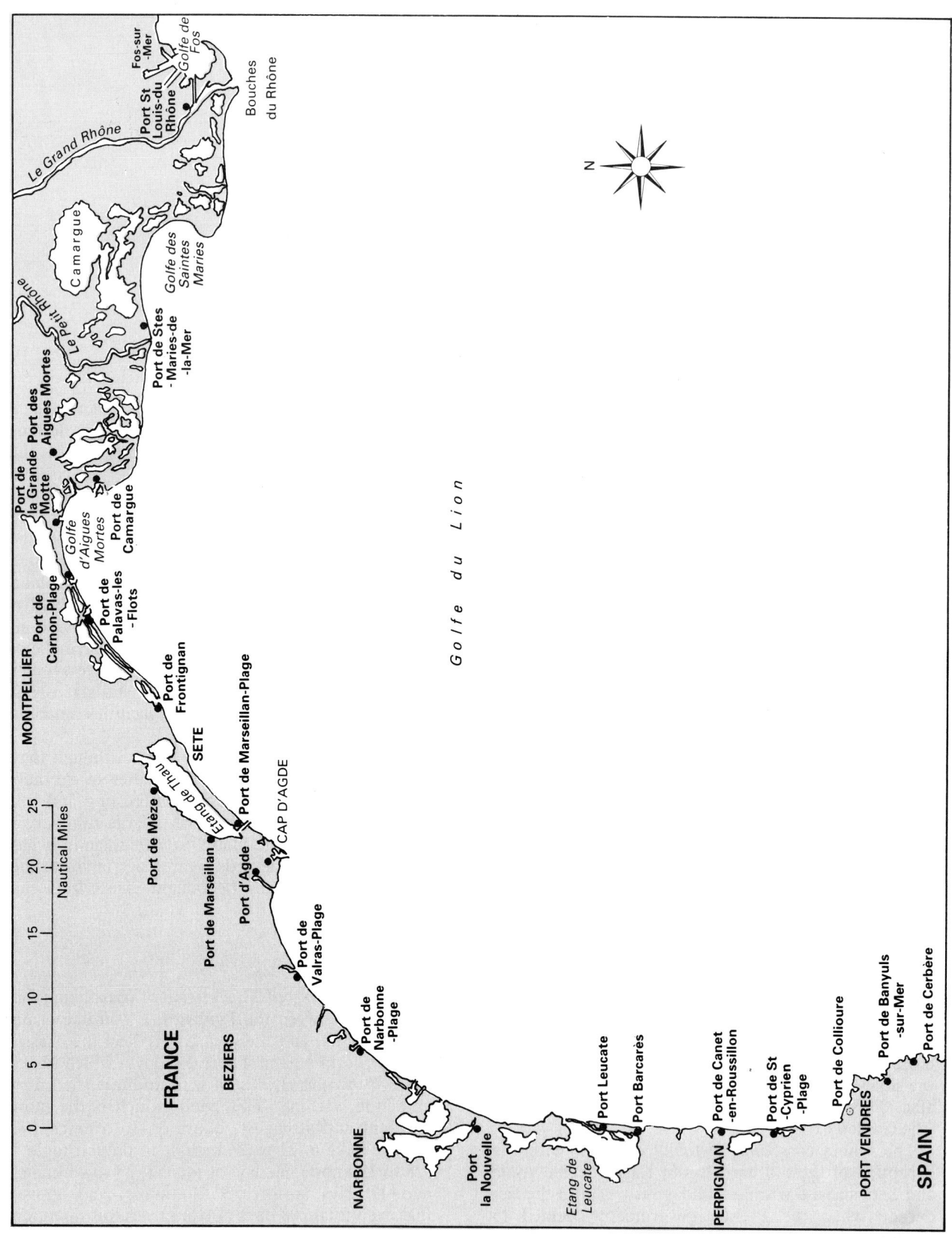

as to the action to be taken. A radio watch should be kept on Radio Marseille at H+03 and H+33 when gale warnings are given. In addition a radio watch should be kept on VHF Ch 9 when within 30M of the coast for warnings of gales and weather forecasts. See also page 16.

A yacht wishing to cross the Golfe du Lion is advised to follow the coast so that shelter can quickly be obtained, this is essential in winter. Away from the land a really vicious sea can develop in a remarkably short time and it will be found impossible to make any headway against the wind and sea. The only course remaining open is to run for the Spanish coast or the Balearic Islands.

If caught by this wind while coasting get as close inshore as the draught will permit and make all speed for the nearest harbour. It should be remembered that the wind usually builds up to gale force in a matter of a quarter of an hour and it is essential to be able to make to windward once inside the harbour mouth. Although the water may be comparatively calm a powerful engine and a handy craft are necessary to be able to do this. Many craft which do not have powerful enough

FLAGS	LIGHTS	WIND STRENGTHS
One Green Flag	No Light	Force 0 to 3 0 to 10 knots 0 to 0.50 metre waves
One Red Flag	Interrupted Quick Flashing 10 seconds	Force 4 and 5 11 to 21 knots 0.50 to 1.25 metre waves
Two Red Flags	Interrupted Quick Flashing 4 seconds	Force 6 to 8 22 to 40 knots 1.25 to 2.50 metre waves
One Black Flag	Quick Flashing	Force 8 and greater Waves over 2.50 metres

Ports du littoral Languedoc-Roussillon
Signals of wind speed (measured at the port)

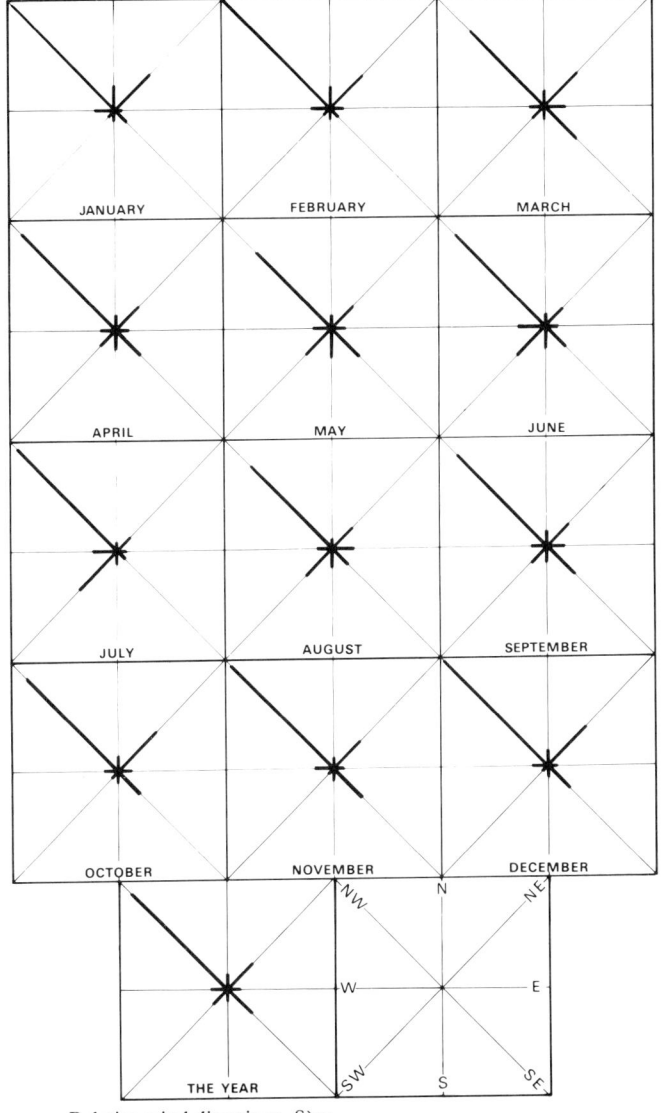

Relative wind directions. Sète

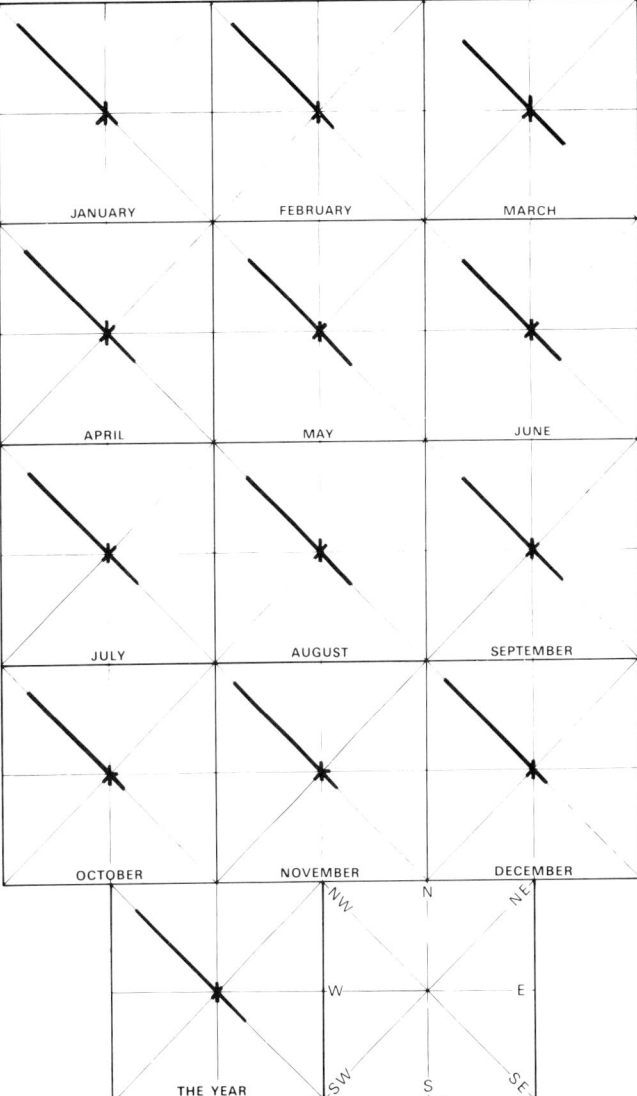

Relative wind directions. Cap Béar

engines or which are not sufficiently handy to make to windward in confined waters in a gale come to grief in the mouth of the harbour or fail even to enter and have to spend a miserable time at sea until the wind drops, which has been known to take longer than a week though more usually three days.

Shallow-draught craft caught out in one of these winds should consider the advisability of running the craft ashore onto a sandy beach and taking mooring lines and chain to any solid object available. Larger craft have been known to do the same in an emergency. Note that in general an offshore wind will lower the sea level and an onshore wind raise the level.

NE–E–SE Marin Because this is a gently shelving sandy shore without any offshore obstructions, swell generated by winds from the NE–E–SE can reach a dangerous state some distance offshore and after strong and prolonged winds from a seaward direction, breaking waves may be encountered as far out as the 20m contour line some 2M offshore.

In these conditions it is quite impossible to approach and enter the majority of the new harbours. Even the big old ports of Port Vendres, La Nouvelle and Sète may be closed, and yachts should keep well out to sea away from the lee shore until the swell diminishes sufficiently for them to enter a large port. Happily the duration of these winds is usually short.

Shelter in harbour from wind and sea Virtually every harbour on this coast offers shelter from the seas once entered, though some may become uncomfortable owing to the swell finding its way around the jetties or to a short chop developing due to a large area of open water. Details are given in the section dealing with the port concerned.

Shelter from the wind, especially the NW *tramontane*, is more difficult to find. The ports of Sète and Vendres offer fair shelter but most of the new harbours offer very little though this is improved as buildings are erected. Shelter is very necessary for yachts wintering in the area, as wind speeds of 120 knots, well over force 12 (64 knots), have been recorded and houses, trains and bridges have been blown over.

Restricted areas

Collioure There is a firing range just NW of Collioure for the commandos stationed there. A red flag is hoisted on a mast at the fort when this is in use.

L'Aude A firing range exists about 6M SW of the mouth of l'Aude. When it is in use two red flags are hoisted on a mast to S of la Maison de Pêch Rouge.

Leucate An air-to-sea firing range extends 13M along the coast and 12M out to sea at Cap Leucate.

Palavas A firing range exists in front of Palavas. Firing is announced by four shots from a gun. There is also an air-to-sea firing range in the same area. Special announcements are made if this range is to be used.

Anchoring and fishing are prohibited within an area about 1½M wide at its centre about 2M offshore between Banyuls and Canet. Navigation is also restricted or controlled in the approaches to Port la Nouvelle, Sète and Pte de l'Espiguette where tankers have special access channels.

Artificial reefs 15,000 cubic metres of concrete blocks with a height of 4·5m have been sunk in areas along the Languedoc–Roussillon coast in about 25m depth for breeding areas for fish and crustaceans – see charts for location.

Data

Charts The area charts for this section of coast are as follows:
Admiralty 1705
French 7008, 6951. Large scale charts are listed with the ports concerned.
Spanish 876, 49
Navicarte 507, 508, 509, 510, 511

Tides The tidal range in this part of the Mediterranean reaches a maximum of 0·15m (0·5ft) at springs and is barely detectable at neaps. For all practical purposes, tidal height and streams can be disregarded.

Currents There is a permanent current that flows along this coast in a W-going direction of 0·5 to 1 knot. In the Golfe d'Aigues Mortes a small clockwise circulation is produced by the Pointe d'Espiguette. This normal current when reinforced by the wind blowing in the same direction can reach 4 knots off points and headlands. Conversely it is slowed down by winds from other directions. The current tends to follow the coast so its direction changes to SW and S further along the coast.

Sea levels Strong winds from the SE raise the sea level up to 1m (3ft). Similarly strong NW winds can lower the level by 0·5m (1·5ft) below mean level. This change in level which can take place in a few hours causes very strong currents in the *graus* and canals leading to the *étangs* which may reach 5 knots.

Navigational warnings Keep a radio watch on VHF Ch 9 for warnings of navigational importance when within 10M of the coast.

Marine radiobeacons
Cap Béar BR (— ··· / — ·) 313·5kHz 50M
Sète SÉ (··· / ·· — ··) 287·5kHz 50M
Cap Couronne CR (— · — · / · — ·) 295·5kHz 50M
Porquerolles PQ (· — — · / — — · —) 314kHz 200M

Air radiobeacons
The following air radiobeacons operate in the area but may not transmit continuously:
Nice, Mont Leuza LEZ (· — ·· / · / — — ··) 399kHz 75M
43°43'·52N 7°19'·63E

VHF Direction-finding service

This service is for Emergency use only. Each VHF direction-finding station is remotely controlled either by a Regional Operational Centre for Surveillance and Rescue (CROSS)[1], Signal Station or Naval Lookout Station.

1For operational details of CROSS stations see *Admiralty List of Radio Signals Vol 3 NP 283* and *Vol 6(1) NP 286(1)*

CROSS Stations watch on Ch 16, 11; 67, (when a maritime rescue operation is already underway on Ch 11).

Signal stations and lookout stations keep a priority watch on Ch 16. Also available are 7 additional frequencies retained in memory (scanner sweeping) from amongst the following channels:

1-29	156·050MHz –157·450MHz
36	162·400MHz
39	162·550MHz
48	121·500MHz
50	155·525MHz
52	155·625MHz
55	155·775MHz
56	155·825MHz
60-88	156·025MHz – 157·425MHz

Ship transmits on Ch 16 (distress only) or Ch 11 in order that the station can determine its bearing.

Ship's bearing from the station is transmitted on Ch 16 (distress only) or Ch 11.

Hours of watch continuous. Controlled by Sig Stn unless otherwise stated.

La Garde RG Controlled by CROSS 43°06.3N 5°59.5E
Cap Bèar RG 42°30′·8N 3°08′E
Cap Leucate RG 42°55′·1N 3°03′·7E
Sète RG 43°23′·8N 3°41′·5E

Coast radio stations

St Lys (FFL-FFS-FFT)

R/T watch on 4366, 8806, 13152, 17323, 22771kHz Continuous. The above coast radio station operates on this coast but it is normally only used for commercial purposes. Traffic lists on 4366, 8806, 13152, 17323, 22771kHz every H+03 and H+30 (0700–2230) so far as possible. See *Admiralty List of Radio Signals Vol. 1 NP 281(1)* for full details also WT(MF) service of stations listed below.

Perpignan
VHF Ch 02, 16 Continuous. Call *Marseille Radio.*

Marseille (FFM)
R/T 1671, 1906, 1936, 1939, 2625, 2628, 3792, 3795, 2182kHz 1kW. Traffic lists on 1906kHz at every odd H+10.
VHF Ch 16, 24, 26 Continuous. Call *Marseille Radio.*

Martigues
VHF Ch 16, 27, 28 Continuous. Call *Marseille Radio.*

Sète
VHF Ch 16, 19. Continuous. Call *Marseille Radio.*
Details for automatic calls see *Admiralty List of Radio Signals Vol. 1 NP 281(1).*

Weather forecasts

This section of coast is covered by Area No. 521 Golfe du Lion and the most effective weather forecast is from Marseille (FFM). This station also broadcasts storm warnings every odd H+10. Weather forecasts by radio are available as follows:

Marseille (FFM) 1906kHz at 0103, 0705, 1220, 1615 UT and on request. VHF Chs 24, 26.
Radio France-Marseille 675kHz 150M at 0555, 1905
Perpignan VHF Ch 02 at 0633, 1133 UT[1]
Sète VHF Ch 19 at 0633, 1133 UT[1]
Agde (CROSS) Pic de Neoulos VHF Ch 09 at 0715, 1730

UT[1] Agde VHF Ch 09 at 1720, 1735 UT[1]. This station operates July and August only
[1]Transmits one hour earlier during summer time (DST)

Weather forecasts By phone are available as follows:

Perpignan Station météo, aerodrome, ☎ 68 61 03 38 and 68 61 03 39, automatic pre-recorded forecast ☎ 68 61 03 92.
Montpellier Station météo, aerodrome, ☎ 68 92 91 41, automatic pre-recorded forecast ☎ 68 92 90 30.

Major light and fog signals

Cabo Creus Fl(2)W.10s87m20M White round tower on dwelling. Fog siren Mo(C)40s. (Aeromarine light)
Cap Béar Fl(3)W.15s80m30M RC Pale red pyramid tower, grey corners Vis 146°-056°
Perpignan-Rivesalte Aero Mo(X)W.8·5s58m33M Pylon
Cap Leucate Fl(2)W.10s66m20M White pyramidal tower, red top, grey corners
Ilot Brescou Fl(2)WR.6s22m13/10M White tower, red top. 113°-R-190°-W-133°. 2 F.R on radio masts 1·9M NW
Sète Mont Saint-Clair Fl.W.5s93m29M White 8-sided tower, green lantern. W (unitens) 013°-104° (91°)
Pointe de l'Espiguette Fl(3)W.15s27m24M White square tower, black top
Beauduc Fl(2)R.10s26m16M White and black tower, white cupola
Faraman Fl(2)W.10s41m23M Black tower white bands.

Visits

Local places of interest to visit are detailed in the section dealing with the harbour concerned. There are also many other places further inland that can be visited by bus, rail or taxi. Details of these can usually be obtained from the nearest office of the Syndicat d'Initiative which should always be visited when any length of time is spent in a port as more comprehensive details of the harbour and its surroundings together with a street map can usually be obtained free and this can make the stay more interesting.

A few of the places of special interest situated some distance inland are listed below:

Elne The pre-Roman capital of Roussillon which has many very old buildings and a world-famous cloister.
Perpignan The present capital of Roussillon which has many interesting 14th to 17th-century buildings.
Salses Where there is a magnificent castle.
Narbonne The Roman capital of the province which has many old and attractive buildings and excellent museums.
Carcassonne A fortified medieval town that has been fully restored and is one of the wonders of France.
Montpellier The capital of Languedoc and of ancient origin. There are a large number of ancient buildings to be seen.
Nîmes One of the original Roman towns which still has a fantastic amphitheatre that could hold 20,000. There are also numerous other Roman remains.

There are many other equally interesting places to visit in addition to those mentioned above.

History

To write even a brief history for this section of the coast is almost impossible because of its series of seaborne invasions, conquests and occupations by the Ligurians (1000 BC), the Greeks (600 BC), the Romans (100 BC), the Saracens (800 AD), the landborne invasions of the Barbarians including the Vandals, Suèves, Alains (409 AD) and Visigoths (413 AD), not to mention the fraternal internecine wars between the various powerful nobles and landowners. Over and above all this was a long series of wars and skirmishes between France and Spain over their frontiers, as often as not conducted by local nobles and their private armies. Because of the size of the area many of these events were of a local nature and affected only one town or department. The result is that the history of one town or area is quite different from another that of not so far away.

Some details of the history of various ports and harbours have been given in the section dealing with the place concerned and more details are usually available from the information bureau of the Syndicat d'Initiative.

Planning guide

Ports, harbours, anchorages, headlands, islands, passages and special features

Note This guide lists features in a NE direction from the Spanish frontier to l'Embouchure du Rhône. There are other fair weather anchorages to be found which are not listed below; additional anchorages are detailed in the sections dealing with the various harbours and ports.

Distances	Headlands and features	Ports, anchorages and landings Spanish frontier	Open to winds from
	Cabo Falco		
		⚓ *Plage du Mineral*	NE–E–SE–S
	Cap Cerbère		
½M		⚓ *Plage d'el Canu*	N–NE–E
		⚓ *La Cova*	NE–E–SE
		1 Port de Cerbère 4–3–4 page 43	
		⚓ *NE of harbour breakwater*	NE–E–SE
	Cap Canadell		
		⚓ *Anse de Terrambou*	NE–E–SE
	Cap de Peyrefite		
		⚓ *Anse de Peyrefite*	NE–E–SE
3M	Cap Réderis		
		⚓ *NE of Cap Réderis*	NW–N–NE–E–SE
		⚓ *S of Cap de l'Abeille*	NW–N–NE–E–SE
	Cap de l'Abeille		
		⚓ *300m to E of Cap du Troc*	NW–N–NE–E
	Cap du Troc		
		⚓ *Plage du Troc*	NW–N–NE–E
		2 Port de Banyuls-sur-Mer 4–3–4 page 47	
	Cap d'Osne		
		⚓ *Below Cap d'Osne*	N–NE–E–SE
		⚓ *Plage des Elmes*	N–NE–E–SE
	Cap des Elmes		
		⚓ *Plage N of Cap des Elmes*	NE–E–SE
	Large hospital		
	Cap Castell		
1½M		⚓ *Very small to N of Cap Castell*	NE–E–SE
		⚓ *to S of Cap Oullestrell*	NE–E–SE
	Cap Oullestrell		
		⚓ *Plage d'el Forat*	N–NE–E
		3 Port Pierre Méry (projected) page 51	
		⚓ *Anse de Paullilles*	N–NE–E–SE
		⚓ *Plage de Bernardi*	NE–E–SE
3M		⚓ *Plage Balanti*	NE–E–SE–S
		⚓ *Anse Ste Catherine*	NE–E–SE
	Cap Béar		

		4 Port Vendres 2–3–2 page 52	
	Cap Gross	⌇ *Anse de la Mauresque*	N–NE–E
		⌇ *Plage d'en Baux*	NW–N–NE
1M		⌇ *Plage de l'Huile*	NW–N–NE
	Punta del Raguès	⌇ *Anse del Raguès*	NW–N–NE
		5 Port de Collioure 2–3–4 page 58	
		⌇ *Plage de l'Ouille*	NW–N–NE–E
		⌇ *Anse de Portell*	NW–N–NE
1½M		⌇ *Le Racou Plage*	NW–N–NE–E
		6 Port d'Argelès-Plage 3–2–3 page 61 **(Racou)**	
	Grau de la Ribérette	*Etang de Leucate (Salses)*	
5M	Rivière le Tech		
	Grau de Etang de Canet (St-Nazaire)		
5M		**7 Port de St-Cyprien-Plage** 3–2–3 page 64	
5M		**8 Port de Canet-en-Roussillon** 3–2–3 page 68 **(St-Nazaire)**	
1M	Rivière la Têt		
		9 Port de Ste Marie-la-Plage 3–4–3 page 71 **(La Mer)**	
	Etang de Leucate (Salses)		
	Grau et Rivière		
	Bourdigoul		
5M	Rivière l'Agly		
		10 Port Barcarès 3–3–3 page 75 **(Le Grau St-Ange)**	
4½M	*Lydia* ship on beach		
		11 Port Leucate 3–3–2 page 78	
	Grau de Leucate (Port Ostreicole)		
8M	Cap Leucate		
		⌇ *NW Cap Leucate*	NW–N–NE–E–SE
		⌇ *La Franqui Plage*	N–NE–E–SE
	Grau de Etang de Ayrolle	**12 Port la Nouvelle** 2–3–3 page 83	
5½M			
		13 Port la Nautique 3–3–3 page 87	
		14 Port de Gruissan-Vieux 2–4–4 page 90 **(Barberousse)**	
1M			
		15 Port de Gruissan-Neuf 3–3–2 page 93	
4M	Les Ayguades (Grau de Pêch Rouge)		
		16 Port de Narbonne-Plage 3–3–3 page 98 **(St-Pierre-sur-Mer)**	
3M	Rocher St-Pierre	⌇ *St Pierre-la-Mer*	NE–E–SE–S
		17 Port des Cabanes de Fleury 3–3–4 page 100 **(Embouchure de l'Aude)** **(Grau de Vendres)**	
3M			
		18 Port de Valras-Plage 3–3–3 page 104 **(Port de l'Orb)**	
	La Grand Maire		
6M	Ancien Grau de Libron		
	La Tramarissiere		
		19 Port de Grau d'Agde 3–3–3 page 108	
2M			
		20 Port d'Agde 2–3–2 page 110	
3M	Ilot et Fort Brescou	⌇ *Rade de Brescou*	E–SE–S–SW–W
		21 Port de Cap d'Agde 2–2–2 page 113	
1½M			
		⌇ *SW of Cap d'Agde*	NE–E–SE–S
	Cap d'Agde		
		⌇ *La Conque*	NE–E–SE–S
		⌇ *Roquitte*	NE–E–SE–S

2M		**22** **Port Ambonne** 3–3–3 page 118 **(Port Nature)**
1½M	Etang de Thau (Bassin de Thau)	**23** **Port de Marseillan-Plage** 4–3–4 page 124
		⚓ *Anchorage possible in most areas of the Etang*
1M	Pointe des Onglous (Canal du Midi)	**24** **Port des Onglous** 4–3–4 page 127
	Pointe de Montpenèdre	**25** **Port de Marseillan-Ville** 2–3–4 page 129
3M		
2½M	Cap de Tourre	**26** **Port le Mourre-Blanc** 4–3–4 page 131
		27 **Port de Mèze** 2–3–3 page 132
3M		
2M	Pointe de Balaruc (Roquerols beacon)	**28** **Port Bouzigues** 3–3–3 page 135
		29 **Port de Balaruc-les-Bains** 4–3–4 page 137 **Port de Balaruc-les-Usines**
1½M	Basin des Eaux Blanches (Canal de Rhône à Sète)	
		30 **Ports de Barrou Maritime and** **Base Nautique** 4–3–4 page 141
2½M	Base Nautique Pointe de Barrou	
		31 **Port des Quilles** 4–3–4 page 142
		⚓ *Off les Quilles* SW–W
	Pointe du Lazaret	⚓ *Crique de l'Anau* E–SE–S–SW
2M	Cap de Sète	**32** **Port de Sète** 2–2–2 page 145
3M		**33** **Port de la Peyrade** 4–3–3 page 151
1½M		**34** **Port de Frontignan** 3–3–3 page 153
9M		⚓ *Les Bancs de Maguelonne* NE–E–SE–S–SW
		35 **Port de Palavas-les-Flots** 4–3–3 page 157 **(Grau du Palavas)**
2M		**36** **Port de Carnon-Plage** 3–3–3 page 161 **(Grau de Perois)**
4M	Petit Tavers tower and air radiobeacon	
		37 **Port de la Grande Motte** 3–2–2 page 165
2M		⚓ *Etang du Ponant* SW
		38 **Port de Grau du Roi** 3–2–3 page 168
3M		**39** **Port des Aigues Mortes** 1–3–3 page 172
4M		**40** **Port de Camargue** 2–2–3 page 175 **(Port de l'Espiguette)**
	Pointe de l'Espiguette	
7M		**41** **Port de Grau d'Orgon** 3–4–3 page 179 **(Mouth of the Petit Rhône)**
1M	Golfe des Saintes Maries La Gacholle Lt Ho	
		42 **Port Gardia** 3–3–3 page 182 **(Port des Stes-Maries-de-la-Mer)**
		⚓ *Beauduc. Golfe des Saintes Maries.* SW–W–NW *Delta du Rhône*
25M	Pointe de Beauduc Lt Ho Faraman Lt Ho Mouth of Le Grand Rhône They de la Gracieuse	
		Part III. West Côte d'Azur
2M		**43** **Port de Carteau** 4–4–5 page 197
		44 **Port St-Louis-du-Rhône**

Pilotage

Cabo Falco

A high rocky cliffed conspicuous headland with isolated rocky outcrops. The French-Spanish frontier runs inland from its highest point; there is a small white building on the top of this headland (170m).

⚓ Plage du Mineral

In a small bay S of Cap Cerbère open to NE–E–SE–S. Some rocks and rocky bottom. Cave in the cliff.

Cap Cerbère

A prominent conspicuous pointed headland (89m) with rocky cliffs and a few isolated rocky islets. The coastal road runs along the crest. A disused light tower (89m) is located on top and an operational light (55m) is situated on the point.

⚓ Plage d'el Canu

A small anchorage on the N side of Cap Cerbère open to N–NE–E.

1 PORT DE CERBERE

66750 Pyrénées Orientales

Position 42°26'·5N 3°10'·2E
Minimum depth   in the entrance 10m (33ft)
                                in the harbour 5 to 1m (16 to 3ft)
Width of the entrance 90m (30ft)
Number of yacht berths 150
Population 1726 (approx)
Rating 4–3–4

General

A small deep *calanque* (creek) which has a small quay with pontoons and space to anchor. It gives some protection from the NW *tramontane* but is open to the NE–E and in these winds becomes dangerous. Approach and entrance are easy. Only limited facilities exist. Although this is the nearest harbour to the Spanish frontier, inwards or outwards customs clearance cannot be carried out here and yachts must clear at Banyuls or Port Vendres.

Data

Charts   Admiralty 1705
            French 6843
            Spanish 876
            Navicarte E03

Magnetic variation 2°09'W (1994) decreasing by about 6' each year.

Speed limit 5 knots.

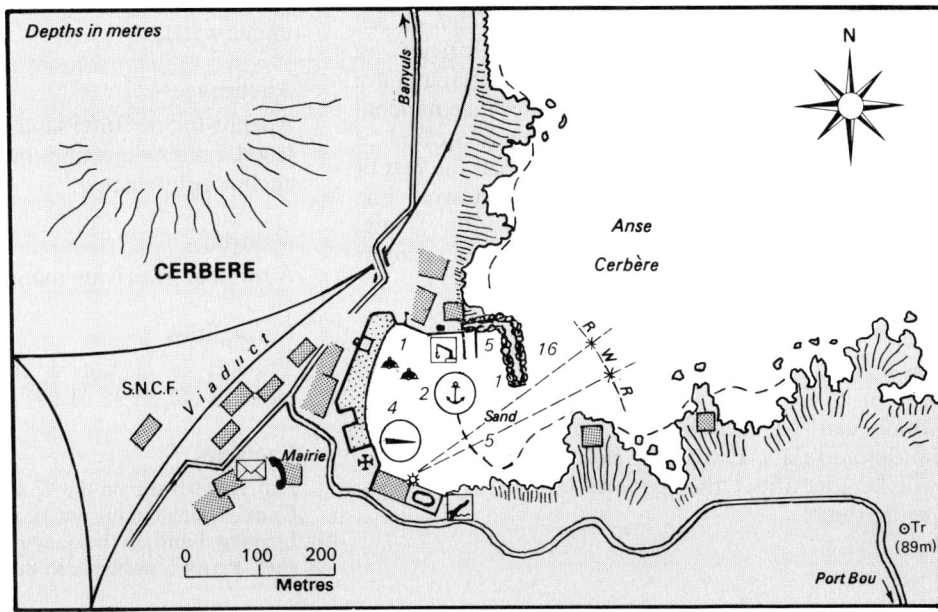

Port de Cerbère

Pontoon Berths

Port de Cerbère looking W

Lights

Cap Cerbère Fl.W.4s55m15M Grey pyramidal tower, red top

Port de Cerbère Fl(2)WR.6s12m9/6M. Red post 202°-W-237°-R-202°

Buoys There are two small yellow conical buoys marking sewage outfalls.

Warning

This harbour being wide open to NE–E is dangerous and must be left at once should winds develop from this direction.

Approach by day

From S Cross the deep Bahía de la Selva and follow the very broken coastline backed by high mountains. There is a series of small deep bays with high-cliffed promontories between which it is difficult to distinguish. Cabo Falco has a triangular shape and a small white hut on top where the international frontier runs. Cap Cerbère may be identified if coasting close in as it projects further than the rest of the headlands and has a lighthouse and tower. The Calanque de Cerbère can be identified by a long railway viaduct on which there is a large customs shed with double arches below.

From N Round the very prominent Cap Béar which has a lighthouse, signal station, radio tower and old fort on it. Cross the wide and deep Baie de Banyuls which can be identified by the concentration of houses and flats. If coasting close in the Cap Cerbère will be identified; the harbour lies in the *calanque* just to the N.

Approach by night

Using the following lights navigate to a position where the harbour lies W 400m:
Cap Béar Fl(3)W.15s30M
Punta Sernella Fl.W.5s13M
Cap Cerbère Fl.W.4s15M

Entrance

By day Approach in the centre of the *calanque* on a SW course.

By night Enter with care in the white sector of Fl(2)WR.6s between 202° and 237°.

Berths

Berth stern to small quay or pontoon in NW corner from bow. Beware of projecting quay wall and rocks under water.

Anchorage

Anchor in 5m (16ft) sand in N corner of the *calanque*. Good holding ground but use an anchor trip line, anchor light/shape.

Moorings

A number of private moorings.

Formalities

Though it is not a customs clearance harbour, customs (☎ 68 38 41 60) may visit yachts.

Facilities

Slip A small slip on the W side of the harbour.
Crane A small crane on the quay.
Landing Land on the quay or sandy beach.
Fuel Petrol is available in the village.

Port de Cerbère looking NE

Water From a small café on the sea front.

Provisions Some shops to SW of the harbour.

Post office The PTT office is on the street which is the concreted bed of a dry river.

Information office In the season the Syndicat d'Initiative has an office in the town hall which is on the way to the post office. (☎ 68 38 42 36)

Visits The Tour de Ker'Roig, a little distance inland, was built in 55 BC.

Beaches A small sandy beach at the W side of the harbour and a swimming pool to SW.

Hotels Two ** and two * hotels.

Restaurants A few small restaurants and some café/bars.

Communications Bus and rail.

Lifeboat Runabout type (☎ 68 38 41 60).

⚓ Just to NE of the harbour breakwater open to NE–E–SE. Coast road and railway on top of cliffs. A few isolated rocks.

Cap Canadell

A rounded cape with rocky cliffs, an offlying group of islets and a marine farm at its foot. Coastal road along the cliff tops. Open to N–NE–E–SE.

⚓ Anse de Terrambou

A large bay open to NE–E–SE. Rocky sides with outliers. Anchor in sand 9m near centre of bay. Coastal railway and road inland. There are two other anchorages in this bay at N and S sides.

Cap de Peyrefite

A lower pointed headland with rocky outcrops on its SE side. A yellow light buoy (Fl.Y.4s) ½M to E marks the SE corner of a marine reserve area.

⚓ Anse Terrambou

⚓ Anse de Peyrefite

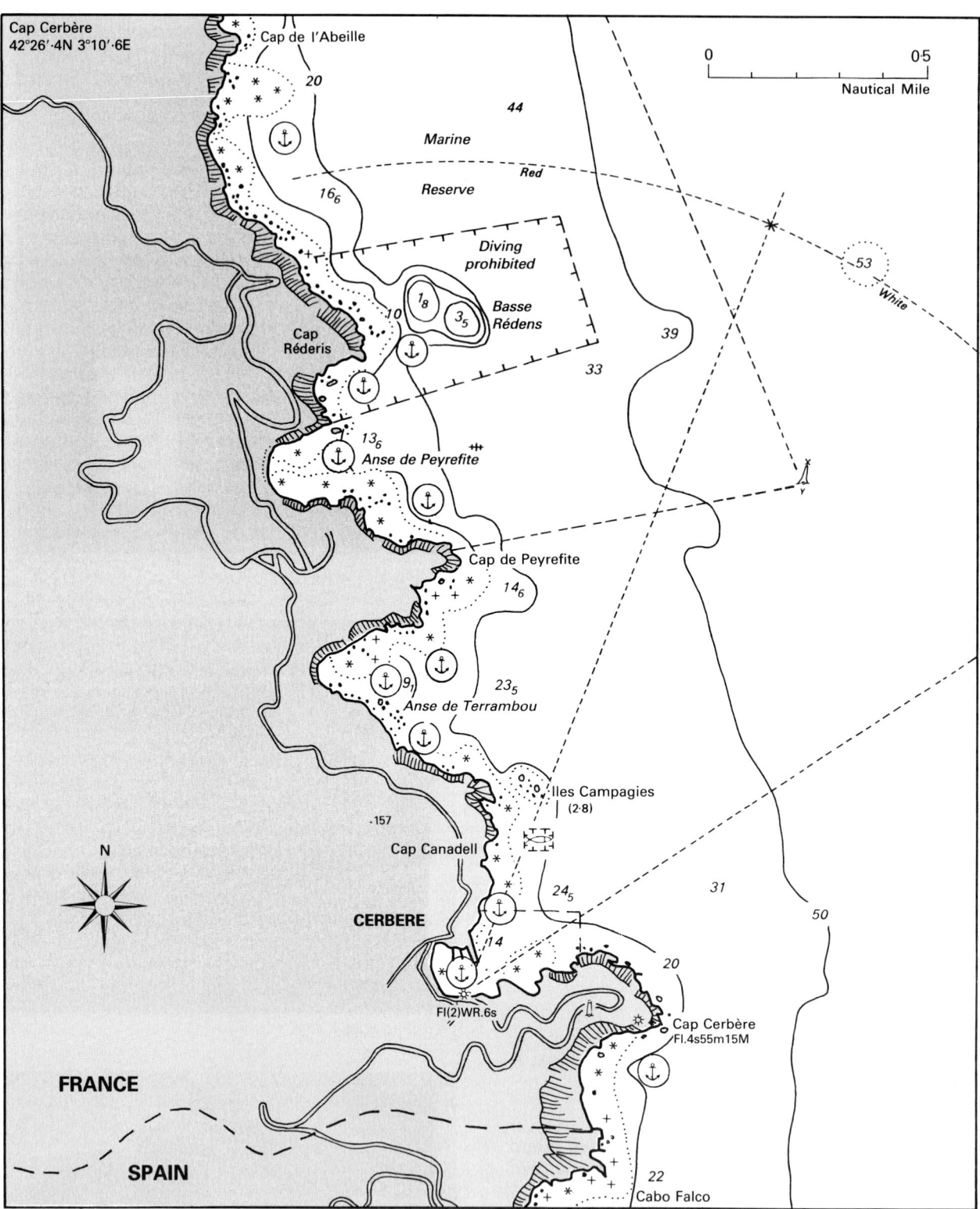

Anchorages north of Cerbère

⚓ Anse de Peyrefite

A large wide bay open to NE–E–SE with two anchorages off sandy beaches. Road and rail close inland. Wreck in about 20m off the centre of the bay's mouth.

Cap Réderis

A small cliffed point with offlying shallows 1·8 and 3·5m to NE. The coast is fringed with rocks on its NE side.

⚓ NE of Cap Réderis and behind the two shallow patches. Subaqua diving is not permitted here. Open to NW–N–NE–E–SE.

Cap de l'Abeille

A prominent high (64m) rocky cliffed point. The coast is lined with rocks. A yellow light buoy Fl.Y.4s lies ½M to NE marking the NE corner of a marine reserve.

⚓ Anchorage to S of Cap de l'Abeille open to N–NE–E–SE. Anchor in 10m mud and sand 500m to S of the Cap. Many rocks close inshore.

⚓ Anchorage 300m to E of Cap du Troc open to NW–N–NE–E.

Cap du Troc

A small point with rocky cliffs; coast road behind. Isolated rocks. Fishing not permitted in the area.

⚓ Small anchorage off Plage du Troc to W of Cap du Troc, sandy beach. Anchor in the middle of the bay 10m sand. Fishing not permitted in the area. Open NW–N–NE–E.

---

2 PORT DE BANYULS-SUR-MER

66650 Pyrénées Orientales

Position 42°29'·9N 3°08'·0E
Minimum depth in the entrance 5m (16ft)
in the harbour 4 to 1·5m (13 to 5ft)
Number of berths 400
Maximum length overall 12m (39ft)
Population 4600 (approx)
Rating 4–3–4

General

A newly-developed yacht harbour in a sheltered bay beside a pleasant town in attractive surroundings. Approach and entrance are easy but would be difficult and dangerous in heavy N–NE–E winds and seas. In these conditions the berths near the harbour entrance become uncomfortable. There are only fair facilities available. Shelter from the seas of the NW *tramontane* is possible here but not from the wind itself.

Data

Charts Admiralty 1705
French 7002
Navicarte 511

Currents A S-going current of 0·5 to 1 knot crosses the mouth of the bay.

Magnetic variation 2°09'W (1994 decreasing by about 6' each year.

Radiobeacon Cap Béar lighthouse BR(— ··· / — ·) 313·5kHz 50M

Weather forecasts These are posted twice daily at the *bureau du port*. Prerecorded forecast (☎ 36 68 08 08 and 36 68 08 66).

Port radio VHF Ch 9. 24hrs.

Speed limit 5 knots within 300m of the shore, 8 knots in the marine reserve area.

Storm signals Storm signals are displayed from the signal station at Cap Béar.

Lights
Ile Petite Fl.WG.4s10m10/7M White tower, dark green top 193°-W-247°-G-193°
Jetée N Est head Oc(2)R.6s10m White column, red top
Jetée N Ouest head Iso.W.4s1m Strip light

Buoys There is a black and yellow buoy about 800m E of Isle Grosse.

Warning

E winds can send very heavy swells into this bay and under these conditions it is not advisable to approach or try to enter the harbour.

During summer months a line of small yellow buoys is laid across the mouth of the Anse de la Ville. Anchorage is to seaward of this line.

A marine nature reserve extends ¾M to seawards just S of Banyuls. It is marked by yellow light buoys (Fl.Y.4s). Fishing, diving and anchoring are forbidden within this area – see chart.

Approach by day

From S Cross the wide Bahía de la Selva and close the coast so that the more prominent Cap Cerbère can be identified from a number of similar promontories with small bays between. In the bay to N of Cerbère will be seen the small harbour of Cerbère which is backed by a long rail viaduct, the N end being on two tiers of arches. Follow the coast around at ½M outside some rocky shallows and from E of Banyuls the houses and blocks of flats will be seen. Approach down the centre of the bay and do not cut the corner but keep clear of Ile Grosse by at least 50m.

From N Round Cap Béar, a very prominent sloping point with a conspicuous lighthouse signal station, radio masts and an old fort. The houses and flats of Banyuls will be seen from afar; set course towards them. In the closer approach the harbour wall will be seen.

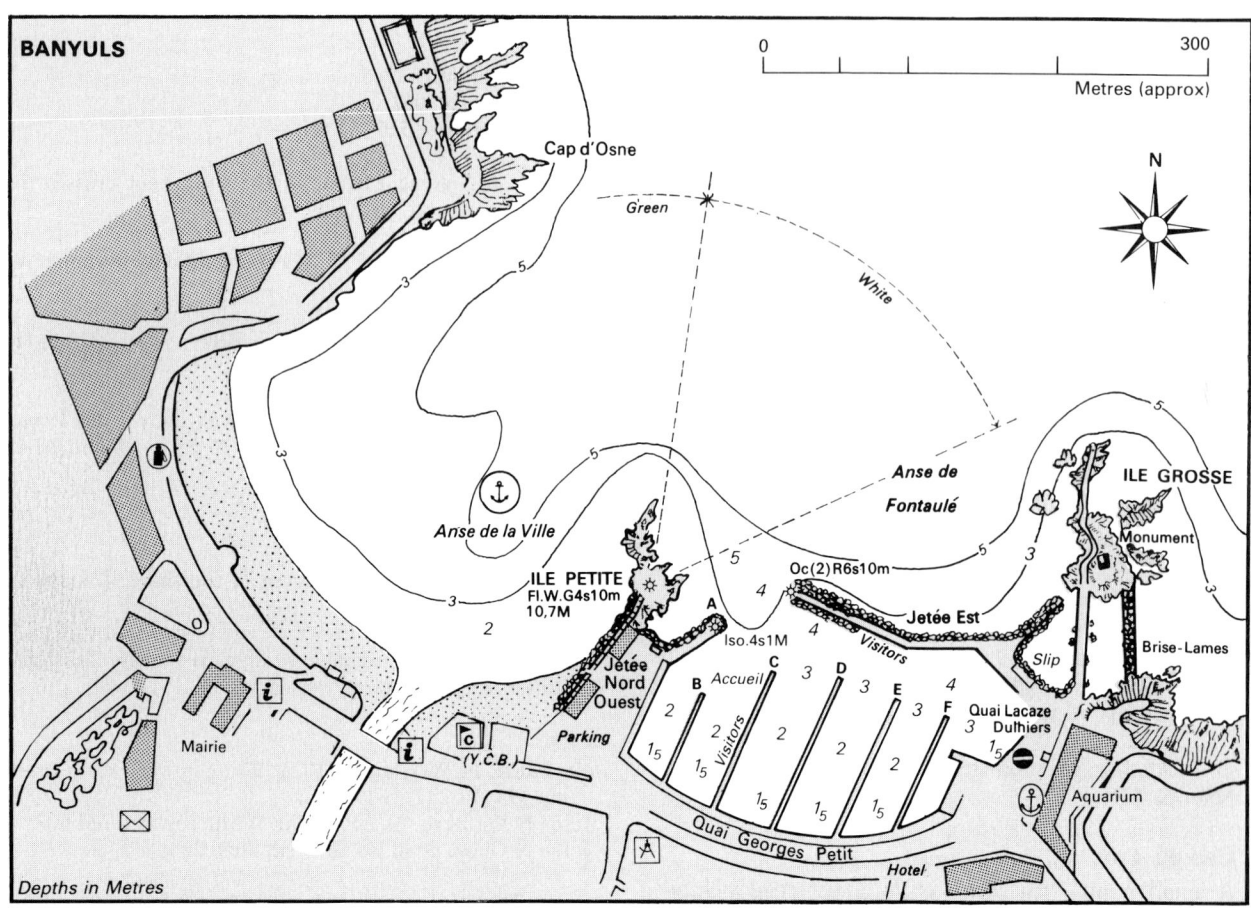

Port de Banyuls-sur-Mer

Port de Banyuls-sur-Mer. Entrance looking S

Approach by night

Using the following lights navigate to where the harbour bears SW at 500m:

Cap Béar Fl(3)W.15s30M
Punta Sernella Fl.W.5s13M
Cap Creus Fl(2)W.10s20M
Cap Cerbère Fl.W.4s15M

Anchorage in the approach

Anchor 200m to the N of the harbour entrance in 9m (30ft) sand, mud and weed. This anchorage is unpleasant in an E wind and could be dangerous.

Entrance

By day Approach the centre of the Anse de la Ville on a SW course until the tall white light tower with red top at the head of the Jetée Est is 20m to port

and turn to port leaving the inner side of the Jetée Est 20m clear. Secure to pontoon C.

By night Approach the Anse de la Ville on a SW course in the white sector of Fl.WG.4s. When Oc(2)R.6s is due S turn and approach this light. Round it at 20m to port into the harbour leaving the Fl.WG.4s and an Iso.W (line) to starboard. Secure to pontoon C.

Berths

Secure alongside pontoon C and await allocation of a berth.

Formalities

Report on arrival to the *bureau du port* (☎ 68 88 30 22), open summer 0900–1200, 1400–1800 and winter

Entrance

Port de Banyuls-sur-Mer looking **W**

0800–1300, 1400–2100, at the end of the harbour. If from a foreign port also report to the customs (☎ 68 88 31 48) in the office next door, open Tuesday, Thursday and Saturday, for clearance.

Harbour charges

There are harbour charges.

Facilities

Hard A hard standing at the E side of the harbour.
Slipway 8-ton.
Crane A mobile crane is available. 8-tonne crane and 10-tonne lift at E side of the harbour.
Fuel Diesel (*gasoil*) and petrol are only available from a service station 200m along the sea front towards the town. Open summer 0700–1900 and winter 0800–1800.
Water Water points on the quays and pontoons.
Electricity Supply points for 220v AC on the pontoons and quays.
Provisions A number of shops of most types including a *supermarché* in the town, and a market on Wednesday and Saturday.
Ice Ice is delivered outside the town hall at 10 o'clock every day in the season and is also available from the yacht club.

Garbage Rubbish bins at the ends of the pontoons.
Chandlery A ships' chandler at the S of the harbour.
Repairs Simple repairs can be undertaken by local shipyards and garages.
Post office The PTT is located at the back of the town.
Hotels One ★★★, seven ★★, three ★ and four unclassified hotels.
Restaurants Nineteen restaurants and café/bars.
Yacht club The Yacht Club de Banyuls-sur-Mer (YCB) (☎ 68 88 32 97) has a clubhouse at the *bureau du port*.
Showers Bureau du port. 10 WCs, four showers.
Information office The Syndicat d'Initiative (☎ 68 88 31 58) has an office in the town hall (*mairie*) which is on the front.
Visits A visit to the *caves* where the local wine is bottled is worthwhile. The 13th-century church is also of interest. There is an aquarium to E of the harbour which should be visited. The view from Cap de l'Abeille is excellent.
Beach A fine sandy beach to W of the harbour.
Communications Bus and rail services.

Port de Banyuls-sur-Mer

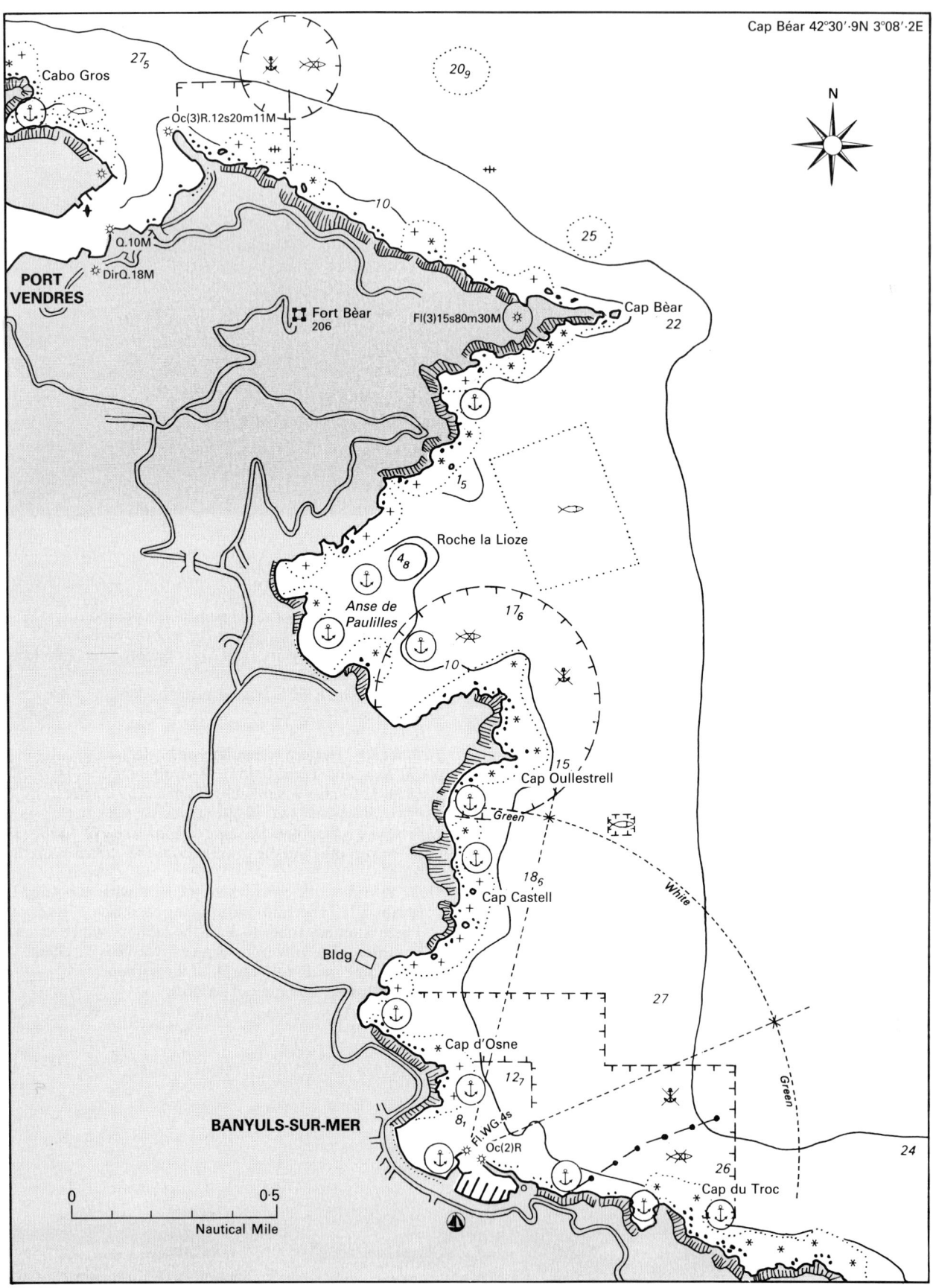

Anchorages N of Banyuls

Future development

This harbour has some of the ancillary developments which still remain to be completed. It is occasionally dredged. There are plans to enlarge the harbour on its E side.

History

Aristide Maillol (1861–1944), the famous sculptor, was born and worked here. A large memorial to the war dead seen near the *mairie* is an example of his work. A statue to the three nymphs at the Tate Gallery, London, is another. Details of the town's complex history from the information bureau (in English).

Cap d'Osne

A small headland with rocky feet. Coast road on archways at top of the cliff where there are houses.

⌁ A small anchorage below Cap d'Onse open N–NE–E–SE.

⌁ Anchorage to NW of Cap d'Osne in a medium-sized bay with rocky sides. Anchor at head of the bay off the Plage des Elmes; coast road behind and a large convalescence hospital building. Open N–NE–E–SE.

⌁ to NW of Cap d'Osne

Cap Castell

A very small rocky cliffed point. Marine farm ½M to NE of the point.

⌁ Small anchorage to N of Cap Castell. Open NE–E–SE.

⌁ Small anchorage to S of Oullestrell. Open NE–E–SE.

Cap Oullestrell

A rocky cliffed point (52m) with offlying rocks.

⌁ Anse de Paullilles

A large deep bay with four anchorages in sand, Plage d'el Forat, Anse de Paullilles, Plage de Benardi, Plage Balanti, Anse Ste Catherine. A disused explosives factory with chimney and coast road ashore. Fishing not permitted in the area. Open N–NE–E–SE.

---

3 PORT PIERRE-MERY (Not yet built)
66660 Pyrénées Orientales

Position 42°30'·3N 3°7'·5E

General

A new yacht harbour and marina yet to be constructed in the Baie de Paullilles under the auspices of Port Vendres. 470 berths, two hotels and a residential village are planned. This will replace the old disused explosives factory. Details are not yet available so approach with caution.

The outline plan of construction calls for a lake of 8 hectares to be dug out behind the beach with a canal and jetty cut through to the sea. The lake will have three long islets with small houses and another canal which will lead to a yacht harbour.

Port Pierre Méry looking W

⌁ Anchorage to SW of Cap Béar in a small bay, Anse Ste Catherine, with one awash rock, coast road near by. Open NE–E–SE. A very useful anchorage if caught out by a *tramontane/mistral*.

Cap Béar

An important major headland. The point slopes down from 206m where there are a fort and buildings to a 9m black rocky cliff. On the crest are a pink lighthouse (56m), a white signal station and a black and red radio pylon.

Cap Béar looking NW

Cap Béar looking SW

Cap Béar looking S

4 PORT VENDRES

66660 Pyrénées Orientales

Position 42°31′·4N 3°07′·1E
Minimum depth in the entrance 10m (33 ft)
 in the harbour 6 to 1·5m (20 to 5 ft)
Width of the entrance 330m
Maximum length overall 40m (131 ft)
Number of yacht berths 250
Population 5332
Rating 2–3–2

General

A large commercial and fishing harbour located in a natural *calanque* which has been improved by the provision of a breakwater and quays. Approach and entrance are usually easy but in a strong NW *tramontane* they can be difficult due to breaking seas in the entrance. Good shelter is obtained in the Nouvelle Darse but heavy swell from N and NE render it uncomfortable. There are fair facilities for yachtsmen. The town that surrounds the harbour is pleasant and the mountainous area around is attractive.

Data

Charts Admiralty 1506
 French 7002
 Navicarte 511

Current There is a permanent SW-going current in the area of 0·5 to 1 knot.

Magnetic variation 2°09′W (1994) decreasing by about 6′ each year.

Radiobeacon Cap Béar lighthouse BR(— ···/ — ·) 313·5kHz 50M

Weather forecasts The weather forecast is posted each day on a board at the *bureau du port* in the S corner of the harbour. Recorded forecast ☎ 36 68 08 08 and 36 68 08 66.

Speed limit 5 knots.

Traffic signals Displayed from a red and white metalwork tower on Pointe Fanal.
(*Note* Commercial vessels under radio control may disregard these traffic signals.)

Day	Night	Meaning
3 balls vertical	3 red lights vertical	Entrance absolutely prohibited
A cone point up between 2 balls	A white light between 2 red lights	Entrance prohibited
2 cones points together above one ball	A white light between a red and a green light	Entrance and departure prohibited
2 cones points together above a cone point down	A white light between 2 green lights	Departure prohibited

Port radio (Yacht harbour) VHF Ch 9, 16.
(*Commercial harbour) and pilots* Ch 12 and 16.

Storm signals Storm signals are shown from Cap Béar and from Pointe Fanal.

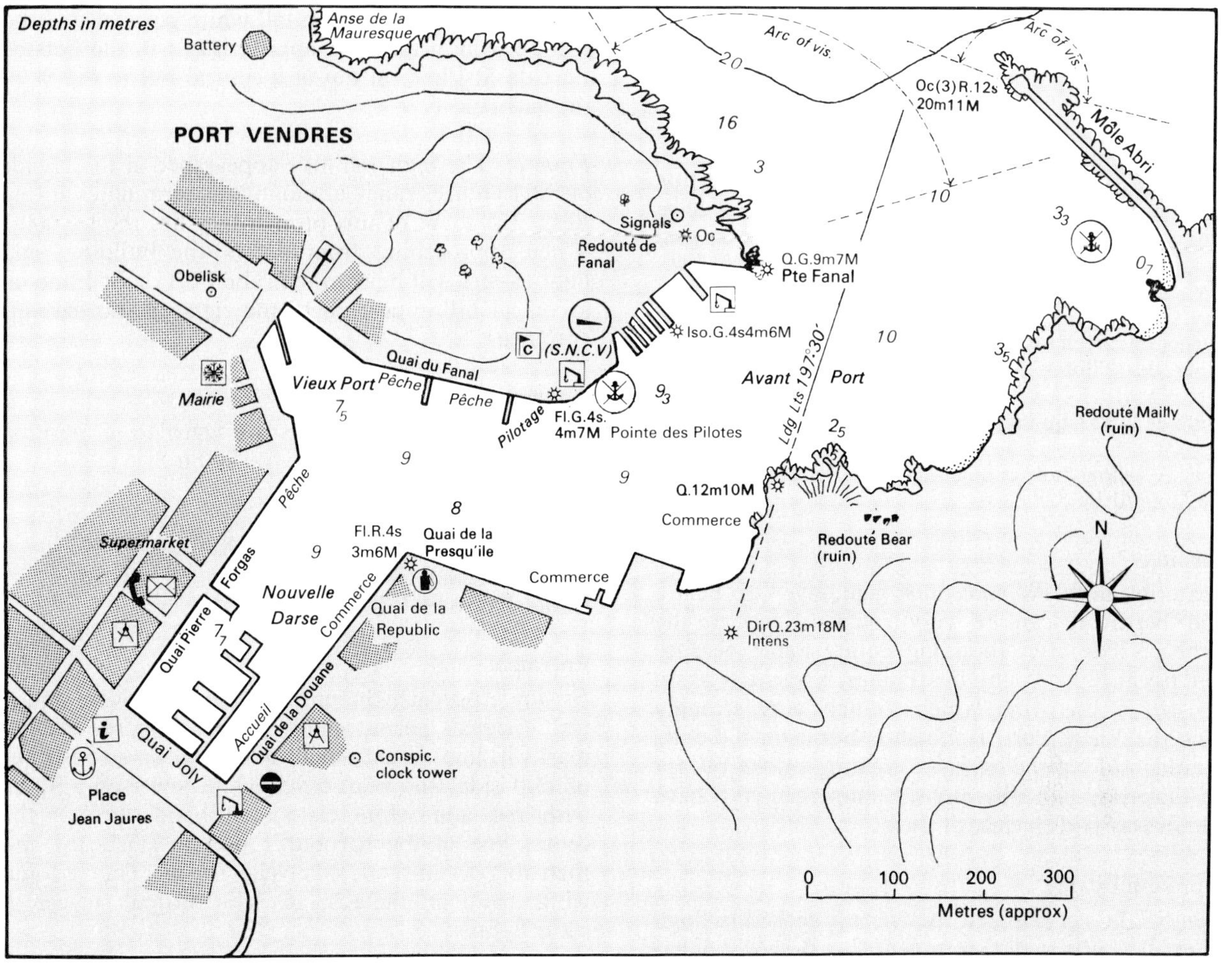

Depths in metres

Battery

Anse de la
Mauresque

PORT VENDRES

Obelisk

Mairie

Vieux Port

Pêche

Pêche

Pêche

Pêche

Supermarket

Forgas

Nouvelle
Darse

Quai Pierre

Commerce

Accueil

Quai de la Douane

Quai Joly

Place
Jean Jaures

Signals

Redouté de
Fanal

Quai du Fanal

(S.N.C.V.)

Iso.G.4s4m6M

Oc

Pte Fanal
Q.G.9m7M

Oc(3)R.12s
20m11M

Môle Abri

Pilotage

Fl.G.4s.
4m7M   Pointe des Pilotes

Avant Port

Commerce

Redouté Mailly
(ruin)

Q.12m10M
Commerce

Redouté Bear
(ruin)

Fl.R.4s
3m6M   Quai de la
Presqu'ile

Quai de la
Republic

Commerce

DirQ.23m18M
Intens

Conspic.
clock tower

N

0   100   200   300
Metres (approx)

Port Vendres

Pontoons

Port Vendres looking SW

Lights

Redoute du Fanal W side Oc.G.4s29m8M White square tower, dark green house 147°-vis-264°

Pointe Fanal Q.G.9m7M White tower, green top

Môle Abri head Oc(3)R.12s20m11M Six-sided hut on white column with red top. 110°-vis-287°

Redoute Béar Leading Lts 197°30' *Front* Q.W.12m10M Red metal structure on white hut, grey base. *Rear* 200m from front Dir.Q.W.23m18M White tower, red top, red and white chequered band. Intensified 196°-199°. Synchronised with front light

Anse Gerbal jetée head Iso.G.4s4m6M White framework structure, green top

Pointe des Pilotes Fl.G.4s4m7M White metal column, green top

Pointe de la Presqu'île Fl.R.4s3m6M Red metal structure

Buoys A yellow buoy is moored 400m 075° from the head of Môle Abri.

Warning

If entering in a NW *tramontane* gale, give Cap Béar a good berth; it can be very rough. Keep to the starboard side after rounding Pointe Fanal because after passing the Pointe des Pilotes, a yacht is again exposed to the wind which funnels very strongly down the Vieux Port. Rubbish is burnt on the cliffs on either side of the entrance creating smoke by day and flickering lights by night. Commercial craft have right of way – keep clear of them.

Approach by day

From S The very broken rocky coast backed by high mountains ends at the prominent Cap Béar which has a conspicuous lighthouse, signal station, radio masts and an old fort. Steep rocky cliffs line the coast from Cap Béar to this harbour. The Môle Abri with a remarkable light tower on tall white posts at its head will be seen in the close approach as will the isolated Fort de St-Elmo on top of a conical hill to the W of the harbour.

From N The high wall-like appearance of the N side of the Pyrénées range of mountains terminates at Cap Béar. 1M to W of this promontory lies the harbour. When approaching from the N the buildings and light towers will be seen with the Fort de St-Elmo on a conical hill appearing to the right of the harbour entrance.

Approach by night

Using the following lights navigate to a position where the harbour entrance lies 200m S:

Cap Béar Fl(3)W.15s30M
Cap Leucate Fl(2)W.10s20M
Perpignan-Rivesaltes Aero Mo(X)W.8·5s33M
Collioure Iso.G.4s8M
Canet-Plage Fl(4)W.12s15M

Entrance

By day Approach the entrance on a S course and if traffic signals permit enter on 197° with the leading marks in line. Front: small white hut on stone tower on cliff side, and rear: small white tower on a house with red and white chequered band. Follow the centre line of the harbour round to starboard and then to port into the Nouvelle Darse. The red and white band on the rear mark is difficult to see in some lights.

By night Approach the entrance on a S course and line up Q.W synchronising with Q.W intensified on 197°30'. Enter between Oc(3)R.12s to port and

Front leading light  *Rear leading mark (light)*

Port Vendres. Leading marks

Port Vendres looking SW up the harbour to pontoons

Oc.G.4s and Q.G to starboard. Then turn SW leaving Iso.G and Fl.G to starboard; when the latter is abeam turn to a W course and then SW to leave Fl.R.4s to port.

Berths

Berth stern-to a pontoon, or to Quai Pierre Forgas near the head of the Nouvelle Darse with bow-to mooring buoy, or alongside Quai de la Douane or Quai de la Republic.

Note A berth on Quai Pierre Forgas costs half as much as a pontoon berth.

Moorings

A few private moorings for yachts near the Pointe des Pilotes, details from the yacht club.

Anchorage

Anchoring inside the harbour is not permitted.

Formalities

On arrival report to the *bureau du port* on 3 Quai Joly on S side of the harbour (☎ 68 82 12 00, 68 82 12 00 or 68 82 08 84 or Telex 500 125 CECOMEX) or *Fax* 68 82 29 51. Open 0800–1200 and 1400–1800. If from a foreign country and report to customs (☎ 68 82 00 90) which office is in the SE corner of the harbour.

Harbour charges

There are harbour charges to be paid.

Facilities

Hard A small hard standing near the yacht club.
Slipways A large 300-tonne slip to NW of the *avant port*; a 150-tonne travel-lift is also installed here.
Cranes A 4-tonne crane and a 150-tonne travel-hoist at the yacht club, and a large 20-tonne mobile crane is available.
Fuel Diesel *(gasoil)* and petrol are available from fuel point on the E side of the Nouvelle Darse, open summer 0800–2000, winter 0800–1800 (☎ 68 82 00 25). If a commercial ship is alongside the fuel will be delivered by bowser.
Water Many water points along the quays at the *bureau du port* and on the pontoons.
Electricity Outlets 220v AC and pontoons (three can supply 30 amps).
Provisions Many shops of all kinds nearby including *supermarchés*.
Ice A small ice plant for local fishermen at the SW side of the Vieux Port where, as a kindness, it may be possible to buy ice, also available from the *bureau du port*.
Duty-free goods It is possible to obtain duty-free goods here. Place orders with the supermarket nearby. They will make all the necessary arrangements for delivery on board under the supervision of the customs. New rules are expected.
Garbage Rubbish containers on the quay at the S side of the Nouvelle Darse.
Chandlery Two ships' chandlers, one each side of the Nouvelle Darse.
Repairs Repairs can be carried out by two shipyards to NW of *avant port* and local mechanics can carry out minor engine repairs. Sailmaker and electricians available. A small yard specialises in wood craft.
Post office On the Quai Pierre Forgas.
Hotels One ★★★, three ★★, five ★ and some unclassified.
Restaurants Eighteen restaurants and some café/bars.
Yacht club The Société Nautique de la Côte Vermeille (SNCV) (☎ 68 59 80 46, 68 89 20 46 and 68 82 04 78) has a clubhouse with a bar and showers on the NE side of the *avant port*.
Showers Public showers at S end of the harbour. Eight WCs, eight showers.
Information office The Syndicat d'Initiative has an office to SW of the Nouvelle Darse (☎ 68 82 08 84).
Lifeboats An all-weather lifeboat is stationed here (☎ 68 82 11 46).
Visits The view from Fort de St-Elmo is worth the climb. Collioure should also be visited; it is an attractive place.
Beaches Two small beaches on the NE side of the *avant port* and a few sandy coves to NW.
Communications Bus and rail services. There are ferry boats to Algiers and Morocco. Airport at Perpignan (15M).

ading marks (light)   *Vieux Port*   *Shipyards*   *Redouté Fanal (lighthouse)*

Port Vendres looking W–NW–N from near Redouté Bear

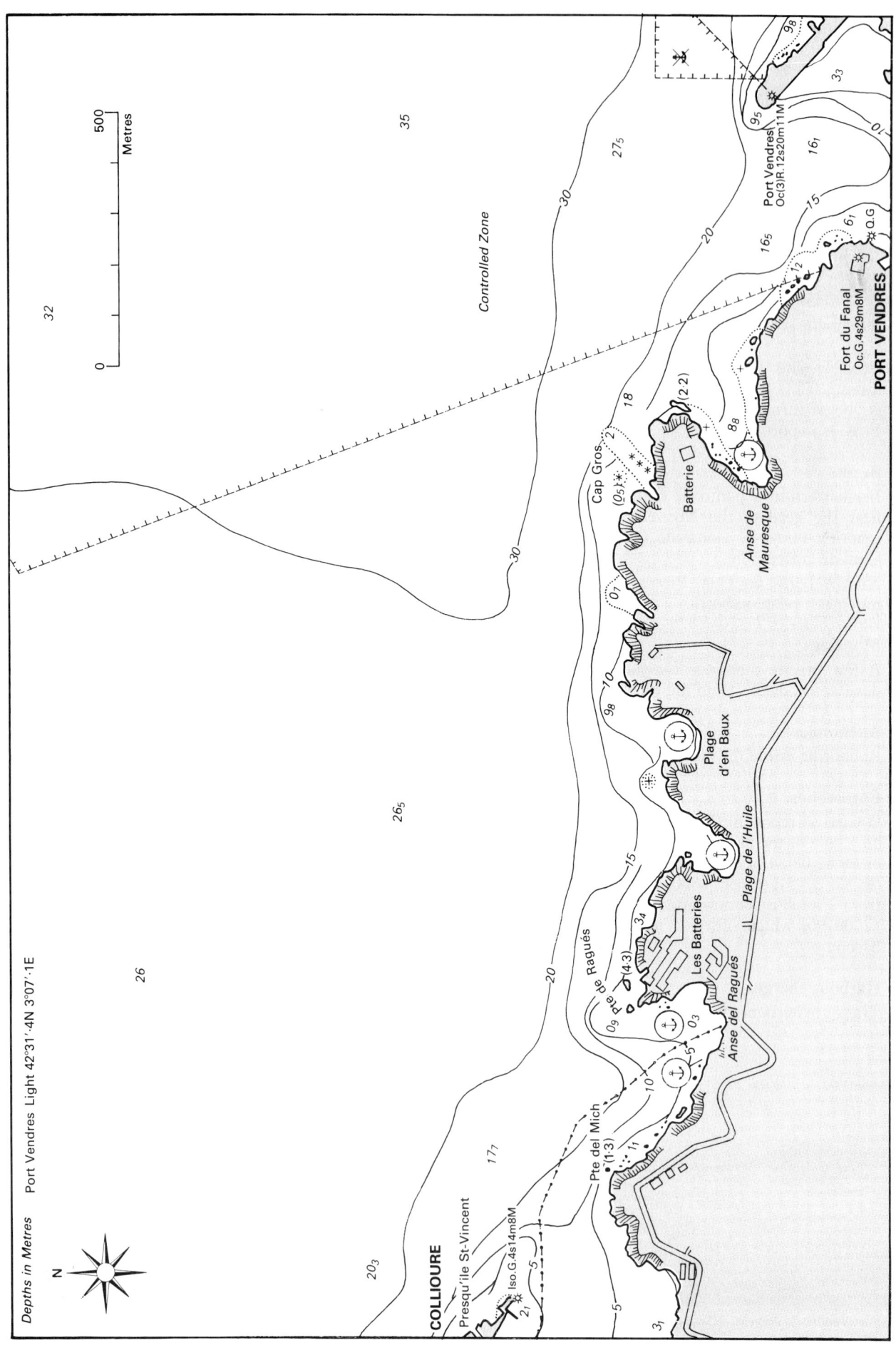

Depths in Metres   Port Vendres Light 42°31'·4N 3°07'·1E

500

Metres

0

32

26

26₅

35

27₅

Controlled Zone

30

30

20

20

15

17₇

20₃

COLLIOURE

Presqu'île St-Vincent

Iso.G.4s14m8M

2₁

5

3₁

Pte del Mich
(1·3)
11

10

5

0·9

Anse del Ragués

0·3

(4·3)

3·4

Pte de Ragués

Les Batteries

Plage de l'Huile

Plage
d'en Baux

9₈

10

0₇

18

2

Cap Gros

(0·5)

(2·2)

Batterie

8₈

Anse de
Mauresque

16₅

16₁

15

9₅

98

33

01

Port Vendres
Ocl(3)R.12s20m11M

6₁

Q.G

1·2

Fort du Fanal
Oc.G.4s29m8M

PORT VENDRES

56

Port Vendres looking W over the Nouvelle Darse

Future development

More pontoons may be established in the Nouvelle Darse. A new harbour is to be built at Port Pierre Méry (see page 51). This is under the control of Port Vendres.

History

This natural harbour has been in use since pre-Roman times. The Romans when they occupied it called it Port Veneris (Port Venus). The harbour was not fortified until 1679 when the first fortifications were begun under the supervision of Maréchal Vauban and these works were not completed until 1851. The town and harbour were badly damaged during the last war.

⚓ **Anse de la Mauresque**

A bay with low rocky cliffs and a few rocks. Old Batterie de la Mauresque on N side and signal station (24m) to SE. Tracks to road. Open N–NE–E.

Cap Gros

A large rounded headland with outlying rocks and two reefs 0.7 and 2m. Slopes up to 28m where there are some buildings. Batterie de la Mauresque on the E crest.

⚓ **Plage d'en Baux**

A small anchorage in a cliffed bay with sandy beach. Anchor in mid bay sand. Houses and track to road ashore. Open NW–N–NE. Half covered rock to W.

⚓ **Plage de l'Huile**

A small rocky cliffed bay with sandy beach. Houses and an old *batterie* ashore, track to road. Open NW–N–NE. Half covered rock to E.

Punta del Raguès

A rocky cliffed point with two outlying islets and a few rocks. Houses on the crest with roads.

⚓ **Anse del Raguès**

A small bay with sandy beaches, houses and roads above the rocky cliffs. 0·3m rock in centre of bay. A pipeline comes ashore in S corner. Open to NW–N–NE.

⚓ Anse del Raguès

Anchorage Anse de la Raguès between Port Vendres and Collioure looking E. Strong NW tramontane/mistral blowing.

5 PORT DE COLLIOURE

66190 Pyrénées Orientales

Position 42°31′·7N 3°05′·3E
Minimum depth in the entrance 8m (26ft)
          in the harbour 4 to 0·5m (13 to 1·5ft)
Width of inner harbour entrance 15m (49ft)
Number of yacht berths 90
Maximum length overall 6·5m (21ft)
Population 2741 (approx)
Rating 2–3–4

General

A most picturesque old natural harbour surrounded by beautiful old buildings with a backdrop of high mountains. Approach and entrance are easy and there is shelter from all directions except the NE–E. It may be necessary to change berth should the wind alter because in some conditions the swell can make the harbour uncomfortable. Facilities for yachtsmen are limited.

Data

Charts Admiralty 1705
      French 7002
      Navicarte 511

Magnetic variation 2°09′W (1994) decreasing by about 6′ each year.

Radiobeacon Cap Béar lighthouse BR(−···/·−·) 313·5kHz 50M

Speed limit 5 knots.

Weather forecast Recorded (☎ 36 68 08 08 and 36 68 08 66).

Lights
Mole head Iso.G.4s14m8M Structure on green round hut. 135°-vis-278°
Fishing lights 2F.W.11m5·9M to NNW

Buoys Mooring buoys in the bay.

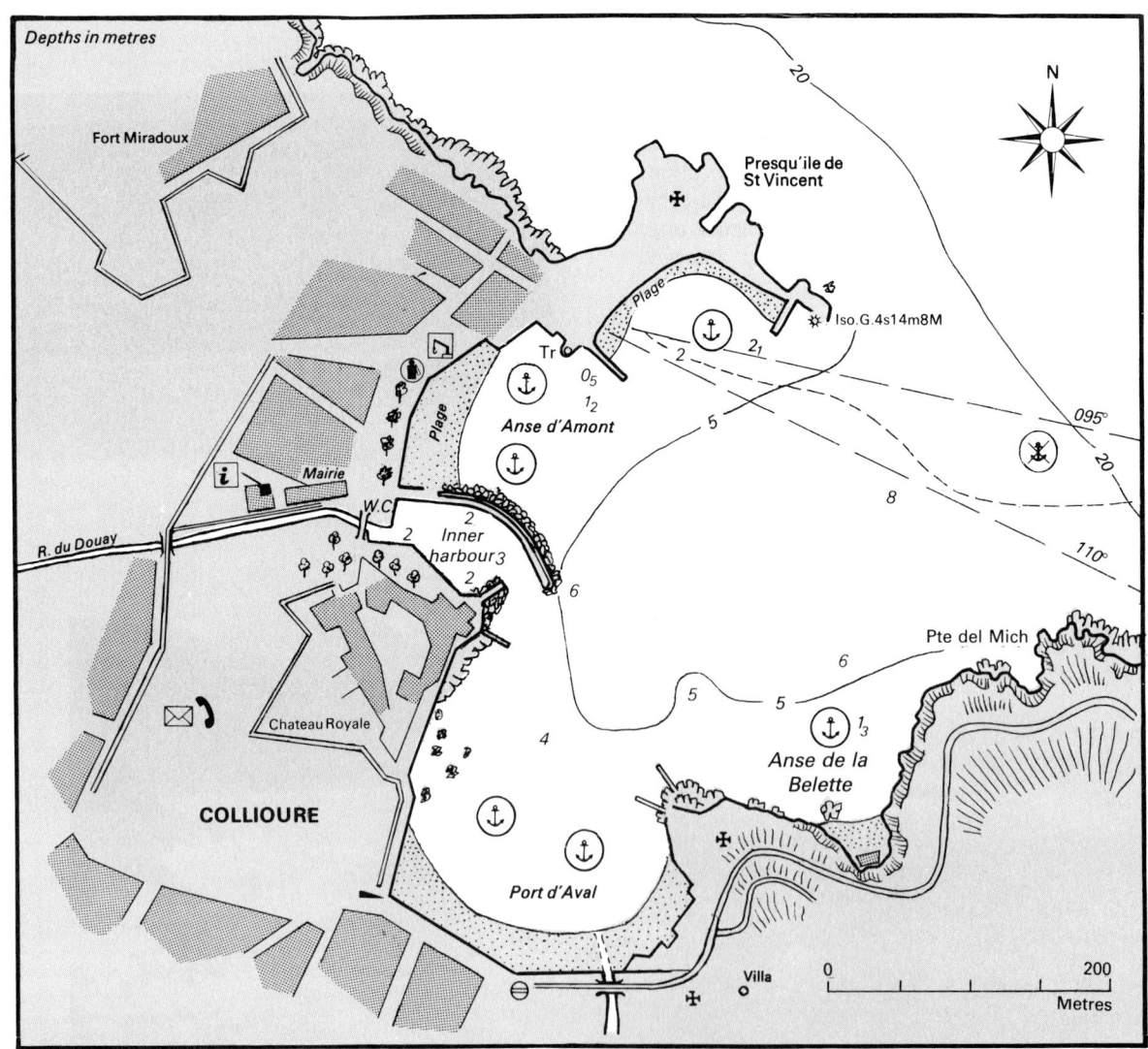

Port de Collioure

Inner harbour

Port de Collioure looking SW

Warnings

There is a military training area around this harbour and a firing range to N where a commando unit is stationed. If the range is in use a red flag is displayed on Fort Carré. In strong winds from NW–N–NE a considerable swell enters the bay. Underwater pipes are laid between two broken lines shown on the plan; anchorage is not permitted in this area.

Approach by day

From S Round the very prominent Cap Béar with its conspicuous lighthouse, signal station, radio masts and an old fort. Follow the steep high cliffs in a WNW direction passing the entrance to Port Vendres which has a large mole with a remarkable light tower on posts at its end. The coast now becomes broken with small bays between rocky headlands. The church and mole of Collioure are visible in the closer approach.

From N The miles of low flat sandy coast running in a N–S direction suddenly end at a wall-like range of high mountains – the N face of the Pyrénées, running eastwards and terminating at Cap Béar. Collioure lies about 2M to E of this junction of coasts, nearly halfway to Cap Béar. The town buildings and those of Port Vendres, together with Fort de St-Elmo on its conical hill between them, can be seen from afar. In the closer approach the church and the mole will be seen.

Approach by night

Using the following lights navigate to a position where the mole lies 200m to SW:
Cap Béar Fl(3)W.15s30M
Cap Leucate Fl(2)W.10s20M
Port Vendres Oc.G.4s8M

Perpignan-Rivesaltes Aero Mo(X)W.8·5s33M
Canet-Plage Fl(4)W.12s15M

Entrance

By day Approach on a SW course and leave the mole head 50m to starboard.

By night Approach Iso.G.4s of a SW course and leave 50m to starboard. Inner harbour is not lit but street lights give some illumination.

Berths

Berths for smaller yachts may be available in limited numbers on N side of the inner harbour, if not required by fishing craft. Secure and report to the *capitaine*.

Moorings

Some private mooring buoys and a few belonging to the harbour authorities in the bay, some of which may be vacant.

Anchorage

Anchor where indicated on the plan to suit direction of the wind but be prepared to move if the wind direction should change. In a NW *tramontane/mistral* anchor in Port d'Amont or behind the mole close inshore with a line ashore to a strong point.

Formalities

Report to the port captain at the *mairie* (☎ 68 82 05 66) open 0800–1200 1400–1800. Customs Port Vendres (☎ 68 82 00 90).

Charges

There are harbour charges. One hour is free.

Port d'Aval   Inner harbour   Port d'Amont   Môle

Port de Collioure looking NW from Pointe de Mich

Inner harbour Entrance

Port de Collioure. Entrance

Port de Collioure. Inner harbour

Facilities

Slip A slip on Plage d'Aval, shallow.

Fuel Diesel (*gasoil*) and petrol can be obtained from pumps on the road at the Port d'Amont.

Water A water point near the bridge over the Ravin du Douay and on the quay.

Electricity 220v AC points on the quays.

Provisions A number of small shops in the old village and to the S of the harbour.

Chandlery A shop in the town.

Post office In the rue de la Republique to W of the harbour.

Hotels One ★★★★, five ★★★, ten ★★, five ★ and several other hotels.

Restaurants Twelve restaurants one of which is ★★★★. Many café/bars.

Yacht club The Société Nautique de Collioure (SNC) (☎ 68 82 06 34) is a sailing school and has a private pontoon.

Showers Four on the beaches.

Information office The Syndicat d'Initiative has an office in the road alongside the Ravin du Douay (☎ 68 82 15 47).

Visits The Museum of Painting at the town hall (*mairie*), the Château Royale, the 17th-century church with its Arab tower and baroque interior and the old 14th-century church are some of the places to visit.

Beaches Several beaches around the harbour.

Communications Bus and rail services. Airport Perpignan (☎ 68 61 22 24).

Future development

It is regrettable to learn that plans exist to turn this most attractive old harbour into a modern yacht harbour. It is bound to be ruined just as St-Tropez, La Ciotat, Beaulieu and St-Jean-Cap Ferrat have been over-developed and over-populated. It already is spoilt by the thousands of tourists and visitors who descend on the village in the summer.

History

The origins of this natural harbour are lost in time. When the Ligurians occupied it they called it Pyrénée after an Iberian princess, and there was a good trade with the Phocaeans. (The Romans changed the name to Cocoliberim when they were in occupation). It was occupied in turn by Greeks, Visigoths and Arabs, followed by the Francs of Charlemagne, the Kings of Aragon who built the beautiful château, the Kings of Mallorca and at various times by the Spanish. It was however spared during the last war. Over the centuries it was captured eleven times and withstood six sieges. It is considered to be one of the birthplaces of modern painting and was a favourite of Mâtisse, Derain, Picasso, Dufy, Juan Gris and others. The old lighthouse was built in the 14th century by the Arabs and the church alongside was built in the 17th century.

⚓ **Plage de l'Ouille**

A small sandy bay with rocky sides, sandy beach with track to the road and a small river usually dry. Open to NW–N–NE–E.

⚓ Plage de l'Ouille

⚓ **Anse de Portell**

An open bay with a sandy beach, road and rail behind, rocks at sides open to N–NE–E.

⚓ **Le Racou Plage**

An open anchorage in 5m sand off the small town of Racou just to S of the Port d'Argelès-Plage. Sandy beach. Open to NW–N–NE–E.

---

6 PORT D'ARGELES-PLAGE (RACOU)

66700 Pyrénées Orientales

Position 42°32'·7N 3°03'·4E°
Minimum depth in the entrance 4m (12ft)
in the harbour 2m to 0m (6 to 0ft)
Number of yacht berths 1500 planned 420 now available
Maximum length overall 24m (79ft)
Population 5753
Rating 3–2–3

General

A half-built new harbour still in the course of construction. Completion was planned for 1984 but this has been delayed by the world-wide recession. See plan for 1991 situation.

Visiting yachts will be accepted into the harbour but should note that facilities are limited.

Data

Charts Admiralty 1705
French 6843
Navicarte 511

Magnetic variation 2°09'W (1994) decreasing by about 6' each year.

Speed limit 3 knots.

Port Radio VHF Ch 9.

Weather forecast Posted once a day. Recorded forecast (☎ 36 68 08 08 and 36 68 08 66)

Lights
NE jetée head Fl.G.4s5m3M Green post
SW jetée head Oc(2)R.6s4M Metal column with gallery

Le Racou   *Port d'Argelès-Plage*

Anchorage off Racou looking NW – strong *tramontane* blowing

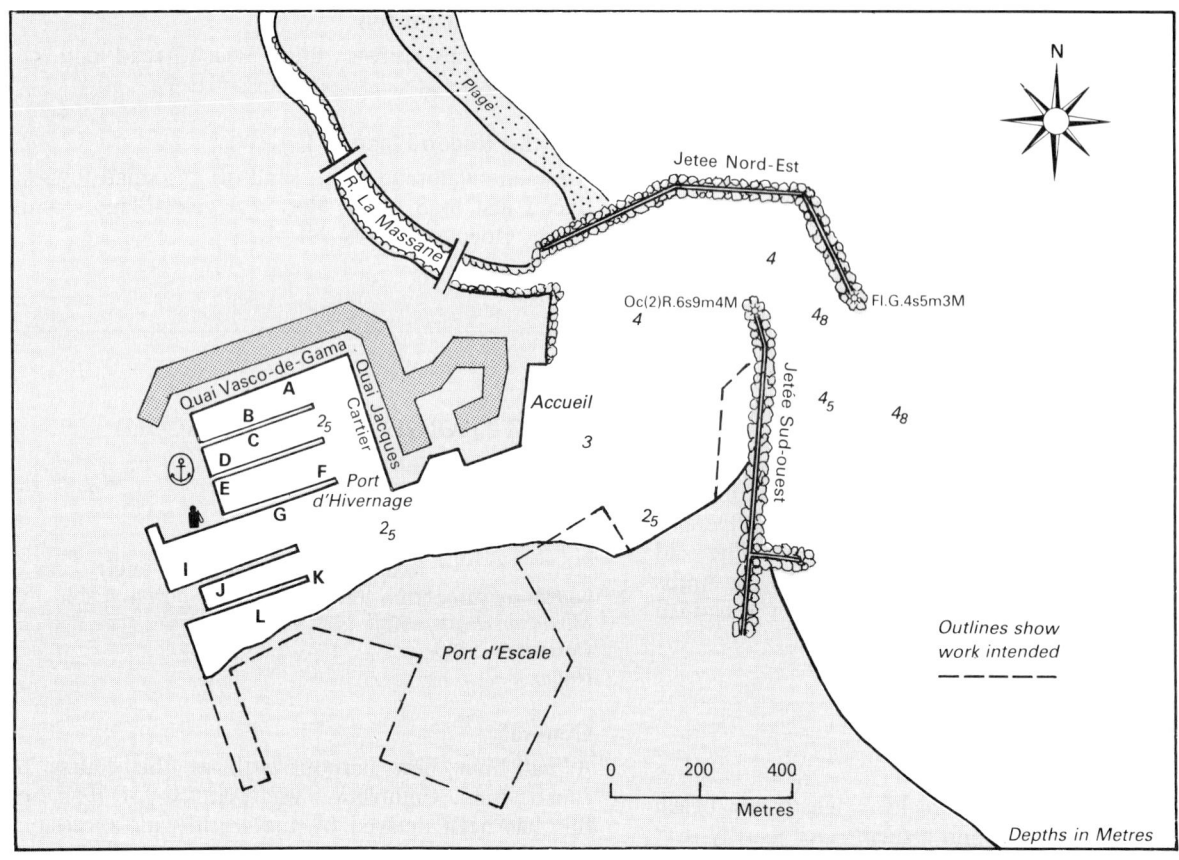

Port d'Argelès-Plage (Racou)

Pontoons

Port d'Argelès-Plage (Racou) looking NW

Cap Béar   Port Vendres

Port d'Argèles-Plage looking E–SE. Note: Shallows in foreground

Port d'Argèles-Plage (Racou). Entrance looking SE

Warning

Due to construction work considerable care should be exercised in approaching, entering and manoeuvring inside the harbour, and changes must be expected. Dredging to 3·5m is expected.

Approach by day

From S Round Cap Béar which has a conspicuous lighthouse, signal station, radio masts and old fort. Follow the rocky-cliffed coast which is steep-to in a W direction passing Port Vendres which has a distinctive lighthouse on its Môle Abri head and then Collioure which has a large old fort and château. Follow the coast for 2M to where the coast turns northwards. The harbour breakwater will be easily observed. Establish a position where the entrance is due W and approach.

From N Follow the coast at ¼M in a S direction. The harbours and buildings of Canet and St-Cyprien-Plage will be easily recognised. The mouth of the Rivière le Tech is not conspicuous; a road bridge may be seen. The high-rise buildings of Argelès-Plage are seen from afar. The harbour lies just over 1M to S of these buildings, the breakwaters are easy to see. Bring the entrance due W and approach.

Approach by night

Use the following lights to navigate to a position when the harbour lies due W:
Cap Béar Fl(3)W.15s30M
Cap Leucate Fl(2)W.10s20M

Port Vendres Oc.G.4s8M
Perpignan-Rivesaltes Aero Mo(X)W.8·5s33M
Carnet-Plage Fl(4)W.12s15M

Entrance

By day Approach on a W course round the head of NE jetée leaving it 10m to starboard and enter. Until harbour is completed use great care and sound carefully.

By night Approach a Fl.G.4s and round it at 15m leaving Oc(2)R.6s to port. Not recommended until harbour is completed without a previous visit by day.

Berths

To be established on pontoons in the Bassin d'Escale. At the moment (1993) secure to the Quai d'Accueil.

Anchorage

In 10m sand 300m to E of entrance. At the moment it is possible to anchor inside the harbour on the port hand.

Formalities

Bureau du port (☎ 68 81 63 27), *Fax* 68 81 69 14, open summer 0900–1200 and 1400–1830, winter 0830–1200 and 1400–1830, is in a hut to W of the harbour. *Douane* at Port Vendres (☎ 68 81 00 44).

To pontoon berths   River mouth

Port d'Argelès-Plage (Racou). Inside the outer harbour looking SE–S–SW

Facilities

Some facilities are now available but at the moment only a few have been established. The following are available at Argelès-Plage 1M to N and Argelès Village 1M to NW.

Travel-lift (26 tonnes) to W of the harbour, and 1-tonne crane.

Fuel Diesel (*gasoil*) and petrol from garage pumps near village (☎ 08 81 63 27) open 0900–1200 and 1500–1800.

Water Water points around the quay.

Electricity 220v AC points on quays and pontoons.

Provisions Supermarket and many small shops in village.

Post office PTT in village.

Hotels Three ★★★, twelve ★★, nine ★.

Restaurants Over 20.

Repairs Mechanic available. Small yard, repair for hull and engines near harbour. Small shop.

Yacht clubs Club de Plaisance d'Argelès-Plage Nord (☎ 68 36 03 37 and 68 81 07 29) open June to September.

Showers Three showers and four WCs.

Information office Municipal du Tourisme, Place des Arones, Argelès-Plage (☎ 68 81 15 85).

Visits 13th-century church is worth a visit, also the old town of Elne.

Beaches Long sandy beaches either side of the harbour.

Communications Bus and rail. Airport at Perpignan.

History

A small fishing port which was fortified in the Middle Ages as an outpost near the frontier of France and Spain. Agriculture and vineyards were the main sources of prosperity until the coast was opened up as a mass tourist area.

7 PORT DE ST CYPRIEN-PLAGE

66750 Pyrénées Orientales

Position 42°37'·2N 3°02'·4E
Minimum depth in the entrance 4m (13ft)
            in the harbour 3m (10ft)
Width of the entrance 50m
Number of yacht berths 2200
              (Port des Capellans 500 berths extra)
Maximum length overall 20m (66ft)
Population 6922
Rating 3–2–3

General

An artificial yacht harbour and a marina with houses and flats. Easy to approach and enter with full shelter from the swell, but not the wind, once inside. Approach and entrance can be dangerous in strong winds and swell from NE–E–SE. All normal facilities for yachtsmen available. The area is flat and uninteresting with the exception of the old town of Elne and the vineyards. Considerable enlargement of the harbour and marina (Port des Capellans) to S and SW is in progress.

Data

Charts Admiralty 1705
        French 6843, 78002
        Navicarte 511

Current There is a S-going current of 0·5 to 1 knot across the entrance.

Magnetic variation 2°09'W (1994) decreasing by about 6' each year.

Port radio VHF Ch 9,16 also CB Ch 30.

Radar A radar with a 48M range at *bureau du port*.

Weather forecasts Weather forecasts are posted three times a day at the *bureau du port*. Pre-recorded forecasts ☎ 36 68 08 08 and 36 68 08 66. Also on VHF Ch 9 each odd hour.

Speed limit 3 knots.

Lights

Jetée Sud head Fl(4)R.15s10m5M White column, red top, on hut. Storm signals
Jetée Nord head Fl.G.2·5s5M White mast, green top

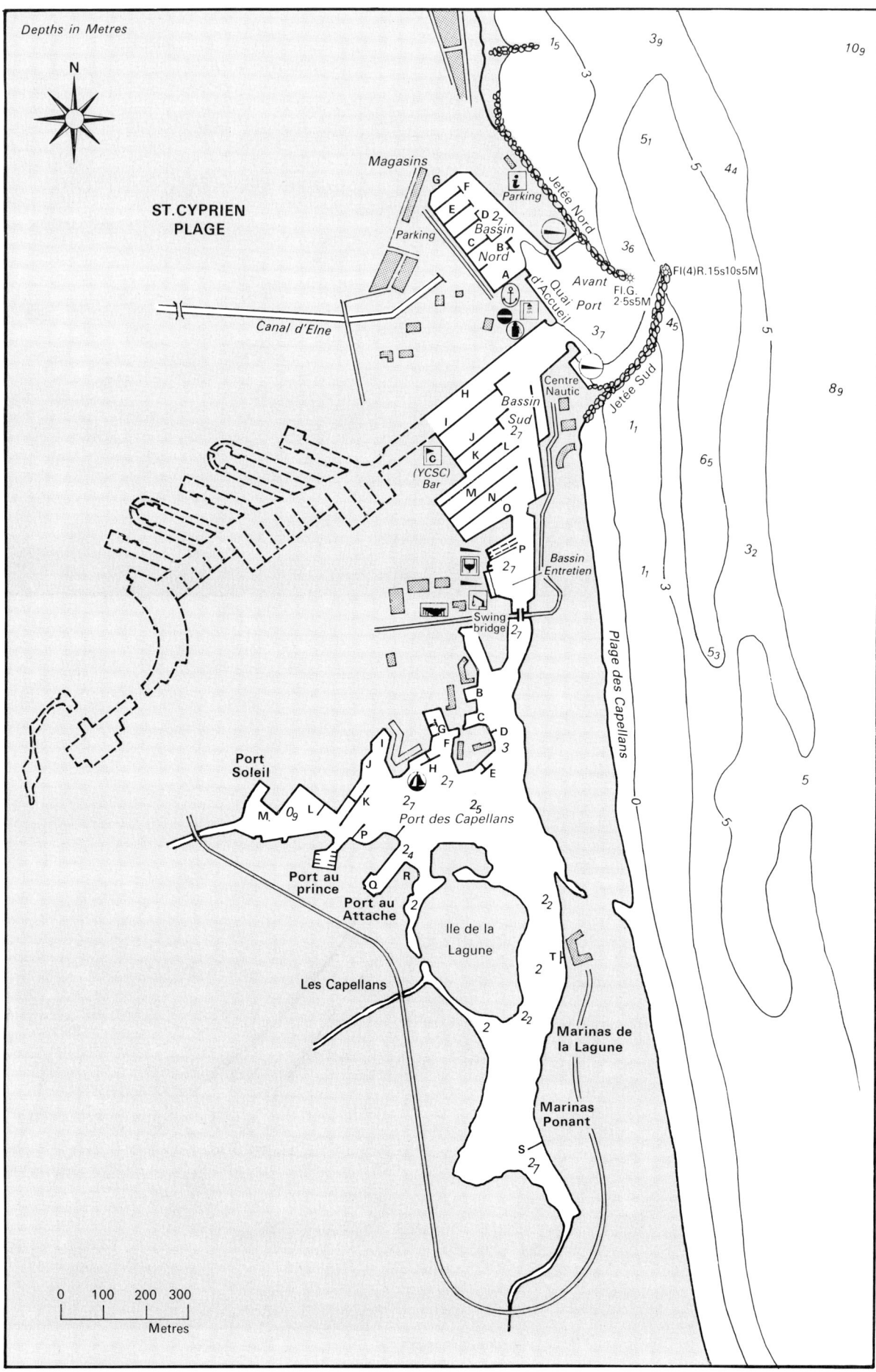

Port de St-Cyprien-Plage

Bureau du port

Port de St-Cyprien-Plage looking W

Ile de la Lagune   *Port des Capellans*

Port de St-Cyprien-Plage. Port des Capellans and Ile de la Lagune looking W

Warning

As this harbour is still under development (1993) changes must be expected. The Roche de St-Cyprien is covered 8m and has an underwater cable running N–S (see chart).

Approach by day

From S From where the coast turns N near Argelès-sur-Mer it becomes low, flat, sandy and featureless. The blocks of flats and houses at St-Cyprien are easily seen. There is a large water tower at St-Cyprien which can be seen from afar. The Jetée Sud will be seen in the closer approach.

From N From Canet-Plage, which can be identified by its harbour, blocks of flats and water tower, the coast is featureless with a low, flat, sandy beach. In the closer approach the Jetée Nord of St-Cyprien will be seen.

Approach by night

Using the following lights navigate to a position where the harbour lies 200m SW:
Cap Béar Fl(3)W.15s30M
Port Vendres Oc.G.4s8M
Cap Leucate Fl(2)W.10s20M
Perpignan-Rivesaltes Aero Mo(X)W.8·5s33M
Canet-Plage Fl(4)W.12s15M

Anchorage in the approach

Anchor 400m to NE of the entrance in 5m (16ft) sand, mud and weed.

Entrance

By day Approach the entrance on a SW course, enter and turn onto a W course.

By night Approach Fl(4)R on a SW course, leave it 25m to port and a Fl.G.2·5s 25m to starboard and then turn onto a W course.

Bridge

Pont du Touman, a turning bridge at the S of the harbour, opens every ten minutes 0830-1920 in summer.

Berths

Secure alongside the Quai d'Accueil near the *bureau du port* and when allocated a berth secure stern-to, bow-to mooring buoy (some berths have fingers). A new harbour, the Port des Capellans, has been established to S of the main harbour; it is approached via the turning bridge. There are some visitors' moorings available in this new harbour.

Formalities

Report on arrival to the *bureau du port* (☎ 68 21 05 97) open summer 0700–2100, winter 0800–1200 and 1400–1800. Customs (☎ 68 21 06 08) are in the same building if clearance from a foreign country is needed.

Entrance

Port de St-Cyprien-Plage. Approach looking NW

Entrance

Port de St-Cyprien-Plage. Approach looking W

Bassin Sud   *Bureau du Port*   *Bassin Nord*

Port de St-Cyprien-Plage. Entrance looking W

Harbour charges

There are harbour charges.

Facilities

Hards Three hard standing areas in the harbour; see plan.

Slips Six slips in the main harbour and seven in the marina of Port de Capellans.

Slipways There are two 100-tonne slipways on the W side of the Bassin d'Entretien.

Cranes There are 30- and 50-tonne travel-lifts and a 1·5-tonne crane in the Bassin d'Entretien.

Fuel Diesel (*gasoil*) and petrol are available, summer 0700–2100, winter 0800–1200 and 1400–1700, from pumps in the Bassin Sud (☎ 68 21 07 98).

Water Water points on all quays and pontoons.

Electricity Electrical outlets are established on quays and pontoons (220v AC 10 amps).

Provisions Most supplies can be obtained from shops and a supermarket near the harbour. There are many other shops at St-Cyprien-Plage about 1M away and at Elne 3M away.

Ice Ice is available in the season from a shop near the harbour and from several machines.

Garbage Rubbish containers are on the quays and pontoons.

Chandlery Six chandlers around the harbour.

Repairs Five major shipyards are established to the S of the harbour where all repairs can be undertaken including electronics, engines, sails, etc.

Post office At St-Cyprien (☎ 68 21 04 25) and at St-Cyprien-Plage, both 1M away.

Hotels One ★★★★, one ★★★, eight ★★ at St-Cyprien and the harbour.

Restaurants 26 on the N side of the harbour and at St-Cyprien.

Yacht club The Yacht Club de St-Cyprien (YCSC) (☎ 68 21 04 25) has a new clubhouse being built to W of the harbour which will have all facilities.

Showers There are twelve showers and ten WCs available at the *bureau du port*.

Information office All information about the harbour and its surroundings is available from the office of the Syndicat d'Initiative to N of the harbour (☎ 68 21 01 33). There are also offices at St-Cyprien and St-Cyprien-Plage.

Visits The ancient cloisters at Elne are world famous and should be visited. There are also other historic buildings nearby. A museum has been established at St-Cyprien. A visit to St-Nazaire is worthwhile.

Beaches Miles of sandy beaches either side of the harbour.

Communications Bus service, and at Elne there is a railway station. There is an airport at Perpignan 20 km away.

Lifeboat 2nd class (☎ 68 21 07 98).

Future development

The harbour is to be expanded in a S and a SW direction, providing more marinas. A new entrance to the sea may be built to E of Port des Capellans.

History

Remains show that the area has been in occupation since the Iron Age and first century BC.

8 PORT DE CANET-EN-ROUSSILLON (ST NAZAIRE)

66140 Pyrénées Orientales

Position 42°42'·5N 3°02'·3E
Minimum depth in the entrance 4·5m (15ft)
in the harbour 3 to 1·5m (10 to 5ft)
Number of yacht berths 1000
Maximum length overall 24m (79ft)
Population 2000 (approx)
Rating 3–2–3

General

An artificial yacht harbour still being enlarged, located in the old mouth of R. la Têt. When completed it will become part of a huge marina interconnected by canals with the yacht harbours to N and S. Approach and entrance are easy, but difficult during strong winds from NE–S–SE. Good shelter is obtained once inside from all seas but not from the wind itself. There are good facilities for yachtsmen which are to be improved further. It is an uninteresting area but the old towns of Perpignan and Elne 5M inland are attractive.

Data

Charts Admiralty 1705
French 6483
Navicarte 511

Current There is a S-going current of 0·5 to 1 knot off this harbour.

Magnetic variation 2°09'W (1994) decreasing by about 6' each year.

Port radio VHF Ch 9 and 16.

Weather forecast Posted three times a day at the *bureau du port*, also weather maps once a day. Transmits forecast on VHF Ch 9 at odd hours. Recorded forecast (☎ 36 68 08 08 and 38 68 06 66).

Speed limit 3 knots.

Lights

Canet-Plage Fl(4)W.12s27m15M White structure
Jetée Sud head Oc.R.4s9m9M White and red column
Jetée Nord head Fl(2)G.6s5m5M White tower, green top

Warning

This harbour is still in the course of development and changes must be expected (1992).

Approach by day

From S The low, flat, sandy coast is featureless. The flats, houses, jetties and water tower of St-Cyprien can be identified, also a road bridge over a dried up river bed leading to the Etang de Canet. The flats and houses of Canet and another water tower can be recognised and in the closer approach the Jetée Sud will be seen.

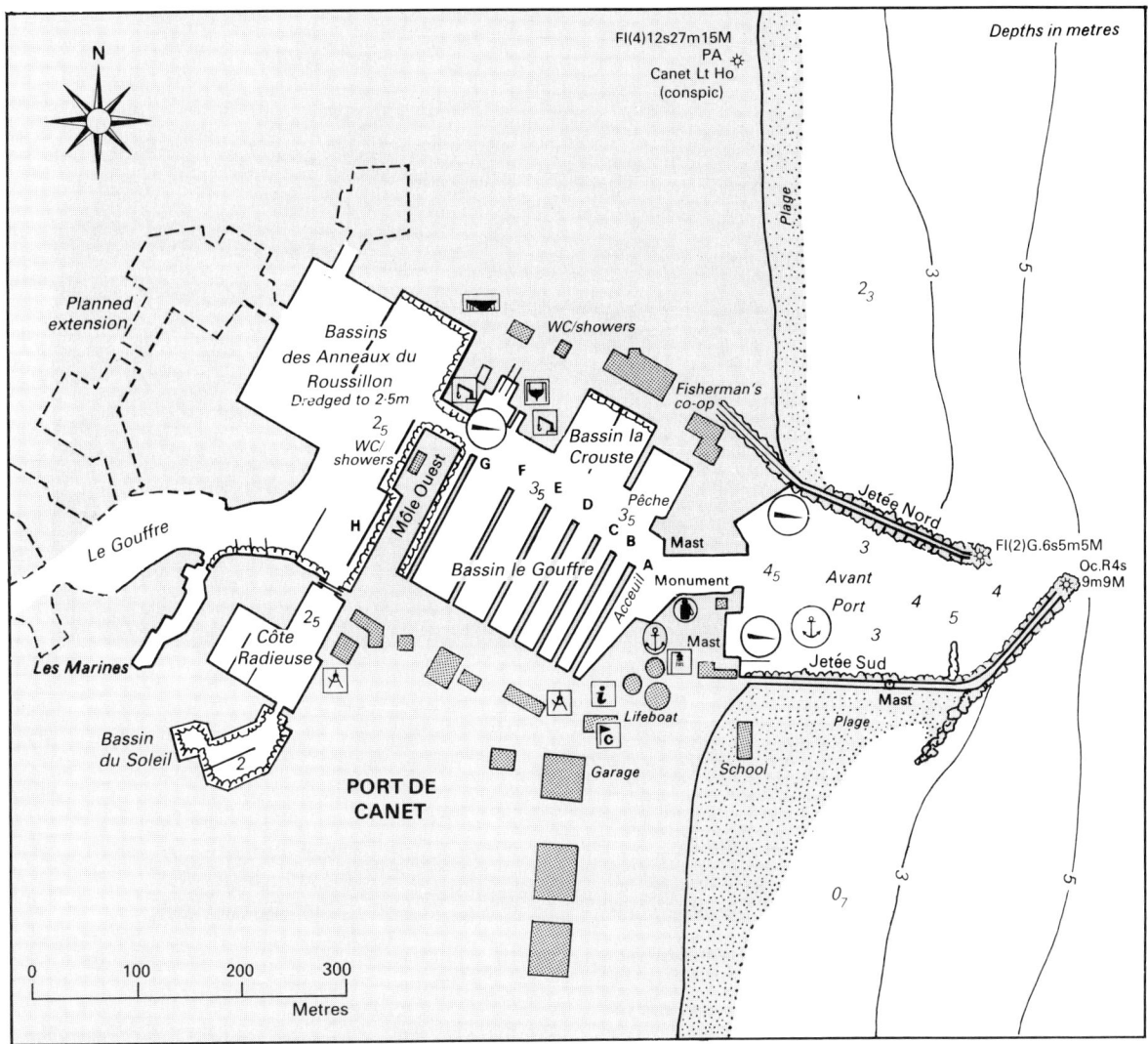

Port de Canet-en-Roussillon (St-Nazaire)

From N From Port Barcarès (Le Grau St-Ange), which can be identified by its jetty and blocks of flats, the low, flat, straight, sandy coast has no conspicuous features. The houses, flats and water tower of Canet can be seen from afar and the jetty can be seen in the closer approach. Canet lighthouse, of unusual design, is conspicuous.

Approach by night

Using the following lights navigate to a position where the entrance is SW at 300m:

Cap Béar Fl(3)W.15s30M
Port Vendres Oc.G.4s8M
Cap Leucate Fl(2)W.10s20M
Perpignan-Rivesaltes Aero Mo(X)W.8·5s33M
Canet-Plage Fl(4)W.12s15M

Anchorage in the approach

Anchor 400m to NE of the entrance in 8m (26ft) sand, mud and weed.

Entrance

By day Approach the entrance on a SW course altering to a W course, enter the inner harbour, and secure to first pontoon to port (A) or near the fuel pumps.

By night Approach Oc.R.4s on a SW course and leave it 25M to port, and Fl(2)G.6s to starboard, then change to a W course and enter the inner harbour. Secure to pontoon A or near the fuel pumps.

Berths

Secure alongside quay just to W of fuel pumps to pontoon A. When a berth is allocated, usually at the first pontoon, secure stern-to, bow-to mooring buoy.

Formalities

Report to the *bureau du port* (☎ 68 80 20 66), open in summer 0800–1830, in winter 0800–1230 and 1330–1830, on arrival, and if necessary report to the customs (☎ 68 80 31 08) in the office nearby.

Port de Canet-en-Roussillon (St-Nazaire) looking W

Port de Canet-en-Roussillon (St-Nazaire). Entrance looking NW

Port de Canet-en-Roussillon looking NW–W

Harbour charges
There are harbour charges.

Facilities
Slips Two slips, one each side of the *avant-port*.
Cranes There are a travel-lift (27 tonnes) and cranes (2·5 and 10 tonnes) to N of the harbour.
Slipway 60 tonnes.
Fuel Diesel (*gasoil*) and petrol are available from pumps near the *bureau du port* (☎ 68 73 58 73). Open in summer 0800–2000, in winter 1000–1200 and 1500–1800.
Water Points are established along quays and pontoons.
Electricity Supply points for 220v AC 6 amps and 12 or 24v DC are to be found on quays and pontoons.

Provisions A few shops near the harbour and many more at Canet-Plage.
Duty-free goods It is possible to obtain duty-free goods here. (A change is expected.)
Ice Obtainable at the moment from the Co-operative de Pêche and also at Taverne du Port, Iceberg and Tino Pêche. Automatic machine.
Garbage Rubbish containers are to be found on quays and pontoons.
Chandlery Two ships' chandlers to W of the harbour.
Repairs Major shipyards and repair workshops are built to the N of the harbour. Repairs to hull, engine, sails, etc. possible.
Post office In Canet-Plage.
Hotels One ***, six **, five * hotels and some eight unclassified.

Restaurants Some 35 in Canet-Plage and a number of café-bars.

Yacht clubs The YC Canet-en-Roussillon (YCCR) (☎ 68 73 58 73). The Club Nautique de Canet-Perpignan (CNCP) (☎ 68 73 33 95) has a small clubhouse just to the S of the harbour entrance. The Sport Nautique Canetois (SNC) is at the *bureau du port* (☎ 68 80 00 66). There are plans for other clubhouses around the harbour.

Showers Eighteen showers and WCs are available at a building near the *bureau du port* and around the harbour.

Information office The Syndicat d'Initiative (☎ 68 73 25 20) has an office by the *bureau du port* and another in Canet-Plage.

Visit The old towns of Perpignan, Elne and St-Nazaire should be visited since there are many interesting buildings to see. A small aquarium and a museum of boats are also interesting.

Beaches Miles of sandy beaches either side of the harbour.

Communications Bus at Canet-Plage, air and rail services at Perpignan 7M.

Lifeboat Vedette, 3rd class (☎ 68 80 20 66).

Bicycles Hire of bicycles for one hour free of charge.

Future development

A considerable amount of work has still to be carried out on this harbour, its surroundings and its facilities, and it will be several years before the existing plans are completed. These plans envisage connecting canals with nearby harbours and the Etang de Canet.

---

9 PORT DE STE MARIE-LA-PLAGE (LA MER)
66470 Pyrénées

Position 43°·5′N 3°3′·5E
Minimum depth in the entrance 2m (6·6ft)
                            harbour 2 to 0·5m (6·6ft to 1·6ft)
Width of the entrance 20m (approx)
Number of yacht berths about 100+
Maximum length overall 12m (40ft)
Population 500 (approx)
Rating 3-4-4.

General

A small yacht harbour recently developed in what was probably an old mouth of the river La Têt which now has its mouth ½M to S. To N of the harbour lies the rapidly expanding seaside town of Sainte-Marie-la-Plage. Approach and entrance to the harbour require care due to shallow depths. In strong winds and swell from NE–E–SE it would be dangerous to enter. Facilities limited to normal everyday requirements.

Data

Charts Admiralty 1705
        French 6844
        Navicarte 511

Currents A S-going current of 0.5 to 1 knot off the entrance to this harbour.

Magnetic variation 2°09′W (1994) decreasing by about 6′ each year.

Warning
This harbour could be expanded and improved with ease and changes must be expected.

Approach by day
From S The long straight flat sandy coast is lacking in easily identified objects, but the ports of Argelès-Plage, St-Cyprien-Plage and Canet-Plage should be recognised from near the 20m contour. 1M to S of the entrance of this harbour the Canet-Plage lighthouse can be recognised.

From N Cap Leucate with its lighthouse lookout and radio towers should be recognised, as should the entrances to Ports Leucate and Barcarès. There is a 14m disused lighthouse at Barcarès de St-Laurent; the entrance is 4M to S of it.

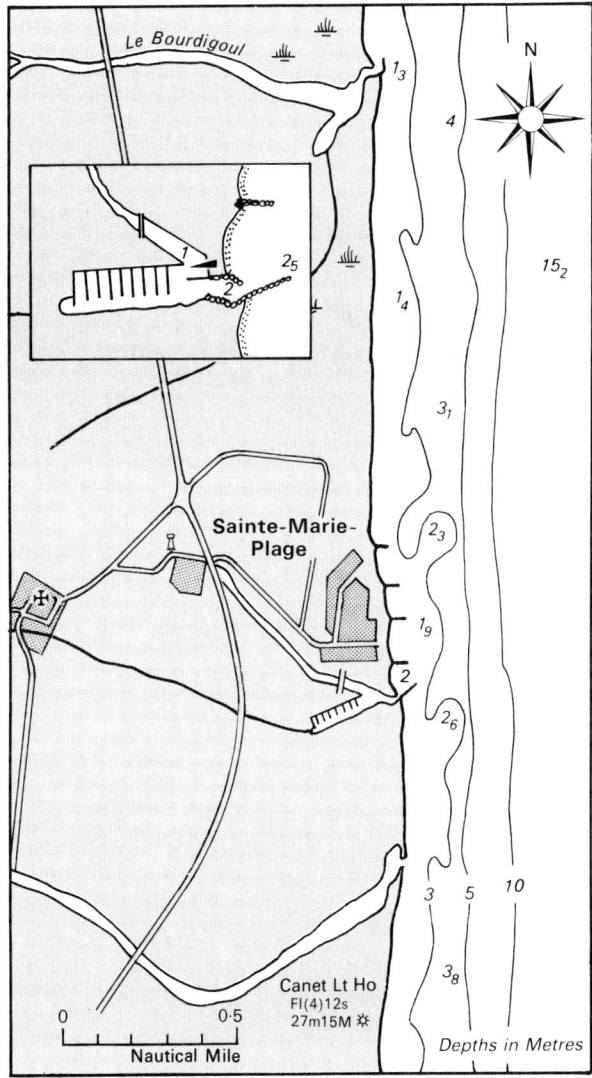

Port de Ste Marie-la-Plage (La Mer)

Port de Ste Marie-la-Plage looking NE

Bureau du port and mast

Port de Ste Marie-la-Plage. Entrance looking W

Approach by night

Not recommended unless a previous visit has been made by day. The lack of navigation lights makes entrance difficult.

Entrance

By day The town of Sainte-Marie-la-Plage has four groins for retaining the sand. The harbour entrance is just to S of the fourth (most S) groyne. Enter close to the short Digue Sud sounding carefully. There are several buoys marking the entrance; keep to the port side. A very tall mast stands beside the entrance.

Berth

Secure in a vacant space and visit the *bureau du port* to be allocated a berth.

Medium sized yachts   *Workshop and café*   *Small yachts*

Port de Ste Marie-la-Plage looking NW up the harbour

Formalities

Bureau du port (☎ 68 80 51 02) is in a temporary cabin near the entrance to the harbour.

Charges

Harbour charges to be paid.

Facilities

Slip One near the *bureau du port.*
Cranes Two 10-tonne mobile cranes.
Dock A small dock for launching.
Water Several taps around the harbour.
Electricity A few points at roots of pontoons
Provisions From the town 1M inland or from shops near the shore.
Garbage Old oil drums.
Chandlery Shop near harbour.
Repairs Engineers and electronic mechanics.
Post office In town.
Restaurants and café/bars Many in the area.
Yacht clubs Association de l'Abri Nautique de Ste Marie (AANSM) (☎ 68 73 36 97) has a cabin near the *bureau du port.*
Information Syndicat d'Initiative office on the sea front.
Visits St-Nazaire, Elne and Perpignan should be visited.
Beaches Good sandy beaches N and S.
Communications Bus service, air and rail at Perpignan.

Future development

It would be easy to enlarge this harbour and to provide more facilities. It is expected that this will occur in the near future.

ETANG DE LEUCATE (ETANG DE SALSES)

General

This large inland lagoon of brackish water is 7M long and 3M wide at the widest place, and has two major harbours, Barcarès and Leucate, and several small marinas.

Entrances

It has three entrances to the sea:

One at Port Barcarès which has a depth of 2m (6·5ft) and a clearance under a bridge of 3·80m (12·5ft).

Another entrance at Port Leucate of minimum depth 3·20m (10·5ft) and a clearance under a road bridge of 18m (59ft).

The third entrance, the Grau de Leucate, further N is not yet fully developed. It is used by small fishing boats.

Depths

The S half is the deepest with depths greater than 2m (6·5ft) quite close to the shore, providing a sheltered area of 4M by 2M where deep-keeled craft can sail. The N half is shallow, 1m (3ft) or less, and a large area in the centre is given over to oyster beds.

Harbours

There are three marina-type harbours in addition to Port Barcarès and Port Leucate already built on the E side of the *étang* and more are planned. The harbours built are Marina (or Cité Lacustre) Nautica, La Coudalière and the Marina des Brigantines. A small harbour is being developed at St Laurent de la Solongue.

Navigation

Other than the line of small white buoys that mark the E side of the channel between the two ports of Barcarès and Leucate and the red and black buoys that mark the entrance to these two ports from the *étang*, there are no navigational aids. The high bridge at Leucate, the block of flats at Barcarès and the water tower at Barcarès de St-Laurent are all conspicuous. Keep clear of any shellfish beds and do not anchor near them.

Seas

Despite the fact that this is sheltered water, it can become very rough and dangerous to small craft when the NW *tramontane* blows.

Ferry

A ferry for tourists carries out a one-hour tour of the *étang*.

Teleski

A teleski is established near the Marina des Brigantines.

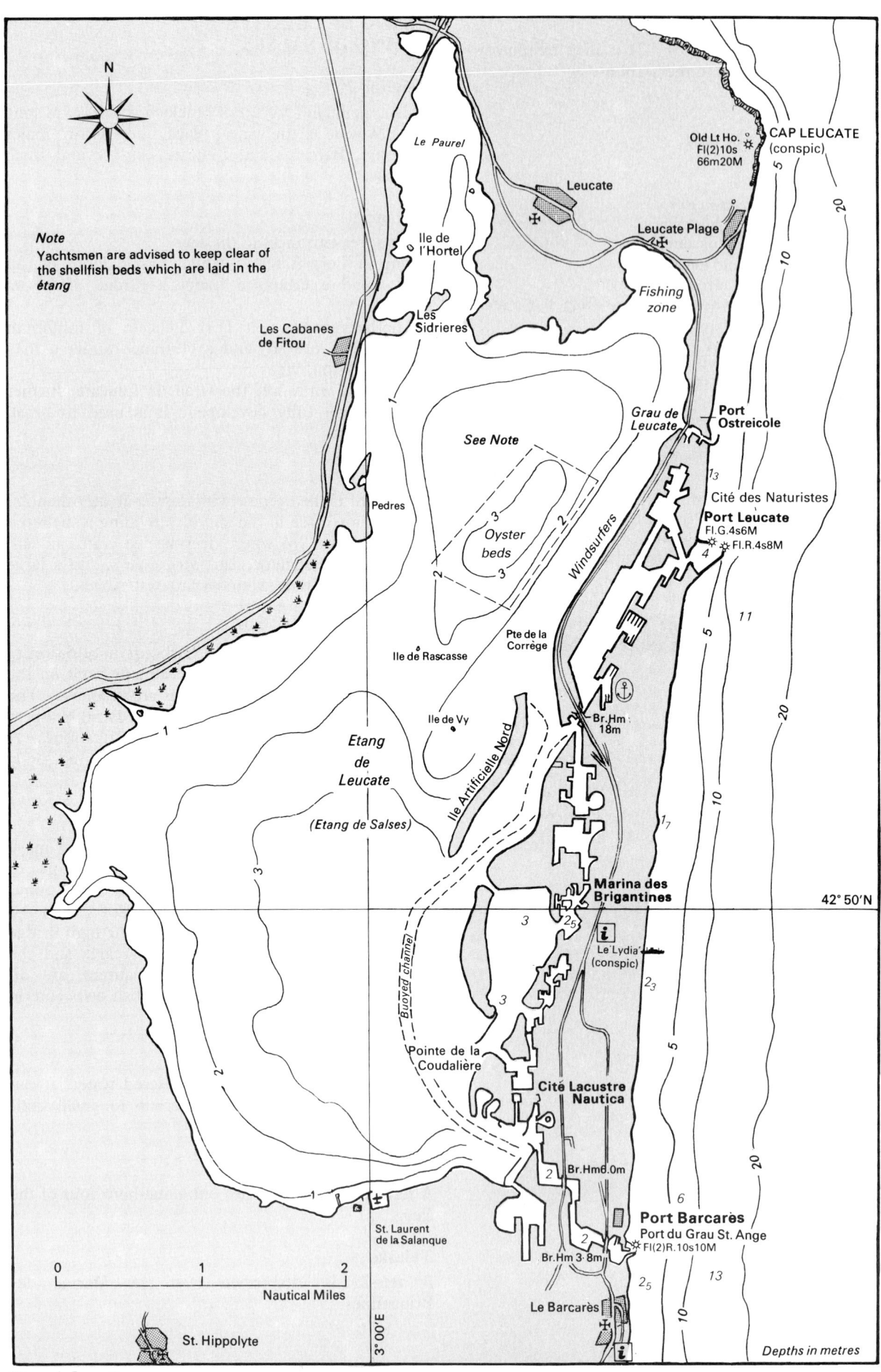

N

Note
Yachtsmen are advised to keep clear of
the shellfish beds which are laid in the
étang

Le Paurel

Leucate

Old Lt Ho.
Fl(2)10s
66m20M

CAP LEUCATE
(conspic)

Ile de
l'Hortel

Leucate Plage

Les
Sidrieres

Fishing
zone

Les Cabanes
de Fitou

See Note

Grau de
Leucate

Port
Ostreicole

1₃

Cité des Naturistes

Port Leucate
Fl.G.4s6M

Pedres

3

2

Oyster
beds

4   Fl.R.4s8M

2

3

Windsurfers

11

Pte de la
Corrège

5

Ile de Rascasse

Ile de Vy

Ile Artificielle Nord

Br.Hm
18m

Etang
de
Leucate

10

(Etang de Salses)

3

20

Buoyed channel

1₇

**Marina des
Brigantines**

3

2₅

42° 50′N

Le 'Lydia'
(conspic)

2₃

3

5

Pointe de la
Coudalière

1

2

**Cité Lacustre
Nautica**

20

St. Laurent
de la Salanque

2

Br.Hm6.0m

6

Port Barcarès
Port du Grau St. Ange
Fl(2)R.10s10M

13

Br.Hm 3·8m

2

2₅

Le Barcarès

10

| 0 | 1 | 2 |

Nautical Miles

St. Hippolyte

Depths in metres

Etang de Leucate

10 PORT BARCARES (LE GRAU ST ANGE)

66420 Pyrénées Orientales

Position 42°47′·9N 3°02′·4E
Minimum depth in the entrance 3m (10ft)
in the harbour 2·5 to 2m (8 to 6ft)
Bridge clearance 3·8m (12·5ft)
Width of the entrance 25m
Number of yacht berths 203
Maximum length overall 13m (43ft)
Population 500
Rating 3–3–3

General

An old *grau* leading to the huge Etang de Leucate which has been developed into a modern yacht harbour by the establishment of jetties, quays and pontoons. The area is still under development. It is connected by canals with harbours to the N. Easy to approach and enter but if there is a swell and the wind is from NE–E–SE entrance is difficult. Facilities are limited at the moment (1993) but in due course will be good. In a NW *tramontane* the harbour offers shelter from the seas but not from the wind.

Data

Charts Admiralty 1705
French 6844
Navicarte 511

Current There is a S-going current of 0·5 to 1 knot off this harbour.

Magnetic variation 2°09′W (1994) decreasing by about 6′ each year.

Weather forecasts Weather forecasts are published three times daily outside the *bureau du port*. Recorded forecasts from ☎ 36 68 08 08 and 36 68 08 66.

Speed limit 3 knots.

Lights
Jetée Sud head Fl(2)R.10s10m10M White column with red top
Jetée Nord F.W.3m Strip light

Warning

This harbour is still in course of construction and changes must be expected.

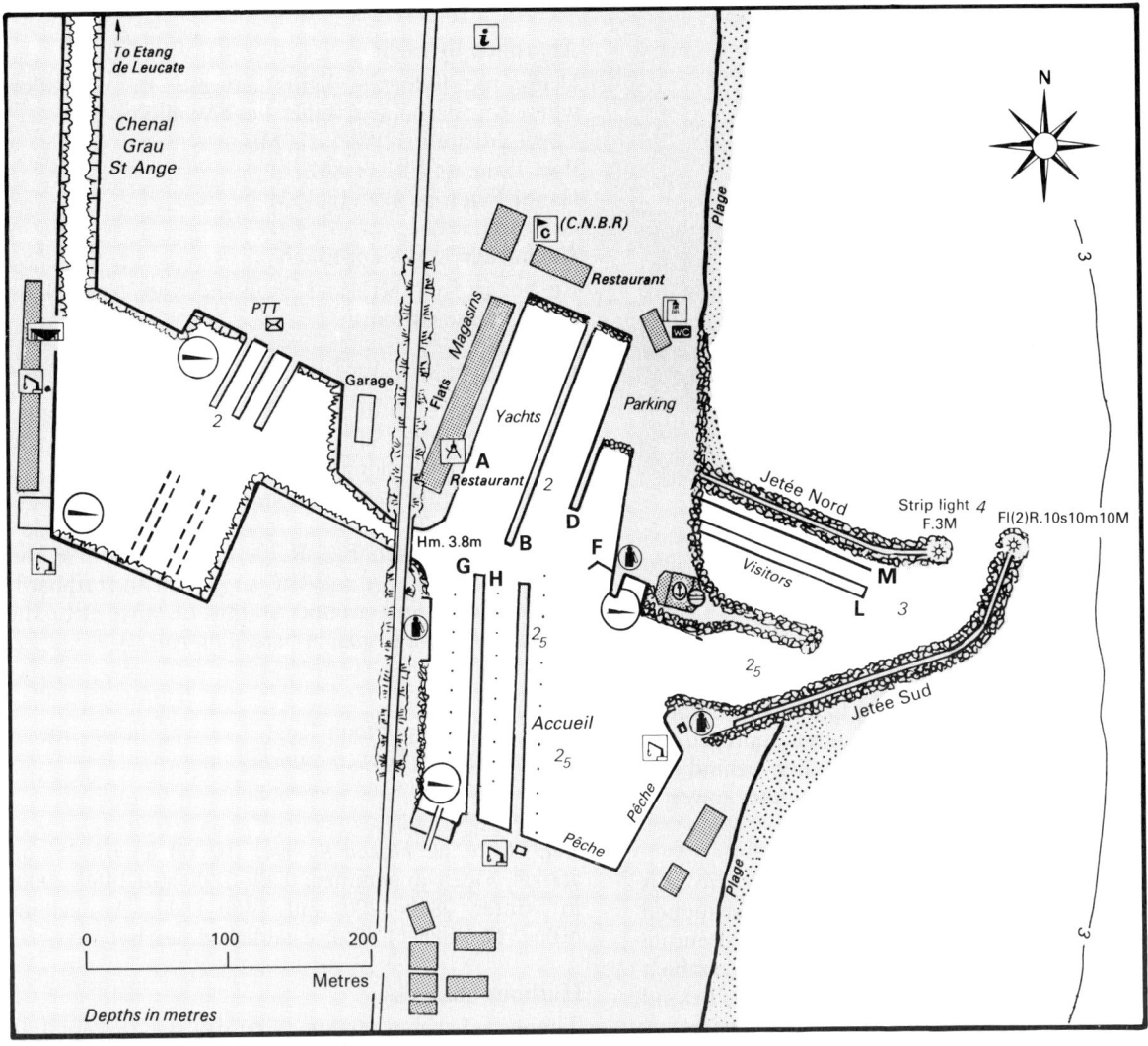

Port Barcarès

Bureau du port   *Visitors*

Port Barcares (Le Grau St-Ange) looking NW

Bureau du port

Port Barcares (Le Grau St-Ange) looking W

Approach by day

From S The low flat sandy featureless coast stretches in a straight line N–S. The concentration of houses and flats and the harbour jetties of St-Cyprien and Canet can be identified. The houses and water tower of Le Barcarès de St-Laurent 1M to S of this harbour may also be recognised. In the closer approach the jetties and the block of flats that lies behind the harbour will be seen. The *bureau du port* tower is very conspicuous.

From N A similar type of coast stretches to this harbour from Cap Leucate which has low flat-topped whitish cliffs. The entrance jetties of Port Leucate are easily recognisable as is the beached steamboat *Lydia* which is painted white. Again the flats behind this harbour, the jetties and the conspicuous *bureau du port* will be seen in the closer approach.

Approach by night

Using the following lights navigate to a position where this harbour entrance lies SW 400m:
Cap Leucate Fl(2)W.10s20M
Port Leucate Fl.R.4s8M
Canet-Plage Fl(4)W.12s15M

Anchorage in the approach

Anchor in 5m (16ft) sand, mud and weed some 400m to NE of the entrance.

Entrance

By day Approach the entrance on a SW course, enter 15m from Jetée Sud head leaving it to port, and follow the jetty along at the same distance into the harbour. Secure to *quai* at *bureau du port.*

By night Approach Fl(2)R.10s on a SW course and leave it 15m to port and FW strip light to starboard. Follow Jetée Sud around at this distance into the harbour. Secure to *quai* at *bureau du port.*

Berths

Berth stern-to pontoon located on the inner side of the Jetée Nord, bow-to mooring buoy.

Formalities

Report to the *bureau du port* (☎ 68 86 07 35) on arrival. Open in summer, 0700–1300 and 1400–2000, in winter 0800–1200 and 1400–1800. A customs office (☎ 68 86 11 88) is established nearby.

Harbour charges

There are harbour charges; first day free (except July and August).

Port Barcarès. SS *Lydia* on the beach 1M to N of the harbour

Port Barcares (Le Grau St-Ange) looking NE–E

Facilities

Slips A slip just inside the entrance on the starboard hand and another on the S side of the harbour.

Slipway A small slipway on the S side of the harbour.

Crane Two 10-tonne cranes and one 4-tonne crane at the S side of the harbour and another at the shipyard under the bridge.

Fuel Diesel (*gasoil*) and petrol pumps near *bureau du port*. Open in summer 0730–1300 and 1400–1930, in winter 0800–1200 and 1400–1800.

Water Water points are available on all quays and pontoons.

Electricity Supply points for 220v AC 5 amp are on the quays and pontoons.

Provisions Limited shops at the harbour but more to be provided. Many shops at Le Barcarès 1M away.

Ice From *bureau du port*.

Garbage Rubbish containers on the quays.

Chandlery A ships' chandler to W of the harbour.

Repairs A shipyard to the W of the harbour where all normal repairs can be carried out.

Post office At Le Barcarès 1M away.

Hotels Three ★★, two ★ and several unclassified hotels.

Restaurants Fifteen restaurants and some café/bars.

Yacht club The Cercle Nautique du Barcarès-Roussillon (CNBR) (☎ 68 86 07 28) has a small modern clubhouse to the NW of the harbour with all normal facilities.

Showers Eight showers and eight WCs in building to N of harbour.

Information office The Syndicat d'Initiative has offices at the town hall (*mairie*) at Le Barcarès (☎ 68 86 16 56) and at the *Lydia*.

Lifeboat Vedette, 2nd class (☎ 68 80 20 66 or 68 86 07 35).

Visits To see something out of the ordinary the *Lydia* should be visited. St-Nazaire, Elne and Perpignan should also be visited.

Beaches There are miles of sandy beaches either side of the harbour.

Communications Bus service and rail and air services at Perpignan.

Future development

It will take a number of years to complete the plans that exist for the development of the area.

History

This was a very small fishing port based on the outlet from the Etang de Leucate.

Pte de la Coudalière   *Village des Pêcheurs*

Entrance to Etang de Leucate from Port Barcarès looking NW to La Coudalière

11 PORT LEUCATE
11370 Aude

Position 42°52'·4N 3°03'·3E
Minimum depth in the entrance 4m (13ft)
                  in the harbour 3m (10ft)
Width of the entrance 60m
Number of yacht berths 1000 (8000 when completed)
Maximum length overall 20m (65ft)
Population 300 (approx)
Rating 3–3–2

General

An extensive complex of yacht harbours and marinas artificially constructed between a very large *étang* and the sea. It is not yet fully completed (1991) but will in due course offer excellent facilities to yachtsmen. The approach and entrance are usually easy, but in strong winds and swell from NE–E–SE become difficult and could be dangerous. The harbour offers protection from the NW *tramontane/mistral* but no real shelter from the wind itself.

Data

Charts   Admiralty 1705
           French 7002
           Navicarte 510, 511

Current A S-going current of 0·5m to 1 knot runs past this harbour entrance.

Magnetic variation 2°09'W (1994) decreasing by about 6' each year.

Port radio VHF Ch 9. Continuous watch in summer, closed in winter 1200–1400.

Speed limit 5 knots

Weather forecasts Weather forecasts are posted twice a day at the *bureau du port* near the shipyard. Recorded forecasts from (☎ 36 68 08 11, 68 40 91 68 and 36 68 08 08. Forecasts are also broadcast on VHF Ch 9 at each even hour.

Lights
Jetée Est head Fl.R.4s8m8M White column, red top
Inner entrance S Oc.R.4s3m6M Red tower
Inner entrance N Oc.G.4s3m6M Green tower
Jetée Ouest head Fl.G.4s8m6M White column, green top
Harbour lights Five F.Rs and two F.Gs mark basin entrances and projecting walls inside the harbour (range 6–8M)

Buoys There is a line of red and green buoys marking the channel beyond the Pont de la Corrètge. There is also a line of buoys marking the N edge of the shallows.

Warning

This harbour is still in the process of development and changes are to be expected (1993). Anchorage inside the harbour is not allowed without good reason.

Approach by day

From S The village of Barcarès, the jetties of Port Barcarès with a block of flats behind, the white steamship *Lydia* stranded ashore and the high Pont

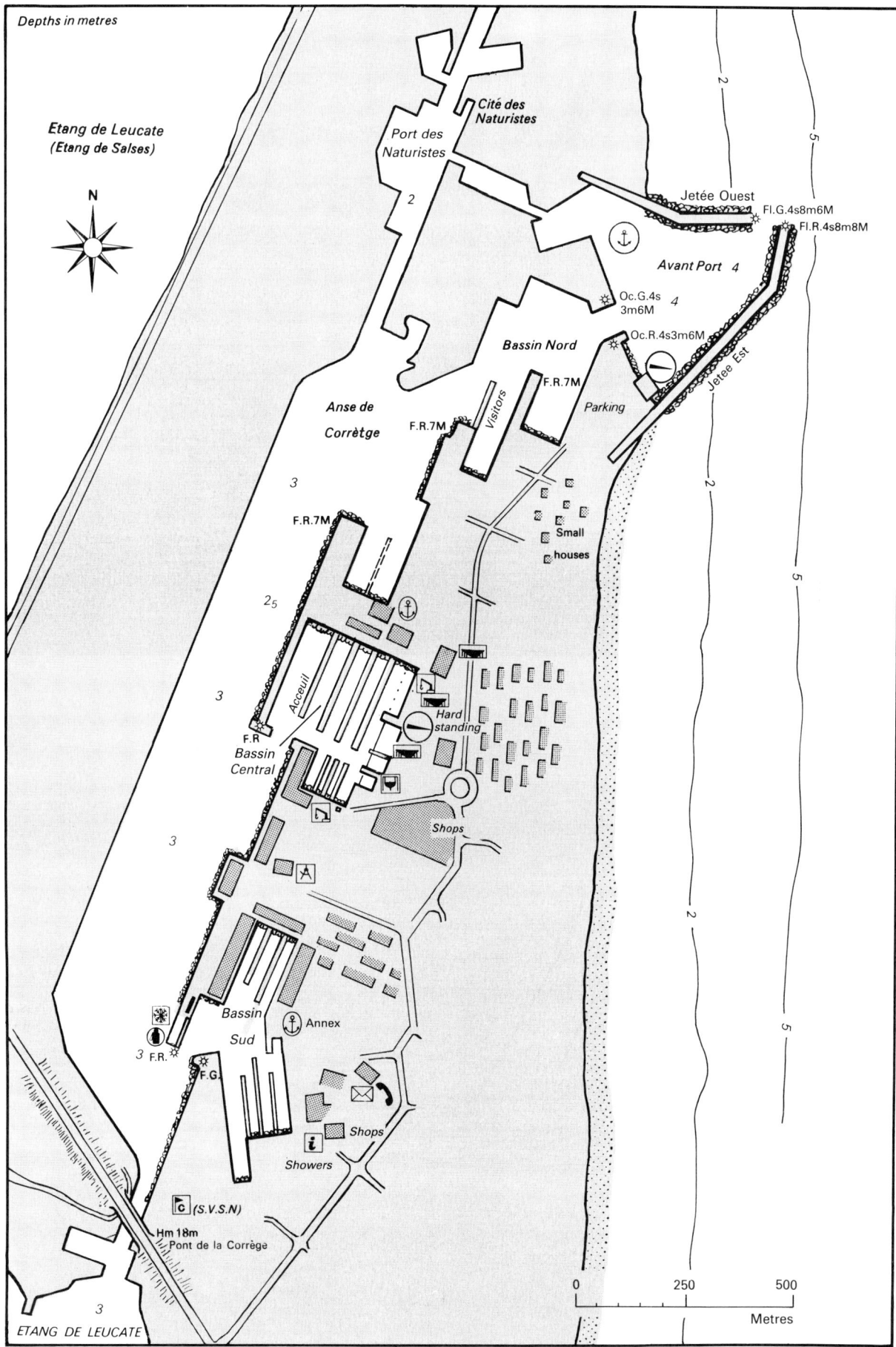

Port Leucate

Visitors   *Bureau du port*   *Cité des Naturistes*

Port Leucate. Entrance looking W

Bureau du port

Port Leucate. Middle section of port looking NW

Port Leucate. Inner entrance looking SW

Grau de Leucate

de la Corrège are all identifiable on the low flat sandy straight coast. In the closer approach the jetties of this harbour will be seen.

From N The flat-topped whitish cliffs of Cap Leucate with its conspicuous lighthouse, radome and old signal station are easily recognised. The jetties of this harbour with their light towers show up well in the closer approach.

Approach by night
Using the lights listed below navigate to a position where the entrance lies 400m SW:
Cap Leucate Fl(2)W.10s20M
Canet-Plage Fl(4)W.12s15M
Port Barcarès Fl(2)R.10s10M

Anchorage in the approach
Anchor in 8m (26ft) sand, mud and weed 400m to NE of this entrance.

Entrance
By day Approach the entrance on a SW course and enter close to the head of Jetée Est where the water is deeper. Cross the *avant-port* and enter the Bassin Nord.

By night Approach Fl.R.4s on a SW course and leave this light 20m to port and Fl.G.4s to starboard. Enter between Oc.R.4s and Oc.G.4s and leave 5 more F.R lights to port.

Berths
Take the S inner entrance (the N entrance leads to Cité des Naturistes) and then proceed down the harbour to the Bassin Central. Secure at No. 9 pontoon marked 'No. 9 Visitors' beside the *bureau du port* for the allocation of a berth. Then secure stern-to quay or pontoon, bow-to mooring buoy where instructed.

Anchorage
A temporary anchorage is available in the *avant-port* in 4m (13ft) sand.

Formalities
Report on arrival to the *bureau du port* (☎ 68 40 91 24, *Fax* 68 40 72 27). Open summer 0800–1200 and 1400–2000, winter 0800–1200 and 1400–1800. There are customs here in the season (☎ 68 40 85 30).

Harbour charges
There are harbour charges.

Facilities
Slips Slips in the Bassin Central and two in the *avant-port*.
Slipways Two slipways.
Cranes A 45-tonne and 6-tonne travel-lift and 1-tonne and 3-tonne cranes at the Bassin Central.
Fuel Diesel (*gasoil*) and petrol are available from pumps at the entrance to the Bassin Sud (☎ 68 40 91 24). Open summer 0900–1300 and 1600–1900, winter 0830–1200 and 1400–1730 on demand.

Water Water points are established at all quays and pontoons.

Electricity Supply points 220v AC 5 amp are established at all quays and pontoons.

Provisions A few shops and a supermarket to the SW of the Bassin Sud.

Ice Ice is available from the fuel stations and also from the *bureau du Port* and café/bars.

Garbage Rubbish containers on all quays and pontoons.

Chandlery A ships' chandler between the Bassin Sud and Central; supplies are also available from the shipyards.

Repairs Three shipyards which can carry out all normal repairs to hull, engines, electronics, etc.

Post office In the season a post office is established near the *bureau du port*.

Hotels Four **, three * and many unlisted are to be built in the area, with more to be constructed.

Restaurants Many restaurants and café/bars in operation and more to be provided.

Yacht clubs The Société Nautique de Port Leucate (SNPL) has a clubhouse at the *bureau du port* (☎ 68 40 72 66). The Société de Voiles et Sports Nautiques (SVSN) (☎ 68 33 10 40) has a clubhouse at the Pont de la Corrège with a bar, lounge and showers. The Société Méditerranée de Yachting (SMY) has a clubhouse near the Bassin Central. There is also the Société Nautique de Cap Leucate (SNCL) (☎ 68 86 00 14) which has an office at the town hall.

Showers Eighteen showers and WCs around the harbour.

Information office There is an information office near the *bureau du port* annex (☎ 68 40 91 31).

Beaches Miles of sandy beach each side of the harbour.

Lifeboat An inshore rescue craft is manned in the season.

Visits The old Fort des Mattes which is in ruins can be visited, but Perpignan is the main place of interest.

Communications Bus service, rail service at Le Franqui 1M and Perpignan, air service at Perpignan 13M.

Future development

It will take a many years to finish the existing plans for the development of this area.

Cap Leucate

This is an isolated flat-topped (52m) whitish-coloured prominent headland. It is cliffed and there are some isolated rocks close in; otherwise it is sheer-to. There are a red-topped lighthouse and a radio tower, both of which are white, located on the crest.

⌁ NW Cap Leucate

An open anchorage tucked in close under the cliffs to NW of the Cap, rocks very close in; open to NW–N–NE–E–SE. Track, road and houses on the cliff top.

Cap Leucate looking NW

Anchorages to NW of Cap Leucate. Strong *tramontane* blowing

⚓ La Franqui-Plage

Two useful anchorages. The first is behind a sand bar 2·4 to 1·7m that runs in a NW direction from Cap Leucate, entered from the N and open to N–NE–E–SE. The second is through a gap in the sandbank close to the village of La Franqui-Plage and short of the road/railway bridges inland. Reconnoitre by dinghy first because changes occur from time to time in both the sand bars and banks. In periods of drought the entrance may dry up or become too shallow to use. Hotel and *club nautique* ashore.

La Franqui Plage

⚓ NW Cap Leucate

12 PORT LA NOUVELLE
11210 Aude

Position 43°00'·8N 3°04'·2E
Minimum depth   in the entrance 6m (20ft)
                  in the harbour 5·8m (19ft)
Width of the entrance 100m
Number of yacht berths 130
Maximum length overall 9m (30ft)
Population 5000
Rating 2–3–3

General

An original *grau* (channel) leading to the Etang de Sigean, now developed by the addition of breakwaters and quays into a commercial and fishing port with a section set aside for yachts. The approach and entrance are easy but in heavy seas and wind from the NE-E-SE it can become dangerous to enter.

Facilities and yacht berths are limited. The Canal de la Robine is connected to this harbour and leads to the Canal du Midi via Narbonne. This harbour offers shelter from the seas of the NW *tramontane/mistral* but only gives protection from the wind to a small extent. It is a harbour of character compared to the new harbours in this area.

Data

Charts   Admiralty 1705
           French 6844, 7002
           Navicarte 510

Water levels NW *tramontane* winds lower the level of water in the harbour by up to 0·5m (1·5ft), and conversely SE winds can increase the level by the same amount. This change of up to 1m (3ft) can take place within 1 to 2 hours.

Currents There is a S-going current off the entrance of 0·5 to 1 knot. When the direction of the wind changes and the levels of the water alter there can be streams of up to 3 knots in the harbour.

Magnetic variation 2°09'W (1994) decreasing by about 6' each year.

Port radio VHF Ch 12, 16.

Weather forecast Posted once a day at the *bureau du port* at 0930. Recorded forecast (☎ 36 65 08 11 and 36 65 08 08).

Speed limit 5 knots.

Traffic signals Shown from a mast 100m to NW of Jetée Sud.

Day	Night	Meaning
Red flag	Red light	Seas are breaking in the entrance. Do not enter

Light

Jetée Sud head Lts in line 292°24'. *Front* Q.W.23m14M. White tower, red top. *Rear* 2M from front Q.W.48m17M Tower
Jetée Nord head Iso.G.4s15m5M White round tower, green top

Buoys An E cardinal light buoy (Q(3)10s), ♦ topmark, marks the extremity of an oil pipeline about 1M E of the entrance. There is also a group of mooring buoys at the pipeline terminal. A red and yellow light buoy (Fl(3)20s) is moored to S of the tanker approach channel, with a yellow spindle light buoy (Fl(3)Y.20s) topmark St Andrew's Cross to seawards.

Warning

Entry or exit should not be attempted when commercial vessels are using the entrance; they have priority inside and outside the harbour. An offshore marine farm marked by two light buoys extends to 1M E of this harbour mouth. SW corner Q(6)+LFl.W.15s ▼ topmark. NE corner Q(3)W.10s ♦ topmark.

Approach by day

From S Cap Leucate, which has vertical whitish cliffs and a flat top with a conspicuous lighthouse and old signal station, is easy to recognise because the rest of the coast is low and flat. A tall factory chimney, white with red bands, will be seen to the W of the harbour and the tall white light towers at the

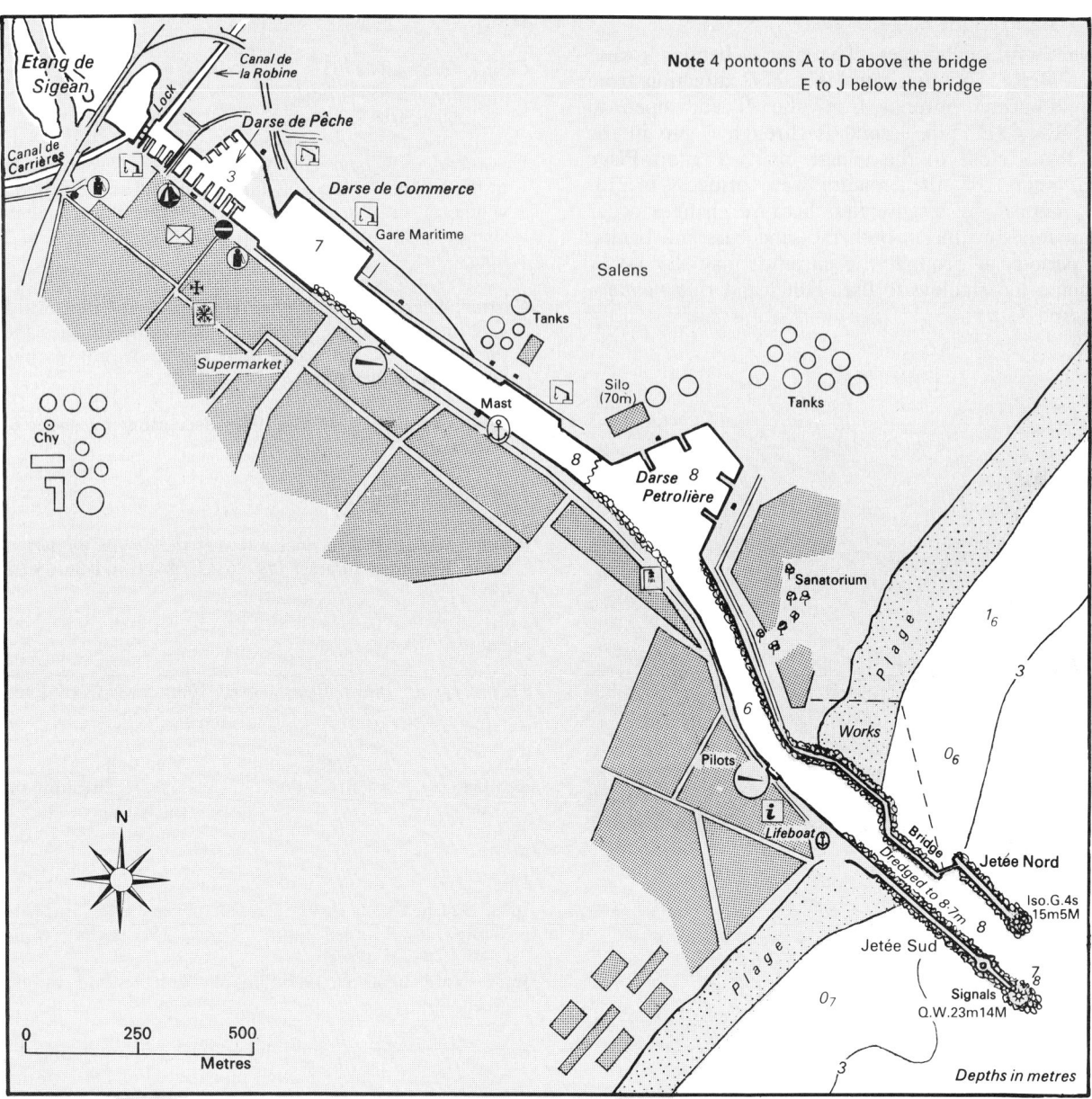

Note 4 pontoons A to D above the bridge
E to J below the bridge

Port la Nouvelle

entrance can be seen from afar. There are a number of large fuel tanks painted silver to the N of the entrance.

From N The town of Valras-Plage can be recognised by its casino building, two high electricity pylons, water tower and harbour jetties. The jetties one (at l'Aude Narbonne-Plage, one at Grau de Pêch Rouge, and two sets at Gruissan) can also be seen from close inshore. The grey hills of Montagne de la Clape a few miles inland will also be seen. The fuel tanks, chimney and light towers described are to be seen from this direction equally well.

Approach by night

Using the lights listed below navigate to a position where the entrance is W at 400m:

Cap Leucate Fl(2)W.10s20M

Port Leucate Fl.R.4s8M
Valras-Plage Fl.G.4s7M

Anchorage in the approach

Anchor 400m to SE of the entrance in 5m (15ft) mud and weed. Yachts must not use the deep water anchorage 3M to SE of the entrance which is marked by yellow buoys.

Entrance

By day Approach on a W course and enter having first ascertained that there are no commercial vessels manoeuvring in the area and that there is no red flag on the signal tower. Follow Jetée Sud at 40m.

By night Approach Q.W in line with Q.W on 292°24' 2M apart; leave 40m to port. After 100m

Bureau du port

Port la Nouvelle. Entrance looking W

leave Iso.G.4s15m to starboard and follow the line of the Jetée Sud in mid-channel.

Harbour pilotage

By day and night Follow the S bank of the canal at 40m for 1¼M as far as a low road bridge which crosses it.

Berths

Yachts secure to one of eight pontoons on the S bank just short of the road bridge. Close to the bank there is only about 1m (3ft) mud but there is 5m (16ft) at the head of the pontoons. Four pontoons for small motor craft lie above the road bridge. Secure stern-to with bow to mooring buoy. There may be a strong stream running in either direction. A temporary berth may be found alongside the quay to port just S of Darse du Commerce at weekends. It is not permitted to secure to any commercial quay or the river bank.

Formalities

Report on arrival to the *bureau du port* (☎ 68 48 17 64, *Fax* 68 40 31 42) or the marina office (☎ 68 32 26 06) which is situated on the S bank. Open 0800–1200 and 1400–1800. There is a customs office (☎ 68 48 01 55) on the S bank near the pontoons, and the officials may visit yachts.

Harbour charges

Harbour charges may be made for long visits. The first five days are free.

Facilities

Slips Two small slips on the S bank.

Cranes The following cranes are available: five of 6 tonnes, ten of 10 tonnes and a 10-tonne elevator capacity on the N bank. These can be hired for removing or stepping masts. Contact *capitaine du port*, at the *bureau du port*, who will direct yachtsmen to the correct office nearby.

Fuel Diesel *(gasoil)* and petrol can be obtained from a garage on the S bank and from another on the way to the station. There is a bulk diesel supply point for canal craft just above the bridge on the N bank where tax-free fuel may be obtained.

Water A water point on the quay by the pontoons.

Provisions A number of shops and a supermarket nearby, and more shops spread around the town.

Ice Ice can be bought from a store to the S of the church and also from the garage on the S bank.

Garbage A broken rubbish container on the quay by the pontoons.

Chandlery Two ships' chandlers on the S bank near the pontoons, but they do not have much yacht equipment in stock.

Repairs Three shipyards that can carry out normal repairs. There are also mechanics who can repair engines.

Post office The PTT is located on the S bank near the pontoons.

Hotels One ★★★, four ★★, two ★ and several unclassified hotels.

Restaurants Three restaurants and a number of café/bars.

Yacht club The nearest yacht club is at Port la Nautique at the N end of the Etang de Sigean. It is the Société Nautique de Narbonne (SNN) (☎ 68 32 26 06) which has a bar, restaurant, lounge and showers.

Information office The Syndicat d'Initiative has an office on the S bank close to the beach.

Chimney   Pontoons

Port la Nouvelle. NW end of the port

Chimney   Silo (conspic)

Port la Nouvelle. Entrance looking NW

Port la Nouvelle looking NW from just inside entrance

Sluice to Etang de Sigean　　　　*Canal de la Robine*

Port la Nouvelle. Entrance to Canal de la Robine and Etang de Sigean

Lifeboat A lifeboat is stationed here, 1st class *vedette* (☎ 67 94 12 02).

Visits Small craft and dinghies can enter the Etang de Sigean which is a vast area of inland water, maximum draught 0·8m (2·5ft). The bridge clearance is 1m (3ft), but dependent on the height of the water at the sluice gates. A short journey by train or bus to the very attractive ancient city of Narbonne is worthwhile.

Beaches Miles of sandy beach either side of the harbour mouth.

Communications There are bus and rail services.

Future development

The facilities may be improved and more pontoons established.

History

This *grau* has been in use since Roman times, being connected by the Etang de Sigean with a canal to the original port at Narbonne, several miles inland which was the capital of central Gaul.

13 PORT LA NAUTIQUE
11100 Aude

Position 43°08'·7N 3°00'·5E
Minimum depth in the entrance 1·5m (5ft)
　　　　　in the harbour 1·5 to 0·5m (4·9 to 1ft)
　　　　　in the *étang* 1·6 to 0m (5·2 to 0ft)
　　　　　at sluice gate 1·10m (4ft)
Overhead clearance at sluice gate 1·0m (3ft)
Maximum length overall 8m (26ft)
Number of yacht berths 200
Population 200 (approx)
Rating 3–3–3

General

This small double harbour at the N end of the Etang de Bages (Sigean) is located near the original Roman harbour for the city of Narbonne. Until recent times the *étang* could be easily entered by large boats via the *grau* at La Nouvelle, but access is now barred by a sluice gate which restricts entry to small boats only. The *étang* measures 10M by 6M and covers 2600 hectares, the greater part being navigable. There are good slips for launching trailed yachts at the harbour and all normal facilities are available. Ideal area for those who prefer lake sailing to the dangers of the open sea.

Data

Charts　Admiralty 1705
　　　　French 6844
　　　　Navicarte 510

Magnetic variation 2°04'W (1994) decreasing by about 6' each year.

Speed limit 3 knots.

Weather forecast At *bureau du port*. Automatic relay (☎ 36 68 08 11)

Warning

A detailed chart of the Etang de Bages (Sigean) is not yet available. The level of the water is affected by heavy winds and rain. Watch out for obstructions

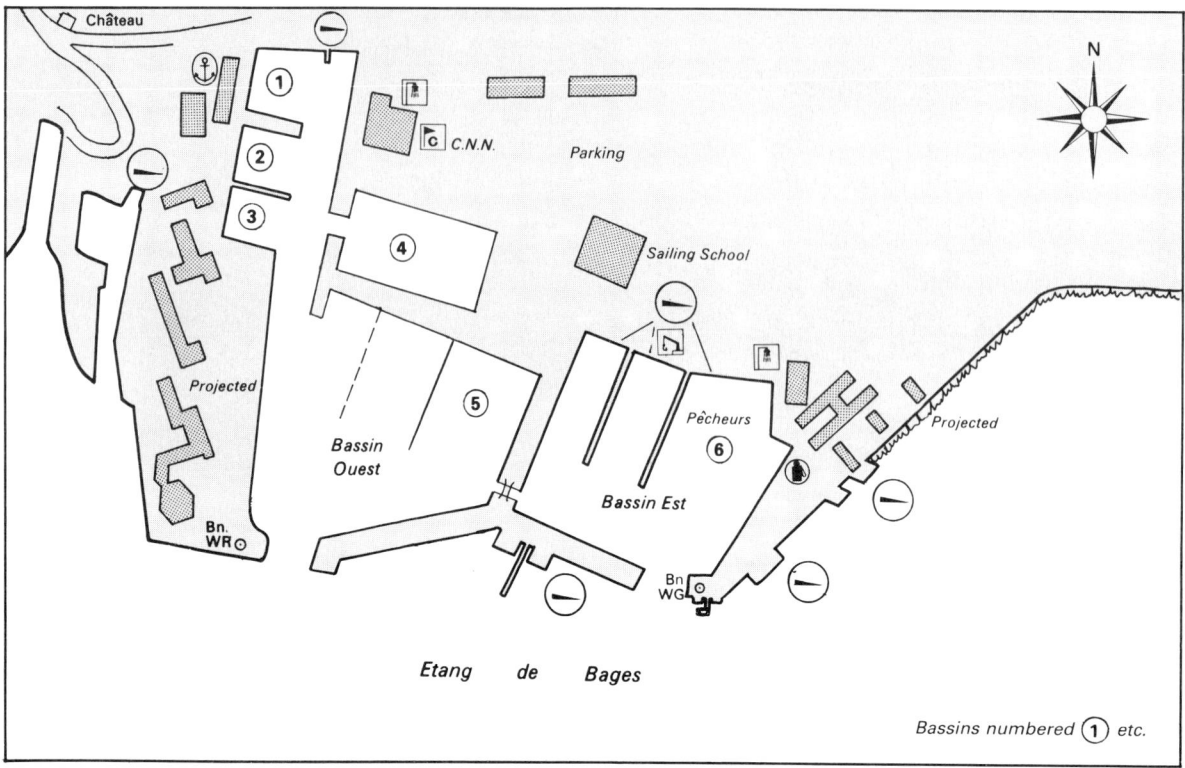

Port la Nautique

created by fish traps in the *étang*. The *étang* bottom is soft mud and weed.

Approach by day

Approach the N end of the *étang* on a N course. The harbour buildings backed by a line of pine trees with the towers of Narbonne in the distance make it easy to recognise. The harbour breakwater is marked by a small white pillar on the starboard side of the E *bassin* (No. 6) entrance and a small white pillar with red band on the port side of the *bassin* (No. 5) entrance. These will be seen in the close approach.

Approach by night

Not recommended due to lack of navigational lights.

Entrance

Enter either *bassin* and secure temporarily; report to the *bureau du port* or yacht clubhouse for berthing instructions.

Formalities

Report to *bureau du port* on arrival (☎ 68 32 26 06). Open 0900–1200 and 1400–1800. Customs at Gruissan (☎ 68 49 00 91) and Port la Nouvelle (☎ 68 48 01 55).

Harbour charges

There are harbour charges but the first day is free.

Facilities

Slips There are five slips for launching small craft.
Hards Hard standing area to N of the harbour.
Crane A 6-tonne crane at N side of E *bassin*.
Fuel Petrol pump at E side of harbour.
Water Water points on quays and pontoons.
Electricity 220V AC points on quays and pontoons.
Provisions From Narbonne 2M to N.
Garbage A few rubbish bins around the harbour.
Repairs Simple repairs possible.
Post office Narbonne.
Restaurants Several local café/bars.

Port la Nautique. Entrance looking W

Port la Nautique. E Basin from the entrance

Port la Nautique. W Basin from entrance

Port la Nautique looking SE–S–SW from the Club Nautique

Yacht club Société Nautique de Narbonne (SNN) (☎ 68 32 26 06) has a bar, terrace and showers.
Showers Three showers and WCs.
Visits The old city of Narbonne (2M) should be visited; it was one of the main capitals of Gaul.
Communications Rail and bus at Narbonne. Air at Perpignan.

Future development

A 200-berth marina is planned, as are major improvements to the existing harbour.

History

This is near the site of the ancient Roman harbour of Narbo-Marcius, which served Narbonne, one of the most important capitals of Gaul.

14 PORT DE GRUISSAN-VIEUX (BARBEROUSSE)
11430 Aude

Position 43°05'·6N 3°06'·8E
Minimum depth   in the entrance 1m (3ft)
in the harbour 2·5m (8ft)
in the canal 1·4m (4ft)
Maximum length overall 13m (43ft)
Number of yacht berths 316
Population 3000 (approx)
Rating 2–4–4

General

An old *grau* leading to the Etang de Gruissan that has been canalised (2400m). A small harbour for yachts and fishing craft has been established at the foot of a most attractive old village which is surmounted by a ruined castle whose tower can be seen from afar. The approach is easy but there is a bar at the entrance that makes entry impossible when there is a swell. There are few facilities and limited accommodation for yachts. Shelter from seas but not from wind is obtainable. The small hill of Gruissan and the Montagne de la Clape do to a certain extent break up the NW *tramontane/mistral* wind.

Data

Charts Admiralty 1705
French 6844
Navicarte 510

Magnetic variation 2°04'W (1994) decreasing by about 6' each year.

Speed limit 3 knots.

Port radio VHF Ch 9

Weather forecast Posted at *bureau du port*.

Lights
Digue Sud Head Fl.R.4s6m3M White mast, red top
Digue Nord Head Oc(2)G.6s6m2M White mast, green top
Epi Central Head Fl.G.2s2m1M Concrete pedestal

Buoys W cardinal light buoy ⚑ Q(9)15s 1M SE of the entrance.

Warning

Huge developments are taking place to the N of this harbour and will affect it in due course. The depth over the bar which is normally 1m (3ft) can be less on occasion. It is dredged to 2m periodically.

Approach by day

From S From the conspicuous entrance to Port la Nouvelle with its two jetties and light towers the coast is low, flat and sandy. There is a small tower by the *grau* into the Etang de l'Ayrolle. The grey barren rocky Montagne de la Clape will be seen in the background, as well as the village of Gruissan on a small pointed hill with a ruined tower on its summit. In the closer approach the two small jetties will be seen.

From N From the small harbour of Narbonne-Plage with its water tower the low flat sandy coast parallels the grey rocky Montagne de la Clape. A breakwater with black tower and yellow band at Grau de Pêch Rouge will be seen. The new and extensive breakwaters and jetties of Port de Gruissan-Neuf are easily seen 1M to N of the entrance to this harbour. There is a mass of small holiday huts of the same shape just N of the entrance.

Approach by night

An approach and entrance by night are not advised due to shallows.

Anchorage in the approach

Anchor some 400m to E of the entrance in 8m (26ft) sand, mud and weed.

Entrance

By day Approach the entrance on a SW course with care and enter between the two jetties, then leave a central spur to starboard. Proceed 1¼M up the Canal de Grazel. The harbour entrance is to port and is 150m short of the bridge.

Berths

Secure stern-to the pontoon, bow-to mooring chain.

Formalities

Report to the *bureau du port* (Gruissan ☎ 68 49 01 37) on arrival. Open 1800–1200 and 1400–1800. Customs (☎ 68 49 01 37).

Facilities

Slip A small slip on N side of the harbour.
Slipway A slipway, 6 tonnes, on N side of the harbour.
Crane A 3·5-tonne crane on the W side of the harbour and a 12-tonne lift.
Fuel Diesel (*gasoil*) and petrol are available from a pump at the W side of the harbour.
Water Water points on the quays.
Electricity 220v AC points along the quays and pontoons.
Provisions Some shops in the village and a large number in Narbonne about 5M away.
Ice From nearby camp site.
Garbage A few rubbish containers around the harbour.
Repairs Motor mechanics here.
Post office The PTT is located to the SE of the town.
Hotels Three **, one *, and several unclassified.
Restaurants A few restaurants and some café/bars.
Yacht club The Cercle Nautique Barberousse (CNB) (☎ 68 49 01 30) has an office at the town hall to E of the church.
Showers Five showers and seven WCs.
Information Syndicat d'Initiative (☎ 68 49 00 22).
Visits In addition to the old village there are some prehistoric caves nearby and the beautiful old city of Narbonne should be visited. The shallow Etang de Gruissan can be visited in a dinghy, 2m (6ft) clearance under the bridge. There is also a unique sailors' cemetery.

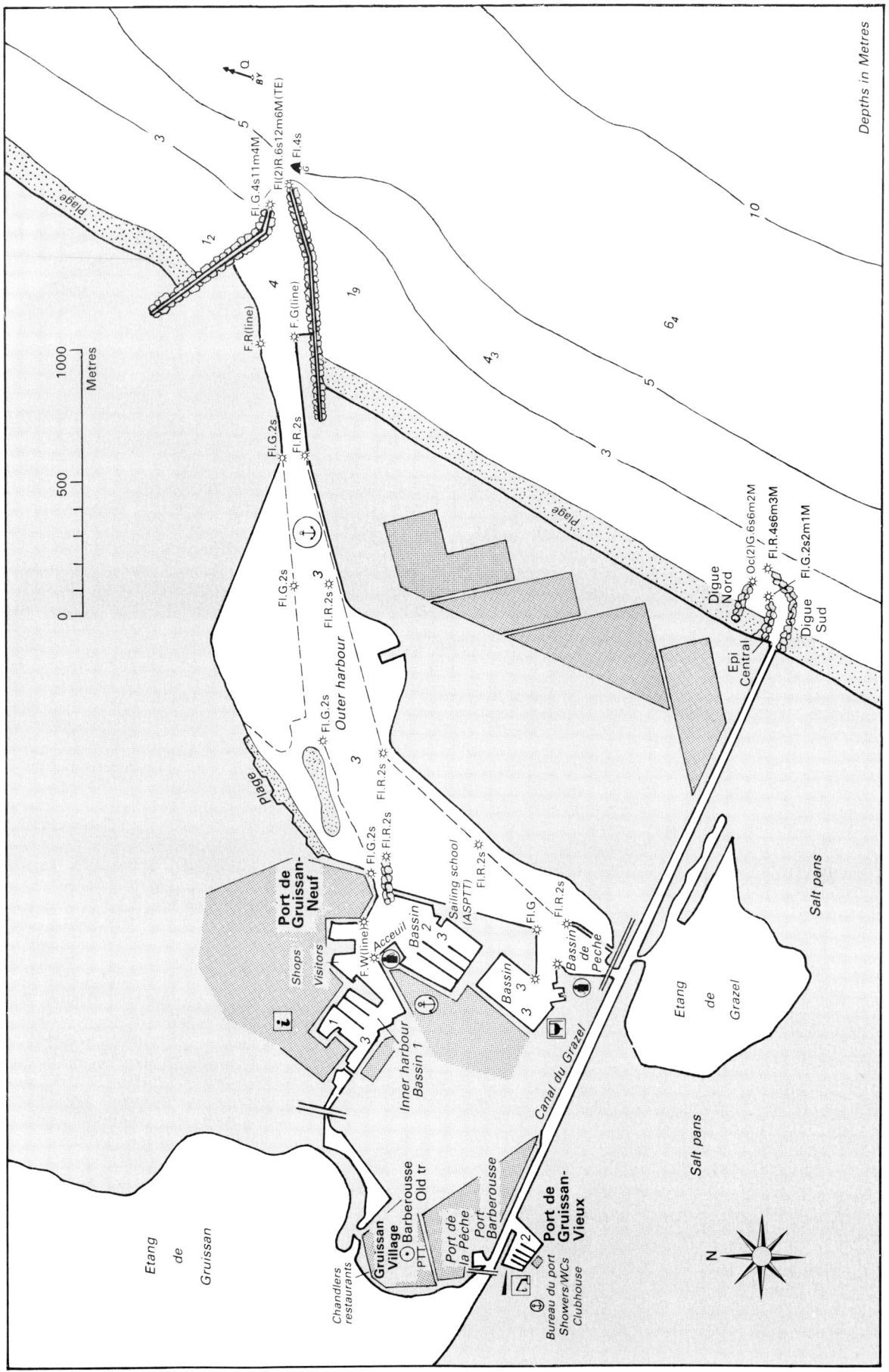

Port de Gruissan

Tour de Barberousse   *Housing estate*

Port de Gruissan-Vieux (Barberousse). Entrance to Canal du Grazel looking W

Harbour   *Tour de Barberousse*   *Port de Gruissan-Neuf*

Port de Gruissan-Vieux (Barberousse). Approach Chenal du Grazel

Road bridge across Canal de Grazel

Port de Gruissan-Vieux (Barberousse) looking W–NW

Port de Gruissan-Vieux (Barberousse). Port de Plaisance looking NW

15 PORT DE GRUISSAN-NEUF
11430 Aude

Position 43°06'·8N 3°07'·9E
Minimum depth in the entrance 3m (10ft)
in the harbour 3m (10ft)
Width of the entrance 40m
Number of yacht berths 700
Maximum length overall 30m (98ft)
Population 2000
Rating 3–3–2

General

A major artificial yacht harbour and marina complex, parts of which are still under construction. Approach and entrance are easy but become dangerous in heavy seas from NE–E–SE. Facilities are good and will be excellent. Shelter from the seas is good and the Montagne de la Clape offers some protection from the NW *tramontane/mistral*. The Avant Port offers a safe refuge in case of a strong *tramontane/mistral*. The access channel is 1M long.

Data

Charts Admiralty 1705
French 6844
Navicarte 510

Magnetic variation 2°04'W (1994) decreasing by about 6' each year.

Port radio VHF Ch 9.

Weather forecast Posted three times a day at *bureau du port*. Recorded forecasts (☎ 36 68 08 08 and 36 68 08 11).

Speed limit 3 knots.

Lights
Jetée Sud head Fl(2)R.6s12m6M Pylon
Jetée Nord head Fl.G.4s11m7M White structure, green top
Inner entrance N side Fl.G.2s3m3M, S side Fl.R.2s1m3M
Entrance to Bassin No. 2 E side Fl.G.2s, W side Fl.R.2s
Entrance to Bassin No. 3 Pêche NE side Fl.G.2s, SW side Fl.R.2s
Entrance to Bassin No.1 E side Fl.W.4s(line)

Port de Gruissan-Neuf. Entrance looking NW

Inner inner entrance

Port de Gruissan-Neuf. Inner inner entrance looking W

Buoys N cardinal light buoy ⬤ (Q) ½M to NE of entrance. The approach channel is marked with light buoys on the lateral system. Three starboard-hand light buoys (Fl.G.2s) and four port-hand light buoys (Fl.R.2s), but they are on posts.

Warning

This harbour is still being enlarged and works, dredging etc. may not be completed for several years. The light tower on the *jetée* has to be rebuilt.

Approach by day

From S From Port la Nouvelle, which has very conspicuous jetties with large light towers on the ends, the coast is low, flat, sandy and featureless. The small jetties at the entrance to the Canal de Grazel, leading to Gruissan Village, can be seen from close to the shore. The village on a pointed hill with a ruined tower on top can also be seen in the hinterland. The larger jetties of Gruissan-Neuf will be seen in the closer approach.

From N Valras-Plage, which has a large casino building, water tower and a pair of tall electricity pylons, can be identified by its jetties. The harbour of Narbonne-Plage will also be seen with the bare, grey, rocky Montagne de la Clape behind. The breakwater at Grau de Pêch Rouge with a black beacon, yellow band, is conspicuous. Again the jetties of this harbour will be seen in the closer approach.

Approach by night

A night approach will be possible using the lights listed below to obtain a position where the entrance lies W at 400m:

Cap Leucate Fl(2)W.10s20M
Port la Nouvelle QW.14M
Sète Mont Saint-Clair Fl.W.5s29M

Anchorage in the approach

Anchor 400m to E of the entrance in 10m (33ft) sand, mud and weed.

Entrance

By day Enter between the breakwater heads on a W course and then between the two arms of the inner entrance. A channel, dredged to 3m, is marked by four green buoys (Nos.1–3–5) to starboard and four red buoys (Nos. 2–4–6–7) to port. These buoys are on posts. The dome-shaped top of the brown *bureau du port* will be seen ahead with the entrance to the inner harbour in line with it. Enter the inner harbour.

By night Enter between light buoy Fl.R.4s to port and Fl.G.4s to starboard and then between a Fl.R (line of light) and Fl.G (line of light). Keep between three pairs of light buoys Fl.R.2s and Fl.G.2s and enter the inner harbour between a Fl.R.2s and a Fl.G.2s.

Bureau du port   *Inner inner entrance*

Port de Gruissan-Neuf looking NW across the harbour

Port de Gruissan-Neuf looking NW across Bassin No 1

Bureau du port   *Fuel berth   Inner harbour*

Port de Gruissan-Neuf looking SW–W–NW from inner entrance

Inner entrance   *Fuel berth*   *Harbour entran*

Port de Gruissan-Neuf. Panorama from bureau du port

Berths

Secure to quay to E of *bureau du port* near the fuel berth and report to the office for allocation of a berth. Berths are usually available for multi-hulls.

Anchorage

Anchor in 3m sand in the outer harbour clear of the centre where the deep-water channel.

Formalities

Report to the *bureau du port* (☎ 68 49 08-20, *Fax* 68 49 11 05). Open in summer 0700–2300 and winter 0100 and 1400–2100. Customs office (☎ 68 49 00 91).

Harbour charges

There are harbour charges.

Facilities

Slips Five slips around the harbour.
Cranes 2-tonne telescopic crane. 12-tonne travel-lift.
Fuel Diesel (*gasoil*) and petrol available from pumps (☎ 68 49 08 20) near the *bureau du port*. Open summer 0800–1900, winter 0800–1200 and 1400–1800.
Water Water points on all quays and pontoons.
Electricity 220v AC 5 amp points on quays and pontoons.
Provisions Limited shops in the area, more planned.
Ice Available at the *bureau du port* and from café/bars.
Garbage Many rubbish bins around the harbour.
Chandlery Shop established.
Repairs Four yacht yards, several mechanics and a sailmaker.
Post office To be provided.
Restaurants Several restaurants, more planned.
Hotels Two hotels, more planned.
Yacht club The Cercle Nautique Barberousse (CNB) has its office at the *mairie*, 3 pontoons. ASOTT de Carcassonne,

Port de Gruissan-Neuf looking SW towards the shipyard

Footbridge

Port de Gruissan-Neuf looking NW up the inner harbour

Bureau du port   *Bassin No 1*

Port de Gruissan-Neuf. Entrance to the inner harbour looking W

office Allée Iéna, 11000 Carcassonne (☎ 68 25 37 84). Clubhouse (☎ 68 49 01 30) at Gruissan.

Showers Near *bureau du port*. Four blocks around the harbour with a total of 25 showers and 20 WCs.

Lifeboat Vedette 1st class (☎ 68 45 04 42).

Laundrette At *bureau du port*.

Information office Centre d'Information (☎ 68 49 09 00). Syndicat d'Initiative (☎ 68 49 03 26) located on N side of area.

Visits The unique old sailors' cemetery and of course Narbonne itself (7M). Small yachts and dinghies will eventually be able to enter the Etang de Gruissan by passing under two bridges with 3m (10ft) clearance. Entrance at the moment is through Canal de Grazel and Gruissan. There is a museum in Gruissan village.

Communications Bus service. Rail service from Narbonne, air service Béziers and Pérpignan.

Future development

There is still a lot of construction work to be carried out, and some facilities remain to be provided.

History

Except for the old fishing village of Gruissan with its Tour de Barberousse, the area, which consisted of salt marshes, *étang*s and a few salt pans, was completely deserted until this new harbour complex was built.

⚓ **Les Ayguades (Grau de Pêch Rouge)**

Difficult to classify. A large *étang* which has two *digues* forming a canalised mouth to the sea which has been allowed to silt up. Anchorage for shallow-draught craft is possible on the seaward side of the entrance. Breakwater head Q(3)W.10s7m3M, black pedestal, yellow band (TE). It would not be difficult to dredge the entrance and the *étang* and to turn it into a harbour again. At the moment it is used by windsurfers and wetbikes.

16 PORT DE NARBONNE-PLAGE (ST PIERRE-SUR-MER)

1110 Aude

Position 43°10'·5N 3°10'·2E
Minimum depth   in the entrance 2m (6ft)
                   in the harbour 1·2m (4ft)
Clearance at bridge height 2·4m (8ft)
                   width 3·7m (12ft)
Width of the entrance 15m
Maximum length overall 12m (37ft)
Number of yacht berths 600
Population 400
Rating 3–3–3

General

A small and shallow harbour for smaller yachts only. It can be entered only in fair conditions due to a bar where onshore waves break. Inside, shelter is obtained but heavy swell from the ESE makes the harbour very uncomfortable. There is limited shelter from the NW *tramontane/mistral* winds by virtue of the low cliffs at the back of the harbour. Facilities are limited but are improving. It becomes very crowded in the summer.

Data

Charts   Admiralty 1705
          French 6864
          Navicarte 509, 510

Current There is a S-going current of 0·5 to 1 knot past the entrance.

Magnetic variation 2°04'W (1994) decreasing by about 6' each year.

Buoys The channel across the *avant-port* to the inner entrance is marked.

Weather forecast Posted daily at *bureau du port*. Also VHF Ch 9 broadcast at each even hour +5 (☎ 36 68 08 11).

Lights

Jetée Sud head Fl.R.4s7m4M Red mast
Jetée Nord head Fl.G.4s7m1M Green mast
Digue Est head Oc.R.4s Strip light
Bassin des Exals Fl(3)W.12s24m15M Grey metal tower 220°-vis-040°

Warning

The bar and entrance of this harbour tend to silt up, and the depths may be different from those shown on

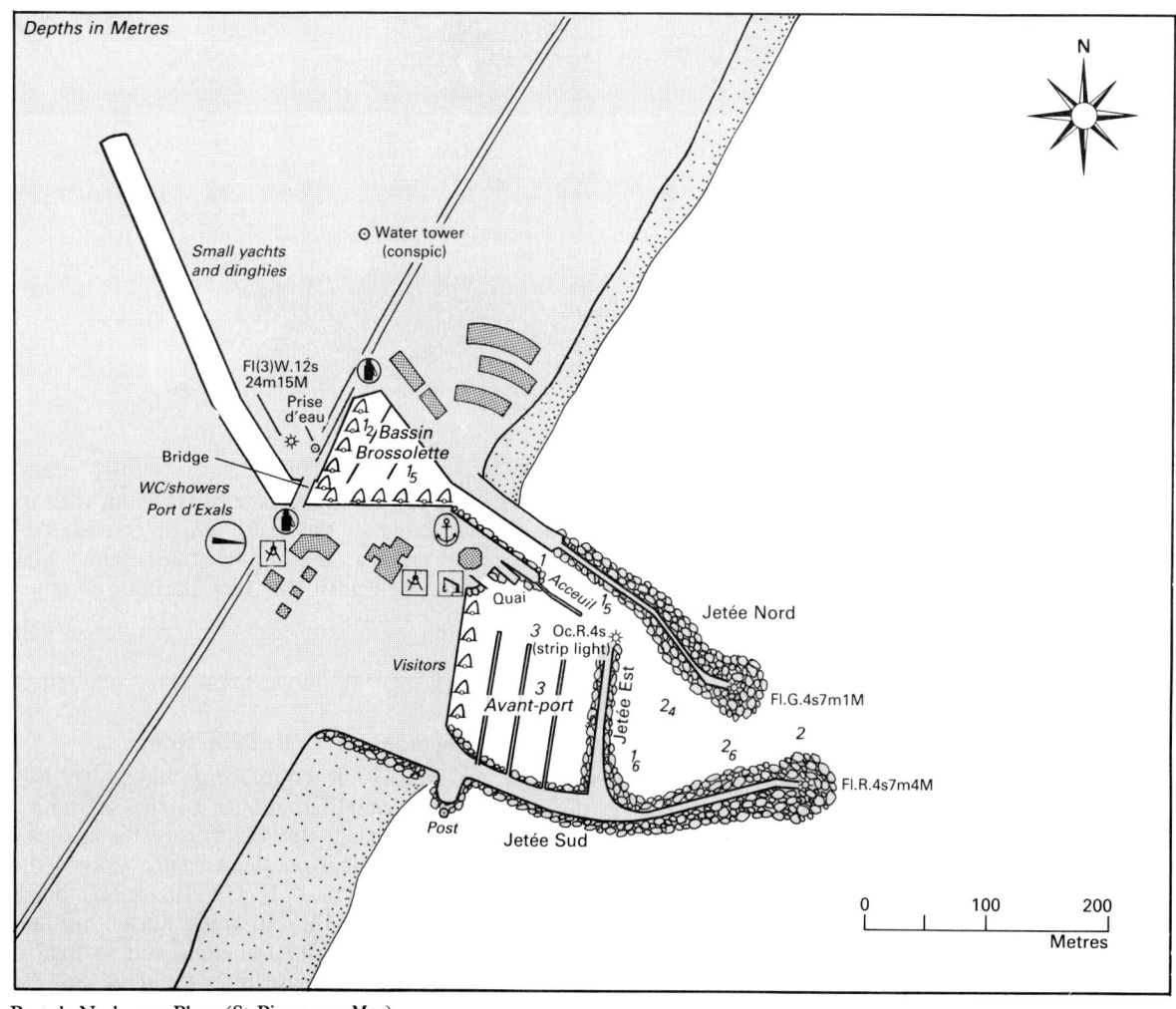

Port de Narbonne-Plage (St-Pierre-sur-Mer)

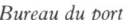

Bureau du port

Port de Narbonne-Plage (St-Pierre-sur-Mer) looking NW

the plan, depending on the time elapsed since the last dredging operation.

Approach by day

From S The small jetties of Port Gruissan-Vieux and the large jetties of Port Gruissan-Neuf 1M to N can be identified, with the old village on a pointed hill and a conspicuous ruined tower lying behind it. The coast remains low, flat and sandy with the bare grey rocky Montagne de la Clape behind. The jetties of this harbour will be seen in the closer approach together with a white water tank on the cliff behind a group of houses and flats. There is a conspicuous TV tower 2M to WNW and two radar domes, one green and the other white, are 2½M to W on the top of a hill 234m (760ft).

From N The town of Valras-Plage, which has a large casino, two high electricity pylons and two jetties, is easily recognised. From close in, the two jetties at the mouth of R. Aude will be seen. Rocher St-Pierre, an isolated low rock, projects from the sandy coast ½M to NE of this harbour in the close approach, and the breakwaters and houses of Port de Narbonne-Plage are easily seen.

Approach by night

Night approach and entrance are not advised unless a recent day visit has been made, due to uncertain depths in the entrance and in the harbour.

Anchorage in the approach

Anchor 400m to SE of the entrance in 4m (13ft) sand, mud and weed.

Entrance

By day Approach the entrance on a SW course at slow speed (there is not much room for manoeuvre) and enter between the breakwater heads, turning to a NW course and towards the inner entrance where there is a pontoon in front of the *bureau du port*; secure here. A bridge, 2·4m (8ft) clearance, 3·7m (12ft) wide, leads NW to the new harbour of Des Exals.

Berths

Secure stern-to quay or pontoon, bow-to mooring buoy, in any vacant berth.

Formalities

Report to the *bureau du port* on arrival (☎ 68 49 91 43), open summer 24 hours, winter 0930–1150 and 1530–1800. Customs (☎ 68 48 01 55) at Port la Nouvelle.

Harbour charges

Harbour dues will be charged but the first day is free.

Facilities

Slips Two small slips near the W corner of the harbour.
Crane 5-tonne mobile crane.
Fuel Petrol from a pump 100m to W of the harbour.
Electrical 220v AC on quays and pontoons.
Water Water points on quays and pontoons.
Provisions A few shops near the harbour and many in Narbonne some 10M away. Special Sunday market 1M to N.
Garbage A few rubbish containers.
Repairs A local artisan can carry out minor repairs to hulls and engines.

Bureau du port   Monument

Port de Narbonne-Plage (St-Pierre-sur-Mer). Outer harbour looking NW

Bridge to inner harbour   Monument

Port de Narbonne-Plage (St-Pierre-sur-Mer) looking W from entrance to inner harbour

Chandlery A shop on S side of the harbour.

Post office A PTT in the village.

Hotels Several from ★★ in the area.

Restaurants Several restaurants and a number of café/bars.

Yacht clubs Circle Nautique de Narbonne-Plage (CNNP) (☎68 32 09 37) has a clubhouse locally.

Showers Five showers and five WCs near the bridge.

Information office The Syndicat d'Initiative has an office open in the season (☎ 68 49 84 86).

Visits A visit by bus or taxi to the very old and attractive city of Narbonne is recommended.

Communications Bus service. Rail Narbonne. Air Béziers.

Future development

This harbour may eventually be included in the huge development at Gruissan or undergo further local expansion.

⚓   **Rocher St-Pierre-la-Mer (5m)**

A very small headland created by an isolated lump of rock surrounded by a disused fort with a village and church behind it. Anchorage is possible off the sandy beach to N and S

17 PORT DES CABANES DE FLEURY (EMBOUCHURE DE L'AUDE) (GRAU DE VENDRES)

11560 Aude

Position 43°12'·7N 3°14'·6E
Minimum depth in the entrance 2m (6·5ft)
　　　　　　　　in the harbour 6 to 5m (20 to 16ft)
Width of entrance 150m
Maximum length overall 15m (49ft)
Population 200 (approx)
Rating 3–3–4

General

A completely unspoilt and undeveloped area around the mouth of the Rivière de l'Aude and therefore attractive in a natural way. New breakwaters and two small yacht harbours have been built recently otherwise; there are only a few quays and short jetties alongside a small village on the SW bank of the river about ½M from its mouth, where it is possible to secure for short periods. The approach is easy but the entrance needs care and is impossible in any strong swell from SE–S–SW. The harbour is also uncomfortable in the NW *tramontane/mistral* as the wind blows straight down the river, creating very rough water. Facilities are limited to a small shop and a water point, but improvements are expected.

Data

Charts　Admiralty 1705
　　　　　French 6844
　　　　　Navicarte 509, 510

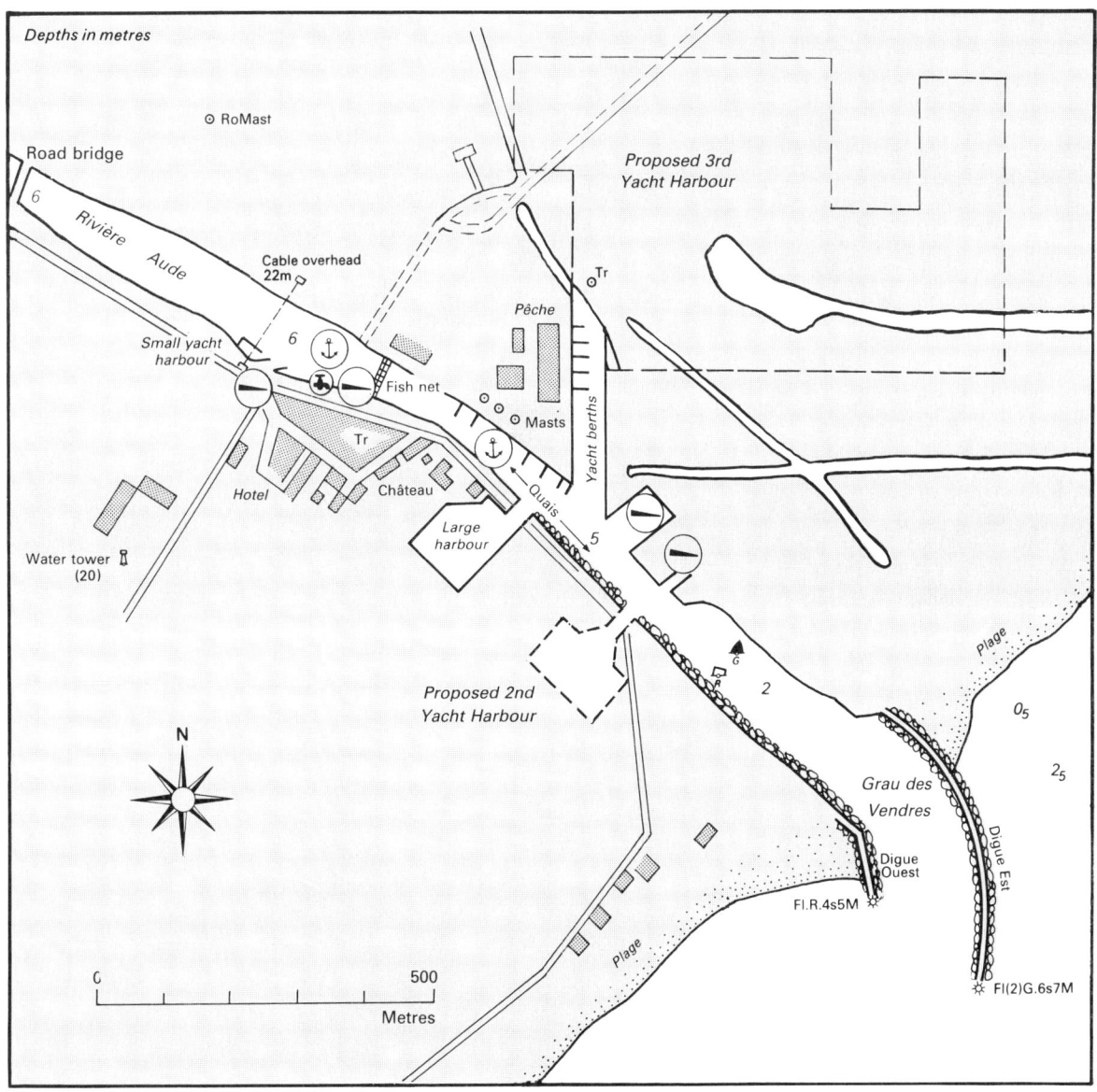

Port des Cabanes de Fleury

Current A S-going current of 0·5 to 1 knot flows past the entrance.

Magnetic variation 2°04'W (1994) decreasing by about 6' each year.

Speed limit 3 knots.

Lights
Digue Est head Fl(2)G.6s10m8M Aluminium column
Digue Ouest head Fl.R.4s7m5M Aluminium tripod

Buoys Fish farm 3M to SE–S of entrance. SW corner VQ(6)+LFl.W.10s9m4M with ⍲ topmark. NE corner VQ(3)W.5s9m4M with ⍲ topmark.

Beacons The river is marked by red and green light beacons with can and conical topmarks.

Warnings

A fishing net may be stretched across the river near the middle of the village. The net is lowered to the bottom when vessels approach. There is an overhead cable 12m (39ft) across the river above the village and a road bridge is 1M further upstream. Changes must be expected as development takes place. Exposed wreck 1M to NE of the entrance, 400m offshore. When in spate the river is dangerous because it brings down debris, trees, etc.

Approach by day

From SW Pass the small jetties at Port de Gruissan-Vieux and continue 1M further N to the larger jetties of the Port de Gruissan-Neuf. Follow the low, flat, sandy coast which is backed by the bare grey rocky Montagne de la Clape. A breakwater with black beacon (yellow band) Q(3)10s7m2M at Grau de Pêche-Rouge will be seen. The small jetties, houses and flats with a white monument behind Port de Narbonne-Plage can be identified. The mouth of this river has two jetties which will be seen in the closer approach, as will the village houses in the background and a water tower to the S of the village.

Port des Cabanes de Fleury. Entrance looking NW

2nd yacht harbour   *Fishing harbour*

Port des Cabanes de Fleury. Inside the entrance looking NW

From NE Valras-Plage will be seen, with its large casino, two electricity pylons and jetties; the coast is low, flat and sandy. In the closer approach the low jetties at the mouth of the river will be seen, along with the houses of the village.

Approach by night
Though there are navigational lights, a night approach and entrance are not advised unless a previous visit by day has been made.

Anchorage in the approach
Anchor some 400m to E of the head of the jetty in 5m (16ft) mud.

Entrance
By day Approach the heads of the two jetties on a N heading. When about 50m from the head of the Digue Est alter course to leave it 20m to starboard. Follow the NE bank at this distance for about 300m then from a slight bend continue in mid stream. It is advised to sound continuously and to enter with care at slow speed as depths are liable to change.

Berths
Secure alongside the SW bank near the village, approaching with care since there are shallows and sloping banks. It is advised to secure temporarily alongside another boat and reconnoitre a suitable berth from land. Alternatively berth alongside the NE side of a short canal that has been dredged just below the village on the opposite (NE) bank of the river, or secure in the first yacht harbour.

Anchorages
Anchorages above or below the village in 5 to 6m (16 to 20ft) mud are possible if the river is not in spate.

Facilities
Slips A large and a small slip at the village, and another beside the short canal on the NE bank.
Water A water point alongside a hut on the river bank by the village.
Provisions A small shop in the village where basic requirements can be obtained.
Repairs A local yard can carry out most repairs.
Chandlers A shop at the yard.
Hotels A small hotel in the village.

Château   *Small yacht harbour*

Port des Cabanes de Fleury looking NW upriver – quays on both sides of river

Entrance to yacht harbour   *Château*

Port des Cabanes de Fleury looking SW towards yacht harbour

Fishing pontoons   *Tower*   *Yacht berths*

Port des Cabanes de Fleury looking N up fishing and yachting harbour

103

Restaurants Several small café/bars in the village.

Visits A number of interconnected waterways that can be explored by dinghy. Small craft can ascend the river as far as Carcassonne depending on the amount of water flowing.

Beaches Excellent sandy beaches either side of the river mouth.

Communications Occasional bus service.

Future development

There exist plans to develop this area into a huge marina for 50,000 people and 1500 yachts, which seems a pity as it is virtually the last harbour that can be visited that has not been 'over-developed'. But it would appear that this scheme has been abandoned or at least postponed. Very little has been done since a first visit in 1973, but there were signs of development in 1991.

---

18 PORT DE VALRAS-PLAGE (PORT DE L'ORB)

34350 Hérault

Position 43°14'·8N 3°17'·9E

Minimum depth in the entrance 3m (10ft)
in the harbour 2m (6·5ft)

Clearance in the river 3m (10ft)
electric cable 16m (52ft)

Width of the entrance 20m

Number of yacht berths 270+5+300=575

Maximum length overall 12m (39ft)

Population 2000

Rating 3–3–3

General

This harbour consists of the canalised mouth of the Rivière de l'Orb which has a series of yacht basins on its SW bank and a number of berths along the river banks. Approach is easy but entrance requires care and is impossible with seas from E–SE–S which break in the entrance. Fair facilities are available. Protection from the NW *tramontane/mistral* seas is obtained here but protection from the wind is only partial. About 3m can be carried 2·5M as far as Serignan where there are two low road bridges.

Data

Charts Admiralty 1705
French 7054
Navicarte 509, 510

Current There is a SW–going current of 0·5 to 1 knot past the entrance to this river. The normal river current is 3 knots which can vary.

Magnetic variation 2°04'W (1994) decreasing by about 6' each year.

Weather forecasts Weather forecasts are posted once a day outside the *bureau du port*, Valras-Plage. Recorded forecast (☎ 36 68 08 34).

Speed limit 5 knots.

Port radio VHF Ch9.

Storm signals Storm signals are flown from a staff at the *bureau du port*, Valras-Plage.

Lights

Digue Nord-Est head Fl.G.4s8m7M White structure, green top

Digue Sud-Ouest head Fl(4)W.12s9m9M Aluminium structure, red top

Entrance to Valras Plage yacht harbour Iso.G.4s2m and Iso.R.4s2m lights on corners of jetty heads – strip lights

Entrance to Bassin Jean Gau F.R and F.G

Warning

The depths in the river and at the entrance can vary with the amount of water flowing in the river and the silt that it brings down.

Approach by day

From SW The grey bare rocky Montagne de la Clape which ends at Narbonne-Plage is followed by the flat, featureless sand coast broken only by the mouth of the Rivière de l'Aude, which has two *digues*. The large casino, houses, two tall electricity pylons and the jetties at the mouth of this river can be seen in the closer approach.

From NE The prominent Cap d'Agde, with its breakwaters and buoys and Fort Brescou with its lighthouse, are unmistakable. The twin *digues* and light towers at Grau d'Agde are likewise easily identified. The houses of Valras-Plage and the two *digues* will be seen in the closer approach.

Approach by night

Using the lights listed below navigate to a position where the entrance lies 40m to NE:

Port la Nouvelle Q.W.14M (extreme range)

Grau d'Agde Oc(2)R.6s7M

Ilot Brescou Fl(2)WR.6s13/10M

Anchorage in the approach

Anchor 400m to E of the head of the jetty in 6m (20ft) mud and sand.

Entrance

By day Approach the entrance on a NW course and enter between the heads of the *digues*. Continue in midstream until past Valras-Plage, then keep nearer to the W bank.

By night Approach Fl.G.4s on a NW course. Leave this light 40m to starboard and a Fl(4)W.12s to port. Continue upriver in midstream but at Port de Valras-Plage keep nearer the starboard-hand bank.

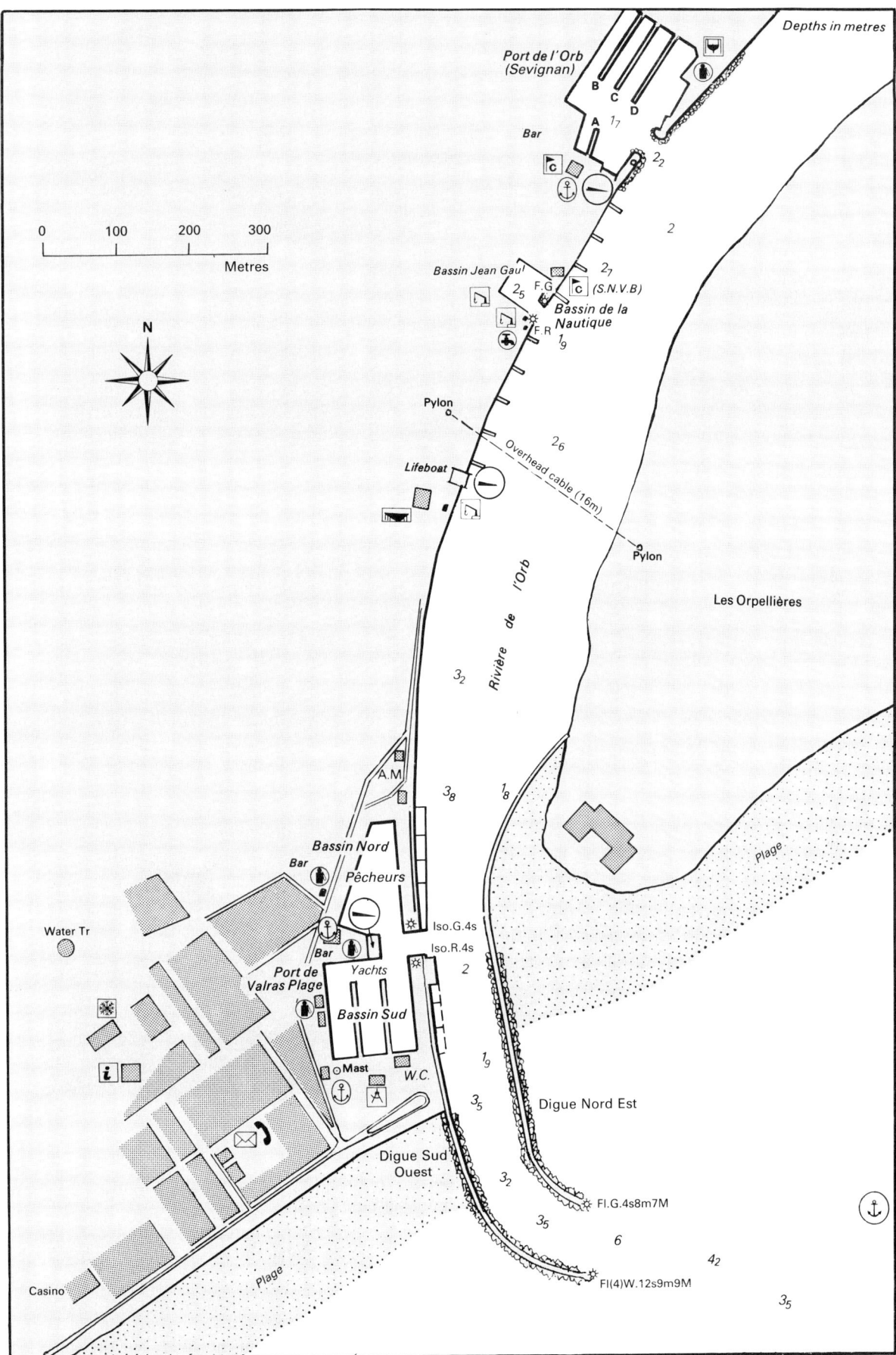

Port de Valras-Plage

Port de Valras-Plage (Port de l'Orb) looking NW

Port de Valras-Plage (Port de l'Orb). Approach looking NW

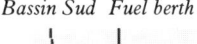

Port de Valras-Plage (Port de l'Orb). Entrance to yacht harbour looking W

Berths

Port de Valras-Plage Secure alongside pontoon outside entrance and await instructions as to which berth to occupy. Secure stern-to, bow-to mooring buoys in this berth.

Bassin Jean Gau (de la Nautique) Secure alongside in entrance and report to clubhouse for allocation of a berth. Secure stern-to quay, bow-to mooring chain.

Port de l'Orb (Serignan) Secure to first pontoon or quay on port hand and await instructions as to which

berth to occupy, then secure stern-to, bow-to mooring buoy.

W bank of the river There are a number of private berthing stages along the river bank which may be vacant.

Anchorage

It is possible to anchor in the river, but the soft mud does not offer a very secure holding ground; use two anchors. Anchor lights and shapes should be shown.

Port de Valras-Plage (Port de l'Orb) looking W

Port de Valras-Plage   *Bassin Jean Gau*   *Port de l'Orb*

Port de Valras-Plage (Port de l'Orb) looking W–NW

Old lighthouse

Port de Valras-Plage (Port de l'Orb). Inside entrance looking NW

Formalities

At Port de Valras-Plage or if secured to W bank report to the *bureau du port* (☎ 67 32 33 64) to the S of the port. Open summer 0900–1600 and 1800–0800 and winter 0800–1200 and 1400–1800. At Bassin Jean Gau report to the yacht club. At Port de l'Orb report to the clubhouse. A customs office (☎ 67 32 27 97) which is in the town in Bvd Jean-Danga.

Harbour charges

There are harbour charges.

Facilities

Slips Three slips, one in Port de Valras-Plage, one near the shipyard on the W bank and one in Port de l'Orb.

Cranes Three cranes of 7 tonnes, one at the shipyard, one at the Bassin Jean Gau and one at Port de l'Orb, also a 10-tonne travel-lift.

Fuel Diesel (*gasoil*) and petrol can be bought from the pumps at Port de Valras-Plage, also from other pumps on the W bank. Open summer 0600–2000 and winter 0800–1200 and 1400–1800.

Water Water points are available at Port de Valras-Plage and de l'Orb on the quays and pontoons and from the yacht clubhouse at Bassin Jean Gau.

Electricity Supply points of 220v AC on quays and pontoons at Port de Valras and de l'Orb.

Provisions A number of shops of various sorts in the town and also a market.

Ice From a shop located to N of the market.

Garbage Containers for rubbish at all ports and basins.

Harbour entrance   Quai d'accueil

Port de Valras-Plage (Port de l'Orb) looking N upriver

Chandlery In the new yacht harbour; another in the town.

Repairs Normal repairs to wood and GRP hulls can be carried out by three shipyards. Engines can also be repaired by several mechanics. Sailmaker.

Laundrette A laundry beside the Port de Valras-Plage.

Post office A PTT in the town.

Hotels One ***, five **, four * and one unclassified hotel.

Restaurants 23 restaurants and many café/bars.

Yacht clubs The Société Nautique Béziers-Valras (SNBV) (☎ 67 32 29 44) has a clubhouse at Bassin Jean Gau with bar, restaurant, lounge, showers, etc. There is also the Yachting Club de Valras-Plage (YCVP).

Showers At the *bureau du port*, Valras Plage. Eight showers and three WCs.

Information office The Syndicat d'Initiative has an office to W of the market (☎ 67 32 36 04).

Lifeboat A lifeboat is stationed here, *vedette* 2nd class (☎ 67 43 80 13 or 67 93 00 23).

Visits A visit to the attractive old town of Béziers and to the recently excavated pre-Roman settlement of Ensérune is worthwhile. A trip up the river in a small motor craft to Serignan is recommended.

Beaches Long sandy beaches either side of the mouth of the river.

Communications Bus service locally and rail service at Béziers.

19 PORT DE GRAU D'AGDE
34300 Hérault

Position 43°16'·7N 3°26'·6E
Minimum depth   in the entrance 4m (13ft)
                in the harbour 5 to 4·5m (16 to 14·5ft)
Clearance   large road bridge 12m(18ft)
(½ way to Port d'Agde) 00m (00ft)
Width of the entrance 60m
Population 2500 (approx)
Rating 3–3–3

General

A small harbour just inside the mouth of the Rivière de l'Hérault consisting of quays and small landing stages on both banks and a small basin with a seaside holiday town on the E bank. The entrance and approach are easy but in heavy swell from the SE–S–SW waves can break on the bar and entrance is then dangerous. Very limited accommodation for yachts and the facilities are only fair. Shelter is to a limited extent obtainable from the NW *tramontane/mistral*, but swell is sometimes troublesome in the harbour from S–SE winds.

Data

Charts   Admiralty 1704
         French 7003, 7004
         Navicarte 509

Current A W-going current of 0·5 to 1 knot crosses the entrance to this river.

Magnetic variation 2°04'W (1994) decreasing by about 6' each year.

Weather forecast Recorded forecast (☎ 36 68 08 08 and 36 68 08 34).

Speed limit 3 knots.

Lights

Jetée Ouest head Oc(2)R.6s14m7M White truncated tower, red top

Jetée Est head Oc.G.4s14m7M Horn 10s White truncated tower, green top

River banks FR and FG as far as Agde

Two radio masts 1·6M to ENE FR

Warning

There is a shoal bank extending some 300m to SSW of the head of Jetée Ouest. If the river is in spate due to heavy rains the current can become very strong and berths dangerous. Much floating debris including whole trees may be carried down the river in these conditions.

Approach by day

From SW Follow the low, flat, sandy coast at 1M past Valras-Plage, which will be recognised by its casino, water tower, two pylons and jetties. The entrance to Grau d'Agde can be seen from afar as the two light towers are conspicuous; there is also a wood to the W of the entrance. Do not cut the corner but keep at least 400m seaward of the heads of the *digues* until they bear N before making the approach.

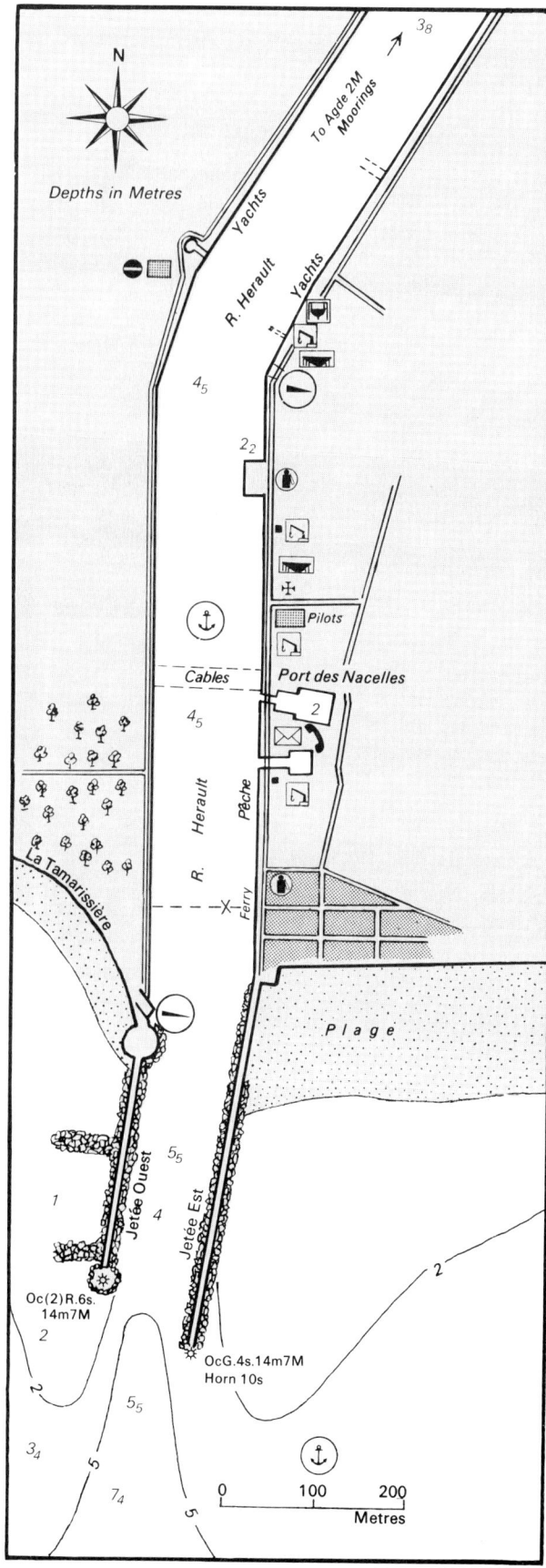

Port de Grau d'Agde

From NE Round Cap d'Agde at 300m outside the very conspicuous Fort and Ilot Brescou. The entrance light towers are easily seen from this direction. Do not sail directly towards them but obtain a position 400m to the S of the entrance before turning and approaching.

Approach by night

Using the lights listed below navigate to a position where the harbour entrance lies 400m to N:
Cap Leucate Fl(2)W.10s20M (extreme range)
Valras-Plage Fl(4)W.12s9M
Ilot Brescou Fl(2)WR.6s22m13M/10M

Anchorage in the approach

Anchor 200m to SE of the head of Jetée Est in 6m (20ft) mud.

Entrance

By day Enter from a point 400m to S of the entrance. When inside the jetties keep to the port-hand side of the channel until level with the first buildings and then follow the centre of the river.

By night Approach Oc(2)R.6s and Oc.G.4s on a N course from a position 400m to the S. Enter between these lights and then keep to the port-hand side of the river, moving over into midstream when level with the first houses.

Berths

It is impossible to berth right alongside the banks as they are sloping, but a berth may be available alongside a private pier or outside a yacht already secured to the banks on either side of the river above the town. 1M upriver are 15 mooring buoys, some of which may be vacant.

Anchorage

Anchor in 4·5m (15ft) mud in midstream 300m above the small Port des Nacelles. Anchorage is prohibited in the area just above this port.

Formalities

Report on arrival to the *bureau du port* (☎ 67 94 78 04 and 67 94 70 28) on the E bank and if necessary to the customs also on the E bank (☎ 67 94 21 68).

Facilities

Hards A hard on the W bank just at the foot of the Jetée Ouest near the ferry terminal.
Slipway A small 10-tonne slip on the E bank above the town at the shipyard.
Cranes Two 2-tonne cranes on the E bank and a travel-lift at the shipyard.
Fuel Diesel (*gasoil*) and petrol from pumps on the E bank.
Water From cafés or shipyard.
Provisions A number of shops in the town which can supply normal requirements.
Chandlery A small shop in the town; also from the shipyard.
Repairs Two shipyards on the E bank above the town and also mechanics who can undertake normal repairs.

Port de Grau d'Agde looking NE

Port de Grau d'Agde. Entrance looking N

Post office PTT in the town.

Hotels One ★, two ★★ and several unclassified hotels.

Restaurants One restaurant and a number of café/bars.

Yacht clubs The Club Nautique Agde-Méditerranée (CNAM) (☎ 67 21 11 37) has an office at La Tramarissiere on the W bank.

Lifeboat A lifeboat is stationed here. Runabout.

Visits Agde itself, where there are many interesting old buildings, should be visited.

Beaches Fine sandy beaches exist either side of this river mouth.

Communications Bus service. Ferry service across the river.

20 PORT D'AGDE

34300 Hérault

Position 43°18′·8N 3°28′·0E

Minimum depth   in the entrance 4m (13ft)
                   in the harbour 3·5 to 0·25m (11 to 1ft)

Clearance   small town road bridge 6m (9ft)
                   large road bridge 12m (18ft)

Width of the river 70m

Population 4000 (approx)

Rating 2–3–2

General

An old and attractive town and river harbour situated some 2·5M up the Rivière de l'Hérault. Accommodation alongside for yachts is somewhat limited. Otherwise facilities are fair. The approach upriver is not difficult. This river connects with the Canal du Midi and there are facilities for stepping and unstepping masts. A large road bridge crosses the river halfway between the town and the sea.

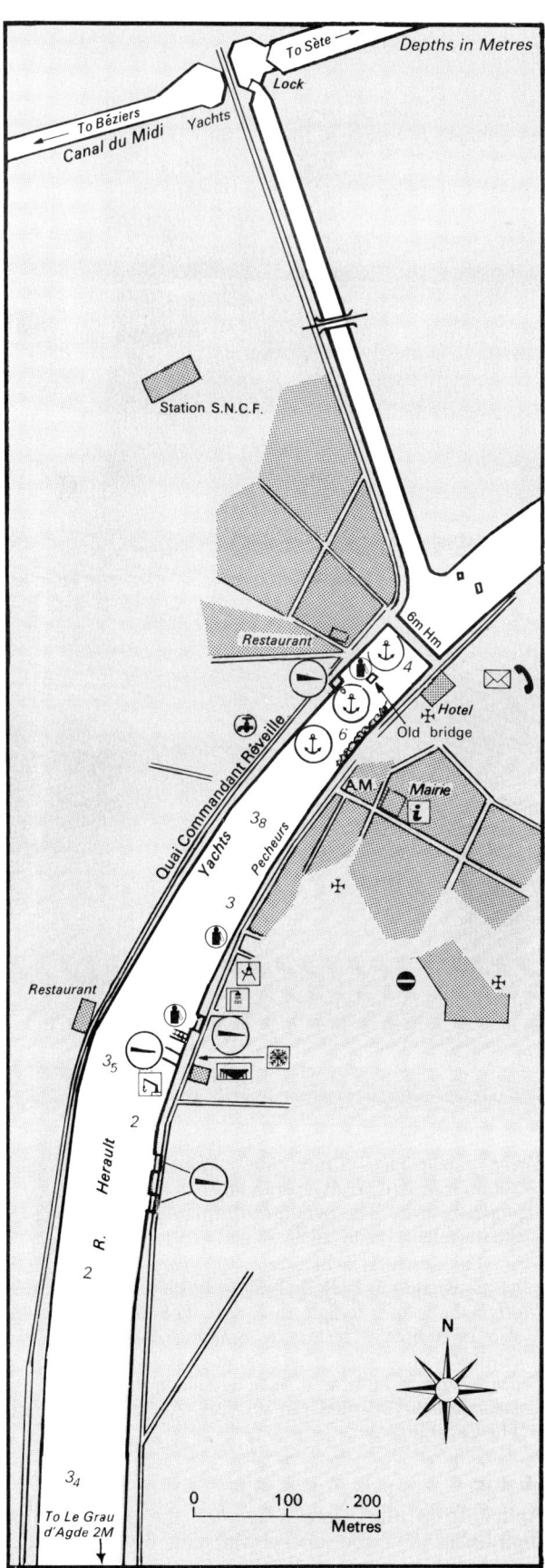

Port d'Agde

Data

Charts   Admiralty 1705
        French 7003, 7004
        Navicarte 509

Warning

Wetbikes and motorskis create a lot of noise and their wash is dangerous, as is that from large fishing boats. Depths in the river can vary with the amount of water flowing and silting can occur especially alongside quays. In the winter and spring when the river is in spate very strong currents can be experienced and the water can rise over the quays. In these conditions much floating debris including whole trees may be encountered in the river. The central pillar of the old road bridge is located in the middle of the river opposite the church.

Approach and entrance

From the sea Port de Grau d'Agde (page 108) first.

From the river by day From Le Grau d'Agde follow the river in midstream keeping towards the outside of bends where there are three white posts.

From the river by night Not recommended for a first entrance. F.R and F.G lights on banks.

From the Canal du Midi, by day A branch canal 600m long from the round lock leads to the Rivière l'Hérault above the town bridge. There is a railway bridge and station half way along this section of canal.

Berths

Berth alongside either bank, bow upstream on the quay between Agde bridge and a point 250m downstream. Check soundings when coming alongside. The E bank in this area has a rocky foot. It may be necessary to use a holding-off anchor. It is also possible to secure in the Canal du Midi to S of the triple (round) lock. There is a quay at the S end.

Moorings

A number of private moorings opposite the shipyard on the E bank below the town. Contact the shipyard.

Anchorage

Anchor just downstream of the large stone island (old road bridge support) that is located in the middle of the river.

Formalities

Report to the *affaires maritimes* (☎ 67 94 78 04 and 67 94 70 28) near the church on arrival. Customs office is on the quay to SW of the church (☎ 67 94 21 68).

Charges

Harbour charges are not made initially but are enforced after three weeks.

Port d'Agde looking NE

Yacht berths   *Fishing and ferry boats*   *Fishing and ferry boats*   *Yacht berths*

Port d'Agde looking NE upriver

Port d'Agde looking downstream from the road bridge

Facilities

Slips Several hards on the E bank.

Slipway Two slipways of 150 tonnes at the shipyard on the E bank below the town.

Crane A 10-tonne crane at the shipyard.

Fuel Diesel (*gasoil*) and petrol are available from pumps on the E bank and to W of the town bridge.

Water Water points on both sides of the river and beside the canal.

Provisions A number of shops and two supermarkets in the town, and a daily market.

Garbage A few rubbish containers on the quays.

Chandlery A ships' chandler in the town. Shipyards have a limited supply.

Repairs Two shipyards on the E bank below the town where repairs can be carried out to hull and engine.

Laundrettes Several laundrettes in the town.

Post office The PTT is located near the bridge on the E bank.

Hotels One ★★★, five ★★ and others which are unclassified.

Restaurants Four restaurants and many café/bars.

Yacht clubs The Club de Motonautisme Agde-Méditerranée (CMAM) has an office at the town hall.

Information office The Syndicat d'Initiative has an office at the town hall. (☎ 67 26 38 58 and 67 94 29 68).

Visits The cathedral, which took 400 years to rebuild after its destruction in 1286, is built of black lava rock on the original site of a temple to Diana. The museum should also be visited. The *mairie* building dates from 11th century.

Beaches Only at Le Grau d'Agde and along the coast.

Communications Bus and rail services. Air at Montpellier. The Canal du Midi.

History

Agde, from the Greek *Agathe* (the Good), was founded at the same time as Marseille by the Greeks, though it was previously in existence as a small Phoenician colony. Later it came under the protection of Rome, only to be captured in 471 by the Vandals, who in their turn lost it to the Visigoths. In 720 the Saracens razed the town; after

Yacht yards

Port d'Agde

being rebuilt, it was again destroyed during the wars of Aragon. After being rebuilt again it remained comparatively undisturbed as a small port and agricultural centre.

⚓ Rade de Brescou

Anchorage in 5m sand lies 400m to N of the very conspicuous island. Approach from SE or SW, giving the island a good berth, because inside the 2m contour there are many awash and covered rocks. All requirements available from Port de Cap d'Agde. Open to E–SE–S–SW–W.

21 PORT DE CAP D'AGDE

34300 Hérault

Position 43°16'·8N 3°30'·3E
Minimum depth   in the entrance 4m (13ft)
                  in the harbour 3 to 2m (10 to 6·5ft)
Width of the entrance 50m
Number of yacht berths 2450
Maximum length overall 25m (82ft)
Population 2450
Rating 2–2–2

General

A vast complex consisting of a very large artificial yacht harbour with several marinas and smaller separate harbours. The harbours and their equipment are completed but there are many acres of building still to be finished. The approach is easy and entrance is not too difficult but would be dangerous in a heavy swell from SE–S. Facilities are good and improvements are planned to a high standard. Protection from the seas of the NW *tramontane/mistral* is obtainable here, as to a certain extent is shelter from the wind itself.

Data

Charts   Admiralty 1705
           French 7003, 7054
           Navicarte 509

Current There is a W-going current of 0·5 to 1 knot off this harbour.

Magnetic variation 2°04'W (1994) decreasing by about 6' each year.

Port radio VHF Call Ch 16, 9 and 12.

Weather forecasts These are posted twice a day at the *bureau du port*. Forecasts by phone from ☎ 36 68 08 34 and 36 68 08 08.

Speed limit 3 knots.

Storm signals Storm signals are displayed from a mast at the *bureau du port*.

Lights
Ilot Brescou Fl(2)WR.6s22m13/10M. White tower, red top on S corner of fort. 113°-R-190°-W-133°. 2 FR on radio masts. 1·9M NW
Digue Est head Iso.G.4s8m9M White column, green top
Digue Ouest head Fl.R.4s8m5M Red and white column Numerous lights inside the harbour
Inner entrance Fl.R and Fl.G
Porte de la Clape entrance Fl.R and Fl.G
Port St-Martin entrance Fl.R and Fl.G

Buoys There are two small buoys marking the fairway into the harbour; leave red buoy (Fl.R) to port and green buoy (Fl.G.) leave to starboard. Just over 1M to S there is a S cardinal light buoy (Q.Fl(6) + LFl) ▼ topmark.

Beacons La Lauze beacon tower is on an isolated danger near the entrance (Fl.G.4s10m6M) aerogenerator (white tower, green top).
Marine Farm W corner VQ(9)W.10s, W cardinal, yellow pile, pivoted black band. N corner Q.W, N cardinal, yellow pile, pivoted. E corner VQ(3)W.5s, E cardinal, black pile. S corner VQ(6)+LFl.W.10s, S cardinal, black pile.

Warning

A strong *tramontane/mistral* can raise uncomfortable seas in parts of the harbour. Only enter the harbour from the E and leave La Lauze beacon tower to starboard. With local knowledge and calm weather it is possible to use the passage to the NW of Ilot Brescou and that to the N of La Lauze. The construction of the harbour is not yet complete and changes should be expected. There is a marine fish farm 2M to NE of Ilot Brescou marked by buoys (see above). See chart for areas of floating obstructions.

Approach by day

From SW Valras-Plage with its casino, jetties and two high electricity pylons and Le Grau d'Agde with its two jetties and twin light towers are both easily recognisable. The Ilot Brescou with its fort and small light tower is likewise conspicuous. Round this island

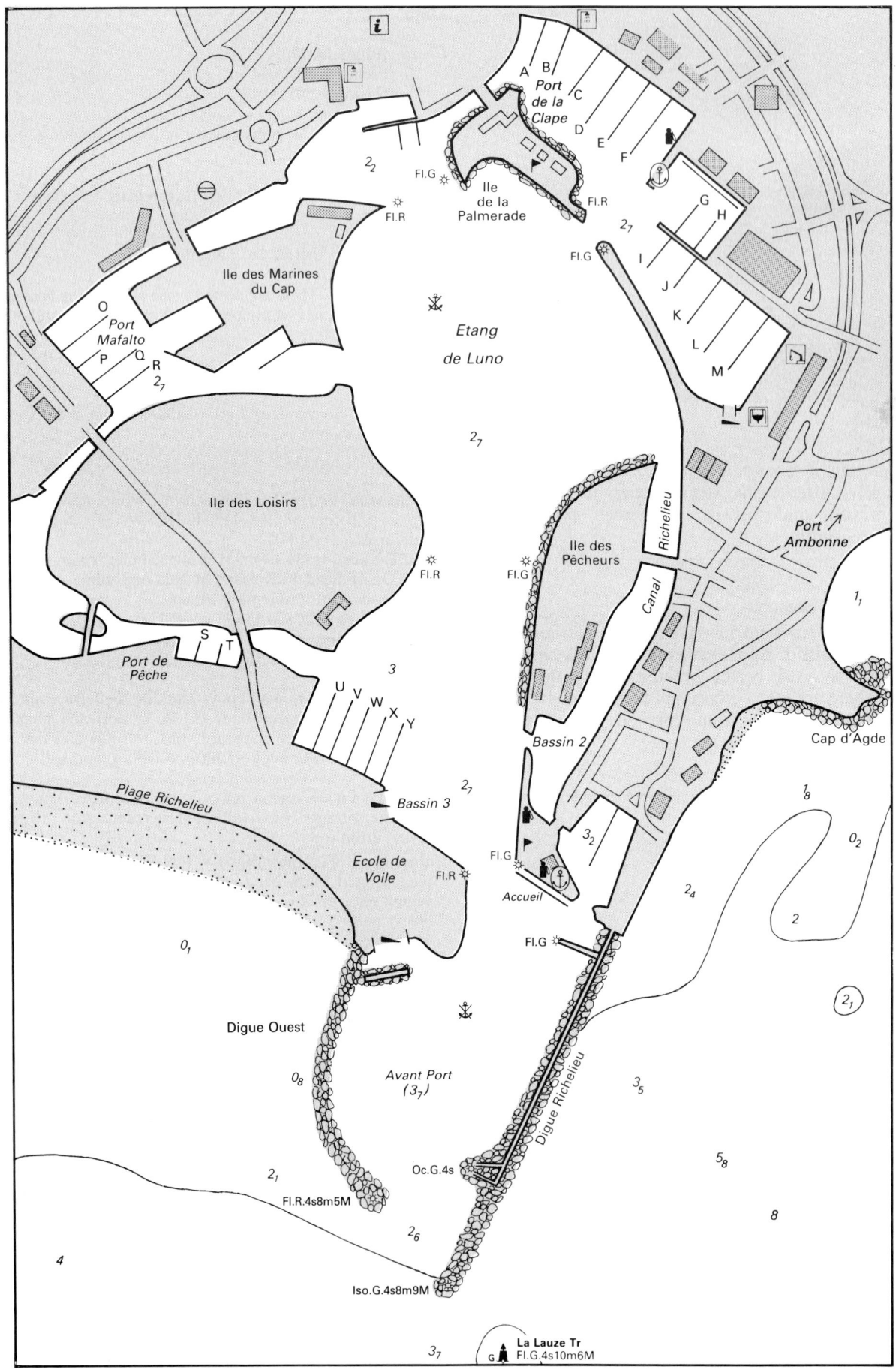

Port de Cap d'Agde

Cap d'Agde

Ilot Brescou   *Monte St Loup*   *La Lauze tower* *Bureau du port*

Port de Cap d'Agde looking N

Ilot Brescou

Mont St Loup · Entrance

Port de Cap d'Agde. Approach looking N

Bureau du port

Port de Cap d'Agde looking NW anchorages in foreground

200m to S and outside the buoys if they are established. Mont St-Loup which is 1M to the N of the harbour has a TV relay station on its top and can be seen a good distance away – it looks at first like an island. Mont St-Loup TV tower between the two breakwaters, bearing 357°, clears all dangers in the approach.

From NE The island-like Mont Saint-Clair at Sète together with its breakwaters and harbour installation are easily recognised. The straight, low, flat and sandy coast is only broken by the short jetties at Marseillan-Plage and Port Ambonne. The low, dark, rocky cliffs at Cap d'Agde, Ilot Brescou and the Mont St-Loup with its TV tower are easily seen. The La Lauze beacon, white tower, green top (Fl.G.4s) in line with Ilot Brescou lighthouse (Fl(2)WR.6s) on 233° clears all dangers in the approach. Mont St-Loupe is also conspicuous from this direction.

Approach by night
Using the lights listed below navigate to a position where Ilot Brescou is 500m to W:

Le Grau d'Agde Oc(2)R.6s7M
Ilot Brescou Fl(2)WR.6s13/10M
Sète Mont Saint-Clair Fl.W.5s29M

Anchorage in the approach
Anchor in the Baie de la Conque 300m from the shore in 5m (16ft) sand, rock and weed. In NW *tramontane/mistral* it is advisable to anchor close inshore. Pay attention to the rocks off Cap d'Agde.

Entrance
By day Approach the entrance on a W course leaving Ilot Brescou 200m to port and La Lauze beacon tower, white tower, green top, aerogenerator, to starboard. When between the two, turn to a N course and enter between the heads of the two jetties.

By night Approach Fl(2)WR.6s on a W course. When Iso.G.4s is N turn towards this light and leave it 20m to starboard and Fl.R.4s20m to port. If the beacon tower (Fl.G.4s) can be seen it will be possible to turn on to a NW course earlier leaving the beacon tower 80m to starboard.

Harbour pilotage
By day Proceed on a roughly N course through the narrows. When in the central Etang de Luno the entrance to the Port de la Clape will be seen ahead. Proceed to the *bureau du port* for instructions. In

summer proceed to the second a *bureau du port* located to starboard near the entrance to Bassin No. 1.

By night Continue on a N course passing between Fl.R to port and Fl.G to starboard then between a Fl.R and a Fl.G buoy. When in the centre of Etang de Luno the entrance to the Port de la Clape will be seen. The entrance is marked by a Fl.R and Fl.G. Report to the *bureau du port*. In summer report to the *bureau du port* (annex) at entrance to Bassin No. 1.

Anchorage

Anchorage is not now permitted inside the harbour.

Berths

Secure stern-to, bow-to mooring buoy or between fingers in the berths allocated in the Port de la Clape.

Formalities

Report to the *bureau du port* (☎ 67 94 78 04 and 67 94 70 28) on arrival. Open in summer 0800–2100 and in winter 0800–1200 and 1400–1800. If necessary the customs from Le Grau d'Agde (☎ 67 94 21 68) will visit a yacht here, usually Wednesday pm and Saturday am. A second *bureau du port* (annex) at Bassin No. 1 (☎ 67 26 00 08) is open in the summer. Secure to pontoon beside this bureau.

Harbour charges

There are harbour charges.

Facilities

Slip A slip in the S corner of Bassin No. 7.
Slipway Two slipways at the S corner of Bassin No. 7.
Cranes Cranes of 5 tonnes and 1 tonne and travel-lifts of 27 and 13 tonnes at the S corner of Bassin No. 7.
Fuel Diesel (*gasoil*) and petrol are from pumps on the SE side of the Port de la Clape Bassin No. 5 and at Bassin No. 1a, open in summer 0800–2000, in winter 0800–1200 and 1400–1800.
Water Water points on all the quays and pontoons.
Electricity Electrical supply points of 220v AC are established on all quays and pontoons.
Provisions A number of shops here. The nearest large shopping centre is at Agde some 2M away. Daily fish market and a full market Tuesday.
Ice Ice can be obtained in the season from the supermarket.
Garbage Rubbish containers on the quays and pontoons.
Chandlery Four ships' chandlers around the harbour.
Repairs Five shipyards are established in the SE corner of Port de la Clape, also sailmakers.
Post office A PTT is located in the shopping area in the season.
Hotels Ten ★★★, seven ★★, one ★ at present and more are being built.
Restaurants Twenty restaurants and café/bars are established around the area.
Yacht clubs The Yacht Club d'Agde et du Cap (YCAC) (☎ 67 26 26 21) has a clubhouse built on an island near the entrance and has all facilities.
Showers Showers and WCs are in six buildings around the harbour.

Information office The Syndicat d'Initiative (☎ 67 26 38 56 summer) (☎ 67 26 00 97) has an office on top of a small hill to the N of the harbour.
Visits The old city of Agde should be visited and a boat trip to Ilot Brescou is of interest.
Beaches Sandy beaches and black rocks are at both sides of the harbour.
Communications Bus service and rail service at Agde. Air service at Montpellier and Béziers.

Future development

This project will take many years to complete.

History

Some five centuries BC the Greeks established a sheltered anchorage in the Etang de Luno which then had an exit to the sea in a WSW direction. They called it *Agathe Nesos* (Good Moorings). However the entrance silted up and it was abandoned. In the course of time Richelieu, appreciating its strategic position, had a mole built and also a fort on Ilot Brescou. He was intending to develop it into a naval base but he died before the project was realised and the area again reverted to its natural state until recent development.

⚓ **Anchorage to SW of Cap d'Agde**

A shallow (2m) anchorage to SE of the *digue est*. Open to NE–E–SE–S. All facilities from the port.

Anchorage Cap d'Agde

Cap d'Agde

A low point sloping inland with cliffs on its NE side and rock and islets 5·7 and 8m around its foot. Inland there are roads and houses.

⌁ to NE of Cap d'Agde

⌁ **La Conque**

A shallow (2m) anchorage in a bay with rocky islets on S side and some rocks on the N side. All facilities at Port de Cap d'Agde. Open to NE–E–SE–S. There is a deep water anchorage offshore in 6m sand.

⌁ **La Roquitte**

A shallow (2m) coastal anchorage 200m offshore, very exposed. Open to NE–E–SE–S.

22 PORT AMBONNE (PORT NATURE)
34300 Hérault

Position 43°17'·5N 3°31'·8E
Minimum depth in the entrance 2m (6·5ft)
in the harbour 2 to 0.5m (6·5 to 1·5ft)
Width of the entrance 20m
Maximum length overall 8m (26ft)
Number of berths 264
Population 500 (approx)
Rating 3–3–3

General

A very small artificial yacht harbour for shallow-draught yachts which has a large complex of flats, houses and camping grounds to NE side for nudists. The harbour is easy to approach and enter but it would be dangerous to attempt to do so in strong winds and swell from the SE. There is shelter from the seas of the NW *tramontane/mistral* inside, but none from the wind. Facilities are limited, and as they are mostly in the naturist area they are only available to members of the naturist clubs, as are the berths.

Data

Charts Admiralty 1705
French 7003, 7054
Navicarte 509

Magnetic variation 2°04'W (1994) decreasing by about 6' each year.

Weather forecast Posted twice a day at the *bureau du port*. Recorded forecast (☎ 67 26 00 21 and 67 26 00 22).

Port radio VHF Ch 9.

Speed limit 3 knots.

Lights
Digue Sud-Ouest head Fl(2)R.6s9m7M White column, red top.
Digue Nord-Est head Oc.W.4s3m Strip light.

Warning

A sand bar (0·5m) sometimes forms in the entrance. See chart for areas of floating obstructions.

Approach by day

From SW Round Ilot Brescou leaving it 200m to port and follow the coast at 400m for 1·5M. The long low blocks of flats of this port and the small jetties will be seen in the closer approach.

From NE From Sète with its isolated Mont Saint-Clair and harbour installations that are easily recognised the coast is straight, flat, low and sandy. The jetties at Marseillan-Plage will be seen and 2M further on are the jetties and blocks of flats of Port Ambonne.

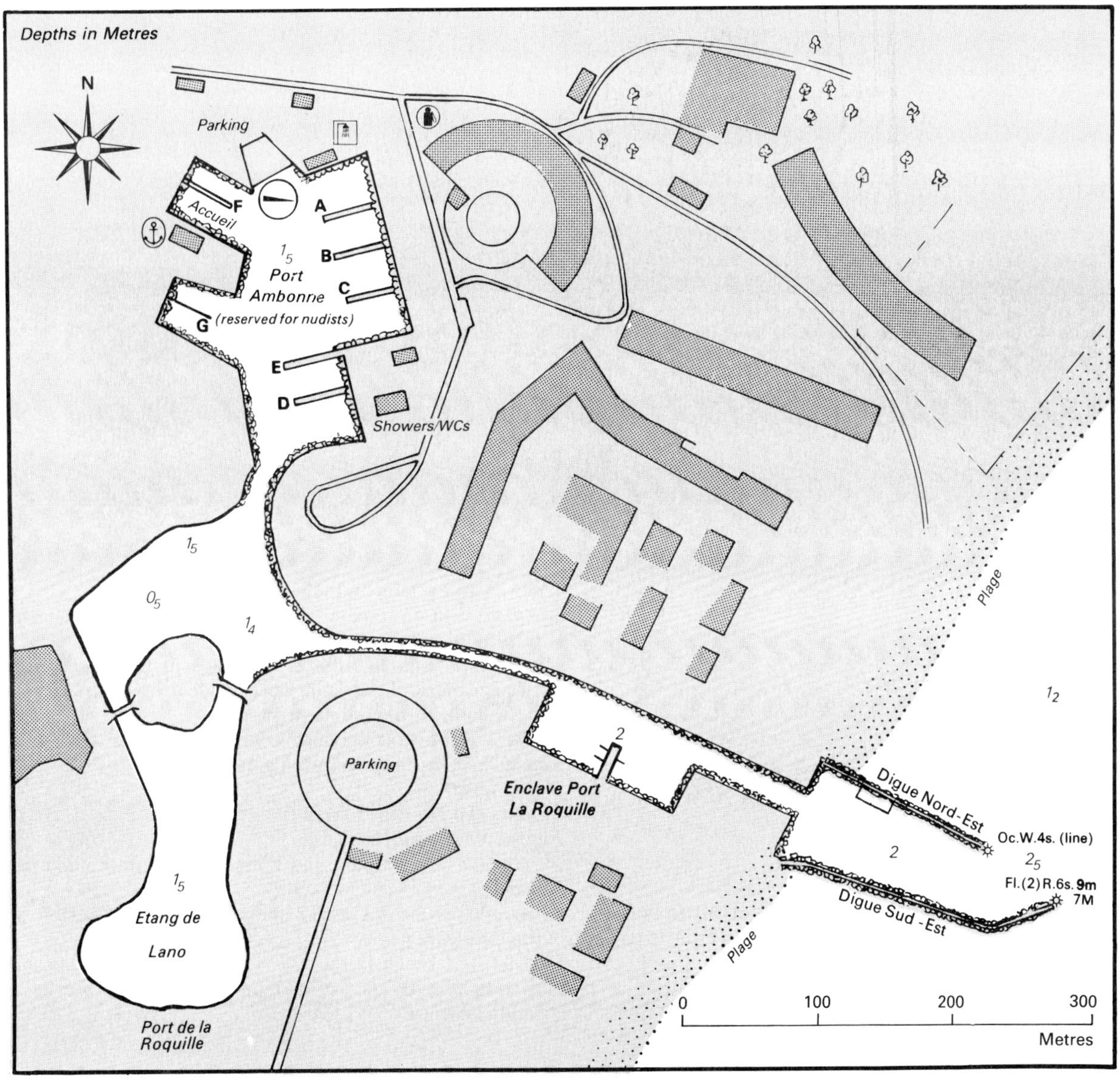

Depths in Metres

N

Parking

Accueil

F

A

Port
Ambonne

B

C

(reserved for nudists)

G

E

D

Showers/WCs

*1*5

*1*5

*0*5

*1*4

Plage

*1*2

Parking

Enclave Port
La Roquille

2

Digue Nord-Est

Oc.W.4s. (line)

*2*5

2

Fl.(2)R.6s. **9m**

Digue Sud -Est

7M

Etang de
Lano

*1*5

Plage

Port de la
Roquille

| 0 | 100 | 200 | 300 |

Metres

Port Ambonne (Port Nature)

Entrance

Bureau du port

Port Ambonne (Port Nature) looking W

Port Ambonne (Port Nature). Entrance looking W

Approach by night

Use the lights listed below:

Ilot Brescou Fl(2)WR.6s13/10M
Marseillan-Plage Fl.R.4s9M
Sète Mont Saint-Clair Fl.W.5s29M

Anchorage in the approach

Anchor 200m to SE of the entrance in 5m (16ft) sand and weed.

Entrance

By day Approach the entrance on a W course and round the head of Digue Ouest at 15m, leaving it to port and turning on to a NW course once inside. Follow the channel around to starboard after 300m.

By night Approach Fl(2)R.6s on W course; round it at 15m leaving it to port and Oc.W (strip light) to starboard.

Berths

Secure stern-to F pontoon berth, bow-to mooring buoy and report to *bureau du port* for instructions.

Formalities

Report on arrival to the *bureau du port* (☎ 67 26 00 23). Open summer 0800–1200 and 1400–1900, winter 0800–1200 and 1400–1800. If intending to make use of the facilities inside the naturist area produce your naturist club card. Cameras are not allowed to be used in or near this area. In summer call *bureau du port* on VHF Ch 9 before entering.

Harbour charges

There are harbour charges and an entrance fee to the nudist area. Free berth for two nights.

Facilities

Slip A slip in the N corner of the harbour.
Crane A mobile crane available.
Fuel There are fuel pumps in the naturist area for cars.

Water Water points on the pontoons and quays.
Electricity Supply points of 220v AC are available on the quays and pontoons.
Provisions A limited number of shops in the large semi-circular block of flats and more inside the naturist area.
Ice Available inside the naturist area.
Garbage Rubbish containers around the harbour.
Laundrette One in the naturist area.
Hotels One *.
Showers To N of the harbours.
Repairs Mechanics available.
Restaurants A restaurant and some café/bars in the naturist area.
Information office All details about the area are available at the *bureau du port*.
Beaches The beach to the NE is reserved for naturists and that to the SW is open to the public. Both are good sandy beaches.

Etang de Thau
(Bassin de Thau)

General

This very extensive inland salt water lagoon is nearly 12M long and in places 2M wide. A large part is suitable for use by yachts and there are several pleasant small harbours to visit. It forms a continuation of the Canal du Midi to Sète and thence to the Canal du Rhône à Sète. There is also a direct connection to the sea at Sète and at Marseillan-Plage. The *étang* is sausage-shaped, the long axis being NE/SW with two deep bays at the NE end, namely the Crique de l'Angle and the Bassin des Eaux Blanches. It is an excellent area for yachtsmen to practise in without exposing themselves to the ocean swell.

Depths

The middle of the *étang* is 6 to 8m (20 to 26ft) deep with a number of shallow spots of 2 to 3m (6·5 to 10ft). The sides shallow regularly and are of mud and sand. The bottom is in general sand with weed.

Levels

The level of the water can increase by up to 0·6m (2ft) after strong and prolonged winds from the S quarter, and decrease by the same amount with winds from the N sector.

Currents

There are no currents in the *étang* but strong currents may be experienced in the canals connecting it to the sea especially when there is a change in the level of water. This can reach 5 knots at times.

Obstructions

There are large areas of oyster beds which are easy to identify by day by means of tall metal stakes sticking out of the water; at night, however, these are very difficult to see. The area allocated for these beds is N of lines joining the beacon tower Rocher de Rôquerols and the Jetée NE head at Mèze, and the Digue E head at Bouzigues to the Jetée et Les Onglous; see chartlet.

Navigation

Despite the oyster beds mentioned above and the shallow sand and mud sides there is little difficulty in navigating this *étang*.

By day Mont Saint-Clair at Sète and Mont St-Loup at Agde are easily recognised from afar. The concentration of buildings and the churches at Marseillan, Mèze, Bouzigues and Balaruc-les-Bains are easily identified, as is the mass of factories and chimneys at Balaruc-les-Usines.

By night There are sufficient lights to allow navigation at night though the powerful light at Mont Saint-Clair is obscured in the NE half of the *étang*.

Seas

A strong NE *tramontane/mistral* can raise a nasty sea in the Etang de Thau, as can strong winds from the SE, but it will not be as bad as the open sea. This should be borne in mind when cruising in the area.

Warnings

Fast motorboats. Most of the shell fishermen use very fast motor launches to tend to their farms and they usually run them at full throttle.

Exits/Entrances

There are four as listed below:

Exit A – to the Canal du Midi. Details are given at 24 Port des Onglous (see page 127).

Exit B – to the Canal de Pisse-Saumes (leading to the sea at Marseillan-Plage. See page 124).

By day Proceed as for Canal du Midi, but 400m short of the head of the Jetée S and its lighthouse, branch to port into a buoyed channel which takes a S course then curves slowly towards the E where it runs between banks of dredged soil. The channel then passes under three bridges of clearance 2·5m (8ft). The canal is dredged to 2m (6·5ft).

By night Night approach and entrance are not advised.

Exit C – to the Canal du Rhône à Sète

By day Leave the beacon tower Rocher de Rôquerols (Fl(2)WR.6s11/8M), red with black bands and red ⁝ topmark, 50m to port and on a course of 105° approach the coast which is just over 1M away. The entrance is just S of a large factory which has a small pier and a chimney. There is a white beacon on the N side of the entrance with a □ topmark and a long jetty on the S side.

By night Night approach and entrance are not advised.

Exit D – to the Canal Latéral, Canal Maritime and Sète

By day Leave the beacon tower Rocher de Rôquerols (Fl(2)WR.6s6m11/8M), red with black bands and a red ⁝ topmark, 50m to port and on a SE course approach the coast 1M away which has a mass of buildings. Leave the beacon tower Barrou (red with cylinder topmark) and Pointe Barrou some 300m to starboard in order to clear some wrecks there. In the closer approach a large lifting rail bridge will be seen, as will the white light towers on either side of the entrance to the Canal Latéral. This entrance leads to the Canal Maritime and thence to Sète and the open sea. For details of Port de Sète see page 145. If the bridge is not open, secure to the NE side of the canal alongside the quay short of the bridge. Phone the *capitaine du port* (☎ 67 74 98 97). When the bridge has been passed turn to port into the Canal Latéral and then, after a second bridge, to starboard into Canal Maritime. The clearance under this bridge and others when closed is 2·2m (7ft). The

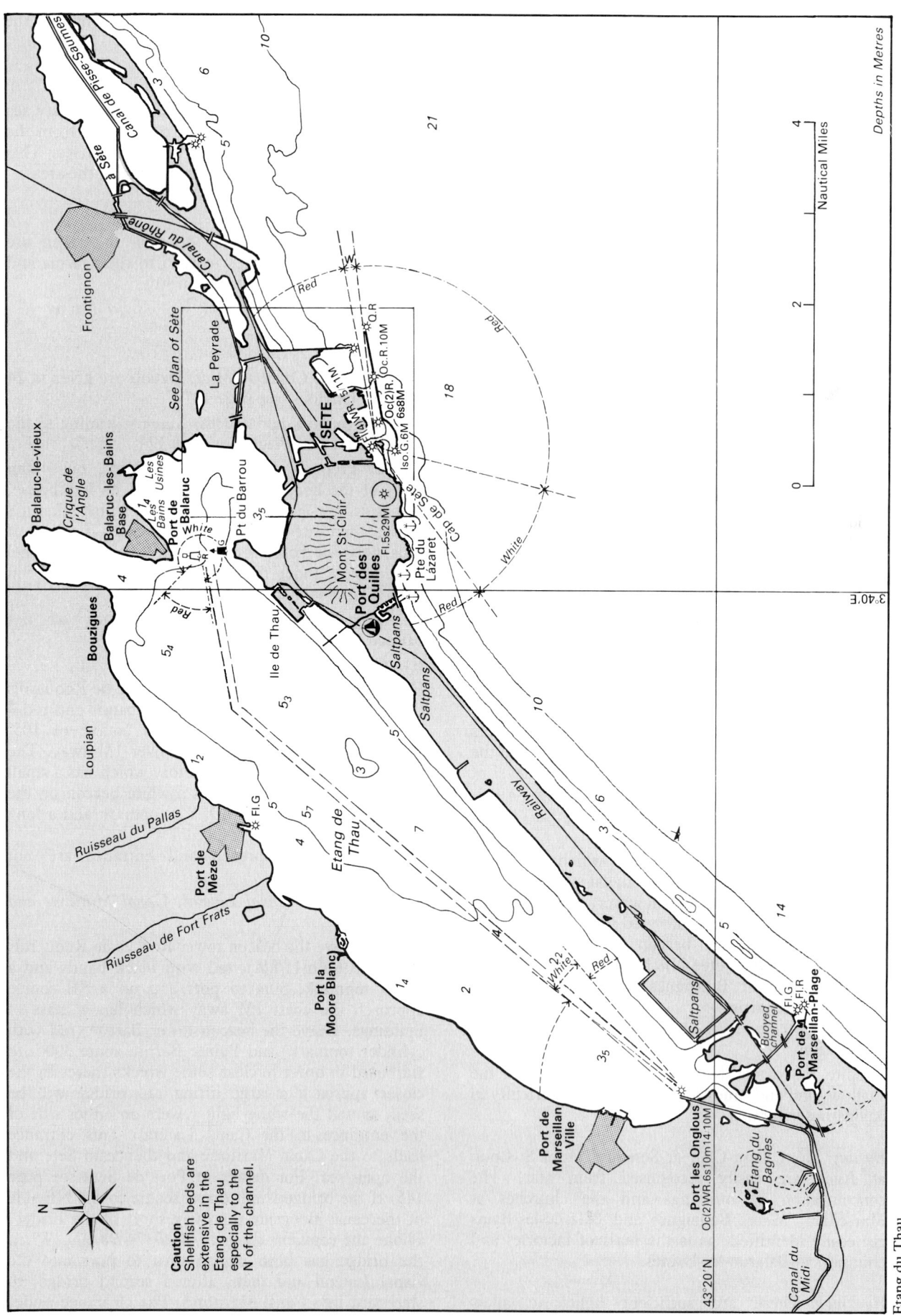

Etang du Thau

Etang de Thau (Bassin de Thau). Rocher du Roquerôls beacon looking E

Etang de Thau (Bassin de Thau). Entrance to Canal Latéral looking SE

bridges are normally opened – sea to *étang* 0815 and 1640; *étang* to sea 0850 and 1700. Arrive one hour early.

By night Approach Fl(2)WR.6s on a NE course and when 100m short of it change to a SE course. Keep on this course for nearly 1M and when a F.R and F.G are S turn to this course and enter between them. Secure to the NE side of the canal short of the bridge. Bridges are not opened at night. The red section from Rocher de Rôquerols is 078°–137°.

⚓   Anchorage in mud and sand 0 to 6m almost anywhere, and any obstructions are easily seen; sound carefully from 2m and less.

Pointe de Onglous
A very low point with the Canal du Midi entrance and a lighthouse at its head. A few buildings to S.

Etang de Thau

PLANNING GUIDE

Ports, harbours, anchorages and landing places

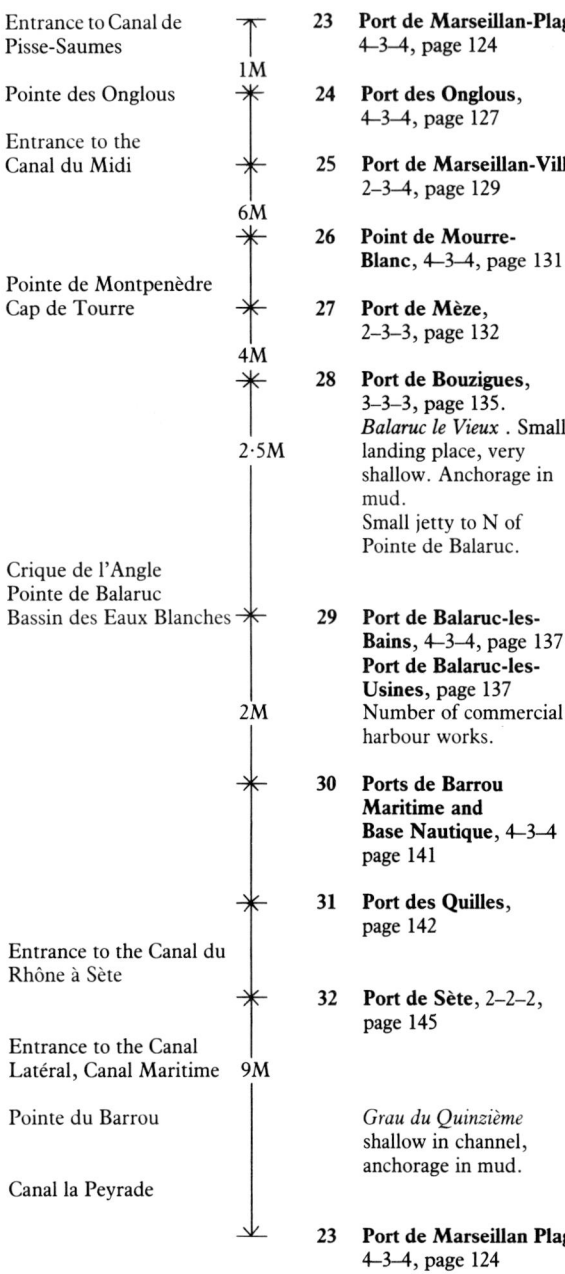
23 PORT DE MARSEILLAN-PLAGE
34340 Hérault

Position 43°19'·1N 3°33'·5E
Minimum depth   in the entrance 3m (10ft)
                           in the harbour 2·5 to 1m (8 to 3ft)
Minimum clearance under bridges 2·5m (8ft)
Number of berths 176
Population 1000 (approx)
Rating 4–3–4

General

This is the new entrance to the Etang de Thau from the sea at its SW end. It is still in the process of construction and facilities are limited. Approach and entrance are not difficult but would be dangerous in heavy swell from E–SE–S. The NW end of the canal is buoyed into the Etang de Thau.

Data

Charts   Admiralty 1705
             French 6839

Water levels The water level in the *étang* can alter by as much as 0·6m (2ft) above or below normal. The NW *tramontane* lowers the levels and creates a SE-going current and wind from the SE raises them and creates a NW-going current.

Currents The currents in the canal can reach 3 knots during a change of the water levels.

Magnetic variation 2°04'W (1994) decreasing by about 6' each year.

Weather forecast Posted once a day. Recorded forecast (☎ 36 68 08 34 or 36 68 08 13).

Speed limit 3 knots.

Port radio VHF Ch 9.

Lights
Digue Ouest Fl.R.4s7m9M White column, red top
Digue Est Fl.G.4s8m5M White column, green top

Warning

As this harbour and canal are still under construction minor changes can be expected. Shelter should be taken under Digue Est during a *tramontane/mistral*. Currents of up to 3 knots can be encountered in the entrance and in the canal. The harbour is dredged each year and depths are uncertain. A sand bar (0·5m) sometimes forms in the entrance.

Approach by day

From the sea from SW Round the conspicuous Ilot Brescou with its fort and lighthouse and follow the flat, low, sandy coast for 4M passing the small jetties of Port Ambonne which have some large blocks of flats behind them. The similar jetties of Port de Marseillan-Plage and a small group of houses at their root will be seen in the close approach, and the large Hotel Richmond (20m) is very conspicuous.

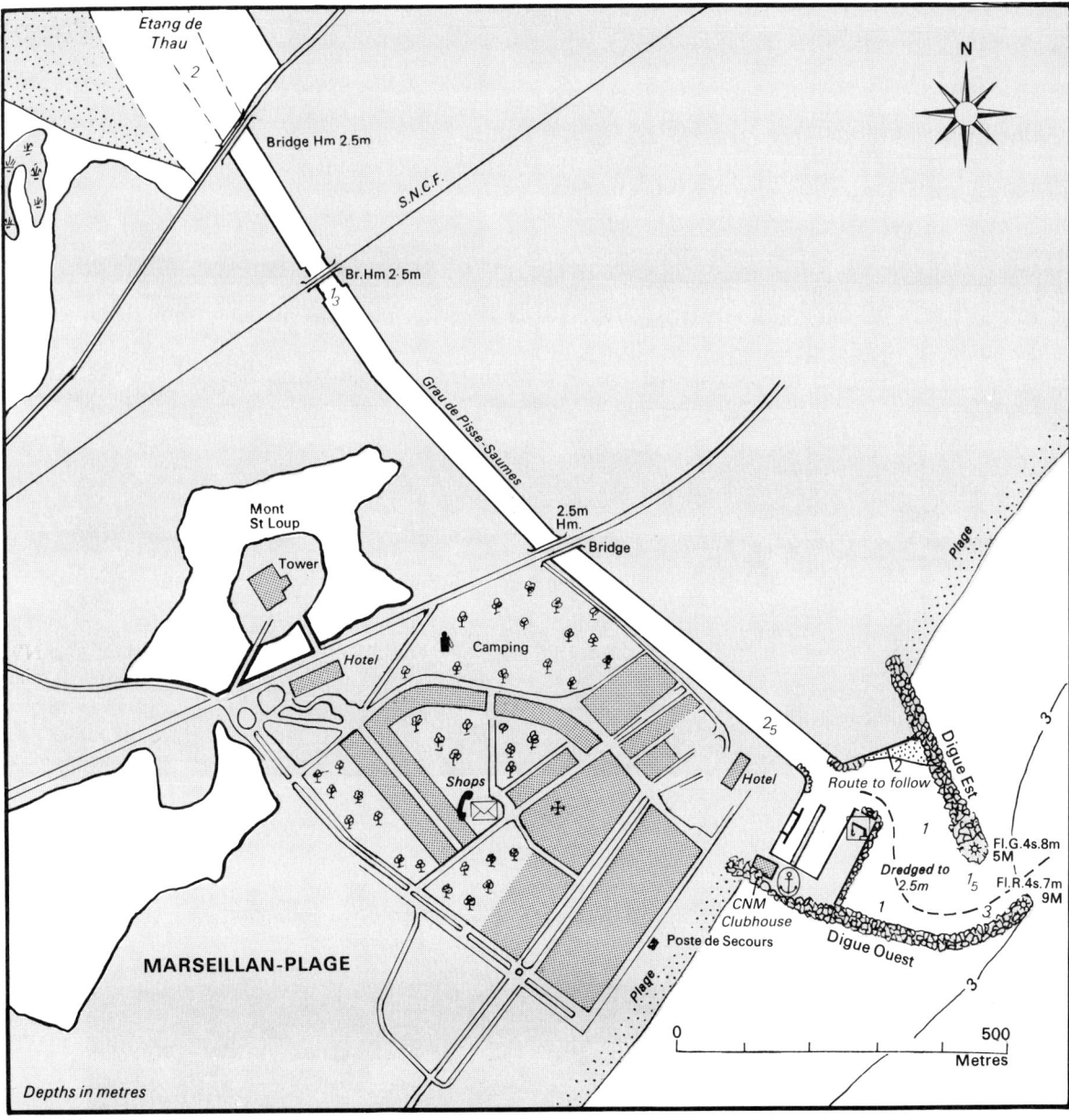

Port de Marseillan-Plage

From the sea from NE From Sète with its very conspicuous Mont Saint-Clair and harbour installations the coast is likewise low, flat and sandy. After 7M the jetties, houses and hotel of the Port de Marseillan-Plage will be seen.

From the Etang de Thau Follow a course towards the light tower at Les Onglous (Oc(2)WR). White and red tower, grey top and bottom, 11m (36ft high) 400m to NE, branch off in a S direction into the buoyed Canal de Pisse-Saumes which passes under three bridges.

Approach by night
Use the following lights:
Ilot Brescou Fl(2)WR.6s13/10M
Sète Mont Saint-Clair Fl.W.5s29M

Anchorage in the approach
At sea Anchor 300m to E of the entrance in 6m (20ft) sand and weed.
In the étang Anchor 400m to NE of the lighthouse at Les Onglous in 2·5m (8ft) mud.

Entrance
By day From sea approach on a W sounding carefully course and round the head of Digue Ouest at 20m leaving it to port and follow it at 10m into the outer harbour until a crane is N; approach it and round it at 10m into the inner harbour.

By night Not recommended until a visit has been made by day.

Onglous

Port de Marseillan-Plage looking NW

Mont St Loup

Port de Marseillan-Plage Entrance looking NW

Anchorage

A temporary anchorage is possible inside the jetties in the N corner.

Berths

Two pontoons provide a limited number of berths for small and medium-sized yachts.

Harbour charges

There are harbour charges but the first day is free.

Formalities

A *bureau du port* (☎ 67 21 99 30) is located on the S side of the harbour. Report here on arrival.

Facilities

Crane 8-tonne crane.

Fuel From service station on main road (RN 108).

Water From pontoons and quays.

Electricity 220v AC points available on pontoons and quays.

Provisions Limited provisions are obtainable in the town.

Ice From a nearby shop.

Post office The PTT is located in the middle of the town.

Chandler In the town.

Hotels Several small pensions and the large Hotel Richmond ★★.

Restaurants Some small restaurants and cafés.

Showers Two showers and two WCs at the *bureau du port*.

Beaches Excellent beaches either side of the harbour mouth.

Communications Bus service and rail 1.5M away.

24 PORT DES ONGLOUS
3430 Hérault

Position 43°20'·4N 3°32'·4E
Minimum depth in the entrance 1·5m (5ft)
in the harbour 1·8m (6ft)
Population 20
Rating 4–3–4

General

A canal-type harbour at the entrance to the Canal du
Midi where it joins the Etang de Thau at its SW
corner. Easy to approach and enter but
uncomfortable in NW–N–NE winds. There are
virtually no facilities but in the season some
assistance may be obtained from the Centre Nautique
de Glénans which has a section here.

Data

Charts Admiralty 2606, 1705
French 6839
Navicarte 509

Currents The current is weak in the canal and is dependent
on the wind direction affecting the level of the *étang*.

Magnetic variations 2°04'W (1994) decreasing by about 6'
each year.

Light
Jetée Est head Oc(2)WR.6s10m14/10M White and red
tower. 217·5°-W-229°-R-217·5°.

Facilities

Water From the Centre Nautique des Glénans or from the
house of the canal staff on the W bank.
Provisions From Marseillan about 1M away where other
facilities are available.
Yacht club Centre Nautique des Glénans (CNG) (☎ 67 77
22 73) has a small clubhouse with bar, lounge and
showers.

Approach and entrance

By day From NE. Keep down the centre of the *étang*
on a SW course with Mont St-Loup (Mont d'Agde)
seen in the distance, fine on the port bow. In the
closer approach the light tower and the Jetée Sud
together with some houses and clumps of trees will
be seen. Approach the light tower leaving it to port
and follow the Jetée Sud at 20m. Leave a small white
beacon on the W bank of the canal to starboard on
entering.

By night From NE. From a position in mid-*étang*
approach Oc(2)WR.6s on a SW course in the white
sector. Leave this light 20m to port and follow the
Jetée Est round into the canal with care as there are
no lights.

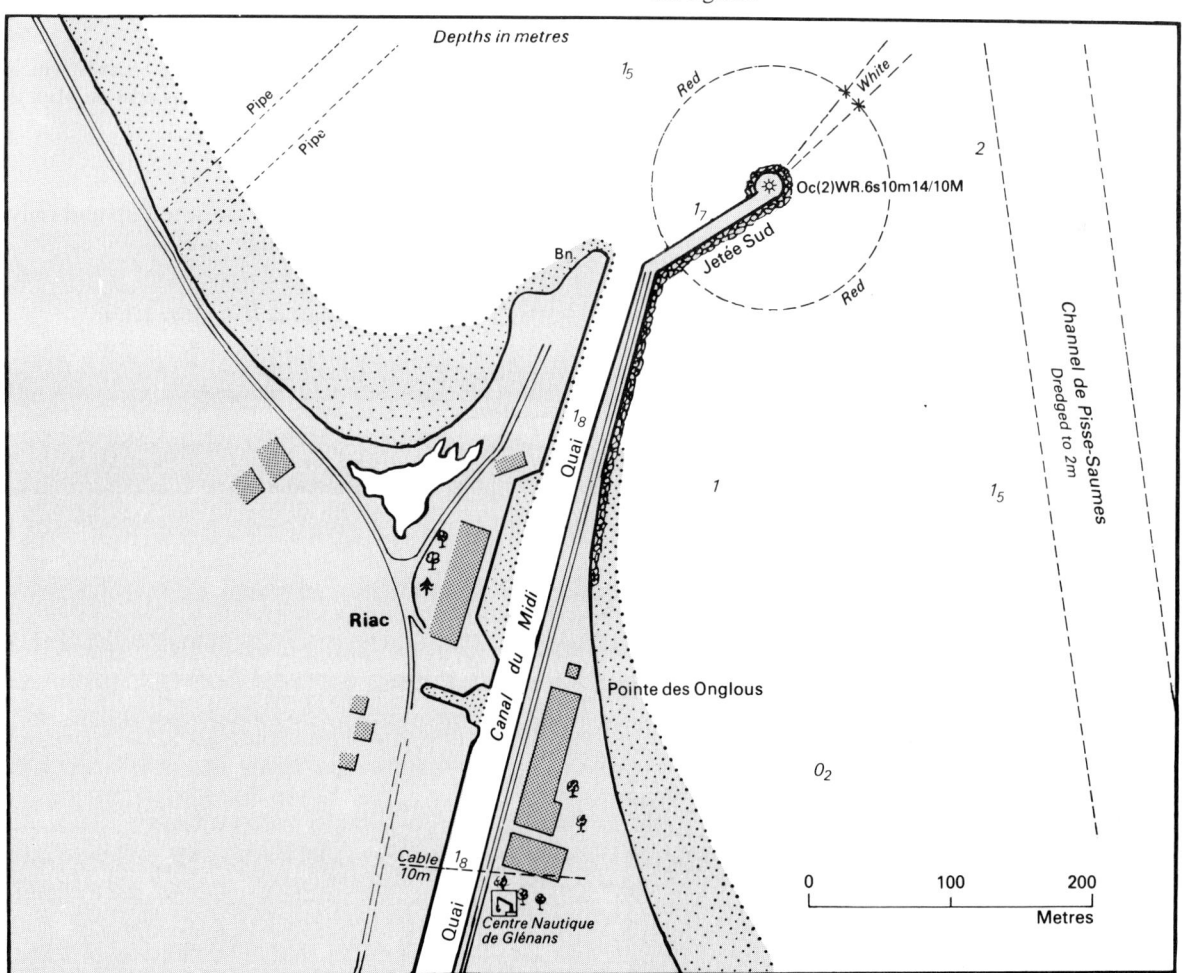

Port des Onglous

Port

Port des Onglous looking W

Port des Onglous looking NE

Berths

Secure alongside the E bank quay some 250m inside the entrance where there are mooring rings.

Buoys The entrance to the Canal de Pisse-Saumes which lies 400m to the E of the entrance to the Canal du Midi is buoyed.

Warning

The two basins on the W bank are silted up and only suitable for small shallow-draught craft.

Entrance to Canal de Pisse-Saumes   *Lighthouse   Canal du Midi   Mont d'Agde*

Port des Onglous looking SW-W

Port des Onglous. Port and quays looking SE

25 PORT DE MARSEILLAN-VILLE
34340 Hérault

Position 43°21'·2N 3°32'·2E
Minimum depth in the entrance 3·5m (11ft)
　　　　　　　in the harbour 2 to 1·0m (6·5 to 3ft)
Width of the entrance 30m
Number of yacht berths 200
Maximum length overall 15m (49ft)
Population 4040 (approx)
Rating 2–3–4

General

A most attractive simple old fishing and yachting harbour which is not normally too difficult to approach and enter, but strong winds from E–SE–S make the entrance difficult and the harbour uncomfortable. Inside, good shelter is obtained.

There is a second harbour, the Port de Pêche (1·5 to 0·6m (5 to 2ft)), to the N of the main harbour, but this is normally reserved for fishing craft, as is the quay to NE of the main harbour.

Data

Charts Admiralty 2606, 1705
　　　French 6839
　　　Navicarte 509

Magnetic variation 2°04'W (1994) decreasing by about 6' each year.

Weather forecast Posted daily. Recorded forecast (☎ 36 68 08 08/36 68 08 34).

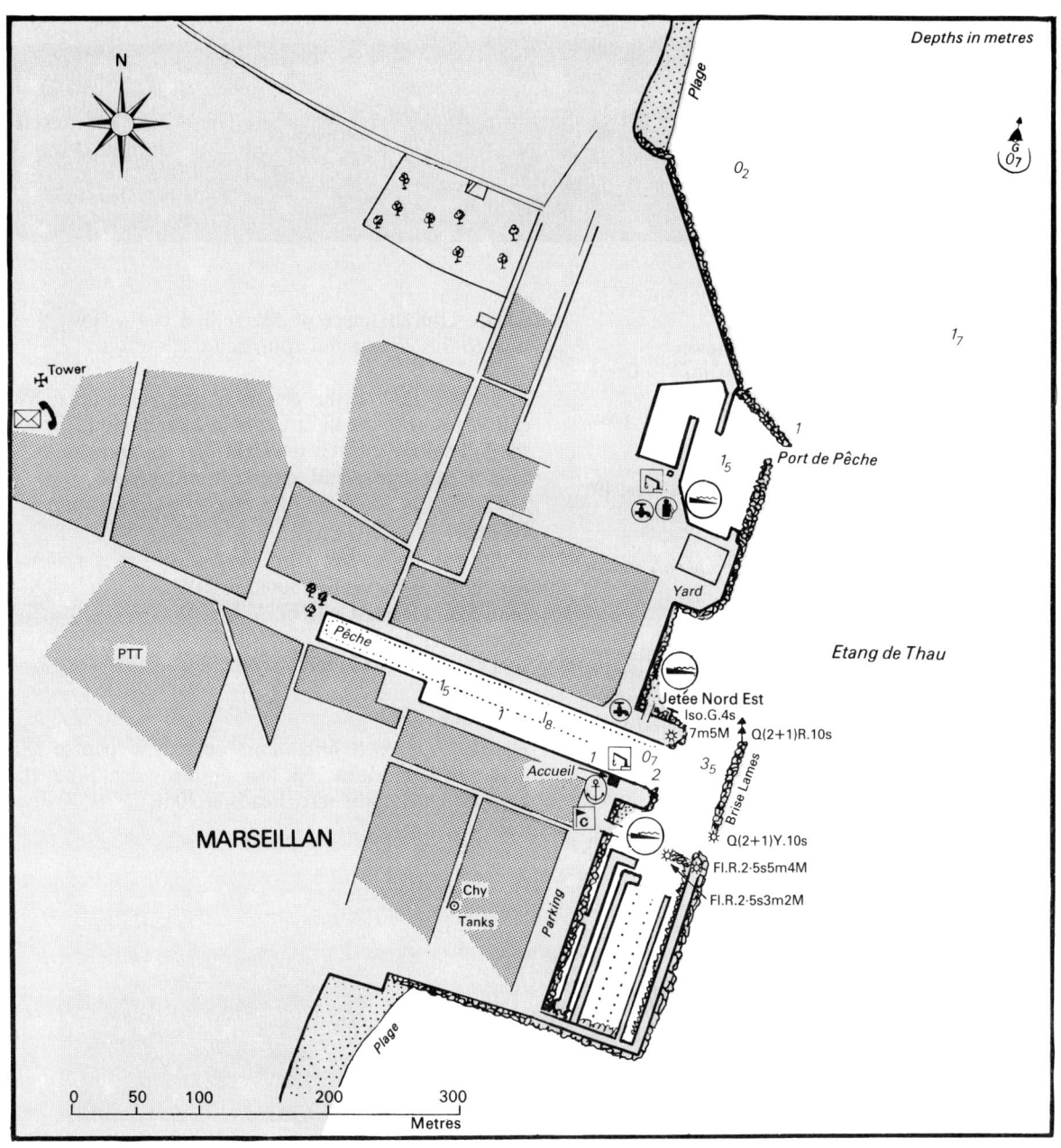

Port de Marseillan-Ville

Port de Pêche

Port de Marseillan-Ville looking NW

Lights

Jetée Nord-Est head Iso.G.4s7m5M Green tower

Brise-Lames Nord head Q(2+1)R.10s5m7M Green column, red band

Brise-Lames Sud head Q(2+1)Y.10s5m5M Grey post, yellow top

Nouvelle Jetée head Fl.R.2·5s5m4M Pylon

Nouvelle Jetée spur Fl.R.2·5s3m2M Pylon 324°-vis-249° (285°)

Beacon A small green beacon tower with topmark ⬥ marks shoal area to N of the entrance.

Warning

There are many oyster beds along the coast which can be seen and avoided by day but not by night. The harbour tends to silt up and is not dredged very often.

Approach by day

From S Leaving the Canal du Midi at Les Onglous, proceed on a NE course for 0.5M until the very tall square church tower of Marseillan bears NW, then turn to this course and approach the harbour.

From NE Follow the centre of the *étang* on a SW course towards the light tower at Les Onglous. When the tall square church tower at Marseillan bears NW turn to this course and approach the harbour.

By night

Using the lights listed below navigate to a position where the entrance lies 500m to NW:

Sète Mont Saint-Clair Fl.W.5s29M

Mèze Fl.G.4s7M

Les Onglous Oc(2)WR.6s14/10M

Entrance

By day Approach *brise-lames* on a NW course and divert to round it at 20m leaving it to port. Enter the harbour leaving the jetty heads at 20m.

Fuel Yacht club *Château* *Church tower*

Port de Marseillan-Ville. Entrance looking W

Top of château   *Entrance to old harbour*   *Sè*

Port de Marseillan-Ville. New harbour looking N

By night Approach Q(2+1)R on a NW course. When 200m from it divert to port to round it at 20m. Then enter leaving Iso.G.4s to starboard.

Berths

Secure to posts and quay on SW side of the harbour near the *bureau du port*. There is only about 0·8m (3ft) alongside the quay but it is deeper near the middle of the harbour. Yachts are usually secured stern-to the quays. Alternative berths in external harbour.

Formalities

On arrival report to the *bureau du port* (☎ 67 77 34 93) at the office to S of the entrance for the allocation of a berth. Open in winter 0830–1200 and 1400–1700. Customs at Agde (☎ 67 94 21 68).

Harbour charges

Harbour charges are levied.

Facilities

Slip A small slip outside the harbour on NE *jetée*.
Cranes Two cranes of 2·5 tonnes, one on the SW quay, the other in the Port de Pêche.
Fuel A fuel pump to SW of the Port de Pêche but diesel (*gasoil*) is not available.
Water From points on quays and pontoons.
Electricity 220v AC points on quays and pontoons.
Provisions A number of shops in the town about 500m away.
Repairs Minor repairs to hull and engine are possible by local artisans. There is also a sailmaker.
Post office In the centre of the town, Rue de la Paix.
Hotels Several hotels in the locality including one ★.
Restaurants A number of small restaurants and café/bars.
Information Syndicate d'Initiative at the *mairie* (☎ 67 77 22 33).
Yacht clubs The Société Nautique de Marseillan (l'Aviron Marseillanais) (SNM) (☎ 67 77 23 69) has a small club-house at the head of the Jetée Sud Ouest. Showers.
Showers Four showers and four WCs.
Beaches Sandy beaches either side of the harbour.
Visits Noilly Prat the vermouth distillers run a tour of their works several times a day. Pezenas, 15M inland, is worth a visit.
Communications Bus service. Rail at Agde. Airport at Montpellier.

History

A small fishing harbour since 535 BC when the Phoenicians founded it. There was no great development until the 17th century AD. It is now well known as a centre for shellfish culture and vermouth production.

26 PORT LE MOURRE-BLANC
34140 Hérault

Position 43°24'·3N 3°34'·6E
Minimum depth   in the entrance 1·5m (5ft)
                  in the harbour 1·5 to 0m (5 to 0ft)
Width of the entrance 15m
Number of yacht berths 6
Maximum length overall 11m (36ft)
Population 6 approx
Rating 4–3–4

General

A small shallow rather complex harbour only suitable for small power and sailing boats. The harbour is used as a base by shell fishermen who keep their fast fishing boats here with their stores and equipment in small huts on the quays. The harbour should only be used in an emergency.

Data

Charts   Admiralty 2606, 1705
           French 6839
           Navicarte 509

Magnetic variation 2°04'W (1994) decreasing by about 6' each year.

Beacons A red can beacon lies 1M to NE.

Approach by day

From SW Leave Les Onglous on a NE course until the tall square church tower of Mèze bears NW. Then follow this course until about ¼M from the outer harbour breakwaters, turn to a SW course and follow the coast for ½M sounding carefully. An isolated rocky patch lies ½M to NE of the harbour.

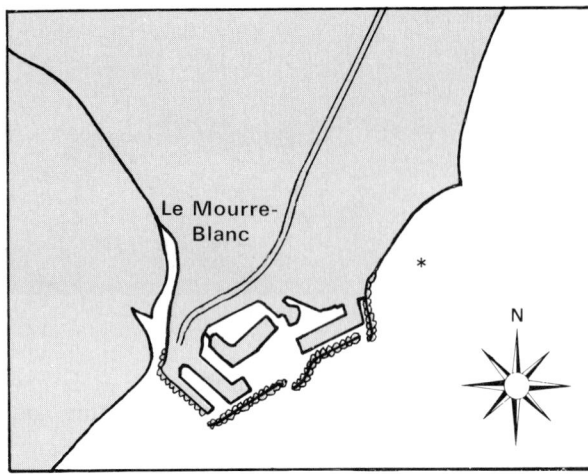

Port le Mourre-Blanc

Entrance

Port de Mourre-Blanc looking SW

From NE Follow the centre line of the *étang* on a SW course until the tall square church tower of Mèze bears NW whenupon proceed as above.

Approach by night

Not advised without a previous visit by day.

Entrance

By day Approach the breakwater on a N course and enter the centre entrance with care using the echo sounder. Note that there are three entrances, one at each end and one in the middle of the harbour.

By night Not recommended without a previous daytime visit.

Berths

Secure in a vacant place or alongside another boat. Be prepared to move if the owner returns.

Facilities

Water A few taps around the harbour.
Provisions From Mèze 2M away.
Ice Normally available from the fishermen.

Future developments

The harbour could easily be enlarged to take yachts.

---

27 PORT DE MEZE

34140 Hérault

Position 43°25′·3N 3°36′·4E
Minimum depth   in the entrance 2·5m (8ft)
                          in the harbour 3 to 0·6m (10 to 2ft)
Width of the entrance 30m
Number of yacht berths 122
Maximum length overall 11m (36ft)
Population 6500 (approx)
Rating 2–3–3

General

A fishing and yachting harbour in the middle of a pleasant old town, easy to approach and enter and with good shelter inside except in E–SE–S winds, which make the entrance difficult and the harbour uncomfortable. There is a second small harbour, the Port des Nacelles (depth 0·6m (2ft), which lies to the NE of the main harbour and is normally reserved for fishing craft. To the SW lies a third small harbour, l'Abri de l'Ecole de Voile le Taurus (depth 1·5m (5ft), which is used by the sailing school, and others but only by special arrangement. The town is the centre of the *étang* oyster trade.

Data

Charts Admiralty 2602, 1705
       French 6839
       Navicarte 509

Magnetic variations 2°04′W (1994) decreasing by about 6′ each year

Lights
Jetée Est head Fl.G.4s8m7M White eight-sided pyramidal tower, green top
Jetée Ouest head Fl.R.4s

Buoys There are a number of unlit mooring buoys in the centre of the harbour. A series of red and green buoys mark the entrance channel to the harbour.

Beacon There is a red beacon with a ▁× topmark marking a rocky bank situated about 0·5M to SW of the harbour.

Warning

The NW half of the *étang* is filled with oyster beds which can be seen by day but are not lit at night. The quays have rocky ledges below water level. Oyster boats leave and enter at high speed. The harbour may silt up but it is periodically dredged.

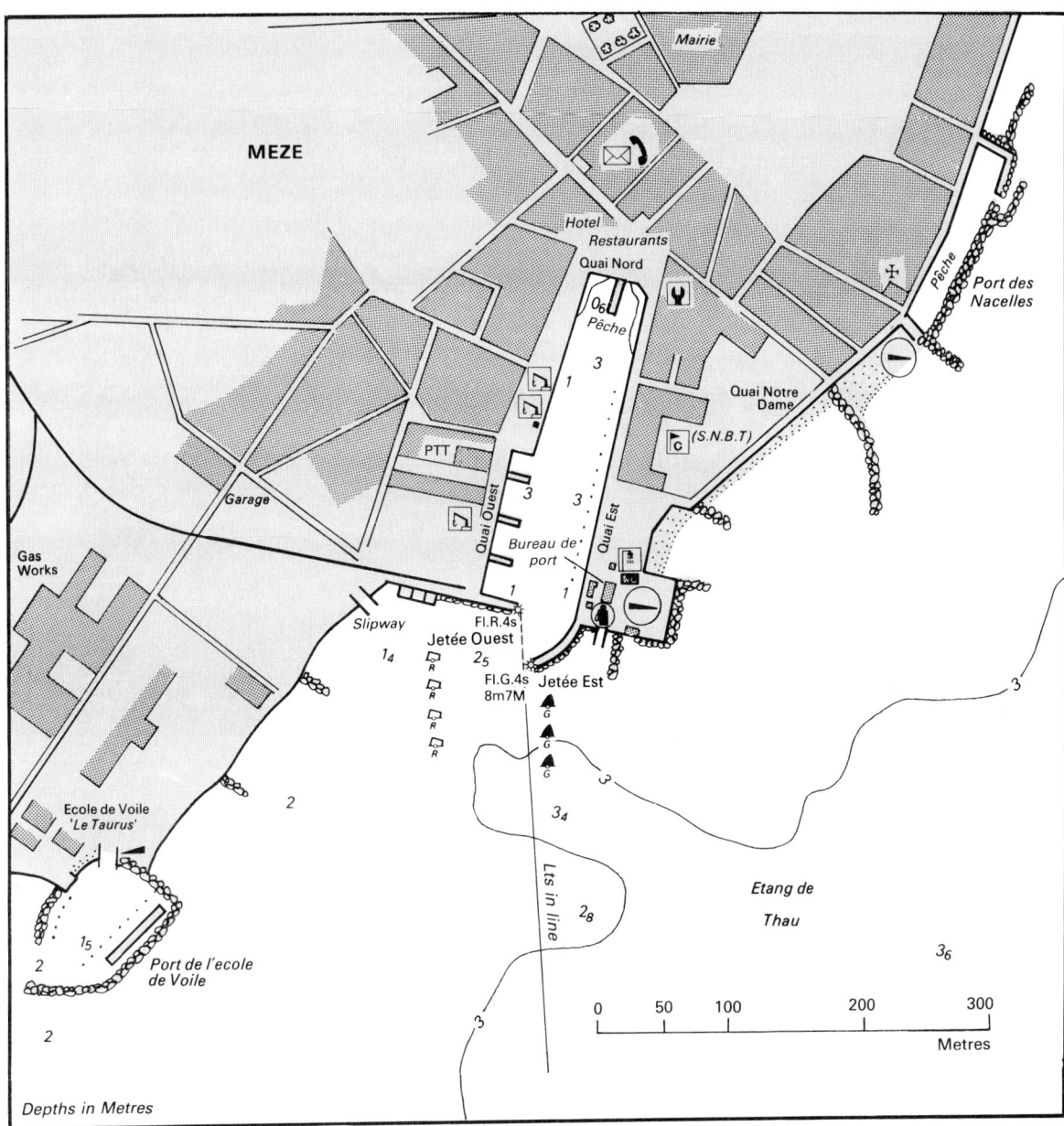

Port de Mèze

Approach by day

From SW Follow the centre axis of the *étang* on a NE course until the square church tower in the town of Mèze is N, then turn to this course and approach.

From NE Follow the axis of the *étang* down the centre on a SW course until the square church tower of Mèze bears NNW, then turn to this course and approach.

Approach by night

Using the lights below navigate to a position where the harbour lies N 1M:
Sète, Mont Saint-Clair Fl.W.5s29M (obscured in the close approach)
Rocher de Rôquerols Fl(2)WR.6s11/8M
Les Onglous Oc(2)WR.6s14/10M

Entrance

By day Approach the head of Jetée Est, which has a white light tower with a green top, on a N course. Leave this head 20m to starboard and then the head of Jetée Ouest 20m to port.

By night Approach Fl.G.4s on a N course and in the closer approach line it up with the Fl.R.4s light located behind. Leave the Fl.G.4s 20m to starboard and round it, then leave Fl.R.4s 20m to port.

Berths

Secure stern-to quay, bow-to mooring post on the E side of the harbour near the entrance. The head of the harbour is reserved for fishing boats. Do not get too close to the quay as it is shallow alongside.

Ecole de Voile   *Port de Mèze*

Port de Mèze looking NW

Port de Mèze. Entrance looking N

Church tower

Port de Mèze looking N

Formalities

Report to the *bureau du port* at the club (☎ 67 43 85 25) on arrival, the harbourmaster is not always on duty, await his return. Open in winter 0800–1900.

Harbour charges

There are harbour charges.

Facilities

Slips A small slip just outside the harbour beside the lifeboat house, but only 0·8m (2·5ft) of water. There is another at the Port des Nacelles.

Slipways A small slipway just outside the harbour to the W.

Cranes A 5-tonne crane on the quay to W of the harbour and two other small ones (1–2 tonnes) nearby.

Fuel Diesel (*gasoil*) and petrol can be obtained from pumps to SE of the harbour.

Water Water points on the quays.

Provisions A number of shops in the town and a market on Sundays. Supermarket outside the town.

Chandlery Obtainable in limited amounts from the shipyard shop.

Repairs Minor repairs to hull and engines can be carried out here by a shipyard and mechanics.

Post office The PTT is located just to the N of the harbour.

Hotels One ★★★ and one ★★.

Restaurants A number of restaurants and café/bars.

Yacht club The Société Nautique de Bassin du Thau (SNBT) (☎ 67 43 83 82) has a clubhouse to the E of the harbour which has showers.

Showers Showers and WCs available in summer.

Information office The Syndicat d'Initiative has an office in the town hall (☎ 67 43 93 08).

Lifeboat A lifeboat is stationed here. It is of the 2nd class type (☎ 67 74 40 00).

Visits The 15th-century church should be visited and also the Abbaye de Valmagne. The Musée de la Conchy culture is of interest as is the village of Pézenas 15M inland.

Beaches Sandy beaches either side of the harbour.

Communications A bus service and the railway station about 1M away.

Future development

The sailing school harbour is to be improved.

History

The history of the town goes back to the Phoenician occupation in the 7th century BC and the Greek occupation in the 5th century BC. The Romans occupied it around 125 AD, when it was called Mansa, and gave the town the name of Mezua from which Mèze has derived. The harbour flourished over the ages and had become by the 19th century one of the largest wine-exporting ports, shipping wine all over the world. In 1930 the culture of oysters commenced and Mèze has now become a renowned centre for these and other shellfish.

28 PORT BOUZIGUES

34140 Hérault

Position 43°24'·8N 3°39'·5E
Minimum depth in the entrance 2m (6·5ft)
in the harbour 1·7 to 0·2m (5 to 1ft)
Width of the entrance 25m
Population 1000 (approx)
Rating 3–3–3

General

A small shallow fishing harbour with few facilities for yachtsmen next to a small old village. Approach and entrance are not difficult but the harbour is silting up. There is a smaller harbour just to the E with 0·6 to 0·4m (2 to 1·5ft) of water used normally by fishing craft.

Data

Charts Admiralty 2606, 1705
French 6839
Navicarte 509

Magnetic variations 2°04'W (1994) decreasing by about 6' each year

Warning

In the NW half of the *étang* there are considerable areas devoted to oyster beds which are easily seen by day but are not lit at night.

Approach by day

From S Navigate to the area of the beacon tower Rocher de Rôquerols Fl(2)WR.6s11/8M, a black tower with red band and ball topmark. From here on course 335° approach the village of Bouzigues. In the closer approach set course for a building to the right of which is a squat round tower with low pointed roof.

Approach by night

Approach and entrance by night not advised owing to the lack of lights.

Entrance

By day Enter on a N course and round the head of Digue Est at 20m, leaving it to starboard.

Berths

Secure stern-to the inner side of the Digue Est, using two posts if available, or an anchor with tripline from the bows if not.

Facilities

Slip A long slip near the crane.
Cranes Two cranes, one of 1 tonne and one of 2 tonnes.
Fuel A fuel point between the two harbours.
Water Points for water on the quayside.
Provisions A limited number of shops provide basic requirements.
Repairs There is a local mechanic.
Post office The PTT is located near the N side of the village.

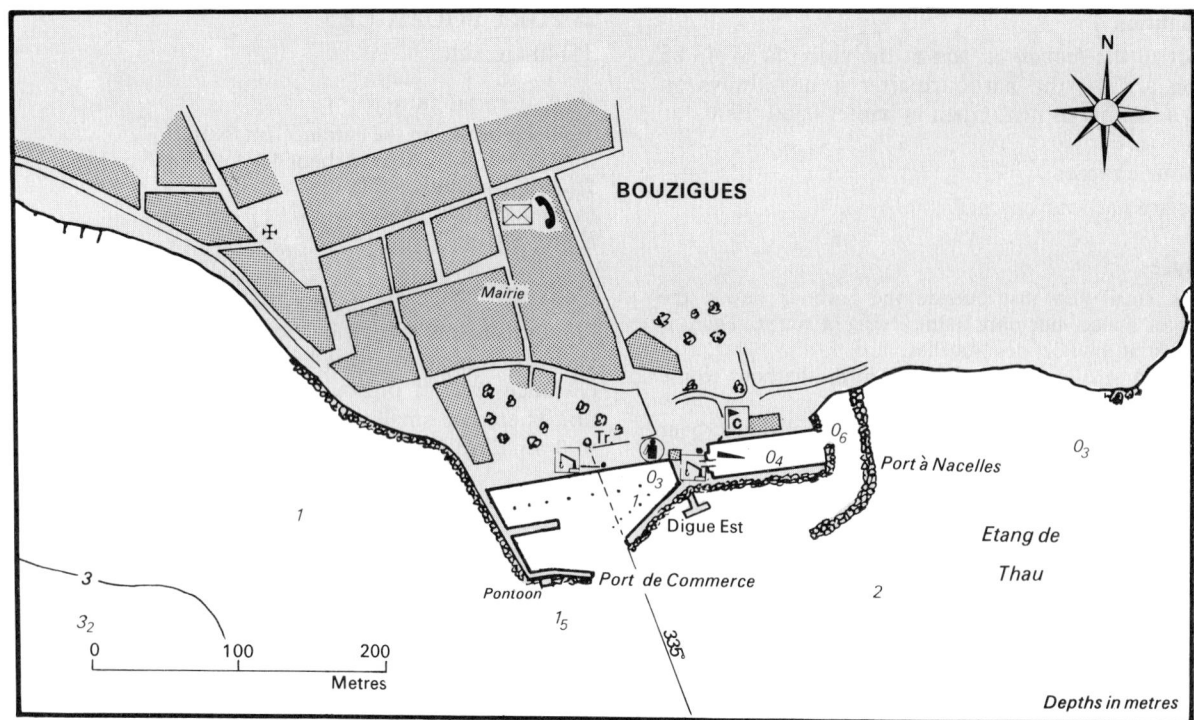

Port Bouzigues

Port de Bouzigues looking NW

Port de Bouzigues. Approach looking NW (335°)

Hotels Some small hotels and one large ★★★ motel.
Restaurants Several small restaurants and café/bars.
Yacht club A branch of the Club Nautique de Frontignan (CNF) operates here.

Information At the *mairie* (☎ 67 78 30 12).
Communications A bus service.
Visits Musée de l'Etang de Thau (☎ 97 78 33 57) open 1000–1900.

Tower

Port de Bouzigues. Entrance looking NW

Point de Balaruc

A pointed headland at the NE end of the Etang de Thau. The headland is covered with houses and there is a tower on the point. La Rôquerols light beacon 700m to S, shallow water near the headland.

29 PORT DE BALARUC-LES-BAINS, PORT DE BALARUC-LES-USINES

34540 Hérault

Position 43°26'·3N 3°41'·5E
Minimum depth   in the entrance Les Bains 1·2m (4ft)
　　　　　　　　Les Usines 1·8m (6ft)
　　　　　　　　in the harbour Les Bains 1 to 0·7m
　　　　　　　　(3 to 2·5ft)
　　　　　　　　Les Usines 1·5 to 0·2m (5 to 1ft)
Number of yacht berths Les Bains 30 Les Usines 150
Maximum length overall Les Usines 20m (66ft)
Population 5047 (approx)
Rating 4–3–4

General

There are two harbours about ½M apart at the head of the Bassin des Eaux Blanches. First is a small harbour for shallow-draught craft in the holiday area of Balaruc-les-Bains, which is open to winds from NE–E–SE. There is a second harbour close to some factories which, though deeper and offering better shelter, is in a disused state. Approach and entrance are not difficult in either case but facilities are limited.

Data

Charts　Admiralty 2606, 1705
　　　　French 6839
　　　　Navicarte 509

Magnetic variation 2°04'W (1994) decreasing by about 6' each year.

Warning

There are a number of commercial installations on the E side of the Etang des Eaux Blanches which may not be used by yachts. Parts of the basin are shallow; sound carefully.

Approach by day
For Les Usines

From SW Cross the Etang de Thau on a NE course down the middle and leave the Rocher de Rôquerols beacon tower Fl(2)WR.6s11/8M, black with red bands and a ball topmark, to port. Proceed on an E course for 1M and join a channel on course 349°, marked by red can buoys square topmarks to be left to starboard and black conical buoys ⚲ topmark to be left to port. Follow the prolongation of this channel towards a pair of diamond-shaped beacons that lead straight into Les Usines harbour.

For Les Bains

Turn to a W course when 200m short of the entrance to Les Usines harbour. This harbour will be seen to the N of an open air swimming pool surrounded by wood pontoons.

Approach by night

Approach and entrance by night are not advised owing to the lack of navigational lights and the shallow water.

Entrance

Les Usines Enter on a N course between two small red buoys and approach with care any quays etc. since there are underwater obstructions near them. Stop in front of a crane on a quay by a large hanger marked 'Citröen'.

Les Bains Approach on a W course and leave an open air swimming pool to port or secure alongside it.

Berths

Les Usines Secure to the landing stage alongside the quay hard to port on entering, stern-to stage, bow-to mooring chain, and report to the Citröen garage, or secure to any other quays using great care because of their damaged state.

Les Bains Secure stern-to *digue* near swimming pool.

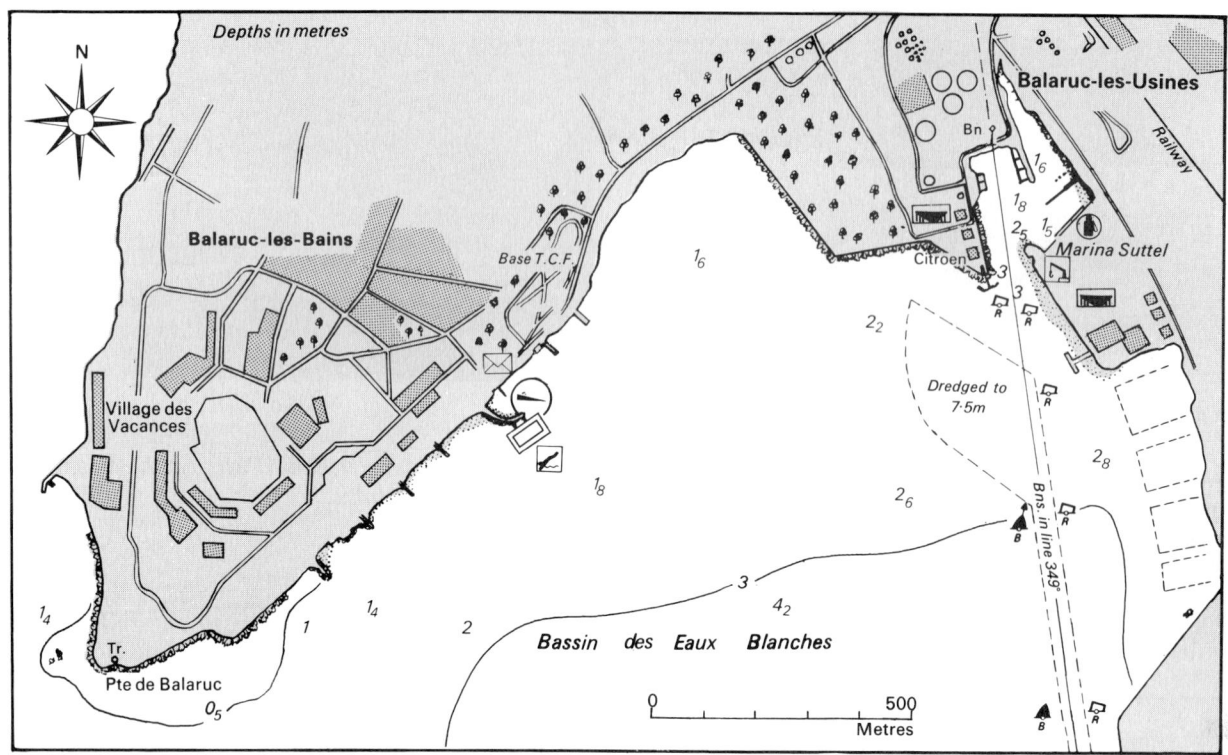

Port de Balaruc-les-Bains and Port Balaruc-les-Usines

Port de Balaruc-les-Bains, Port de Balaruc-les-Usines looking NE

Bureau du port

Port de Balaruc-les-Usines looking NE

Entrance

Port de Balaruc-les-Bains. Entrance looking NW

Facilities

Slips There are two slips near the breakwater at Les Bains.

Crane 3·5 tonnes at Les Usines near the Citröen garage.

Fuel Only from a service station in the town.

Water From supplies at the swimming pool and the camping ground, also at Marina Suttel and Citröen.

Electricity Several 220v AC points.

Provisions A limited number of shops in the town including a supermarket can provide basic requirements.

Ice From service station and supermarket.

Repairs The Marina Suttel has a mechanic who can carry out repairs to hull and engine.

Post office Not far from the harbour at Les Bains.

Hotels A number of small hotels including two ★★★ and one ★★ and a large thermal establishment.

Restaurants A few restaurants and many café/bars.

Yacht club The Club de Yachting à Voile Languedoc-Méditerranée (CYVLM) (☎ 67 74 90 61) is a Touring Club de France base. It has a clubhouse with normal facilities.

Information office The Syndicat d'Initiative has an office at the *mairie* which is open after midday (☎ 67 48 54 34 and 67 48 50 07).

Beaches There are some crowded beaches to SW of the harbour.

Visits The Chapelle Notre Dame des Eaux is interesting (12th century)

Communications Bus service.

History

The thermal baths here have been exploited since the Romans erected bath houses and a temple. Many famous people have come to 'take the waters' here over the centuries. More than 30,000 took a cure in 1990.

Pointe de Barrou

A low point covered with houses and with two small harbours, located to N of Mont Saint-Clair. Some wrecks off the point, and a green can buoy marks a 3m underwater bar 150m offshore; shallow near the point.

Club

Ports de Barrou Maritime and Base Nautique looking E

Ports de Barrou Maritime and Base Nautique looking SE

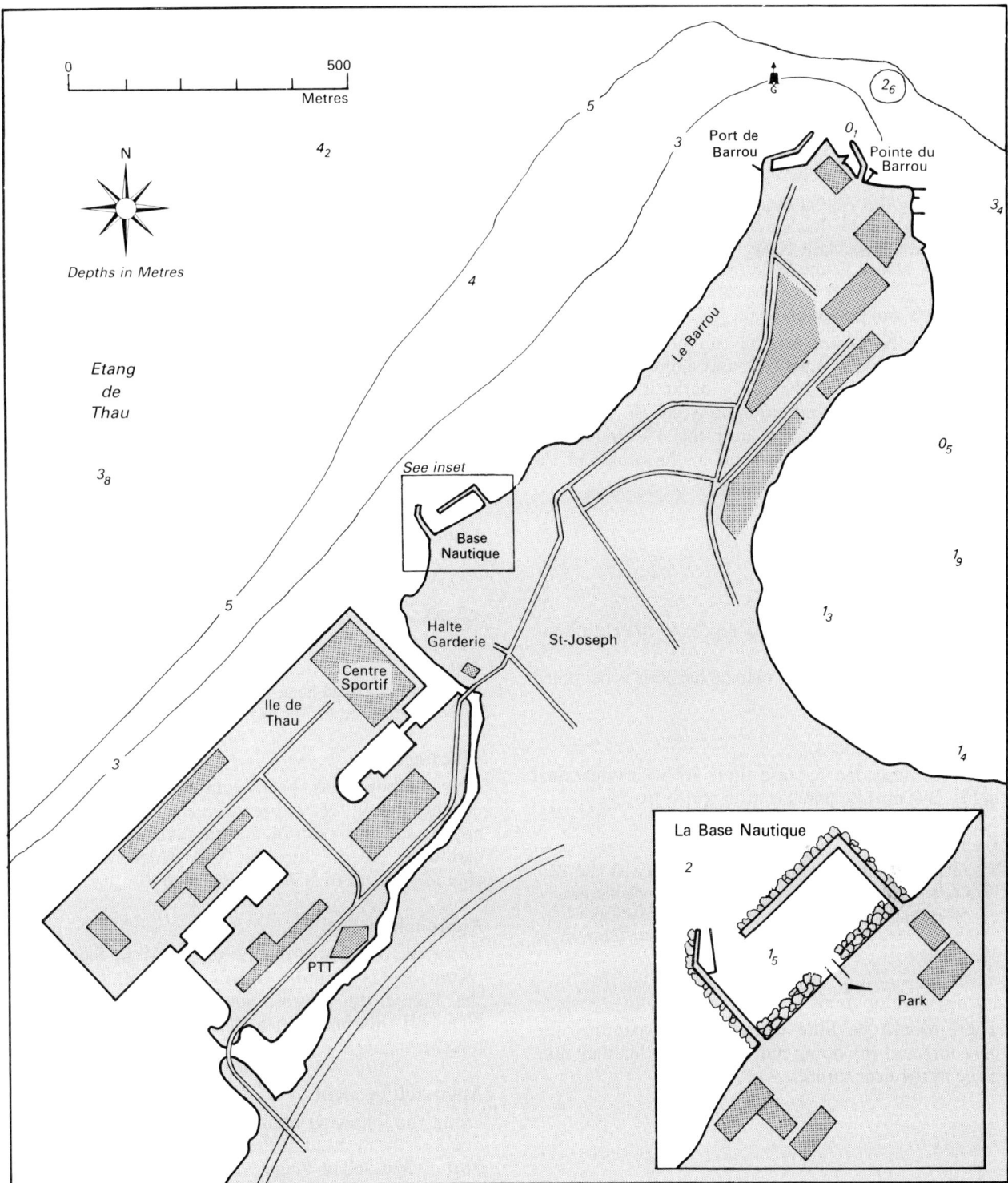

Port de Barrou Maritime and Base Nautique

30 PORTS DE BARROU MARITIME AND BASE NAUTIQUE
34504 Hérault

Position 43°25'·1N 3°40'·1E and 43°25'·N 3°40'·6E
Minimum depth in the entrance 2m (6·6ft)
             harbour 1·5m to 1m (4·9ft to 3·3ft)
Number of berths 20
Maximum length overall 9m (30ft)
Population (Sète) 42,000
Rating 4–3–4

General
Two small artificial harbours built as part of a municipal school of yachting and a marine school for dinghies and small yachts. They are private but nevertheless can be used in an emergency or by prior arrangement with the club (☎ 67 53 55 24), or with previous permission from the authorities. The harbours offer good shelter normally they are only in use from March to December.

Data

Charts Admiralty 2606,1705
French 6839,7054,7072
Navicarte 509,508

Magnetic variation 2°04′W (1994) decreasing by about 6′ each year.

Beacons A green conical beacon lies 100m to NW of the Pointe de Barrou. Rocher de Roquerols, a beacon light tower, red with black bands (F(2)WR.6s6m11/8M) lies 700m to NW of Pointe de Barrou.

Approach and entrance by day

Bring the N Tower on the top of Mont de Sète (Mont Saint-Clair) onto 140° and approach the coast sounding carefully. The rocky harbour jetties with large building behind will be seen in the close approach. The entrance is near the SW end of the jetty of the Base Nautique and in the centre of the breakwater in the marine harbour.

Approach by night

Not advised due to shallows

Berth

Secure to a vacant berth and report to the clubhouse or office.
Note The SW side of the marine harbour is occupied by fishing boats.

Approach by night

Not recommended because there are no navigational lights, but may be possible after a visit by day.

Facilities

There is a clubhouse with showers and WCs at the Base Nautique. Simple everyday requirements available locally. (See also page 145, 32 Port de Sète, for other facilities.)
Communications Bus service to Sète, rail at Sète, air at Montpellier.

Future developments

There would be little difficulty in expanding the harbours and providing more facilities; this may take place in the near future.

31 PORT DES QUILLES
34200 Hérault

Position 43°23′·6N 3°39′·9E
Minimum depth   in the entrance 2m (6·6ft)
harbour 2m to 1·5 (6·6 to 4·9ft)
Width of the entrance 25m
Clearance under bridges 2·5m (8ft)
Population (Sète) 42,000
Rating 3–3–4.

General

This private 'marina' could be used by small motor craft in an emergency or could be converted into a reasonable-sized harbour without too much difficulty. Approach and entrance are not difficult, and good protection is afforded inside the harbour. Facilities very limited. A similar type of private 'marina' exists 1M to N based on the Ile de Thau on the NW side of Mont Saint-Clair.

Data

Charts Admiralty 2606, 1705
French 7054, 7072
Navicarte 509, 508

Speed limit 4 knots,

Light
Brise-Lames Ouest head Fl(3)G.12s8m5M
Jetée Ouest head Fl(3)R.12s6m3M

Warnings

This harbour has been constructed recently and changes may be expected. The depths in the approach and entrance may change – sound carefully. At the moment only small motor craft should proceed to NW of the bridge.

Approach by day

Bring the TV tower on the top of Mont Saint-Clair (Mont de Sète) onto a bearing of 40° and approach the Pointe du Lazaret sounding carefully. When 200m off this point set a W course 50m outside the long *brise-lames*.

Approach by night

Using the following lights navigate to a position ½M due S of the W head of the *brise-lames*.
Port Marsellan-Plage Digue Ouest Head Fl.R.4s9M
Mont Saint-Clair Fl.W.5s29M
Port de Frontignan Digue Ouest Head Fl(2)R.6s7M

Entrance

By day Round the SW head of the *brise-lames* at 20m leaving it to starboard, then turn to port to a NE course and enter between Jetée Ouest and Jetée Est. The shallows in the approach are marked by buoys.

By night Approach Fl(3)G.12s on a N course, and leave it to starboard rounding it at 20m on to a NE

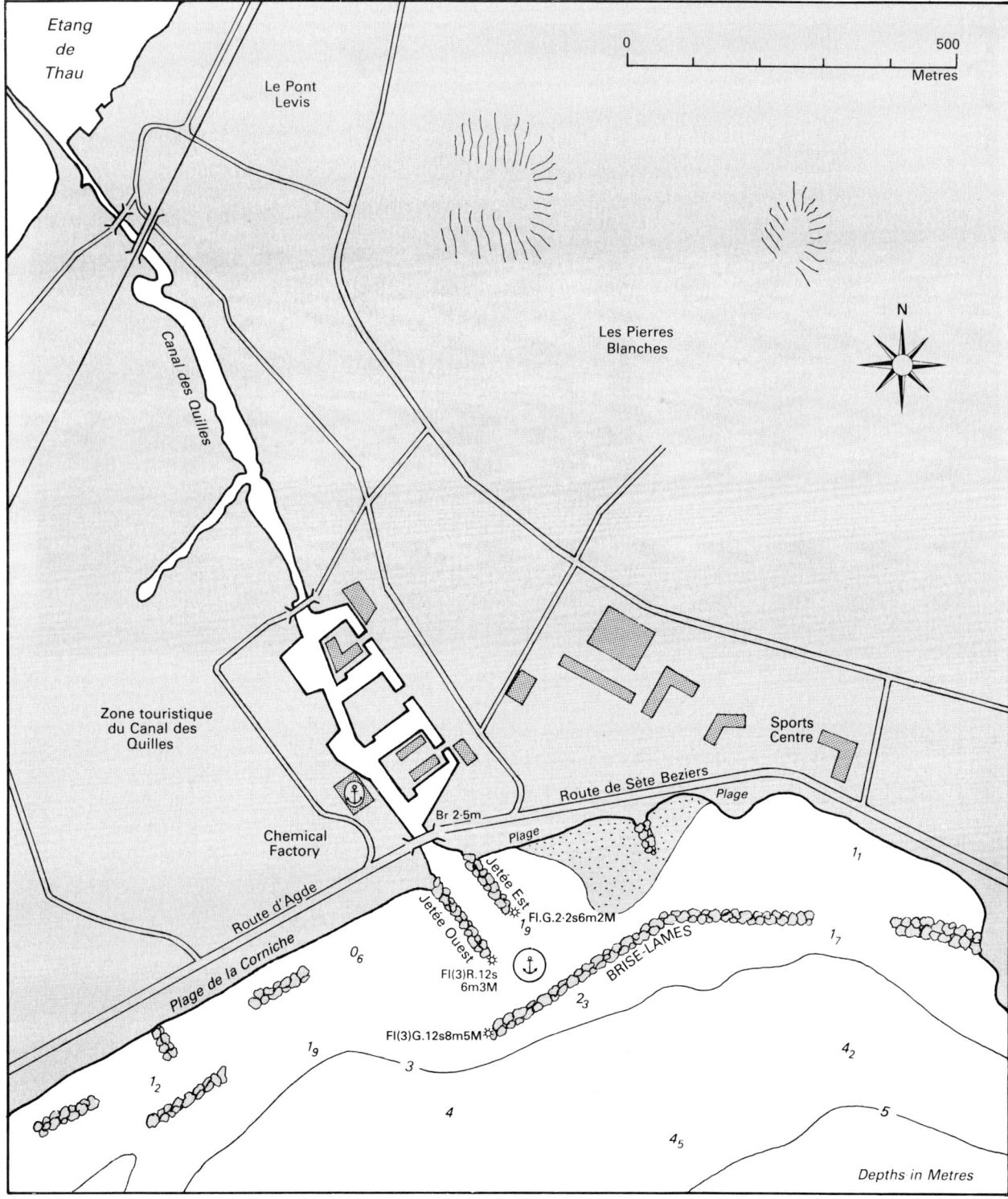

Port des Quilles

course. Leave Fl(3)R.12s to port and Fl.G.2·2s to starboard, entering between on a NW course.

Berths

Secure to poles on the inner side of the Jetée Ouest or the Jetée Est and report to the *bureau du port* on NW side of the bridge for allocation of a berth.

Formalities

Bureau du port (☎ 67 51 13 15) on NW side of the bridge.

Harbour charges

To be expected.

Port des Quilles looking NW

Port des Quilles looking NW. Entrance canal bridge

Facilities

Local shops including a permarket provide normal daily requirements.

Repairs A local yard (☎ 07 43 06 15) can undertake small repairs.

Restaurants and café/bars Many in the area.

Communications Bus service, rail at Sète and air at Montpellier.

Future developments

By using the existing local breakwaters and jetties a large yacht harbour could be constructed with ease. More facilities are expected.

⚓ Off des Quilles behind the outer breakwater at the entrance to the Port des Quilles in 3m sand. Sound carefully – possible silting. Road and houses ashore. Sandy beaches. Open SW–W.

Pointe du Lazaret

A rocky cliffed point to S of Mont Saint-Clair. Large convalescent hospital on the crest and a church (44m).

Cricque de l'Anau

A wide bay with rocky cliffs and a sandy beach. Houses and roads ashore. Anchor in 2 to 3m sand and mud in the middle. Open to E–SE–S–SW.

Cap de Sète

A high large rocky cliffed point with a fort on its NE side and a road running along the crest. Many houses, a lighthouse/radiobeacon and a cemetery on the Mont Saint-Clair.

---

32 PORT DE SETE
34200 Hérault

Position 43°24'·0N 3°42'·5E
Minimum depth   in the entrance Passe Est 15m (50ft)
                   Passe Ouest 5m (16ft)
Clearance under bridges (closed) 2·2m (7ft)
Width of entrance Passe Est 200m
                   Passe Ouest 40m
                   Passe Est 200m
                   Passe Ouest 40m
Number of yacht berths 280 at Société Nautique
Maximum length overall 30m (28ft)
Population 42,000
Rating 2–2–2

General

This is a very old natural harbour that has been developed into a major commercial and fishing port by the addition of breakwaters and quays and is now second in capacity to Marseille on the S coast of France. The town and harbour are picturesque and make a pleasant change from the modern yacht harbours on this part of the coast. It is not overrun by tourists as are the more modern resorts nearby. There are excellent facilities for yachtsmen and good repair workshops. Good shelter from the NW *tramontane* is available here. The approach and entrance are easy and can be taken without too much difficulty in any weather. This harbour is connected with the Canal du Midi and the Canal du Rhône à Sète. Masts can be stepped and unstepped here. The harbour is sometimes dirty and frequently disturbed by the wash of large fishing craft passing at speed. France uses this harbour as the base for her attempts to win the America's Cup; the yachts are also built here.

Data

Charts   Admiralty 2606, 1705
          French 7054, 7072
          Navicarte 508, 509

Currents There is a SW-going current of 1 to 3 knots outside the harbour. In a NW *mistral/tramontane* an E-going current flows inside the outer breakwater; this flow is reversed with a SE wind. With NW *mistral/tramontane* winds, water from the Etang de Thau flows out via this port and with winds from SE the water flows in. The rate of flow can reach 5 knots in the Canal Maritime.

Levels The water level inside the harbour can alter by as much as 1m (3ft) due to the effects of the winds as described above.

Magnetic variation 2°04'W (1994) decreasing by about 6' each year.

Radiobeacons Sète   Mont   Saint-Clair   lighthouse SÉ(···/··—··) 287.5 kHz 50M

Port radio VHF Ch 16, *bureau de port de commerce* Ch 12 and 06. Pilots Ch 16. Yacht harbour VHF Chs 9, 16. Yacht club Ch 9.

Weather forecast The weather forecast is posted once a day outside the club and twice a day at the *bureau du port*. Recorded forecast (☎ 36 65 08 34).

Speed limit 5 knots.

Storm signals Storm signals are flown from a mast on Citadelle Richelieu.

Lights
Môle St-Louis head Fl(4)WR.12s34m15/11M. White truncated tower, red lantern. 014°-W-054°-R-260°-W-264°-R-014°
Mont Saint-Clair Fl.W.5s93m29M White eight-sided tower, green lantern. White (unintens) 013°-104°
Epi Dellon Middle Oc.R.4s21m10M White truncated tower, red top with name 'Epi Dellon' in white 080°-vis-268°
Epi Dellon head Q.R.12m9M White pylon, red top
Epi Dellon W end Oc(2)R.6s15m7M White 8-sided tower, red top and base. 'Brise-Lames' on side
Digue Est head Fl(2)G.6s10m White pylon, green top

Entrance

Port de Sète W entrance

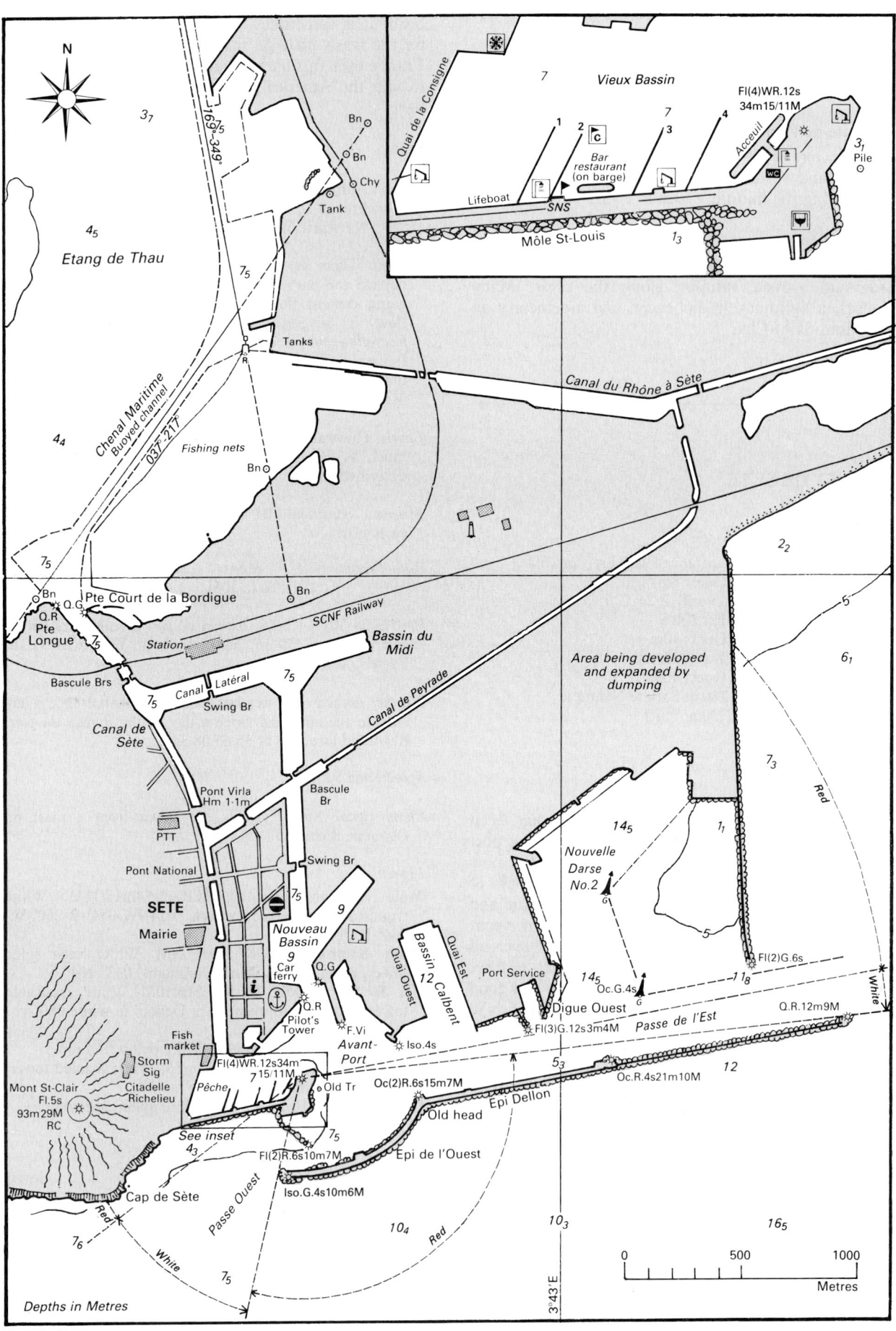

N

3$_7$

Etang de Thau

4$_5$

4$_4$

7$_5$

Chenal Maritime
Buoyed channel

037°-217°

169½-349°

7$_5$

Bn
Bn
Chy
Tank

Fishing nets

Bn

Canal du Rhône à Sète

Tanks

R

2$_2$

5

6$_1$

Bn

Bn

7$_5$

Pte Court de la Bordigue

Q.G
Pte
Longue
Q.R

7$_5$

Bascule Brs

Station

SCNF Railway

*Bassin du
Midi*

Canal de Peyrade

Area being developed
and expanded by
dumping

7$_3$

Red

*Canal de
Sète*

7$_5$

Canal Latéral

Swing Br

7$_5$

Pont Virla
Hm 1·1m

Bascule
Br

PTT

Pont National

Swing Br

7$_5$

14$_5$

*Nouvelle
Darse
No.2*

1$_1$

5

Fl(2)G.6s

SETE

Mairie

9

*Nouveau
Bassin
9*
Car
ferry

Q.G

Q.R

Pilot's
Tower

F.Vi

*Avant-
Port*

Iso.4s

Bassin
Calbent

Quai Ouest

Quai Est

12

14$_5$ Oc.G.4s

11$_8$

White

Port Service

Digue Ouest

Fl(3)G.12s3m4M

Passe de l'Est

Q.R.12m9M

Fish
market

Storm
Sig

Citadelle
Richelieu

Mont St-Clair
Fl.5s
93m 29M
RC

Fl(4)WR.12s34m
15/11M

Pêche

Old Tr

See inset

4$_3$

7$_5$

Fl(2)R.6s10m7M

Epi de l'Ouest

Iso.G.4s10m6M

Oc(2)R.6s15m7M

5$_3$

Epi Dellon

Old head

Oc.R.4s21m10M

12

Cap de Sète

Red

7$_6$

White

7$_5$

Passe Ouest

10$_4$

Red

10$_3$

3°43'E

16$_5$

0   500   1000
Metres

Depths in Metres

--- Inset (Vieux Bassin) ---

Quai de la Consigne

7

Vieux Bassin

Fl(4)WR.12s
34m15/11M

1

2

7

3

4

c

Acceuil

Bar
restaurant
(on barge)

WC

3$_1$
Pile

Lifeboat

SNS

Môle St-Louis

1$_3$

Port de Sète

Digue Ouest head Fl(3)G.12s3m4M White tower, green top

Brise-Lames (Epi de l'Ouest) W end Iso.G.4s10m6M. Green tower

Môle St-Louis Spur Fl(2)R.6s10m7M White cylinder, green top

Jetée de Frontignan Iso.W.4s

Nouveau Bassin Entrance W side Q.R.7m8M. White column, red top

Nouveau Bassin Entrance E side Q.G.6m8M. White column, green top

Digue Est head Fl.G.4s9m7M White column, green top

Bassin aux Petroles E side Iso.W.4s (strip light)

Buoys A group of large mooring buoys for an oil terminal are located 1M to ENE of the E entrance. These buoys have floating pick-up lines attached. There is a yellow and black light whistle buoy (Fl.G.4s and whistle) close to the line of approach to this entrance which marks the S edge of the area. A set of leading marks and lights (FW. intensified) located to the S of a large petrol refinery on a line 18° indicates the area. There is a swell gauge buoy, black and yellow, 1000m to the S of Môle St-Louis. There is a small red conical buoy marking the S side of obstructions in the W pass.

Beacons There is a flare that is permanently burning at the huge petrol refinery at Frontignan 3M to NE of the port which can be seen some distance away.

Warnings

Commercial traffic has right of way, and commercial vessels must not be obstructed by yachts, especially in the entrance and in the Canal Maritime where they may be experiencing difficulties with the currents.

The lights of vessels leaving the harbour at night may not easily be visible against the mass of harbour lights. Do not use the W entrance in very bad weather. Large fishing craft enter and leave at speed by both entrances. There are a number of large buoys to the E and SE of this harbour, some of which are unlit; they mark an oil terminal and the approach route for tankers. Changes are frequently made to the buoys near the oil terminal.

Approach by day

From SW Round Cap d'Agde, a low, dark and rocky promontory, with the conspicuous Ilot Brescou and its fort just offshore. Mont St-Loup with a TV tower on it lies a little way inland. The coast is low, flat and sandy; small jetties at Port Ambonne and Marseillan-Plage can be identified. Mont Saint-Clair (de Sète), which is covered with houses and has an island-like appearance when seen from afar, stands beside the Port de Sète.

From NE The coast from the Golfe d'Aigues Mortes is low, flat and sandy and is broken by the easily distinguishable groups of flats and houses at Le Grau du Roi, La Grande Motte, Carnon and Palavas. There is a large group of dark trees at Frontignan on the coast between Palavas and Sète, and a huge petrol refinery which has a flare and many tanks 2M NE of Sète. The entrances of Frontignan and Peyrade harbours may be seen. Again Mont Saint-Clair can be seen from afar.

Canal de Rhône à Sète. Entrance into the l'Etang de Thau looking E

W entrance   Visitors berths   Mole St-Louis

Port de Sète looking NW

Approach by night

Using the lights listed below navigate to a position just S of a light whistle buoy (Fl.G.4s and whistle) where the entrance lies W at 2M or in good weather where the W entrance lies NE at 2M:

Ilot Brescou Fl(2)WR.6s13/10M
Palavas-los-Flots Oc.G.4s7M
Pointe de l'Espiguette Fl(3)W.15s24M

Anchorage in the approach

Anchor about 400m from the shore in 5m (16ft) mud and sand in a bay on the S side of Mont Saint-Clair – Cap de Sète.

Entrance

When possible yachts should use the W entrance, leaving the E entrance for commercial vessels.

By day E entrance Approach the E head of Epi Dellon on a W course keeping to S of mooring buoys (yellow and black) and light whistle buoy belonging to the oil pipeline. Enter, leaving Epi Dellon 100m to port, and follow it along at this distance. When level with its old W head set course towards the head of Môle St-Louis and round this at 50m leaving it to port. If the visibility is good, approach and enter with the lighthouse at the head of Môle St-Louis (white tower, red top) in line with the lighthouse on Mont Saint-Clair (white eight-sided tower, green top) on 262°.

W entrance Round Cap de Sète at 200m and set course to leave the old W head of Epi de l'Ouest 50m to starboard, then leave the head of Môle St-Louis and a small detached stone warping pile 50m to port.

By night E entrance Approach on 262° with Front Fl(4)WR.12s in the W sector (260°-264°) in line with Rear Fl.W.5s. Leave to port Q.R and the Oc.R.4s and then Oc(2)R.6s. Leave to starboard Fl(2)G.6s, Oc.G.4s Fl(3)G.12s and Iso.W.4s, then alter course to leave Fl(4)WR.12s 100m to port passing into the red sector of this light.

W entrance Approach Fl(4)WR.12s on 034° in W sector (014°-054°). Enter between Iso.G.4s 50m to starboard and Fl(2)R.6s 15m to port, then turn to port, rounding Fl(4)WR.12s in the red sector at 100m crossing into the white sector.

Harbour pilotage

The channel from the Vieux Bassin to the Canal de Sète beyond is not normally used, having a depth of 2·5m (8ft) and a clearance of only 1·5m (5ft) under the fixed bridges. The Canal Maritime leading to the Canal Latéral has a depth of 7·3m (24ft) and a clearance of 2·2m (7ft) with the bridges down. The four bridges are opened from sea to *étang* 0815 and 1640, from *étang* to sea 0850 and 1700 (arrive one hour early), except on holidays, Saturdays and Sundays. It is advisable to phone the *capitaine du port*

Port de Sète. East entrance looking W

Port de Sète. E entrance

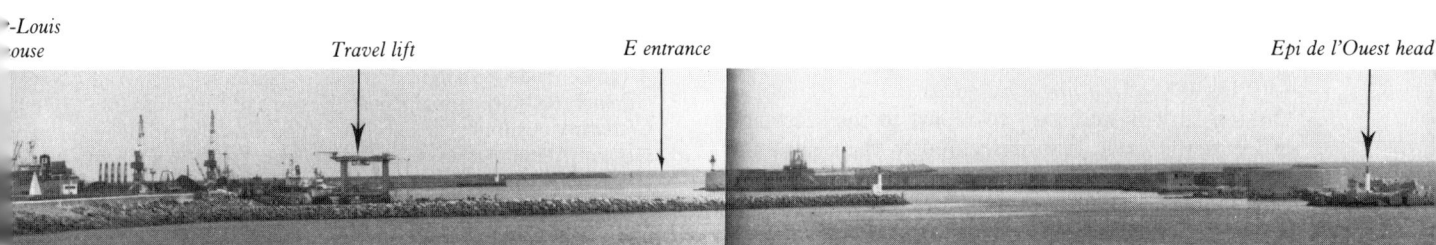

Port de Sète. Inside west entrance looking NE–E–SE

Port de Sète. Close approach to W entrance

Port de Sète. La Vieux bassin and yacht berths

(☎ 67 74 98 97 or VHF Ch 12) in advance if wanting the bridges opened at any other times. For details of this entrance see Etang de Thau page 121.

Berths

Yacht berths are stern-to No 5 pontoon in the Vieux Bassin close to the lighthouse, bow-to mooring buoy. Secure in a vacant berth and report to the yacht club office or hand on duty for the allocation of a berth. Berths may be available alongside the Quai de Bosc and Quai Adolphe Merle at the N end of the Canal de Sète and for large yachts at the Quai d'Alger in the Nouveau Bassin. In these cases report to the *bureau du port* (commercial). Yachts may have to move if commercial vessels arrive.

Formalities

On arrival it is necessary to report to the secretary's office at the yacht club if secured to their pontoons. Open in summer 0700–2100; in winter 0800–1200 and 1400–1800. If secured to other quays report to the *bureau du port* (commercial) (☎ 67 46 00 81 and 67 74 88 20). If necessary report to customs office (☎ 76 74 35 01) at 24 Quai Aspirant Herbert.

Harbour charges

There are club and harbour charges. One day per year is free of charge at the Société Nautique. Visits for a few hours (shopping etc) are free.

Facilities

Slip A small slip at the yacht club and a number to N of Mont Saint-Clair in the Etang de Thau.

Slipway A number of small slipways to N of Mont Saint-Clair. There are other slipways up to 300 tonnes.

Cranes A 6-tonne crane at the yacht club and many of from 2 to 120 tonnes' capacity around the harbour. Masts can be stepped and unstepped at the yacht club or commercial concerns.

Fuel Diesel (*gasoil*) and petrol are available from pumps at the yacht club.

Water Water points on the pontoons and on the Quai d'Alger.

Electricity Electrical supply points of 220v AC on the pontoons.

Provisions Many shops of all types in the town. There is a market that opens every day including Sunday.

Ice An ice supply depot at the N end of the fish auction rooms, or from the clubhouse.

Duty-free goods These are available here and arrangements can be made for supply from three firms.

Garbage Rubbish containers at the roots of the pontoons.

Chandlery A number of excellent ships' chandlers nearby.

Repairs A number of shipyards to the N of Mont Saint-Clair and many mechanics are available. There are five repair shops for electronic equipment.

Laundrettes Several in the town.

Post office The PTT is located near the centre of the town.

Hotels Three ***, 21 **, five * and five other hotels.

Restaurants Some thirty restaurants of all qualities. Local seafood dishes are a speciality. There are a large number of café/bars.

Yacht club The Société Nautique de Sète (SNS) (☎ 76 74 98 97) has a small clubhouse with bar, restaurants, lounge, terrace and showers on the Môle St-Louis.

Showers Sixteen showers and eight WCs on Môle St-Louis.

Information office The Syndicat d'Initiative is located to W of Nouveau Bassin on Quai d'Alger (☎ 67 74 71 71).

Lifeboat A lifeboat is stationed here, all-weather type (☎ 76 43 80 13, 76 74 73 00, 76 74 28 78 or 67 74 40 00).

Port de Sète. Visitors' berths at head of Môle St-Louis

Visits The view from the top of Mont Saint-Clair is worth the climb. The famous Cimitière Marin and the Musée Paul Valéry can be visited on the way. Pézenas, an old village 15M inland, is worth a visit

Beaches The best sandy beach is to the SW of Mont Saint-Clair.

Communications Rail and bus services. Boats to Algeria, Baleares, La Corse and other Mediterranean ports. Air service at Montpellier.

Future development

New docks for petrol tankers are being built to the NE of the port. There are plans for a new yacht harbour to be built to SW of Mont Saint-Clair but these may not be carried out.

History

Sète, a name which has been spelled in a number of different ways through the centuries, originated from the Venetian sailors who called it Settin (a mountain from which one can see far). The first attempt at making a harbour here was on the SW of Mont Saint-Clair in the 16th century and this was a failure. What is now the Vieux Bassin was not built until 1666 and was completed by Paul Riquet of Canal du Midi fame. Since then the port, town and population have grown steadily. The arrival of the French expatriates from North Africa, les pieds noirs (black shoes), has given a considerable boost to the wine and fish trades.

33 PORT DE LA PEYRADE
34110 Hérault

Position 43°25'·2N 3°44'·8E
Minimum depth in the entrance 5·5m (18ft)
　　　　　　　 harbour 5·7 to 3m (19 to 10ft)
Width of the entrance 150m.
Bridges (2) clearance 150m
Population 16,508 (Frontignan)
Rating 4–3–4

General

A new harbour recently constructed for large fishing boats, it also forms a second entrance to the Canal du Rhône à Sète. Approach and entrance are not difficult except with strong winds and swell from NE–E–SE. Facilities are very limited and there is an oil tank farm N of the area which can produce an unpleasant smell with N winds. At the end of the harbour is a huge ice factory coloured white and blue. The small town of Peyrade lies about 1M to NW and can supply normal requirements, the large town of Frontignan is 2M to N. This harbour forms a useful short cut to and from the canal system avoiding Sète and is a good harbour for use in an emergency. Yacht berths may be provided.

Data

Charts
　　Admiralty 2606, 1705
　　French 7072, 7054
　　Navicarte 508

Current There is a permanent SW-going current in the area of 0·5 to 1 knot which may be increased or decreased by prevalent winds. Ingoing and outgoing currents occur when there is a change of level between the sea and the canal system.

Magnetic variation 2°04'W (1994) decreasing by about 6 each year.

Radiobeacon Sète, Mont Saint-Clair lighthouse SÉ (···/··—··) 287·5kHz 50M

Speed limit 5 knots.

Port radio

Lights
Digue Sud head Fl.R.4s8m3M Metal pylon, red top
Digue Est head Fl(2)G.12s9m3M Metal pylon green top

Beacons Digue Ouest Head Red post and can top mark. Digue Est Head Green post and can top mark.

Buoys A series of red and green buoys mark the deep water channel inside the harbour.

Bridges The two bridges (8m clearance) to N of the harbour do not open. Those in the canal beyond open at 0710 and 1430 hours.

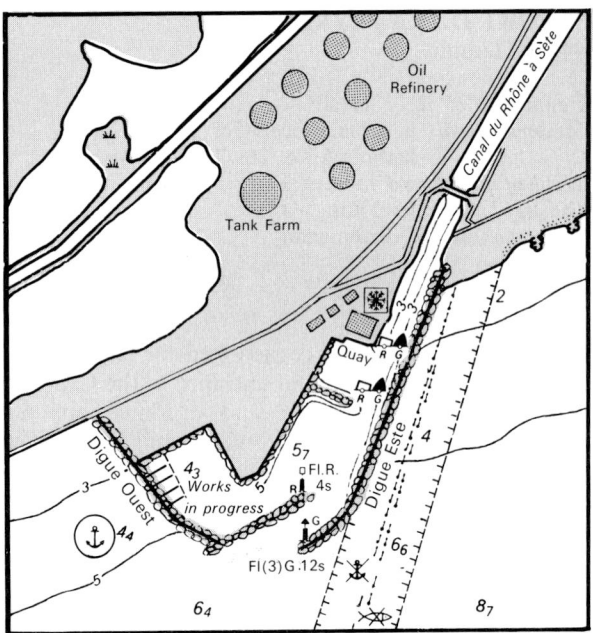

Port de la Peyrade

Warnings

Commercial traffic has right of way. This harbour is in the process of being constructed and changes must be expected.

Approach by day

From SW Follow the coast in a NE direction in depths of 10 to 20m. Mont Saint-Loup and Port Le Cap d'Agde, the Port de Marseillan-Plage and Mont Saint-Clair with the Port de Sète are all easy to recognise. In the close approach the tank farm with its many tanks and several chimneys indicates where the harbour is located.

From NE Having rounded the Point de l'Espiguette giving the coast a 2M berth and passing outside the buoys set a course just S of W for Sète. Mont Saint-Clair (180m) should be seen as an island when halfway across the Golfe d'Aigues-Mortes. In the closer approach the *digues* of the Port de Frontignan and the collection of apartment blocks behind it should be seen, and then the tank farm and chimneys which lie to N of the harbour entrance.

Approach by night

Use the following lights to navigate to a position where the entrance lies 1M to N.
Ilot Brescou Fl(2)WR.6s13/10M
Mont Saint-Clair Fl.W.5s29M
Pointe de l'Espiguette Fl(3)W.15s24M

Anchorage in the approach

Anchor in 4m sand and mud 500m to W of the entrance.

Entrance

By day Approach the entrance on a NE course, sounding carefully. Enter between the two *digues* and keep at least 20m off the head of the Digue Est in order to avoid shallow patches in the area.

Port de la Peyrade looking N

Head of Digue Este

Port de la Peyrade. Entrance looking NE

Ice factory quay and offices   *First bridge*

Port de la Peyrade. looking NE up the harbour

By night Bring the flares from the refinery between a Fl.R.4s and a Fl(2)G.12s and approach on a NE course, entering between the R and G lights (see lights above).

Berths

Follow the inner (NW) side of the Digue Est into the harbour, keeping between a series of red and green buoys to the quay. Secure in a free berth or alongside another vessel.

Facilities

Fuel W side of inner entrance.
Water From large building and quay.
Electricity From quay and pontoons.
Provisions None locally, but everyday requirements available at La Peyrade and Frontignan, 1 and 2M.
Ice From the large building which is an ice factory.
Garbage Some old oil drums.
Showers Showers and WCs on the S side of the ice factory. Apply to the office first.
Hotels In La Peyrade and Frontignan.
Restaurants and café/bars Some in La Peyrade, many in Frontignan.
Visits The two towns are very old and there are some buildings of interest.

Future Development

Much has still to be done to the harbour and its facilities. It will develop very differently if it continues as a harbour devoted to fishing craft. How it will develop if it becomes a harbour shared with yachts is another matter.

34 PORT DE FRONTIGNAN
34110 Hérault

Position 43°25'·2N 3°46'·1E
Minimum depth   in the entrance 3m (10ft)
   in the harbour 3m (10ft)
Width of the entrance 50m (approx)
Number of yacht berths 600
Maximum length overall 18m (89ft)
Population 12,288
Rating 3–3–3

General

This artificial yacht harbour has been constructed by opening up an old *grau* and building a pair of breakwaters seawards. Approach and entrance are easy but would be difficult and perhaps dangerous with a E–SE–SW gale and heavy swell. Facilities at the moment are adequate.

The area around consists of *étangs* and salt-pans with a vast petrochemical works in the background. The beach is lined with small houses, chalets and high apartment blocks.

Data

Charts   Admiralty 2602, 1705
   French 7054
   Navicarte 507, 508

Currents There is a SW-going coastal current of 0·5 to 1 knot and a current of up to 2 knots may be experienced in the inner entrance of the harbour with strong winds from N and SE.

Level The level in the harbour may fall 0·1m (0·3ft) in NW winds and rise up to 0·6m (2ft) in SE winds.

Magnetic variation 2°04'W (1994) decreasing by about 6' each year .

Weather forecasts Published at the *bureau du port* twice a day. Recorded forecast (☎ 36 68 08 34 or 36 68 08 08).

Speed limit 5 knots.

Port radio VHF Ch 16 and 19. Permanent watch on Ch 9.

Lights
Jetée Ouest head Fl(2)R.6s9m7M. Red column
Jetée Est head Fl.G.4s9m7M. White column, green top

Radiobeacon
Sète (Mont Saint-Clair) lighthouse SÉ (···/··—··) 287·5kHz 50M.

Warning

This harbour may be further developed and changes must be expected. There is a sand bank to SE of the head of Jetée Est; do not cut the corner. Depths inside the harbour may vary with periodic dredging.

Approach by day

From SW The conspicuous Mont Saint-Clair at Sète appears as an island from afar. Beside it the town of

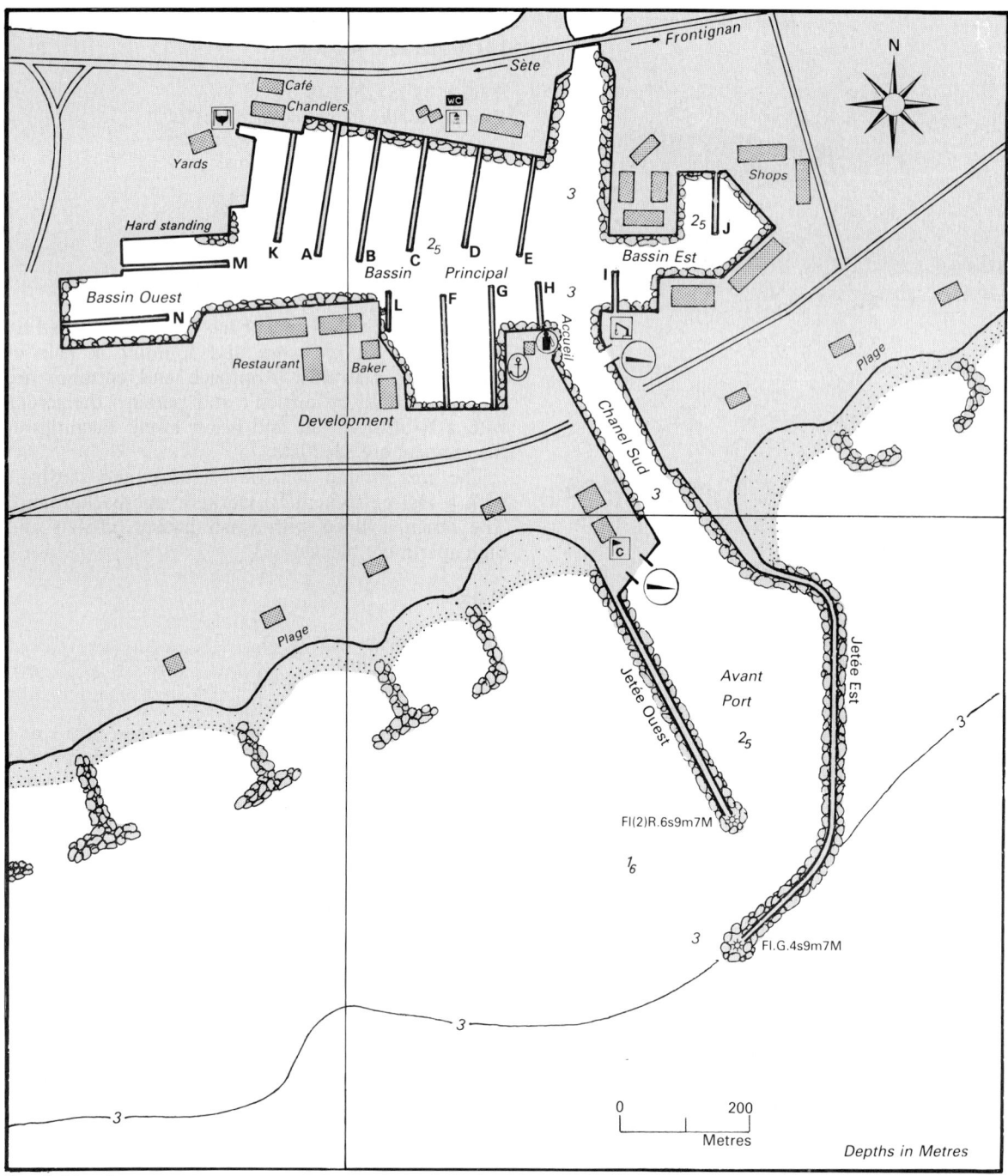

Port de Frontignan

Sète and its long harbour breakwaters are easily recognised. 3M to NE of Sète the breakwaters of Port de la Peyrade will be seen and in the closer approach are seen the breakwaters of Frontignan. The area is backed by a huge petrochemical works where there are a number of flares. Approach the breakwater heads on a NE course. Do not cut the corner around the head of Jetée Est, it has a shallow bank.

From NE From the harbour of Palavas there is a line of buildings 2M long followed by an old tower. After this the coast is featureless for 6M after which the breakwaters of Frontignan will be seen. Pass the breakwater heads on a SW course at 300m then turn and approach these heads on a NE course. Do not cut the corner, there is a shallow bank.

Approach by night
Using the lights listed below navigate to a position where the breakwater head are 400m to W.
Sète, Mont Saint-Clair Fl.W.5s29M
Palavas-les-Flots, Jetée Ouest Fl.R.4s8M
Carnon Jetée SW Fl(4)R.15s7M
Pointe de l'Espiguette Fl(3)W.15s24M

Bureau du port

Port de Frontignan looking NE

Port de Frontignan looking N

Anchorage in the approach

Anchor 200m to SE of breakwater heads in 4m sand.

Entrance

By day From a position about 400m to SW of the breakwater heads approach on a NE course leaving the head of Jetée Est 20m to starboard. Turn on to a N course having passed the Jetée Ouest head. Follow the canal into the harbour basin.

By night Approach Fl(2)R.6s and Fl.G.4s on a NE course, enter between them and turn to port towards a tall lamppost with powerful lights which is located on the port side of the inner entrance.

Berths

Secure to the port hand quay near the fuel pumps just inside the harbour and report to the *bureau du port* nearby for allocation of a berth, usually a pontoon which has fingers.

Formalities

Report to the *bureau du port* (☎ 67 48 75 21) on arrival. It is open in summer 0700–2000, in winter 0800–1200 and 1400–1800. Customs office at Sète (☎ 67 74 35 01).

Harbour charges

There are harbour charges.

Facilities

Slips There is a large slip near the inner harbour entrance on the SW side and another on the W side inside the harbour.

Cranes A 3·6-tonne crane on the NE side of the harbour and a 4·5-tonne travel-lift.

Fuel Pumps just inside the harbour on W side next to the *bureau du port*; there is a large 'Mobile' sign. Open 24 hours (☎ 67 48 75 21).

Water Water points on pontoons and quays.

Electricity 220v AC on pontoons and quays.

Provisions The nearest shops are in Frontignan 1.5M away to NW. Local shops include bakery and fish shops. Supermarket at Frontignan.

Ice From fuel station.

Garbage Rubbish bins around the harbour.

Repairs Limited repair facilities which will be improved.

Post office Frontignan.

Hotels Two in Frontignan and one beside the harbour.

Restaurants Several in Frontignan and four beside the harbour.

Yacht clubs Centre Nautique de Frontignan (CNF) (☎ 67 48 21 72) Clubhouse Frontignan Plage – showers.

Showers On N side of the harbour twelve showers and sixteen WCs.

Information Bureau du Tourisme, Rond Pont de l'Esplanade (☎ 67 48 33 94 and 67 48 94 70).

Visits The 12th-century church at Frontignan is built on the site of an original Roman church. The ancient cathedral of Maguelonne, dating from the second century, has a long and complicated history; it is well worth while making a visit to it by taxi. Museum of History at Frontignan.

Beaches Excellent sandy beaches either side of the harbour.

Communications Occasional local bus service, railway at Frontignan.

Future development

Plans for the expansion of the harbour, also for improved facilities.

History

The area has been in partial occupation since Roman times. In the town there are several Roman remains, and the muscat wines of the area, which are deservedly famous, were imported by the Romans. The *graus* which connected the various *étangs* to the sea were the sites of small fishing communities.

⚓ Les Banc de Maguelonne

An open anchorage in 11m red sand 1M from the shore with Maguelonne church bearing 294°. Open to E–SE–S–SW.

Port de Frontignan. Entrance looking NE

Port de Frontignan. From entrance looking W–NE–N–NE

35 PORT DE PALAVAS-LES-FLOTS
(GRAU DU PALAVAS)

34250 Hérault

Position 43°31'·5N 3°56'·0E
Minimum depth   in the entrance 3m (10ft)
                in the harbour 2·0 to 0·4m (6ft)
                in the *bassin* 1·5 to 0·4m (5 to 1·5ft)
Width of the entrance 26m
Width of the canal 25m
Bridge clearance 2·2m (7ft)
Cable car clearance 6m (20ft)
Number of yacht berths in *bassin* 200
                  in harbour 620
                  in Canal Lez 200
Maximum length overall 14m (46ft)
Population 6000
Rating 4–3–3

General

A large artificial harbour built out from the coast with a basin for shallow-draught craft inland above a road bridge and up the canalised Rivière le Lez.

There are also a number of short piers along the river banks above and below the bridge which are usually occupied by local craft. The town is a typical seaside holiday resort and is crowded in the season. Entrance would be difficult with strong winds and swell from NE–E–SE, and perhaps dangerous. Facilities for yachtsmen are good. There is shelter here from the seas but not from the NW *tramontane/mistral* winds. This river joins the Canal du Rhône à Sète just NW of the yacht harbour on the Rivière le Lez but the passage needs dredging and is only suitable for shallow-draught craft.

Data

Charts Admiralty 1705
          French 7053
          Navicarte 507, 508

Current The current in the river is not strong except after heavy rain. There is a W-going coastal current of 0·5 to 1 knot.

Level The level in the river may fall by 0·1m (0·3ft) in NW winds and rise up to 0·6m (2ft) in S winds.

Magnetic variation 2°04'W (1994) decreasing by about 6' each year.

Weather forecasts Published at the *bureau du port* once a day. Recorded forecast (☎ 36 68 08 34).

Port radio VHF Ch 9 and 16 24 hrs less 13-14.

Speed limit 5 knots.

Storm signals Flown from a mast at the *bureau du port*.

Lights
Digue du Large head Fl.R.4s8m8M White tower, red top marked Palavas Ouest
Jetée Est head Oc.G.4s8m7M White tower, green top marked Palavas Est

Buoys There is a swell gauge ½M ESE of the entrance coloured yellow and red and a red and white light buoy (Fl.W) off the entrance.

Warning

The banks alongside the river slope back and it is impossible to come alongside them. However, private jetties line both banks below the road bridge, and the *bassin* has many above the bridge. Storms from E may raise sea level 2m.

Approach by day

From SW Sète with its island-like Mont Saint-Clair and harbour installations is easily recognised as is the petrol refinery about 2M to NE where there are also the breakwaters of Peyrade and Frontignan. The coast is then low, flat and sandy with no conspicuous features until Palavas, where there is a concentration of houses and a large water tower.

From E The low, flat and sandy Pointe de l'Espiguette has a conspicuous lighthouse behind some trees. Do not cut this corner, since there are extending shoals, but keep outside the buoys. The jetties and buildings of Port de Camargue, Le Grau du Roi and La Grande Motte are easily recognised. Carnon-Plage has some blocks of flats but is joined to Palavas by a line of houses. The water tower at Palavas is conspicuous.

Approach by night

Using the lights listed below navigate to a position where the heads of the jetties are NW 400m:
Sète, Mont Saint-Clair Fl.W.5s29M
Carnon Fl(4)R.15s7M
Pointe de l'Espiguette Fl(3)W.15s24M
Montpellier-Fréjourges Aero Mo(Y)W 12·5s

Anchorage in the approach

Anchor 400m to SE of the entrance in 5m (16ft) sand and weed.

Entrance

By day From a position about 400m to SE of the entrance approach on a NW heading and leave the head of the Digue du Large 30m to port. If entering the yacht harbour follow the inner side of this *digue* into the harbour. If wishing to mount the Rivière le Lez proceed on the NW course between two smaller breakwaters.

By night From a position 400m to SE of the Fl.R.4s proceed on a NW course towards it rounding it as 30m to port. If proceeding to the outer yacht harbour follow the inner side of the Digue du Large into the harbour. If proceeding NW up to the Rivière le Lez follow the inner side of Jetée Est after passing close S of Oc.G.4s.

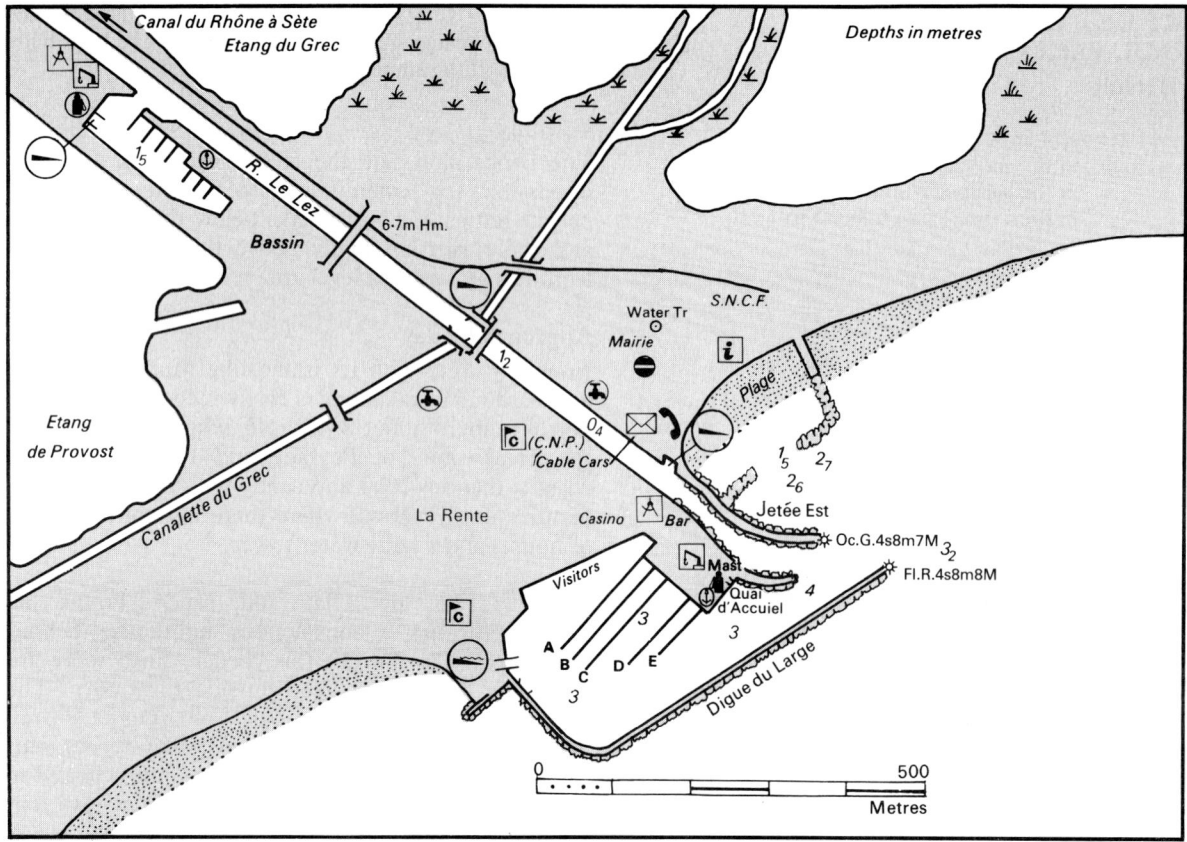

Port de Palavas-les-Flots

Berths

Secure to Quai d'Accueil near fuel pumps in the yacht harbour, or to any vacant small pier, or outside another boat in the canal. As all these berths are private, special arrangements will have to be made with the owners. Alternatively proceed further upstream and under two road bridges to a point ¾M from the sea where there is a small yacht basin on the port-hand bank. Enter and secure to a pontoon beside the *bureau du port*. Report to the *bureau du port* office.

Formalities

Report to the *bureau du port* if in the yacht harbour (☎ 67 07 73 50). Open in summer 0800–2000, in winter 0800–1200 and 1400–1800. If in the *bassin* report to the *bureau du port* (☎ 67 68 05 12) open in summer and winter 0800–1200 and 1400–1800. Customs office at Sète (☎ 67 68 26 75).

Harbour charges

There are harbour charges.

Facilities

Slips A small slip just inside the entrance at the root of the Jetée Est and another at the N side of the yacht harbour.
Slipway A small slipway of 27 tonnes at the yacht harbour, another of 10 tonnes in the yacht basin.
Crane A 15-tonne travel-lift at the N end of the yacht harbour and another of 1·5 tonnes.
Fuel Diesel (*gasoil*) and petrol can be obtained from pumps at the N end of the yacht basin and from the SE side of

the yacht harbour (☎ 67 68 00 90) open in summer and winter 0800–1130 and 1400–1730.
Water Water points on the pontoons and quays in the yacht harbour and yacht basin; also from cafés etc., in the town.
Electricity 220v AC electricity points at the yacht harbour and yacht basin.
Provisions A fair number of shops in the town and also a local market three times a week.
Garbage Rubbish containers around the yacht harbour and yacht basin.
Chandlery Several ships' chandlers in the town, one at the yacht harbour, one at the yacht basin and one on the road to Carnon.
Repairs A shipyard to the NW of the yacht harbour and one to the N of the yacht basin, where normal repairs to hull and engines can be carried out. Also electric and electronic repairs.
Laundrette A laundrette in the town.
Post offices PTT in the town.
Hotels Eighteen hotels in the area including two ***, five ** and five * and six unclassified.
Restaurants 25 restaurants and café/bars.
Yacht club The Club Nautique de Palavas (CNP) has an office in the town (☎ 67 68 97 38).
Showers Four showers at the *bureau du port* in the yacht harbour and others at the yacht basin. Twelve showers and eight WCs around the harbour and yacht basin.
Information office The Syndicat d'Initiative has an office in the town hall, Bvd Maréchal Joffre (☎ 67 88 02 34).
Lifeboat Vedette 2nd class (☎ 67 68 00 09 or 67 68 03 45).
Visits The old city of Montpellier should be visited, also the 11th-century church at Maguelonne.
Beaches Miles of sandy beaches either side of this harbour.
Communications Bus, rail and air services at Montpellier.

Bureau du port

Port de Palavas-les-Flots (Grau du Palavas) looking N

Entrance   *Water tower (conspic)*

Port de Palavas-les-Flots. Approach looking NW

Digue du Large   *Bureau du port Fuel berth*   *Jetée Central*   *River*

Port de Palavas-les-Flots (Grau du Palavas). Entrance to yacht harbour looking W

Aerial railway cable

Port de Palavas-les-Flots (Grau du Palavas). Entrance to river looking NW

Bureau du port

Port de Palavas-les-Flots (Grau du Palavas) looking N

Port de Palavas-les-Flots (Grau du Palavas) looking SE

Future development

Further improvements are to be made to the existing harbours and more facilities provided. There is a three-year plan to construct another harbour to SE of the Digue du Large with berths for 410 more yachts. More short pontoons are to be built in the river near the yacht basin.

36 PORT DE CARNON-PLAGE (GRAU DE PEROIS)

34280 Hérault

Position 43°32'·4N 3°58'·5E
Minimum depth in the entrance 2·5m (8ft)
in the harbour 2·0 to 1m (6 to 3ft)
Width of the entrance 30M
Number of yacht berths 700
Population 2000
Rating 3–3–3

General

A small artificial harbour recently built, surrounded by a large number of blocks of flats which form an excellent barrier against the wind. Easy to approach and enter but dangerous in heavy winds and swell from SE–S–SW. Facilities are good. This harbour offers a certain amount of shelter from the NW *tramontane* winds. There is a connection from this harbour to the Canal du Rhône à Sète for shallow-draught craft only.

Data

Charts Admiralty 1705
French 7004
Navicarte 507, 508

Currents A W-going current of 0·5 to 1 knot follows the coast. There is a weak outgoing current from the harbour which is stronger after rain and with a NW wind.

Levels The water level falls by up to 0·2m (0·7ft) maximum during NW wind and rises up to 0·8m (3ft) in S winds.

Magnetic variation 2°04'W (1994) decreasing by about 6' each year.

Port radio A listening watch is kept on VHF Ch 16 and 9.

Weather forecasts Posted twice a day at the *bureau du port*. Recorded forecast (☎ 36 68 08 34).

Speed limit 3 knots.

Lights
Jetée Sud-Ouest head Fl(4)R.15s9m7M White column, red top
Jetée Est Fl.G.4s8m3M White column, green top

Warning

There are a series of small rocky training walls is either side of the entrance which must not be mistaken for the jetties. A large wreck lies exposed 3·5M to SSE of the light at Pointe de l'Espiguette.

Approach by day

From SW The harbour installations of Sète and the island-like Mont Saint-Clair are unmistakable, as is the petrol refinery to its NE. The coast is then low, flat, sandy and featureless as far as Palavas-les-Flots where there are a concentration of buildings, harbour jetties and a conspicuous high water tower. From this harbour to Carnon there is a continuous line of houses. At Carnon there are high blocks of flats and two water towers further to the NE. The harbour jetties with their small light towers are identifiable in the close approach.

From E Round the low, flat and sandy Pointe de l'Espiguette outside the light buoys. Do not cut the corner as there are extending shoals. The lighthouse partly screened behind a row of low trees is conspicuous. The groups of buildings at Port de Camargue, Le Grau du Roi and La Grande Motte are easily identified. The radiobeacon mast on top of a pink-brown sandstone octagonal tower on the E edge of Carnon Plage are conspicuous from this direction.

Approach by night

Using the lights listed below navigate to a position where the entrance lies NW at 400m:
Sète, Mont Saint-Clair Fl.W.5s29M
Palavas-les-Flots Oc.G.4s7M
Pointe de l'Espiguette Fl(3)W.15s24M
Montpellier-Fréjourges Aero Mo(Y)W.12·5s

Anchorage in the approach

Anchor in 5m (16ft) sand and weed with the entrance 400m to NW.

Entrance

By day From a position 400m to SE, approach the entrance and enter between the jetty heads. Then cross the *avant-port* on a NNW heading towards the canal entrance and follow this in midstream for 300m.

By night From a position 400m to SE of the entrance approach Fl(4)R.15s; round it at 15m leaving it to port and Fl.G.4s to starboard. Cross the *avant-port* on a NNW heading towards a canal and enter, following this canal for 300m in midstream.

Berths

Secure alongside the *bureau du port* and report to the office for allocation of a berth. Then secure stern-to, bow-to mooring posts or buoys as applicable.

Formalities

Report to the *bureau du port* on arrival (☎ 67 68 10 78). Open in summer 0800–1200, in winter 0800–1200 and 1400–1800. Customs at La Grande Motte (☎ 67 56 51 47).

Harbour charges

There are harbour charges.

Facilities

Slips Three slips, one either side of the canal entrance and a large one in the NW corner of the harbour.
Hard A hard standing to W of the footbridge.
Crane A mobile crane of 5 tonnes. A travel-hoist of 13 tonnes and a 1·5-tonne fixed crane.
Fuel Diesel (*gasoil*) and petrol are available from pumps beside the *bureau du port*. Open in summer 0700–1300

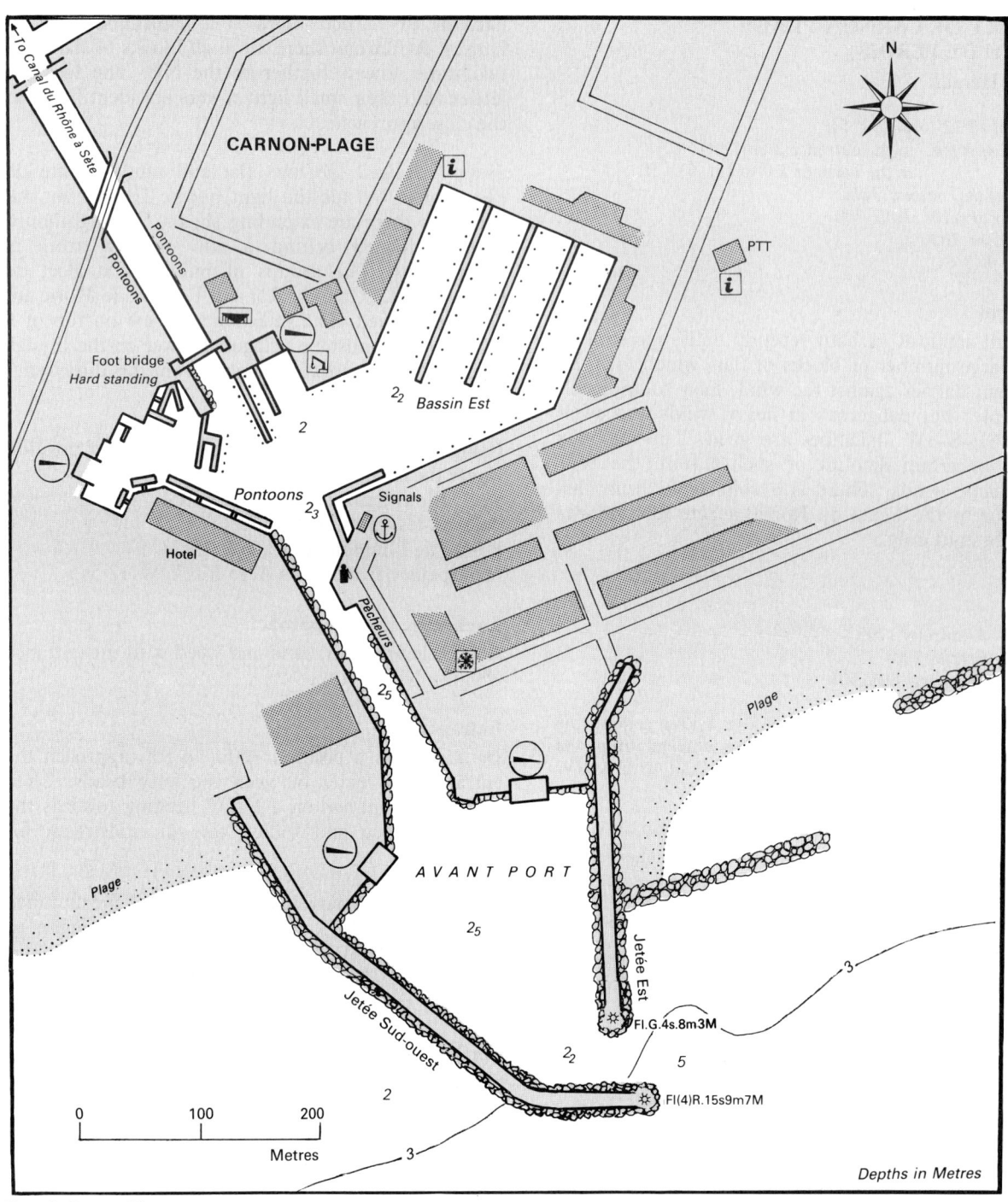

Port de Carnon-Plage

and 1400–2000, in winter 0800–1200 and 1400–1800 (☎ 67 68 10 78).

Water Water points on all quays and pontoons.

Electricity Distribution points for 220v AC on the quays and pontoons.

Provisions A few shops nearby but more are to be found in Carnon-Plage.

Ice From a shop not far from the *bureau du port*.

Garbage Rubbish containers around the harbour.

Repairs Three shipyards where normal repairs to hull and engine can be carried out. Also electronic repairs available.

Post office The PTT is located in Carnon-Plage.

Hotels One ★★★, one ★★, three ★ and four unlisted.

Restaurants 29 in Carnon-Plage and a number of café/bars.

Yacht clubs The Société Nautique Carnon Régates (SNCR) (☎ 67 75 12 44 and 67 50 91 70) has a clubhouse at *bureau du port*. There is also the Yacht Club Languedoc-Méditerranée (YCLM).

Shower Eight showers and eight WCs available at the *bureau du port*.

Lifeboat Vedette 2nd class (☎ 67 68 00 90 and VHF Ch 16).

Information office The Syndicat d'Initiative has an office near the NE corner of the harbour (☎ 67 50 51 15 and 67 68 16 00).

Visits The old city of Montpellier should be visited. Small boats and dinghies can enter the Etang de l'Or and the Etang de Mauguio where there is much wildlife.

Port de Carnon-Plage (Grau de Perois) looking NW

Bureau du port

Port de Carnon-Plage (Grau de Perois) looking N

Port de Carnon-Plage (Grau de Perois). Tower between Carnon-Plage and La Grande Motte

Beaches Good sandy beaches either side of the harbour.
Communications Bus service locally. Rail and air services from Montpellier.

Future development

A further extension of the harbour in a W direction is planned.

Port de Carnon-Plage looking NE

Port de Carnon-Plage. Approach looking NW

Port de Carnon-Plage (Grau de Perois). Entrance looking W

Port de Carnon-Plage. Bureau du port and inner entrance looking N

37 PORT DE LA GRANDE MOTTE
34280 Hérault

Position 43°33′·2N 4°05′·0E
Minimum depth in the entrance 4m (13ft)
     in the harbour 3 to 2m (10 to 6·5ft)
Width of the entrance 90m (300ft)
     inner entrance 50m (164ft)
Number of yacht berths 1364
Maximum length overall 30m (98ft)
Population 5000
Rating 3–2–2

General

The most developed of the new artificial yacht harbours on this coast and also the largest. Many of the buildings are now completed giving a good idea of what this harbour and others of similar design will be like when fully developed. The harbour is easy to approach and enter and provides good shelter, even to a certain extent from the NW *tramontane* winds. In strong swell and winds from SE–S entrance is difficult and could be dangerous. Very good facilities are available for yachtsmen and these are to be improved further.

Data

Charts Admiralty 1705
    French 7053
    Navicarte 507, 508

Current Out to sea there is a W-going current of 0·5 to 1 knot but it is usually circulatory off this harbour and is therefore E-going close inshore.

Magnetic variation 2°04′W (1994) decreasing by about 6′ each year.

Air radiobeacon Montpellier-Fréjourges (43°33′·5N 3°56′E) FG(··−·/−−·) 339kHz. Low power.

Port radio VHF Call Ch 16, work Ch 9. 2182kHz

Weather forecasts Posted three times a day at the *bureau du port*. Recorded forecasts (☎ 36 68 08 08 and 36 68 08 34).

Speed limit 3 knots.

Storm signals Hoisted on a mast at the *bureau du port*.

Traffic signals Hoisted on the mast at the *bureau du port*. The simplified system is used.

Local wind signals Green light: below 10 knots (Force 3). Red light: 10 to 20 knots (Force 4–5). Two red lights: 21 to 33 knots (Force 5–6). No light: above 33 knots (Force 8).

Lights
Digue Ouest head Fl(2)R.6s12m7M Red lantern on wall
Digue Est head Fl.G.4s9m5M White tower, dark green top

Warning

This is a busy harbour in the season and care should be exercised when approaching and entering. A large wreck lies exposed 3·5m to SSE of Pointe de l'Espiguette.

Approach by day

From SW The solid line of buildings at Palavas-les-Flots, which can be identified by its water tower and jetties, joins with those of Carnon, which can be recognised by its blocks of flats and jetties. Between here and La Grande Motte is an octagonal pink-brown sandstone tower with a radiobeacon mast. The unusual pyramid-shaped blocks of flats of La Grande Motte can be seen from afar.

From E Round the Pointe de l'Espiguette outside the buoys. Do not cut the corner since there are extending shoals. This point, which is low, flat and sandy, is identified by its lighthouse partly obscured by trees. The jetties of Port de Camargue, its buildings and the group of buildings at Le Grau du Roi are easily recognisable. Le Grau du Roi has conspicuous water towers, one on each side, and a pair of large jetties. The pyramid-shaped blocks of flats of La Grande Motte are easily visible from this direction.

Approach by night

Using the lights listed below navigate to a position where the entrance is NW at 400m:
Pointe de l'Espiguette Fl(3)W.15s24M
Carnon-Plage Fl(4)R.15s7M
Sète, Mont Saint-Clair Fl.W.5s29M
Montpellier-Fréjourges Aero Mo(Y)W.12.5s

Anchorage in the approach

Anchor in sand 400m to SW of the entrance or 400m to SE.

Entrance

By day From a position about 400m to SE of the entrance, approach and leave the head of Digue Ouest 50m to port. This *digue* has a large 'M' at its head. The head of Digue Est should now be left 50m to starboard. Round it onto a N course and proceed towards the inner harbour. Yachts drawing 2·5m (8ft) must keep in mid-channel and not cut corners.

By night From a position about 400m to SE of the entrance, approach Fl(2)R.6s keeping Fl.G.4s open to starboard. Leave Fl(2)R.6s which also has a large illuminated 'M' below, 50m to port. Now leave Fl.G.4s 50m to starboard and round it onto a N course. Approach the entrance to the inner harbour.

Berths

Secure alongside the quay or pontoon beside the *bureau du port* for allocation of a berth which will be stern-to a pontoon or quay, bow-to mooring buoy or posts.

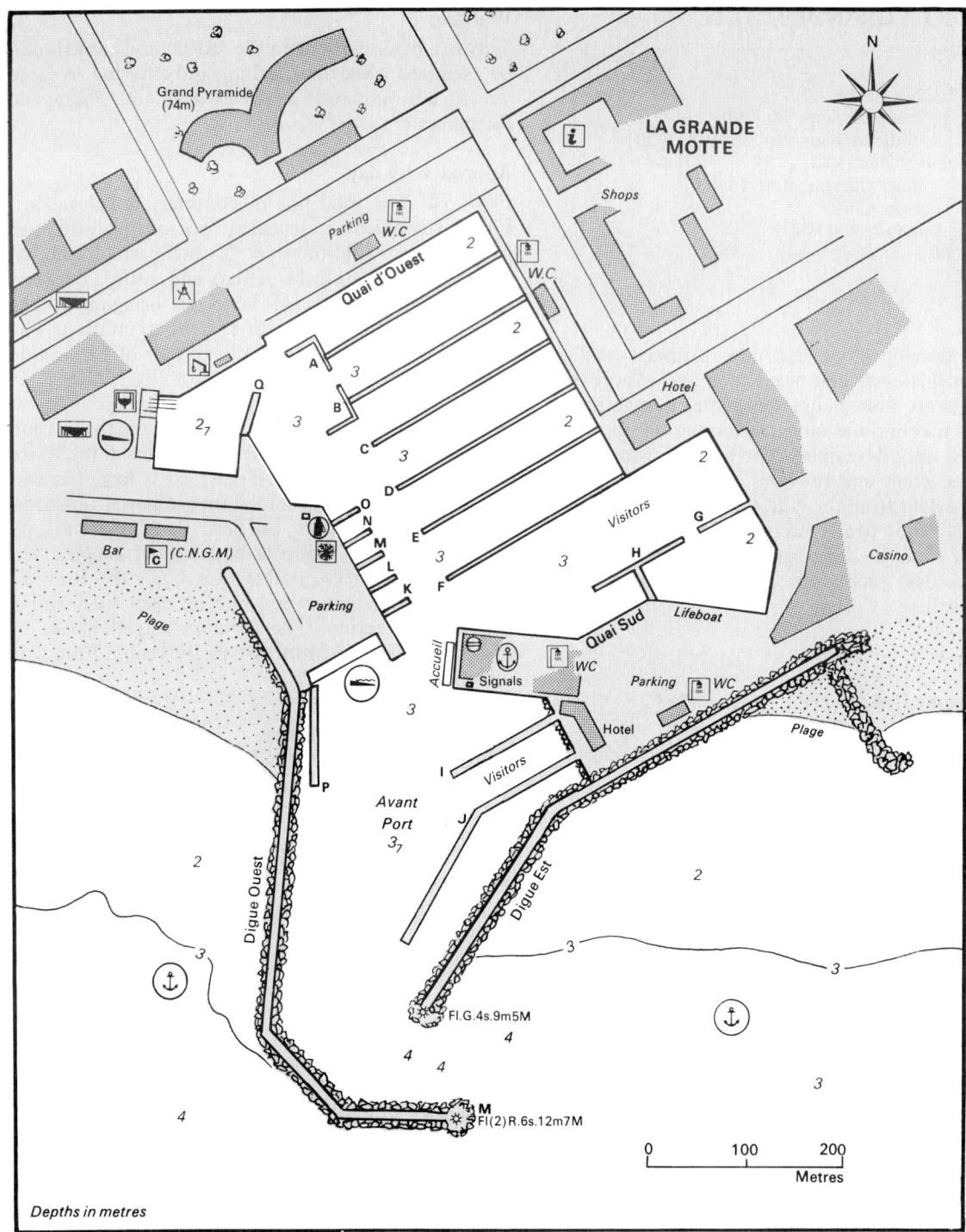

Port de la Grande Motte

Formalities

On arrival report at once to the *bureau du port* (☎ 67 56 50 06) and if necessary to the customs office which is in the same building (☎ 67 56 51 47).

Harbour charges

There are harbour charges.

Facilities

Slips A slip on the NW side of the *avant-port* and another in the W corner of the inner harbour.

Cranes A three-tonne crane and another of 27 tonnes, draught 2·60m (8·5ft) and travel-lifts of 50 and 9 tonne maximum beam 5m (16ft). All in the workshop corner to NW.

Fuel Diesel (*gasoil*) and petrol are available from pumps at the W side of the inner harbour (☎ 67 56 50 94). Open in summer 0500–2100, winter 0800–2000, closed Tuesday. Maximum draught 2·6m(8·5ft).

Water Water points on all pontoons and quays.

Electricity Points for the supply of 220v AC are on pontoons and quays.

Port de la Grande Motte. Entrance to Etang de Ponente

Bureau du port

Port de la Grande Motte looking N

Inner entrance   *Bureau du port*

Port de la Grande Motte. Inside entrance looking N

Port de la Grande Motte Harbour looking N

Provisions A number of shops to the NE and NW of the inner harbour which can provide normal requirements. Duty-free goods are available.

Ice Ice is available from the fuel station.

Garbage Rubbish containers on all quays and pontoons.

Chandlery Several ships' chandlers to the NW of the harbour.

Repairs A number of shipyards to the NE of the inner harbour where all normal repairs to hull and engine can be carried out. Electronic equipment can also be repaired. A sailmaker is available.

Laundrette Two laundrettes.

Post office A PTT in the shopping area.

Hotels There are six hotels, four being ***, one **.

Restaurants 21 restaurants and café/bars.

Yacht club The Société des Régates de la Grande Motte (SRGM) (☎ 67 56 19 10) has a clubhouse to W of the harbour with bar, restaurant, lounge and showers. Yacht Club de la Grande Motte (YCGM) (☎ 67 56 50 21).

Showers Showers are available in the same building as the *bureau du port* and sixteen showers with twenty WCs are located in two blocks..

Information office The Syndicat d'Initiative has an office to N of the inner harbour (☎ 67 56 62 62).

Lifeboat A lifeboat is stationed here, a *vedette* of 9m (☎ 67 56 60 06 or 67 56 03 01).

Communications Bus service. Rail and air services at Montpellier.

Future development

There is still much to be finished in and around this harbour and extra pontoons, extra facilities and accommodation are to be provided. An entrance into the Canal du Rhône à Sète has been opened up and an extra 350 berths are to be established in the Etang du Ponente.

38 PORT DE GRAU DU ROI

30240 Gard

Position 43°32'·1N 4°07'·9E

Minimum depth in the entrance 4m (13ft) in the canal up to the swing bridge 4 to 3m (13 to 10ft) in the Port de Pêche 3m (10ft) in the Canal Maritime 2 to 1·3m (6·5 to 4·5ft)

Clearance under swing bridge 2m (6ft) sliding bridge 2m (9ft)

Width of the entrance 50m

Number of yacht berths 182

Population 5300 (approx)

Rating 3–2–3

General

An old commercial and fishing harbour at the mouth of Le Rivière Vidourle where the Canal Maritime from Aigues-Mortes and the Canal du Rhône à Sète also meet the sea. It is a pleasant holiday and fishing centre and fair facilities are available. Unfortunately vacant berths are impossible to find below the bridge, all piers being privately owned and the banks too sloping to bring up alongside. Permission is usually given to lie alongside a fishing boat while waiting for the bridge to open.

Berths can sometimes be obtained in the port de pêche above the bridge or a space may be found on the starboard hand between the two bridges. Approach and entrance are not too difficult but become dangerous in strong winds and swell from S–SW–W due to a 2·4m (8ft) shallow patch in front of the entrance to the canal.

Data

Charts   Admiralty 1705
                  French 7053
                  Navicarte 507, 508

Currents There is a W-going current of 0·5 to 1 knot in the offing but it is circulatory and SE-going off the entrance. The current in the *grau* is normally outgoing at 1 knot but it can increase to 4 knots after heavy rain inland.

Magnetic variation 2°04'W (1994) decreasing by about 6' each year.

Weather forecasts Posted twice a day at the Marine Pompiers (☎ 96 68 08 30).

Port radio VHF Ch 11, 16 12.

Speed limit 5 knots.

Lights

Jetée Est head Fl(3)G.15s10m10M White column, dark green top, marked Grau du Roi Est

Jetée Ouest head Oc(2)R.6s9m7M White tower, red top.

Warning

There is a shoal patch 2·4m (8ft) 150m directly in front of the entrance which should be avoided in bad weather. If there is a heavy swell at the same time as the river is in spate, the waves may break in the entrance. A large wreck lies exposed 3·5M to SSE of the light at Pointe de l'Espiguette. Do not cut the corner around the Pointe de l'Espiguette – keep outside the buoys.

Approach by day

From SW From Palavas and Carnon, which are connected by a line of houses, the coast is low, flat and sandy and there is a radiobeacon aerial on an octagonal pink-brown tower between these two harbours and La Grande Motte, which is easily identified by virtue of the unique pyramid-shaped blocks of flats. Le Grau du Roi has a water tower on either side of the town and a pair of long jetties with conspicuous white light towers at their head. An old disused lighthouse will be seen at the root of the jetty.

From E Round the Pointe de l'Espiguette, a low, flat and sandy promontory with a conspicuous lighthouse, outside the buoys. It is most important not to cut the corner because of extending shoals. Only when the old lighthouse at the foot of the jetties at Le Grau du Roi is clear of the heads of the jetties at Port de Camargue should a course be shaped towards the entrance. Port de Camargue will be recognised by its blocks of flats. The water towers on either side of Le Grau du Roi are clearly visible in this approach.

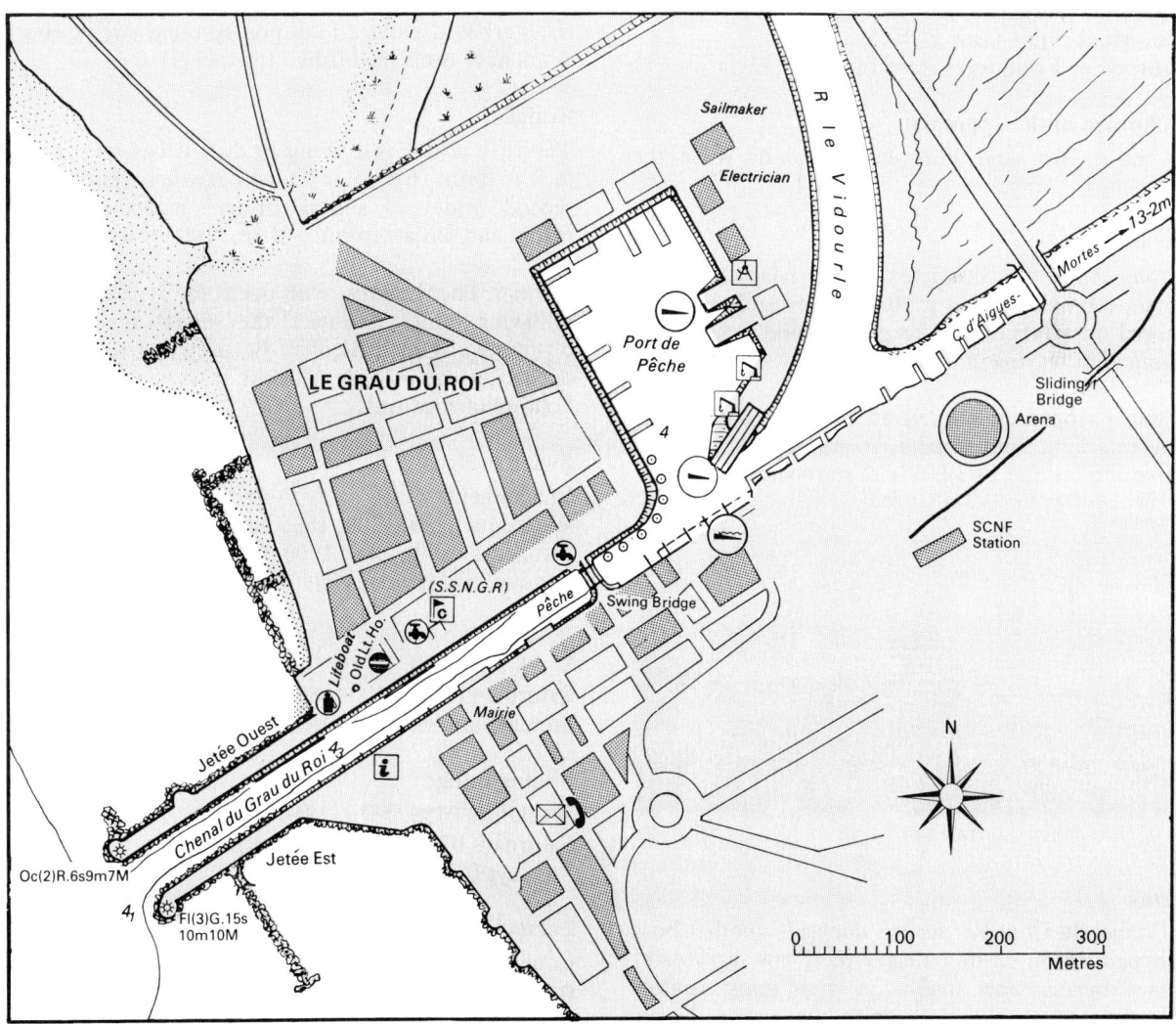

Port de Grau du Roi

Old lighthouse   Salins

Port de Grau du Roi looking E

Approach by night

Using the lights listed below navigate to a position where the entrance is 400m to E:

Pointe de l'Espiguette Fl(3)W.15s24M
La Grande Motte Fl(2)R.6s7M
Sète, Mont Saint-Clair Fl.W.5s29M
Montpellier-Fréjourges Aero Mo(Y)W.12·5s

Anchorage in the approach

Anchor in 5m sand and weed 400m to W of the entrance.

Entrance

By day Approach the Jetée Ouest head on an E course, round it leaving it 20m to port and enter the channel on a NE course keeping a good lookout for fishing craft leaving at speed.

By night Approach Oc(2)R.6s on an E course and leave this light 20m to port, rounding it onto a NE course and leaving Fl(3)G.15s to starboard.

Old lighthouse

Port de Grau du Roi. Entrance looking NE

Berths

In Chanel du Grau Roi secure alongside another boat with permission or to a vacant pier, bow upstream. These berths can only be temporary unless arrangements can be made with the owner. Never leave the yacht without crew on board and be ready to move if required. Two berths on the pontoon near the old lighthouse are sometimes available.

In the *port de pêche* above the bridge berths may be available on short pontoons established there or at the shipyards. Just below the second bridge and on the starboard hand a long pontoon and twelve short spurs have been established for yachts.

Bridges

The first bridge is a swing bridge; it has a clearance of 2 to 1·5m (6·5 to 5ft) under it when closed. The second bridge, a sliding bridge, is 500m further inland and has a clearance of 3m (10ft) when closed.

Timings The bridges will open on request at the following times. Contact the *mairie* or Syndicat d'Initiative if in difficulty. Be prepared to pass the opened bridge directly it opens so as to minimise the hold-up of road traffic.

Swing bridge

In summer
Weekdays 0800, 1300, 1800 hours
Saturdays 0800, 1300, 1700 hours
Sundays and holidays 0830, 2000 hours

In winter
Weekdays 0800, 1100, 1715 hours
Saturdays 0800, 1100, 1630 hours
Sundays and holidays closed

Sliding bridge

Weekdays 0750, 1310, 1810 hours
Saturdays 0745, 1315, 1715 hours
Sundays 0815, 2015 hours

Formalities

Contact *bureau du port* at Maison de la Mer (*mairie*) rue des Lamparos. Open in summer 0830–1200 and 1330–1730. (☎ 66 53 54 55 and 66 51 40 05) for information. There is an office for the customs here

Port de Grau du Roi. Swing bridge in the town

Port de Grau du Roi. Sliding bridge across Canal d'Aigues Mortes above the town. Note: Lines to fishing nets across canal

Entrance to Port de Pêche   *Yacht berths*

Port de Grau du Roi. Above the swing bridge looking NE

Yards

Port de Grau du Roi. Port de Pêche looking SE-S

but the official is stationed at Aigues-Mortes (☎ 66 51 95 13).

Harbour charges

Harbour charges may be levied.

Facilities

Slips A muddy stone slip above the bridge on the SE bank and two others at the shipyards.

Slipways Two slipways at the shipyards, maximum length 25m (82ft), beam 5·5m (18ft) and draught 3m (10ft).

Crane Two 18-tonne cranes at the shipyard. Travel-lift 14 tonnes.

Fuel Diesel (*gasoil*) and petrol are available from pumps at Quai du 19 Mars 1962, open in summer 0700–2000 and winter 0800-2000 on the NW bank near the root of the Jetée Ouest.

Water Several points for water on the NE bank and on the pontoons.

Provisions A number of shops in the town of most types.

Ice An ice factory on the road to Aigues-Mortes or from Quai Colmont.

Chandlery Several ships' chandlers in the town.

Repairs Three shipyards can carry out most repairs to hull and engine. There is also a sailmaker and repairs can be made to electronic equipment as well.

Post office In the town there is a PTT.

Hotels Six ★★★, eight ★★, three ★ and four other hotels.

Restaurants 45 restaurants and a number of café/bars.

Yacht club The Société Nautique de Grau du Roi (SNGR) (☎ 66 51 43 83) has a clubhouse on the NW bank with bar, lounge and showers. There are several other clubs.

Information office The Syndicat d'Initiative has an office at the town hall (*mairie*) (☎ 66 51 67 70).

Lifeboat A lifeboat is stationed here (☎ 66 51 43 09).

Visits A visit by bus or boat to Aigues-Mortes should be made.

Beaches 18km of fine sandy beaches on either side of the harbour.

Communications Bus service and rail service for goods only. Rail and air at Montpellier.

Future development

The possible improvement of the area above the bridge to provide berths for yachts.

History

The first canal from the port of Aigues-Mortes to the sea was built in 1340 by enlarging the existing *grau* which drained the salt lakes. Over the ages other canals were dug in the area to replace sections which had silted up. The present Canal Maritime was dug in 1725 as a connection between Aigues-Mortes and the sea. The town itself did not develop until 1806 when the harbour at Aigues-Mortes finally silted up. The Jetée Ouest was built in 1822 and the village was commenced in 1830; by 1850 the population was 500.

39 PORT DES AIGUES-MORTES
30220 Gard

Position 43°34'·0N 4°11'·3E
Minimum depth   in the entrance and the Canal Maritime
2 to 1·3m (6·5 to 4·5ft)
in the harbour 2 to 1·3m (6·5 to 4·5ft)
Number of yacht berths 100
Maximum length overall 12m (40ft)
Population 52,000
Rating 1–3–3

Note The canal and harbour are occasionally dredged to greater depths but often silt up.

General

A very old small harbour some 3M inland up a canal from Le Grau du Roi lying beside a fabulous medieval fortified town with its original walls and fortifications virtually intact. There are fair facilities for yachtsmen and complete shelter is obtainable in the harbour. The approach up the canal and the entrance to the harbour are straightforward though both canal and harbour tend to silt up with very soft mud. Because the mud is so liquid it is often possible to drive the yacht through it. There is a connection here to the Canal du Rhône à Sète. A useful port for wintering in fresh water. Mosquitoes can be bad. This harbour is controlled by Port de Camargue *bureau du port*.

Data

Charts   Admiralty 1705
French 7004, 7053
Navicarte 507, 508

Current There is normally a weak outgoing current which increases after heavy rains.

Levels The levels can increase by up to 0·6m (2ft) above normal after strong winds from SE–S.

Magnetic variation 2°04'W (1994) decreasing by about 6' each year.

Weather forecast Port de Camargue *bureau du port* (☎ 66 51 43 09). Recorded forecast (☎ 36 68 08 13).

Port radio La Camargue VHF Ch 9, 12 16

Speed limit 3 knots.

Warning

There is an overhead electric power cable only 16m (53ft) in height about 1M from the town.

Approach by day

From SW The turning bridge and sliding bridges at Le Grau du Roi only open at certain hours – see page 168. The clearance below the turning bridge when closed is 2 to 1·5m (6·5 to 5ft) and below the sliding bridge when closed the clearance is 3m (10ft). Wait for the bridges to open secured bow upstream alongside another boat with the owner's permission.

Be ready to pass the bridges directly they open and proceed up the canal in midstream. The banks slope in and are soft mud. Where small streams enter a mudbank may be found just below them.

Approach by night

Night approach and entrance are not advised due to lack of navigational lights.

Entrance

By day Enter the harbour basin nearer the starboard-hand side as it is shallow near the NW bank.

Berths

Bow-to quay that lies parallel to the town walls, stern-to mooring buoy. It is shallow near the quays due to silting.

Formalities

No local *bureau du port* as the harbour is controlled from Port de Camargue. Officials from the *bureau du port* there will visit yachts. There are customs here and their office (☎ 66 51 95 13) is near the tower.

Harbour charges

There are harbour charges.

Facilities

Slip A small slip at one of the shipyards.
Cranes Two cranes (6 and 10 tonnes) at the shipyards.
Fuel A petrol service station beside the canal to N of the town.
Water Water points along the quay.
Electricity 220v AC supply points alongside the quay.

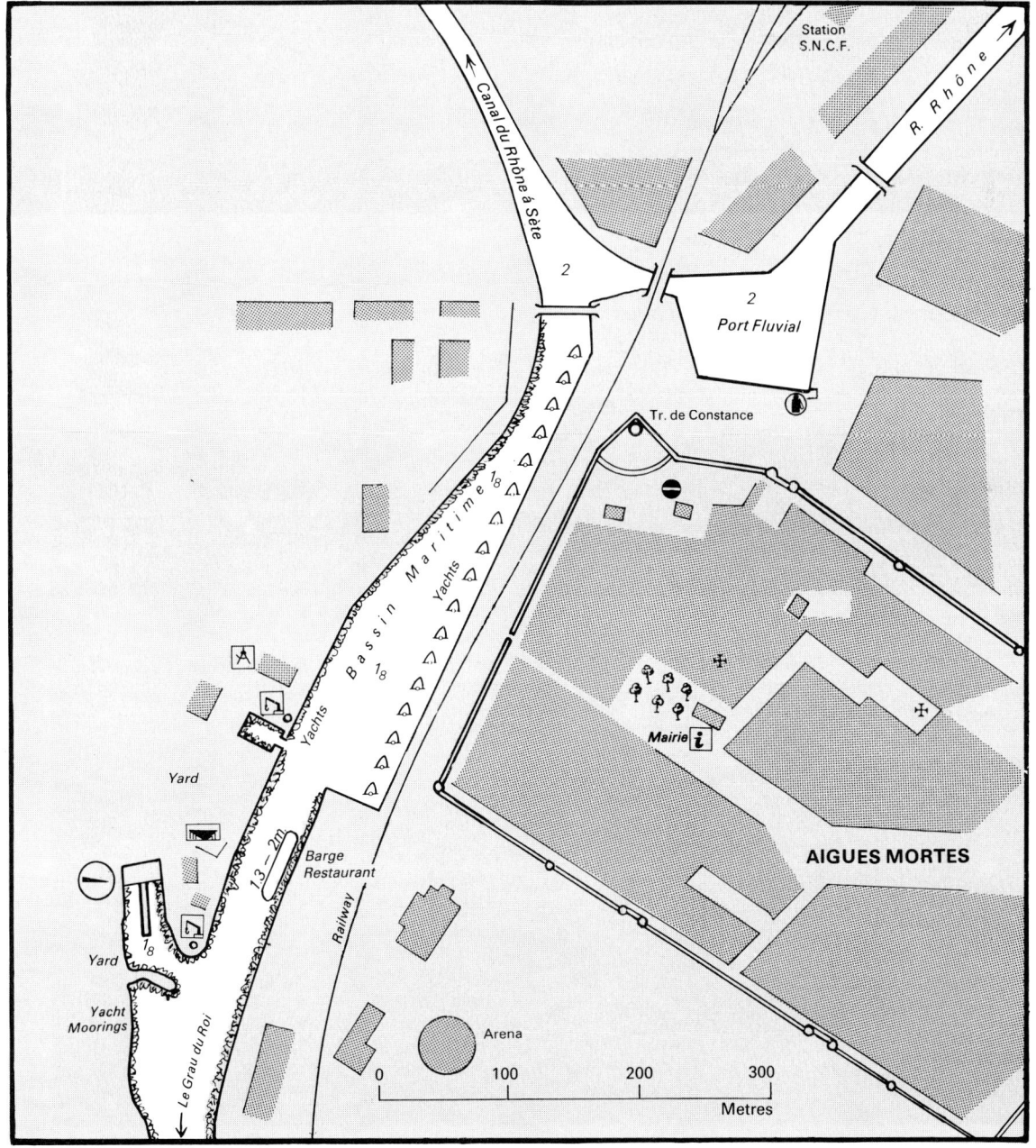

Port des Aigues Mortes

Canal du Rhône à Sète   *Yacht quay*   *Yacht yards and berths*

Port des Aigues Mortes looking NE

Tour de Constance

Port des Aigues Mortes, Port Fluvial looking S

Town walls   *Entrance to Canal d'Aigues-Mortes à Grau du Roi*

Port des Aigues Mortes – Basin Maritime looking S

Provisions A number of shops in the town and a daily market. There is a special market on Sunday and Wednesday.

Ice From shop in the town.

Garbage Rubbish containers on the quays.

Chandlery A certain amount is available from the shipyards and two shops.

Repairs The two shipyards can repair hulls and there is a mechanic for engine repairs.

Post office The PTT is located in the N half of the town.

Hotels Two ★★★, four ★★ and two ★, and some unlisted.

Restaurants 21 restaurants of various types.

Yacht club The Club Nautique Hauturier d'Aigues-Mortes (CNHAM) has an office at Chantier Pfister.

Information office The Syndicat d'Initiative has an office at the town hall (☎ 66 53 73 00).

Visits There are a number of interesting old buildings in this town and in the area around. A walk around the walls is recommended and a visit to the Tour de Constance should be made.

Communications Bus service and goods rail service locally. Rail and air service at Montpellier and Nîmes.

History

This 13th-century town has had a long and complicated history. Many French kings took a great interest in the place and two crusades were mounted from here in the 12th and 13th centuries. The Tour de Constance and the town walls were built between 1290 and 1300 and the tower was used to hold a series of important prisoners over the years. The tower and town changed hands several times between 1421 and 1789. Many improvements were made to the town's defences during the following years.

40 PORT DE CAMARGUE (PORT DE L'ESPIGUETTE)

30240 Gard

Position 43°31'·0N 4°08'·0E
Minimum depth in the entrance 4m (13ft)
in the harbour 3m (10ft)
Width of the entrance 15m
Number of yacht berths 4340
Maximum length overall 24m (79ft)
Population 1000 (approx)
Rating 2–2–3

General

The most northeasterly of the series of new yacht harbours being developed on this coast and in a late stage of development. It is a large harbour with a considerable area devoted to marinas. It has excellent facilities for yachtsmen. The harbour offers good protection and is easy to approach and enter in all weathers except strong winds and swell from the S–SW–S. Some care is necessary when approaching from the E to keep outside the extending shoals off the Pointe de l'Espiguette. A second harbour entrance has been developed to the SW of the main harbour but this is only for residents with small boats. The buildings in Port de Camargue are much lower than those of La Grande Motte, which makes it a more attractive and pleasant harbour to be in.

Data

Charts Admiralty 1705
French 7004, 7053
Navicarte 507, 508

Current The current in the offing is W-going 0·5 to 1 knot but is circulatory in the Golfe d'Aigues-Mortes and is therefore S-going off the entrance to this harbour.

Magnetic variation 2°04'W (1994) decreasing by about 6' each year.

Port radio VHF Calling Ch 16, working Chs 9 and 12. 2182kHz

Port de Camargue (Port de l'Espiguette) looking E up Canal Sud

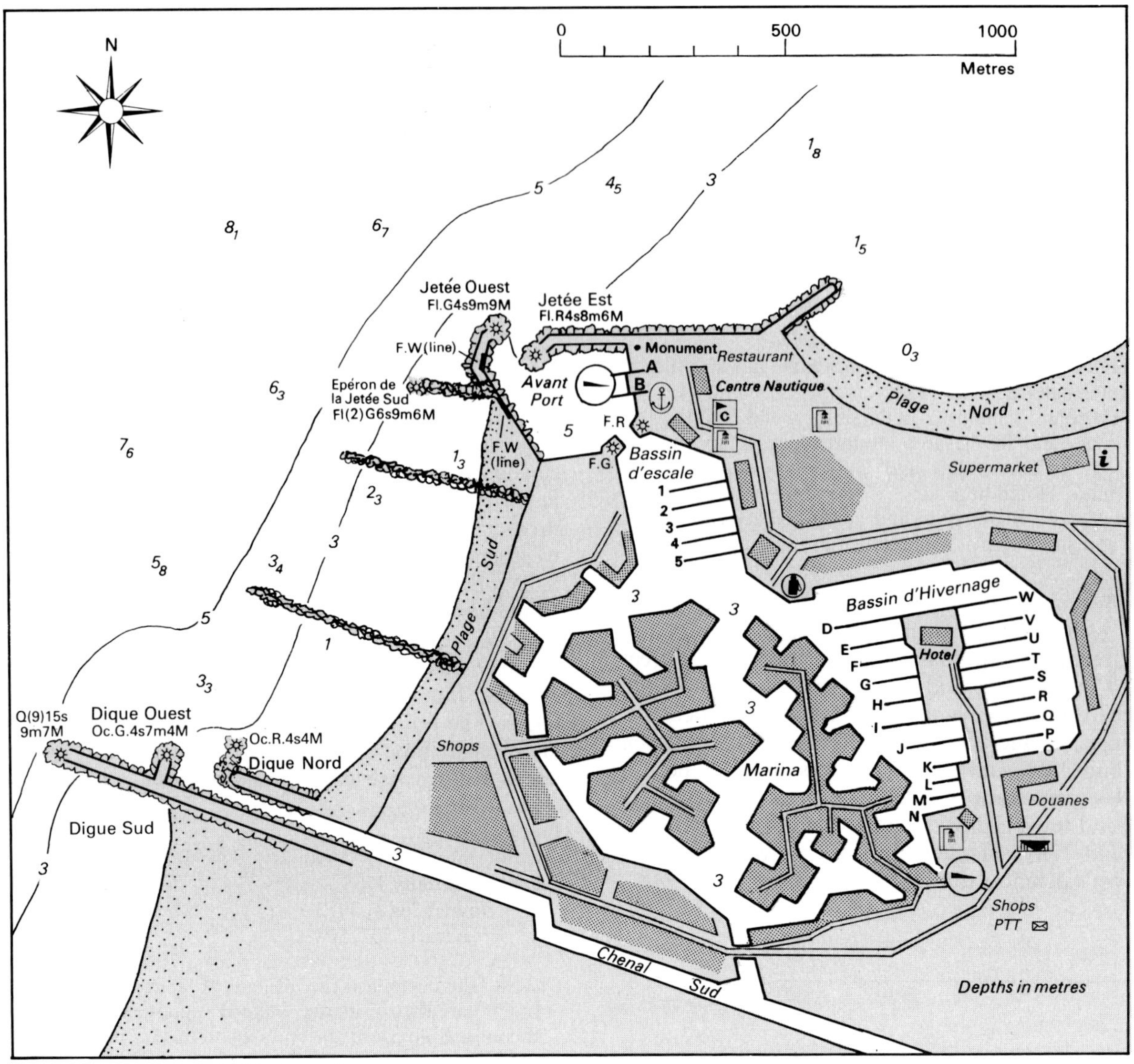

Port de Camargue (Port de l'Espiguette)

Weather forecasts Posted twice a day at the *bureau du port*. Recorded forecast (☎ 36 68 08 30 and 66 51 80 81).

Traffic signals Shown from the mast at the *bureau du port*.

Day	Night	Meaning
Red flag	Red light	Entry forbidden
Green flag	Green light	Exit forbidden
Red and green flags	Red and green lights	Entry and exit forbidden

Storm and wind signals Shown from mast at the *bureau du port*. Storm signals are as diagram in Part I page 118.

Wind force and sea signals state:

Pendant flag	Meaning			
	Wind	Beaufort scale	Sea	Mer
Green	0 to 10 knots	0 to 3	0 to 0·5m	*Calme à belle*
Red	11 to 21 knots	3 to 5	0.5 to 1·25m	*Peu agitée*
Two red	20 to 40 knots	5 to 8	1·25 to 2·5m	*Agitée*
Black	Above 40 knots	Above 8	Above 2·5m	*Fort à très fort*

Port de Camargue entrance.

Speed limit 5 knots.

Lights

Pointe de l'Espiguette Fl(3)W.15s27m24M White square tower, black top

Digue d'Arrêt head VQ(9)W.10s9m9M ⟨ topmark, yellow column, black band

Jetée Ouest head Fl.G.4s9m9M White column, green top. FW strip lights on two corners of jetty

Jetée Est head Fl.R.4s8m6M White column, red top

Channel S. Digue d'Arrêt head Q(9)W.15s9m7M. ⟨ topmark on yellow dolphin, black band

Digue Ouest head Oc.G.4s7m4M White structure, green top 059°-vis-345°

Digue Nord head Oc.R.4s4M White structure, red top 063°-vis-345°

Avant-port SW side 2 F.W line lights.

Entrance to Bassin d'Escale F.R and F.G

Buoys Pointe de l'Espiguette: W cardinal light and whistle buoy, ⟨ topmark, yellow, black band, 1·5M to SW of lighthouse VQ(9)10s.

Pointe de l'Espiguette oil terminal: A number of unlit mooring buoys 1.7M to S of lighthouse marked by N cardinal light buoy, ⟨ topmark, black over yellow, 1.5M to S of lighthouse (QW).

S cardinal light buoy, ⟨ topmark, yellow over black, 2M to S of lighthouse (VQ(6)+LFl.W.10s).

Harbour entrance Green light buoy marks edge of extending sand bank (Fl.G.2s).

Restrictions Windsurfers, wetbikes etc. are not allowed in this harbour.

Warning

This harbour is still in the final stages construction and alterations may be expected. The harbour entrance is subject to silting and depths of only 1.0m have been recorded N of Jetée Ouest; this is corrected by periodic dredging. Yachts under sail inside the harbour do not have automatic right of way. A large wreck lies stranded 3·5M to SSE of Pointe de l'Espiguette lighthouse.

Approach by day

From SW Pass the long line of houses that connects Palavas with Carnon, and also the radiobeacon tower between them and La Grande Motte, which can be identified by its high pyramid-shaped blocks of flats. Le Grau du Roi can be identified by water towers on each side of the town and by twin jetties with light towers at their extremities and a disused lighthouse at their root. The conspicuous blocks of flats of Port de Camargue will be seen in the closer approach.

From E Round the low, flat and sandy Pointe de l'Espiguette to S of S cardinal light buoy (VQ(6)+LFl.10s) and outside the cardinal W light buoy (VQ(9)10s Whistle). Do not cut the corner as there are extending shoals. When the disused lighthouse at Le Grau du Roi can be seen clear to the W of the heads of the jetties at Port de Camargue it is safe to approach, but not before.

Approach by night

Using the lights listed below navigate to a position where the entrance is 400m to S of the harbour entrance:

Pointe de l'Espiguette Fl(3)W.15s24M

La Grande Motte Fl(2)R.6s7M

Sète, Mont Saint-Clair Fl.W.5s29M

Entrance Bureau du port Inner entrance   *Epéron de la Jetée Sud*

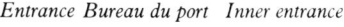

Port de Camargue (Port de l'Espiguette) looking SE

Anchorage in the approach
Anchor in 5m (16ft) sand with the entrance 400m to S.

Entrance
By day Enter on a SE course between the heads of the jetties and round the head of Jetée Est at 20m, leaving it to port, onto a SE course. Proceed on a SE course across the *avant-port* to the entrance to the *bassin d'escale*.

By night From a position where the entrance is 400m to S approach Fl.R.4s on this course, leave it 20m to port and round it onto a SE course leaving Fl.G.4s to starboard. Cross the *avant-port* towards F.R and F.G leaving two F.W (strip lights) to starboard.

Berths
Secure alongside the quay beside the *bureau du port* to receive instructions. Then berth stern-to quay, bow-to mooring buoy or pair of posts where directed.

Formalities
Report to the *bureau du port* (☎ 66 51 43 09) on arrival. Open in summer 0800–2000, in winter 0800–1800. The customs are at Aigues-Mortes (☎ 66 51 67 57). They have an office at the *bureau du port* for use in summer.

Harbour charges
There are harbour charges.

Facilities
Slip A large slip on the NE side of the *avant-port*.
Cranes A crane of 3 tonnes and travel-lifts of 5·15 and 45 tonnes.
Fuel Diesel (*gasoil*) and petrol are available from pumps on the NE side of the inner harbour (☎ 66 51 44 54). Open in summer 0630–2200, winter 0800–2000.
Water Water points are to be found on all quays and pontoons.
Electricity Supply points for 220v AC 5 amps are on all quays and pontoons.
Provisions A limited number of shops in the harbour area, including a *supermarché*, and many more at Le Grau du Roi 2M away.
Ice Ice can be obtained from the fuel station.
Garbage Rubbish containers on all quays and pontoons.
Chandlery A ships' chandler in the extreme SE corner of the harbour.

Bureau du port   *Inner entrance*   *Epéron de la Jetée Sud*

Port de Camargue (Port de l'Espiguette) looking SE from Avant port

Head of Jetée Ouest *Head of Jetée Est* *Bureau du port* *Epéron Jetée Sud*

Port de Camargue (Port de l'Espiguette). Approach looking E

Port de Camargue (Port de l'Espiguette). Harbour looking N

Repairs Eleven shipyards in the extreme SE corner of the harbour where hulls and engines may be repaired. Electrical and electronic repairs also possible.

Hotels Three ***, eight ** and three * hotels and more to be built.

Restaurants 45 restaurants at the moment.

Yacht club Société des Sports Nautique du Grau du Roi-Port de Camargue (SSNGRPC) (☎ 66 51 43 82 and 66 53 29 47) has a clubhouse with all facilities including showers.

Showers Showers and WCs at the *bureau du port* and nine blocks around the harbour near shipyards.

Lifeboat A lifeboat is on duty here. *Vedette* 1st class (☎ 66 51 43 09).

Beaches Miles of sandy beaches either side of this harbour.

Communications Bus service, rail service Nîmes and Grau du Roi, air service Nîmes and Montpellier.

Information office The Syndicat d'Initiative has an office to NW of the harbour (☎ 66 51 74 78, 66 51 71 68 and 66 51 67 70).

Future development

It will take a few years finally to fulfill the plans that already exist.

Pointe de l'Espiguette

Built in 1873, a large low flat point with a sandy beach and sand dunes backed by trees. On the SW side are a conspicuous lighthouse (24m) and a lookout building. Depths around the point are shallow and unreliable as the whole area is slowly extending by about 10m a year. Keep to the 20m contour and outside the light buoys, and do not cut the corner.

Old signal station

Pte de l'Espiguette lighthouse

41 PORT DE GRAU D'ORGON (PETIT RHONE)

13200 Bouches du Rhône

Position 43°26′·6N 4°24′·0E
Minimum depth in the entrance 1·50m (4·9ft)
              in river 4 to 9m (13 to 29ft)
Width of entrance 100m (approx)
Population 2244
Rating 3–4–3

General

A series of small harbours has been established 2M inside the entrance of the Petit Rhône on the E bank l'amarrer above the rear landing light and at Port Dromar. There are in addition many small private pontoons alongside the same bank located both above and below Port Dromar. This river is only suitable for small to medium-sized yachts and can only be entered in calm conditions. With winds from SE–S–SW the waves break across the entrance making entrance and exit difficult if not dangerous. Facilities are very limited and there is very little development to be found away from the coastline where there is a campsite and a number of houses have been built. The area is very suitable for those who prefer the simple life away from all the facilities and civilization of the modern yacht harbours. A large shallow draught tourist boat makes several trips each day up the river from Port Gardian.

Data

Charts Admiralty 1705
      French 6693
      Navicarte 507

Current The current in the offing is 0·5 to 1 knot W-going but is subject to strong winds. In the river it rarely exceeds 2 knots.

Magnetic variation 2°04′W (1994) decreasing by about 6′ each year.

Lights

Le Petit Rhône leading lights 337° *Front* DirQ.G.6m14M Green pylon with banded black and white topmark marked Petit Rhône in green. Intensified 335°-339°. *Rear* DirQ.G.13m14M 650m from front Green pylon with black and white diagonal striped topmark. Intensified 335°-339°

Buoys Grau d'Orgon light buoy, red and white stripes, ball topmark, Iso.W.4s located 4·50M to SSE of the river mouth. River channel buoyed inside the mouth.

Beacons River mouth E side: green up-pointed cone, W side: red cylindrical topmark.

Warning

This river mouth should be approached and entered with care sounding continuously because of shifting sand banks. Seek advice as to the current situation from the *bureau du port* at Port Gardian first. Some 3M upstream is a cable ferry with 2·7m (9ft)

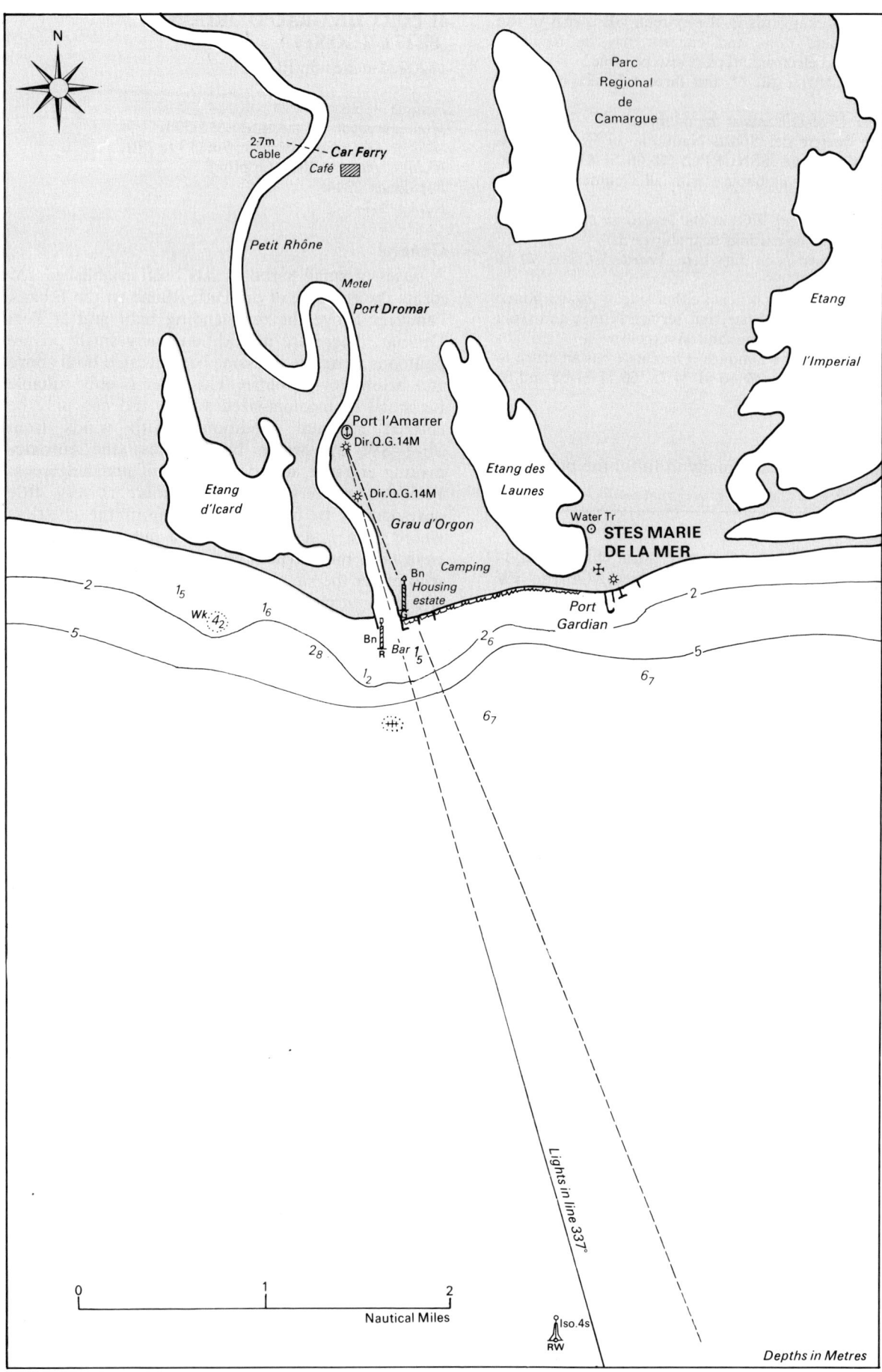

Port de Grau d'Orgon (Petit Rhône)

clearance. The bar at the river mouth is about 400m long and about 1·6m (5·5ft) deep.

Approach by day

From W The pyramid-shaped buildings at La Grande Motte, the group of houses, two water towers and the old lighthouse de le Grau du Roi, and the mass of low buildings at Port de Camargue, are all easily recognised. Round the Pointe de l'Espiguette outside the W cardinal light buoy and the light buoys off the oil terminal. The coast is flat and featureless until near the harbour when the church and houses of Stes-Maries-de-la-Mer will be seen. Follow the 20m sounding to the Grau d'Orgon light buoy, red and white stripes, ⁑ topmark, (Iso.W.4s) where turn to 340° and approach the coast.

By 8m depth the leading lights of the entrance should be seen with a group of houses to the E. Bring the two light towers into line and approach. Pay attention to a wreck just to port, there is another further away (2M approx.)

From E Follow the line of buoys which marks the shallows of the River Rhône delta from the Golfe de Fos to the Pointe de Beauduc. These are located near the 20m contour. The coast is flat and featureless but the lighthouses of Faraman and Beauduc should be seen. When the Pointe de Beauduc has been passed follow the 20m contour to the Grau d'Orgon buoy and proceed as detailed in the *From W* section above.

Approach by night

Using the lights listed below navigate to the Grau d'Orgon buoy (Iso.W.4s) whence the leading lights DirQ.G.14M should be observed. Bring them into line on 337° and approach. Entrance at night for a first visit is not advised.

Pointe de l'Espiguette Fl(3)W.15s24M
La Gacholle Fl.WRG.4s13-10M
Pointe de Beauduc Fl(2)R.10s16M
Faraman Fl(2)W.10s23M

Note The change of La Gacholle sectioned light from white to red on 065° crosses the line of the leading lights 2M from the coast.

Anchorage in the approach

Anchor 1M from the shore in 6m sand and mud to the E of the leading lights.

Entrance

By day Follow 337° with the two leading light beacons in line until two short rocky training walls are reached. Enter the mouth about 15m off the E training wall leaving it to starboard and follow it into the river which is buoyed. In general the deep water is to be found on the outer sides of bends. The seaward ends of the two training walls are submerged.

By night Not recommended without local knowledge due to lack of lights in the river. Anchor off the coast until dawn.

Entrance   *Front leading mark/light*

Port de Grau d'Orgon (Petit Rhône). Approach looking NE

Rear leading light   Front leading light

Port de Grau d'Orgon (Petit Rhône). Inside the entrance looking N

Berths

Secure with bow upstream to a vacant pontoon and ask locals if it is free. Or enter one of the small harbours on the E bank and enquire about a possible berth.

Formalities

None.

Facilities

Cranes A mobile crane (3 tonnes).
Water Tap near small harbour; also at hotel.
Provisions From Stes-Maries de la Mer 3M away.
Hotels A small hotel and others nearby.
Restaurants Many restaurants and café/bars in the area.
Visits A visit to Stes-Maries-de-la-Mer is recommended. It is possible to ascend the Petit Rhône for 3M as far as a ferry at Sauvage where a cable with 4m (13ft) clearance

Rear leading mark   Pont l'Amarrer   Port Dromar   Front leading mark

Port de Grau d'Orgon (Petit Rhône). ½M up the river looking N

Port Dromar   Rear leading light   Pont l'Amarrer

Port de Grau d'Orgon (Petit Rhône). 1M further up the river

crosses the river; above this there are no further obstructions.

Future development

Coastal development is taking place and it may result in a demand for more harbours and easier entrance to the Petit Rhône. However the area is a part of the Parc Régional de Camargue and developments are likely to be controlled. A small harbour has just been constructed to the S of Port Dromar and more harbours are expected.

42 PORT GARDIAN
(PORT DES STES-MARIES-DE-LA-MER)
13460 Bouches du Rhône

Position 43°26'·8N 4°25'·7E
Minimum depth   in the entrance 3m (10ft)
                          in the harbour 2·50m (8ft)
Maximum length overall 17m (56ft)
Number of yachts 415
Population 2120
Rating 3–3–3

General

A new yachting and fishing harbour beside Stes-Maries-de-la-Mer located on the coast of the Camargue close to the mouth of Le Petit Rhône. It is a most useful stopping place near the centre of the 45M stretch of coast between the Golfe d'Aigues-Mortes and the Golfe de Fos where there are no other harbours available. The harbour is easy to approach and enter but would be difficult with strong winds from SE–S–SW and could be dangerous.

Data

Charts   Admiralty 1705
              French 6693
              Navicarte 507

Magnetic variation 1°59'W (1994) decreasing by about 6' each year.

Weather forecast Recorded forecast posted up at *bureau du port* daily (☎ 36 68 08 08 and 36 68 08 13).

Currents The normal coastal current is W-going 0·5 to 1 knot but this may be increased by strong winds from E or conversely decreased by those from the W. There is a S-going current of 1 to 2 knots off the mouth of Le Petit Rhône.

Levels On-shore winds especially from SW raise levels in the harbour by up to 0·6m (2ft) while offshore winds may lower the levels by 0·1m (0·3ft).

Speed limit 3 knots.

Port radio VHF Chs 16 and 9.

Lights
Digue Ouest head Fl.R.4s8m5M Red structure
Digue Est head Fl.G.2.5s8m5M Green structure. 140°-vis-326°
Digue Ouest elbow F.W

Warning

Strong onshore winds and swell will make entering this harbour difficult and perhaps dangerous. Because the harbour has just been built changes must be expected. The coastal depths are constantly changing and charts will not be up to date, so the frequent use of an echo-sounder is advised.

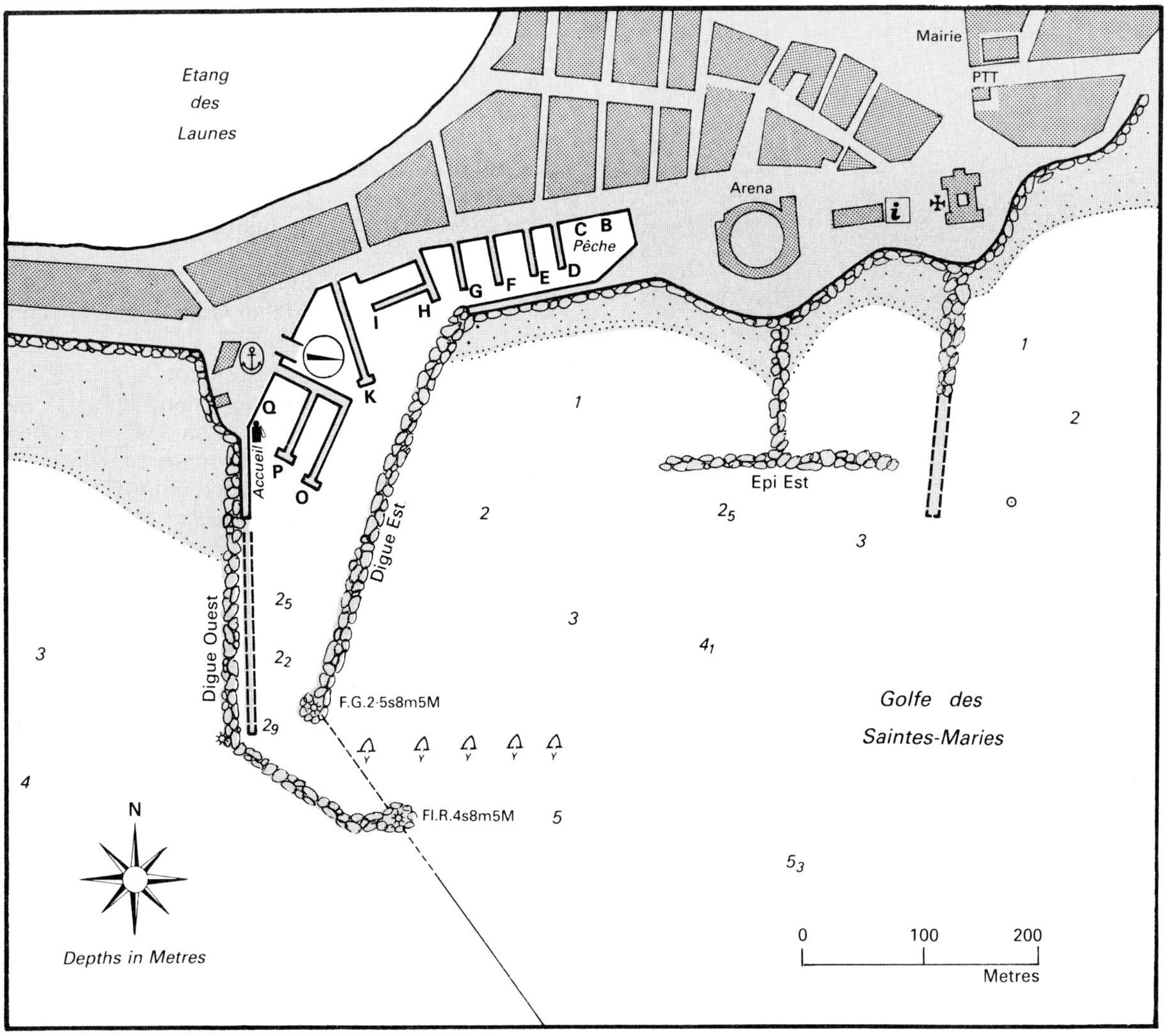

Port Gardian

Port Gardian (Port des Stes-Maries-de-la-Mer) looking NW

Port Gardian (Port des Stes-Maries-de-la-Mer). Entrance looking W

Breakwaters to E of this harbour and two training walls at the mouth of Petit Rhône have submerged heads.

Approach by day

From W The group of harbours at La Grande Motte, Le Grau du Roi and Port de Camargue is easily recognised as is the white square tower, black top (27m) of the lighthouse at the Pointe de l'Espiguette. Keep outside Espiguette cardinal W light buoy, ⚑ topmark, yellow black band (VQ(9)10s). Also keep outside the outer of the two oil terminal light buoys, a cardinal S light buoy, ⚑ topmark, yellow over black (VQ(6)+LFl.10s).

Thence follow the 10m depth contour which lies about 1M offshore. The coast is very flat with no conspicuous features. A mast may be seen on the coast 4M to E of the oil terminal buoy. The buildings and church of Stes-Maries-de-la-Mer (30m) can be seen from afar. Remain at least 1M offshore until the mouth of Le Petit Rhône has been passed and only approach the harbour on a N heading.

From E Cap Couronne with its conspicuous white tower, red top lighthouse and the village and harbour of Carro are easily recognised. Cross the Golfe de Fos on a W heading passing S of the two buoys off the mouth of the Rhône, Roustan Est, a cardinal S light buoy, ⚑ topmark, yellow over black (Q(6)+LFl.15s), and Roustan Ouest, a cardinal S, whistle buoy.

Keep in at least 20m of water on a general W heading passing near Piémanson cardinal S light buoy, ⚑ topmark, yellow over black (Q(6)Fl.10s) and Faraman, cardinal S light and whistle buoy, ⚑ topmark, yellow over black (Q(6)+LFl.15s). The coast is flat and featureless but the Faraman lighthouse (41m), black and white bands, may be observed when between Piemanson and Faraman buoys.

The 20m depth contour may be followed on a general WNW heading from Faraman to Beauduc cardinal W light buoy, ⚑ topmark, yellow with black band (VQ(9)10s). The Beauduc lighthouse (26m) white tower should be seen from here and Stes-Maries-de-la-Mer should be seen when halfway across this *golfe*; a direct course may then be shaped towards the harbour.

Approach by night

The following lights will assist in navigating to the Grau d'Orgon light buoy, ball topmark, red with white stripes (Iso.4s5M):
Pointe de l'Espiguette Fl(3)W.15s24M
La Gacholle Fl.WRG.4s13-10M, 300°-G-019°-W-065°-R-085°
Pointe de Beauduc Fl(2)R.10s16M

Note The sectored light of La Gacholle helps considerably in locating the Grau d'Orgon light buoy.

From the Grau d'Orgon light buoy approach the coast on a N heading until the leading lights to the Petit Rhône (DirQ.G) are in line on 337° and follow this line into 10m depths. From here when the harbour lights have been identified approach may be made to the harbour, otherwise anchor until dawn.

Port Gardian (Port des Stes-Maries-de-la-Mer) looking N. Visitors' berths

Anchorage in the approach

Anchor in 5m mud off Stes-Maries-de-la-Mer. Holding is not always very good so keep an anchor watch.

Entrance

By day Approach the head of the Digue Ouest, round it at 20m onto a NW course leaving a line of yellow buoys to starboard, and enter between breakwater heads. Do not confuse the harbour breakwaters with coastal defence works on either side of the harbour.

By night Not recommended without previous visits by day.

Berths

Secure to vacant berth on first two pontoons, P or O (yachts of 11m(+) use O and those of 10m(−) use P) and report to *bureau du port* for allocation of berth.

Formalities

Report to *bureau du port* (☎ 90 97 85 87 and ☎ 90 97 82 45). Open in summer 0800–2200, in winter 0800–1200 and 1400–1800. Customs in the same building (☎ 90 96 07 43).

Harbour charges

There are harbour charges.

Facilities

Hard A large hard standing near the *bureau du port*.
Slip A large slipway near the *bureau du port*.
Cranes To be provided. Travel-hoist 14 tonnes.
Fuel At root of Digue Ouest. Open 0800–1145 and 1400–1700.
Water Water taps on all pontoons and quays.
Electricity 220v AC points on all pontoons and quays.
Provisions All normal supplies available from nearby shops and supermarket in the town.
Ice Available from shop in Rue Frédéric Mistral and from the *bureau du port*.
Garbage Rubbish bins around the harbour.
Chandlery Two chandlery shops in the town.
Repairs Minor repairs possible to engines.
Post office In the town.
Hotels Nine **, one * and many others in the area including one *** and eight **.
Restaurants 25, and many café/bars.
Yacht clubs A yacht club is established in the clubhouse at the *bureau du port*.
Showers At the *bureau du port*. Eighteen showers and thirteen WCs. To use apply to *bureau du port* for code numbers.
Laundrette In the town.
Lifeboat 2nd class *vedette* (☎ 90 97 83 07).
Information office The Syndicat d'Initiative is located in the town to E of the Arena (☎ 90 97 82 55).
Visits A visit should be made to the church and the museum in Baroncelle. If time is available a tour of La Camargue by taxi or horse is well worthwhile. A day's visit to Arles is also advised.
Beaches Sandy beaches to E and W of the harbour.
Communications Bus service to Arles. Rail service at Arles and air service at Nîmes, Montpellier.

Future development

There is some construction work still to be completed and many facilities are still to be provided. Pontoons M, O and P to be extended.

History

Stes-Maries-de-la-Mer has a fascinating history. According to Provençal tradition, in about 40 AD the Jews of Jerusalem put Mary (the Virgin's sister) wife of Cleophas, known as Marie Jacobe, Mary (the mother of the apostles James and John) styled Marie Salomé, Mary Magdalene and her sister Martha into a small boat together with Lazarus, St Maximin, St Sidonius and a black servant, Sarah. The boat had no sails, oars or provisions. They were miraculously carried by the currents and wind to this spot and landed on what was a small island where there was a pagan temple. Leaving the two old Marys behind with Sarah, the others set out to convert Provence to Christianity. Stes-Maries became a place of

Port Gardian (Port des Stes-Maries-de-la-Mer) looking NE. Visitor's berths

pilgrimage and when the gypsies arrived in the 15th century they adopted Sarah as their patron saint. Each year on 23rd May gypsies from all over Europe arrive to celebrate the event by an all night vigil followed a few days later by sports, processions and dances.

⚓ Beauduc Golfe des Saintes Maries

A large (5M wide) bay with sandy beaches and a lighthouse, La Gacholle, on a black and white square tower (17m). Anchor in the SE corner in 8m sand open to S–SW–W.

⚓ Anchorage is also possible along the 12M of sandy beach as far as the mouth of the Petit Rhône.

Pointe de Beauduc

Similar to Pointe de l'Espiguette (page 179) except that the point is fronted by banks of sand which are extending at 15m a year. The banks have radar reflectors. The conspicuous lighthouse (26m) is painted black and white. Round the point in 20m depth to S of the light buoy.

Beauduc lighthouse

Mouth of the Grand Rhône

Not a real headland but developing into one at a rate of 30m a year. The sandy coast nearby is low and flat and marked by radar reflectors and a radar beacon. Many caravans and tents line the beaches. The area is very dangerous due to shifting sand bars. Keep in 20m or more and pass to S of the two light buoys Roustan Ouest and Este.

DELTA DU RHONE

The section of coast that lies between the Golfe d'Aigues-Mortes and Golfe de Fos merits a separate description on two counts. Firstly it is by far the longest section of the southern French coast with only one harbour, and secondly by virtue of its ever – extending shoal waters and featureless coast it is probably the most dangerous.

Topographical

The whole area has been built up and is still being built up by the silt brought down by the River Rhône and deposited when it reaches the sea. This has resulted in a vast area of flat lands, shallow lakes and *étangs*. A large part of this is the famous Camargue, a completely deserted area with its wild grey horses and pink flamingoes, now declared a National Park.

Coast

The coast is low, flat and sandy-beached, backed by dunes. The sea bed shelves fairly regularly out to sea, but little reliance should be placed on charted depths as they are continually changing, usually becoming more shallow.

Data

Charts Admiralty 3414, 1705
French 6684
Navicarte 507

Magnetic variation 1°59′W (1994) decreasing by about 9′ each year.

Currents The normal current is W-going 0·5 to 1 knot but strong SE winds can increase this and NW winds decrease and reverse this flow. There is a marked SSE-going current near the mouth of the Grand Rhône.

Lights

Pointe de l'Espiguette Fl(3)W.15s27m24M White square tower, black top
La Gacholle Fl.WRG.4s17m13-10M Black and white square tower, white lantern and hut. 300°-G-019°-W-065°-R-085°
Port Gardian Digue Ouest head Fl.R.4s8m5M Red structure
Digue Est head Fl.G.2·5s8m5M Green structure
Le Petit Rhône Leading lights 337° *Front* DirQ.G.6m14M Green pylon with banded black and white topmark, Petit Rhône in green. Intensified 335°-339°. *Rear* DirQ.G.13m14M Green pylon with black and white diagonal striped topmark. Intensified 335°-339°
Pointe de Beauduc Fl(2)R.10s26m16M White and black tower, white cupola
Faraman Fl(2)W.10s41m23M Black tower, white bands

Buoys Espiguette light buoy, yellow with black band, ⚑ topmark, VQ(9)10s.
Outer oil terminal light buoy, yellow over black, ⚑ topmark, VQ(6)+LFl.10s (missing 1991.)
Inner oil terminal light buoy, black over yellow, ⚑ topmark Q.W (missing 1991)
Beauduc light buoy, yellow with black band, ⚑ topmark, VQ(9)10s.

Delta du Rhône. W Roustan whistle buoy

Faraman lighthouse

Delta du Rhône. E Roustan light buoy

Faraman light and whistle buoy, yellow over black, ⚑ topmark, Q(6)+LFl.15s.
Piémanson light buoy, yellow over black, ⚑ topmark, VQ(6)+LFl.15s.
Roustan Ouest whistle buoy, yellow over black, ⚑ topmark.
Roustan Est light buoy, yellow over black, ⚑ topmark, Q(6)+LFl.15s.
Balancelle Est light buoy, black, yellow band, ⚑ topmark Fl(3)5s

Beacons Groups of radarbeacons mark the mouth of the river Rhône. One on the E bank, They de Roustan, carries a Racon, 3 and 10cm, 270°-090°. The Racon signal appears as a succession of 8 dots. The distance between each pair of dots corresponds to 0.3M.

Warning

The coast is extending at the mouth of the Grand Rhône at the rate of 30m a year, off the Pointe de Beauduc at 15m a year and off the Pointe de l'Espiguette at 10m a year. Heavy swells from the SE–S–SW can break as far out as the 20m depth contour. The low coast is difficult to see unless visibility is very good and even so it is difficult to judge the distance off due to the lack of any recognisable features.

Route

From the SW Take a departure from the two buoys at the oil terminal checking the current flowing when passing them. Allowing for this, plot a course outside the Beauduc buoy. The church at Stes-Maries-de-la-Mer may be seen in clear weather and later the white lighthouse tower at Beauduc. The 20m contour line follows this course and provides a check. The new buoy off Stes-Maries may also be seen. After location of Beauduc buoy, in calm weather the coast may be followed but in any swell it is essential to keep to seaward of the series of buoys around the mouth of the Grand Rhône. When crossing the mouth of this river a vessel will be set to seaward by the flow of water and it is always advisable to pass outside the buoys here. On no account should any attempt be made to enter the mouth of this river which is filled with constantly changing and unmarked sandbanks.

From the E Similar problems to those mentioned above occur and the foregoing section should be read. Approach the mouth of the Grand Rhône, following the 20m depth contour and passing outside Balancelle and the two buoys at the mouth of the river. Again keep outside the next three buoys, Piémanson, Faraman and Beauduc, if there is any swell running. From abreast of Beauduc, course can be set for the oil terminal buoys off Pointe de l'Espiguette making due allowance for any current. Having reached this group of buoys do not try to cut the corner, but stand on as far as the Espiguette buoy before turning towards Le Grau du Roi.

Anchorage

Anchorage is possible in calm weather or offshore winds virtually anywhere along the coast, but in particular in the Golfe des Stes-Maries, which is well protected from the E winds.

Plans for bad weather

Before proceeding along this section of coast obtain an up-to-date forecast, and keep a listening watch at H+03 and H+33 on Marseille Radio and VHF Ch 26 for storm warnings while at sea. Keep a contingency plan in mind so that should a NW *tramontane/mistral* blow up or a SE swell develop no time will be lost debating what to do. In general should a *tramontane/mistral* occur it will bring good visibility and the coast can be closed into shallower and calmer water. It may be necessary to run the yacht almost ashore and to anchor there until the weather improves. On the other hand it is vital to stand out into deeper water if there is a heavy swell from seawards which usually indicates the E–SE winds.

PART III
West Côte d'Azur

Introduction

General description

This 140M section of the French Mediterranean coast is very different from the miles of straight, low and flat sandy beaches of Languedoc-Roussillon that lie to its W; quite suddenly to the E of les Bouches du Rhône rocky hills and mountains arise which stretch as far as the Italian frontier. In this area the coast and harbours are more interesting and picturesque and the facilities are better. On the whole the towns are not spoilt by tourism and although in the season there are swarms of summer visitors, the pressure is not so great as it is on the coast further eastward. A special feature of this section of the coast is the large number and variety of anchorages available. Many are described herein but there are many others for readers to discover for themselves.

The Golfe de Fos, which forms the E side of the delta of the Rhône, is shallow on its W side with a flat low coast and sandbanks which must be avoided, but on the E side it has low rocky cliffs and deep water within half a mile of the coast. There are several major commercial ports in the Golfe as well as a canal to the Etang de Berre and to the River Rhône.

From Cap Couronne to Marseille, the coast referred to as la Côte Bleue, the coastal hills are of a bare whitish rock and there are a number of small indentations wherein lie a few small harbours separated by the coastal hills, la Chaîne de l'Estaque, there is a huge inland lagoon, l'Etang de Berre, which has a number of harbours of its own and offers the attractive alternative of lake sailing to seagoing vessels.

On the further side of the huge port complex of Marseille, the Côte des Calanques is bounded by even higher white hills of a very rugged nature where there are to be found a number of most attractive, very deep and narrow creeks or *calanques* that penetrate some distance inland and form ideal anchorages. There are few harbours along this spectacular part of the coast.

Offshore to the S and SE of Marseille lie scattered groups of rugged islands composed of the same bare white rock as the mainland; some anchorages and a few harbours are to be found amongst them. Further eastward the high rocky cliffs and hills increase in size as far as Bec-de-l'Aigle, an extraordinarily shaped rocky prominence that has the appearance of an eagle's head from certain directions. Nearby the cliffs are the highest in France and are most impressive.

From Bec-de-l'Aigle the coast consists of a number of bays with lower and less rugged cliffs around them various harbours are to be found in these bays.

The coast between Ile des Embiez, one of another group of islands, and Cap Sicié about 4½ miles SE, contains a number of islets close inshore, Cap Sicié itself being a high rocky promontory which is easy to identify by virtue of its size and a conspicuous TV tower at its summit.

The isolated Ile de Planier and La Cassidaigne reef, with their light towers are the only offshore dangers, apart from the islands mentioned above. It is possible in fair weather to coast close to the shore in deep water, though there are some places where piles of rocky debris have fallen from the cliffs, and these may extend some 50m out. Sandy shallows are to be found near the heads of the various bays, notably those of Bandol, Sanary and Le Brusc.

Warnings

Winds and seas The predominant and strongest winds, as shown in the diagram, are normally from either NW (the *mistral*) or from SE (the *marin*) with an occasional E wind (the *levant*). When cruising offshore these winds should be kept in mind and contingency plans made as to where to seek shelter should they arise. It should be possible to enter any of the large deep water ports in a sound seagoing yacht under most conditions but no attempt should be made to approach and try to enter any of the smaller harbours unless the wind is blowing offshore. Shelter can often be obtained in the lee of the high cliffs, but the narrow *calanques* should not be used as not only does the wind funnel down them but they can become traps if the wind direction should change. Heavy seas occasioned by these strong winds can become dangerous in the following areas:

NW *mistral*
To the E of Cap Couronne
Off Cap Croisette
To the SW of the islands
Off Cap Sicié

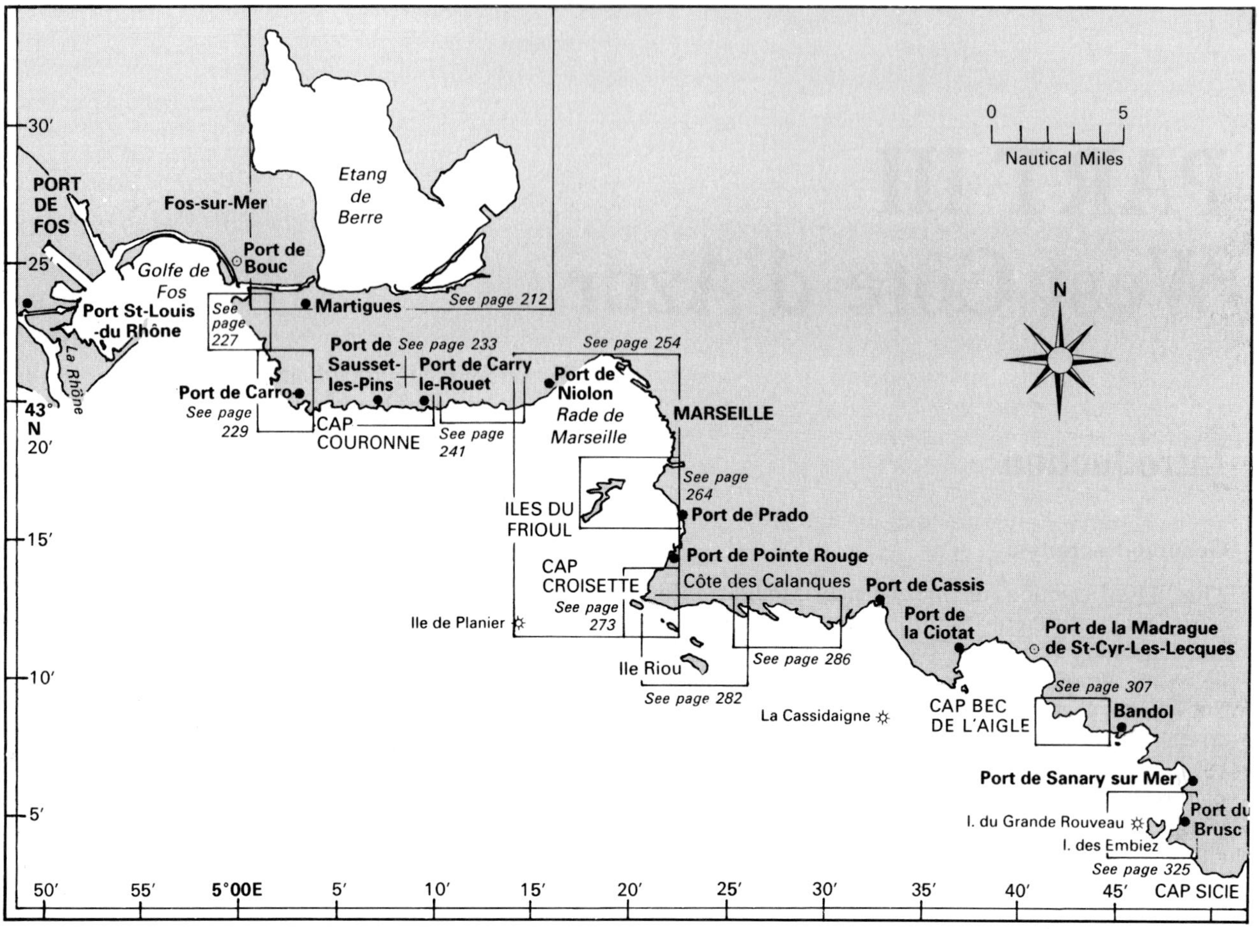

SE *marin* or *céruse* and E *levant*
Off les Bouches du Rhône
S of Cap Croisette
Baie de Cassis
Baie de la Ciotat
Off Cap Sicié

Virtually all the harbours offer shelter from the seas caused by these winds but it may be necessary to shift berth to a more sheltered position within the harbour. Only a few harbours offer shelter from the wind itself.

Restricted areas

Anchoring, mooring and fishing are not permitted in the following areas which are shown on Admiralty and French charts:

a. An area to the S of the entrance to Port de Bouc
b. Around the entrance to Port de Fos
c. On most of the Canal de Caronte
d. Between Ile Pomègues and the mainland extending some 6M to SE and around to W
e. A small area to E of Ile Riou
f. Baie de Cassis and some 4M to S
g. A small area to SE of Ile des Embiez

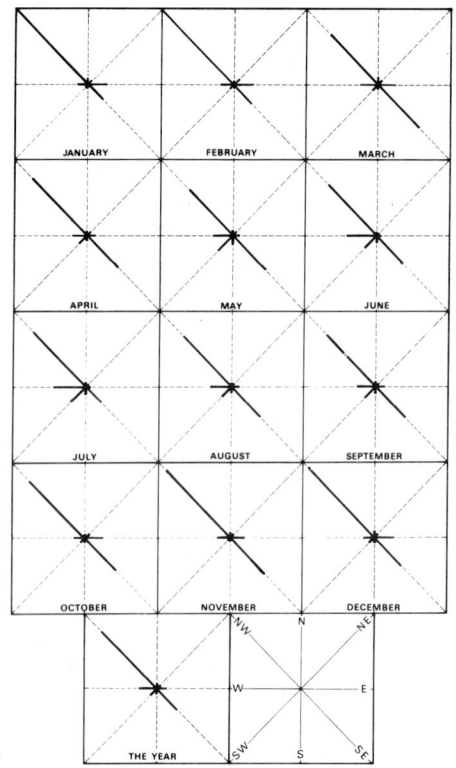

Relative wind directions

Firing notices If any area is to be used for firing practice this is announced on Marseille Radio (FFM) 1906kHz at H+10.

Data

Charts The following small-scale charts cover this section of coast:
Admiralty 1705, 2164, 3498
French 6951
Spanish 49
ECM 504, 505

Tides and heights The tidal range in this part of the Mediterranean reaches a maximum of 0·15m at springs and is hardly detectable at neaps; for all practical purposes, therefore, tidal heights and streams can be disregarded.

Currents On the other hand, currents are important and can reach rates of 2 knots or more off promontories in strong winds. The basic Mediterranean circulatory current around this part of the coast is W-going at about 1·5 knots and this is increased in strong winds from E to SE. Winds from the NW tend to slow down and reverse this basic current, especially along SW, W and N facing coasts, off promontories and in gaps between islands.

Sea levels In very strong winds from the SE the water rises up to 1m above the normal levels and during strong winds from the NW the level falls about 0·5m.

Marine radiobeacons
Cap Béar BR (−···/·−−) 313·5kHz 50M
Sète SÉ (···/··−··) 287·5kHz 50M
Cap Couronne CR (−·−·/·−·) 295·5kHz 50M
Porquerolles PQ (·−−·/−·−−·) 314kHz 200M

Air radiobeacons
The following air radiobeacons operate in the area but may not transmit continuously:
Nice, Mont Leuza LEZ (·−−·/·/−−··) 399kHz 75M
43°43'·52N 7°19'·63E
Ajaccio, Pointe de la Parata IS (··/···) 341kHz 50M
41°54'N 8°36'·9E
Pointe de Senetosa SNE (···/−/·−·) 394·5kHz 15M
47°33'·50N 8°47'·90E
Solenzara SZA (···/−−−·/·−) 349·5kHz 80M 41°55'·9N
9°23'·7E. Bearings may be unreliable 080° to 120°.
Bastia, Poretta BP (−···/·−−·) 369kHz 50M 42°25'·7N
9°32'·2E

VHF Direction-finding service
This service is for emergency use only. Each VHF direction-finding station is remotely controlled either by a Regional Operational Centre for Surveillance and Rescue (CROSS)[1], Signal Station or Naval Lookout Station.
[1]For operational details of CROSS stations see *Admiralty List of Radio Signals Vol 3 NP 283* and *6(1) NP 286(1)*
CROSS Stations watch on Ch 16, 11; 67, (when a maritime rescue operation is already underway on Ch 11).
Signal Stations and Lookout Stations keep a priority watch on Ch 16. Also available are 7 additional frequencies retained in memory (scanner sweeping) from amongst the following channels:
1-29 156·050MHz –157·450MHz
36   162·400MHz

39   162·550MHz
48   121·500MHz
50   155·525MHz
52   155·625MHz
55   155·775MHz
56   155·825MHz
60-88 156·025MHz – 157·425MHz

Ship transmits on Ch 16 (distress only) or Ch 11 in order that the station can determine its bearing.
Ship's bearing from the station is transmitted on Ch 16 (distress only) or Ch 11.
Hours of watch continuous. Controlled by Sig Stn unless otherwise stated.
Cap Couronne RG 43°20'·1N 5°03'·3E
Pomègues RG 43°16'N 5°17'·7E
Bec de l'Aigle RG 43°10'·5N 5°34'·6E
Cap Cépet RG Controlled by Lookout Stn 43°04'·8N 5°56'·5E
Porquerolles RG 43°00'N 6°13'·7E
Cap Camarat RG 43°12'·1N 60°40'·5E
Cap du Dramont RG 43°24'·8N 6°51'·2E
La Garoupe RG 43°34'N 78°08'·2E
Cap Ferrat RG 43°41'·2N 7°19'·5E

Coast radio stations
St Lys (FFL-FFS-FFT)
R/T watch on 4366, 8806, 13152, 17323, 22771kHz Continuous. The above coast radio station operates on this coast but it is normally only used for commercial purposes. Traffic lists on 4366, 8806, 13152, 17323, 22771kHz every H+03 and H+30 (0700–2230) so far as possible. See *Admiralty List of Radio Signals Vol. 1 NP 281(1)*for full details also WT(MF) service of stations listed below.

Marseille (FFM)
R/T 1671, 1906, 1936, 1939, 2625, 2628, 3792, 3795, 2182kHz 1kW. Traffic lists on 1906kHz at every odd H+10.
VHF Ch 16, 24, 26 Continuous. Call *Marseille Radio*.
Martigues
VHF Ch 16, 27, 28 Continuous. Call *Marseille Radio*.
Sète
VHF Ch 16, 19. Continuous. Call *Marseille Radio*.
Toulon
VHF Ch 16, 25, 62. Continuous. Call *Marseille Radio*.
Grasse (TKM)
R/T Transmits 1746, 2649, 3719, 3722, 2182kHz. Receives 2045, 2048kHz (for foreign registered vessels), 2051, 2054, 2057, 3168, 2182. 2090 working frequency for French registered vessels. Continuous. Traffic lists on 2649kHz every even H+33. VHF Transmits Ch 02,18 (0630–2100) Ch 16 continuous.
Cavalaire VHF Ch 04, 05 (0600–2100) and Ch 16 continuous, remotely controlled from Grasse.
Monaco (3AC, 3AF)
R/T Transmits 4363, 6504, 8728, 13146, 17260, 22750kHz. Receives 4071, 6203, 8204, 12299, 16378, 22054kHz. Traffic lists on all frequencies every H+03 (0503–2203). VHF Ch 16, 20, 22, 86. Continuous. Traffic lists Ch 16 every H+03 (0700–2300) UT.

Details for automatic calls see *Admiralty List of Radio Signals Vol. 1 NP 281(1)*.

Coast signal stations Signal stations are located at Cap Couronne, Ile Pomègues and Cap Sicié where communications may be established by means of radio, the international code of signal flags, or lamp.

Weather forecasts This section of the coast falls inside weather area No.522 Provence, and the most effective weather forecast is from Marseille (FFM) which also broadcasts storm warnings at every odd H + 10. Weather bulletins and forecasts are transmitted regularly as follows:

Marseille (FFM) VHF Chs 24, 26 at 0633, 1133.,

Grasse (TKM) VHF Ch 02 at 0633, 1133

Paris (France Inter) 164 kHz, 1829m at 0555, 1905 UT[1]

Marseille (Radiodiffusion Française) 674 kHz, 445m at 0018–0043, 0718–9745, 1210–1243, 1830–1900 UT

Sud Radio 819 kHz, and VHF Ch 09, 366m at 0800, 1300, 1930 UT[1]

Radio Monte Carlo 218, 1466kHz at 0800, 1900 UT[1]

Marseille Bureau météo, Direction de Port ☎ 91 91 90 66, but not weekends and holidays. Automatic prerecorded forecast ☎ 91 90 35 00 Ext 336

Marignane Aerodrome Station météo ☎ 42 88 42 88. Automatic prerecorded forecast.

Istres Aerodrome Station météo ☎ 42 56 30 24.

[1] Broadcasts given 1 hour earlier during DST.

Major lights and fog signals

Pointe de Beauduc Fl(2)R.10s26m16M White and black tower, white cupola

Faraman Fl(2)W.10s41m23M Black tower, white bands

Port de St-Louis-du-Rhône. Tour St-Louis DirQ.W.16m19M Grey square tower, red top intens 262°-265°

Pointe de St-Gervais IQ(7)WRG.12s45m25-21M Black framework tower 323°-G-340°-W-348°-R-007°

Cap Couronne Fl.R.3s34m20M White tower, red top RC Reserved light range 13m

Ile de Planier Fl.W.5s68m26M White tower Obscured by Ile de Riou and adjacent islets when less than 284°

Château d'If Fl(2)W.6s27m11M White tower, red top, obscured by Iles de Pomègues and Ratonneau 054°-152°

Ile du Grand-Rouveau Oc(2)W.6s45m15M White square tower, black lantern. Obscured by Ile des Embiez 255°-317° unintens 225°-297°

Ile Tiboulen de Maire Fl.WG.4s58m11/8M White column, black top 142°-G-327°-W-142°

Cap Cépet Fl(3)W.15s59m21M White square tower, black lantern

Visits

In addition to local places of interest which are mentioned under *Visits* for each harbour, there are many places further inland which should be seen if time permits and details of these are available from the office of the nearest Syndicat d'Initiative. The following are especially worthy of note: Arles, which is full of magnificent Roman remains and Romanesque churches, St-Rémy-de-Provence, an ancient Gallo-Roman town with many remains from the 1st century BC to the 1st century AD, Salon-de-Provence, the town of Nostradamus, which also has a fine 13th to 15th century fort, and Aix-en-Provence, the ancient capital town of Provence, with many attractive old buildings and streets. Les Baux-de-Provence, a small town in a fantastic setting dating from before AD 981, is also worth a visit.

History

Recorded history of the area starts around 1000 BC with the Ligurians in occupation; in 600 BC the Greeks founded Marseille and during the next 200 years established outstations along the coast. However, the Celts invaded the area and in 125 BC an appeal for help was made to Rome, who then defeated the invaders and established themselves there, founding Aix in the process as the capital of the area.

The Roman general Marius defeated a Teuton invasion some time later and in 49 BC Julius Caesar captured and destroyed Marseille because the city sided with his rival Pompey. The Roman occupation lasted until the 4th century AD during which time many 'new' towns were founded. Between the 4th and 6th centuries the area suffered successive invasions by Vandals, Burgundians, Visigoths, Ostrogoths, Francs and finally in the 8th century by the Saracens.

During the time of Charlemagne, the Saracens, who established themselves in Les Maures to the NE of Toulon, brought terror to the area for over a century. Between the 8th and 15th centuries it changed hands many times as the influence of the various noble families rose and fell, becoming in turn a part of the estates of Lothaire, Provence, Anjou and Savoie. In 1486 Provence was united to the French crown.

The region suffered during the religious wars of 1563 and was invaded by the Prince of Savoie in 1707. In 1720 the plague that was to sweep across Europe decimated the inhabitants of the area. During the revolution of 1790 Marseille sent a detachment of 500 to Paris and their song, the *Marseillaise*, became in due course the French national anthem. Until the end of the 18th century the coast was subject to constant attack by seaborne raiders; Moors, Corsairs, Saracens and pirates of all nationalities landed without warning to loot, pillage and burn, frequently capturing local inhabitants to man their galleys.

Recent history is one of continued expansion of farming, industry and tourism with a consequent considerable increase in the population. See also page 29.

Planning guide

Ports, harbours, anchorages, headlands, islands, passages and special features

Notes

1. This guide is listed in an W to E direction from the the mouth of the River Rhône.
2. There are many other fair weather anchorages to be found which are not listed below.
3. Additional anchorages are detailed in the sections dealing with the various port and harbours.

Distances	Headlands and features	Ports, anchorages and landings
		Mouth of Rhône
		⚓ *Mouillage de Carteau*
8M		**43 Port de Carteau** 4–4–5 Part II
2M	They de la Gracieuse	
5M		**44 Port St-Louis-du-Rhône** 4–3–4 page 200
		Port de Fos-sur-Mer – huge commercial port
3M		**45 Port de St-Gervais (Fos-sur-Mer)** 2–2–3 page 205
2M	Golfe de Fos	**46 Port de Bouc** 4–3–2 page 207
6M	L'Etang de Berre	**47 Port de Martigues** 2–2–2 page 214
	Pointe St-Pierre	⚓ *Anse de Ranquet*
		48 Port des Heures Claires (Istres-St-Martin) 3–3–4 page 217
	Pointe Monteau	⚓ *Baie de St-Chamas*
4M		⚓ *Port de Miramas, a very small shallow harbour for dinghies*
		49 Port de St-Chamas (Vieux) 2–3–4 page 219
0.1M		**50 Port de St-Chamas (Neuf)** 2–3–3 page 220
	Riv. la Touloubre Canal de la Durance	
3½M		⚓ *La Pointe*
		51 Port du Canet (Beau Rivage) (EDF) 3–2–4 page 221
2M		**52 Port de Sagnas (Marveille Mauran)** 4–3–4 page 222
		⚓ *Shelter jetty at les Cabanes, very shallow*
	Pointe de Berre	Port petrolier de la Pointe de Berre, a large mole for petrol tankers with offlying light buoys ▲ 5M (Fl.G.4s) and sectored light (Fl(4)WR.12s12m12/9M)
		Port du Passet, a very small shallow canal from saltpans
		53 Port de Berre-l'Etang 4–3–3 page 223
		Port de Raffinerie de pétrole Small commercial harbour
		Port de Rognac, a small shallow harbour behind two 3M jetties, only 1·2m depth

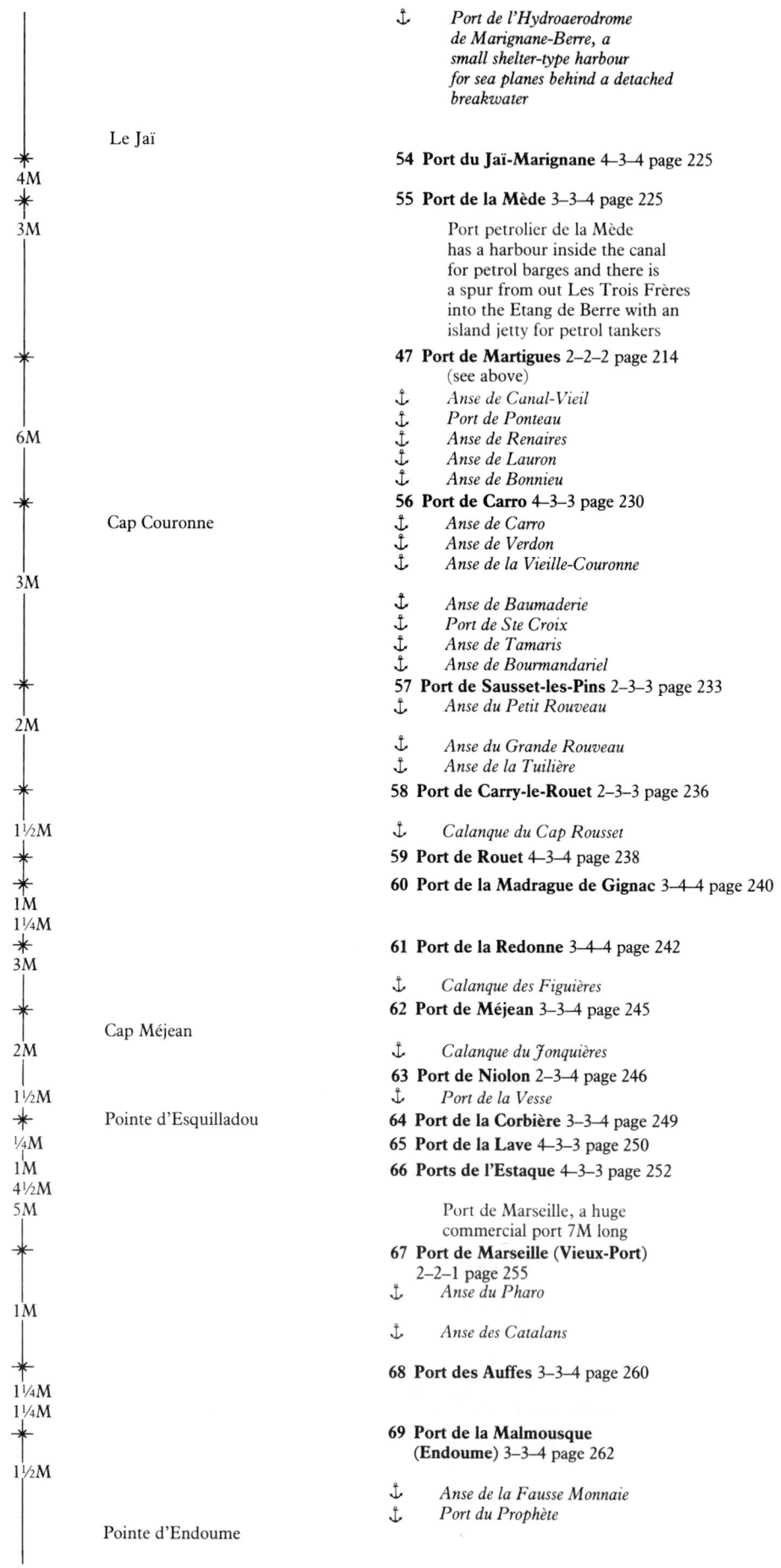

$⌁$ Port de l'Hydroaerodrome
de Marignane-Berre, a
small shelter-type harbour
for sea planes behind a detached
breakwater

Le Jaï

4M

54 Port du Jaï-Marignane 4–3–4 page 225

3M

55 Port de la Mède 3–3–4 page 225

Port petrolier de la Mède
has a harbour inside the canal
for petrol barges and there is
a spur from out Les Trois Frères
into the Etang de Berre with an
island jetty for petrol tankers

47 Port de Martigues 2–2–2 page 214
(see above)

6M

$⌁$ Anse de Canal-Vieil
$⌁$ Port de Ponteau
$⌁$ Anse de Renaires
$⌁$ Anse de Lauron
$⌁$ Anse de Bonnieu

56 Port de Carro 4–3–3 page 230

Cap Couronne

$⌁$ Anse de Carro
$⌁$ Anse de Verdon
$⌁$ Anse de la Vieille-Couronne

3M

$⌁$ Anse de Baumaderie
$⌁$ Port de Ste Croix
$⌁$ Anse de Tamaris
$⌁$ Anse de Bourmandariel

57 Port de Sausset-les-Pins 2–3–3 page 233

$⌁$ Anse du Petit Rouveau

2M

$⌁$ Anse du Grande Rouveau
$⌁$ Anse de la Tuilière

58 Port de Carry-le-Rouet 2–3–3 page 236

1½M

$⌁$ Calanque du Cap Rousset

59 Port de Rouet 4–3–4 page 238

60 Port de la Madrague de Gignac 3–4–4 page 240

1M
1¼M

61 Port de la Redonne 3–4–4 page 242

3M

$⌁$ Calanque des Figuières

62 Port de Méjean 3–3–4 page 245

Cap Méjean

2M

$⌁$ Calanque du Jonquières

1½M

63 Port de Niolon 2–3–4 page 246

$⌁$ Port de la Vesse

Pointe d'Esquilladou

64 Port de la Corbière 3–3–4 page 249

¼M

65 Port de la Lave 4–3–3 page 250

1M
4½M
5M

66 Ports de l'Estaque 4–3–3 page 252

Port de Marseille, a huge
commercial port 7M long

67 Port de Marseille (Vieux-Port)
2–2–1 page 255

$⌁$ Anse du Pharo

1M

$⌁$ Anse des Catalans

68 Port des Auffes 3–3–4 page 260

1¼M
1¼M

69 Port de la Malmousque
(Endoume) 3–3–4 page 262

1½M

$⌁$ Anse de la Fausse Monnaie
$⌁$ Port du Prophète

Pointe d'Endoume

3M

11M 3M

3M

1M

1M   Pointe de Montredon

1M

1M

1M   Cap Croisette

2M

Bec Sormiou

8M

Cap Devenson

Pointe de Castel-Vieil

Pointe de Cacau

1½M

5M

Bec-de-l'Aigle

1¼M

2½M   Cap des Moulins

1M

70 Port du Prado (Roucas Blanc)
3–3–4 page 263
⚓   *Plage du Grande Roucas Blanc*

Plage du Prado
(Details of islands to SW
of Marseille, page 265)
71 Port du Frioul, Ile Ratonneau
2–2–3 page 267
72 Port de Pointe Rouge 3–2–1 page 270

**73 Port de la Madrague de
Montredon** 3–3–3 page 272

⚓   *Calanque de Samena*
⚓   *Calanque du Mauvais Pas*
74 Port de l'Escalette 3–5–5 page 275
Calanque Blanche
Calanque des Trous
75 Port des Goudes 3–3–4 page 276
⚓   *Anse de la Maronaise*
(Details of islands to S
of Marseille page 265)
Anse de Baume Rousse
76 Port de Callelongue 3–4–4 page 279
⚓   *Calanque de la Mounine*
⚓   *Calanque de Marseilleveyre*
⚓   *Calanque des Queyrons*
⚓   *Calanque de Podestat*
⚓   *Calanque de Cortiou*

⚓   *Calanque de Sormiou*
⚓   *Calanque de la Triperie*
⚓   *Calanque de Morgiou*

(Details of islands to SE
of Marseille page 265)
⚓   *Calanque de Sugiton*
⚓   *Calanque des Pierres-Tombées*
⚓   *Calanque de St-Jean de Dieu*

⚓   *Calanque du Devenson*

⚓   *Calanque de l'Oule*
⚓   *Calanque d'En Vau*
⚓   *Calanque de Port-Pin*

77 Port Miou 4–2–4 page 289

78 Port de Cassis 2–3–3 page 291
⚓   *Anse de Ste Magdeleine*
⚓   *Anse de l'Arène*
⚓   *Calanque de Figuerolles*
⚓   *Anse du Sec*
⚓   *Anse du Petit-Mugel*
⚓   *Anse du Grand-Mugel*
⚓   *Calanque St-Pierre (Ile Verte)*
⚓   *Calanque Seynerolles (Ile Verte)*
⚓   *Grande-Calanque (Ile Verte)*

79 Port de la Ciotat 3–2–2 page 297
Port des Capucins (or des
Flot Bleus) a small private
fishing harbour

80 Port de St-Jean 3–3–4 page 301

81 Port de St-Cyr-les-Lecques 3–3–2 page 302

**82 Port de la Madrague de
St-Cyr-les-Lecques** 3–4–4 page 305

⚓   *N of of Pointe des 3-Fours*
⚓   *Baie des Nations*

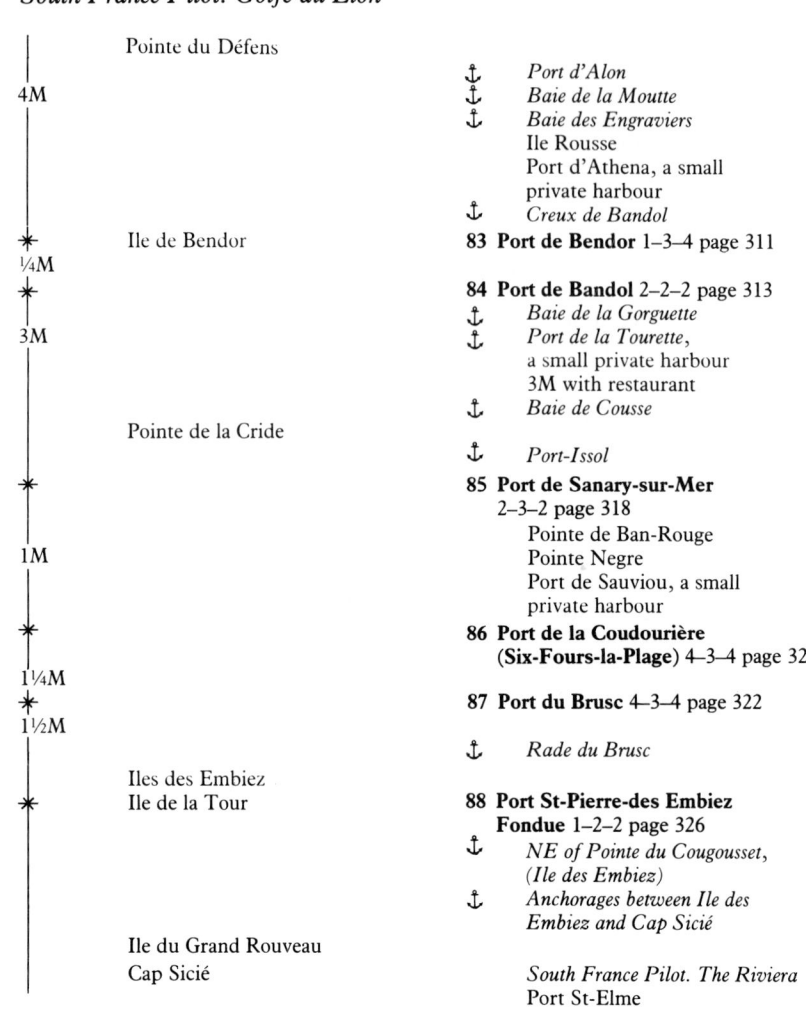

Pointe du Défens

4M

⚓ *Port d'Alon*
⚓ *Baie de la Moutte*
⚓ *Baie des Engraviers*
Ile Rousse
Port d'Athena, a small
private harbour
⚓ *Creux de Bandol*

✳ Ile de Bendor
¼M
✳
3M

83 Port de Bendor 1–3–4 page 311

84 Port de Bandol 2–2–2 page 313
⚓ *Baie de la Gorguette*
⚓ *Port de la Tourette*,
a small private harbour
3M with restaurant
⚓ *Baie de Cousse*

Pointe de la Cride

⚓ *Port-Issol*

✳
85 Port de Sanary-sur-Mer
2–3–2 page 318
Pointe de Ban-Rouge
Pointe Negre
Port de Sauviou, a small
private harbour

1M

✳
86 Port de la Coudourière
(Six-Fours-la-Plage) 4–3–4 page 321

1¼M
✳
1½M

87 Port du Brusc 4–3–4 page 322

⚓ *Rade du Brusc*

✳ Iles des Embiez
Ile de la Tour

88 Port St-Pierre-des Embiez
Fondue 1–2–2 page 326
⚓ *NE of Pointe du Cougousset,*
(Ile des Embiez)
⚓ *Anchorages between Ile des*
Embiez and Cap Sicié

Ile du Grand Rouveau
Cap Sicié

South France Pilot. The Riviera
Port St-Elme

Pilotage

Golfe de Fos

General

This gulf 4M wide and 6M deep lies between the mouth of the Grand Rhône and Cap Couronne. It accommodates the huge new commercial Port de Fos, the older commercial harbours of Port de Bouc, Saint-Louis-du-Rhône and Lauron, the fishing harbour of Carteau and the two yacht harbours of Carro and Saint-Gervais. Saint-Louis and Port de Bouc also have small yacht harbours inside the main port.

Saint-Louis has direct access to the Rhône via a lock, Port de Bouc offers access to the Etang de Berre via the Canal de Caronte, and the Canal d'Arles à Fos enters Darse No.1 of the Port de Fos. This canal enters the Rhône at Arles.

There are several anchorages around the gulf, especially on the hilly E side. The NW, N and NE sides have a large number of commercial and petrochemical concerns. The W and NW sides are very flat and low and the coast is difficult to distinguish in poor visibility.

Charts Admiralty 3498
French 6684

Warning

The banks around the mouth of the Rhône are extending by about 50m a year. There are restricted areas off Port de Bouc and Cap Couronne, see chart. On no account attempt to enter the mouth of the Rhône or, having descended the river, to enter the Mediterranean by this route. There are many unmarked shallows.

Depths

Sound carefully as there is much silting in the Golfe de Fos.

Blue and white hanger

Seas Strong SE–S–SW winds send in heavy seas, especially the SE wind off Cap Couronne.

Currents The S outflow from the mouth of the Rhône extends several miles to SE and with a NW wind creates an E flow across the mouth of the gulf.

⚓ Mouillage de Carteau

A spacious anchorage behind the They de la Gracieuse, well protected from seas from all directions except strong NE winds. The coast is low and flat and virtually deserted. Anchor in 6m sand and mud 1M to SE of the head of the Digue Saint-Louis or further inshore as draught permits.

---

43 PORT DE CARTEAU
13230 Bouches du Rhône

Position 43°23'·1N 4°52'·2E
Minimum depth in the entrance 3m (9·84ft)
in the harbour 6·3 to 0m (20·5 to 0ft)
Width of the entrance canal 80m
Population 20 (approx)
Rating 4–4–5

General

This small undeveloped fishing harbour is located in one of the old channels of the Grand Rhône delta. It is approached by a 1M dredged channel and offers good protection from all directions. Approach is easy but the entrance requires care and good visibility. Local facilities are non-existent but normal supplies and facilities are available at St-Louis-du-Rhône 2M away. This harbour would attract those who would like to get away from the normal type of yacht harbour.

Port de Carteau. Outer buoys and canal looking SW

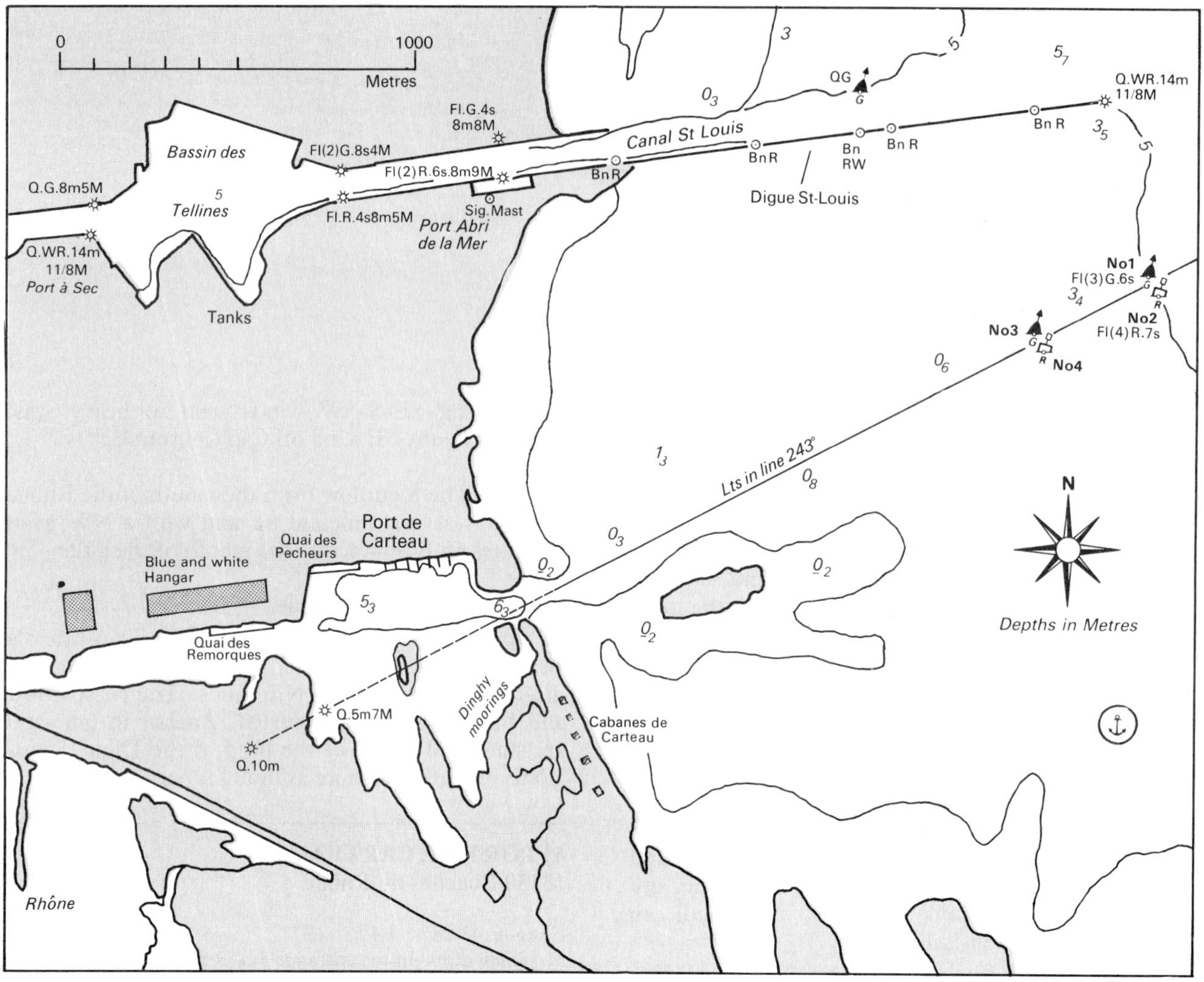

Port de Carteau

Data

Charts Admiralty 2164, 3498
French 6684
Navicarte 505, 507

Magnetic variation 1°59′W (1994) decreasing by about 6′
each year.

Marine radiobeacons Cap Couronne CR(—·—·/·—·)
295·5kHz 50M

Lights
Canal St-Louis Digue St-Louis head Q.WR.14m11/8M
White tower and cupola 072°-W-267.5°-R-072°
Port de Carteau. Leading lights 243° *Front*: Q.W.5m7M
Rear: 277m from front Q.W.10m. White pylons

Buoys Entrance to dredged channel. Outer pair: green
conical buoy, conical topmark, No.1, and red can buoy,
can topmark, No.2. Inner pair: 400m WSW similar to
outer pair but numbered 3 and 4. The outer pair may be
lit.

Currents An outgoing current of up to 2 knots may be
experienced in the entrance with N–NW winds, and an
ingoing current of up to 1·5 knots with E–SE winds.

Warnings

Considerable development is taking place in the area
and changes are to be expected. There may be a
number of large ships in the approach which have
right of way. Deep-draught ships show 3F.R(vert)
plus 3F.W(vert) plus black ball over black cylinder.

Leading marks/lights *Blue and white hanger* *Quay*

Port de Carteau, looking SW–W–NW

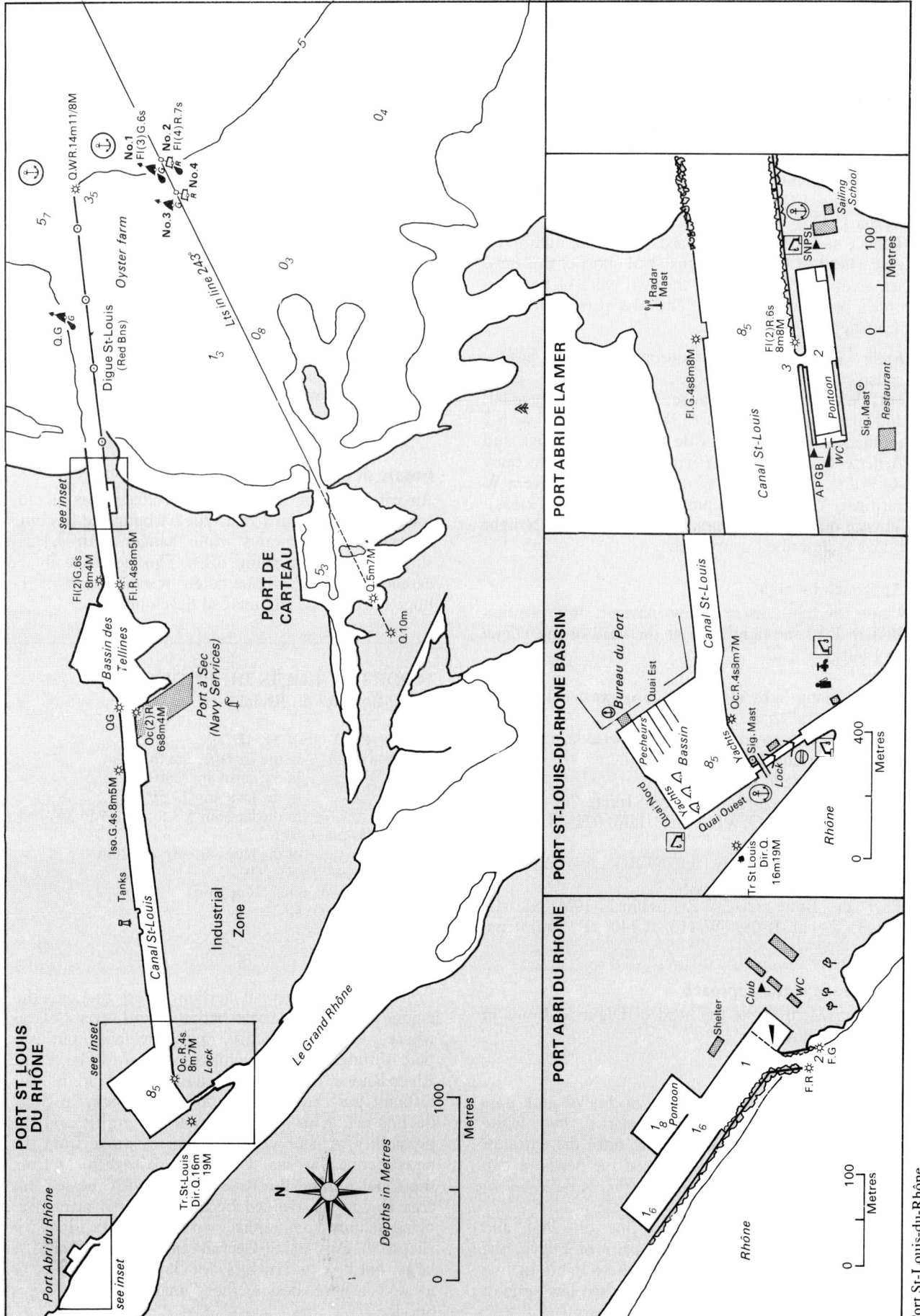

PORT ST LOUIS DU RHÔNE

Port Abri du Rhône

see inset

see inset

Tr. St-Louis
Dir.Q.16m 19M

Oc.R.4s.
8m 7M
Lock

Iso.G.4s.8m5M

Canal St-Louis

Tanks

QG

Oc(2)R
6s8m4M

Port à Sec
(Navy Services)

Bassin des
Tellines

Fl(2)G.6s
8m4M

Fl.R.4s8m5M

see inset

Industrial
Zone

Le Grand Rhône

**PORT DE
CARTEAU**

Q.5m7M

Q.10m

N

Depths in Metres

Metres

QWR.14m11/8M

No.1
Fl(3)G.6s

No.2
Fl(4)R.7s

No.3

No.4

Q.G

Digue St-Louis
(Red Bns)

Oyster farm

Lts in line 243°

PORT ABRI DU RHONE

Rhône

Pontoon

Shelter

Club

WC

F.R
F.G

Metres

Port St-Louis-du-Rhône

PORT ST-LOUIS-DU-RHONE BASSIN

Bureau du Port

Quai Nord

Quai Est

Pecheurs

Yachts

Bassin

Yachts

Quai Ouest

Sig.Mast

Lock

Oc.R.4s3m7M

Canal St-Louis

Tr St Louis
Dir.Q.
16m19M

Rhône

Metres

PORT ABRI DE LA MER

Radar
Mast

Fl.G.4s8m8M

Canal St-Louis

Fl(2)R.6s
8m8M

Pontoon

APGB

WC

Sig.Mast

Restaurant

SNPSL

Sailing
School

Metres

199

Approach by day

From SW Round the mouth of the Grand Rhône keeping outside the two S cardinal buoys, YB with ⚑ topmarks; Roustan E buoy is a light buoy (Q(6)+LFl.15s), and W buoy is a bell buoy, R then outside the following light buoys (see general chart page 199):

Balancelle E cardinal, BYB with ♦ topmark, VQ(3)5s; Annibal Est as above but Q(3)10s; GE as above but VQ(3)5s; GN N cardinal, BY with ⬥ topmark, Q.

Thence set a W course towards the white lighthouse at the head of Digue St-Louis. ¾M short of this head set a course 243° towards the two pairs of entrance buoys sounding carefully. The first pair of buoys is near the 5m depth contour.

From E Round Cap Couronne which has a conspicuous white lighthouse with a red top. Keep outside the restricted area (see general chart page 00) and then pass outside Carro W cardinal, YBY with ⬥ topmark, light and whistle buoy (VQ(9)10s) and Arnette W cardinal, YBY with ⬥ topmark, light buoy (Q(9)15s). Then in a NW direction to the Lavéra W cardinal, YBY with ⬥ topmark, light buoy (Q(9)15s). Thence on a WNW course outside GE and GN light buoys as described in approach.

Approach by night

Using the lights listed below, navigate to a position ¾M to E of the lighthouse at the head of the Digue St-Louis.

Notes

1. The many light buoys will also assist navigation. (See general chart.)
2. The three sectored lights give a useful lead into the area and valuable intersections.

Faraman Fl(2)W.10s41m23M

Tour St-Louis DirQ.W.16m19M Intens 262°-265°

Digue St-Louis Q.WR.14m11/18M 072°-W-267·5°-R-072°

Pointe de St-Gervais IQ(7)WRG.12s45m25-21M. 323°-G-340°-W-348°-R-007°

Port de Bouc Oc(2)WRG.6s30m13-10M 321°-G-343°-W-040°-R-087°-W-112°-R-140° R (unintens) 140°-230°

Anchorage in the approach

Anchor 1M to SE of the head of Digue St-Louis in 6m sand and mud.

Entrance

By day Locate the two pairs of buoys and pass between keeping the leading marks, two white latticework towers in line on 243° until the entrance to the harbour which lies between the heads of two low spits of land is reached.

By night Bring two Qs into line on 243° and approach passing between two pairs of buoys, the first of which may be lit. Keep these lights in line until the harbour entrance between two low spits of land has been passed.

Berths

There are no specific yacht berths but one may be found on the fishermen's quay with their permission.

Anchorage

Just inside the harbour on the starboard hand in 6m mud clear of the entrance channel. Careful sounding is advised.

Formalities

None.

Harbour charges

None for a short visit.

Facilities

Hard Rough hard of sand, stones and mud at NE side of harbour.

Water Perhaps available from fishermen's shacks.

Provisions Only available from St-Louis-du-Rhône 2·5M (see page 197).

Future development

An earth-moving and dredging concern has already established itself further up the harbour and has built a very large grey and white hangar with a quay suitable for ocean-going tugs. This could easily be extended or the harbour taken over as a part of the huge Port de Fos commercial development.

---

44 PORT ST-LOUIS-DU-RHONE
13230 Bouches du Rhône

Position 43°23'·3N 4°51'·1E
Minimum depth in the entrance 2m (6·6ft)
in the canal 8m (26ft)
in the lock 4m (14·5ft)
in the harbour 5·8 to 1m (19 to 3ft)
Width of the canal 60m
of the harbour entrance 20m
Number of yacht berths 260
Maximum length overall 14m (46ft)
Population (1990) 8,624
Rating 4–3–4

General

Primarily a commercial harbour, Port St-Louis-du-Rhône also has two yacht harbours and several places where yachts may secure, being the most southerly port through which yachts can enter or leave the River Rhône. The approach and entrance are not too difficult but careful navigation is necessary in Golfe de Fos owing to shoals, commercial traffic and the possibility of poor visibility due to smoke from the petrochemical works. Unless on passage to or from the canal linking the River Rhône with the sea this area should be avoided because it is not attractive, being mainly commercial, with limited facilities for yachts in Port de St-Gervais and Port de Bouc. A large hard with hangars for laying up yachts is located ashore beside the Canal St-Louis (Navy Service).

Data

Charts Admiralty 2164, 3498
French 6693
Spanish 49
Navicarte Nos 505, 507

Magnetic variation 2°11′W (1994) decreasing by about 6′ each year.

Marine radiobeacons Cap Couronne CR($-\cdot-\cdot/\cdot-\cdot$) 295·5kHz 50M. Continuous.

Port radio and pilots Port call on Ch 16, work on Ch 30. Pilots call on Ch 16 and work on 14.

Traffic signals Shown from a latticework mast to SW of the canal yacht harbour and from a mast located in the SW corner of the Bassin Commercial.

By day	By night	Meaning
Red flag	Red light	Entrance prohibited
Green flag	Green light	Exit prohibited
Red over green flag	Red over green light	Entrance and exit prohibited.

Shown from each end of lock:

Day and night	Meaning
Two red lights	Access forbidden, lock closed
One red and one green light	Access forbidden, lock opening
Two green lights	Access allowed, lock open

Shown from mast at N side of entrance to Port de Fos and from a mast at Port de Bouc:

Day and night	Meaning
One white light between two red lights	Keep clear of all channels as deep-draught vessel is approaching

Lights
Canal St-Louis Jetée Sud head Q.WR.14m11/8M White tower and cupola 072°-W-267.5°-R-072°
Tour St-Louis DirQ.W.16m19M Grey square tower, red top Intens 262°-265°
Port de Carteau leading lights 243° *Front*: Q.W.5m7M *Rear*: 227m from front Q.W.10m White pylons

Port St-Louis-du-Rhône. Entrance to Canal St-Louis looking W

Port St-Louis-du-Rhône. Harbour at E end of Canal St-Louis looking S

In the canal
N side
Green conical light buoy, ▲ topmark, Q.G
No.1 Fl.G.4s8m8M Green pylon marked I 264°-vis-144°
No.3 E Fl(2)G.6s8m4M White column, green top
No.3 W QG.8m5M White column, green top
No.5 Iso.G.4s8m5M White column, green top
S side
Q.WR.14m11/8M White tower and cupola
No.2 Fl(2)R.6s8m8M Red pylon marked 2
No.4 Fl.R.4s8m5M White column, red top
No.6 Oc(2)R.6s8m4M White column, red top
No.8 Oc.R.4s8m7M Red pylon 080°-vis-268°

Buoys There are numerous buoys in the Golfe de Fos which are best seen from the chart, the majority are light buoys. Due to developments, they are sometimes altered.

Beacons A small beacon tower marks the head of the underwater section of training bank on the N side of the Canal St-Louis entrance and there are four beacons, can topmarks, along the Jetée St-Louis. The delta of the River Rhône has a series of radarbeacons along the coast.

Currents In River Rhône 1 to 3 knots, in canal 1 knot, E-going.

Levels In the canal the water level drops as much as 0·5m in N to NW winds and can rise up to 0·5m in SE winds.

Warnings
On no account should an attempt be made to enter or leave the River Rhône by its mouth. There is a dangerous bar with constantly shifting sandbanks and shoals and this area is not buoyed. Care should be taken to keep well clear of the They de la Gracieuse, a long low inconspicuous sandbank which extends 5M to NE of the mouth of the River Rhône.

Large vessels that cannot leave the dredged channels show a black ball over a black cylinder and three white lights by day, and three red lights and three white lights by night both vertically. Considerable development is taking place around the new Port de Fos and its approaches, and buoys are

Buoy *Arnette*

frequently moved. Because the surrounding area is very flat the NW *mistral* is very strong and makes manoeuvring difficult. Industrial haze or fog is often present.

Approach by day

From SW Round the mouth of the Grand Rhône keeping to the S of two S cardinal buoys, YB with ▼ topmarks; the W buoy is a bell buoy marked R and the E buoy a light buoy marked Roustan (Q(6)+LFl.15s), then pass to E of the following buoys:

Balancelle E cardinal, BYB with ♦ topmark, VQ(3)5s;

Annibal Est as above but Q(3)10s;

GE as above but VQ(3)5s.

Then to the N of GN N cardinal light buoy, BY with ▲ topmark, Q. From here the white lighthouse (Q.WR.14m11/8M) on the head of the Jetée St-Louis at the entrance of the Canal St-Louis will be seen. Set a W course towards it.

From E Round Cap Couronne which has a conspicuous white lighthouse with a red top on the headland. Keep over 800m to S of this lighthouse to avoid a restricted area (see general chart). Then pass to W of Carro W cardinal, YBY with ⟨ topmark, light and whistle buoy (VQ(9)10s) and also the similar Arnette light buoy (Q(9)15s). Proceed in a NW direction to Lavéra W cardinal, YBY with ⟨ topmark, light buoy (Q(9)15s). Thence on a WNW course to N of GE and GN light buoys as described in *Approach by day. From SW*.

Approach by night

Using the lights listed below, navigate to a position ¾M to E of the lighthouse at the head of Jetée St-Louis.

1. There are many light buoys which will also assist the navigator (see general chart).
2. There are three sectored lights which give a useful lead into the area and provide helpful intersections.

Faraman Fl(2)W.10s41m23M

Tour St-Louis DirQ.W.16m19M Intens 262°-265°

Jetée Sud St-Louis Q.WR.12s14m11/8M 072°-W-267·5°-R-072°

Pointe de St-Gervais IQ(7)WRG.12s45m25-21M 323°-G-340°-W-348°-R-007°

Port de Bouc Oc(2)WRG.6s30m13-10M 321°-G-343°-W-040°-R-087°-W-112°-R-140° R (unintens) 140°-230°

Port Abri du Rhône

Port St-Louis-du-Rhône looking NE.

R. Rhône   *Entrance to lock*   *Quay and yard*

Port St Louis-du-Rhône. Entrance to lock, looking NW

Canal   *Lock/bridge*

Port St Louis-du-Rhône Basin and canal, looking E

Port St Louis-du-Rhône. Port Abri du Rhône, looking NW

Anchorage in the approach

Anchor 200m to SE or NE of head of Jetée Sud St-Louis in 5m mud, or in spacious Mouillage de Carteau 1M to SE of the head of Jetée Sud St-Louis in 6m sand and mud.

Entrance from sea

By day Approach on 260° with the Jetée Sud St-Louis in line, leave the head of this jetty with its white light tower 20m to port and follow its line at this distance.

By night Approach on 260° with white light at Jetée Sud St-Louis head (Q.WR.14m11/8M) in line with the directional light on Tour St-Louis (DirQ.W), leave Jetée Sud St-Louis head 20m to port and keep between pairs of red and green lights as listed above. Note the white intensive boundary of light at Tour de St-Louis is 262°-265°.

Entrance from river

By day Follow the E bank southwards at 50m, prepare to turn 160° shortly after passing the Tour St-Louis into the entrance to the lock. Do not cut the corner as underwater obstructions extend some 30m from the point.

By night This is not advised.

Lock The lock is manned 0500–2100 but is normally only opened for commercial traffic (☎ 42 86 02 04). Strong currents may be experienced in the lock.

Berths

In the canal St-Louis

1. Alongside S bank just to W of entrance to the canal yacht harbour in 4m mud. Care is needed due to the wash made by large ships passing.
2. In the Port Abri de la Mer (Port de Plaisance de Carteau) in 2m. There are 40 berths here and the harbour is very crowded. Do not mistake this harbour for the real Port de Carteau (see page 00). Maximum length overall 10m.
3. On the S bank of the canal just short of Bassin Commercial near or alongside a barge in 4m. Apply to the *bureau du port*.
4. Port à Sec (Navy Service). Very large hard standings both open (30,000m²) and covered (20,000m²) plus quays for 23 yachts up to 90m and catamarans up to 12m. Supermarket, workshops etc. available. Located on S side of the Canal St-Louis opposite Bassin des Tellines. Phone (☎ 42 86 39 80) for reservations and terms.

In the harbour and nearby

5. Probably the best place is alongside the quay just to SE of the lock and alongside the small yard either side of the tall yellow crane is the best area.
6. Alongside the E bank of the Rhône level with the lock, do not go too far upstream as there are projecting stones with dolphins. River barges normally secure here. With permission lie alongside one.

7. In the river yacht harbour (Port Abri du Rhône). Apply to the guardian (mornings only) for a vacant berth in 2–1·5m. There are 80 berths here and the harbour is usually very crowded.

In the Bassin Commercial Yachts may berth to pontoons according to length (see plan) obtain permission of the *bureau du port* usually on the NW and SE sides on the new pontoons.

Prohibited anchorages

Anchoring in or near a dredged channel is not permitted.

Formalities

If near Bassin Commercial report to the *bureau de port* (☎ 42 86 09 63) which is to the NE side of the lock. If at the yacht harbours report to the guardians, open 0900–1800. The customs office (☎ 42 06 22 26, 42 06 63 39, 42 86 39 59) is to the W of the lock. The lock-keeper requires duplicate copies of yachts' particulars and will wish to examine or collect the necessary documents from those entering or leaving the river. Lock control office (☎ 42 86 02 04) open 0500–2100.

Charges

There are harbour charges and in the canal yacht harbour there are club charges. The first two hours are free.

Facilities

Slips There are small slips in each yacht harbour.

Slipways One small slipway in each yacht harbour, maximum length 12m overall.

Dry docks 25m length overall, 9m beam at Navy Service (Port à Sec).

Cranes A small crane (6 tonnes) in the Port Abri-de-le Mer, a number in the Bassin Commercial of up to 8 tonnes, and one at the yard for masting/demasting.

Travel-lift 50 tonne at Navy Service (Port à Sec).

Fuel Pumps for diesel and petrol are beside the quay below the lock but are out of action (1986). Fuel can be delivered by tanker lorries (☎ 42 86 11 32).

Water In the canal yacht harbour from a tap near the hard. Also at the lock, from the quays in the Bassin Commercial and at the River Yacht Harbour.

Provisions From shops to the NW of Bassin Commercial, and a small supermarket near the yard.

Garbage A few rubbish sacks at yacht harbours.

Chandlery A limited amount from two shops in the town.

Repairs Two shipyards, one by the lock and the other at the river yacht harbour, can carry out repairs to hull and engines.

Post office In St-Louis.

Hotels There are six hotels, one overlooking the river.

Restaurants There are 22, and a number of café/bars.

Yacht clubs The Société Nautique de Port St-Louis (SNPSL) has a clubhouse at the E end of the canal yacht harbour with shower and lounge (☎ 42 86 02 04) open 0800–1800.

Information office Located at the *mairie* on Quai Bonnardel (☎ 42 86 90 00 and 42 86 01 21).

Lifeboat There is a lifeboat stationed here.

Beaches There are some rather muddy beaches either side of the entrance to the Golfe de Fos.

Communications Rail and bus services. River services to Arles and Lyon. Sea services to North Africa and Mediterranean ports.

Visits The Musée la Mer Fortress and the old town are worth a visit.

History

The Tower St-Louis was built in 1837 and the Canal St-Louis was dug in 1871. The harbour was opened in 1881.

Port de Fos/Canal d'Arles à Fos

This huge commercial harbour which has several entrances to NW of the Golfe de Fos should not be confused with Port de St-Gervais which is sometimes referred to as Port de Fos. This commercial harbour is not for yachts; however, the entrance to the Canal d'Arles à Port de Bouc lies at the NW end of Darse No.1 and yachts are permitted to pass through this *darse*, always provided that they do not interfere with the movement of commercial shipping. The Canal d'Arles à Port de Bouc is the old Canal d'Arles à Fos, which has been enlarged to take ships of up to 5000 tonnes. It is an alternative route to the entrance at St-Louis-du-Rhône and bypasses the lower reaches of the Rhône.

45 PORT DE SAINT-GERVAIS (PORT DE FOS-SUR-MER)

13270 Bouches du Rhône

Position 43°25'·6N 4°56'·5E
Minimum depth   in the entrance 3m (9·84ft)
                  in the harbour 3·0 to 1·5m (9·84 to 5ft)
Width of the entrance 40m
Maximum length overall 17m (56ft)
Number of yacht berths 612
Population 12119
Rating 2–2–3

General

A pleasant small yacht harbour located near the attractive old village of Fos but unfortunately also near a huge petrochemical works. Easy to approach and enter and there is good protection inside. Fair facilities at the harbour and in the village.

Data

Charts   Admiralty 2164, 3498
           French 6684, 6767
           Spanish 49
           Navicarte 505, 507

Magnetic variation 1°59'W (1994) decreasing by about 6' each year.

Marine radiobeacons Cap Couronne   CR(—·—·/·—·)
295·5kHz 50M

Lights
Pointe de St-Gervais IQ(7)WRG.12s45m25-21M Black framework tower 323°-G-340°-W-348°-R-007°
St-Gervais Digue Sud head Fl.G.4s7m White pylon, green top

Buoys A line of three yellow can buoys and a line of two yellow conical buoys mark the entrance channel.

Port radio VHF Ch 09, 16, 12.

Weather forecast Posted daily at *bureau du port* which also has a wind speed meter. Recorded forecast (☎ 35 65 08 13)

Warnings

Large commercial ships have right of way in the gulf. Deep-laden ships display 3F.R(vert)+3F.W(vert)+ black ball over black cylinder.

Approach by day

From W Pass the mouth of the Rhône outside the two S cardinal buoys, YB with ▼ topmarks; the E buoy Roustan is a light buoy (Q(6)+LFl.15s) and the W buoy R is a bell buoy. Then continue on an ENE course passing outside Balancelle E cardinal light buoy, BYB with ♦ topmark, VQ(3)5s. When near the middle of the gulf, steer due N towards the head of the gulf. The conspicuous tall concrete light tower (45m) at Pointe de St-Gervais is easily recognised, steer towards it.

From E Round Cap Couronne which has a conspicuous white lighthouse with a red top, keep outside the restricted area (see general chart) and then pass outside Carro W cardinal, YBY with ✕

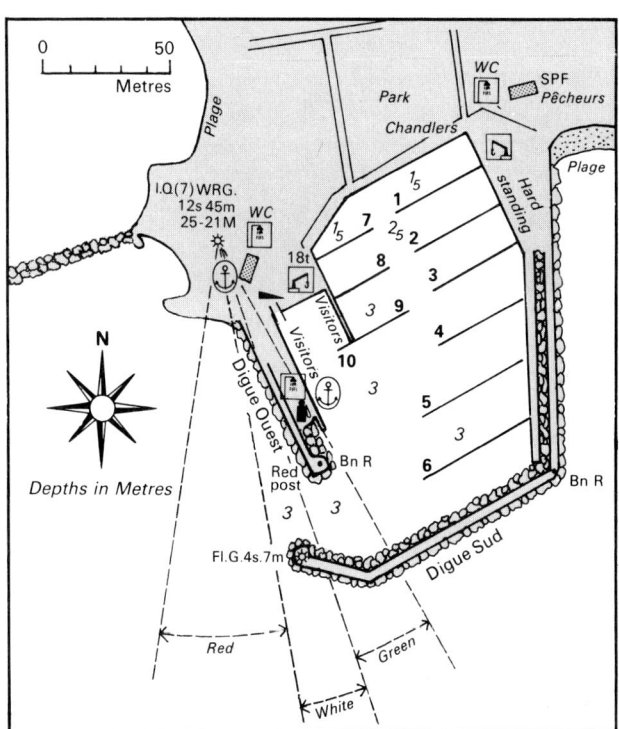

Port de St-Gervais

Conspicuous tall lighthouse

Port de St-Gervais (Fos-sur-Mer) looking N

Lighthouse   *Bureau du port*   *Entrance*

Port de St-Gervais (Fos-sur-Mer). Entrance looking N.

topmark, light and whistle buoy (VQ(9)10s) and Arnette W cardinal, YBY with ⚑ topmark, light buoy (Q(9)15s). Thence onto a NW course towards the centre of the gulf. The conspicuous tall concrete light tower at Pointe de Saint-Gervais is easily recognised; steer towards it.

Approach by night

Use the following lights to obtain a position near the centre of the gulf and then follow the white sector towards Pointe de St-Gervais light:
Faraman Fl(2)W.10s41m23M
Tour St-Louis DirQ.W.16m19M Intens 262°-265°

Jetée Sud St-Louis Q.WR.14m11/8M 072°-W-267·5°-R-072°
Pointe de St-Gervais IQ(7)WRG.12s45m25-21M 323°-G-340°-W-348°-R-007°
Port de Bouc Oc(2)WRG.6s30m13-10M 321°-G-343°-W-040°-R-087°-W-112°-R-140° R (unintens) 140°-230°

Anchorage in the approach

Anchor 300m NW of harbour entrance in 4m mud and sand.

Entrance

By day Approach the head of Digue Sud, leave it 15m to starboard, round it on to an E course and enter rounding the head of Digue Ouest at 15m and leaving it to port. Keep between yellow can and conical buoys. Secure near the *bureau du port* on the inner side of the Digue Ouest near its head.

By night Approach IQ(7)WRG.12s45m25-21M in the white sector and in the closer approach a Fl.G.4s7m will be seen, approach this and round it leaving it 15m to starboard and continue on an E course, then round the head of the Digue Ouest, unlit but with a red beacon, at 15m leaving it to port. Secure near the *bureau du port* on the inner side of this *digue* near its head.

Berths

A pontoon berth will be allocated by the *bureau du port*, usually in the W section of the harbour.

Formalities

Report to the *bureau du port*, open 24 hours a day, on the Digue Ouest (☎ 42 06 21 01 and 42 06 21 02). Customs at Port de Bouc (☎ 42 06 21 35).

Harbour charges

These are made.

Facilities

Hard Hard standing to NE.

Slip NW corner of the harbour.

Crane An 18-tonne semimobile crane in NW corner of the harbour and two small slips.

Fuel Diesel and petrol pumps on Digue Ouest near its head open winter 0800–1130, 1400–1700 and summer 0800–1200 and 1400–1800.

Water Taps on quays and pontoons.

Electricity Outlets 220v AC 10 amps on quays and pontoons.

Telephone Several public telephone boxes.

Garbage Rubbish containers near roots of pontoons.

Provisions Small local shops, more in Fos-sur-Mer ¼M to N.

Ice Available at *bureau du port* and in village during the season.

Chandler One shop near the harbour and one 1½M to N at Les Carabins.

Repairs Two yards can carry out normal repairs to yachts and engines, the one beside the harbour can also carry out electronic repairs. The other yard is located 1½M to N at Les Carabins.

Yacht clubs Centre Fossén de Voile (☎ 42 05 32 90), Club de Voile de Fos-sur-Mer (CFV), a dinghy club (☎ 42 50 70 33), and Société de Pêcheurs de Fos (SFP) with small clubhouse to NE of harbour (☎ 42 05 41 21).

Showers/WCs Seven by *bureau du port* and two to N of the harbour.

Laundrette In the village.

Post office In the village.

Hotels One ***, five **, two * and some unclassified.

Restaurants Four beside the harbour, others in the village.

Information office At Fos-sur-Mer (☎ 42 47 71 90).

Visits The old buildings in the village are worth a visit and there is a museum in the chapel.

Beaches Rather muddy sandy beach to E of the harbour.

Future development

Because the harbour is already full, expansion is planned to W of the harbour.

History

An old Roman harbour of the first century BC. It was an important town in VII to XII centuries and the vast petro-chemical industries of today have restored this ancient importance.

---

46 PORT DE BOUC

13110 Bouches du Rhône

Position 43°23'·6N 4°59'·2E
Minimum depth in the entrance 13·4m (44ft)
in the harbour 8 to 1m (26 to 3ft)
Width of the entrance 200m
of the inner entrance 80m
Number of yacht berths 600
Maximum length overall 16m (52ft)
Population 14,080
Rating 4–3–2

General

A large and busy commercial port with numerous berths for petrol tankers. A large modern yacht harbour is located near the town. There is a small harbour for fishing boats and yachts just inside the main entrance to the port which is also in constant use by pilot boats and tugs. Approach and entrance require some care owing to the traffic and a confusing number of buoys and lights. This port is connected to the Etang de Berre by the Canal de Caronte and to the Canal d'Arles à Port de Bouc. Facilities are good and major repairs can be undertaken. The commercial harbours, Anse Aubran, Port pétrolier de Lavéra, and the small harbour to E of Fort de Bouc should only be entered in an emergency.

Data

Charts Admiralty 2164, 3498
French 6907
Spanish 49
Navicarte 505, 507

Magnetic variation 1°59'W (1994) decreasing by about 6' each year.

New yacht harbour   *Canal de Bouc à Fos*   *Canal de Caronte*

Port de Bouc, looking N–NE

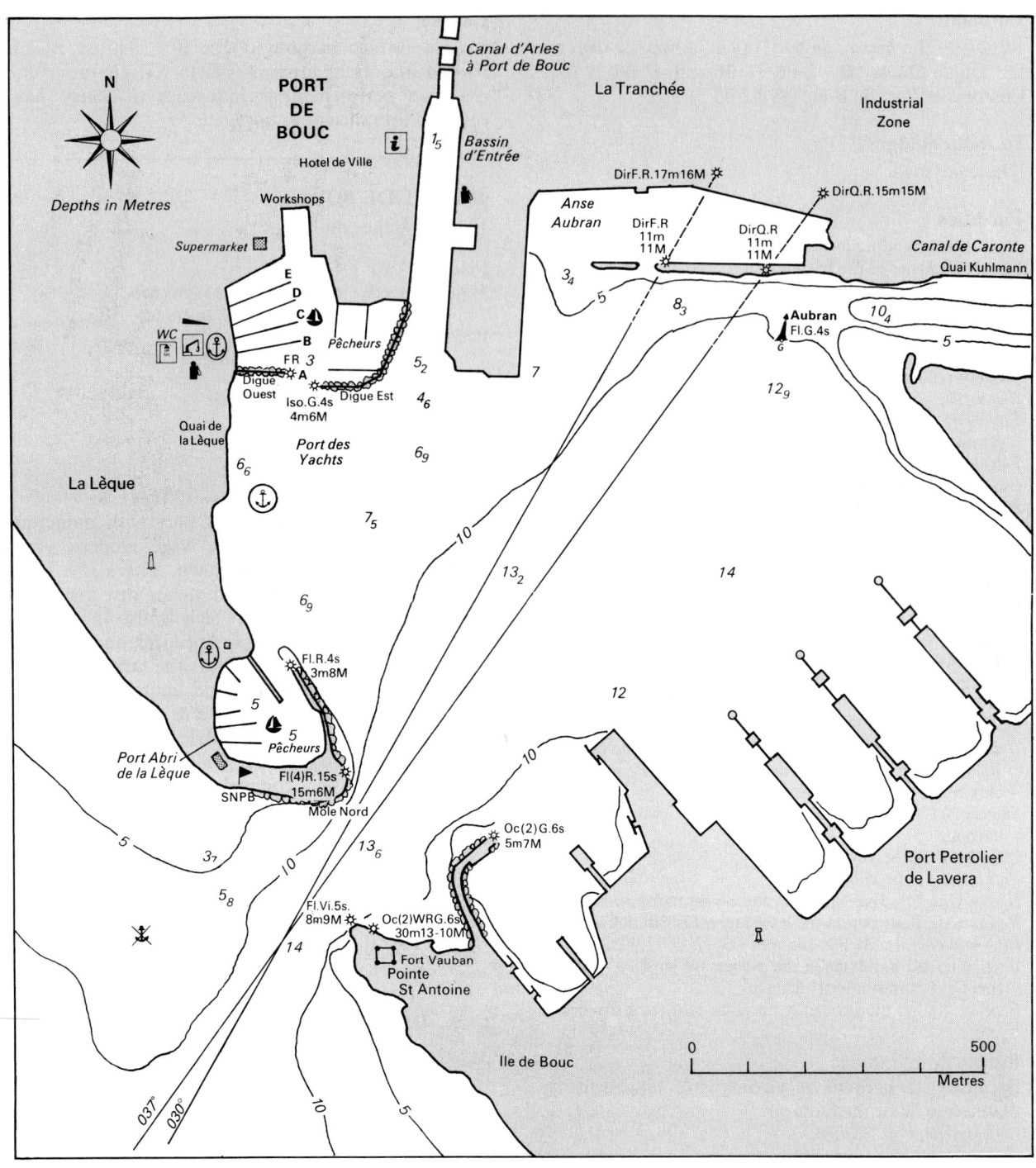

Port de Bouc

Marine radiobeacons Cap Couronne CR(— · — · / · — ·)
295·5kHz 50M Continuous.

Port radio Call on VHF Ch 16, work on Ch 9, 12, 0700 to
2100 hours only (local time), Pilots Ch 09.

Lights

Pointe de St-Gervais IQ(7)WRG.12s45m25-21M Black
framework tower 323°-G-340°-W-348°-R-007°

Fort On S side of entrance Oc(2)WRG.6s30m13-10M Grey
turret on a white square tower, red gallery 321°-G-343°-
W-040°-R-087°-W-112°-R-140° R (unintens) 140°-230°
F.W light is shown from a tower 4¼M NW

Pointe Saint-Antoine Fl.Vi.5s8m9M White column, dark
green top.

Môle Nord head Fl(4)R.15s15m6M Red pylon
E leading lights 037° *Front*: DirQ.R.11m11M White
oblong, red stripe on red pylon, intens 035°-039° *Rear*:
167m from front DirQ.R.15m15M White oblong, orange
stripe on red pylon, intens 026°-048°.
W leading lights 030° *Front*: DirF.R.11m11M Black
oblong, yellow stripe, red and white pylon, intens 020°-
040° *Rear*: 184m from front DirF.R.17m16M White
oblong, yellow stripe, intens 019°-041°
Commercial Basin Môle head Oc(2)G.6s5m7M White
pylon, dark green top
Port Abri de la Lèque. (Yacht/fishing basin) Môle head
Fl.R.4s3m8M White hut with red top
Port des Yachts Digue Est head Iso.G.4s4m6M
Port des Yachts Digue Ouest head. F.R.

Bureau du port

Port de Bouc. Entrance looking NE

W set   Front   Rear   *E set in line*

Port de Bouc. Leading marks

Currents Currents in the entrance and in the Canal de Caronte are very variable, being subject not only to prevalent and recent winds but also to the river outflow from the power station and factories. The current is normally outgoing and can reach 4 knots.

Warnings

There are a number of unlit mooring buoys in the area. In SW winds there may be heavy seas just outside the entrance. Commercial shipping must be allowed unobstructed passage in this area. Much development is taking place.

Approach by day

From W Round the River Rhône delta at least 1M from the coast and outside the two S cardinal buoys, YB with ▼ topmarks; the W buoy is a whistle buoy marked R and the E a light buoy marked Roustan (Q(6)+ LFl.15s). Pass near Balancelle (VQ(3)5s) E cardinal, BYB with ▲ topmark, and Lavéra (Q(9)15s) W cardinal, YBY with ⟊ topmark, light buoys and then on 010° to Tasques red can light buoy, red square topmark (Iso.R.4s). From here the large square tower on Fort de Bouc on the SE side of the entrance and the tall block of the harbour offices (*capitainerie*) some 600m to NW of the entrance will be seen. Approach on 035° leaving Tasques to port.

Front   *Rear*

Port de Bouc. E set of leading marks

Bureau du port

Port de Bouc looking NE

Entrance

Port de Bouc. Approach to new yacht harbour, looking N

Port de Bouc. Entrance to old yacht harbour, looking SW

From E Round Cap Couronne which has a conspicuous white lighthouse with a red top on the headland. Keep over 800m to the S of this lighthouse to avoid the restricted area (see general chart). Then pass to W of Carro W cardinal, YBY with ⍊ topmark, light and whistle buoy (VQ(9)10s) and also the similar Arnette light buoy (Q(9)15s). Proceed in a NW direction to Lavéra W cardinal, YBY with ⍊ topmark, light buoy (Q(9)15s). A large electricity works with four tall red and white banded chimneys and a huge petrol refinery with flares will be passed on this stretch of coast. Keep the tall harbour building just to the W of the tower of Fort de Bouc.

Approach by night

The whole area is illuminated by the flares and lights of the many industrial concerns. There are many light buoys which are best seen from the chart (page 208). The major lights in the approaches are:
Faraman Fl(2)W.10s41m23M to the W of the Rhône Delta
Ile de Planier Fl.W.5s68m26M to the SW
Cap Couronne Fl.R.3s34m20M on the E side of the entrance to Golfe de Fos
  The light at Pointe de St-Gervais (IQ(7)WRG. 12s45m25-21M) and the Port de Bouc leading lights help in the close approach.

Anchorage in the approach

Anchor about 400m S of Fort de Bouc in 10m mud and sand. There is a restricted area ½M to S of the harbour entrance where anchoring is forbidden. See general chart and page 208.

Entrance

By day Enter on a heading of 035° between Fort de Bouc to starboard and Môle Nord head to port. There are two sets of leading marks on the far side of the harbour but they are difficult to see. The E set

on 037° has a white rectangle with an orange stripe on a red metalwork tower. The W on 031° has a yellow stripe on a black rectangle. When inside the harbour proceed on a N course and round the head of the *môle* protecting the Port Abri de la Lèque (Fl.R.4s3m8M) at 20m onto a S course. Watch out for tugs and pilot vessels leaving at speed, and proceed to NW corner of the main harbour where lies the yacht harbour. Enter between the head of Digue Est and that of Digue Ouest.

Berths

Secure stern-to pontoon with bow-to mooring buoy in a vacant space in the W part of Port Abri de la Lèque in 1·5-4m. This is an uncomfortable harbour due to the wash of passing boats and during a *mistral* it can become quite rough. It is far better to go to the Port des Yachts and to secure to a vacant berth on the first pontoon in 3m. An alternative is to lie alongside or outside a barge in the N end of the Bassin d'Entrée au Canal de Port de Bouc à Fos in 1·5-2·9m. A temporary berth is possible alongside a disused dredger on the Quai de la Lèque.

Anchorages

It is possible to anchor some 300m N of the entrance to Port Abri de la Lèque opposite the harbour office in 7m sand. Anchorage not permitted near commercial basins.

Prohibited anchorages

There is a large area about half a mile to the S of the entrance to the port where anchoring is forbidden (see chart).

Formalities

If in the Port Abri report to the guardian at the Société Nautique de Port de Bouc (☎ 42 09 20 18). If secured in the Port des Yachts report to the

Port de Bouc. Port des Yachts looking N

capitainerie on the W side (☎ 42 06 22 29). If secured elsewhere report to the *bureau du port* open 24 hours (☎ 42 06 38 50) on the Quai de la Lèque. Customs (☎ 42 06 21 35) are at rue Charles Nedellec.

Harbour charges

There are harbour charges.

Facilities

Slips Four slips, one on the W side of Port Abri.

Slipways There are a number of large slipways for commercial craft.

Cranes There are two small cranes in the Port Abri of 2 to 6 tonnes, and several in the commercial port with capacity of up to 12 tonnes, also a 16-tonne travel-lift.

Fuel Diesel and petrol are obtainable from pumps on the E side of Bassin d'Entrée au Canal de Port de Bouc à Fos or by tanker lorry (0800–1100 and 1500–2000).

Water From taps on pontoons and quays.

Electricity 220v AC 15-35 amps. Points on quays and pontoons.

Provisions Many shops in Port de Bouc on the N side of the harbour.

Garbage There are rubbish sacks near the clubhouse and at roots of pontoons.

Repairs The shipyards that work on commercial vessels may be of service to yachtsmen. In addition there are a number of firms who can carry out normal yacht repairs.

Post office In the town S of railway station.

Chandlers Two shops nearby have a limited supply.

Hotels One ★★ and seven others.

Restaurants Fourteen restaurants and many café/bars.

Showers Ten showers/WCs around the harbour.

Yacht club The Société Nautique de Port de Bouc (SNPB) has a small clubhouse to the W of Port Abri with bar, lounge, showers, etc. Visiting yachtsmen are welcome (☎ 42 09 20 18).

Lifeboat An all-weather type stationed here.

Information The Syndicat d'Initiative is located at the *mairie* (town hall) (☎ 42 06 26 15) to NE of the yacht harbour.

Information office The Syndicat d'Initiative is located at the *mairie* to W of Bassin d'Entrée au Canal de Port de Bouc à Fos and to NE of the Port des Yachts. This office can supply a useful map and history of the area (☎ 42 06 26 15).

Visits There are fine views of the Golfe de Fos and the surrounding area from the hills nearby. The Tour de Bouc (13th century) and inside the 17th-century fort (Fort Vauban) are worth a visit.

Beaches Those nearby are of poor quality.

Communications There are both rail and bus services from the town.

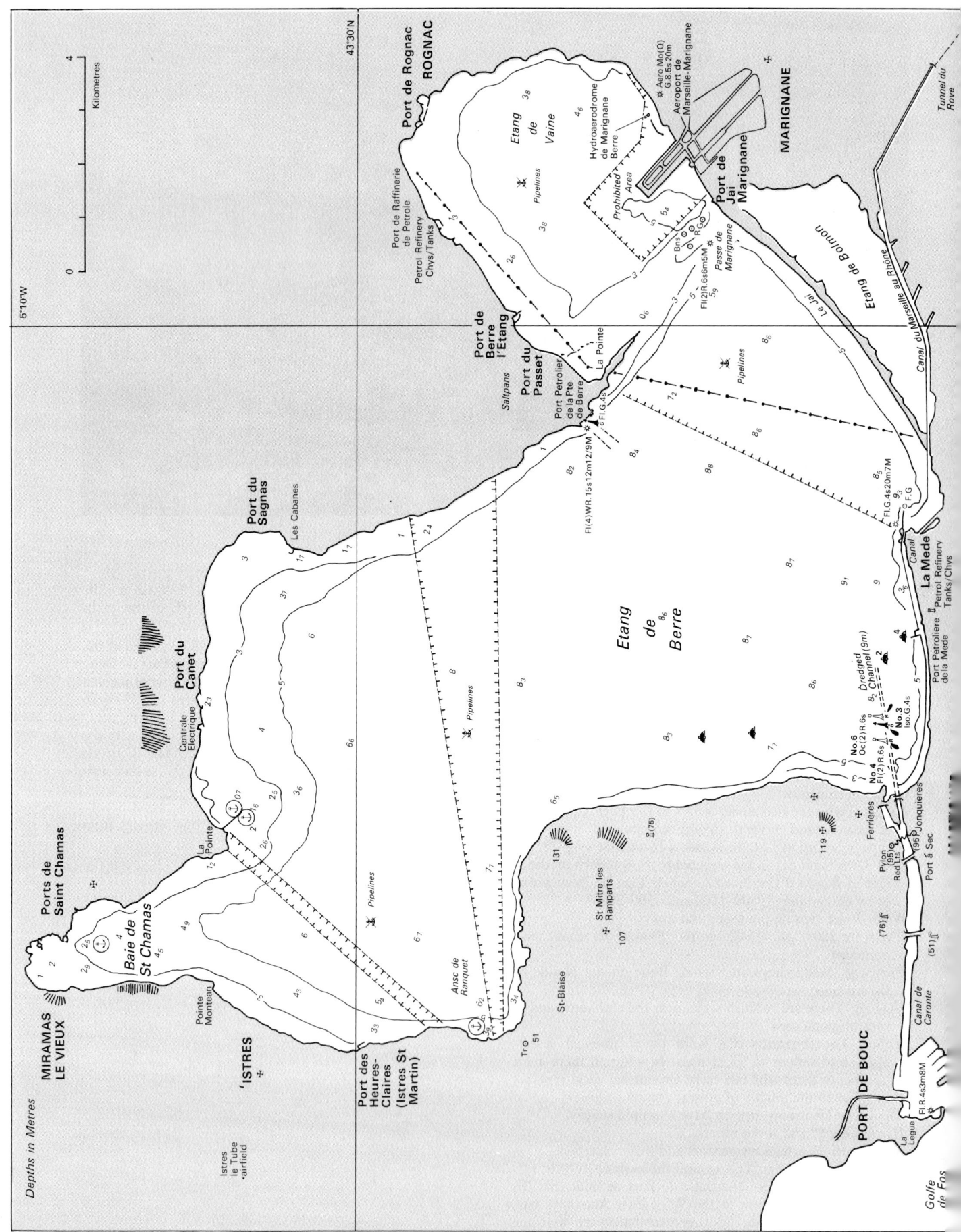

Depths in Metres

L'Etang de Berre

General

This huge salty inland lake of 15,000 hectares is over 9M long and 10M wide. It is entered through the Canal de Caronte, which runs from Port de Bouc to Martigues in the SW corner of the *étang*. Though parts have been ruined by commercial use, there being two huge petrochemical works, a power station, an airfield, an explosives factory and other factories in the area, there are still many parts of l'Etang de Berre which are pleasant to visit in a yacht. The coast to S and W is hilly, the rest is flat and there are few dangers to navigation apart from the shallows to the S of St-Chamas and those off Berre as well as the rocks Les Trois Frères which lie about 400m off the coast to the N of La Mède. There are depths of from 9–5m over almost the whole of the *étang* and these depths are decreasing by 1m every 60 years. The bottom being of weed and mud, it is possible to anchor virtually anywhere, but heavy anchors are recommended to cut through the weed. The villages around the area are very old and some date back thousands of years BC. In general this *étang* forms an excellent area for the not so experienced skipper and crew to practise under less arduous conditions than those found at sea.

Data

Charts   Admiralty 1705, 2164
French 6907
Spanish 49
Navicarte 505, 507

Magnetic variation 1°59′W (1994) decreasing by about 6′ each year.

Port radio Martigues VHF. Call on Ch 16, work on Ch 12.

Lights

Istres-le-Tubé Aero Mo(F)(··—·)W.4s59m23M Water tower

Port Pétrolier de la Pointe de Berre Jetée head Fl(4)WR.5s12m12/9M White pylon, red lantern 012°-W-057°-R-012°

Port de Berre-l'Etang W jetty head Fl.R.4s4m4M Hut

Marignane airfield Aero Mo(Q)(———·)G.8·5s20m House (43°26′·8N 5°13′·0E)

Passe de Marignane entrance. W side Fl(2)R.6s6m5M White dolphin, red lantern

Port de la Mède Les Trois Frères Fl.G.4s20m7M White tower, dark green top F.R and F.G lights along embankment

Port St-Chamas (neuf) entrance Fl.G.4s Metal pedestal

Port de Berre L'Etang entrance F.G. Cement tower

Buoys A green conical light buoy (Fl.G.4s) 500m to the S of the mole at Port de la Pointe de Berre. The following buoys mark the entrance to Martigues:

N side
No.2 Red can light buoy, red square topmark (Fl.R.4s)
No.4 Red can light buoy, red square topmark (Fl(2)R.6s)

No.6 Red can light buoy, red square topmark (Fl(3)R.12s)
S side
No.1 Green conical light, buoy ▲ topmark (Fl.G.4s)
No.3 Black conical light, buoy ▲ topmark (Iso.G.4s)

Beacons A red beacon with a can topmark, a green beacon with a ▲ topmark and two black beacons mark the pass into the Etang de Vaïne. A G starboard beacon marks the Digue Nord head.

Currents In addition to the normal outgoing current from the rivers which varies with the time of year and flow from the hydroelectric power station, there is an additional current created by the wind. A S wind causes a reduction or reversal of this outgoing current and a N wind increases its outward flow. These currents which are strong in the canal are only experienced near the canal and river entrances and here some tidal effects may also be felt.

Winds Due to the local topography, the NW *mistral* blows from N to NNE. In summer S or SW winds often bring rain.

Warnings

Due to the shallowness of the water, dangerous seas can get up very quickly in very strong winds. This applies particularly during the NW to NNE *mistral* and should this wind arise immediate shelter under a windward coast or in harbour must be sought. Commercial vessels have right of way in l'Etang de Berre. There is an area near the Aerodrome de Marseille-Marignane to which entry is forbidden and outside this a further area where it is forbidden to stop (see chart page 212). Ferries showing F.R by day and Q by night have a right of way. Japanese seaweed has become established in the shallow water around the coastline and heavy weed covers the muddy bottom in deeper water.

Planning guide

Ports, harbours, anchorages and landing places

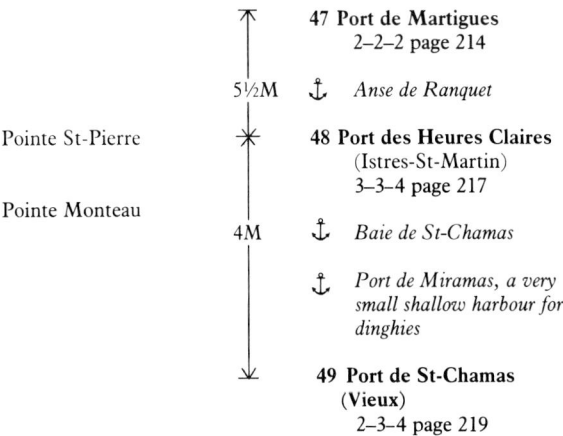

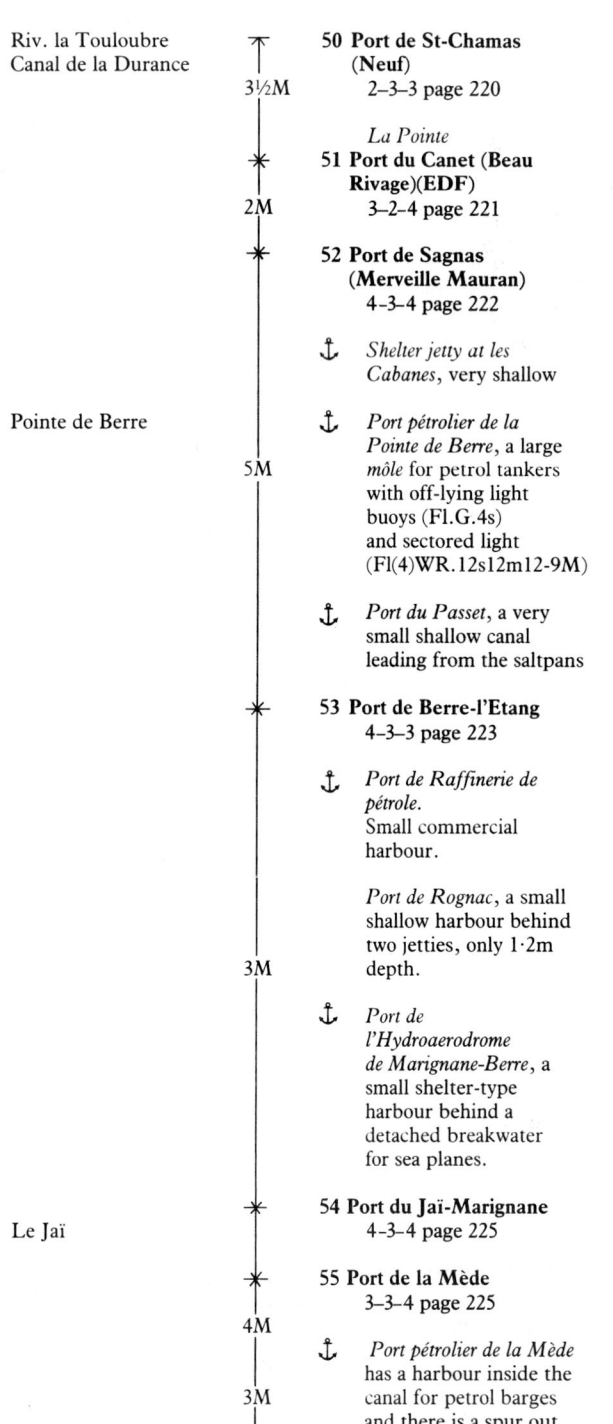

Riv. la Touloubre
Canal de la Durance

3½M

50 Port de St-Chamas (Neuf)
2–3–3 page 220

La Pointe

51 Port du Canet (Beau Rivage)(EDF)
3–2–4 page 221

2M

52 Port de Sagnas (Merveille Mauran)
4–3–4 page 222

⚓ *Shelter jetty at les Cabanes*, very shallow

Pointe de Berre

⚓ *Port pétrolier de la Pointe de Berre*, a large *môle* for petrol tankers with off-lying light buoys (Fl.G.4s) and sectored light (Fl(4)WR.12s12m12-9M)

5M

⚓ *Port du Passet*, a very small shallow canal leading from the saltpans

53 Port de Berre-l'Etang
4–3–3 page 223

⚓ *Port de Raffinerie de pétrole.* Small commercial harbour.

Port de Rognac, a small shallow harbour behind two jetties, only 1·2m depth.

3M

⚓ *Port de l'Hydroaerodrome de Marignane-Berre*, a small shelter-type harbour behind a detached breakwater for sea planes.

54 Port du Jaï-Marignane
4–3–4 page 225

Le Jaï

55 Port de la Mède
3–3–4 page 225

4M

⚓ *Port pétrolier de la Mède* has a harbour inside the canal for petrol barges and there is a spur out into Etang de Berre with an island jetty for petrol tankers.

3M

Les Trois Frères

47 Port de Martigues
2–2–2 page 214

47 PORT DE MARTIGUES

13500 Bouches du Rhône

Position 43°24'·2N 5°03'·5E
Minimum depth   in the entrance 8m (27ft)
                  in the harbour 10 to 1·5m (33 to 5ft)
Width of the canal 50m
Number of yacht berths 300 + 100 + 145 + 1000 = 1545
Population 45,000
Rating 2–2–2

General

This old and attractive harbour town is located where the Canal de Caronte enters the Etang de Berre. Unfortunately it is now surrounded by massive blocks of high-rise buildings and has what must be the most ugly *hôtel de ville* in France. It is easy to approach from the *étang*, but care is needed when approaching from Port de Bouc by the canal. It has good facilities for yachtsmen but berths are not easy to find. The harbour forms a good base from which to explore the *étang*.

Data

Charts   Admiralty Nos 2164, 3498
           French 6907
           Spanish 49
           Navicarte 505, 507

Currents Currents of up to 4 knots flow in the Canal de Caronte, usually in a W direction. There is a factory on the N bank of the canal at the Port de Bouc end that sometimes discharges a considerable volume of water across the channel.

Magnetic variation 1°59'W (1994) decreasing by about 6' each year.

Weather forecasts Recorded forecasts (☎ 36 05 08 08).

Port radio Call on VHF Ch 16, work on Ch 12. Also CB Ch 12.

Traffic signals On the parapet at the side of the lifting bridge at Martigues:

Day and night	Meaning	Applicable to
Fl.G	Bridge open, passage permitted	High vessels
Fl.R or F.R	Bridge closed, passage forbidden	High vessels
F.Y	Bridge about to be opened	All vessels
Fl.Y and R	Passage of low vessels under bridge permitted	Low vessels
Fl.Y	Passage of low vessels under bridge not permitted	Low vessels

Bridge The lifting bridge at Martigues will not open between the following hours: 0545–0600, 0645–0715, 0745–0830, 1100–1240, 1310–1400, 1730–1900. Request to open should be made to the harbour master at Port de Bouc in person or on port radio between 0600–2000 hours on weekdays. At other times to the control cabin at the end of the bridge. Clearance when closed 5.8m.

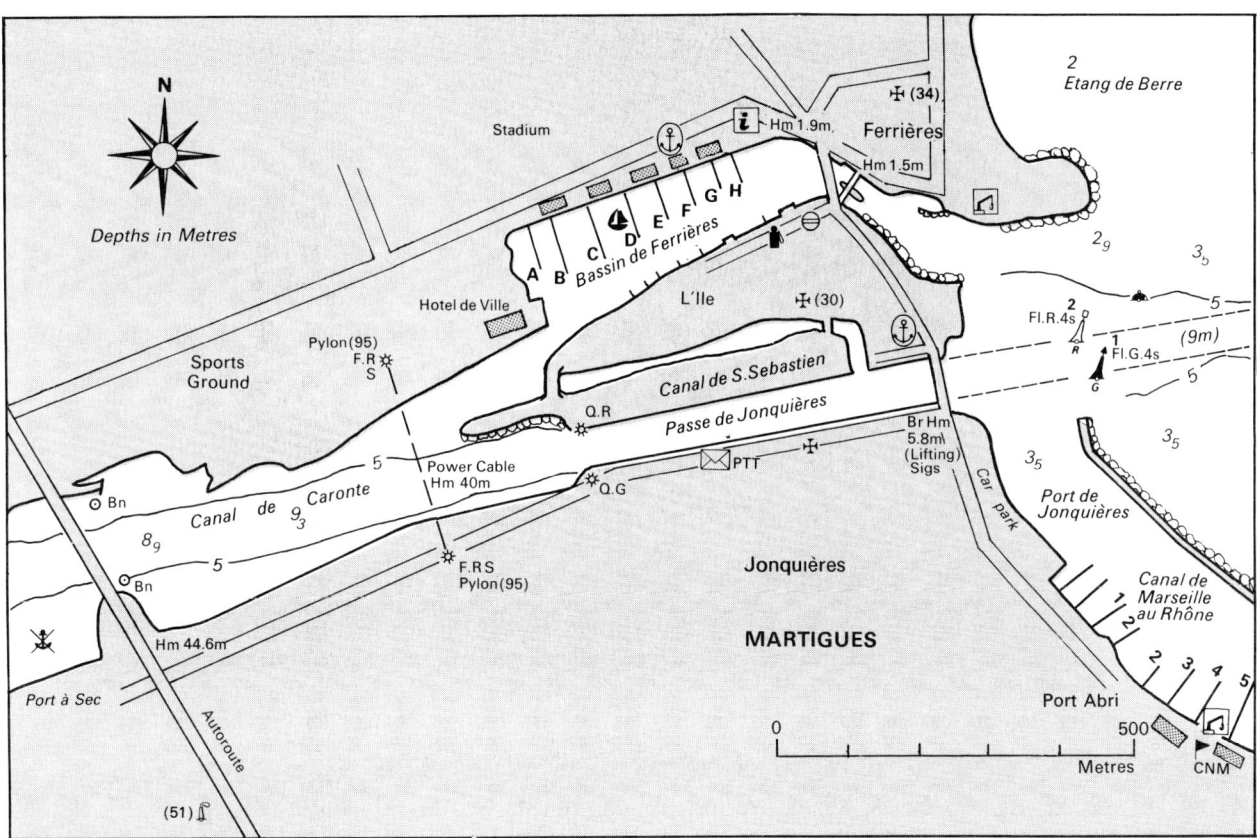

Martigues

Lights

Canal de Caronte
N bank Q.R.9m7M From a mast.

La Gafette N side Fl.R.4s9m8M Red mast

S bank No.1 Q.G.5m6M From a grey dolphin, white tank, green lantern

No.3 Fl.G.4s5m6M From a white dolphin, dark green lantern

No.5 Q.W.5m8M N cardinal topmark ⚑ on yellow dolphin, black top

No.7 Q(9)W.15s5m8M Yellow round tank, black bands on grey dolphin

Traversée de Martigues
N bank Q.R.8m8M Red mast 198°-vis-078° R lights on pylons 275m SW, 300m NW

S bank Q.G.9m8M Dark green mast

Buoys At the W end of the canal, Aubran, a green conical light buoy with ▲ topmark (Fl.G.4s). Red and green light buoys (F. or Iso.R and G) mark the approach channel from Etang de Berre. See page 00.

Warnings

Commercial vessels have priority in the canal and approaches. During a NW *mistral* manoeuvring is difficult due to heavy gusts of wind.

Approach by day

From Port de Bouc Cross the port on 037° towards the E set of leading marks, white rectangles painted with yellow stripe on red latticework towers (F.R intens) until some 40m from the front mark when the canal should be fully opened up. Turn to 093° and follow the N bank of the canal at 50m leaving Aubran green conical light buoy, green ▲ topmark (Fl.G.4s) the same distance to starboard. Do not cut this corner as there are mud banks. At times strong outgoing currents are experienced here. Pass under a high railway swing bridge (clearance 21m) by the N arch, under a cable 65m followed by the *autoroute* bridge (clearance 44.6m), then under some power lines supported by tall pylons (clearance 40m). Here the canal divides, the N branch leads to Bassin de Ferrières in Martigues and also the Canal de St-Sebastien, the S branch leads straight into the Etang de Berre after passing a lifting bridge (closed clearance 5·8m at its centre, 4·4m at the side). The lifting bridge is manned continuously.

From Etang de Berre Martigues lies in the SW corner of this *étang* and can be recognised by two tall pylons, the *autoroute* bridge and the church spires. The lifting bridge and the training wall of broken rocks enclosing the Canal de Marseille are seen in the closer approach. The channel axis 260° to the bridge is marked by pairs of light buoys. leave red buoys with red square topmarks to starboard and green buoys with green cones to port.

Approach by night

There are adequate lights, marks and buoys (see light list above) to make night approach possible, in addition there is considerable background illumination from industrial plants at Port de Bouc and at Martigues.

Port de Bouc

Port de Martigues, looking W

Inner harbour   *Canal to Etang de Berre*

Port de Martigues. Approach from W, looking E

Port de Martigues.
Entrance to inner harbour

Entrance to Miroir aux Oiseaux

Martigues from the
lifting bridge looking NE

Anchorage in the approach

This is not advised in the Canal de Caronte and for most of its length is forbidden, anchorage is however possible virtually anywhere in the Etang de Berre clear of marked channels in 5–9m weed over mud, and outside prohibited areas.

Entrance. By day

Port de Jonquières From 150m E of lifting bridge, enter the Canal de Marseille au Rhône, keep about 50m from its NE bank of broken rocks for some 300m then turn SW towards the pontoons.

Bassin de Ferrières Fork to port from the main canal after passing under the overhead power cables and follow the port-hand bank at 25m until past the entrance to Canal de St-Sebastien, then follow the starboard-hand bank until level with the ultra-modern *hôtel de ville* and then enter the *bassin*.

Berths

Port de Jonquières Secure stern-to pontoons, bow-to mooring chain, near the fuelling pontoon in any vacant space and as near to the end of the pontoon as possible in 2m. Report to the guardian or club official for allocation of a berth.

Bassin de Ferrières Secure stern-to pontoon with bow-to mooring chain in vacant space in 4–1m. Caution is necessary owing to silting.

Canal de Caronte Berth temporarily alongside the quay some 150m short of the lifting bridge on either side of the canal. Care is necessary here as passing vessels create a tremendous wash and turbulence. Small craft drawing under 1·5m may find a berth in Le Miroir aux Oiseaux or Canal St-Sebastien.

Port à Sec A very large hard standing with places for 1,000 yachts of 6 to 15m length overall, maximum draught 3m, maximum weight 16 tonnes. Slip and travel-hoist, water and 220v AC electric power. ☎ 42 07 00 00 for reserved places and terms. Located on the S side of the Canal de Caronte to SW of the *autoroute* bridge. Buoyed route to the waiting pontoon. All normal facilities of a normal port.

Formalities

Report to the club if berthed in Port de Jonquières. If in Bassin de Ferrières report to *bureau du port* (☎ 42 80 10 20) located near the N end of the lifting bridge. There is a customs office near the E end of Bassin de Ferrières (☎ 42 80 52 53) but the main office is in Port de Bouc.

Harbour charges

There are harbour charges.

Facilities

Slips There is a small slip in the Port de Jonquières.
Slipway A small slipway in the Port de Jonquières.
Cranes There are two cranes at Port de Jonquières, one of 3 tonnes and one of 6 tonnes. There is a 3-tonne crane at Bassin de Ferrières. To S of Martigues there is a 1000-berth yacht park with 16-tonne travel-hoist (☎ 42 07 00 00).

Fuel Diesel and petrol are available from pumps at head of pontoon in Port de Jonquières and also at SE side of Bassin de Ferrières and by tanker lorry from Lavéra (☎ 42 06 60 34).
Water From pontoons at Port de Jonquières.
Provisions From the many shops which are distributed around the town.
Garbage A few rubbish containers at Port de Jonquières.
Chandlery There are two shops in the town in the Place des Martyrs and in the industrial zone.
Repairs Repairs to hull, sails and engine are possible.
Post office On the S bank of the Canal de Caronte.
Hotels Three★★★, two ★★, three ★ and eight others.
Restaurants There are seven restaurants and many café/bars.
Yacht club The Club Nautique de Martigues et de l'Etang de Berre (CNM) has a clubhouse by the pontoons at Port de Jonquières with bar, lounge and showers (☎ 42 07 30 54). Also Cercle de Voile de Martigues (CMV) (☎ 42 80 12 94).
Information office The Syndicat d'Initiative is located at the N side of the Bassin de Ferrières (☎ 42 90 30 72).
Visits The canals, churches and old houses of l'Ile should be seen and there is a museum at Ferrières.
Communications There is a bus service.

History

From the time of the Roman occupation there were three villages, Ferrières, l'Ile and Jonquières, separated by the canals leading to the Etang de Berre. In 1223 they were ruled by the Comte de Provence. However in 1509 the three villages were combined as Martigues under the Crown. By 1721 as a result of constant wars and the ravages of the plague, the population had dwindled to some six or seven thousand, at which level it remained until the end of the last century when the industrialisation of the area commenced. The area has been a favourite of French painters and Martigues has been painted by many famous artists.

⚓ **Anse de Ranquet**

Anchor close inshore in N half of this bay. Pipelines laid in S half. 3m sand and mud. Sheltered SE–S–SW–W–NW. Some houses and road ashore up hill. Chandler at St-Mitre les Ramparts.

---

48 PORT DES HEURES CLAIRES (ISTRES-ST-MARTIN)
13800 Bouches du Rhône

Position 43°29'·9N 4°59'·9E
Minimum depth   in the entrance 3·4m (11ft)
                             in the harbour 2·4 to 1·5m (8 to 5ft)
Width of the entrance 20m
Number of yacht berths 280
Maximum length overall 12m (40ft)
Population 30,360
Rating 3-3-4

Port des Heures-Claires. Approach

Port des Heures-Claires, looking SE

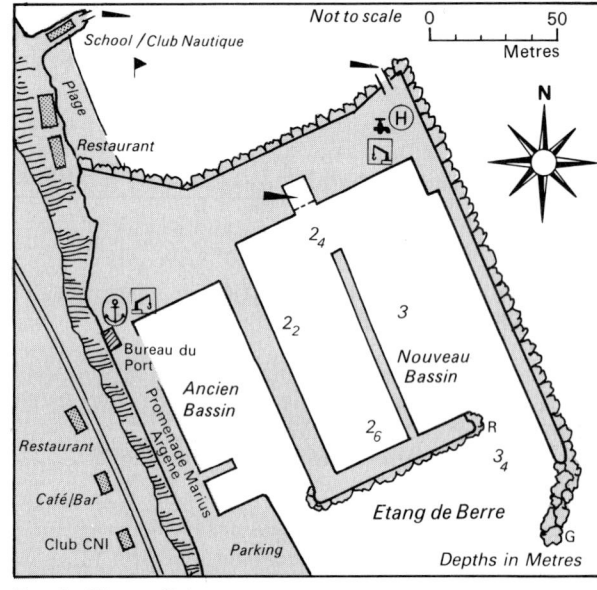

Port des Heures-Claires

General

A small artificial yacht harbour added onto an old harbour, situated some 4 kilometres from the town and occupying a favoured position in the *étang*. Entrance is not difficult but facilities are somewhat limited.

Data

See l'Etang de Berre page 212.

Port radi VHF Ch 09 and 16

Weather forecast Posted at *bureau du port*. Recorded forecast (☎ 36 68 08 08 and 36 68 08 13).

Lights

The harbour is floodlit. There are red and green reflectors at the entrance.

Approach and entrance by day

Approach on a NW course, the low rocky harbour wall and a large blue crane will be seen in the close approach. A series of small white buoys leads on a N course to the entrance. Well sheltered from the NW *mistral*.

Berths

Secure stern-to the pontoon or quay in a vacant berth in the Nouveau Bassin.

Formalities

Report to *bureau du port* on W side of the harbour on arrival (☎ 42 55 51 73 and 42 56 09 72). Open 0800–1700.

Harbour charges

There are harbour charges.

Facilities

Slips There are slips at the N end of the new basin.
Cranes There is a 12-tonne crane at the N end of the Ancien Bassin.
Fuel At Istres.
Water A water point is at the N end of Nouveau Bassin and at various places on the quays.
Provisions At Istres.
Post office At Istres.
Information office At Istres, 30 allée Jean Jaurès (☎ 42 55 23).
Hotels Three ★★, one ★ and six others.
Restaurants Eighteen restaurants, three of which are near the harbour.
Yacht club The Club Nautique d'Istres (CNI) (☎ 42 55 51 73 and 42 56 09 72) and Association Nautique Omnisport Istrienne (ANOI) at the NW end of the harbour beside the road which runs above the harbour.
Showers Showers and WCs.
Visits The 12th-century Chapelle St-Auprice and the wild area of La Crua can be visited, as can the Musée de Vieil Istres.
Beaches There is a series of small sandy beaches on either side of the harbour.
Communications Bus and rail services. Helicopter landing spot at NE corner of the harbour.

History

There is evidence of occupation of the area 15 to 20 centuries ago, but historical records do not predate 1216 AD after which the town suffered a series of invasions, occupations and changes of rulers similar to those of neighbouring towns; however, by isolating themselves in 1720, the inhabitants were able to escape the disasters of the plague which raged in the area at that time. In 1917 the first school of aviation in France was founded at Istres-Le-Tubé, the military airfield nearby.

⚓ **Baie de St-Chamas**

An anchorage in shallow water near the N end of the Baie de St-Chamas. Anchor in mid-bay in 2–2·3m off St-Chamas in sand and mud. Sheltered from W–NW–N–NE–E.

⚓ **Port de Miramas**

A very small harbour behind a breakwater, very shallow, suitable for dinghies.

49 PORT DE ST-CHAMAS (VIEUX)

13250 Bouches du Rhône

Position 43°33′N 5°01′·5E
Minimum depth   in the entrance 2m (6·6ft)
                                in the harbour 2m (6·6ft)
Width of the entrance 30m
Number of yacht berths 60
Population 5157
Rating 2–3–4

General

A charming small harbour with limited facilities in an attractive setting but unfortunately the entrance channel is silting up and may carry less than 2m so entrance could be difficult. Inside good shelter is obtained.

Data

See l'Etang de Berre, page 212.

Warning

There is a government explosives factory 1·5km to S which must not be approached.

Approach and entrance by day

Following a N course up the centre of the Baie de St-Chamas until the town and a long arched viaduct are NE, when approach on this course and enter the harbour with great care, sounding frequently.

Berths

Berth stern-to quay or alongside.

Formalities

Report to *bureau du port* on arrival (☎ 90 50 80 00).

Harbour charges

There are harbour charges.

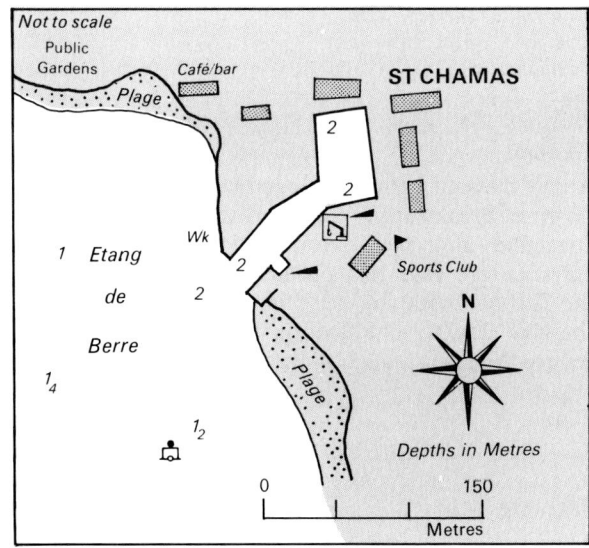

Port de St-Chamas (Vieux)

Port de St Chamas (Vieux) looking SW–W–NW

Facilities

Slips There is one on the S side of the entrance channel and a similar one to S side of the harbour.

Cranes There is a crane of 5 tonnes capacity on the S side of the harbour.

Water From points on the quay.

Electricity There are 220v AC points on the quay.

Provisions Obtainable from nearby shops.

Post office In the village.

Hotels One unclassified.

Restaurants Six and some café/bars.

Information office The Syndicat d'Initiative has an office at Montée des Pénitents (☎ 90 50 90 54).

Visits The old Roman bridge, Pont Flavian, should be seen. The area is very attractive and has many interesting historical remains.

Beaches On either side of the harbour.

Communications Bus and rail.

---

50 PORT DE ST-CHAMAS (NEUF)

13250 Bouches du Rhône

Position 43°32'·8N 5°01'·9E

Minimum depth   in the entrance 2·1m (7ft)
      in the harbour 2 to 1·2m (6·6 to 4ft)

Width of the entrance 12m

Number of berths 205

Population 5157

Rating 2–3–3

General

A new harbour being developed behind two detached floating breakwaters close to the town which is attractive and has fair facilities. Approach and entrance are easy and protection is afforded inside the harbour with the exception of the wind effect of the NW *mistral*. The floating breakwaters effectively reduce the seas created by this wind.

Data

See l'Etang de Berre, page 212.

Warnings

The waters are shallow, sound carefully. The N entrance is blocked and cannot be used.

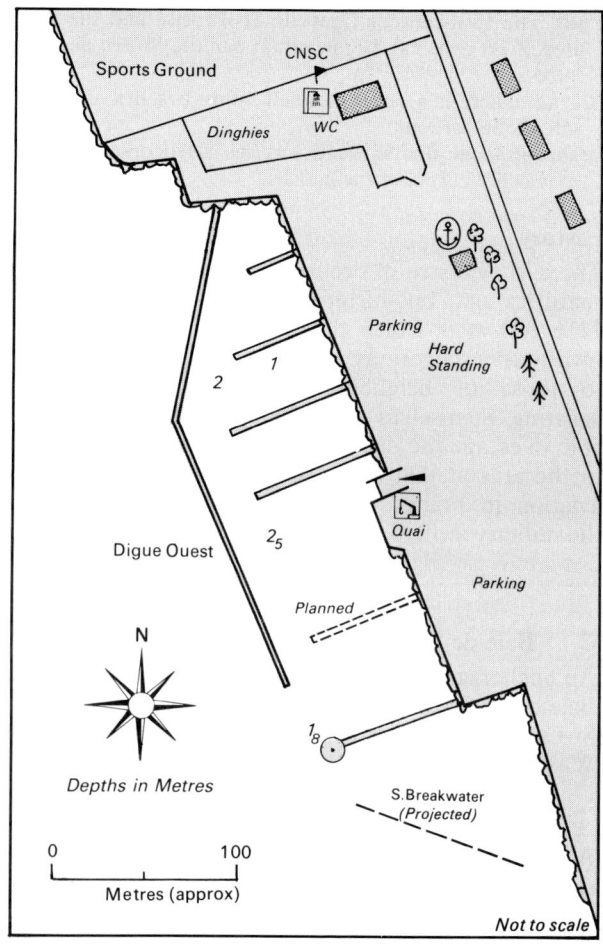

Port de St-Chamas (Neuf)

Port de St-Chamas (Neuf)

Approach and entrance by day
Proceed up to the centre of the Baie de St-Chamas in a NNW direction. A ridge of high land lies parallel to the E shore. On its crest will be seen a small chapel (64m). The harbour lies below this mark. Approach on an E heading and enter between the ends of the two detached breakwaters.

Berths
Secure to nearest vacant berth and report to *bureau du port* for allocation of a berth.

Formalities
Bureau du port to N of the harbour; report here (☎ 90 56 80 00).

Harbour charges
There are harbour charges.

Facilities
Slips A slip on E side of harbour near the quay.
Water From taps on the pontoons.
Electricity From points on the pontoons, 220v AC.
Provisions From shops in St-Chamas ½M away.
Post office In village.
Hotels One unclassified.
Restaurants Six and some café/bars.
Yacht club Club Nautique de St-Chamas (CNSC) has a clubhouse attached to the *bureau du port* (☎ 90 56 80 00). Lounge, WC, shower and bar.
Information office The Syndicat d'Initiative has an office at the Montée des Penitents (☎ 90 50 90 54).
Visits The old Roman bridge, Pont Flavian, is one of the many places of interest in the area.
Beaches Rocky and rather muddy beaches to S.

Future development
The S breakwater is to be moved S and the S end of the W breakwater extended, providing room for another pontoon.

⚓ La Pointe
A long low training wall offers a shallow anchorage either side of its S end to suit wind direction, in 1·6 to 1.0m mud. Area is silting up.

EDF breakwater
The discharge of fresh water from the conspicuous *centrale électrique* (generating station) takes place behind a short breakwater 1M E of La Pointe. Not suitable for anchoring.

---

51 PORT DU CANET (BEAU RIVAGE) (EDF)
13250 Bouches du Rhône

Position 43°31'·6N 5°04'·8E
Minimum depth   in the entrance 2·0m (6·6ft)
                    in the harbour 2·0 to 0·5m (6·6 to 2ft)
Width of the entrance 18m
Number of yacht berths 110
Population 200 (approx)
Rating 3–2–4

General
A small artificial harbour in a comparatively deserted and attractive area, easy to approach and enter and offering good protection. Facilities are limited and it is 3M from the shops etc. at St-Chamas.

Port du Canet, looking SE–S

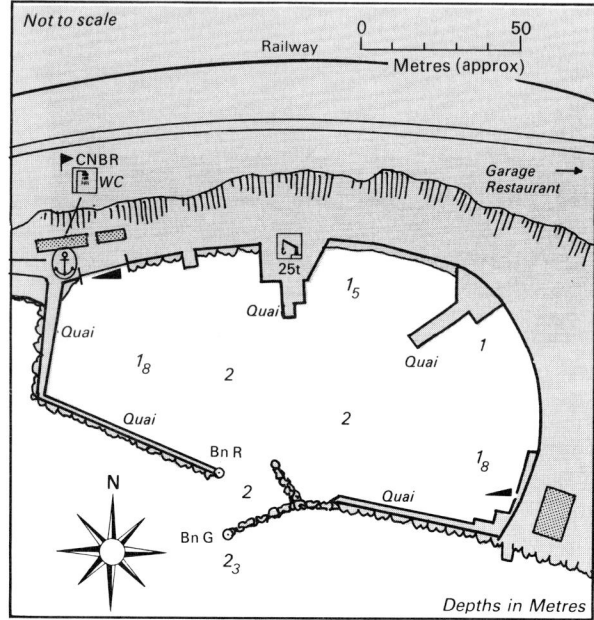

Port du Canet

Data

See l'Etang de Berre, page 212.

Lights
The harbour and entrance are floodlit.

Approach and entrance by day

Approach the N end of the Etang de Berre in mid-*étang*. The tall tower S of the *centrale électrique* (generating station) and the three huge water pipes running down the hill to a large white building should be seen from afar. The harbour lies ½M to E and is not conspicuous but the many yacht masts should be seen in the closer approach. Enter between the two breakwater heads which are marked with two small beacons, one red and the other green. Note that an inner breakwater must be avoided by making a turn to port having passed the outer breakwater. The entrance is floodlit at night.

Berths

Secure in any vacant berth and report to the *bureau du port*. Berths are stern-to quays.

Formalities

The *bureau du port* is at the NW corner of the harbour (☎ 90 50 92 17).

Harbour charges

There are harbour charges to be paid.

Facilities

Slips There are three slips on the N side of the harbour, one is used for sailing dinghies.
Cranes There is a 25-tonne crane on the N side of the harbour.
Fuel From garage to E of harbour on the main road.
Water Water taps around the harbour.
Electricity Several points (220v AC) are by the crane.
Repairs Minor repairs possible.
Provisions At St-Chamas.
Restaurants One to E of harbour on main road.
Yacht club Club Nautique de Beau Rivage (CNBR). Clubhouse at NW corner of the harbour, WC, showers, etc. (90 50 92 17).
Beaches A diving-board on E breakwater.
Visits The Roman bridge and arches at St-Chamas should be visited.

Future development

Electricity points and water taps are being installed on all quays. The harbour is to have a new outer breakwater which will provide more deep water berths.

---

52 PORT DE SAGNAS (MERVEILLE MAURAN)

13250 Bouches du Rhône

Position 43°30'·9N 5°07'·1E
Minimum depth in the entrance 2m (6·6ft)
in the harbour 2 to 1m (6·6 to 3ft)
Number of yacht berths 60
Population 500 (approx)
Rating 4–3–4

General

A small shallow harbour in a little bay to be found about 600m N of the mouth of the river l'Arc, not difficult to enter but with few facilities. The area is rather desolate, flat and marshy.

Data

See l'Etang de Berre, page 212.

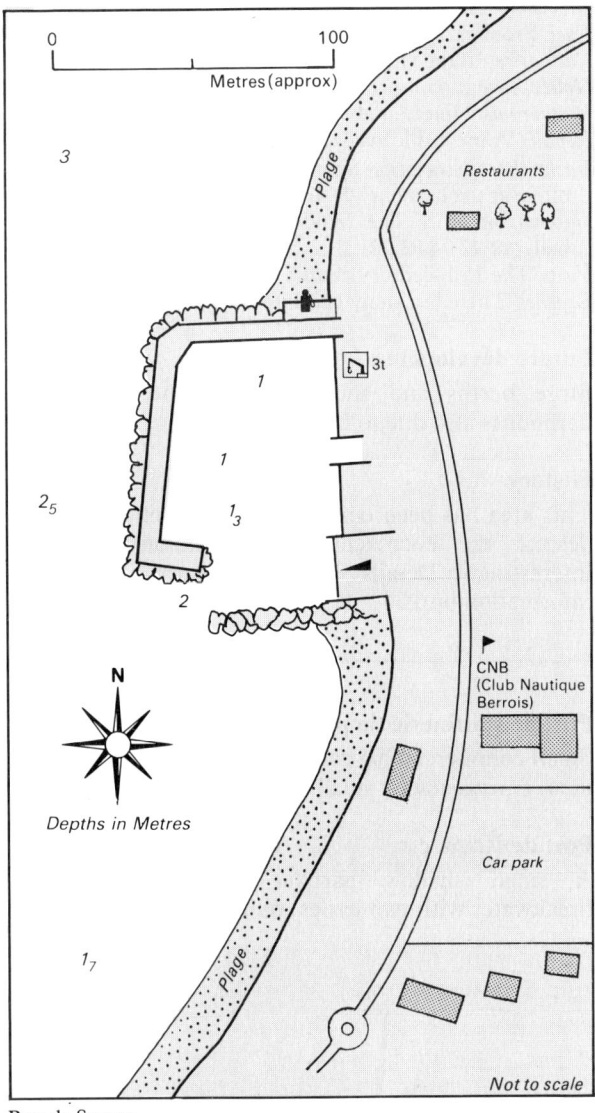

Port de Sagnas

Approach and entrance by day

Approach the extreme NE corner of the Etang de Berre sounding with care. The small jetty will be seen in the close approach and a large blue and white hangar behind, it should not be mistaken for the breakwater near the mouth of l'Arc.

Berths

Secure stern-to quay in a vacant place.

Facilities

Slips There are two.
Crane There is a 3-tonne crane and a 6-tonne mobile crane.
Fuel Diesel pump on quay.
Water Tap 100m to S and at Club Nautique.
Provisions Limited facilities in the village.
Yacht club 300m to S. Club Nautique Berrois (CNB).
Restaurants Two simple restaurants nearby.

⚓ **Shelter jetty les Cabanes just S of the mouth of l'Arc**

Very shallow.

Port pétrolier de la Pointe de Berre

A small commercial oil tanker port dredged to 8m, only for use in an emergency. Offlying green light buoy, green ▲ topmark (Fl.G.4s) and a light on jetty head (Fl(4)WR.15s12m12-9M). White metal framework tower, red lantern, 012°-W-057°-R-012°.

Port du Passet

Discharge canal from salt pans, not a harbour.

---

53 PORT DE BERRE-L'ETANG

13130 Bouches du Rhône

Position 43°28'·3N 5°10'·2E
Minimum depth in the entrance 1m (3ft)
          in the harbour 1·5 to 1m (5 to 3ft)
Number of yacht berths 100
Population 12,650
Rating 4–3–3

General

A small harbour protected by a jetty and breakwater. Very shallow due to silting and too close to the huge petrochemical works to be very attractive for visitors. Entrance is easy except during E winds. Facilities are limited.

Data

See l'Etang de Berre, page 212.

Lights
Entrance F.R. Harbour floodlights.

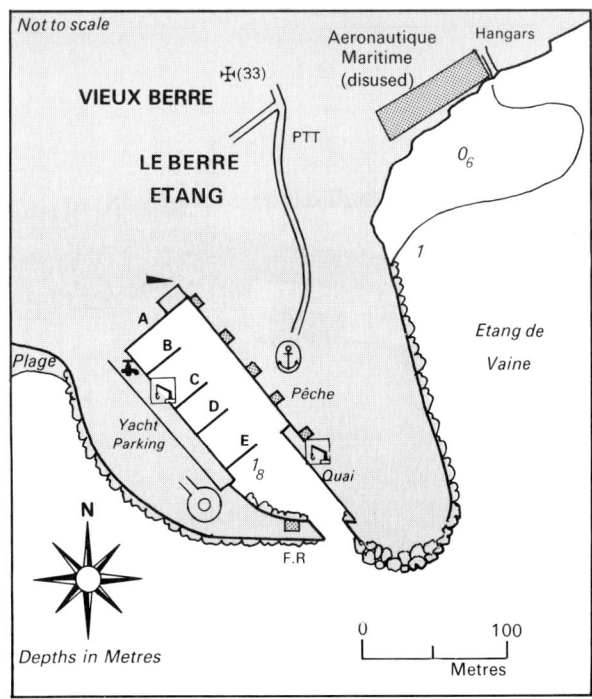

Port de Berre-l'Etang

Approach and entrance by day

Enter Etang de Vaïne by the pass, 450m long 60m wide, in its S corner (Passe de Marignane). This is marked by two green posts with green ▲ topmarks on the starboard side, and on the port side a dolphin (Fl(2)R.6s) and a red post with red can topmark. Enter between these on a NE course and then take a NNW course towards the village and church of Berre, which lie to the SW of the massive petrochemical works and some large hangars. The harbour jetty and *môle* will be seen in the closer approach. Enter on a NW course.

Berths

Secure stern-to quay or pontoon near head of harbour.

Formalities

Report to *bureau du port* on NE side of harbour on arrival (☎ 42 85 40 48 and 42 85 44 70) open 0900–1200 and 1400–1600.

Harbour charges

There are harbour charges.

Facilities

Slips There is one to the NW of the harbour.
Cranes There are two cranes, one of 1·5 tonnes and the other of 8 tonnes, and also a mobile crane of 6 tonnes.
Water A point near W corner of shops in the village, also on pontoons.
Electricity 220v AC on pontoons.

Provisions A limited number of shops in the village.
Fuel From garage in town.
Post office In the village.
Hotels Seven.
Restaurants Nineteen of varying quality.
Repairs A mechanic available.
Yacht club Association Sportive de Berre (ASB) has a club office at the harbour (☎ 42 95 47 16).
Information office The Syndicat d'Initiative at the town hall. (☎ 42 74 93 00)
Visits The 15th-century church is worth a visit.
Beaches There is a stony beach to W of the harbour.

Future development

More berths and showers are to be built. The harbour is also due to be dredged.

History

This area has been occupied since ancient times and despite the encroaching industrialisation is still interesting. Details of its history from the information bureau.

Port de Raffinerie de pétrole

Small commercial harbour, very shallow, for use only in an emergency by small craft.

Port de Rognac

A small shallow harbour behind a detached breakwater with two jetties, only 1·2m deep or less.

Port de Berre-l'Etang, looking NW

⚓ Port de l'Hydroaerodrome de Marignane-Berre

A detached breakwater shelter harbour for seaplanes, located on NE side of the airport runway. Only for use in an emergency; 2·5m deep.

---

54 PORT DU JAI-MARIGNANE
13200 Bouches du Rhône

Position 43°26'·3N 5°11'·5E
Minimum depth   in the entrance 1m (3ft)
                 in the harbour 1m (3ft)
Number of yacht berths 30
Population 22,311
Rating 4–3–4

General

A very small shallow harbour close to the channel into the Etang de Vaïne and to SW of the airport, only suitable for very small yachts. Entrance is simple but facilities at the harbour are limited.

Data
See l'Etang de Berre, page 212.

Approach and entrance by day

The harbour should be approached and entered on a SE course having first entered the Etang de Vaïne.

Berths

Very limited, secure stern-to in a vacant space.

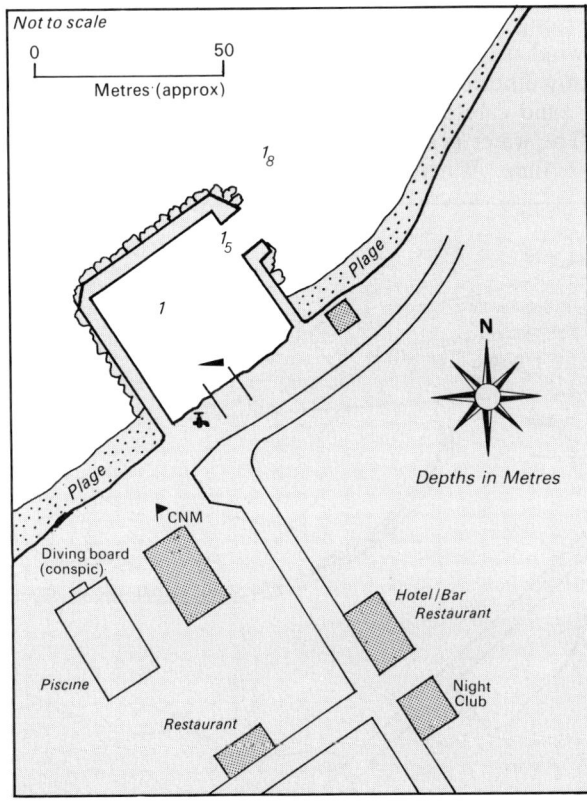

Port de Jaï Marignane

Facilities
Slips There is a small slip.
Water Tap in SW corner of the harbour.
Provisions Normal provisions can be obtained at Marignane 1½M away.
Post office PTT in the Bd Jean-Mermoz, Marignane.
Hotels Two ★★★ and six others.
Restaurants Twelve around the area, two near the harbour.
Yacht club The Club Nautique Marignanais (CNM) has an office and clubhouse here (☎ 42 09 02 18). Showers and WC etc, and swimming pool.
Information office Syndicat d'Initiative has an office in Cours Mirabeau.
Beaches There are good beaches to the SW of the harbour.
Communications The airport is 1½M away. There are bus and rail services.
Visits The *château* of the Barons de Marignane, now owned by the town, is worth a visit.

History

Marignane was founded by the Roman general Marinius in 600 AD and has been inhabited ever since.

---

55 PORT DE LA MEDE
13220 Bouches du Rhône

Position 43°24'·2N 5°07'·4E
Minimum depth   in the entrance 4m (14·5ft)
                 in the harbour 2m (6·6ft)
Number of yacht berths 30
Population 6789
Rating 3–3–4

General

An old barge harbour in the Canal de Marseille au Rhône entered through a gap in the canal bank which lines the S side of the Etang de Berre. Entrance is not difficult, facilities are very limited.

Data
See l'Etang de Berre, page 212.

Approach and entrance by day

Approach the S shore of the *étang* about 400m to the E of Les Trois Frères rocks; the most eastern rock has a green lantern on a white stone tower 20m high. Set course for the head of the mole which has a small green metal framework tower ▲ topmark, round this at 30m and leave it to starboard. Enter the harbour on a W course.

Berths

Secure stern-to the N quay or if space to quays next to town. An alternative for yachts without masts is to carry on 3M along the canal in an E direction and secure in one of the two basins just before Marignane. Care is necessary as the canal has been disused since the Tunnel du Rove became blocked. There are many half-sunken old barges.

Facilities
Water Water tap on quay.

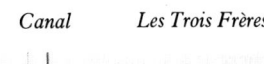

Canal   *Les Trois Frères*   *Head of brea*

Port de la Mède, looking NE

Electricity Electricity point (220v AC) on quay.

Repairs Normal repairs possible.

Provisions These are obtainable in La Mède.

Post office This is to be found in La Mède.

Hotels There are five hotels.

Restaurants There are four restaurants.

Yacht club Nautique Club Mèden (NCM). Clubhouse with WC/showers (☎ 42 81 14 22).

Information office The Syndicat d'Initiative at the town hall.

Beaches There is a sandy beach at Le Jaï to E of harbour.

Communications There is a bus and rail service. The airport is 4½M away.

History

The town has been in occupation since before the 10th century and there are a number of old buildings around the area.

Port Pétrolier de la Mède

A small harbour inside the canal with spur outside the canal for petrol tankers. Two groups of mooring buoys and an oil terminal island jetty lie off the spur. Harbour only for use in an emergency.

47 Port de Martigues, *see page 214*

Les Calanques

The hard limestone hills which stretch along the coast from the Golfe de Fos to Cap Sicié have become weathered and washed away by the elements, leaving behind high cliffs broken at intervals by deep narrow high-sided creeks (*calanques*) and a myriad of large and small bays; in addition a number of islands are to be found near the coast. The sun has bleached the rocks to a very light grey colour, in fact almost white which, coupled with the blue sky and transparent water, makes a most attractive visual effect. The most spectacular area exists between Marseille and Cassis, where the *calanques* are larger and there are several groups of offshore islands. In general these *calanques* are very deep at their entrance with a rocky bottom sloping up towards the head of the creek where the bottom becomes broken rock, stones and weed, and finally a shingle or sand beach. A narrow valley usually continues inland.

At first sight these anchorages appear to be threatening and dangerous, as indeed they are with strong onshore winds and swell, especially if the wind is blowing directly into the *calanque*, but with any other conditions they are quite safe. On entering sound carefully and have a lookout posted forward. The water is so clear that dangers will be easily seen in time. When anchoring, remember that a strong

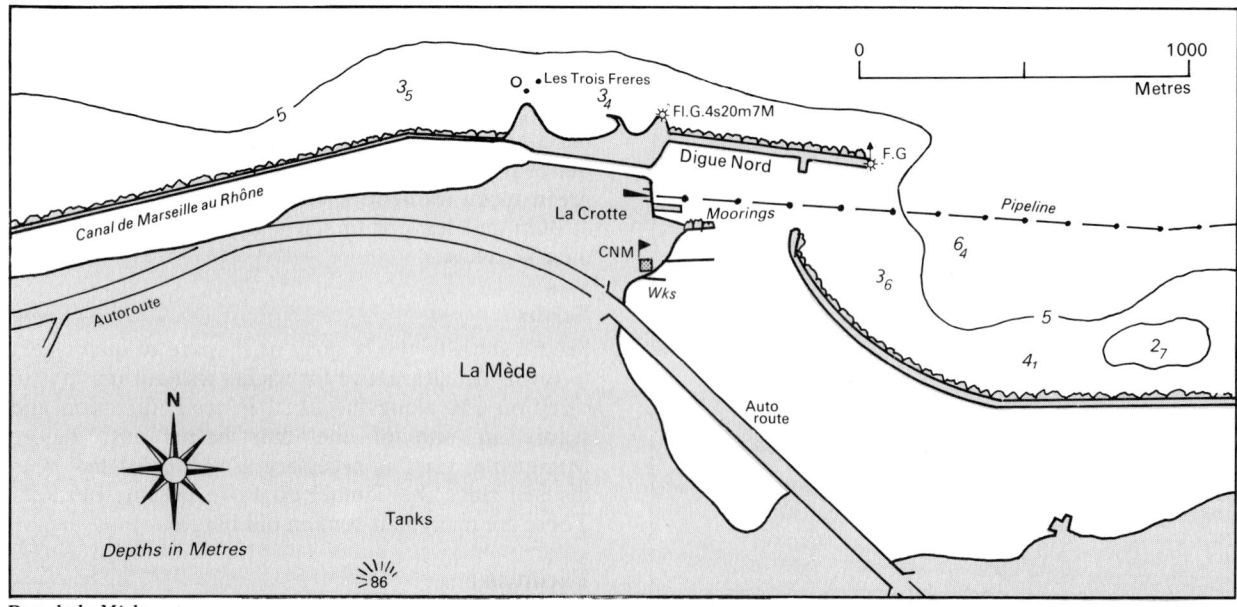

Port de la Mède

wind can blow down the valley, and that if the valley faces NW, the *mistral* can be dangerous. Falling stones are also possible during strong winds. The major and some minor *calanques* have been detailed but there are many others to be found.

⚓ **Canal-Vieil**

Anchorage in a smallish creek, open to SW–W–NW, with rocky sides. There is a power station on the S side, road at head. A single tall chimney on the power station is conspicuous. A second anchorage in Anse de Lavéra.

⚓ **Port de Ponteau**

Small harbour, shallow (1m) at head where there are two rocky breakwaters, shallow sides, chalets and small workshops on N side, also a road, old fort on N point. Open to SW–W–NW. Shallow water either side of the entrance, sound carefully.

⚓ Port de Ponteau looking E

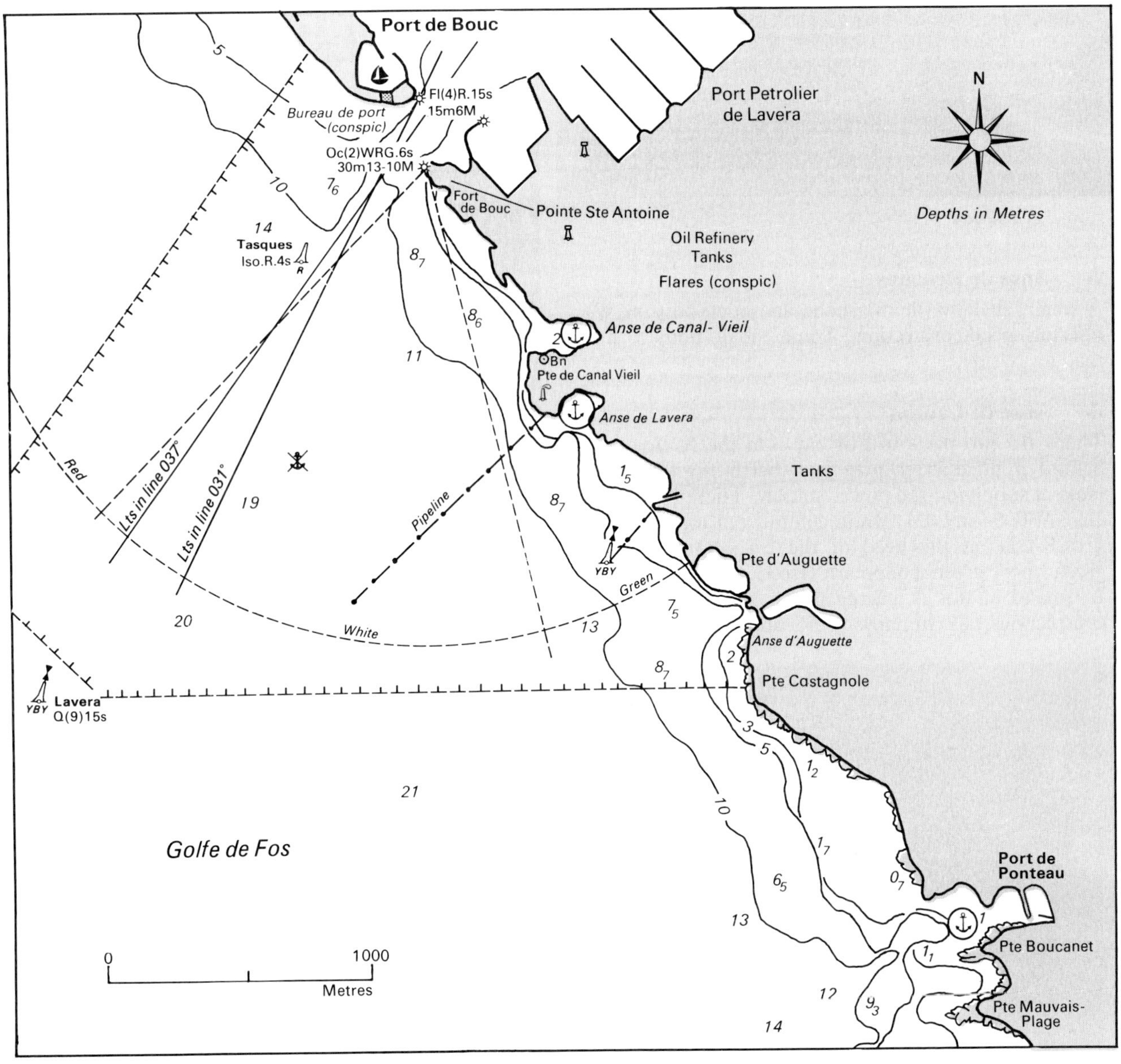

Anchorages S of Port de Bouc

Anse de Renaires, looking NE

⚓ Anse de Renaires

⚓ Anse de Renaires

A small, shallow (0.6m) anchorage open only to W, offering good protection. Some small houses and road on N side.

⚓ Anse de Lauron

There are two parts to this bay. On the N side and behind a breakwater/quay is a berth for small oil tankers supplying the power station. There is a light, Oc(2)WR.6s7m9/6M, white column red top 000°-W-110°-R-000° at the head of the breakwater, and a green buoy, green ▲ topmark (Iso.G.4s) in the bay to E. Inland of this is a large power station with four conspicuous tall chimneys (F.R) and some large fuel

tanks. On the SE side of the buoy in a creek are moorings for small yachts, with a small number of houses around it, also a road. A sandy beach lies on E side. Anchor in 6 to 1·5m sand and boulders in the centre of the bay, open to SW–W–NW. This was a Roman port (100–700 AD) and the original jetty has been found.

⚓ Anse de Bonnieu

Anchorage in a deep shallow creek 5 to 1m sand and rocky boulders. A road but no buildings except a small stone tower. Open to W–NW–N.

⚓ Anse de Bonnieu

⚓ Anse de Lauron

Semaphore   *Cap Couronne lighthous*

Buoy *Carro*

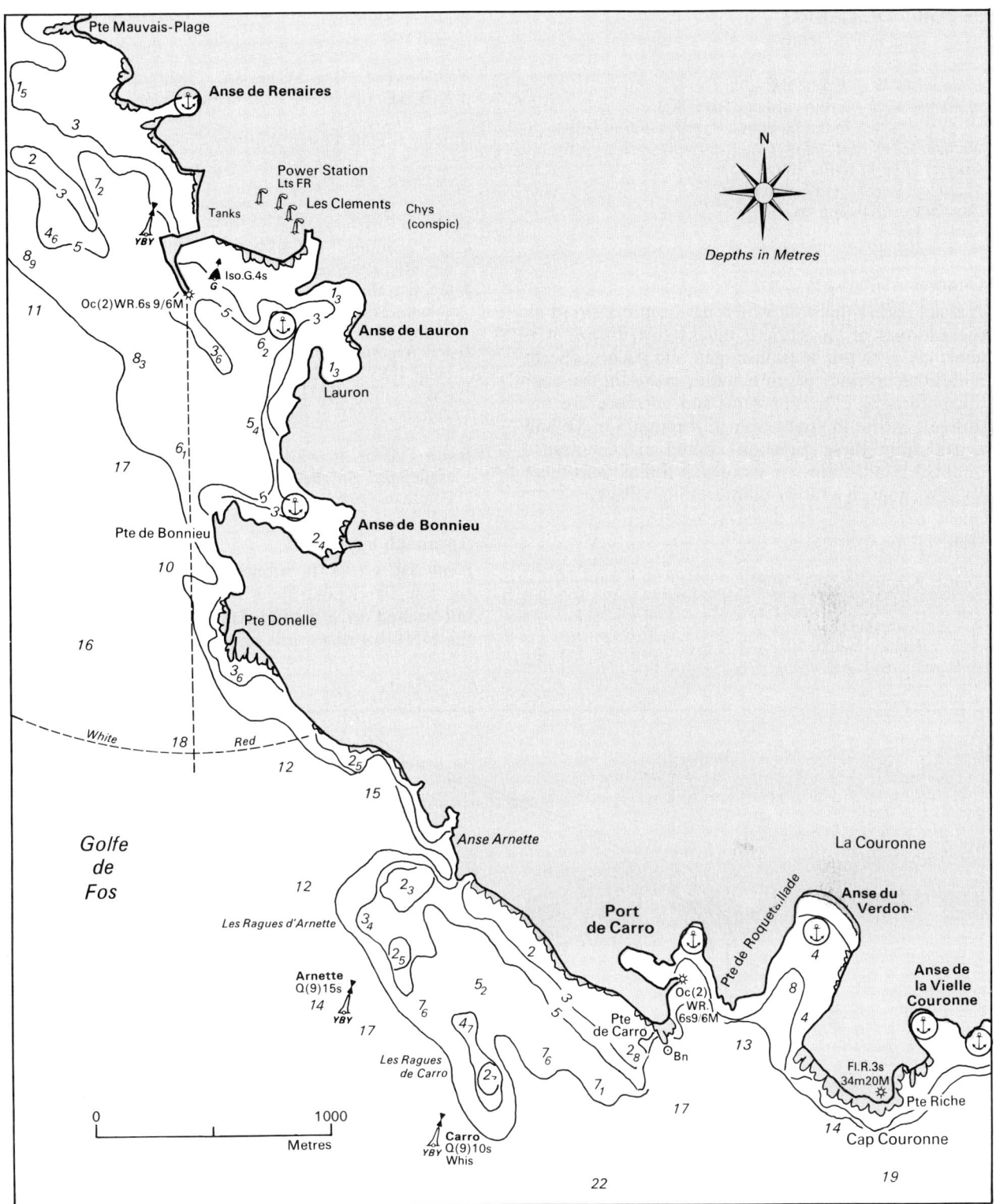

Pte Mauvais-Plage

1₅

3

Anse de Renaires

2

3

7₂

3

4₆

5

8₉

11

Power Station
Lts FR

Tanks

Les Clements

Chys
(conspic)

YBY

Iso.G.4s
G

Oc(2)WR.6s 9/6M

5

1₃

3

Anse de Lauron

3₆

6₂

8₃

1₃

Lauron

17

6₁

5₄

Pte de Bonnieu

5

3

Anse de Bonnieu

10

2₄

16

Pte Donelle

3₆

*Golfe
de
Fos*

White

18

Red

12

15

2₅

Anse Arnette

La Couronne

12

2₃

3₄

Anse du
Verdon

Les Ragues d'Arnette

2₅

Pte de Roquerallade

Anse de
la Vielle
Couronne

Arnette
Q(9)15s

14

YBY

17

5₂

7₆

4₇

Port
de Carro

4

8

4

*Les Ragues
de Carro*

2₇

2

3

5

Oc(2)
WR.
6s9/6M

Pte
de Carro

2₈

Bn

13

Fl.R.3s
34m20M

Pte Riche

7₆

7₁

17

14

Cap Couronne

0

1000

Carro
Q(9)10s
Whis

YBY

22

19

Metres

N

Depths in Metres

Anchorages W of Cap Couronne

56 PORT DE CARRO
13620 Bouches du Rhône

Position 43°19′·7N 5°02′·6E
Minimum depth   in the entrance 5m (18ft)
           in the harbour 2 to 0·5m (6·6 to 1·5ft)
Width of the entrance 25m
Number of yacht berths 200
Maximum length overall 11m (36ft)
Population 2000 (approx)
Rating 4–3–3

General
A small natural harbour which has been improved by
the addition of an artificial breakwater, but as it is
generally very full of fishing craft and yachts a berth
is difficult to find. SE to E winds make the harbour
uncomfortable. The approach and entrance are not
difficult except in winds from E through S to SE and
a gale from these directions would make entrance
impossible. Facilities are somewhat limited and there
are few shops in a rather uninteresting village.

Data

Charts   Admiralty 2164, 3498
        French 6767
        Spanish 49
        Navicarte 505, 507

Magnetic variation 1°59′W (1994) decreasing by about 6′
each year.

Radiobeacons Cap Couronne lighthouse (43°19′·5N
5°03′·1E) CR(— · — · / — ·) 295·5kHz 50M

Weather forecast Posted at *bureau du port* in summer.

Speed limit 3 knots.

Lights
Cap Couronne Fl.R.3s34m20M. White tower with red
top. RC. Reserve light 13M
Jetée Est Head Oc(2)WR.6s8m9/6M Red top and white
column 322°-W-355°-R-322°

Buoys Arnette W cardinal, YBY with ⌁ topmark, light
buoy (Q(9)15s8M). Carro, a similar light and whistle
buoy (VQ(9)10s8M). These two light buoys mark
shallows WSW of the harbour.

Beacons A small white square masonry beacon tower
established on the rocks to the S of the entrance on
Pointe de Carro.

Approach by day
From SW Cross the mouth of the Golfe de Fos from
the low flat Rhône delta on its W side towards the
hill-backed coast behind Cap Couronne. The coast to
the NNW of this *cap* is lined with factories including

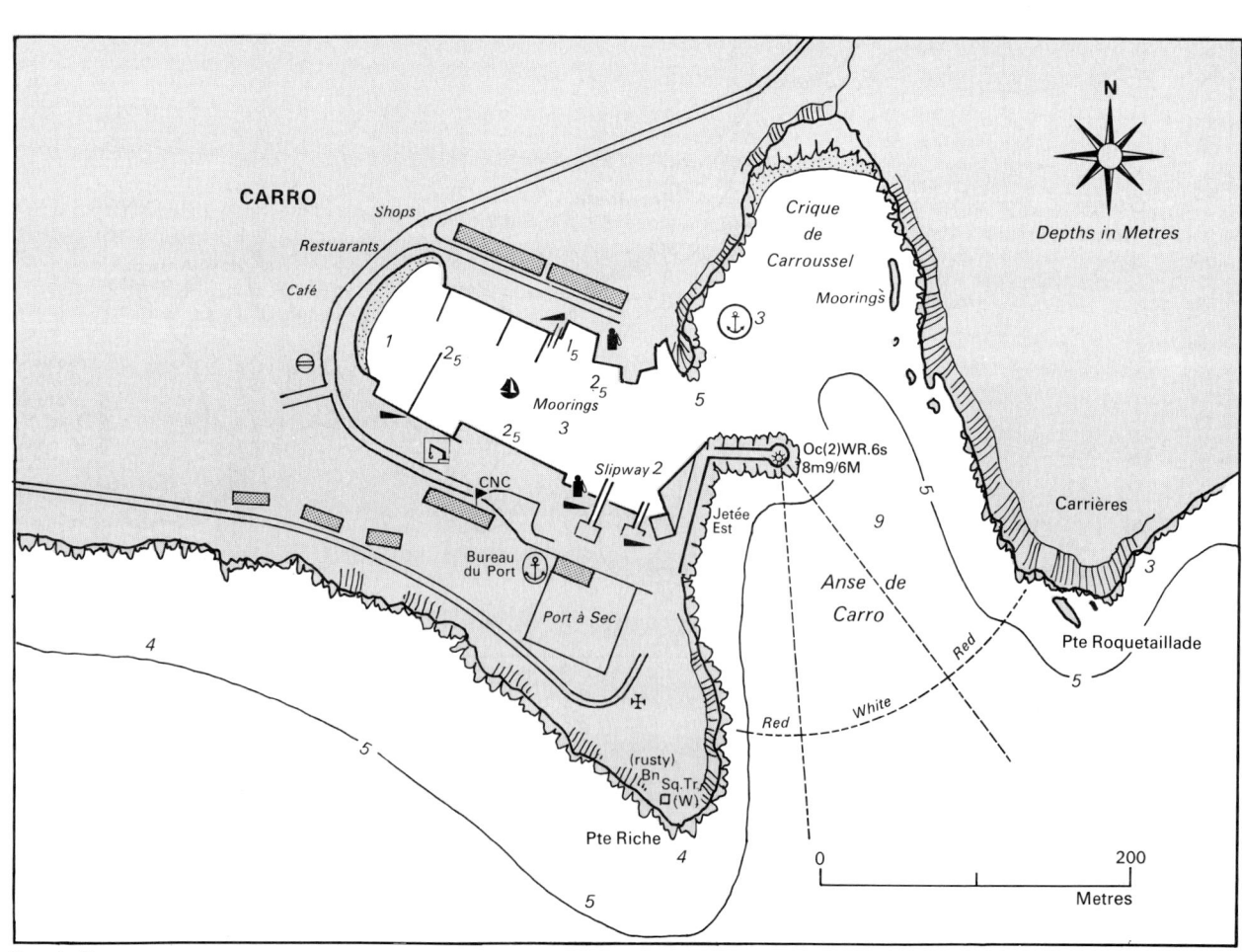

Port de Carro

4 Chimneys Entrance   La Couronne lighthouse

Port de Carro. Entrance and Anse du Lauron chimneys looking NNW. Le Couronne lighthouse

a power station with four tall red and white banded chimneys and a refinery with flares. The lighthouse, white with a red top, which is just beyond the harbour, is conspicuous. Pointe de Carro at the entrance to the harbour is marked by a small square white masonry tower. There are two W cardinal light buoys in the approach (see *Buoys* above) which must be left to port. The jetty is not visible until S of the entrance.

From NE Follow the broken coastline which is backed by a ridge of hills called La Chaîne de l'Estaque. The small isolated Ile Aragon 2M short of

the harbour is conspicuous as is the red-topped white lighthouse at Cap Couronne. Just past this *cap* the entrance to the harbour opens up.

Approach by night
Use the main lights:
Cap Couronne Fl.R.3s34m20M
Faraman Fl(2)W.10s23M to W of the harbour
Ile de Planier Fl.W.5s26M to the SE
   The light buoys of Arnette and Carro (see *Buoys* above) will also help.

Anchorage in the approach
Anchor in the Anse de Verdon, 300m to E of the harbour in 5m of sand or just outside the harbour in the Crique de Carroussel in 3m sand.

Entrance
By day Enter the Anse de Carro on a NNW course towards the head of the Jetée Est and its small white tower with a red top, round this at 20m, leaving it to port.

By night Approach Oc(2)WR.6s in white sector on a course between 322° and 355°. Round it at 20m leaving it to port.

Berths
Secure stern-to inner section of Jetée Est with bow-to buoy in any vacant space in 2m.

Port de Carro looking N   *Port à Sec at bottom left*

Moorings

There are many moorings, the majority belonging to fishing craft; however, three are yacht moorings which may be free. Seek local advice.

Formalities

Bureau du port on S side of the harbour (☎ 42 80 76 28) open 0500–2100 in summer, 0800–2000 in winter.

Facilities

Slips There are two to S of the harbour.
Slipway There is a slipway on the S side of the harbour, 40 tonnes max.
Cranes There is a 6-tonne crane on the S side of the harbour.
Fuel Diesel and petrol are available from pumps on the S side of the harbour (☎ 42 80 74 40) 0800–1200 and 1400–1700.
Water There are several taps around the harbour.
Electricity 220/380v AC available.
Provisions There are a few small shops in the village which can supply simple requirements.
Repairs There is a shipyard and engineer on the S side of the harbour where normal repairs may be carried out.
Post office In the village.
Hotels There are six unclassified hotels in the area.
Restaurants There are fifteen unclassified restaurants and many café/bars.
Yacht club The Club Nautique de Carro (CNC) has an office to the S of the harbour.
Information office At the town hall annex.
Lifeboat A lifeboat is stationed here. Alongside the boathouse is the grave of the French nobleman who was responsible for the development of this service in the area.
Visits The town of La Couronne about half a mile inland has an interesting old church.
Beaches Fine sandy beaches at Verdon and a number of smaller sandy coves along the coast.
Communications Railway at La Couronne and bus services.

Future development

More pontoons to be laid.

History

The area was in occupation in the seventh century BC and was visited by ships from Greece and Italy. By the first century BC it was occupied by the Romans. Tradition has it that the Christian missionaries Lazare, Trophime and Maximin landed here to convert Gaul.

⚓ **Anse de Carro (Crique de Carroussel)**

A small anchorage open to S, with houses at the head and on E side. Port de Carro on W side, sandy beach at head, rocky sides. 3m sand near head.

⚓ **Anse du Verdon**

Anchorage in a deep bay surrounded by low cliffs lined with houses, open to SW. Popular sandy beach at head of bay. Road to Carro. Anchor in 4m sand.

⚓ **Anse de la Vieille-Couronne**

Anchorage open to SE–S. Anchor in 2m sand and rock. Houses on shore and road to La Couronne.

⚓ **Anse de Baumaderie**

A very open anchorage, rocky shore, isolated rock in centre of bay. Not recommended. Anchor in 2m sand.

⚓ **Port de Sainte-Croix**

Another open anchorage, rocky shore, but more suitable for use in offshore winds. Houses and road to E. Anchor in 2m sand.

⚓ **Anse de Tamaris**

A small anchorage surrounded by houses. In approach pay attention to Ile Aragon (the beacon has been washed away 1991). Road ashore to Tamaris – small breakwater. Open S–SW. Anchor in 2m sand.

Semaphore

Lighthouse Cap Couronne

Old Semaphore

Anse du Verdon, looking N

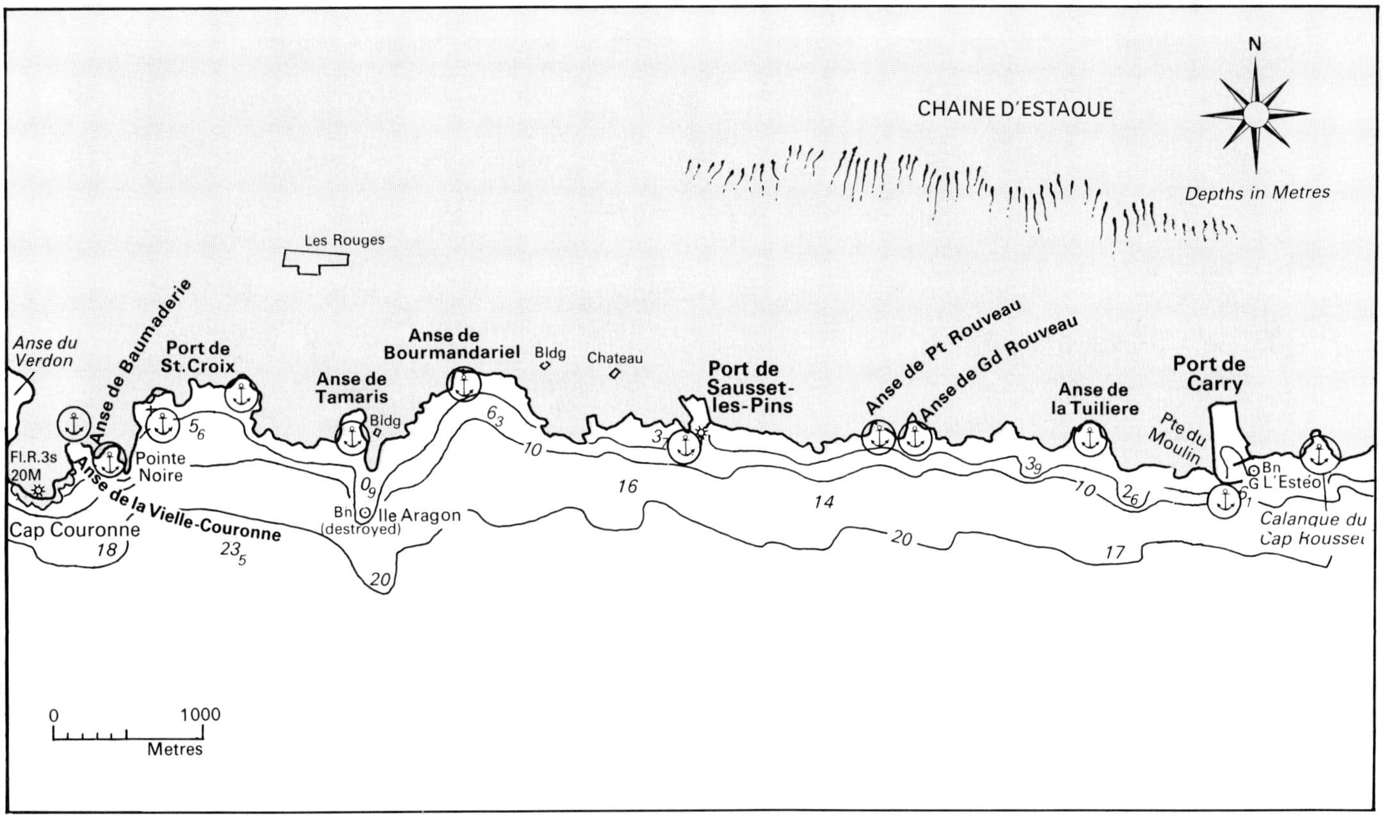

Anchorages E of Cap Couronne

Pointe Noire

Port de Ste Croix, looking N and
Anse de Baumanderie, looking NE

⚓ Anse de Bourmandariel

A very wide anchorage open SE–S–SW. Rocky cliffed shore, road and houses on E side – small breakwaters. Anchor in 4m sand.

⚓ Anse de Bourmandariel and Anse de la Grand Nid

57 PORT DE SAUSSET-LES-PINS
13960 Bouches du Rhône

Position 43°19′·7N 5°06′·5E
Minimum depth   in the entrance 4m (14·5ft)
                in the harbour 3 to 1m (10 to 3ft)
Width of the entrance 40m
Number of yacht berths 294
Maximum length overall 14m (46ft)
Population 3876
Rating 2–3–3

General

A natural fishing harbour which has been improved by the construction of a series of breakwaters, pontoons and quays and has become an excellent yacht harbour. Space along the quays is very limited and is usually taken up by local fishing craft but there are visitors' spaces on the pontoons. Approach and entrance are simple but with heavy winds from SE through S to SW can become dangerous. The harbour and village are pleasant in a simple way and the surrounding countryside is attractive.

Bureau du port

Port de Sausset-les-Pins looking N

Data

Charts   Admiralty 2164, 3498
            French 6767
            Spanish 49
            Navicarte 505

Magnetic variation 1°54′W (1994) decreasing by about 6′ each year.

Speed limit 3 knots.

Port radio VHF Ch 16, 09

Weather forecast Posted daily at *bureau du port*.

Lights
Jetée Ouest head Oc(3)R.12s10m9M Truncated tower
Crête de Sainte Croix Aero Fl.R.2·3s318m

Approach by day

From W Pass half a mile S of Cap Couronne, a low rocky promontory which has a conspicuous white lighthouse with a red top, and outside Ile Aragon, a small isolated rocky island; take care as the beacon has been washed away (1991). The block of flats to the E of this harbour, its Château Gabriel on a small tree-covered hillock inland to the NW and the Jetée Est with a light tower, white with a green top, are all conspicuous.

From NE The coast from Carry, which can be recognised by its very tall block of flats, is of low broken rocky cliffs with many small inlets and bays as far as Sausset. The same features mentioned above are easily seen from this direction.

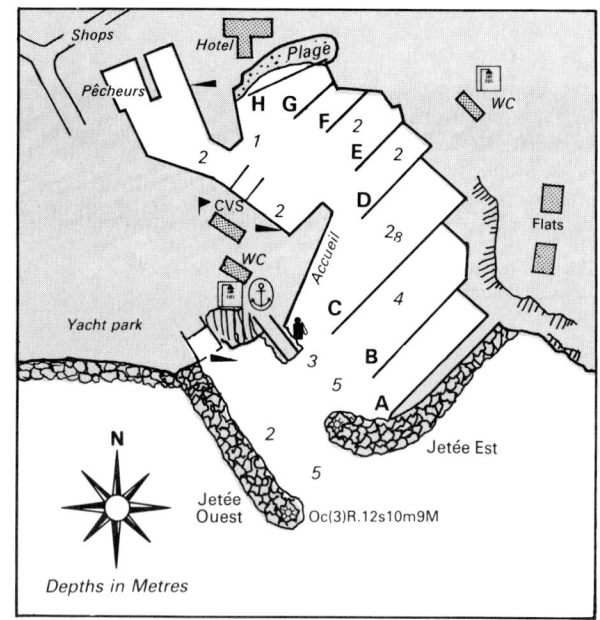

Port de Sausset-les-Pins

Approach by night

Use the major lights:
Cap Couronne Fl.R.3s20M
Ile de Planier Fl.W.5s26M to the SE
Crête de Sainte Croix Aero Fl.R.2·3s318m to N
  There is a minor light on the coast to the E, Ile de l'Elevine Q(6)+LFl.W.15s28m9M.

Château   Entrance

Sausset-les-Pins. Entrance looking NW

Anchorage in the approach

Anchor 100m S of entrance in 10m sand or in the Anse de Bourmandariel 1M to W in 4m sand.

Entrance

By day Approach on a N course leaving the head of Jetée Est to starboard and enter on a NW course rounding on to a NE course and leaving the fuelling jetty to port.

By night Approach Oc(3)R.12s10m9M on a N course and leave it to port, rounding it onto a NE course.

Berths

Secure to Quai d'Accueil or fuelling jetty and report to the *bureau du port*. Berths are stern-to pontoons or quays.

Formalities

Report to the *bureau du port* which is located close to the Quai l'Accueil. Open summer 0800–1200, 1400–2000 and winter 0800–1200, 1400–1800 (☎ 42 44 55 01).

Facilities

Slipway Near Club de Voile.
Slips There are slips both in the inner harbour by the yacht club and in the *avant-port* behind the Jetée Ouest. Another is located beside the hotel.
Travel-lift 16 tonnes.
Cranes One small 3·5-tonne crane to W of the inner harbour.
Fuel Diesel and petrol from pumps just inside the harbour.
Water There are water points on all pontoons and quays.
Electricity 220v AC outlets on all pontoons and quays.
Provisions There are a few shops in the village where supplies may be obtained.
Garbage There is a rubbish bin near the *bureau du port* and near pontoons.
Repairs Limited repairs to engines by a local engineer.
Post office In the village.
Chandlery A shop in the village.
Hotels One ★★, one ★ and six unclassified.
Restaurants There are eight restaurants and a few café/bars.
Yacht club The Club de Voile de Sausset-les-Pins (CVS) has a clubhouse to the W of the inner harbour (☎ 42 45 23 33).

Showers Three showers and WC beside the *bureau du port* and on NE side of the harbour.
Information office The Syndicat d'Initiative is located at the town hall (☎ 42 44 51 51).
Visits A number of prehistoric remains are to be seen inland from this harbour.
Beaches There are sandy coves on either side of the harbour and a small shingle one in the harbour itself.
Festivals A musical week is held during the last week of July.
Communications There are rail and bus services. Airport at Marignane.

⚓ Anse du Petit Rouveau

A small anchorage open to SE–S surrounded by houses on low cliffs, small stony beach. 1 to 2m sand and rocks.

⚓ Grande and Petit Rouveau looking N

⚓ Anse de la Tuilière looking N

⚓ **Anse du Grande Rouveau**

Slightly larger, with rocks on W side of entrance; otherwise similar to above.

⚓ **Anse de la Tuilière**

A wide bay open to SE–S–SW. Road and houses ashore, sand and stone beach at head, rock at head and on E side of the entrance, launching slip. 2m sand and stones.

---

58 PORT DE CARRY-LE-ROUET

13620 Bouches du Rhône

Position 43°19'·7N 5°09'·3E
Minimum depth in the entrance 3m (10ft)
in the harbour 2 to 0·6m (6·6 to 2ft)
Width of the entrance 25m
Number of yacht berths 500
Maximum length overall 15m (49ft)
Population 5241
Rating 2–3–3

General

A medium-sized yacht and fishing harbour in a wide cove that has been improved by the addition of breakwaters. The approach and entrance are not difficult but would be so in strong winds from SE–S–SW and could become dangerous. Facilities are limited but there are a good number of shops etc. in the town which to a large extent is devoted to the summer tourist trade.

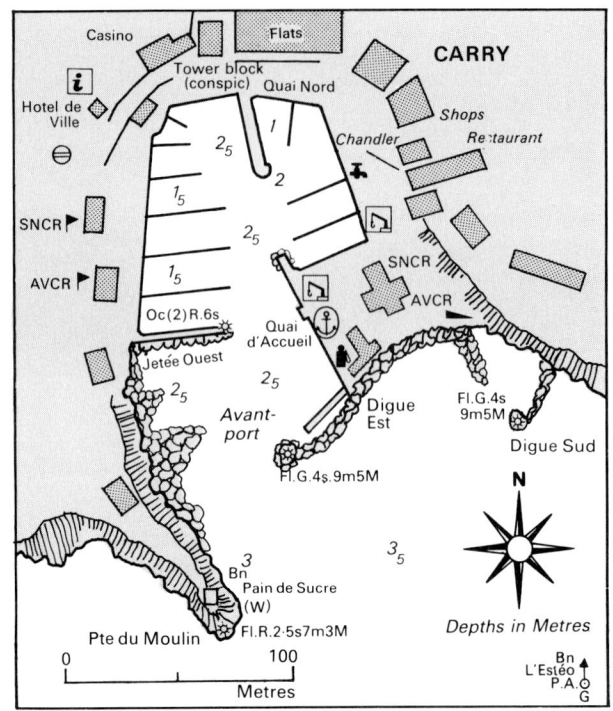

Port de Carry

Port de Carry-le-Rouet looking N

Data

Charts Admiralty 2164
French 6767
Spanish 49
Navicarte 505

Magnetic variation 1°54′W (1994) decreasing by about 6′ each year.

Speed limit 3 knots.

Port radio VHF Ch 16 and 09.

Lights
Digue Est head Fl.G.4s9m5M Green post

Beacons **Pain de Sucre** White truncated conical beacon, red top on Pointe du Moulin Fl.R.2·5s7m3M.
L'Estéo Green beacon, ▲ topmark, W side of rocky shallows.

Weather forecasts Displayed daily at the *bureau du port*. Recorded forecast (☎ 36 68 08 13 and 36 68 08 08).

Warnings

This harbour is in the final stages of reconstruction, and changes are to be expected. A protected subaqua zone exists to SE off this harbour where diving and fishing are prohibited. It is marked by four yellow light buoys, X topmark. A dangerous rocky shallow, L'Estéo, lies to SE of the entrance marked by a ▲ green buoy.

Approach by day

From W Pass ½M to S of Cap Couronne, a low rocky promontory and conspicuous white lighthouse with a red top, and outside the small Ile Aragon (beacon washed away). Port de Sausset will be recognised by some blocks of flats, an isolated *château* and the breakwater. The white tower beacon Pain de Sucre on the Pointe du Moulin will be seen in the close approach to Carry as will the very tall tower block of flats behind the harbour.

From E From Cap Méjean there are four almost equally spaced deep coves all with buildings around their heads. Carry is the fourth and can be identified by the very tall tower block of flats and the white beacon Pain de Sucre on Pointe du Moulin.

Approach by night

Use the following major lights:
Cap Couronne Fl.R.3s34m20M
Ile de Planier Fl.W.5s26M
and minor lights:
Sausset-les-Pins Oc(3)R.12s9M
Ile de l'Elevine (Q(6)+LFl.W.15s9M).

Anchorage in the approach

Anchor about 200m to S of entrance in 7m sand. Day and night anchor shapes/lights to be displayed.

Entrance by day

Approach from a position at least a quarter of a mile offshore on a N course. Leave L'Estéo green beacon

Outer entrance

Port de Carry-le-Rouet looking N–NE–E

Beacon Pain de Sucre   *Entrance*   *Tower block*

Port de Carry-le-Rouet. Approach looking NE

Port de Carry-le-Rouet looking N–NE–E

to starboard and on a NNW course approach the head of the Digue Est, round this and then leave the head of the Jetée Ouest to port. Secure alongside *bureau du port* to starboard.

Berths

Berth stern-to or alongside the club pontoons as directed.

Formalities

Report to the harbourmaster on arrival. The *bureau du port* is located on the starboard side of the entrance and is open winter 0800–1230, 1400–1700, summer 0800–1900 (☎ 42 45 25 13).

Harbour charges

There are harbour charges but a 12-hour stay by day is free.

Facilities

Slips There is a small slip at the N end of the harbour and another in the SE corner.

Cranes There is a 10-tonne crane at the E side of the harbour and another near the *bureau du port*.

Fuel Diesel and petrol from pumps on the E side of the entrance near the *bureau du port*. Open summer 0600–2100, winter 0800–1200 and 1400–1800 (☎ 42 45 25 13).

Water From pontoons and a few places on the quays.

Electricity 220v AC points on pontoons.

Provisions From a supermarket and a number of other shops.

Chandlery A shop on E side of the harbour.

Garbage There are a few rubbish bags on the quays.

Post office In the town.

Hotels One ★★★, two ★★, one ★ and five others.

Repairs Mechanics and one small yard.

Restaurants There are fifteen restaurants and many café/bars.

Yacht club The Société Nautique de Carry-le-Rouet (SNCR) has a clubhouse W of the harbour with bar, lounges and showers (☎ 42 45 13 12). Association de Voile de Carry-le-Rouet (AVCR) also at W side of the harbour (☎ 42 45 47 07).

Showers Six showers and WCs at the *bureau du port*.

Information office Syndicat d'Initiative which is located next to the town hall at the N end of the harbour (☎ 42 45 49 72).

Lifeboat A small lifeboat is kept here.

Beaches There are other small sandy coves to the E along the road.

Festivals The local feast day is 15th August.

Communications There are bus and rail services. Airport at Marignane.

Future development

A plan exists for considerable expansion of the port to almost double its size but there is much local opposition to this development.

History

About 2000 years ago the port of Carry extended some 800m further inland as far as the present position of the railway station. It was used by both the Greeks and the Romans as a place to load the rose-pink stone blocks from a nearby quarry. Some of these were used in the construction of buildings at Marseille. Large saltpans existed to E of the harbour until they were washed away in 1863. There is a statue to Fernandel the famous French comic of world renown.

⚓ **Calanque du Cap Rousset**

A useful anchorage 500m to E of Pont de Carry-le-Rouet with small beach, open to SE–S–SW. Approach with care avoiding L'Estéo rocks.

---

59 PORT DU ROUET

13620 Bouches du Rhône

Position 43°20'·0N 5°10'·5E
Minimum depth in the entrance 2m (6·6ft)
in the harbour 2 to 1m (6·6 to 3ft)
Width of the entrance 20m
Population 146
Rating 4–3–4

General

A small shallow artificial harbour at one end of a large sandy bay, which is very crowded in the season and is more suitable for small day cruisers and runabouts than for yachts. The harbour is open to winds from SE to S.

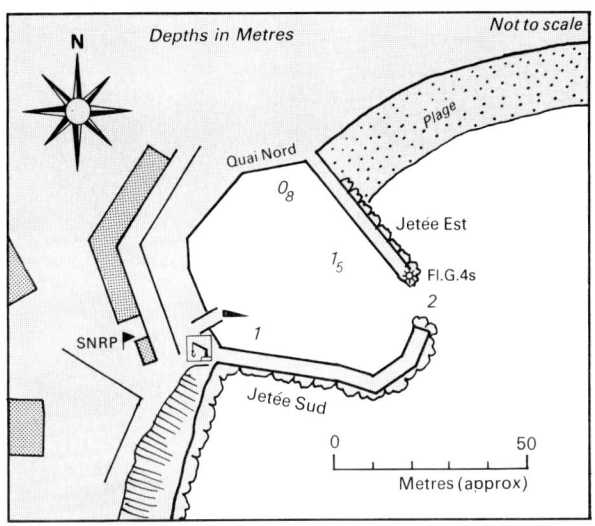

Port du Rouet

Data

Charts Admiralty 2164
French 6767
Spanish 49
Navicarte 505

Magnetic variation 1°54′W (1994) decreasing by about 6′ each year.

Lights
Digue Est head Fl.G.4s9m5M Green mast

Warning

There are rocky dangers off the headlands at each side of the bay.

Approach by day

From W Pass the harbour of Carry with its very tall block of flats behind and follow the broken coastline to the next wide sandy bay, which is backed by a

Port du Rouet. Approach looking NW

Port du Rouet. Entrance looking W

Port du Rouet, looking E

large car park and a group of houses with a ruined church at the E end. The harbour lies on the W side and the jetties become visible from S of the bay.

From E Follow the broken coastline from the conspicuous rail viaducts near Cap Méjean passing the three inlets of Méjean, Figuières and Gignac. The harbour will be seen at the far side of a wide sandy bay behind which is a large car park.

Approach by night

There are no navigational lights and a night approach is therefore not advised.

Anchorage in the approach

Anchor near the middle of the bay in sand, not near either headland, where the bottom is rocky.

Entrance by day

Approach the entrance on a N course and round the head of Jetée Sud at 20m leaving it to port. Enter in mid-channel.

Berths

Secure stern-to Jetée Sud or quay. The area near Quai Nord is shallow.

Facilities

Slips There is a small slip in SW corner.
Crane Small crane in SW corner.
Water Water taps on quays.
Provisions There are a few shops in the village and some that cater for the daily visitors to the beaches.
Restaurants There are several beach café/bars.

Yacht club Société Nautique du Rouet Plage (SNRP) in SW corner of the harbour.
Beaches There is a very good but crowded sandy beach.
Communications A bus service passes near the beach.

---

60 PORT DE LA MADRAGUE DE GIGNAC
13700 Marignane, Bouches du Rhône

Position 43°19′·9N 5°11′·9E
Minimum depth in the entrance 6m (20ft)
　　　　　　　　in the harbour 5 to 1m (18 to 3ft)
Width of the entrance 35m
Population 2772
Rating 3–4–4

General

An attractive small natural harbour which has been improved by some simple harbour works. Approach is easy but some care is necessary in entering due to rocks. The harbour is exposed to E–SE–S winds and in these conditions approach could be dangerous. There are limited facilities.

Data

Charts　Admiralty 2164
　　　　　French 6767
　　　　　Spanish 49
　　　　　Navicarte 505

Magnetic variation 1°54′W (1994) decreasing by about 6′ each year.

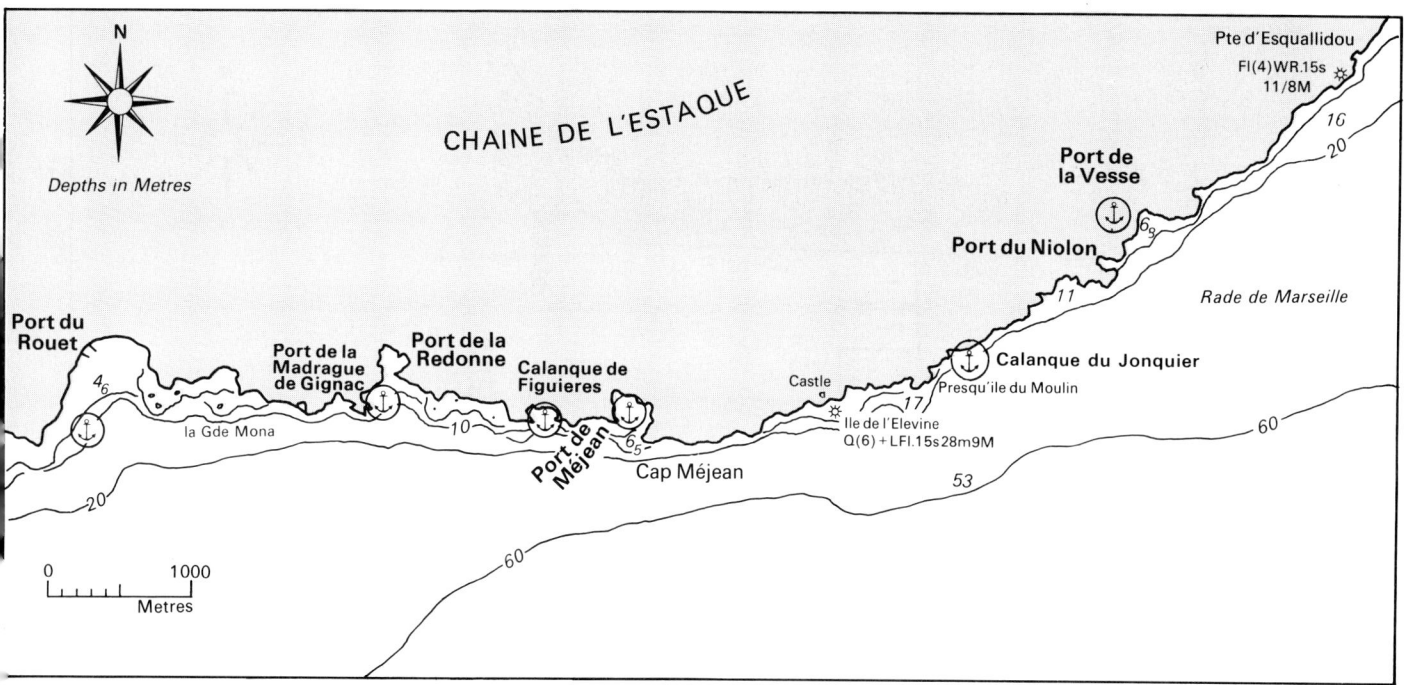

Anchorages W of Rade de Marseille

Warning

In SE winds leave this harbour and take refuge in La Redonne or Carry.

Approach by day

From W Follow the rocky broken coast past Carry with its breakwaters and conspicuous high-rise building. The bay of Le Rouet is identified by the small harbour with a breakwater at the W end of a wide sandy beach with a large car park behind. La Madrague de Gignac lies in the next inlet to the E, which has two railway viaducts behind it, one with six arches. There are a number of rocky dangers extending up to 200m from the coast.

From E Cap Méjean has a small rocky island off its E side (Ile de l'Elevine) on which there is an

Port de la Madrague de Gignac looking NW

Port de la Madrague de Gignac. Approach looking N

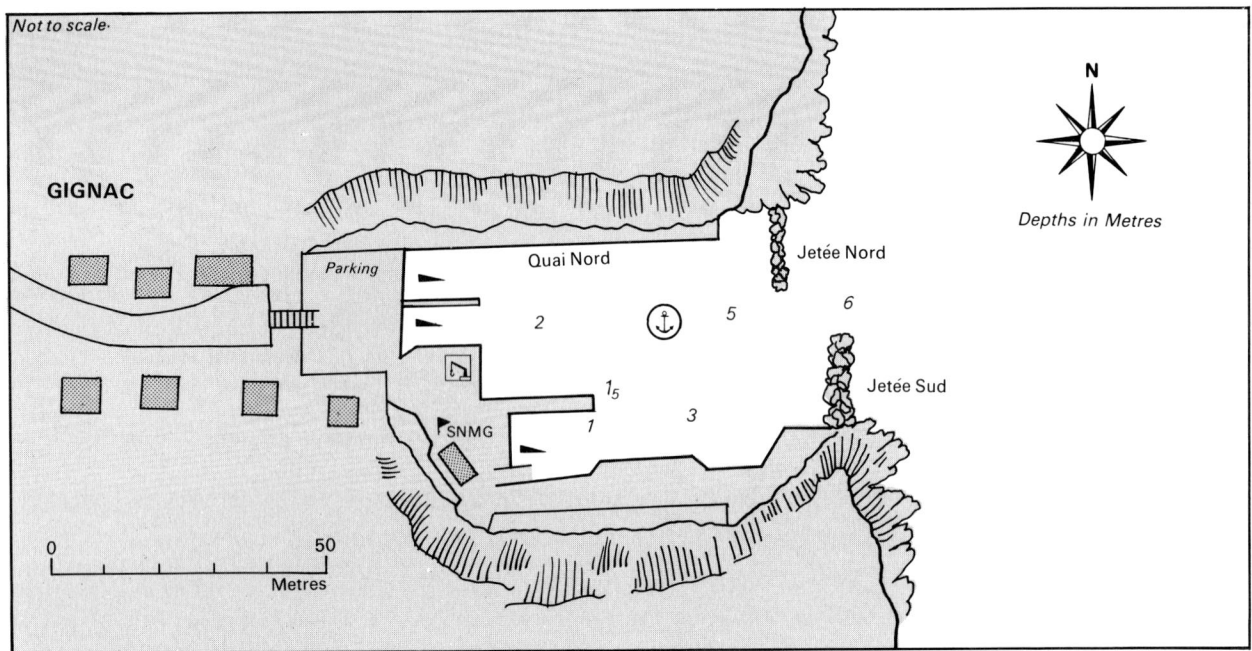

Port de la Madrague de Gignac

inconspicuous lighthouse, S cardinal, black tower, yellow top with ꝟ topmark (Q(6)+LFl.15s28m9M). Round the *cap* and pass Méjean inlet which is deep and Figuières which is small. Calanque de la Redonne and Calanque de Gignac are in the next inlet 1M to W. The railway viaduct behind is also conspicuous from this direction. There are rocky outliers extending some 200m along the coast.

Approach by night

Approach by night is not recommended owing to the lack of navigational lights.

Anchorage in the approach

Anchor in the middle of the bay NE of the harbour entrance in 5m sand.

Entrance by day

Approach the centre of the inlet on a N course. When the Jetée Sud head of La Madrague de Gignac is due W turn to this course and enter between the heads of the Jetée Nord and the Jetée Sud.

Berths

Berths for smaller craft are very limited in number and usually fully occupied. Larger yachts secure to Quai Nord if there is space.

Anchorage

Anchor near the centre of the harbour in 4–5m sand if there is space, otherwise anchor outside to NE of the entrance.

Formalities

Bureau du port at Redonne. Report on arrival.

Harbour charges

There are harbour charges.

Facilities

Slips One large slip and one small at the W end of the harbour.
Cranes There is a 2-tonne crane at the W end of the harbour.
Fuel Petrol is available at La Redonne.
Water There is a water point at the W end of the harbour.
Provisions A limited supply from small shops nearby.
Restaurants Several restaurants and café/bars which cater for the many visitors to the beaches.
Yacht club The Société Nautique de la Madrague de Gignac (SNMG) has a clubhouse to the W of the harbour.
Beaches There are some small rocky beaches nearby.

---

61 PORT DE LA REDONNE

13700 Marignane/Bouches du Rhône

Position 43°20′W 5°12′E
Minimum depth in the entrance 5m (18ft)
in the harbour 5 to 1m (18 to 1ft)
Width of the entrance 40m
Population 2772
Rating 3–4–4

General

An attractive old fishing harbour which has not yet been overdeveloped, easy to approach and enter and offering good protection from all directions except S. Facilities are limited.

Data

Charts Admiralty 2164
French 6767
Spanish 49
Navicarte 505

Magnetic variation 1°54′W (1994) decreasing by about 6′ each year.

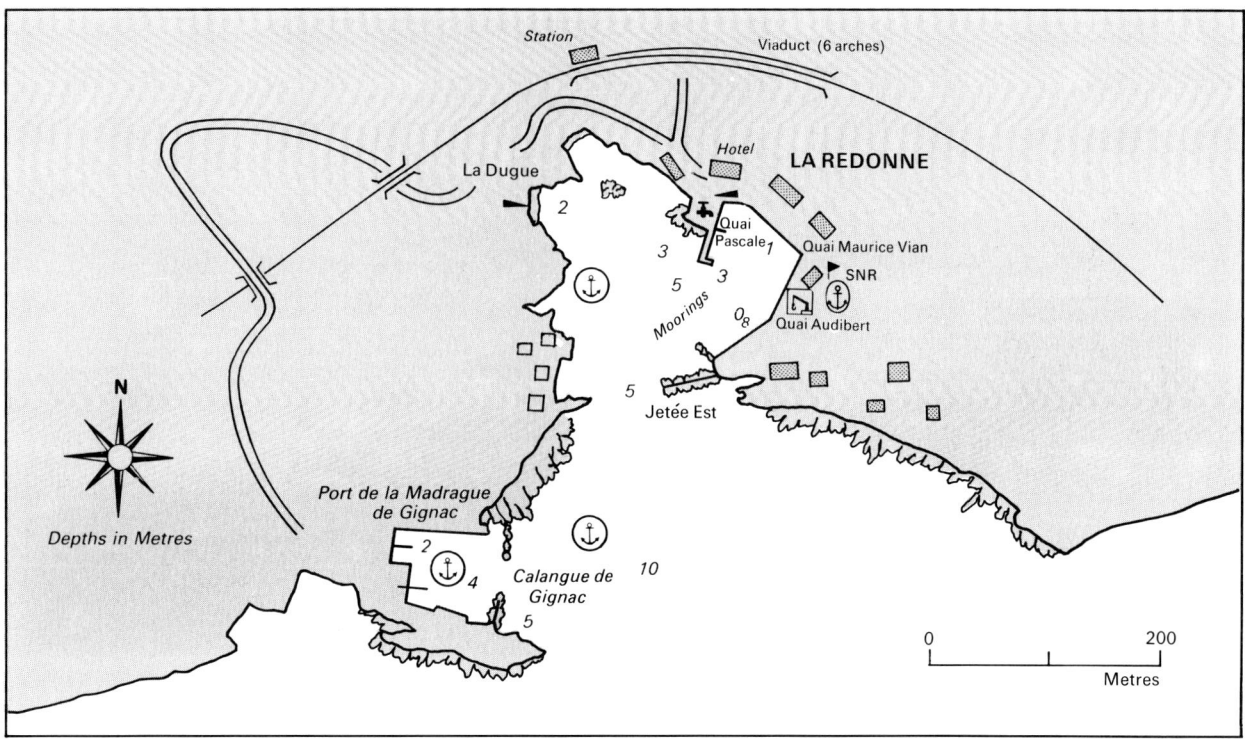

Port de la Redonne

Warning

There are rocky feet to many of the quays.

Approach by day

From W The high-rise tower block of flats at the head of Port de Carry is easily recognised; the Port de Rouet will be seen at the W end of a wide sandy bay. There are a number of exposed and covered rocks lining the coast extending out to 200m. The inlet where this harbour is located is just over 1M to E of Rouet, and can be recognised by a 6-arch viaduct lying behind the harbour.

From E Cap Méjean has a small rocky island ½M to its E which has an inconspicuous lighthouse, S cardinal, black tower, yellow top with ▼ topmark (Q(6)+LFl.15s 28m9M) which can be recognised. Round this *cap* and pass a narrow deep inlet and one small inlet. The coast has rocky outliers extending up to 200m. This harbour lies 1M to W of Cap Méjean and the viaduct is visible in the close approach.

Approach by night

Approach and entrance by night are not recommended due to the lack of navigational lights.

Anchorage in the approach

Anchor in the middle of the bay to S of the harbour entrance in 5m sand.

Entrance by day

Enter the *calanque* on a N course and leave Port de la Madrague de Gignac 150m to W. Approach the entrance of La Redonne also on a N course, and enter, leaving Jetée Est 15m to starboard.

Berths

Berths for yachts are very limited and care is necessary because of the rocky feet near the quays and pontoons. Lie outside a fishing boat until allocated a berth.

Moorings

A number of private moorings exist, and some may be available, apply to *bureau du port*.

Anchorage

It may be possible to find a place to anchor in the W side of the harbour but proceed with care due to rocks.

Formalities

Bureau du port at E side of the harbour.

Harbour charges

There are harbour charges.

Facilities

Slips Large slip at N side of the harbour but approach is shallow (1.0m).
Crane A 3-tonne crane on E side of the harbour.
Fuel Diesel and petrol from the service station near Ensuès-la-Redonne 1½M inland.
Water Taps at E side of harbour and on central Quay Pascale.
Provisions Limited supply locally, more 1½M inland.
Chandlery Shop 1½M inland.
Repairs Engineers 1½M inland.
Restaurants Several around the harbour.
Yacht club The Société Nautique de la Redonne (SNR) has a clubhouse to E of the harbour.
Beaches Two small sandy beaches.
Communications Railway station just behind the harbour up the hill.

Port de la Redonne looking NE

Port de la Madrague de Gignac

Port de la Redonne, looking S

Dinghy harbour

Calanque des Figuières, looking NE–E

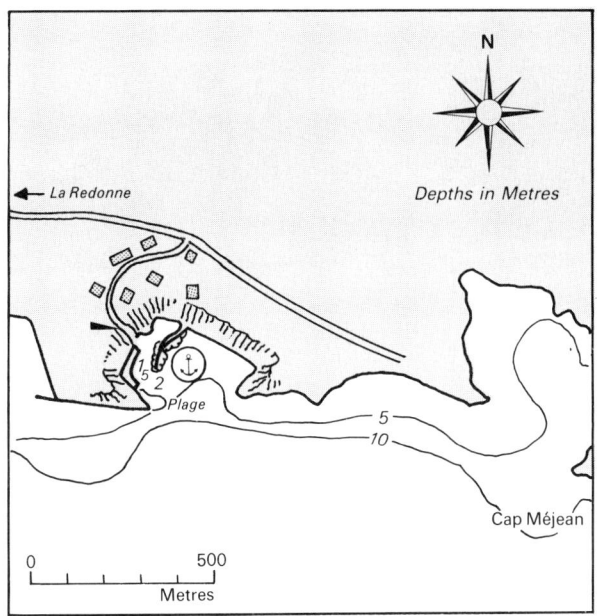

Calanque de Figuières

⌁   **Calanque des Figuières**

This small attractive *calanque* provides good protection from all directions except SE–S–SW. Anchor in mid-*calanque* in 6m sand. There is a small dinghy harbour on the N side from where a road runs inland. There are a number of large houses in the area, which is heavily wooded.

62 PORT DE MEJEAN
Bouches du Rhône

Position 43°19′·8N 5°13′·1E
Minimum depth   in the approach 5m (18ft)
                          in the harbour 3 to 1m (10 to 3ft)
Width of the entrance 30m
Population 200 (approx)
Rating 3–3–4

General

Two small undeveloped harbours, Grand and Petit Méjean, the larger of which is on the E side of a wide *calanque* surrounded by rocky cliffs, and is attractive and suitable for small yachts. The smaller harbour is on the W side and is equally attractive but only has one large slip/hard and quay for dinghies. The approach and entrance are easy and good protection is offered from all directions except S and SW though swell may be experienced from SE. Facilities are very limited.

Data

Charts Admiralty 2164
            French 6767
            Spanish 49
            Navicarte 505

Magnetic variation 1°54′W (1994) decreasing by about 6′ each year.

Approach by day

From W The Port de Carry is easily recognised by the high-rise tower building at the head of the harbour and Port de Rouet will be identified at the W end of a large sandy bay. Keep 200m off the coast because of numerous outlying rocky islets. La Madrague de Gignac at the W side of the entrance to the Calanque de Redonne and the smaller Calanque des Figuières should be recognised. Port de Méjean is located just W of Cap Méjean.

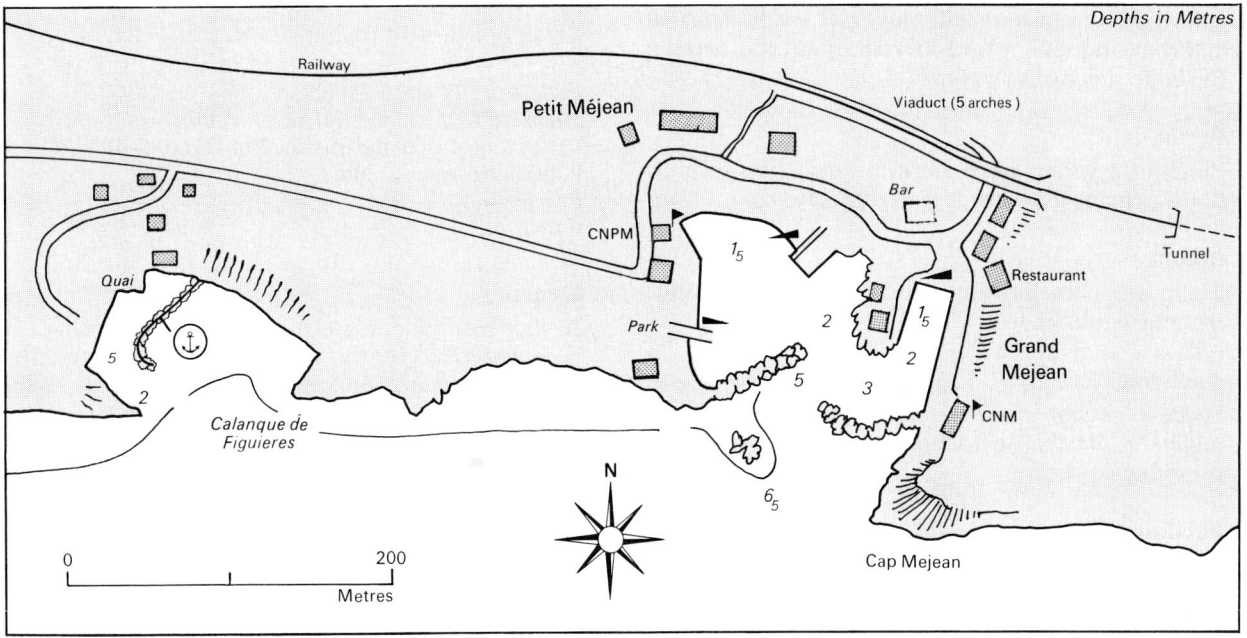

Port de Méjean

Port de Méjean, looking E

From E The cliffed coast from the Port de l'Estaque has only a few *calanques* but Port de la Vesse with a five-arched viaduct, and Port de Niolon with a four-arched viaduct and a number of houses with a square watch tower on the W side of the entrance, should be recognised. The small Ile de l'Elevine has an inconspicuous S cardinal lighthouse tower, black with yellow top and topmark (Q(6)+ LFl.15s28m9M). ¾M to W lies Cap Méjean and just beyond it is the entrance to the Calanque de Méjean.

Approach by night

Not advised due to lack of navigational lights, and rocky dangers.

Entrance by day

Approach the centre of the *calanque* with caution on a N course and keep closer to the starboard side. A rocky islet should be seen to port. Round the small rocky breakwater at the entrance to Grand Méjean leaving it 10m to starboard and enter the harbour on a NW course. A forward lookout is advised because the bottom is rocky in places.

Berths

Berth in a vacant place stern-to quay, bow-to buoy but watch out for rocky feet to the quay.

Moorings

There are a few private moorings and it is possible that one might be free.

Anchorage

Space to anchor inside the harbours is limited but it might be possible to anchor behind one of the two rocky breakwaters.

Facilities

Slips Three slips around the harbour.
Hards Large hard at slips of each harbour and a small one at the SW corner.

Water From clubs or restaurants near the harbour.
Restaurants Several restaurants and café/bars around the harbour.
Yacht club The Club Nautique de Méjean (CNM) has a clubhouse at SE corner of the harbour. The Club Nautique de Petit Méjean (CNPM) has a clubhouse at the W side of the harbour.

Future development

It would not be too difficult to turn this as yet unspoilt harbour into a fair-sized yacht harbour.

⚓   **Calanque du Jonquières (Rade de Moulon)**

An open anchorage in a bay to NE of Presqu'île du Moulon which is open to NE–E–SE–S. Three railway arches, stony beach.

---

63 PORT DE NIOLON

13740 Bouches du Rhône

Position 43°20'·4N 5°15'·6E
Minimum depth in the entrance 3m (10ft)
in the harbour 3 to 1m (10 to 3ft)
Width of the entrance 20m
Population 90
Rating 2–3–4

General

A very small and attractive natural harbour that has been improved by the construction of a small jetty. The harbour is really only suitable for small yachts but it is possible to anchor close in with a larger vessel. The approach and entrance require care as there is not much room to manoeuvre. This harbour is open to strong winds from E, SE and S and is then untenable. There are limited facilities. In the season the old fort is used as a subaqua school and base.

Lighthouse

Lighthouse Cap Méjean (Ile l'Elevine)

Port de Méjean

Cap Méjean, looking NE

Data

Charts Admiralty 2164
French 6739, 6767
Spanish 49
Navicarte 505

Magnetic variation 1°54'W (1994) decreasing by about 6'
each year.

Approach by day

From W Follow the rocky broken coast backed by a
range of hills, La Chaîne de l'Estaque, which become
higher in an E direction. Round Cap Méjean which
has the small Ile de l'Elevine just to the E with an
inconspicuous S cardinal tower, black with yellow

top and ▾ topmark (Q(6)+LFl.15s28m9M). There is
a railway viaduct just SW of the harbour with four
arches. The point just before the harbour has an old
fort with battery on its summit and a watch house.

From E Follow the long and conspicuous outer
breakwater of the commercial port of Marseille in a
NW direction at 1M distance, and when the NW
entrance to the *avant-port* is abeam change to a W
course. Niolon harbour lies in a little cove between
two railway viaducts and is difficult to locate from
afar. The rocky jetty, watch house and small groups
of houses will be seen in the close approach.

Approach by night

Due to the lack of navigational lights approach and
entry by night are not recommended.

Port de Niolon, looking W

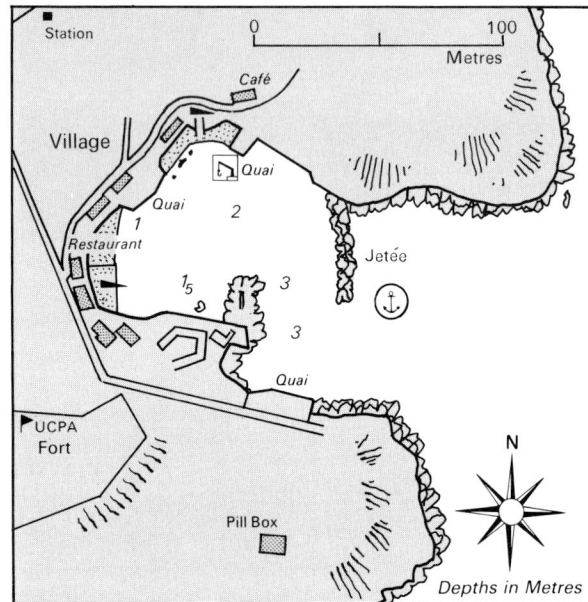

Port de Niolon

Anchorage in the approach

Anchor just outside the entrance in 15m sand and equidistant between the two headlands.

Entrance by day

Approach the head of the jetty on a W course. Enter with care leaving the jetty about 8m to starboard.

Berths

Secure in a vacant space alongside the quay on the starboard hand on entering, or if necessary stern-to.

Moorings

There are a few moorings but they are private and unlikely to be free.

Facilities

Slips There is a sand and concrete slip on the W side of the harbour.

Cranes There is an old 2-tonne crane at the N side of the harbour.

Water There is a tap near the hard.

Provisions There are a few small shops in the village which can supply normal requirements.

Repairs Simple repairs are possible. There is also an engine mechanic.

Restaurants There are a few restaurants which cater for visitors from Marseille, also some café/bars.

Yacht club Centre UCPA de Niolon, based in the fort (☎ 91 46 90 16). Open Easter to end of October.

Beaches There is a stony beach to the NE of the harbour.

Communications There are bus and rail services.

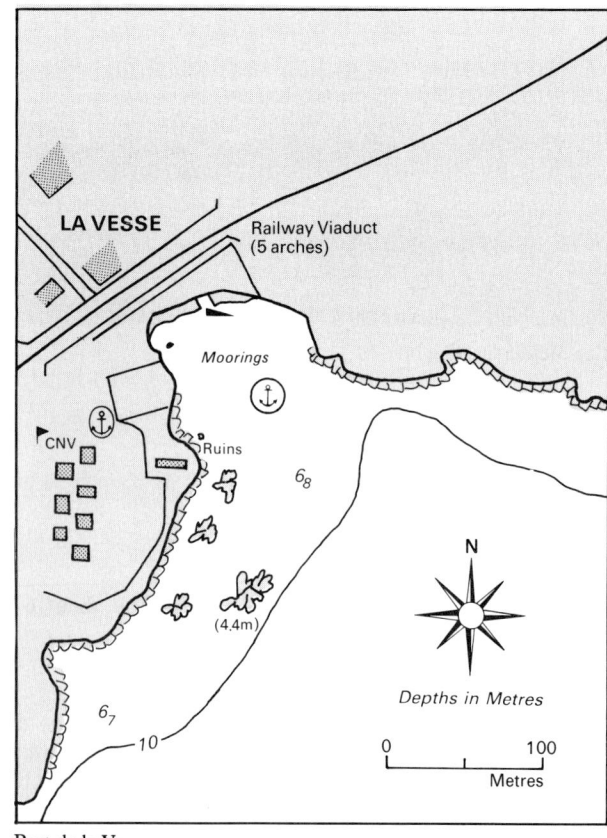

Port de la Vesse

Port de la Vesse looking NW

⚓ Port de la Vesse

Though called a port it is really only an anchorage open to E–SE–S with a place to haul smaller boats ashore. A few moorings have been put down. There is a small village with restaurants and café/bars to N of the viaduct. The Club Nautique de la Vesse (CNV) has a small clubhouse near the hard. Approach on a NW course towards a viaduct with five arches. Pay attention to rocks and rocky islets on the W side of the bay. This bay could be developed into a small harbour.

64 PORT DE LA CORBIERE

13016 Bouches du Rhône

Position 43°21'·5N 5°17'·9E
Minimum depth in the entrance 5m (18ft)
              in the harbour 3 to 1m (10 to 3ft)
Width of the entrance 100m
Population (L'Estaque) 1700 approx
Rating 3–3–4

General

This is a disused commercial harbour once used for loading rock, sand etc. It is now used as a base for a sailing school. It has silted up in parts and care must be taken when using it. Approach and entrance are

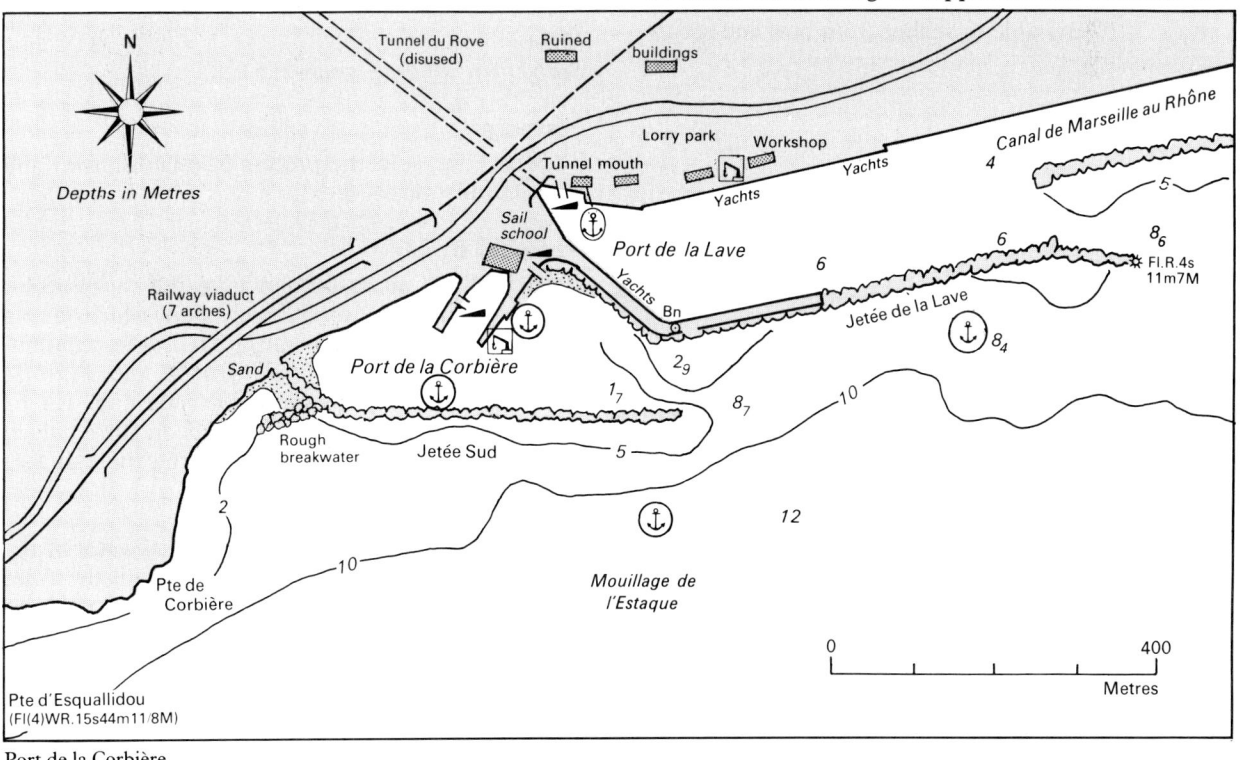

Port de la Corbière

easy, and shelter is provided from all winds except SE–S. No local facilities, but there are good shops and facilities at l'Estaque 1M away.

Data

See 66 Ports de l'Estaque, page 252.

Approach by day

From W Follow the coast along at 200m range. In the closer approach the lighthouse (Fl(4)WR.15s44m11/8M, white column, red top) at Pointe d'Esquilladou will be identified, the Jetée Sud will then be observed, and the large mouth of the Canal du Rove tunnel in the cliff face can be seen when close in.

From S Follow the outer breakwater of Marseille harbour in a general NW direction at ¼M until the Anse de l'Estaque is reached when the large mouth of the Canal du Rove tunnel in the cliff face will be observed. Set course towards this tunnel mouth and the harbour entrance will then open up.

Approach by night

Not recommended.

Anchorage in the approach

Anchor 150m S of the head of Jetée Sud in 10m sand and weed.

Entrance by day

Enter on a W course nearer to the head of Jetée Sud than to the Jetée de la Lave. Have a lookout posted forward and sound carefully.

Berths

Uncomfortable berths alongside the disused loading jetties. It is advisable to anchor from bow and secure stern-to jetty.

Port de la Corbière looking E

Anchor

Anchor to suit draught and wind direction, see chart.

Facilities

Provisions Supermarket nearby.
Repairs Workshop and sailmaker.
Restaurant Café/restaurant to W of the harbour.
Beach Small sandy beach to W of the harbour.
Communications Bus on main road behind the harbour. Rail at l'Estaque.

Future development

This harbour could easily be dredged and converted into a useful yacht harbour.

---

65 PORT DE LA LAVE

13016 Bouches du Rhône

Position 43°21'·5N 5°18'·3E
Minimum depth   in the entrance 8m (26ft)
                  in the harbour 4m (13ft)
Width of the entrance 80m (260ft)
Population 15 (approx)
Rating 4–3–3

General

This is the original barge port where barges manoeuvre before or after using the Tunnel du Rove. The tunnel is now disused due to rock falls and the port is being converted into a spacious yacht harbour. It is well protected except from a swell from SE–S. Entrance is possible direct from the sea or direct from the Ports de l'Estaque via the Canal de Marseille du Rhône.

Data

See 66 Ports de l'Estaque page 252.

Warning

This harbour is in the process of establishment and changes must be expected.

Approach by day

From W Keep at least 200m from the rocky-cliffed shore, passing Pointe d'Esquilladou which has a lighthouse (Fl(4)WR.15s44m11/8M, white column, red top). The rocky Jetée Sud of the Port de Corbière and the Jetée de la Lave beyond will be identified. The mouth of the Tunnel du Rove, which has a large area of ruined buildings on the cliff face above it is easily recognised.

From S Follow the 4M-long outer breakwater of the Port de Marseille in a NW direction until the Anse de l'Estaque is reached. The harbour mouth is 1M in a NW direction from the NW end of the Port de Marseille outer breakwater. A lighthouse (Fl.R. 4s11m7M, white tower, red top) at the head of the Jetée de la Lave is easily seen, as is the Tunnel du Rove, described above.

Approach by night

Not advised without a previous visit by day.

Entrance

Identify the white lighthouse with red top and round the head of the Jetée de la Lave, leaving it 30m to port, on to a W course.

Anchorage in the approach

Anchor 100m to S of Jetée de la Lave in 8m sand and mud.

Berths

Secure to the quay on the N side of the harbour near the head of the harbour in a vacant place and report to the *bureau du port* for the allocation of a berth.

Harbour charges

There are harbour charges.

Facilities

Slipway 25-tonnes slipway (in need of repair).
Cranes Tall crane (18 tonnes).
Provisions Supermarket ½M.
Repairs Mechanic available.
Communications Bus and rail services.

Future developments

Many facilities still to be provided.

Port de la Lave. Tunnel du Rove entrance

Port de la Lave looking E

Main entrance   *Alternative entrance*   *Entrance to commercial harbour*

Port de l'Estaque, looking SE–S

66 PORTS DE L'ESTAQUE
13016 Bouches du Rhône

Position 43°21′·5N 5°19′·0E
Minimum depth in the entrance 5m (18ft)
in the harbour 2 to 0·5m (6·6 to 2ft)
Width of the outer entrance 25m
of the inner entrance 10m
Total number of yacht berths 1504
SNEM 650
Circle de l'Aviron 150
Les Pescadous de l'Estaque 250
Lou Sard 254
Port Autonome 200
Maximum length overall 14m
Population 1709 (approx)
Rating 4–3–3

General

Five small artificial harbours are hidden away in the extreme NW end of the huge commercial port of Marseille with a complex of other smaller harbours devoted to fishing and commercial craft. The approach and entrance are easy except in strong SE winds and accompanying swell. Complete protection is available when inside. Local facilities are fair and they are very good in Marseille itself. The surroundings are not very attractive as this is a commercial area. There are some excellent fish restaurants.

Data

Charts Admiralty 150
French 6739, 6767
Spanish 49
Navicarte 504, 505

Magnetic variation 1°54′W (1994) decreasing by about 6′ each year.

Speed limit 3 knots

Weather forecast Posted daily at SNEM. Recorded forecast (☎ 36 68 08 08 and 36 68 08 13).

Lights
Port de la Lave môle head Fl.R.4s11m7M White tower, red top
Passe de l'Estaque Q.R.11m6M White column, red top. F.R lights are shown from a radio tower 1·8M to NNE of this light
Passe des Chalutiers W side Fl(3)R.12s8m6M White and red tank
E side Fl.G.4s.8m6M White column, green top
Detached breakwater W end Q(9)W.15s5m3M Yellow column, black band, with yellow ⵣ topmark
E end Q(2)R.5s4m1M. Red structure
Môle I. W end Iso.G.4s8m8M White metal column, green top 030°-vis-210°
Digue de Saumaty W head UQ(2)W.1s21m16M White pylon, red top

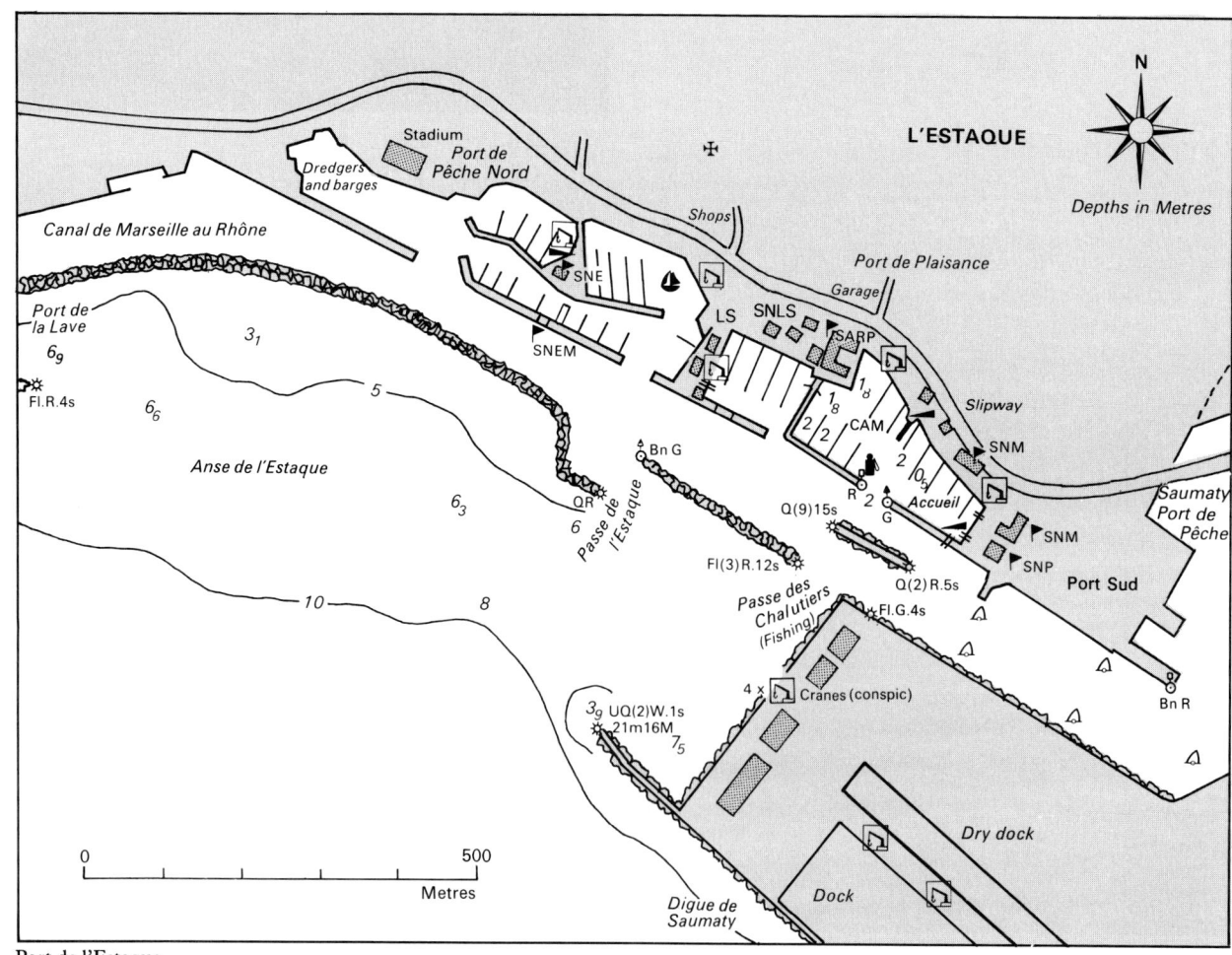

Port de l'Estaque

Port de l'Estaque. Entrances looking NE

Passe Nord Digue du Large N end Fl.G.5s15m8M White tripod, green top

Digue de Saumaty head Fl(2)R.6s12m5M White tower, red top

Forme de radoub No.10 Series of 4 F.W lights on dolphins

Passe de Saumaty. Mourepiane Ouest Fl(3)G.12s7m8M Green column, on dolphin.

Radio tower 5·3M 064° F.R

Warnings

Harbour works are in progress near this yacht harbour and alterations must be expected. Large ships manoeuvring in the area have absolute right of way.

Approach by day

From W The range of whitish rocky hills, La Chaîne de l'Estaque, turns NE at Cap Méjean where there are a series of conspicuous railway viaducts. There is a tall TV tower 1·8M to NNE (F.R) resembling a lighthouse on the hills behind this harbour.

From S Ile Pomègues and Ile Ratonneau are conspicuous, being easily recognisable by their bare white rocky surfaces, as is the large mass of buildings of Marseille surmounted by the church of Notre Dame de la Garde. Pass either side of the islands and approach the extreme N corner of the Rade de Marseille on a N course. The TV tower is also conspicuous from this direction.

Approach by night

Approach and entrance by night are not advised for a first visit owing to the complex layout and harbour works in the area.

Anchorage in the approach

Anchor 220m NW of the entrance in 10m sand.

Entrance by day

Entrance is by the Passe de l'Estaque or Passe des Chalutiers. When using the Passe de l'Estaque leave the outer breakwater and the commercial harbour to starboard. The small red tower marking the entrance will be seen in the closer approach, enter in mid-channel on a NW course and make a U-turn to starboard around the head of the breakwater which has a green beacon, up-pointing cone, leaving it at 20m. Follow this breakwater in a SE direction and enter the inner harbour.

If using the Passe des Chalutiers follow the NW side of the commercial harbour on a NE course and enter between a white and red tank with light and a white post, green top with light. Round the small detached breakwater at its SE end where there is a red light structure.

This entrance is used by large fishing boats, often at speed.

Harbours

The SE Port Plaisance should be entered first, secure near the fuel berth. If no berths are available try the other three yacht harbours or Ports de la Lave or de Corbière.

Berths

Berth stern-to pontoons, with bow-to mooring buoy where there is space.

Anchorage

Anchoring inside the harbour area is not permitted.

Formalities

Bureaux du port

1. Port Autonome Nord (PAN) (☎ 91 91 90 66 and 91 91 20 17 also VHF Chs 16, 2).
2. Société Nautique d'Estaque Mourepiane (SNEM) (☎ 91 46 01 40).
3. Circle d'Aviron de Marseille (CAM) (☎ 91 46 00 66).
4. Lo Pescadou de l'Estaque (LPE) (☎ 91 09 23 90).
5. Lou Sard (LS) (☎ 91 46 23 39).

Report on arrival to the secretary at the yacht clubhouse in the area of the harbour concerned.

Harbour charges

Free of charge for one day. There are harbour charges.

Facilities

Slips There are three small slips in the SE corner of the SW Port Plaisance.

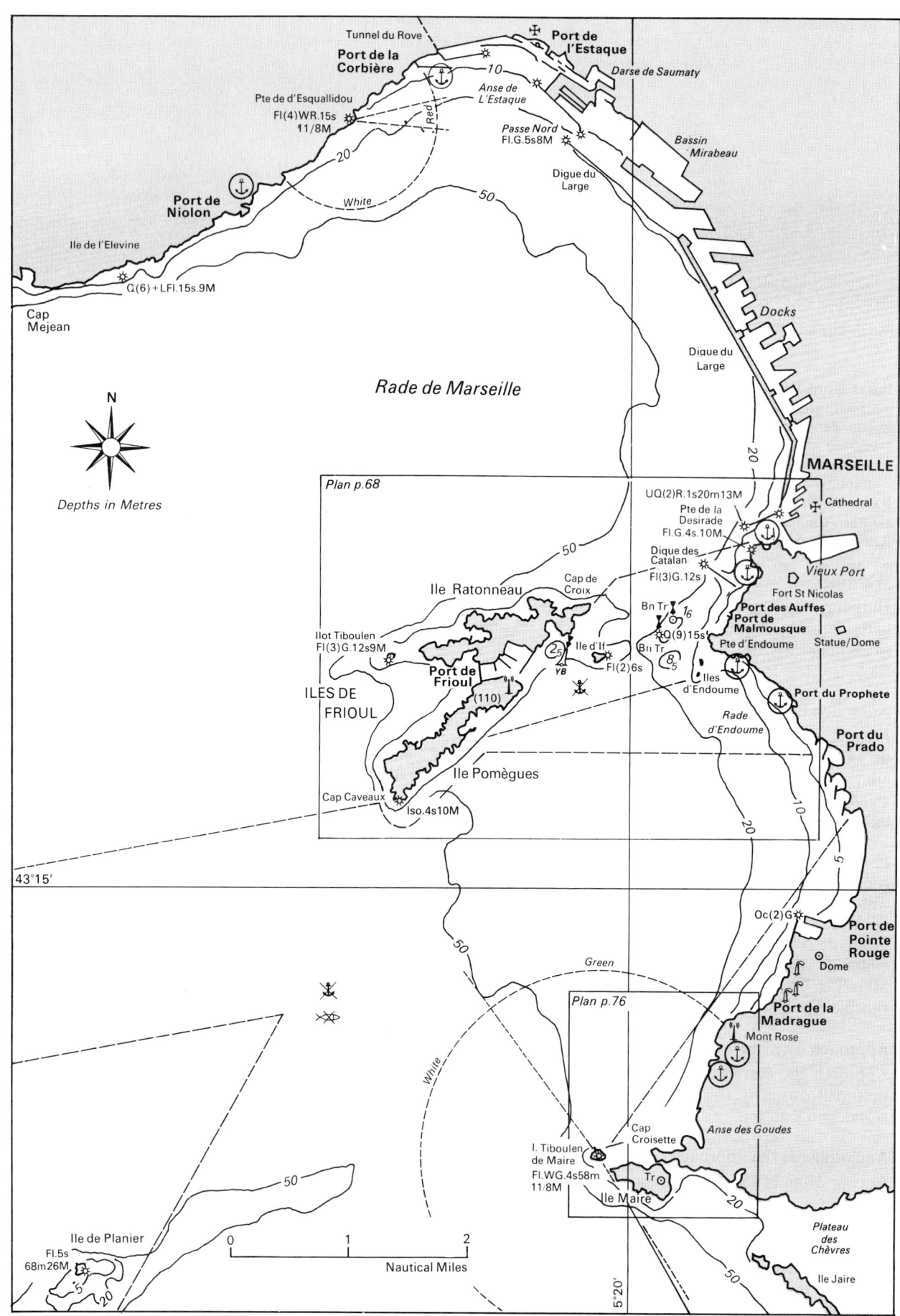

Rade de Marseille

Slipways There are two slipways on the E side of the SW Port Plaisance, one of 25-tonne capacity.

Cranes There are a number of cranes from 3–6 tonnes.

Fuel There are pumps for petrol and diesel at the NW side of the entrance to the SW Port Plaisance. Open 0900–1130 and 1400–1600, Saturdays only. (☎ 91 46 04 72)

Water There are water points on the pontoons and on the quays.

Electricity Points for 220v AC 16 amps at the end of the pontoons.

Provisions A few shops in the village nearby can provide essentials.

Ice Available.

Garbage There are rubbish containers on the quayside.

Chandlery There is a small ironmonger/chandler in the village.

Repairs A mechanic works behind the clubhouse and there are others around the harbour who can carry out minor repairs to hull and engine.

Post office This is in the village.

Restaurants There are a number of restaurants, some of which specialise in seafood.

Showers and WCs Available.

Yacht clubs The Cercle Aviron Marseille (CAM) (☎ 91 46 00 66) was originally a rowing club but now includes yachting. It has a bar, lounge, showers etc. and is on the E side of the inner harbour. The Société Nautique d'Estaque-Mourepiane (SNEM) (☎ 91 46 01 40) has two buildings at the SE end of the inner harbour with similar facilities. There are a three other smaller clubs.

Communications There are rail and bus services.

Future development

A new slip of 40 tonnes is to be constructed at the NW end of the harbour.

Port de Marseille (Commercial)

This huge port complex stretches for 6M in a SE direction, lying behind a detached breakwater. Not for use by yachts.

---

67 PORT DE MARSEILLE (VIEUX-PORT)
13000 Bouches du Rhône

Position 43°17'·6N 5°21'·2E
Minimum depth in the entrance 7m (25ft)
in the harbour 5·6 to 4m (18 to 14·5ft)
Width of the entrance 70m
Number of yacht berths 3200
Population 878,689
Rating 2–2–1

General

A vast complex of docks, basins and harbours make up the largest port in France which stretches along the coast for 5½M from the Anse de l'Estaque, where there is a yacht harbour (see page 252), to the original and natural harbour which has several yacht basins. Visiting yachts usually make use of the Vieux-Port where there are excellent facilities, and where the approach and entrance are easy and can be

taken in any weather. Despite the considerable destruction of the town during the war it is still a fascinating place to visit and there is much to see. The traditional idea that Marseille is a dirty and wild city is inaccurate and although the water in the harbour may be oily, most of the town is smart and fashionable.

Data

Charts Admiralty 150, 2164
French 6739, 6767
Spanish 49
Navicarte 504, 505

Currents and sea levels In stormy conditions sudden surges and currents can be experienced in the entrance, with up to 0·2m changes in sea level.

Magnetic variation 1°54'W (1994) decreasing by about 6' each year.

Port radio Call on VHF Ch 12. Tugs work on Ch 6. Pilots on Ch 8. Local clubs Ch 24, 35, 81, 82, 90, 91, 96. 2049, 1939kHz

Coast radio Marseille (FFM) on 1671, 1906, 1936, 1939, 2625, 2628, 3792 3795, 2182kHz, also VHF 16, 24, 26

Weather forecasts Posted daily in the clubs and *bureau du port*. Recorded forecast (☎ 36 68 08 08 and 36 68 08 13)

Speed limit 4 knots.

Traffic signals Displayed on a mast at the elbow of Digue Ste-Marie and refer to vessels entering Bassin de la Grande Joliette and its *avant-port* but should be noted by yachts entering or leaving the Vieux-Port so as not to interfere with commercial traffic.

By day	By night	Meaning
⦙	3 R Lts, vertical	Entrance absolutely prohibited; port closed
● ▲ ●	R Lt above W Lt above R Lt	Entrance prohibited
▼ ▲ ●	G Lt above W Lt above R Lt	Entrance and departure prohibited
▼ ▲ ▼	G Lt above W Lt above G Lt	Departure prohibited

Lights

Digue des Catalans NW head Fl(3)G.12s7m5M White pylon, green top Ra reflector

Pointe de la Désirade Fl.G.4s13m10M White tower, green lantern 003°-vis-271°

Digue Ste-Marie SW end UQ(2)R.1s20m13M White and red pylon

Root Oc(3)R.12s7m7M Red tower 195°-060.5°

Digue du Fort St-Jean head Oc(3)G.12s7m6M Dark green tower 001·5°-vis-299° unintens, 001·5°-009° and 277°-299°

Fort St-Jean. N side of entrance Q.R.11m7M Red pylon

Fort St-Nicolas S side Iso.G.4s8m7M White column, dark green top

255

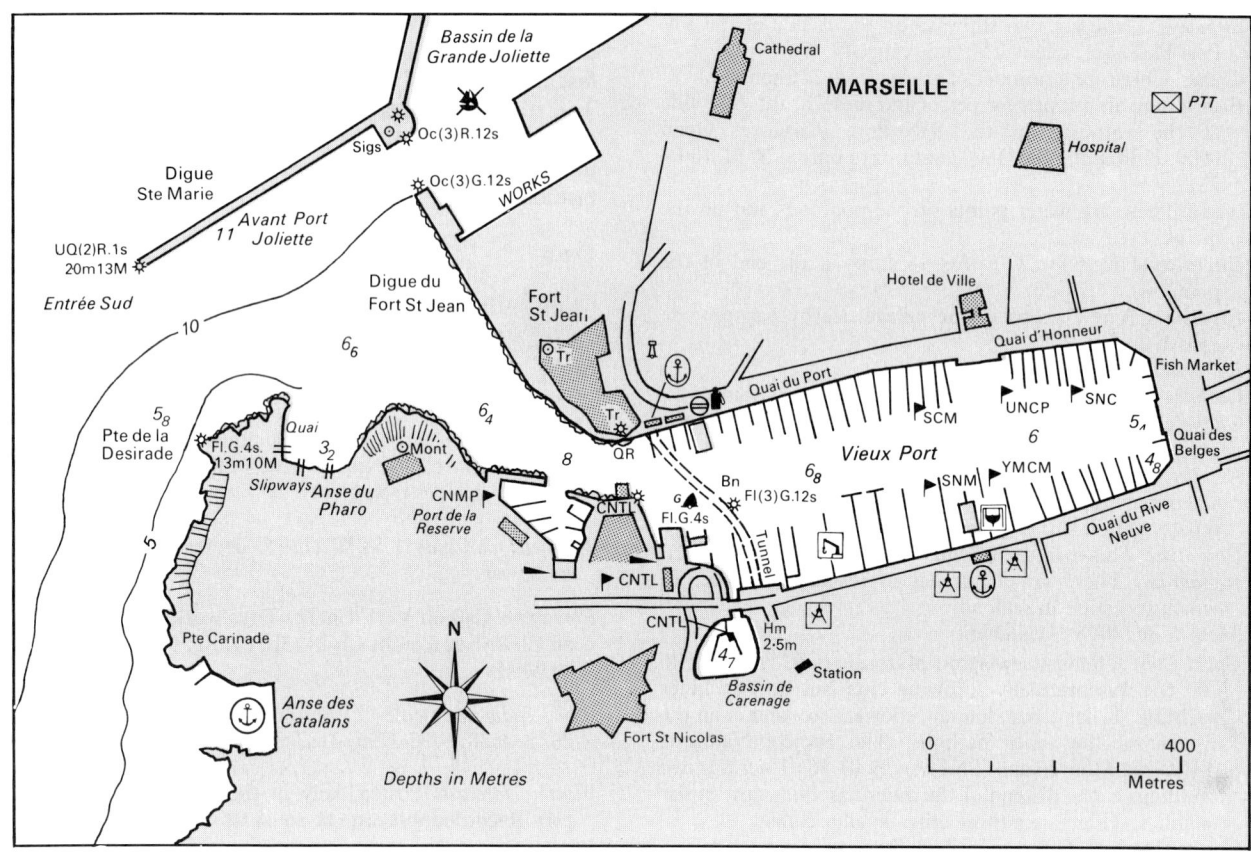

Port de Marseille (Vieux Port)

Port de Marseille. Approach looking E

Port de Marseille. Approach. Isle and Château d'If, looking NW

Port de Marseille (Vieux Port) looking up the harbour

Dolphin W Fl.G.4s5m5M marked 'Tunnel Ouest' in white, green top
Dolphin E Fl(3)G.12s5m5M marked 'Tunnel Est' in white, green top
There are other navigational lights in the commercial part of the port.

Beacons There are two W cardinal, YBY with ⲭ topmarks, beacon towers 1M to SW of this port which can be passed 50m to E or W: Sourdaras, (Q(9)15s13m8M) and Canoubier, (no light).

Warnings
Commercial traffic including ferries have the right of way over yachts in the approach, entrance and interior of this port. Yachts must observe the traffic signals and keep well out of the way of large merchant vessels, and when entering and leaving the Vieux-Port must do so under engine. Mist, fog and industrial haze are all prevalent in this area except when there are strong winds.

Approach by day
From W The bare white rocky Iles Ratonneau and Pomègues can be seen from afar as can the mass of buildings of Marseille surmounted by a pointed hill with Notre Dame de la Garde at the summit, the latter has a gilded statue on the spire which is illuminated at night. Make towards the head of Digue Ste-Marie at the S end of the long breakwater which lies outside the port.

From E Having rounded the very prominent white rocky Cap Croisette outside Ile Maire, set a N course towards two W cardinal, YBY with ⲭ topmarks, beacon towers, Sourdaras (Q(9)15s13m8M) and Canoubier, a similar tower with no light. Pass either side of these towers but leave Ile et Château d'If to port and the small Iles d'Endoume, one of which has a little fort, to starboard. On a NNE course leave Digue des Catalans (Fl(3)G.12s7m5M) to starboard and approach the head of Digue Ste-Marie.

Approach by night
Use the major lights:
Cap Couronne Fl.R.3s20M
Ile et Château d'If Fl(2)W.6s11M
Ile de Planier Fl.W.5s26M
There are many other minor lights which could be used. The Château d'If is floodlit as is Notre Dame de la Garde which has a statue on top.

Anchorage in the approach
Anchor 300m N of head of Digue Ste-Marie in 20m mud and gravel. Holding is not very good.

Entrance
By day Enter on an ENE course leaving the head of Digue Ste-Marie 200m to port, observe the traffic signals. Cross the *avant-port* Joliette turning onto a SE course to pass between the two forts of St-Jean to port and St-Nicolas to starboard, then leave a green light buoy and a green dolphin to starboard.

By night Enter on an ENE course leaving UQ(2)R.1s 200m to port and Fl.G.4s 100m to starboard, observe traffic signals. Keep to this course which is towards Oc(3)R.12s and Oc(3)G.12s until Q.R and Iso.G.4s

257

Traffic signals   *Commercial harbour*

Port de Marseille. Entrance looking NE

Vieux Port

Port de Marseille. Entrance to Vieux Port

appear on the beam then turn to a SE course towards these lights and then between them, leaving Fl.G.4s and Fl(3)G.12s to starboard.

Berths

On entering, small yachts berth stern-to the pontoons of Centre Nautique Touristique du Lacidon (CNTL) which has the first four pontoons on the starboard hand on entering the Vieux-Port.

Large and medium-size yachts secure stern-to the pontoons of Société Nautique de Marseille (SNM), which lie beyond the fishing boats halfway up the harbour on the starboard hand. The clubhouse is a houseboat painted with blue and white bands.

Very large yachts, having booked a berth in advance, secure stern-to Quai d'Honneur halfway up the harbour on the port side opposite the *hôtel de ville* (town hall).

Prohibited anchorages

There is a large area to SW of the entrance where anchoring is not permitted, and it is not permitted inside the harbour either.

Formalities

If using the SNM or CNTL pontoons report to the secretaries concerned, if using the Quai d'Honneur report to the *bureau du port* (☎ 91 56 15 00, 91 33 73 55 or 91 33 05 84) open 0700–1900, 23 quai de Rive-Neuve, on S side of the Vieux-Port. Affaires Maritimes, 23 rue des Phocéens (☎ 91 90 39 65), *douanes* (customs) 48 avenue Robert Schumann (☎ 91 91 90 05).

Charges

There are harbour charges.

Facilities

Slips At the shipyards.

Cranes The SNM has a 10-tonne lift and a 6-tonne crane, the Union Nautique Marseillaise (UNM) has one of 6 tonnes and there are many other smaller cranes. In the commercial port there are many more of up to 150 tonnes.

Fuel Diesel and petrol are available from pumps at the NW corner of Vieux-Port, 0700–1930.

Water From pontoons and quays.

Electricity 220v and 500v AC from points on the pontoons.

Provisions There are very many shops of all types in the town and a number in the back streets just S of the Vieux-Port. There is also a market here.

Ice From an ice factory 400m to the S of SNM clubhouse during mornings only.

Duty-free goods Apply to the secretary of the yacht club who will advise.

Garbage Rubbish containers on pontoons and quays.

Chandlery Very many shops just to S of Vieux-Port.

Repairs There are many shipyards which have works in Port de la Réserve and Anse du Pharo and which specialise in yacht repairs. Just S of the Vieux-Port are a number of workshops where engines may be repaired. There is a sailmaker who can repair sails, and two firms repair electronic equipment. Virtually all repairs can be carried out at this port.

Laundrette To the S of Vieux-Port.

Post office This is to the NW of Vieux-Port in Rue Barbusse.

Hotels One *****, three ****, forty-three **, seven * and many other unclassified hotels.

Restaurants Over one hundred restaurants of all types and many café/bars. Get local advice because many cater only for tourists and give poor value for money.

Yacht clubs There are a number of yacht clubs and societies in Marseille, the most important and oldest being the Société Nautique de Marseille (SNM) (☎ 91 33 05 84 and 91 33 73 55) which has a floating clubhouse with blue and white bands on the S side of the Vieux-Port providing a bar, lounge, restaurant, showers, WCs etc. This club has been in existence since 1887. The Union Nautique de Marseille (UNM) (☎ 91 52 59 71), with a modern clubhouse in the Port de la Réserve has similar facilities. The Yacht Motor Club de Marseille (YMCM) (☎ 91 54 16 42) has a small clubhouse at the S end of the Vieux-Port with showers. The Centre Nautique de Tourisme de Lacidon (CNTL) (☎ 91 33 44 84) has a small office in the Bassin de Carénage. There are many others.

Consul The British Consul resides at 24 avenue du Prado, 13 Marseille 6e (☎ 91 37 68 54).

Information office The Syndicat d'Initiative has an office in La Canebière to E of Vieux-Port (☎ 91 55 11 11).

Visits There are many places to visit including a 12th-century church, Greek and Roman remains and thirteen of museums. Full details are available from the information office.

Beaches The beaches are to the SW of the town but they are very crowded.

Communications Marseille is the centre of a communication network and bus, rail, air and sea passages are available to most places in the Mediterranean and to major cities.

Vedettes (ferries) cross the Vieux-Port at frequent intervals.

Future development

A number of ideas to enlarge the harbour for yachts have been proposed, the latest being studied is the removal of the quays in the Grand Bassin Joliette located to NE of the Vieux-Port and to establish a yacht harbour there.

History

The port was founded in about 600 BC by the Greeks from Asia Minor who used it as a centre from which to colonize the coasts between Agde and Nice; they called it 'Massilia', or 'Massala' from which the modern name has been derived. It is of interest that the seafarers of Marseille voyaged to England and beyond, among them Pytheas who was the first navigator to reach Britain and name it in about 400 BC. Before long the Greeks were joined by the Phoenicians and their republic flourished, but by 200 BC rivalries were such that when there was a Celtic invasion an appeal was made to Rome and after three years of strife the area became part of the Roman Empire.

The city was destroyed in 49 BC by Julius Caesar because it sided with Pompey in his rebellion and with the fall of the Empire the port suffered constant invasions by the Barbarians, but survived to become a part of the Kingdom of France in 1481. Down the centuries Marseille suffered many troubles as it usually supported the side with a lost cause. During the last war large parts of the old town were destroyed by the Germans when they were unable to find resistance groups hiding in the area, as well as by American bombing prior to the invasion of Europe. Many well known artists have painted pictures of the area around Marseille.

Entrance

Port de Marseille (Vieux Port). Entrance looking E at Fort St-Jean

Anse du Pharo, looking W

⚓ Anse du Pharo

Though really a part of the Vieux-Port, it is separated by a large headland from the rest of the harbour and makes a useful anchorage, protected from all directions, but subject to swell from NW. Ashore are the slips and quays of several yards with roads connecting them to the town.

⚓ Anse des Catalans

Only a fair-weather anchorage off a very crowded small sandy beach open to SW–W–NW. Anchor as close inshore as draught permits.

68 PORT DES AUFFES
13000 Bouches du Rhône

Position 43°17'·3N 5°21'E
Minimum depth   in the entrance 4m (14·5ft)
                          in the harbour 3 to 2m (10 to 6·6ft)
Width of the entrance 25m
Population (Marseille) 878,689
Rating 3–3–4

General

An attractive old fishing boat harbour in a *calanque* ¾M to SW of the Vieux-Port de Marseille, only suitable for small craft and very crowded. The entrance is unique, being under a road bridge. Anchorage inside the *avant-port* is possible. Open to NW *mistral* and dangerous with this wind.

Data

See 67 Port de Marseille, page 255.

Port des Auffes. Entrance looking E

Approach by day

From W Pass to the N of Ile Ratonneau and on an E course leave the two W cardinal, YBY with topmarks, beacons Canoubier (no light) and Sourdaras (Q(9)W.15s13m8M) to starboard and the detached breakwater Digue des Catalans (Fl(3)G.12s7m5M) to port. The harbour breakwater and road bridge (three arches) will be seen close S of the conspicuous Monument aux Morts d'Orient which is shaped like a gateway.

From S Cross the wide Baie d'Endoume on a N course leaving Iles d'Endoume (7m) 200m to starboard then Sourdaras and Canoubier 200m to port. Pay attention to the foul ground to N of Pointe d'Endoume. The monument described above is also conspicuous from this direction. Approach on an E course.

Entrance

By day Enter on an E course 15m from the head of the breakwater because there is an awash rock off the small point which forms the port side of the entrance.

By night Entrance not recommended without a previous visit by day.

Berths

Not usually available.

Anchorage

Anchor in *avant-port* in 3m sand and mud with rock patches.

Formalities

Report to *capitaine de port* if securing inside the harbour.

Charges

Harbour charges are made.

Facilities

Hards Along SW side of harbour.
Slips At head of harbour and at head of *piscine*.
Crane 4-tonne crane at SE corner of the harbour.
Water A few taps around the harbour.
Provisions Small shops nearby in Endoume.
Hotel One.
Restaurant Well known fish restaurants L'Epuisette, Chez Fonfon and others near the harbour.
Beach No beach, but a basin used as a swimming pool on S side of the entrance.
Communications Main coast road with bus service. Rail and air services.

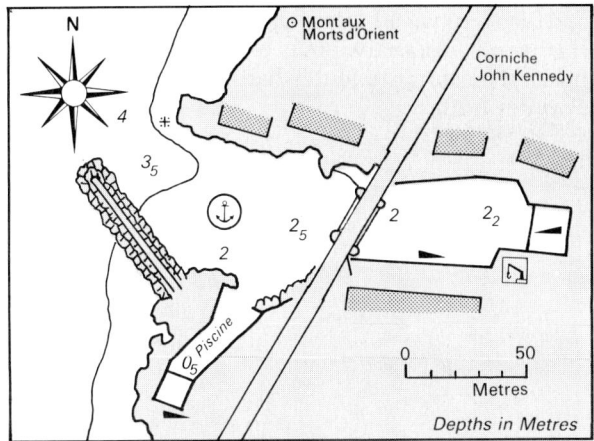

Port des Auffes

PASSAGE BETWEEN ILES D'ENDOUME AND THE COAST

An easy passage with 5·4m minimum depth, and 80m wide taken in a SE or NW direction. The Ecueil des Cent Francs has a fort-like building and a cross while the isle to N is bare rock 7m high.

Beacon towers between Ile Ratonneau and Pointe d'Endoume

Iles d'Endoume passage

Passage between Iles d'Endoume and the coast, looking NW

69 PORT DE LA MALMOUSQUE (ENDOUME)
13000 Bouches du Rhône

Position 43°17'·1N 5°20'·9E
Minimum depth in the entrance 2m (6·6ft)
in the harbour 2 to 1m (6·6 to 3ft)
Width of the entrance 20m
Population (Marseille) 878,689
Rating 3–3–4

General

A very small fishing harbour in a *calanque* surrounded by houses. The entrance requires care, being behind a group of rocks. Open to NW *mistral* and dangerous, all boats are hauled ashore during this wind. Attractive but only suitable for small boats. The entrance to this harbour lies 200m to S of Port des Auffes.

Data

See 67 Port de Marseille, page 255.

Approach by day

From W Pass to the N of Ile Ratonneau and on an E course leave the two W cardinal, YBY with topmarks, beacons Canoubier (no light) and Sourdaras (Q(9)15s13m8M) to starboard and the detached breakwater Digue des Catalans (Fl(3)G.12s7m5M) to port. Port des Auffes breakwater and road bridge (3 arches) will be seen close S of the conspicuous Monument aux Morts d'Orient which is shaped like a gateway. From a position 100m off the entrance to Port des Auffes, proceed on a S course passing equidistant between Ile des Pendus (5m), which has a small white beacon tower, and the mainland, leaving a rock (awash) 10m to starboard.

Entrance   *Beacon*

Port de Malmousque (Endoume). Entrance, looking SE

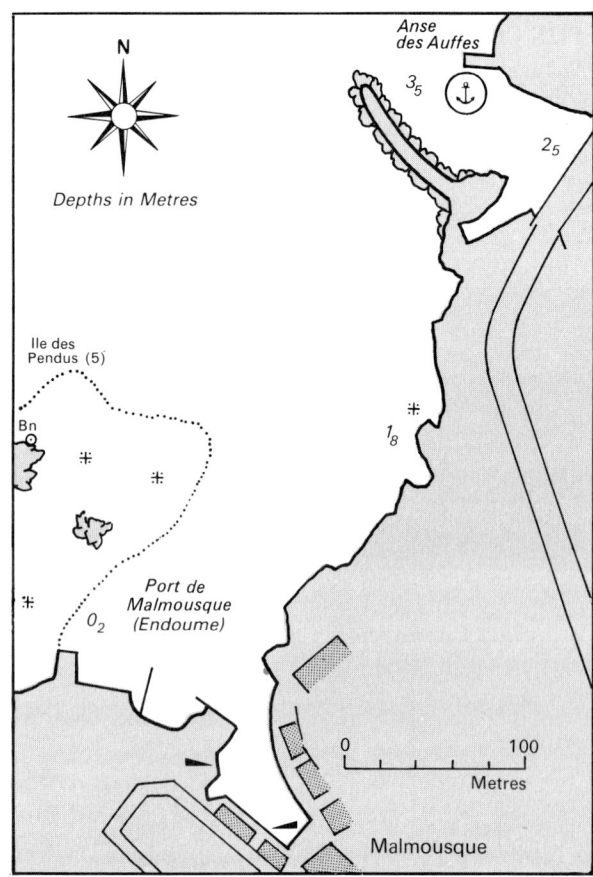

Port de Malmousque

From S Cross the wide Baie d'Endoume on N course leaving Iles d'Endoume (7m) 200m to starboard, then Sourdaras and Canoubier 200m to port. Pay attention to the foul ground to N of Pointe d'Endoume. The monument described above is also conspicuous from this direction. Approach on an E course.

Approach by night

Not recommended.

Entrance by day

Enter with care and a forward lookout, in mid-channel. Secure to any vacant berth and ask if any are available.

Berths

A vacant berth is often difficult to find due to overcrowding.

Moorings

Moorings are sometimes available.

Formalities

Report to *capitaine de port*.

Facilities

Provisions Shops in Malmousque 100m inland.
Restaurants Fish restaurant ashore.
Beach Small beach to S of harbour.
Communications Main coast road inland with bus service.

⚓ **Anse de la Fausse Monnaie**

A small anchorage surrounded by old houses, 2–3m sand open to S–SW. Road ashore.

⚓ **Port du Prophète**

Not a port but a breakwater to collect sand to make a beach, some shelter to N for small craft.

---

70 PORT DU PRADO (ROUCAS BLANC)
13000 Bouches du Rhône

Position 43°16′N 5°22′·1E
Minimum depth   in the entrance 4m (14·5ft)
                              in the harbour 3 to 0·5m (10 to 2ft)
Width of the entrance 100m
Population (Marseille) 878,689
Rating 3–3–4

General
An artificial yacht harbour built to provide a protected area for dinghies and sailboards to practise in and as a private harbour for the Hotel Palm Beach. The pontoons and facilities on the N side of the harbour may only be used by permission of the hotel. Anchorage is possible in the centre of the harbour. Facilities are limited. Exhibitions are sometimes held here and the harbour will be closed.

Data
See 67 Port de Marseille, page 255.

Light
Jetée Ouest head Fl(2)R.6s

Warning
This harbour has been dredged recently to 4m.

Approach by day
From W Round Cap Caveaux at the S end of Ile Pomègues onto an E course. The line of rocky breakwaters will be observed in the closer approach. Proceed towards the N end of the breakwaters where a monument consisting of a single blade of a giant propeller will be seen at the side of the cliff road, just S of this a long low hotel building will be observed which is located at the NE side of the harbour.

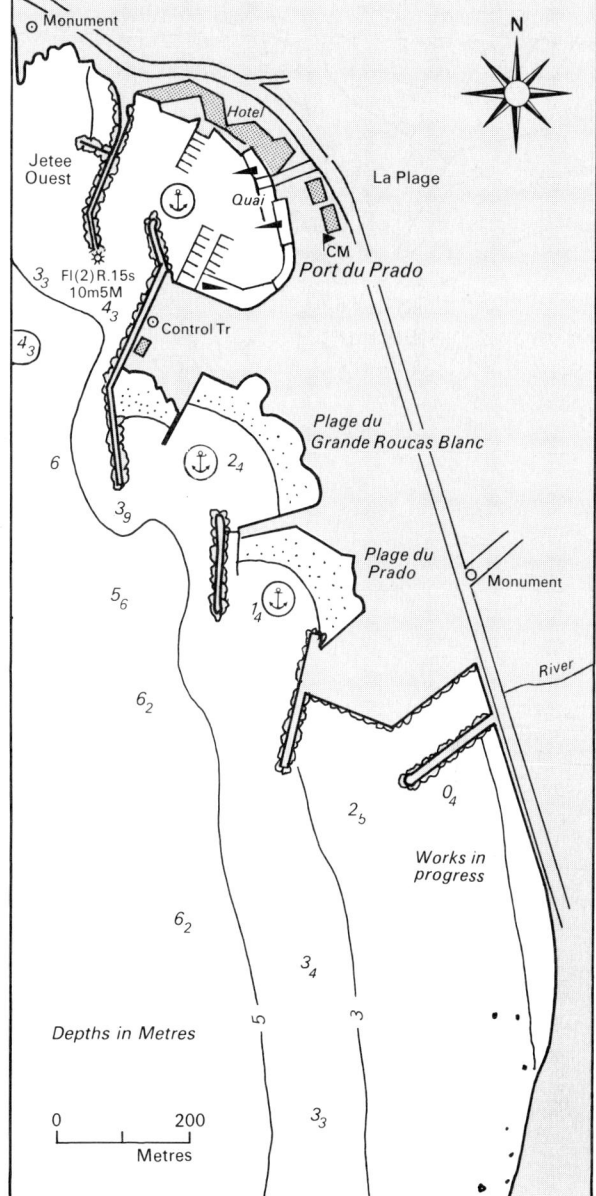

Port du Prado

Port du Prado. Entrance, looking NE

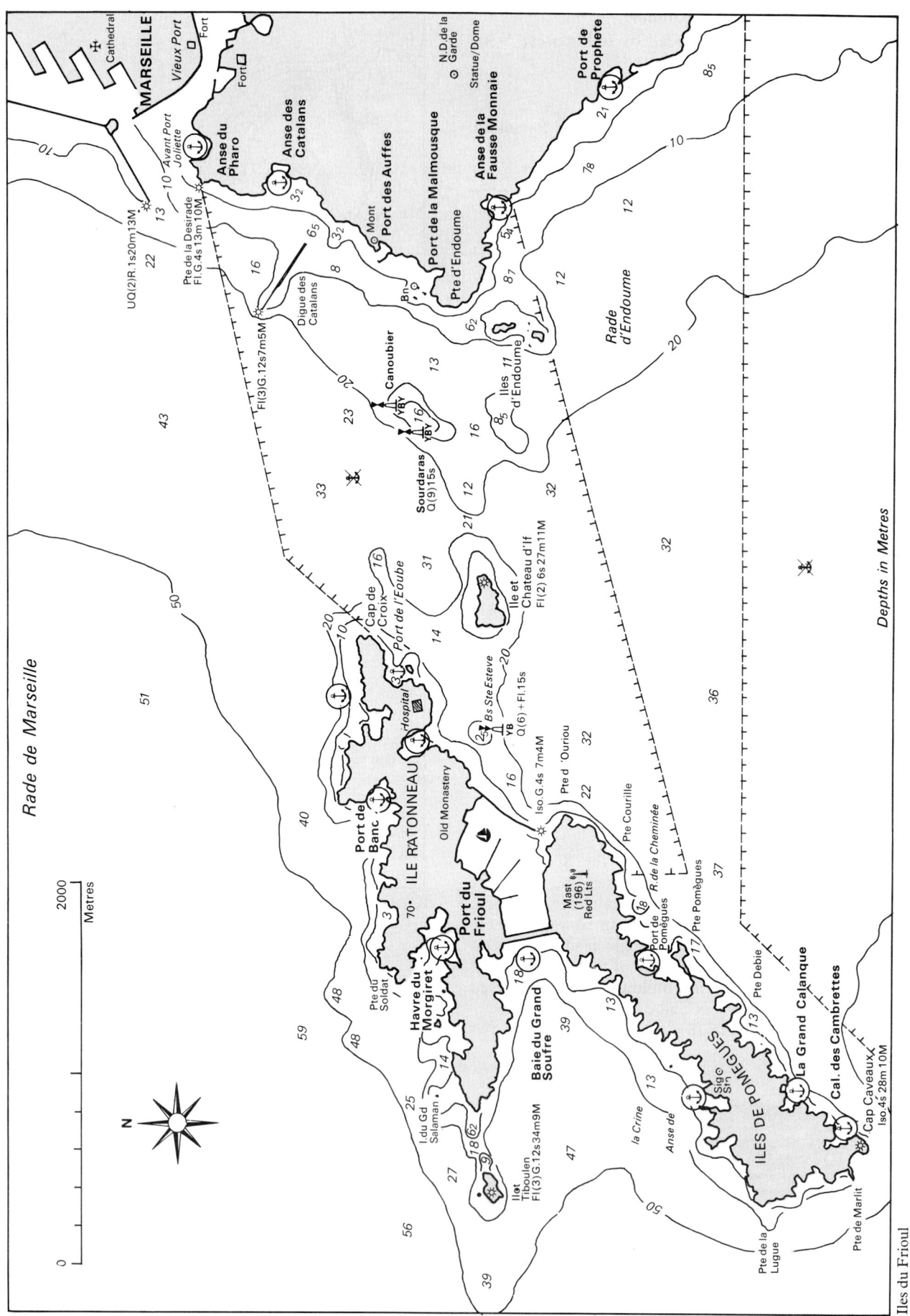

Depths in Metres

Rade de Marseille

MARSEILLE

Cathedral

Vieux Port

Fort

Fort

Avant Port
Joliette

UQ(2)R.1s20m13M

Pte de la Desirade
Fl.G.4s13m10M

Anse du
Pharo

Anse des
Catalans

Port des Auffes

Port de la Malmousque

Anse de la
Fausse Monnaie

Port de
Prophete

N.D.de la
Garde

Statue/Dome

Mont

Pte d'Endoume

Bn

Digue des
Catalans

Fl(3)G.12s7m5M

Canoubier

YBV

YBV

Sourdaras
Q(9)15s

YBV

Iles
d'Endoume

Rade
d'Endoume

Cap de
Croix

Port de l'Eoube

Ile et
Chateau d'If
Fl(2) 6s27m11M

Bs s Ste Esteve

YB
Q(6)+Fl.15s

Pte d 'Ouriou

Iso.G.4s 7m4M

Port de
Banc

Hospital

ILE RATONNEAU

Old Monastery

Pte Courille

R. de la Cheminée

Mast
(196)
Red Lts

Port de
Pomègues

Pte Pomègues

Pte du
Soldat

Havre du
Morgiret

Port du
Frioul

Baie du Grand
Soufre

Pte Debie

ILES DE POMEGUES

La Grand Calanque

Cal. des Cambrettes

I.du Gd
Salaman

Ilot
Tiboulen
Fl(3)G.12s34m9M

la Crine

Anse de

Sig
Sn

Cap Caveaux
Iso.4s 28m 10M

Pte de la
Lugue

Pte de Marlit

N

Metres
2000

0

Iles du Frioul

Entrance

Port du Prado, looking SW

From S and E Round Cap Croisette, Ile Maire and Ile Tiboulen de Maire and follow the coast at ½M in a NE direction. Identify Port de Point Rouge; Port du Prado is 1¼M to N of this harbour. The hotel buildings and monument will also be seen from this direction.

Entrance

By day Approach the head of Jetée Ouest which has a red light tower near its head on a course between SE and NE, round it at 20m and enter.

By night Approach a Fl(2)R.6s on a course between SE and NE, round it at 20m and enter. The hotel and shore lights make it difficult to identify navigational lights at a distance but provide good harbour illumination on entrance.

Berths

With permission of the hotel on the pontoon.

Anchorage

Anchor in 3m sand near centre of harbour.

Formalities

Report to secretary of yacht club on arrival.

Facilities

Hards On the S side of the harbour.
Slips Three slips on E side of the harbour.
Fuel Service station with diesel and petrol nearby.
Water From clubhouse and pontoons.
Provisions Supermarket ¼M to S, other small shops nearby.
Hotel The Hotel Palm Beach ★★★★ (☎ 91 76 20 00).
Restaurants Several in the area.
Yacht club Centre Municipal de Voile (CMV) (☎ 91 76 31 60). Open 15 February to 15 December. Clubhouse at E side of the harbour.
Beaches Large beach inside the harbour, two others to S. Both crowded in the season.
Communications Main coast road with bus service behind the harbour.

⚓ **Plage du Grande Roucas Blanc**
A series of breakwaters to collect sand for beaches, some shelter for small craft. Do not mistake for entrance to Port du Prado.

⚓ **Plage du Prado**
Further S a huge area is being filled in for pleasure gardens, etc.

Islands to SW of Marseille

Iles du Frioul (Ile de Planier, Ile et Château d'If, Ile Ratonneau, Ilot Tiboulen and Ile Pomègues)

General

A group of rugged rocky islands bare of vegetation 3M to SW of the Vieux-Port of Marseille which have many anchorages and also include the Port du Frioul (see page 267). The islands are of white rock and their highest point is 86m. Their coasts are very broken and deep water is close to the shore in most places, but there are a few isolated offshore rocks (see chart). The islands are deserted, with the exception of some houses, cafés, shops and a pilot base around the Port du Frioul. There is a signal station on Pomègues.

ILE DE PLANIER

A small low flat island (3m) with white light tower, red top (66m) and some buildings. Landing on NW side, difficult in bad weather. Foul ground to E and SW. (Fl.W.5s68m26M White tower, red top.)

ILE D'IF

Landing on small quay and pier for launches from the Vieux-Port on N side, no anchorages. The famous Château d'If (conspicuous), constructed by François I for the defence of Marseille, was used as a prison for political and religious prisoners and was made famous by Alexandre Dumas' book *Le Comte de Monte-Cristo*. Light on E side of the island (Fl(2)W.6s27m11M White tower, red top.)

Havre de Morgiret, looking SW

Port de Pomègues, looking SW

ILE RATONNEAU

Once used as a quarantine base with a large conspicuous hospital now in ruins on a hilltop at the NE end. The major anchorages, all deserted, are:

⚓ Baie du Grand Soufre
⚓ Havre de Morgiret
⚓ Port de Banc
⚓ Port de l'Eoube
⚓ Mouillage de Ribolles (to NE of island)
⚓ Calanque de Ratonneau
⚓ Calanque de St-Estève

There are many others, mostly unnamed.

ILOT TIBOULEN

A small rocky island (30m) to W of Ile Ratonneau. Landing difficult. Small lighthouse, white column, green top (Fl(3)G.12s34m9M). Do not confuse with Ile Tiboulen de Maire off Cap Croisette.

ILE POMEGUES

The signal station and the TV tower are conspicuous. There is a mussel farm at the head of the anchorage at Port de Pomègues. The limits are marked by yellow buoys. The major anchorages, all deserted, are:

Ile Pomegues looking NE. Note many small craft around the island (Photo taken at weekend)

⚓ Anse de la Crine
⚓ Calanque des Cambrettes
⚓ La Grande Calanque
⚓ Port de Pomègues

There are many others, mostly unnamed. (Cap Caveaux Iso.W.4s28m10M White structure, black top.)

71 PORT DU FRIOUL

Position 43°16'·7N 5°18'·8E
Minimum depth in the entrance 3·9m (13ft)
in the harbour 6 to 1·6m (20 to 5ft)
Width of the entrance 500m
Number of yacht berths 1500
Population 200 (approx)
Rating 2–2–3

General

This harbour has been created by joining together the two islands, Ratonneau and Pomègues, with a breakwater and by constructing a long *môle* extending from the northern island to protect the harbour entrance on the eastern side. Regrettably these beautiful and once virtually deserted islands have been desecrated by the establishment of a large yacht harbour, a holiday village and a sports centre. However, a large part of the islands still remains untouched and a visit is recommended. Approach and entrance are easy and good protection is afforded inside. Facilities are limited to everyday requirements.

Port du Frioul, Ile Ratonneau looking E

Data

Charts Admiralty 150
French 6739
Spanish 49
Navicarte 504, 505

Magnetic variation 1°44'W (1994) decreasing by about 6' each year.

Speed limit 4 knots.

Lights

Môle Est head Iso.G.4s7m4M Platform on tank, green top, white base. A F.R is shown from a radio tower on Fort de Pomègues 0·26M to SSW

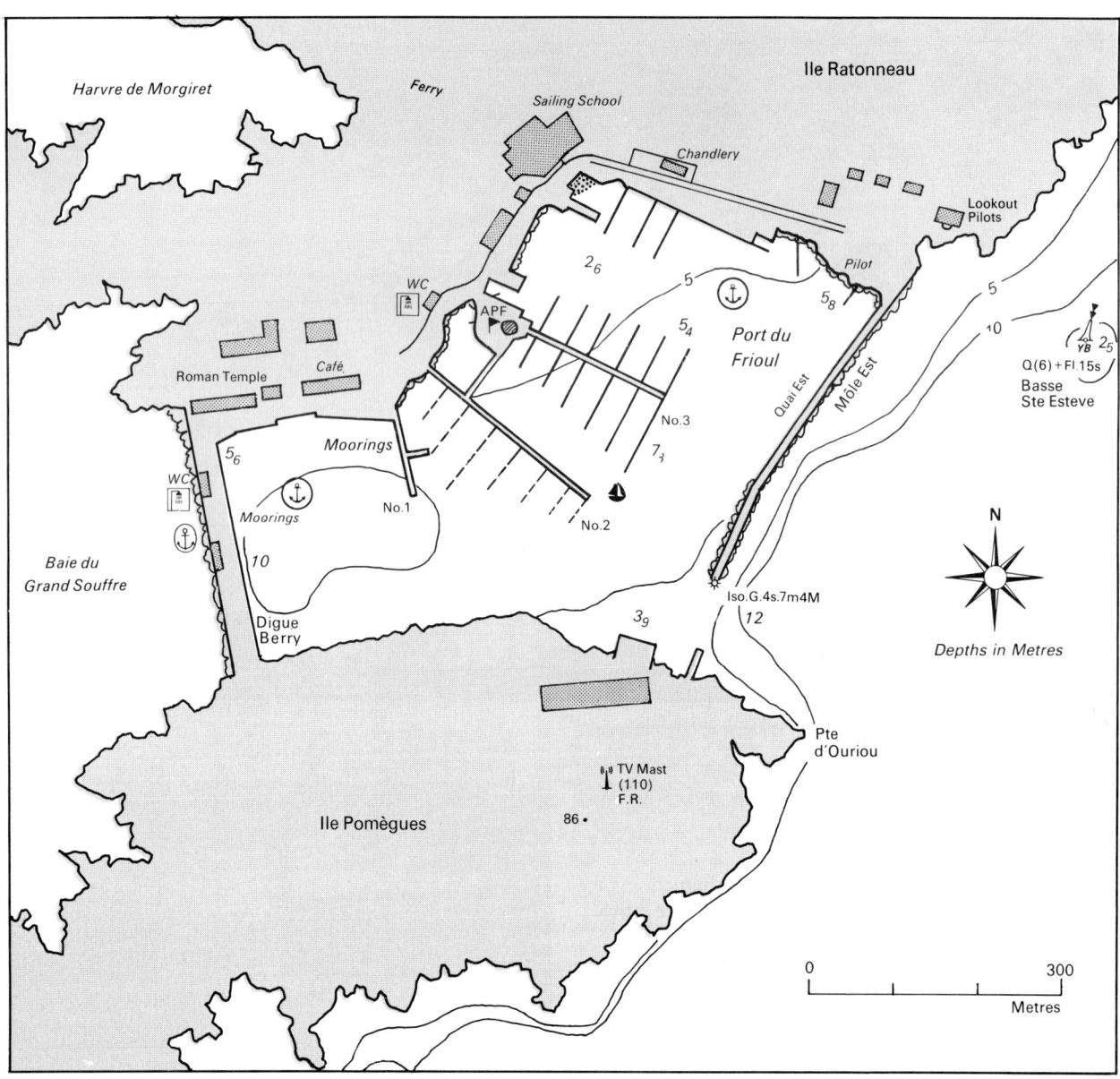

Port du Frioul

Cap Caveaux Iso.W.4s28m10M White structure, black top
Light buoy A small S cardinal light buoy, YB with ▼
   topmark, Basse St-Estève, Q(6)+LFl.15s, lies to S of a
   shallow patch situated 500m to NE of the entrance

Port radio VHF Ch 9 and 16, 24 hours.

Weather forecast Posted at *bureau du port*. (☎ 36 68 08 13
   and 36 68 08 08)

Warning

The quay on the inner side of the Môle Est is in a
bad state of repair and should be approached with
caution owing to fallen stones and other underwater
obstructions. Additional changes are to be expected
and more pontoons are expected to be established.
With strong E winds a heavy swell enters the
harbour.

Approach by day
From W Approach the white rocky islands of

Ratonneau and Pomègues which are very
conspicuous, and round on N or S as convenient.
From S follow the coast of Ile Pomègues at 300m in a
NE direction. The white pilot's house at the N end
of Môle Est, constructed to resemble a ship, is easily
seen, the entrance only appearing in the closer
approach. If rounding the N end of Ile Ratonneau
follow the coast at 300m in a SW direction leaving
the conspicuous Ile et Château d'If to port and the
Basse St-Estève S cardinal light buoy, YB with ▼
topmark, (Q(6)+LFl.15s) to starboard. Môle Est and
the entrance are easily seen from this direction.

From SE Round Cap Croisette and the offlying Ile
Maire and Ile Tiboulen de Maire, then shape a N
course towards Ile Pomègues. In the closer approach
the white ship-like pilot's house will be seen at the N
end of the Môle Est.

Approach by night
Use the main lights:

Digue des Catalans at the S entrance to Marseille
Fl(3)G.12s7m5M
Ile et Château d'If Fl(2)W.6s11M
Cap Caveaux Iso.W.4s10M at the S extremity of Ile
Pomègues

There are many other lights which can be used,
especially if approaching from the N. See chart.

Entrance

By day Enter on a WNW course.

By night Approach Iso.G.4s on a WNW course and
leave some 50m to starboard.

Berths

Berth alongside the inner side of Môle Est or
alongside Quai Berry, the rebuilt breakwater at the
W end of the harbour. The jetties near the pilot's
house must not be used, nor must the E side of
pontoon No.1 where the *vedettes* secure.

Moorings

There are a few moorings which may be available.

Anchorage

There are a number of anchorages which are shown
on the chart.

Prohibited anchorages

Anchoring outside the harbour is prohibited.

Formalities

Bureau du port, centre of Quai Berry at W side of
harbour (☎ 91 59 01 82), open 24 hours.

Bureau de Port

Port du Frioul. Just inside entrance, looking W

Entrance

Port du Frioul, looking SW

Port du Frioul, looking N

Facilities

Cranes A 33-tonne crane and 22-tonne mobile crane.
Fuel N side of harbour (☎ 91 59 01 44).
Water From points on quays and pontoons.
Electricity 220v AC 10 amp points on quays and pontoons.
Provisions Limited supply from shops.
Ice Available from shops.
Showers WC/showers on Quai Berry and near clubhouse.
Chandlery One shop at N side of harbour.
Repairs A small yard to N side of harbour.
Restaurants Several restaurants and many café/bars.
Hotels To be provided.
Yacht clubs Association de Plaisanciers du Port du Frioul (APF) has a clubhouse on an island at the root of pontoon No.3 with four showers and WCs.
Visits There are many interesting caves, coves, old forts and buildings to explore and some wonderful bathing from the rocks.
Communications There are ferries to Marseille.

Future development

The islands have been bought from the military by the authorities of Marseille who plan to develop the area. 800 additional berths are to be provided in a harbour to be built to NE or W of the existing harbour.

72 PORT DE POINTE ROUGE
13008 Bouches du Rhône

Position 43°14'·8N 5°21'·9E
Minimum depth in the entrance 7m (25ft)
in the harbour 6 to 3m (20 to 10ft)
Width of the entrance 50m
Number of yacht berths 1204
Maximum length overall 16m (52ft)
Population 4000 (approx)
Rating 3–2–1

General

An artificial yacht harbour of considerable size which is situated in the bay to the S of Marseille. Approach and entrance are easy but there are bad seas near the entrance with W and NW winds. Facilities are excellent, as is to be expected in a modern garage-type harbour. The harbour is very full and sometimes visitors have to be turned away.

Data

Charts Admiralty 2164
French 6739, 6767
Spanish 49
Navicarte 504, 505

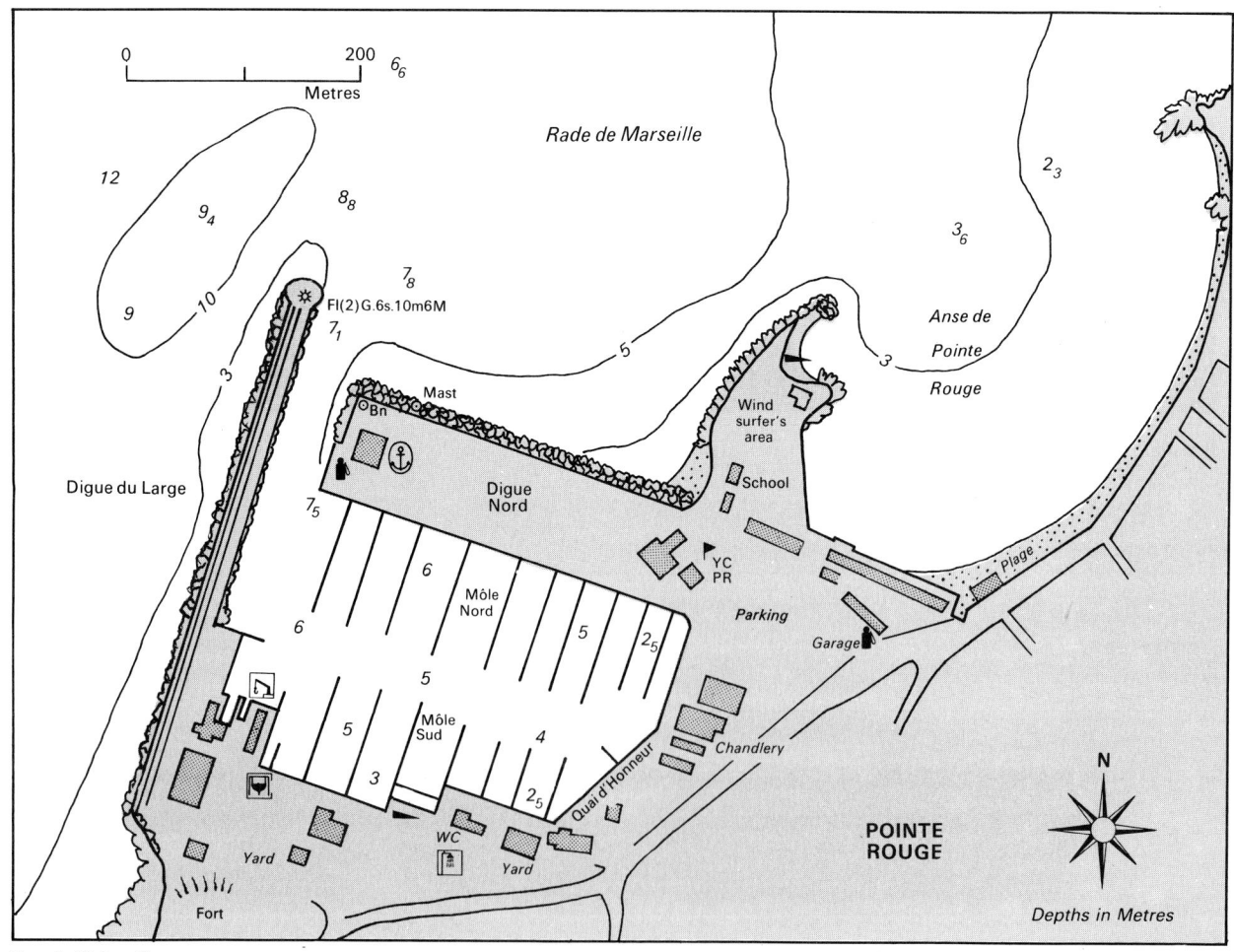

Port de Pointe Rouge

Entrance

Port de Pointe Rouge. Entrance looking SE

Port de Pointe Rouge looking SE

Magnetic variation 1°44′W (1994) decreasing by about 6′ each year.

Port radio VHF Ch 9.

Weather forecasts Posted several times a day at the *bureau du port*. Recorded forecasts (☎ 36 68 08 08 and 36 68 08 13). Broadcasts Marseille FM Ch 24 and 26.

Speed limit 4 knots.

Storm signals From mast at *bureau du port*.

Lights
Digue Ouest môle head Fl(2)G.6s10m6M White column, green bands and top.

Buoys A black/yellow buoy is located 300m W of the entrance.

Warning
Considerable land recovery and reconstruction is taking place on the coast to N of this harbour and the harbour is to be expanded. The many town lights make it very difficult to spot navigational lights.

Approach by day
From W The high bare white rocky Iles Ratonneau and Pomègues with the small Ile et Château d'If to their E are easily identified. These islands can be rounded on the S side the harbour being 105° from Cap Caveaux, or on their N side when passage should be taken to E of Ile et Château d'If leaving the two W cardinal, YBY with ⟁ topmark, beacons Sourdaras (Q(9)15s13m8M) and Canoubier (no light) to port. The harbour lies 140° from here and can be recognised by groups of large flats and a concentration of buildings.

From E Round Cap Croisette, a very prominent feature with the offlying high white rocky Ile Maire and the smaller Ile Tiboulen de Maire, follow the coast in a NE direction at ½M. In the closer approach the *digue* will be seen.

Approach by night
Use the major lights:
Ile Tiboulen de Maire Fl.WG.4s58m11/8M 142°-G-327°-W-142°

Ile et Château d'If Fl(2)W.6s11M
Ile de Planier Fl.W.5s26M

Entrance

By day Approach the head of the *digue* on an E course, round it at 20m leaving it to starboard and enter on a S course.

By night Approach Fl(2)G.6s on an E course, leave 20m to starboard and round on to a S course.

Berths

Berth alongside fuel berth at head of Digue Nord for allocation of a berth.

Prohibited anchorage

Anchoring in or near the harbour entrance is prohibited.

Formalities

On arrival report to the *bureau du port* (☎ 91 73 13 21), open 24 hours, situated at the NW side of the harbour near the fuel berth. Night staff may not receive visiting yachts.

Charges

There are harbour charges.

Facilities

Slips There is a large slip at the S end of the harbour.
Hards Hard standing for 350 yachts.
Travel-lift There is a travel-lift (30 tonnes) at SW corner of the harbour.
Cranes There is a small crane (1·5 tonnes) near the travel-lift.
Fuel Diesel and petrol from pumps at head of Digue Nord to port of the entrance. Open summer 1700–1200, 1330–1830 and winter 0600–1200, 1300–1730 (☎ 91 72 40 87).
Water There are taps on quays and pontoons.
Electricity 220v AC 3kw points on pontoons.
Provisions A number of shops in the village provide everyday requirements. A supermarket is located 500m to NE of the harbour.
Ice This is delivered daily in the season to the *bureau du port* by van.
Garbage Rubbish containers at the roots of all pontoons.
Chandlery There are three chandlers based at the harbour and another in the town. The petrol station also has a small stock of chandlery.
Repairs A comprehensive service for all types of repair is available.
Restaurants There are many restaurants and café/bars in the town.
Yacht club The Yachting Club de Point Rouge (YCPR) (☎ 91 73 06 75) has a clubhouse building in the E corner of the harbour with bar, lounges, restaurant, showers and WCs.
Beaches There is a sandy beach to the NE of the harbour.
Communications No. 19 bus service to Marseille.

Future development

Plans exist to build a second harbour to the NE of the existing harbour with all the necessary ancillary facilities for 800 berths.

73 PORT DE LA MADRAGUE DE MONTREDON
13008 Bouches du Rhône

Position 43°14'·1N 5°21'·2E
Minimum depth   in the entrance 5m (18ft)
               in the harbour 3 to 1m (10 to 3ft)
Width of the entrance 20m
Number of yacht berths 50
Population 10,000 (approx) (Residential area for Marseille)
Rating 3–3–3

General

A small fishing and yachting harbour in a *calanque* 1M to S of Port de Point Rouge, suitable for small yachts. Approach and entrance are not too difficult but would be dangerous during a NW *mistral*. Facilities are limited.

Data

See 72 Port de Point Rouge, page 270.

Approach by day

From W Round Cap Caveaux at the S end of Ile Pomègues and set a SE course. In the closer approach Mont Rose, a rounded hill (83m) near the coast with a radio station on its summit, will be observed. The harbour lies just N of it. There is a factory chimney standing behind it.

From S and E Round Cap Croisette, Ile Maire and Ile Tiboulen de Maire onto a NE course. Mont Rose (83m) with the radio station on its summit is easily seen. Follow the coast at 200m to a position off the harbour.

Approach by night

Not recommended without a previous visit by day.

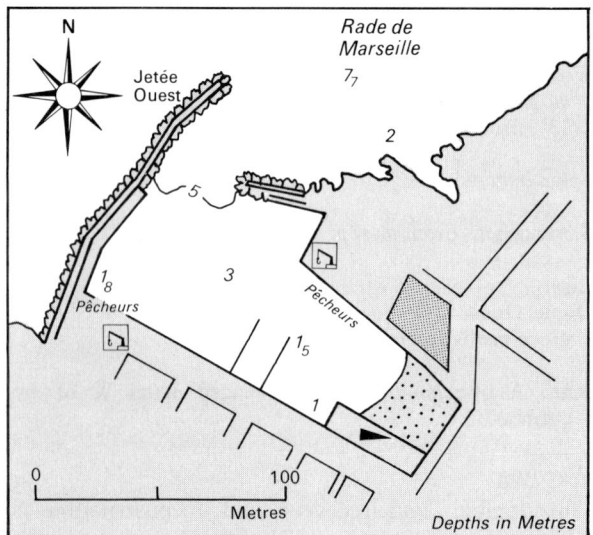

Port de la Madrague de Montredon

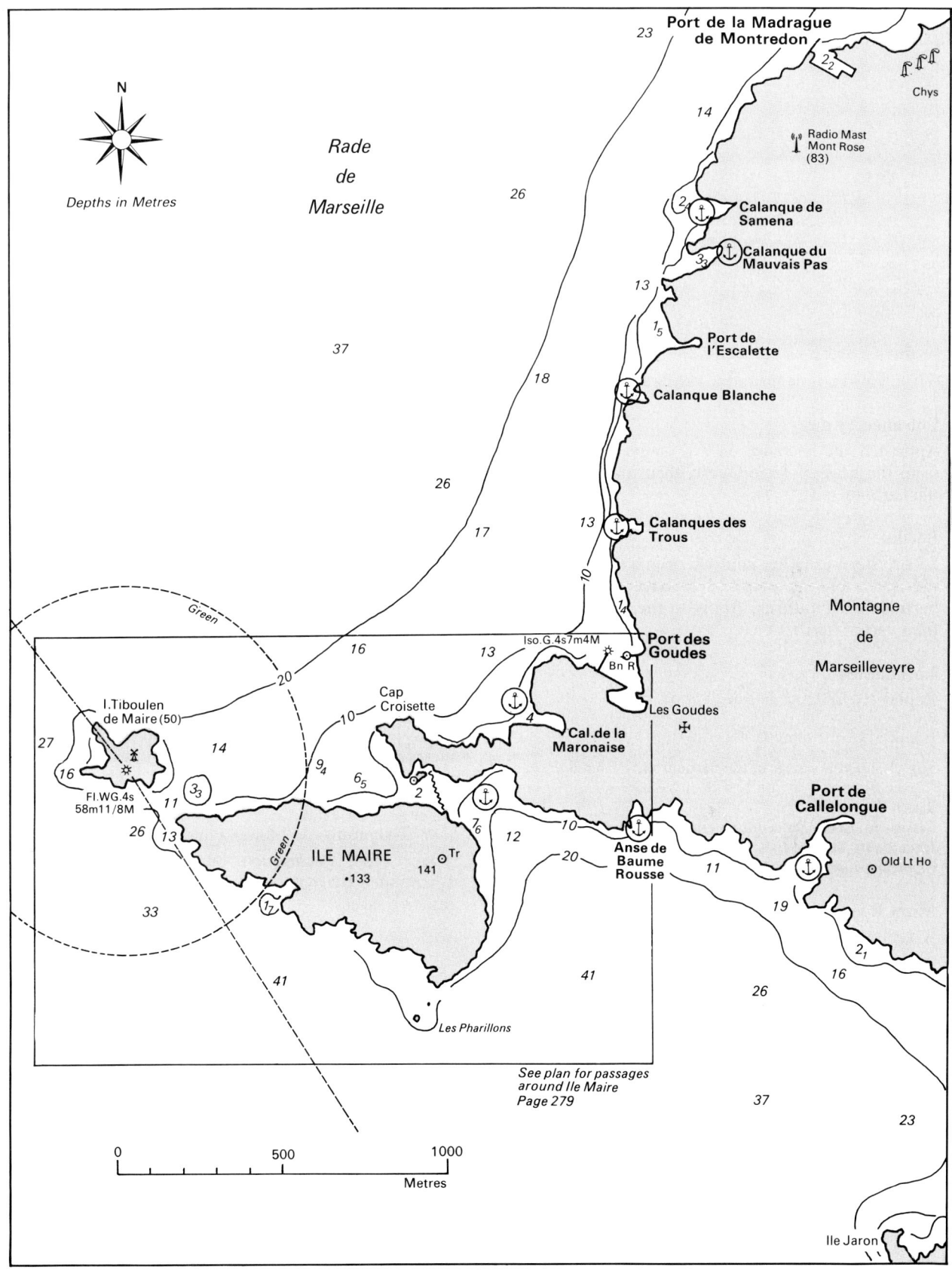

Port de la Madrague de Montredon

23

22

Chys

14

Radio Mast
Mont Rose
(83)

2 Calanque de
Samena

33 Calanque du
Mauvais Pas

13

1 5

Port de
l'Escalette

Calanque Blanche

13 Calanques des
Trous

10

1 4

Montagne

de

Marseilleveyre

*Rade
de
Marseille*

26

37

26

17

18

N

Depths in Metres

16

20

Green

I.Tiboulen
de Maire (50)

27

16

Fl.WG.4s
58m11/8M

11

3 3

26

13

Green

14

9 4

10

Cap
Croisette

6 5

2

ILE MAIRE

• 133

Tr
141

1 7

41

Les Pharillons

13

Iso.G.4s7m4M

Bn R

**Port des
Goudes**

4

**Cal.de la
Maronaise**

Les Goudes

7 6

12

10

20

Anse de
Baume
Rousse

11

41

**Port de
Callelongue**

Old Lt Ho

19

2 1

16

26

37

23

*See plan for passages
around Ile Maire
Page 279*

0   500   1000

Metres

Ile Jaron

Anchorages around Ile Maire and Cap Croisette

273

Entrance

Port de la Madrague de Montredon, looking SE

Entrance by day

Approach the entrance on a S course and enter 7m from the head of Jetée Ouest, then turn to port into the harbour.

Berths

Secure stern-to either pontoon or in a vacant place on the quay, but be prepared to have to leave if the berth's owner returns. Apply to the *capitaine de port* for a vacant berth.

Formalities

Report to *capitaine de port*.

Facilities

Slip A slip at S corner of the harbour only 1·0m deep.
Cranes 5-tonne crane on N side of the harbour.
Water Taps on quays.
Provisions Everyday requirements from local shops.
Restaurants Several fish restaurants around the harbour.
Communications Main coast road inland with bus service.

Mont Rose

A very conspicuous conical coastal hill (83m) with a coast radio station on the top.

⌁ Calanques de Samena and du Mauvais Pas

Two small *calanques* open to SW–W–NW surrounded by rocky cliffs, road at the top. Use only in fair weather.

Mont Rose Marseille radio station

Calanque de Samena

274

Marseille radio station

Calanque Mauvais Pas, looking NE

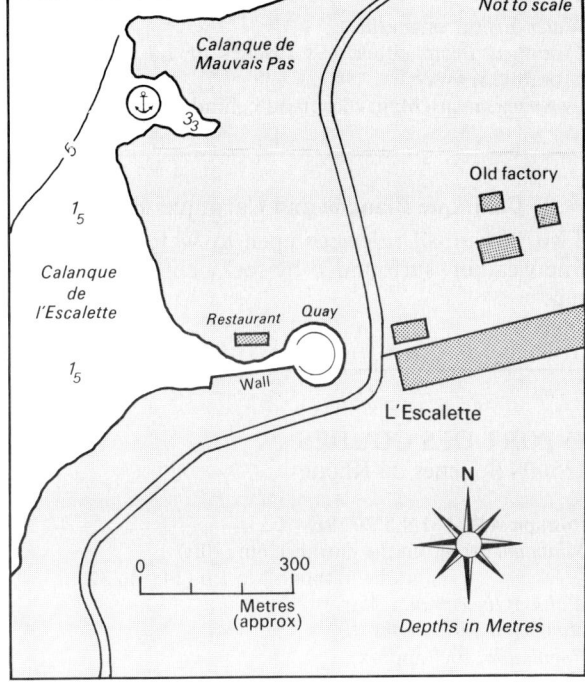

Calanque de l'Escalette

74 PORT DE L'ESCALETTE
13008 Bouches du Rhône

Position 43°13′·6N 5°20′·9E
Minimum depth in the entrance 4m (14·5ft)
in the harbour 2m (6·6ft)
Width of the entrance 15m
Population 20 (approx)
Rating 3–5–5

General
This unique small harbour is shaped like a keyhole and was built for a nearby factory (now disused). It has a narrow entrance channel 40m long running between rock cliffs and a high rocky wall to a circular basin and quay surrounded by a high stone wall. Even with a strong NW *mistral* which prevents any entrance or exit, the waters in the basin remain reasonably calm. Facilities are limited. A few houses on the main road. Only suitable for small yachts.

Data
See 72 Port de Point Rouge, page 270.

Warning
The entrance is dangerous with heavy onshore seas. The harbour should only be used in settled weather. 1·5m shallows to NW.

Entrance

Port de l'Escalette. Entrance, looking E

Calanque Blanche, looking E

Approach by day

From W Approach the coast on a SE course from Cap Caveaux and in the closer approach Mont Rose (83m) with its radio station will be recognised. The harbour lies just under ½M to S and will only be recognised when the entrance opens up.

From S and E From Cap Croisette follow the coast at 200m in a N direction. The Port des Goudes will be recognised by its breakwater and houses. This harbour is ½M further N and will be identified when the entrance is abeam and opens up.

Approach by night

Not recommended.

Entrance by day

Enter in mid-channel and follow it to the circular basin.

Berths

Secure bow or stern-to chains on the quayside and also secure to a buoy.

Facilities

Water From restaurant.
Provisions From either Les Goudes or La Point Rouge, both ½M away.
Communications Main coast road behind the harbour.

⚓ Calanque Blanche and Calanque des Trous

Two very small *calanques* open to W for use only in fine weather, surrounded by rocky cliffs with road at top.

---

75 PORT DES GOUDES
135008 Bouches du Rhône

Position 43°13'·1N 5°20'·8E
Minimum depth in the entrance 6m (20ft)
in the harbour 4 to 1m (14·5 to 3ft)
Width of the entrance 45m
Number of yacht berths 100
Population 400 (approx)
Rating 3–3–4

General

A small natural harbour improved by two jetties for fishing boats and yachts. Easy to approach and enter with offshore winds but dangerous in a NW *mistral*. The harbour tends to be crowded, especially in the high season. Facilities are somewhat limited but there are some good restaurants.

Data

See 72 Port de Point Rouge, page 270.

Light
Digue Ouest head Iso.G.4s7m4M White hut, green top

Beacon tower Red beacon tower, red can topmark, at head of Digue Est.

⚓ Calanques between Mont Rose and Port des Goudes

Entrance

Port des Goudes, looking SE

Approach by day

From W Pass S of Cap Caveaux and set a SW course towards the conspicuous Ile Maire (133m). In the closer approach Ile Tiboulen de Maire (50m) with a small white lighthouse, black top (8m), will also be identified. Cap Croisette is difficult to recognise, being only 12m high. The harbour lies ¾M to ENE of Ile Tiboulen de Maire and in the closer approach the Anse des Goudes will open up. An old fort may be observed on a hill 300m to E of this harbour.

From E Round Ile Maire and pass between it and Ile Tiboulen de Maire or round Ile Tiboulen de Maire. Approach the coast on a NE course, the Anse des Goudes will open up when 200m from the coast.

Approach by night

Not recommended unless a previous visit by day has been made.

Entrance by day

Approach the head of the Digue Ouest on an E course round it at 10m onto a S course and enter.

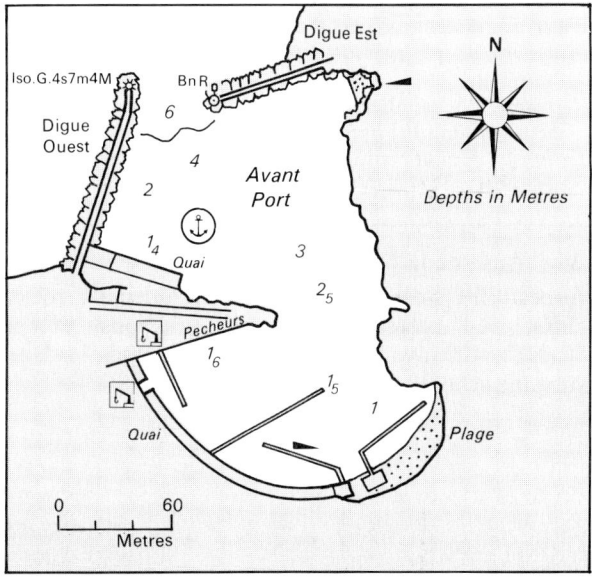

Port des Goudes

Port des Goudes looking N

Berths

A vacant berth may be found on the pontoons, secure and report to the *capitaine de port* for the allocation of a vacant berth.

Anchorage

Anchorage in 4m sand may be possible in the *avant-port*, but this is subject to heavy swell with a NW *mistral*.

Formalities

Report to *capitaine de port* on arrival.

Charges

There are harbour charges.

Facilities

Hard Hard at S side of the harbour.
Slip NE corner.
Cranes Two 3-tonne cranes at W side of harbour.
Water Some water points around the harbour.
Provisions Simple everyday requirements can be bought in the village.
Restaurants A number of restaurants specialising in fish menus around the harbour.
Yacht club Union Nautique des Goudes (UNG). Clubhouse near port.

⚓ Anse de la Maronaise

A beautiful small anchorage, surrounded by rocky cliffs, well protected from all directions, except W–NW. 400m walk to Les Goudes. A track leads to subaqua school.

Islands to S of Marseille

ILE MAIRE AND ILE TIBOULEN DE MAIRE

There are two bare white rocky deserted islands off Cap Croisette. The smaller, Ile Tiboulen de Maire (50m), has a lighthouse (8m), Fl.WG.4s58m11/8M, white/black tower with aerogenerator. The larger island is 141m high and has some ruined towers. It also has two small rocky islets, Les Pharillons (4m high), 150m off the SE corner of its coast.

PASSAGE BETWEEN ILE MAIRE AND ILE TIBOULEN DE MAIRE

A narrow (80m) passage exists between a rock (covered 3·3m) off Ile Maire and the steep-to Ile Tiboulen de Maire. Take this 11m-deep passage in a NE/SW direction one third from Ile Tiboulen and two thirds from Ile Maire.

PASSAGE BETWEEN MAINLAND AND ILE MAIRE

This 60m wide passage, 2m deep, is only for shallow-draught craft in fair weather. It should be taken in a WNW or ESE direction in mid-channel, but slightly nearer the mainland when halfway through. A small harbour for dinghies lies by a cross to SE of Cap Croisette. There are a subaqua school and a restaurant here.

⚓ Ile Maire – NE side

A fine-weather anchorage to the NE of Ile Maire but only protected from N–NE winds.

⚓ Anse de la Baume Rousse

Small shallow anchorage open to SE–S, track to main road.

Fort

Anse de la Maronaise, looking SE

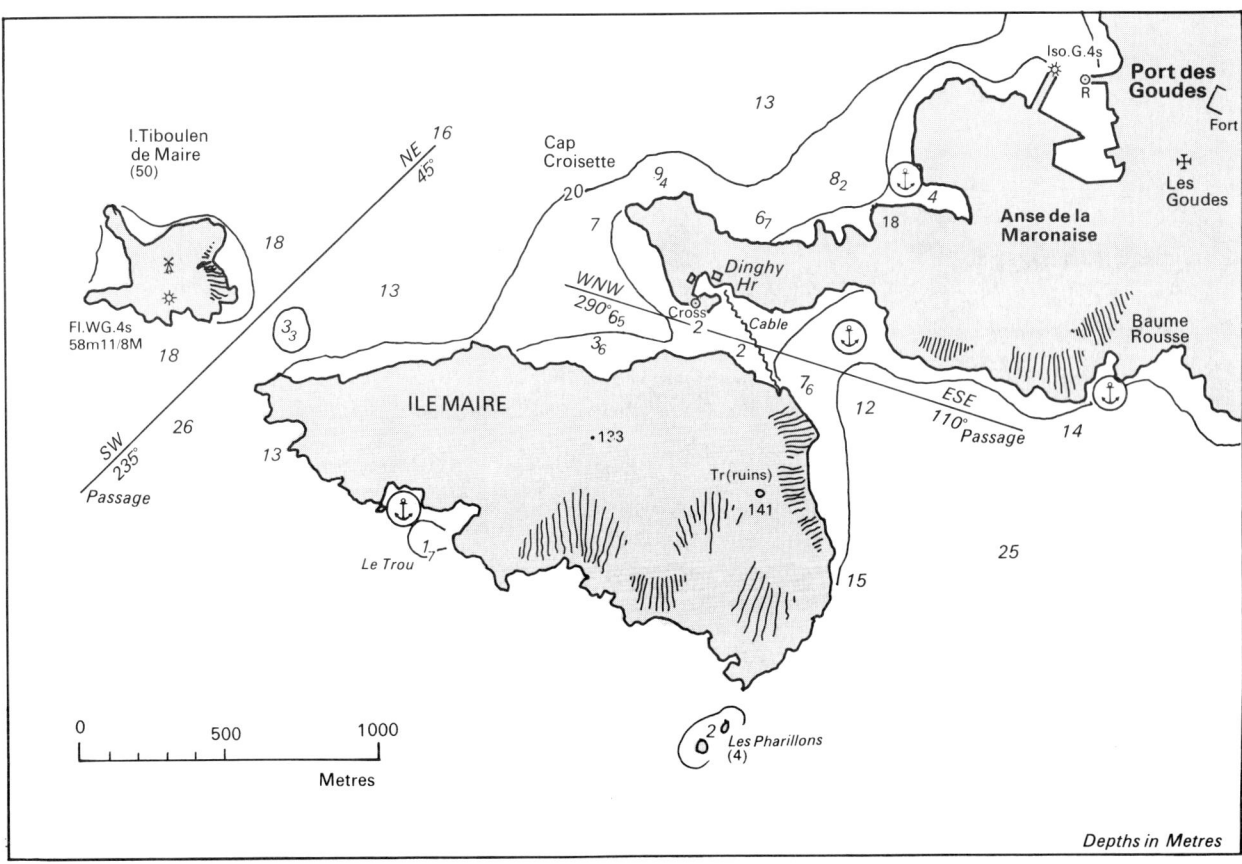

Passages around Ile Maire

Ile Maire and Cap Croisette, looking W

76 PORT DE CALLELONGUE
13008 Bouches du Rhône

Position 43°12′·7N 5°21′·1E
Minimum depth in the entrance 5m (18ft)
in the harbour 3 to 1m (10 to 3ft)
Width of the entrance 100m to 12m
Population 20 (approx)
Rating 3–4–4

General
An attractive but very small harbour in extremely rugged surroundings, only suitable for small craft. Inside the harbour is usually crowded. Limited facilities available. Entrance difficult with strong SE–S–SW winds and swell.

Data

See 72 Port de Point Rouge, page 270.

Passage between Ile Maire and Ile Tiboulen de Maire, looking NE

Dinghy harbour   *Old Semaphore*

Passage inshore of Ile Maire

Dinghy harbour   *Ile Tiboulen de Maire*

Passage inshore of Ile Maire, looking W

Warning

With strong onshore winds and seas this harbour is dangerous to enter and it should only be used in settled weather.

Approach by day

From W From the S of Ile Pomègues set a SE course to Ile Maire (133m), round it or the Ile Tiboulen de Maire 50m) and follow the SW coast of Ile Maire. Round the two isolated beacon-like rocks, les Pharillons, which lie 120m off the S of Ile Maire. From this point the harbour lies ¾M in a NE direction. In the closer approach one or two houses will be seen. A deserted signal station may be seen on the hill to E of this harbour.

From E Follow the coast along at 200m. When Cap de Jarre, the NW point of Ile Jaron, lies SSE, the harbour will open up and some houses will be observed.

By night

Not recommended.

Entrance by day

Enter with care in mid-channel on a NNE course, and round the small breakwater on the port side, the harbour then bends and curves to an ENE direction and is very narrow. Pay attention to a small rock 0·5m deep halfway up the harbour.

Berths

Berth bow or stern-to the quay on port-hand with outer end to a buoy, if a vacant space can be found.

Anchorage

Anchorage is possible in the entrance in 5m sand. Take a line to the shore, so as not to obstruct traffic. This is NOT a secure anchorage in strong winds.

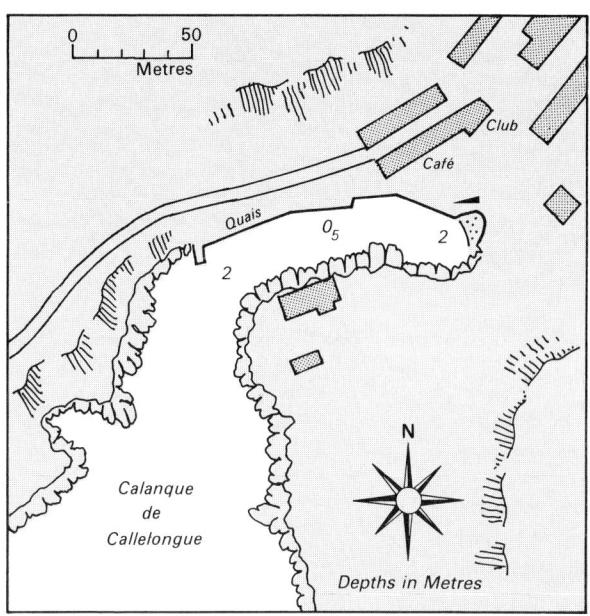

Port de Callelongue

Entrance

Port de Calanque de Callelongue. Approach looking N

Port de Calanque de Callelongue, looking N

Facilities

Slip Small single slip at head of the harbour.
Water From café or restaurant.
Yacht club Club Nautique de Callelongue (CNC) in village at SW end of Avenue des Pebrons.
Restaurant Small restaurant and a café.
Communications Road to Les Goudes and thence to Marseille.

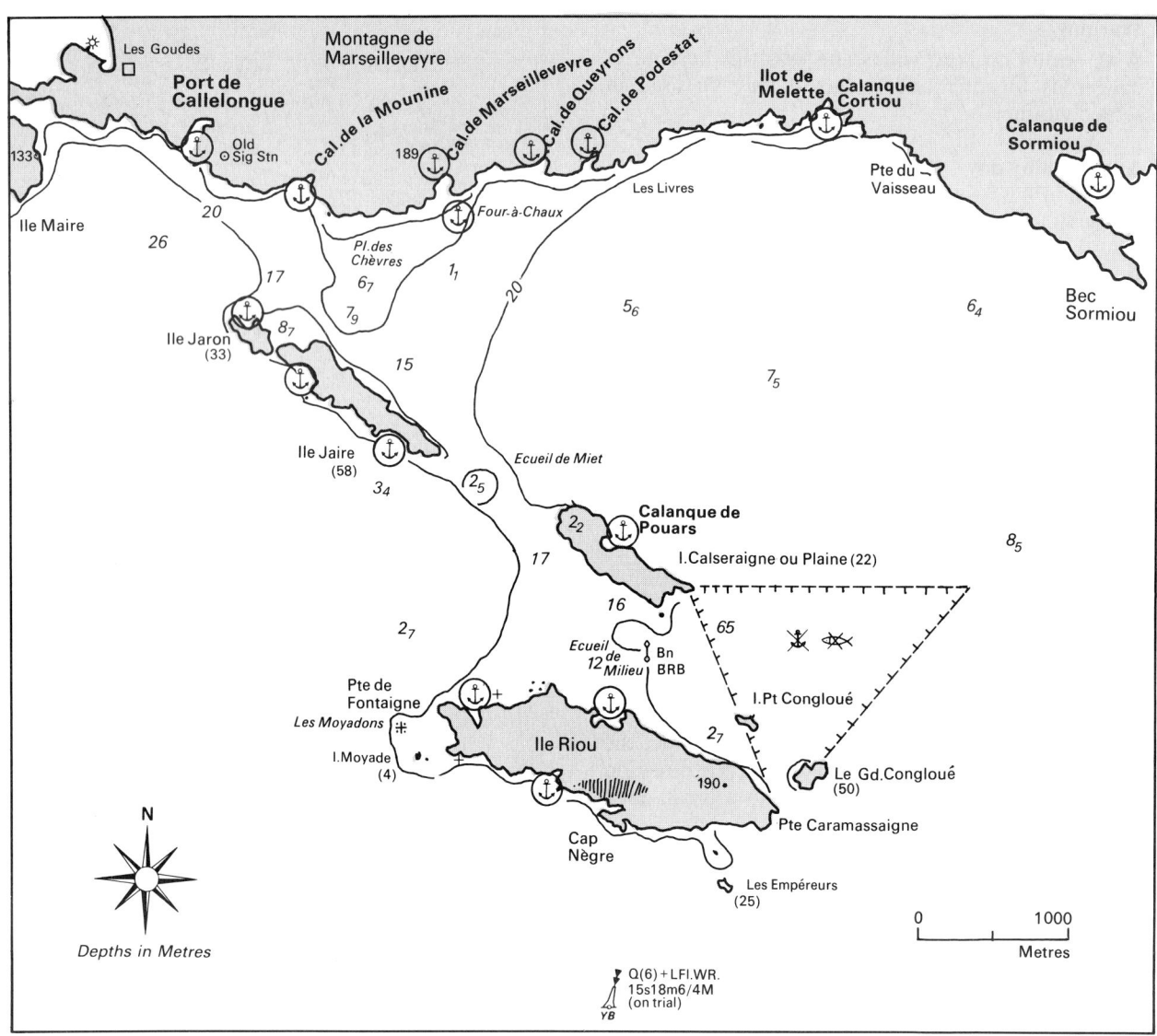

Ile Riou anchorages

⚓ **Calanque de la Mounine**

A very narrow *calanque* leading off a wide bay, shallow, open to S. Valley at head, track inland.

⚓ **Calanque de Marseilleveyre**

A pleasant anchorage with some small holiday buildings and a restaurant around a sandy beach at its head, also an old fort on S side, open only to SE–S. Steep and long track to main road inland after crossing a small flat area. Old battery on point to E. A deep-water (6·7 to 20m) anchorage, Four-à-Chaux between this *calanque* and Ile Jaïre on Plateau des Chèvres.

⚓ **Calanque des Queyrons**

An anchorage open to S–SW, with rocky sides leading to a steep valley. Coastal footpath inland.

⚓ **Calanque de Podestat**

A deep narrow *calanque*, stony beach and house at head with long steep track inland. Steep sides to this open to S. Not very deep, sound carefully.

⚓ **Calanque de Cortiou**

Not recommended because there are three large drains from sewage farms just to E of this *calanque* which discharge raw sewage.

⚓ **Calanque de Sormiou**

A large *calanque* with two hamlets at its head and a small harbour for dinghies, runabouts and small fishing craft. Surroundings are very attractive. A popular anchorage in season and because visitors also come by car to use the sandy beaches, these can become crowded. Several café/bar/restaurants have

Calanque de la Mounine, looking N

Calanque de Marseilleveyre, looking N

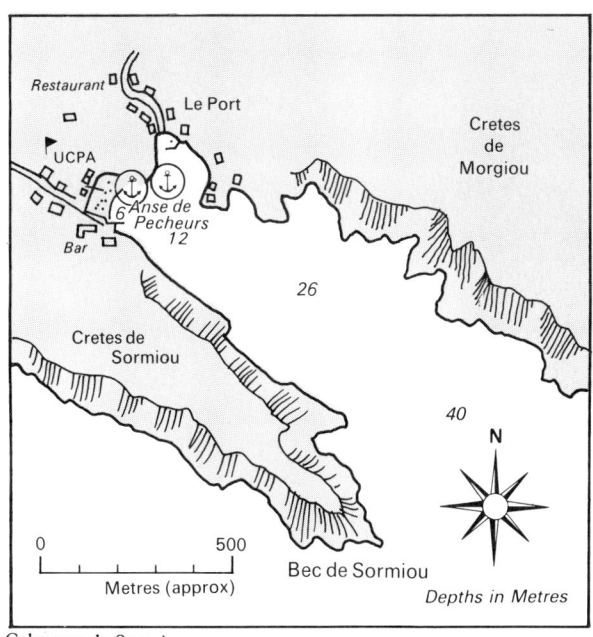

Calanque de Sormiou

Calanque de Sormiou looking NW

Calanque de Sormiou, looking NE

Calanque de Sormiou. Dinghy harbour

⚓ Calanque de Morgiou looking NW

Calanque de Morgiou, looking NW

been established and also a sailing and subaqua school. The anchorage is only open to SE seas. The NW *mistral* is channelled down the valley and can produce strong gusts in the area, causing anchors to drag. The holding in the sandy bottom is not very good due to continual use. Telephone kiosk at NW end of car park. A well, but water not drinkable.

⚓ Calanque de la Triperie
A deep bay behind Cap Morgiou, steep-cliffed sides, open to S–SW. Track inland to Morgiou and Sormiou. Anchor close to shore in 20m rock. Use only in good conditions.

⚓ Calanque de Morgiou
Another large popular *calanque* anchorage in attractive surroundings with a small village at its head, complete with a sandy beach and a harbour, bar/restaurant, telephone, fuel, two cranes (3 and 6 tonnes) and slip. It is protected from all directions except SE. The NW *mistral* is channelled down a valley into this *calanque* and heavy gusts may be experienced causing anchors to drag; the holding ground is sand which has been broken up by much use and is poor holding. There is a narrow road to the main road and an occasional bus service.

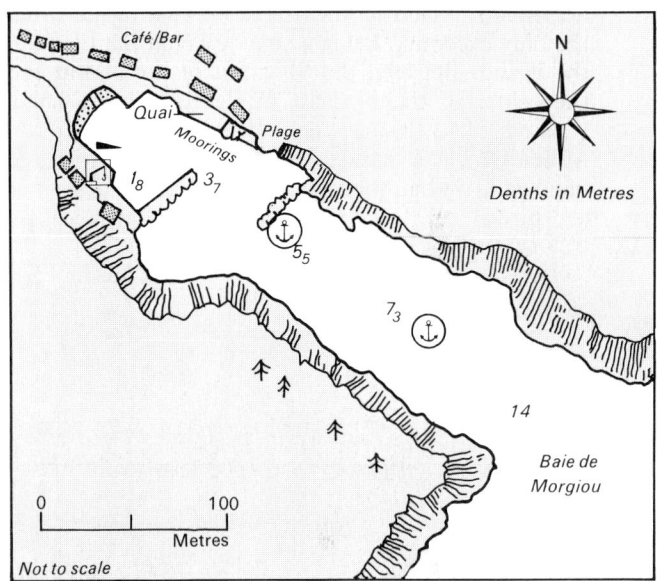

Calanque de Morgiou

Islands to SE of Marseille

ILE JARON, ILE JAIRE, ILE CALSERAIGNE, ILE RIOU (See page 286)

General

A group of three large islands, four smaller islets and a number of isolated rocks. All are of white limestone, virtually bare of vegetation and deserted. They were owned by the armed services but have recently been handed over to the town of Marseille. A triangular area where anchorage and fishing is prohibited lies to W of the group of islands (see chart).

ILE JARON

A small 33m-high island at the NW end of the group. It is just separated from Ile Jaïre by a small gap. A fine-weather anchorage in 5m on N side of the island near Cap de Jarre. It was here that the infamous ship the *Grand St-Antoine* was burnt and sunk after bringing the plague from Syria to Marseille in 1720, causing the death of over 50,000 inhabitants.

ILE JAIRE (JARROS)

The large island to NW of the group is 58m high and 1400m long. Except for two small creeks on the SW side, there are no good anchorages and these two should only be used in good weather. The isolated rock Ecueil de Miet (2·5m deep) lies midway between the SE corner of this island and the NW corner of Ile Calseraigne.

ILE CALSERAIGNE OR PLANE

This island is only 22m high and 1000m long. The top is flat and the coast has vertical cliffs which are very broken. There is an excellent anchorage in the Calanque de Pouars which is only open to NE–E. It is difficult to land on this island because of the cliffs, the only exception being a small quay at the E end of the island. Between the SE point of this island and the centre of the N coast of Ile Riou lies a small isolated rock, Rocher de l'Estéou and Ecueil du Milieu which is marked by a black beacon with red band and two ball topmarks.

ILE RIOU

The largest of these islands, Ile Riou, 190m high and 2400m long, supports a few patches of vegetation. It also has a pleasant sandy beach. On the N coast there is a small anchorage to NE of Pointe de Fontagne, open to NW–N–NE, for use in fine weather. Halfway along the N side is Abri de Riou which has the best sandy beach between Port de Point Rouge and Cassis. It is well sheltered by a rocky point and anchorage is available in 5–7m sand. There are a few huts ashore with the only valley of the island behind them. On the opposite side of this island is Calanque du Contrebandier, a narrow twisty creek only suited to dinghies and yachts of 8m or less. It can only be used in very calm conditions. This spectacular place is ideal for special publicity photos.

At the W end of this island are Ilot Mayade (4m) and Les Moyadons, a series of rocks usually above water but which sometimes cover. Another unnamed group exists on the NW coast to W of Le Monastério (see chart). To N of Pointe Caramassaigne lie Le Grand (50m) and Le Petit (36m) Congloué, while to S of the same point lie Les Empéreurs, one 11m and the other 25m high. An experimental S cardinal light buoy, YB with ▼ topmark, (Q(6)+LFl.15s) lies 1200m to S of this island.

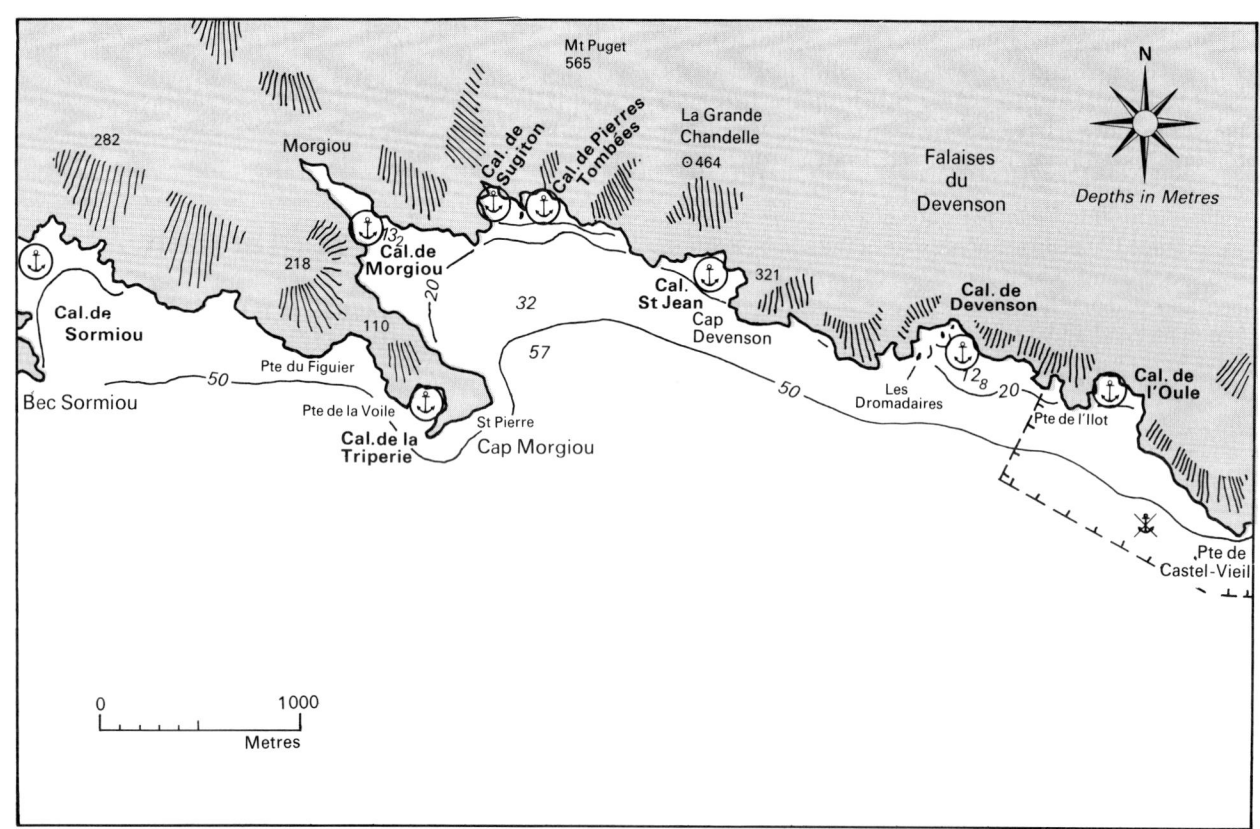

Calanques between Bec Sormiou and Pte de Castel-Vieil

⚓ Calanques de Sugiton and des Pierre-Tombées

⚓ Calanque de l'Oule

⚓ Calanque de Sugiton

A smaller but similar type of *calanque* to Morgiou but deserted and very attractive. A large rock, Le Torpilleur, divides it from the smaller Calanque des Pierres-Tombées to NE and there is a small pine wood. A very steep and long footpath leads inland.

⚓ Calanque des Pierres-Tombées

One of the most spectacular of the *calanques*, with huge piles of broken rocks ashore and steep cliffs leading up to 420m, completely deserted.

⚓ Calanque de St-Jean de Dieu (L'Oeil de Verre)

A wide *calanque* which is open to S–SW and well sheltered from the E. Quite deserted with a very steep footpath inland and to W. Sound carefully when approaching because parts are shallow.

⚓ Calanque du Devenson

A wide *calanque* open to SE–E–SW with steep sides and a very steep footpath inland. Use a trip-line on the anchor, the bottom is of broken rock.

⚓ Calanque de l'Oule

A wide, completely deserted *calanque* open to SE–S–SW but well sheltered from E by high cliffs. A steep footpath leads inland. Cliffs have the appearance of organ pipes on a gigantic scale.

Calanque d'En Vau looking NW

⚓ Calanque d'En Vau

One of the most popular *calanques* but spoilt by the many tourist boats from Cassis visiting it during the hours of daylight. Nevertheless very beautiful and spectacular, with high steep sides. Anchor as far up the creek as draught permits on the starboard side with a line to the shore. This *calanque* is open to E–SE. The bottom is rock and weed in the outer part with sand further in. A wide sandy beach at the head of the *calanque* with a footpath to Cassis.

⚓ Calanque de Port-Pin

In every way similar to Calanque d'En Vau, except that it is open to S, it is deeper and the sandy beach is smaller. Being closer to Cassis it is subject to more day visitors. Small wreck at head of *calanque*. Bottom rocky with weed in outer part, sandy further up *calanque*.

Le Torpilleur rock

Calanque de Sugiton and Calanque de Pierres-Tombées, looking NE

Calanque de l'Oule, looking N

Calanque d'en Vau   *Calanque de Port Pin*

Calanques d'en Vau and Port Pin, looking NW–N

77 PORT MIOU
13260 Bouches du Rhône

Position 43°12'·3N 5°30'·9E
Minimum depth   in the entrance 18m (59ft)
               in the harbour 14 to 1m (46 to 3ft)
Width of the entrance 150m
Number of yacht berths 600
Population 10 (approx)
Rating 4–2–4

General

This was once a beautiful natural harbour, which has been developed to its maximum capacity as a yacht harbour; in addition one side has been quarried away, thereby depriving it to a large extent of its beauty. It is easy to approach and enter and offers complete protection from wind and seas once inside. Facilities are very limited and berthing space is difficult to find but anchorage is usually available in the outer part of the harbour. A recent forest fire has destroyed most of the trees in the area, exposing the bare white rocks.

Data

Charts   Admiralty 2164
          French 6612, 6882
          Spanish 49
          Navicarte 504

Magnetic variation 1°46'W (1994) decreasing by about 6' each year.

Warnings

The seas off the harbour can be severe in strong SE winds but inside the entrance they quickly subside. If blasting is taking place at the quarry a siren is sounded.

Approach by day

From W Follow the high rugged white rocky coast from the prominent Cap Croisette with its group of outlying islands, past the two large inlets of Sormiou and Morgiou to the high Pointe Castel-Vieil, around which will be seen the narrow entrance to the small Calanques d'En Vau and de Port-Pin. Round the prominent Pointe Cacau. Pass a group of disused concrete stone tips on the cliffs. The entrance will open up just beyond these tips. Follow the coast round into the entrance of Port Miou.

From E Round the remarkable Bec-de-l'Aigle and follow the very high rocky cliffs on which there is a conspicuous signal station. When the harbour of Cassis is seen, set course for a point on the coast about 1M further SW. In the closer approach the disused concrete stone tips on the cliffs will be seen, the entrance to the harbour lying just to NE of them.

Approach by night

Approach and entrance for the first time is not recommended owing to the absence of navigational lights.

Port Miou looking N

Entrance by day

Enter on a NW course in mid-channel and follow the cliffs round to starboard, keeping a lookout for yachts and commercial traffic leaving.

Berths

Due to shelving sides in the inner part of the harbour secure bow-to bank and stern-to buoy in mid-channel. There are catwalks along each side of the harbour, parts of which are in a bad state of repair.

Moorings

Not normally available but some private moorings might be vacant.

Anchorage

Anchor inside the entrance below the area where yachts are moored. Anchor in mid-*calanque* stern line to the shore, there are many mooring rings along the shore.

Facilities

Slips Three around the harbour.
Slipways There are two slipways on the NW side, one of 20 tonnes, depth 2m, 11m length overall.
Water There are some water taps near the YCCC clubhouse.
Provisions None locally but available at Cassis 1M away .
Repairs There are two small yards on the NW side of the harbour.
Yacht clubs The Yachting Club des Calanques de Cassis (YCCC) has a small clubhouse on the NW bank (☎ 42 01 77 32) and the Club Nautique de Port Miou (CNPM) has another on the opposite bank (☎ 91 37 61 31).
Visits The area around this harbour is very rugged with excellent rough walking for those who like cross country walking.
Communications A bus passes the head of the inlet on the way to Cassis which is 1M away and where many other facilities exist.

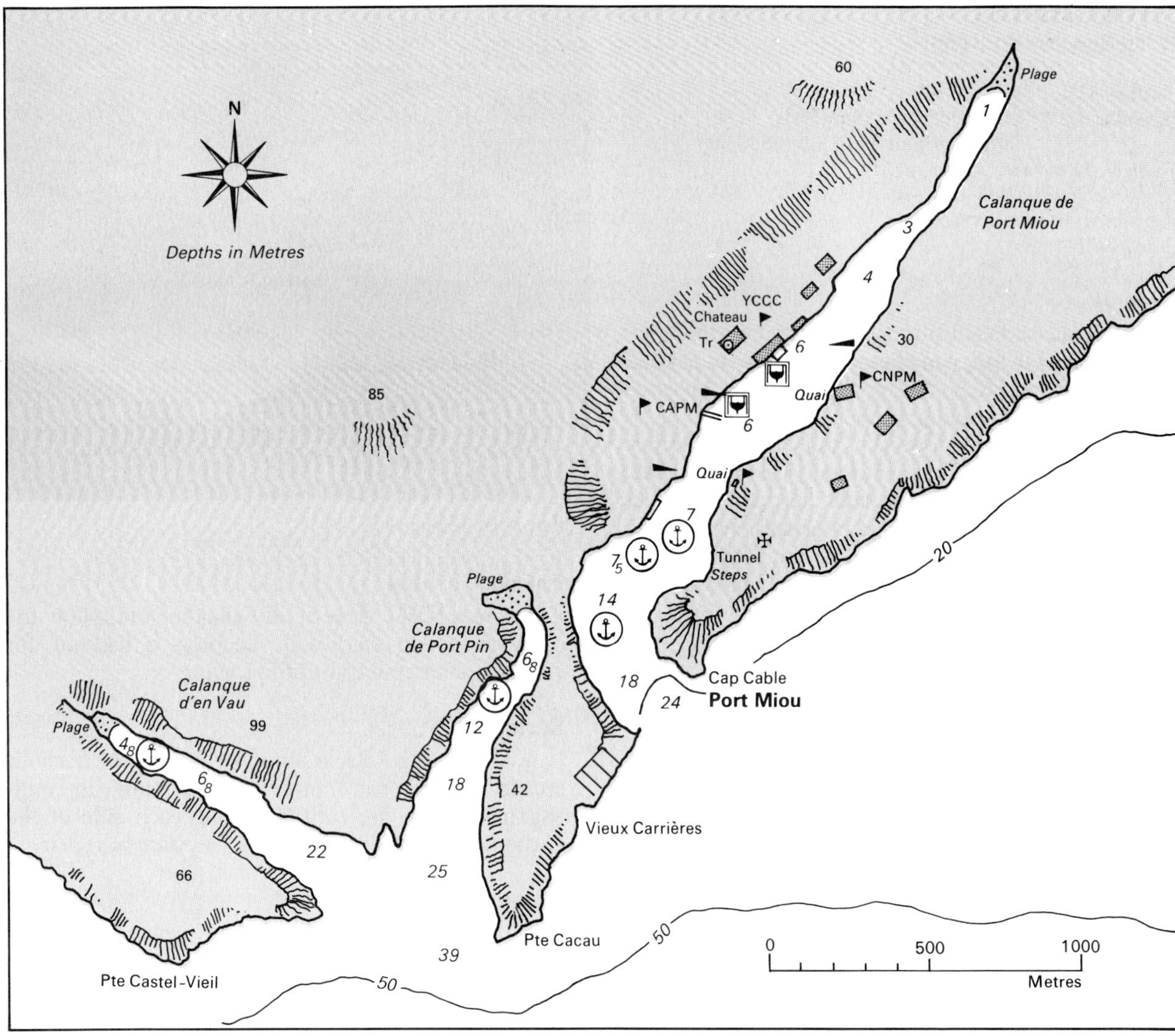

Port Miou

Port Miou. Entrance, looking NE

Port Miou, looking NE–E–SE

78 PORT DE CASSIS
13260 Bouches du Rhône

Position 43°12'·8N 5°32'·0E
Minimum depth   in the entrance 5m (18ft)
                  in the harbour 4·5 to 2m (15 to 6·6ft)
Width of the inner entrance 30m
Maximum length overall 20m (65ft)
Number of yacht berths 450 (+)
Population 7916
Rating 2–3–3

General
A small and very attractive yachting and fishing
harbour surrounded by hills and a pleasant small
town with fair facilities and good shops. It is easy to
approach and not too difficult to enter except in
conditions of strong SE–S–SW winds. The harbour is
very crowded and berths are difficult to find; it is
also expensive in the season.

Data
Charts Admiralty 2164
          French 6612, 6882
          Spanish 49
          Navicarte 504

Currents There can be a strong outgoing current of fresh
   water through the harbour mouth from a spring on the
   N side.

Magnetic variation 1°46'W (1994) decreasing by about 6'
   each year.

Weather forecast Posted daily at the *bureau du port* at 0900.
   Recorded forecast (☎ 36 65 08 09 and 36 65 08 08).

Speed limit 3 knots.

Storm signals Flown from the signal station on the top of
   Cap Canaille.

Port radio VHF Ch 9, 16.

Lights
Môle Neuf head Oc(2)G.6s17m6M White tower, green top
Batterie des Lèques Fl.R.4s12m6M Red column on hut
   248°-vis-068°
Baoue de la Saoupe 3F.Rs. Pylon 1·2M ESE

Warning
Shallow water exists to the E of the lighthouse and
there is a submerged rock (7·1m deep) 50m to S of it.
In bad weather there is a strong scend (surge) inside
the harbour.

Approach by day
From W From Cap Croisette, the high bare white
rocky cliffs are broken by a series of *calanques* and
the rocky islands offshore of similar appearance are
unique. The large *calanques* of Sormiou and Morgiou
are easily identified as is the prominent Pointe
Castel-Vieil with its wooded top, NE of which is a
double and then a single *calanque*. The wide Baie de
Cassis then opens up and the town will be seen at the
head of the bay. The white lighthouse with a green
top located at the entrance of the harbour is
conspicuous as are the blocks of flats in front of a
cemented cliff face, and also the group of *château*
buildings on top of the high cliffs at Pointe des
Lombards.

From E Round the remarkable Bec-de-l'Aigle,
having just passed the small Ile Verte. Follow the
very high rocky cliffs past the small Calanque de
Figuerolles and the conspicuous signal station on the
cliff top, the town of Cassis will then open up. Make
a course across the bay to its W side about half a mile
SW from the harbour and approach it from this
position in order to avoid the rocky shallows off
Pointe des Lombards. The high cliffs to the W of
Bec-de-l'Aigle deflect NW winds and cause a very
short choppy sea.

Approach by night
Use the major lights:
Ile Tiboulen de Maire Fl.WG.4s58m11/8M to the
W
Banc de la Cassidaigne Fl(2)W.6s8M to the S
La Ciotat Oc(2)R.6s13M to E

Anchorage in the approach
Anchor in the Anse de Grand Mer 150m S of the
large *hôtel de ville* in 5m sand and weed.

Entrance
By day Approach on a NE course following the W
side of the bay at 100m; when the entrance opens,

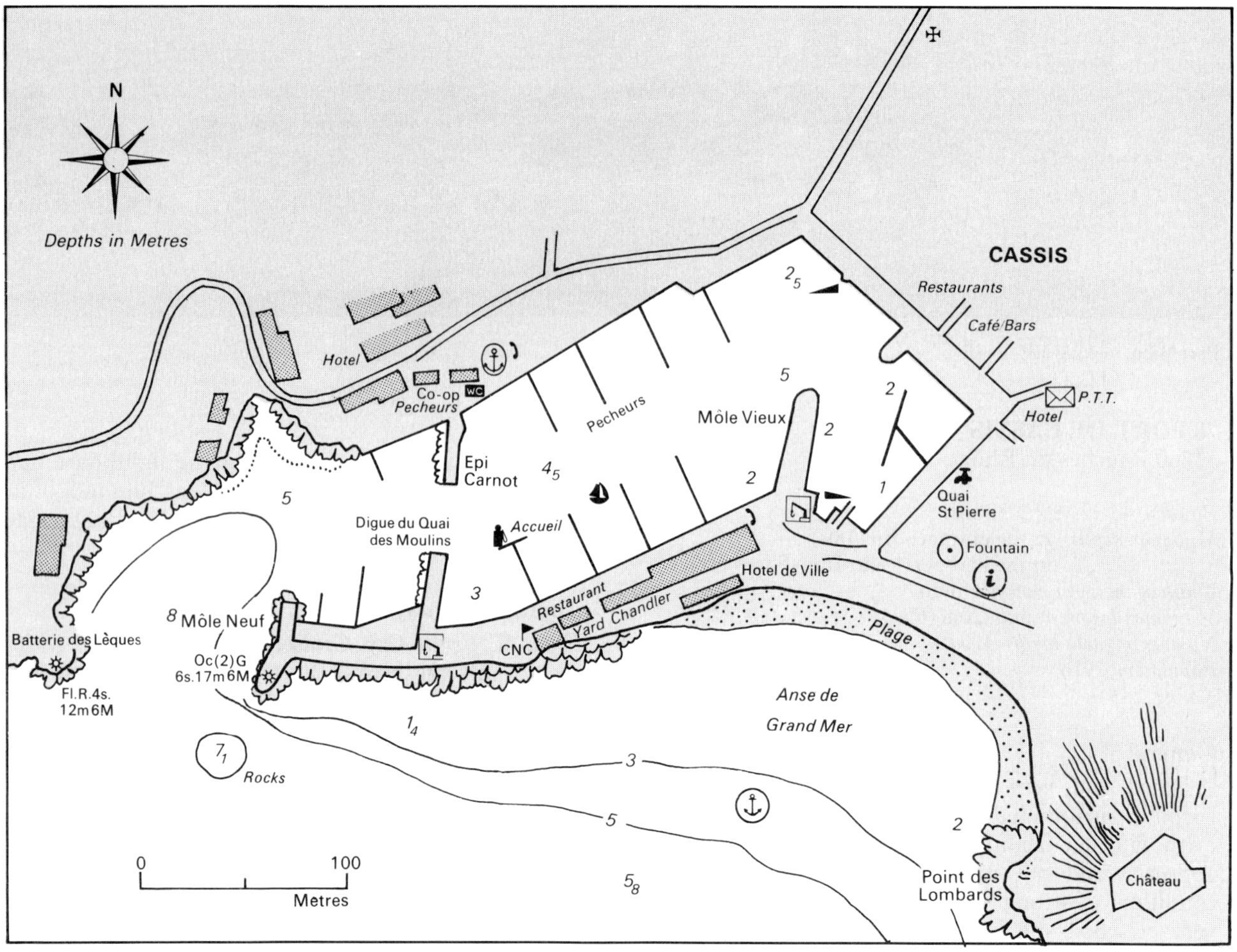

Port de Cassis

Port de Cassis. Approach looking NE

Port de Cassis. Entrance, looking NE

Fuel berth

Port de Cassis. Inner entrance, looking NE

round the Batterie des Lèques with its small red light tower at 30m onto a NNE course leaving the large white lighthouse, green top, at the head of Môle Neuf 60m to starboard. Head then onto a NE course and enter between the inner Epi Carnot and Digue du Quai des Moulins which are only 30m apart.

By night Approach Fl.R.4s on a N course, when Oc(2)G.6s is NE enter between them.

Berths

Berth alongside the fuel berth or, if space is not available there, to a pontoon.

Moorings

None.

Formalities

Report to the *bureau du port* (☎ 42 01 03 73) and to the Cercle Nautique (☎ 42 01 79 04) on arrival. Customs, Place Mirabeau (☎ 42 01 77 32) (Friday mornings only).

Charges

There are harbour charges.

Facilities

Slips There are hards at the E end, and SE and SW corners of the harbour.
Slipways There is a slipway for 25 tonnes at the SE corner of the harbour, but only 1·5m depth in approach.
Cranes There is one 6-tonne crane near the slip and another of 4 tonnes is near the Cercle Nautique.
Fuel Diesel and petrol from pumps at the head of the first pontoon to starboard nearest the entrance.
Water There are taps on the quays and pontoons.
Electricity 220v AC points on pontoons and some quays.
Provisions There is a good selection of shops of all types nearby in the town.
Ice Available from two grocery shops in the town about 200m to NE of the harbour.
Garbage A few rubbish containers around the harbour.
Repairs There is a small shipyard on the Quai des Moulins next to the Cercle Nautique. There are engineers in the town.
Chandlers Next to shipyard.

Post office At the back of the town in a NE direction opening onto a public garden.
Hotels Seven ***, seven **, three * and four others.
Restaurants 55 restaurants and many café/bars.
Yacht clubs The Cercle Nautique de Cassis (CNC) has a small clubhouse on the Quai des Moulins with showers, WCs, restaurant and bar alongside (☎ 42 01 70 40 and 42 01 71 71). Association Nautique Cassidaigne (ANC), Place Grand Carnot (☎ 42 01 24 95).
Information office The Syndicat d'Initiative has an office in the small square to E of the harbour (☎ 42 01 71 17).
Visits If possible the nearby *calanques* should be visited by boat or on foot. There are fourteen well known vineyards in the area.
Beaches There are small sandy beaches either side of the harbour.
Communications There is a bus service, and a railway station is some 2M away.

Future development

Plans exist for the enlargement of the harbour and for the development of a new yacht harbour called Carcon on the other side of Pointe des Lombards. Many minor improvements to the existing harbour are in hand.

History

This little port has been made famous by the poet Mistral, who wrote 'Qu'a vist Paris e noun Cassis a ren vist' (He who has seen Paris but not Cassis has seen nothing), and by the painters Dufy, Vlamink and Matisse. It has also been used as a location for many films. It is famous for its blackcurrant liqueur and for wines from the area.

La Cassidaigne Rock

A dangerous offshore rock, just covered, with 3·6m rocky shallows stretching 300m to SE. It lies 2¾M to WSW of Bec-de-l'Aigle and is marked by a black lighthouse with red bands showing a light (Fl(2)W.6s 25m8M).

Port de Cassis, looking W

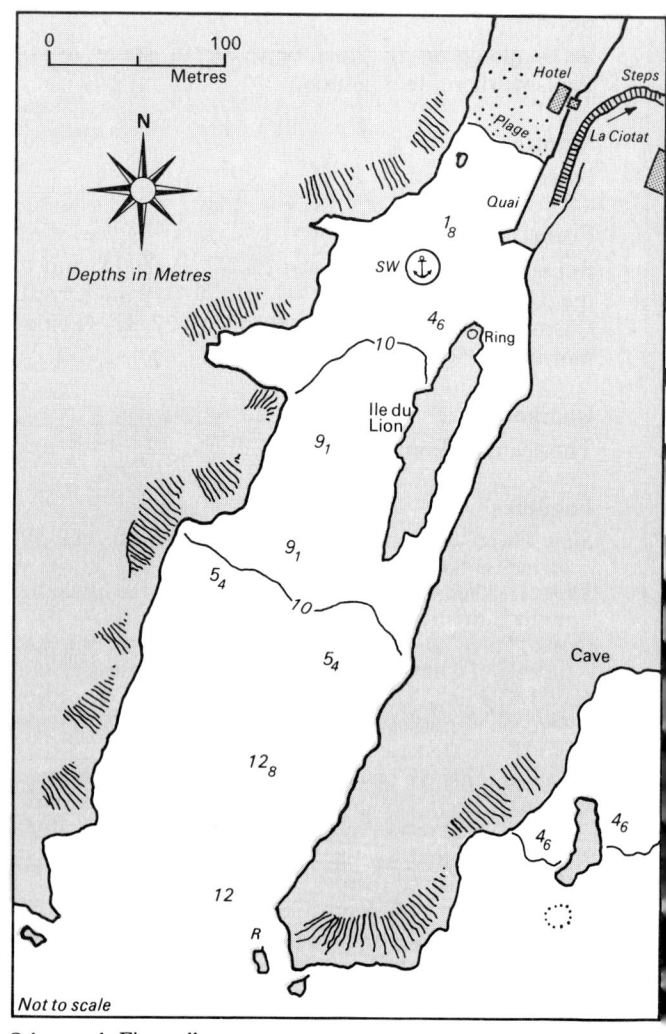

Calanque de Figuerolles

⚓ **Anse de Ste Magdeleine**

An open anchorage facing SW which forms a useful alternative to Port Miou when Cassis is full. Rocky cliffs with a shingle beach at head, houses around it and a road inland. Conspicuous tower on Pointe Corton. Rocky bottom. (A new harbour may be built here.)

⚓ **Anse de l'Arène**

Similar to the above anchorage but with a rocky shore and no beach. Bottom rocky with weed.

⚓ **Calanque de Figuerolles**

A spectacular anchorage between high cliffs. W side of entrance has a small Bec-de-l'Aigle (eagle's beak) not unlike that on the headland to E. Open to S and to gusts of wind from N. The long thin island, Ile du Lion, has a mooring ring on its N end. At the head of the *calanque* is a shingle beach with a small quay and a hotel, restaurant and bar. Steps lead up to the main road. The bottom is rock near the entrance becoming stones and weed further in. There is a deep cave to E of the entrance.

Bec-de-l'Aigle

A spectacular, high-cliffed (155m) rocky promontory surmounted by a rock not unlike the beak of an eagle (Bec-de-l'Aigle), very conspicuous and easily recognised from afar. The point is steep-to.

Cap Bec de l'Aigle, looking NW

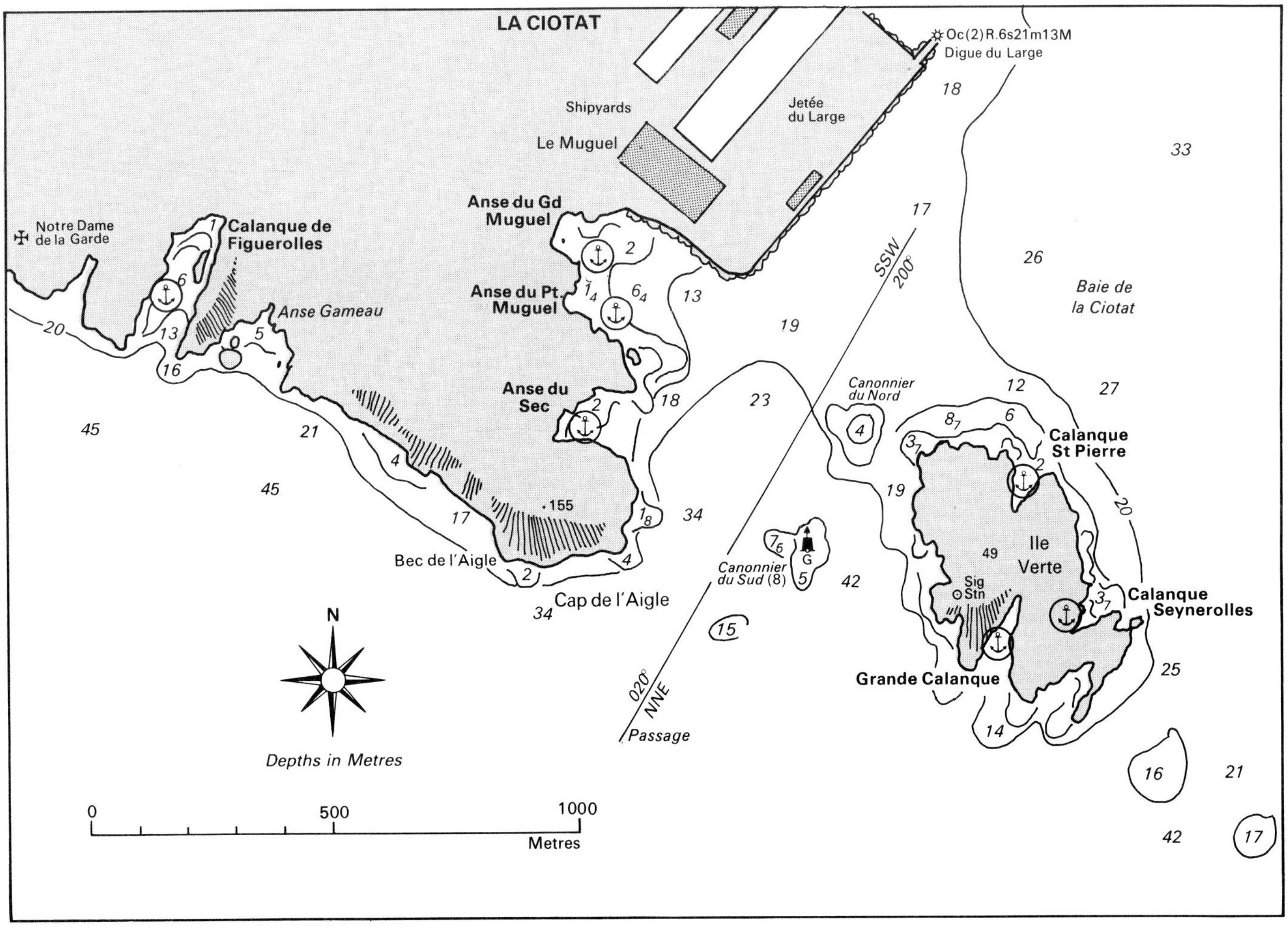

LA CIOTAT

☀Oc(2)R.6s21m13M
Digue du Large

Shipyards

Jetée
du Large

Le Muguel

18

33

Notre Dame
de la Garde

**Calanque de
Figuerolles**

**Anse du Gd
Muguel**

17

26

*Baie de
la Ciotat*

6

2

Anse Gameau

**Anse du Pt
Muguel**

1₄

6₄

13

19

13

0 5

16

20

**Anse du
Sec**

2

18

23

*Canonnier
du Nord*

12

27

45

21

4

17

•155

1₈
8

34

19

4

Bec de l'Aigle

2

4

N

34 Cap de l'Aigle

34

*Canonnier
du Sud (8)*

7₆
6

G
5

42

3₇

8₇

6

**Calanque
St Pierre**

2

*Ile
Verte*

49

*Sig
Stn*

20

3₇

**Calanque
Seynerolles**

25

Depths in Metres

15

SSW
200°

020°
NNE

Passage

Grande Calanque

14

16

21

0   500   1000

Metres

42

17

Anchorages S of La Ciotat

⚓ Calanque de Figuerolles looking NE

Bec-de-l'Aigle looking E

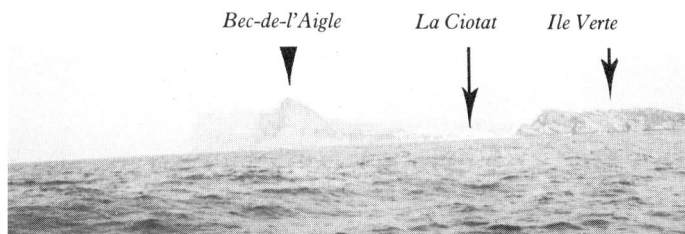

Bec-de-l'Aigle looking W

PASSAGE BETWEEN BEC-DE-L'AIGLE AND ILE VERTE

Deep (14m) passage 220m wide in a N–S direction between Bec-de-l'Aigle and the Canonnier du Sud, marked by a green beacon tower (8m) with up-pointed cone. A narrower (60m) passage exists between this beacon and Ile Verte in a NNE/SSW direction. This passage has a 4m deep rock (Canonnier du Nord) to NE of its N end (see chart). At night the lights on the harbour extensions assist.

⚓ **Anse du Sec**

A small anchorage tucked away to N of Bec-de-l'Aigle. Rock in middle of bay, enter and anchor on S side. Few houses and a road ashore. Open to E.

⚓ **Anse du Petit-Mugel and Anse du Grand-Mugel**

Two small bays with greatly improved protection due to construction of La Ciotat harbour works. Open to E and to some extent to NE and SE. Rock, sand and weed bottom, small beach, road, houses, hotel at head.

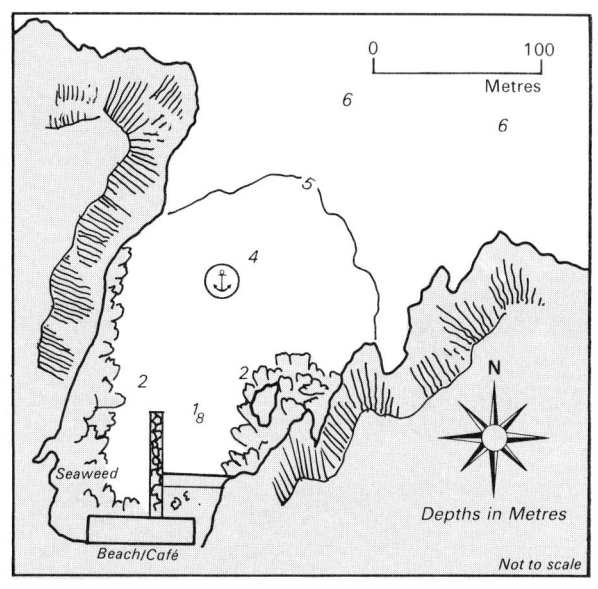

Calanque St-Pierre

Passage between Cap Bec-de-l'Aigle and Ile Verte, looking N

Grand and Petit Mugel, looking W

Calanque Seynerolles, Ile Verte, looking SW

ILE VERTE

Ile Verte is a small deserted island 79m high with a deep *calanque* on its S side and several smaller ones on its N and S sides. It has several anchorages, see chart page 00.

⚓ Calanque St-Pierre

A small *calanque* on the N side of the island, open to N–NE, small jetty for ferries from La Ciotat, large beach, restaurant.

⚓ Calanque Seynerolles

Similar to Calanque St-Pierre but with no facilities.

⚓ Grande-Calanque

Open to S and dangerous with wind from this direction. 11m deep with steep sides, shallows at head. Rocky bottom.

79 PORT DE LA CIOTAT

13600 Bouches du Rhône

Position 43°10'·5N 5°36'·7E
Minimum depth   in the entrance 7m (25ft)
                              in the harbour 4 to 1·5m (14·5 to 5ft)
Width of the entrance 30m
Number of yacht berths 850
Maximum length overall 15m (49ft)
Population 31,727
Rating 3–2–2

General

An old natural harbour which has been improved by the addition of breakwaters and the construction of two yacht harbours nearby. The harbours are easy to approach and enter but strong winds from SE can make the approach difficult. There are good facilities in the area but the yacht harbours tend to be crowded. The old town and port are interesting and are unspoilt by the vast shipbuilding complex on the S side of the harbour.

Data

Charts   Admiralty 2164
              French 5325, 6612, 6882
              Spanish 49
              Navicarte 504

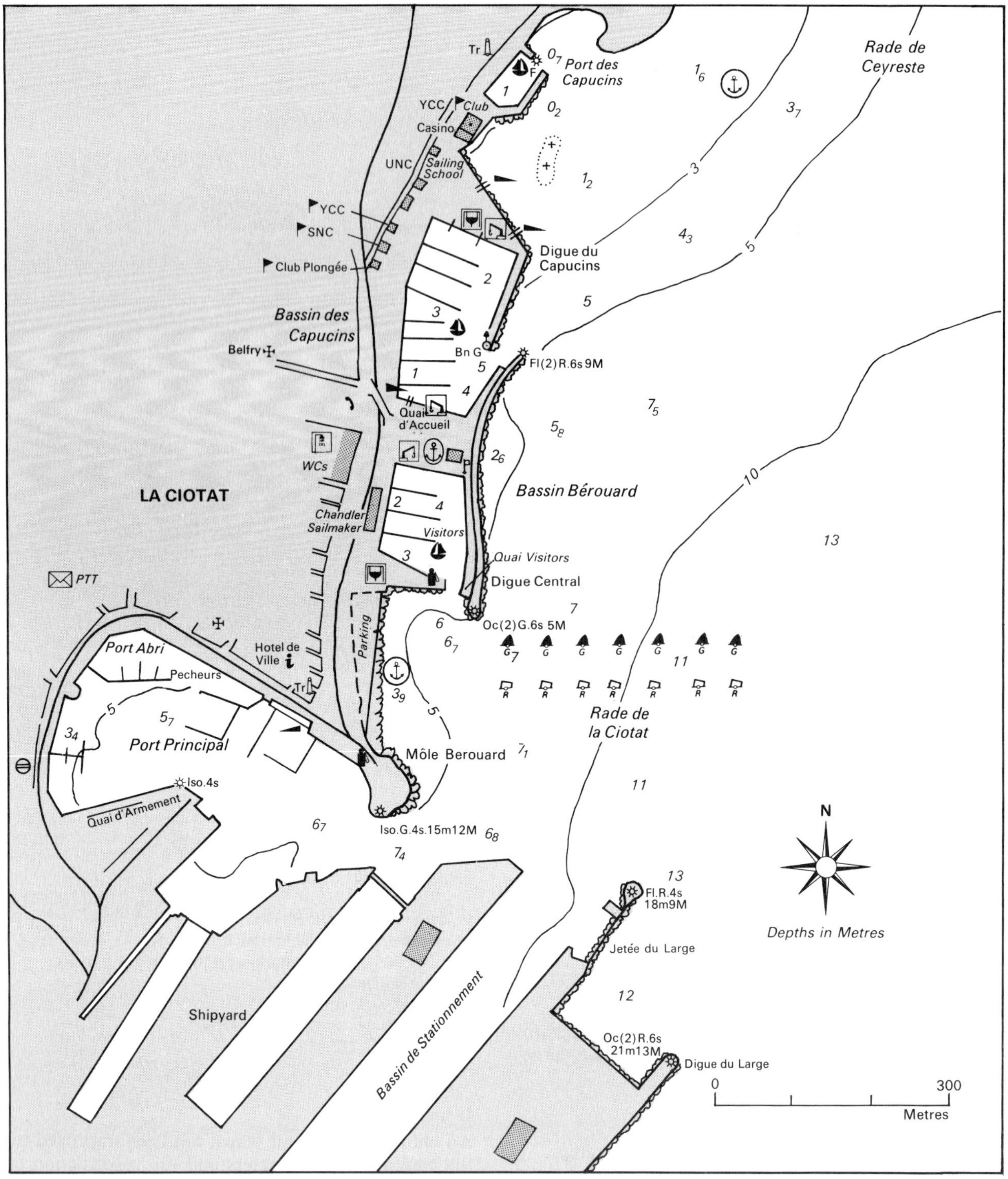

Tr ▯
Port des
Capucins
0₇
F
YCC Club
Casino
1
0₂
UNC Sailing
School
1₆ ⚓
Rade de
Ceyreste
3₇
YCC
SNC
Club Plongée
Digue du
Capucins
1₂
3
3
4₃
5
*Bassin des
Capucins*
Belfry ⛨
2
3
1
4
Bn G
5
5
Fl(2)R.6s 9M
5
5₈
7₅
Quai
d'Accueil
2₆
Bassin Bérouard
WCs
*Chandler
Sailmaker*
2 4
Visitors
3
Quai Visitors
Digue Central
5₈
10
13
PTT
7
6
6₇
6₇
Oc(2)G.6s 5M
G₇ G G G G G
11
Rade de
la Ciotat
Port Abri
Pecheurs
Hotel de
Ville
Tr
3₉
5
R R R R R R R

Port Principal
5
5₇
3₄
⊖
Iso.4s
Parking
Môle Berouard
7₁
11
6₇
Quai d'Armement
Iso.G.4s.15m12M
6₈
7₄
13
Fl.R.4s
18m9M
LA CIOTAT

N

Depths in Metres

Jetée du Large
12
Oc(2)R.6s
21m13M
Digue du Large

Shipyard
Bassin de Stationnement

0   300
Metres

Port de la Ciotat

Port de la Ciotat looking W

Head of Jetée du Large   *Entrance Bassin Bérouard*

Port de la Ciotat, looking NW

Light at head of Digue du Large   *Light at head of Jetée du Large*

Port de la Ciotat, looking W

Entrance Bassin des Capucins

Port de la Ciotat, looking SW

Magnetic variation 1°46′W (1994) decreasing by about 6′ each year.

Port radio VHF Ch 9. Radio watch 0800–1200 and 1400–1700.

Weather forecast Posted twice a day at the *bureau du port* between the two yacht harbours. Also available Ch 9.

Speed limit 5 knots within 300m of harbours, 2 knots inside harbours.

Storm signals A black ball hoisted on a mast by the *bureau du port*.

Lights

Jetée du Large E head Oc(2)R.6s21m13M White structure, red top

Jetée du Large head Fl.R.4s18m9M White metal framework tower, red top

Môle Bérouard head Iso.G.4s15m12M White truncated tower, green top 134·5°-G-228·5°-G(unintens)-134·5°

Digue Central Sud head Oc(2)G.6s8m5M White structure, green top

Digue Central Nord head Fl(2)R.6s7m9M White tower, red top

Buoys Seven port and seven starboard hand buoys mark the entrance channel to Bassin Bérouard.

Beacons A pole used as a race mark is established 100m to the E of the entrance to Bassin des Capucins.

Warnings

With strong SE winds and the NW *mistral*, strong currents can be encountered between Ile Verte and the coast and can be felt as far as the entrance to this harbour. There are two unlit mooring buoys to the N of Ile Verte.

Approach by day

From W Follow the very high rocky cliffs that line the E side of the Baie de Cassis, passing the conspicuous signal station on the top and the small Calanque de Figuerolles, as far as the remarkable Bec-de-l'Aigle. In fair weather round this onto a NNE course passing halfway between the coast and a green beacon tower (Canonnier du Sud) with ▲ topmark, thence on a course towards the head of the Jetée du Large, which will be seen ahead. In very bad weather it is necessary to keep well clear of the coast and to round Ile Verte, leaving it some 300m to port before approaching the harbour (see page 00).

From E Round the yellow-cliffed Pointe du Défens (or Cap d'Alon) and on a WNW course cross the Baie de la Ciotat leaving Ile Verte to port. The large cranes and gantries at the S side of the harbour are very conspicuous from this direction. In the closer approach the rocky Digue Central will be seen and the long Jetée du Large with two lighthouses on its NE ends.

Approach by night

Use the major lights:
Ile du Grand-Rouveau Oc(2)W.6s15M to the E
La Cassidaigne Fl(2)W.6s8M to the W

Anchorage in the approach

Anchor 200m to NE of the entrance to the Bassin des Capucins in 5m sand and mud or 100m to S of the entrance to Bassin Bérouard.

Entrance by day

Bassin Bérouard Leave the S head of Digue Central 20m to starboard and round onto a N course, leaving a low rocky wall to port.
Bassin des Capucins Round the N head of Digue Central at 20m onto a SSW course, leaving it 20m to port and enter between the two harbour walls.
Port Principal (Vieux-Port) Enter between the head of Môle Bérouard marked with a lighthouse, and the head of the Quai d'Armement after passing the heads of Jetée du Large and Nouvelle Jetée to port.

Approach by night

Bassin des Capucins Approach Fl(2)R.6s on a W course, leave it 20m to port and round onto a SSW course.
Bassin Bérouard Approach Oc(2)G.6s on a W course and round it onto a N course, leaving it 20m to starboard.

Berths

Yachts normally berth stern-to the Quai d'Accueil which lies at the N end of Bassin Bérouard and the S end of Bassin des Capucins. Berths in the Port Principal are stern-to the outer side of the jetties enclosing the Port Abri but vacant places are unlikely.

Formalities

Report to the *bureau du port* (☎ 42 08 62 90 and 42 08 43 84) on arrival; this is located between the two *bassins*. Open 0800–1200 and 1400–1730. Customs, Quai Stalingrad (☎ 42 08 05 81).

Harbour charges

There are harbour charges.

Facilities

Slips There are three slips at the N end of the Bassin des Capucins and one at the S end of the Bassin Bérouard.
Cranes One crane of 6 tonnes on the S side of the Bassin des Capucins and one of 6 tonnes on the N side; there is also a 10-tonne crane on the W side of Port Principal (Vieux-Port).
Fuel Diesel and petrol from pumps at the W side of the entrance to the Bassin Bérouard, also from the SW side of the Môle Bérouard. 0700–2000.
Water There are water points around the two *bassins* and in the Port Principal(Vieux-Port).
Electricity Electricity points, 220v AC, around the Bassin des Capucins and Bassin Bérouard.
Provisions Many shops of all types in the nearby town.
Ice Available.
Garbage A number of rubbish bins and barrows around the harbour.
Chandlery There is a shop to SW of the *bassins* not far from the town hall and two more are beside the Bassin Bérouard.
Repairs There are several shipyards in the town and a very large concern that deals with commercial vessels. There are also a number of engineers and electricians and a sailmaker.
Laundrette There are several in the town.
Post office To the NW of the Port Principal (Vieux-Port).
Hotels Three ★★★, nine ★★, five ★ and eleven others.
Restaurants There are 73 restaurants and very many café/bars.
Showers There are five showers and WCs near the *bureau du port* open 0700–1200 and 1300–1900.
Yacht clubs The Société Nautique de la Ciotat (SNC) has an office in the NW corner of the Bassin des Capucins. Alongside it are the clubhouse restaurant, bar, etc. of the Union Nautique de la Ciotat (UNC). The Yachting Club Ciotaden (YCC) (☎ 41 08 50 28) has a clubhouse at N end of harbour.
Information office The Syndicat d'Initiative has an office near the root of the Môle Bérouard, 2 quai Ganteaume (☎ 42 08 43 80 and 42 08 61 32).
Lifeboat A lifeboat is stationed here.
Visits There is a fantastic view from the signal station to the SW of the town near to which is the Chapelle de Notre-Dame-de-la-Garde. There is a 7th-century church and there are many old buildings in the town.
Beaches There are sandy beaches 1M to NE.
Communications There are bus and rail services.

Future development

More shops and other services are to be developed around the two *bassins*. Plans are being made to build a huge edifice over the shipyard and docks, designed by Melville Mark an English architect.

History

The area has been occupied since Neolithic times, and Neolithic remains and those of the Romans can be seen. The Vieux-Port was built in 1835. The brothers Lumières who invented the cinema were born and worked here.

Port des Capucins (Flots Bleus)

A small private fishing harbour just to N of Bassin des Capucins, 1m deep for small boats. Crane 6 tonnes, hard and fresh water.

---

80 PORT DE SAINT-JEAN
13600 Bouches du Rhône

Position 43°11'·2N 5°37'·7E
Minimum depth in the entrance 2m (6·6ft)
in the harbour 2 to 1m (6·6 to 3ft)
Width of the entrance 15m
Number of yacht berths 125
Population (La Ciotat) 31,727
Rating 3–3–4

General

A small artificial harbour tucked away on the SW side of Cap des Moulins suitable for smaller yachts and power boats. Approach and entrance are easy except in strong winds from SE–S–SW, when seas can break in the approach. Local facilities are limited, but La Ciotat is only 1M away where most requirements can be met.

Data

See 79 Port de la Ciotat, page 297.

Warning

Do not mistake the several rocky beach breakwaters, which lie between La Ciotat and this harbour, for the harbour breakwater itself.

Port de St Jean looking NE

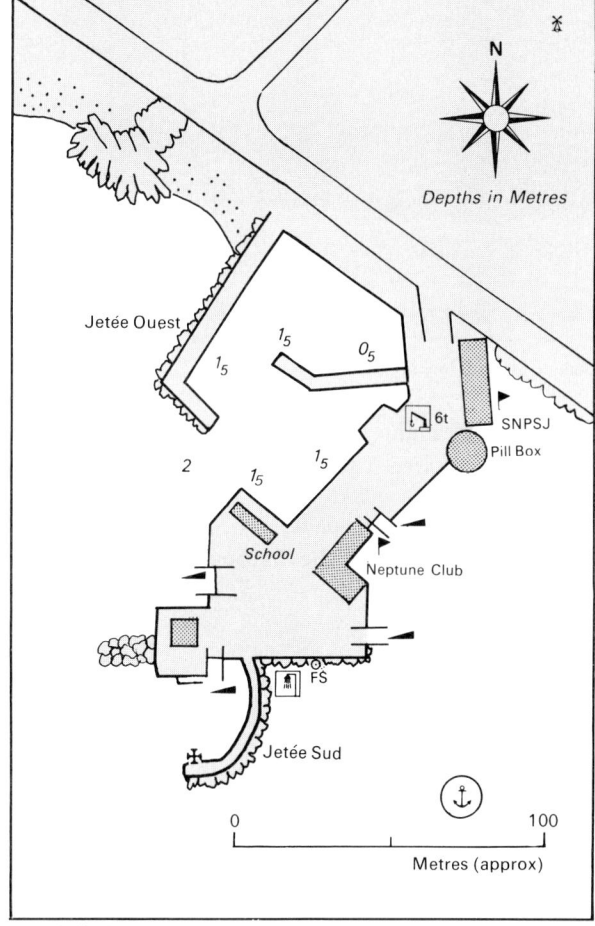

Port de St-Jean

Approach by day

From W Round the conspicuous and prominent Bec-de-l'Aigle and pass inside (see page 296) or outside the Ile Verte onto a NNE course. Having passed the huge shipyard and the twin yacht harbours, look for a low tree-covered point with a windmill and several large houses in the trees. The harbour lies in front of these and the breakwater will be seen in the close approach.

From E Round Point du Défens and set a NW course across the Baie de la Ciotat. In the closer approach the windmill and houses in the trees, described above, will be seen but the windmill is partly screened by the trees from this direction and the breakwater is hidden behind the Cap des Moulins.

Entrance   Windmill

Port de St-Jean, looking N

Approach by night

Not recommended without first visiting it by day.

Anchorage in the approach

Anchor 300m SW of the harbour entrance in 4m sand and some weed.

Entrance by day

Approach the entrance with care due to shallow water on a NE course. The windmill in line with the clubhouse gives a good approach course. The entrance is between a building on a quay left to starboard and the head of the long rocky Jetée Ouest left to port.

Berths

Berth in a vacant space and contact the *capitaine de port* for allocation of a berth.

Facilities

Slips Four small slips on S side of the harbour.
Cranes A 6-tonne crane on S side of the harbour.
Water A few taps around the harbour.
Provisions From La Ciotat.
Showers One on S side of the harbour.
Yacht club Société Nautique du Port de St-Jean (SNPSJ) has a clubhouse on NE side of the harbour (☎ 42 83 26 97). The Neptune Club de la Ciotat-Plage also has a clubhouse in this harbour.
School Sailing and motor-boat school.
Restaurants Several nearby and the Neptune Club at the harbour.
Hotels One ★★★ nearby.
Beaches Good sandy beach to SW.
Communications Coastal road with bus service. La Ciotat railway station 1M inland.

81 PORT DE SAINT-CYR-LES-LECQUES

83270 Var

Position 43°10′.7N 5°41′.0E
Ancien Port
Minimum depth   in the entrance 2m (6·6ft)
in the harbour 1·2 to 0·5m (4 to 2ft)
Width of the entrance 25m
Maximum length overall 8m (26ft)
Nouveau Port
Minimum depth   in the entrance 6m (20ft)
in the harbour 5 to 1m (18 to 3ft)
Width of the entrance 40m
Number of berths for yachts 631
Maximum length overall 15m (49ft), but 8m (26ft) only in Ancien Port
Population (St-Cyr-sur-Mer) 7000
Rating 3–3–2

General

A small shallow artificial fishing and yacht harbour (Ancien Port) has had a new extensive yacht harbour (Nouveau Port) constructed alongside it which is suitable for larger and deeper-draught yachts. Approach and entrance present no problem except with strong winds and swell from SE–S–SW. Good protection once inside but heavy swell from SW is felt in the Nouveau Port. Facilities are good and there are some excellent restaurants.

Data

Charts   Admiralty 2164
French 6612, 6882
Spanish 49
Navicarte 504

Speed limit 3 knots.

Magnetic variation 1°46′W (1994) decreasing by about 6′ each year.

Port radio VHF Ch 9.

Lights
Jetée Sud NE head Fl(2)R.6s8m7M Red framework on white and grey base
Jetée Sud SW head Iso.G.4s10m9M White pylon, green top
Contre-Jetée Ouest head Q.R.3m7M Red post

Weather forecast Posted daily at the *bureau du port*. Recorded forecast (☎ 36 65 08 08 and 36 65 08 09).

Port de St-Cyr-les-Lecques looking NW

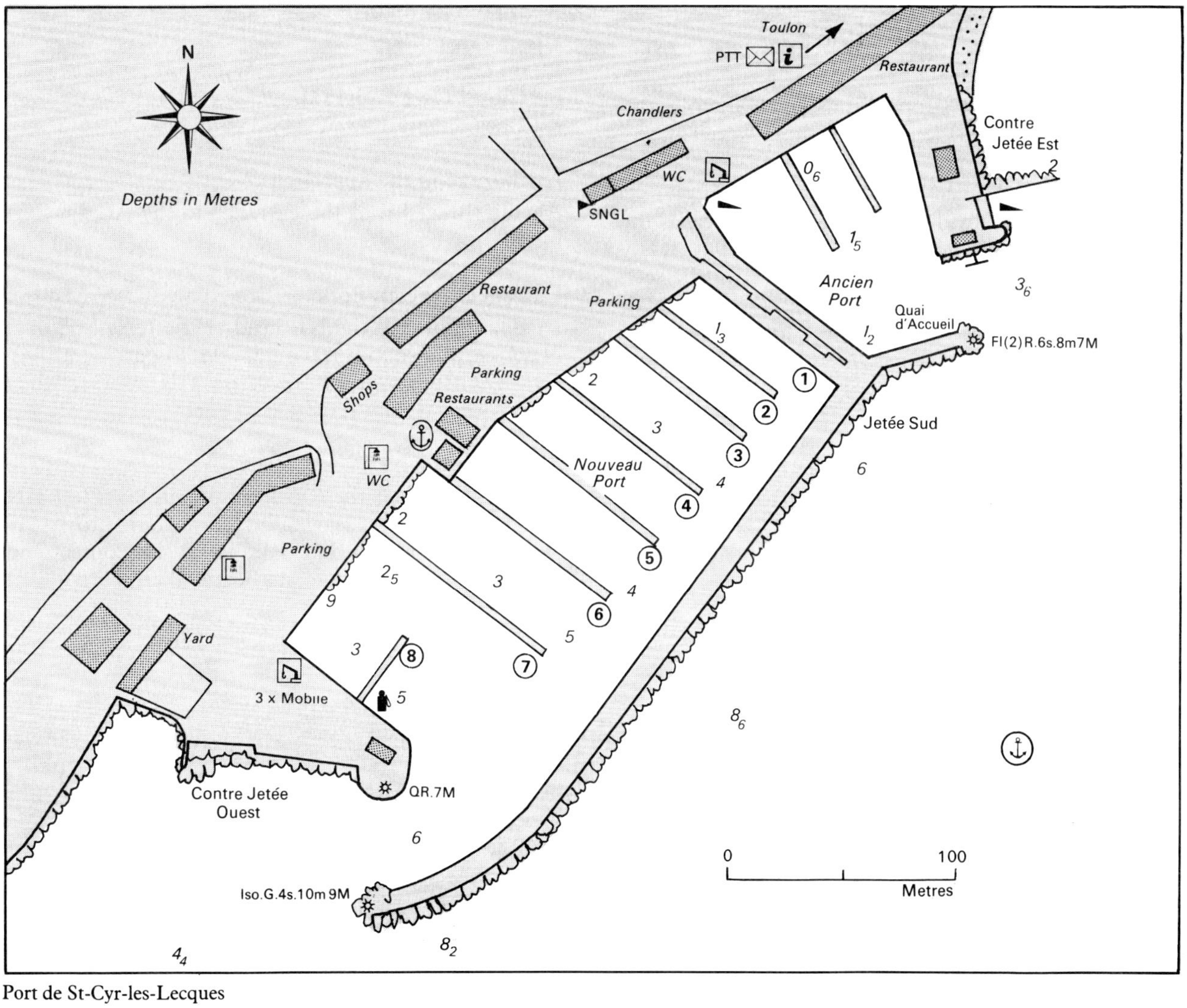

Port de St-Cyr-les-Lecques

Entrance Vieux Port

Port de St Cyr-les-Léques, looking N

Entrance Nouveau Port

Port de St Cyr-les-Léques, looking NE

Warning
A dangerous breaking sea can occur in the approach to this harbour with strong winds from SE to S and SW. The Ancien Port tends to silt up in winter.

Approach by day
From W Cross the wide Baie de la Ciotat towards the NE corner where there is a long low flat sandy stretch of beach. At the NW end of this will be seen the houses of Les Lecques and the rocky harbour breakwater. Cap St-Louis, a low rocky headland topped by dark trees, can be recognised in the close approach.

From E Round the yellow rocky Pointe du Défens (or Cap d'Alon) and pass along the rocky cliff-lined coast at 300m as far as Pointe Grenier, then cross the Baie des Lecques on a N course towards the houses of Les Lecques with its rocky harbour wall which will be seen in the closer approach.

Approach by night
Use the major lights:
Ile du Grand-Rouveau Oc(2)W.6s15M to the SE
La Ciotat Oc(2)R.6s13M
La Cassidaigne Fl(2)W.6s8M to the W

Anchorage in the approach
Anchor 100m SE of the entrance to the Ancien Port in 5m sand and weed.

Entrance. Ancien Port
By day Approach the NE head of the Jetée Sud on a N course and round, leaving it 20m to port.
By night Approach Fl(2)R.6s on a N course, when close round at 20m leaving it to port.

Nouveau Port
By day Approach the SW head of Jetée Sud on a N course and round it leaving it 20m to starboard.
By night Approach Iso.G.4s on a N course and round, leaving it 20m to starboard, then leave a Q.R 20m to port.

Port de St Cyr-les-Léques. Vieux Port, looking SE

Berths

Secure stern-to Quai d'Accueil of Ancien Port just inside the entrance on the port hand with bow-to mooring line. In the Nouveau Port secure to the fuel jetty which is to port on entering.

Formalities

Report to the *bureau du port* on arrival (☎ 94 26 21 98) on N side of Nouveau Port, open 0700–1200 and 1430–2030, or in the Ancien Port (☎ 94 29 47 13) open 0900–1700.

Harbour charges

These are levied but the first 2 hours are free.

Facilities

Slips There is a small slip in the NW corner of the Ancien Port and another on the exterior of Contre-Jetée Est.

Cranes There is a small 2-tonne crane in the E corner of the Ancien Port and a 10-tonne crane at SW end of Nouveau Port.

Fuel From pumps near head of Contre-Jetée Ouest (☎ 94 26 53 39).

Water Several taps around the harbour and on the pontoons.

Electricity Points for 220v AC on pontoons and some quays.

Chandlery There is a shop to the N of the harbour, and two others are nearby.

Repairs Repairs can be carried out by local shipwrights and engineers at the yard on W side of the harbour.

Post office At St-Cyr about 1M away.

Hotels One ★★★, three ★★, four ★ and two others.

Restaurants There are seventeen restaurants and a number of café/bars in the area.

Showers Four showers near W end of the harbour.

Yacht club The Société Nautique de Golfe des Lecques (SNGL) (☎ 94 26 17 55) has an office to the NE of the harbour.

Information office The Syndicat d'Initiative has an office on the front to the N of the harbour (☎ 94 26 13 46).

Visits The Roman museum of Tauroentum and the Moulin à Huile are worth a visit.

Beaches There is a long sandy beach to the SE of the breakwater.

Communications A bus service and railway, the station being 1M away.

Future development

Plans exist for the improvement of the present harbours.

---

82 PORT DE LA MADRAGUE DE ST-CYR-LES-LECQUES
83270 St-Cyr, Var

Position 43°10'·0N 5°41'·6E
Minimum depth in the entrance 3m (10ft)
  in the harbour 2 to 1m (6·6 to 3ft)
Width of the entrance 30m
Number of yacht berths 400
Maximum length overall 8m (26ft)
Population 7083
Rating 3–4–4

Port de Sanary-sur-Mer

General

A small artificial yacht harbour for use only by vessels of shallow draught. Approach requires care and would be impossible in winds from SW, W and NW. Protection from the NW *mistral* is not good and there are only limited facilities.

Data

Charts Admiralty 2164
  French 6612
  Spanish 49
  Navicarte 504

Magnetic variation 1°46'W (1994) decreasing by about 6' each year.

Lights
Jetée Nord Est head Fl(4)G.15s4M
Jetée Sud Ouest head Fl.2s3M (Intended).

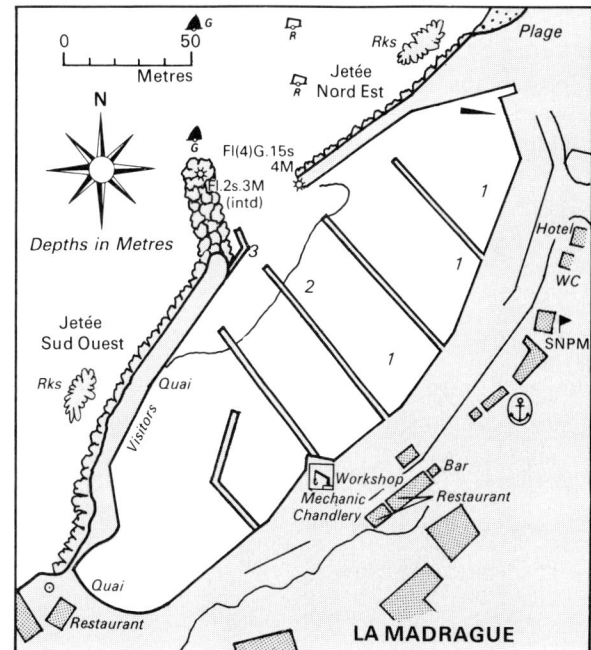

Port de la Madrague de St-Cyr-les-Lecques

Entrance

Port de la Madrague, looking SE

Warning
There is a 1·4m sandbank 300 metres to the SW of the entrance.

Approach by day
From W Cross the wide Baie de la Ciotat towards the low flat sandy coast in the NE corner of the bay. The harbour lies about a quarter of a mile to S of where the sandy coast gives way to rocky cliffs which are topped by dark trees. In the closer approach the rocky jetties will be seen.

From E Round Pointe du Défens and follow the yellow rocky cliffs at 300m as far as Pointe Grenier when the rocky jetties of the harbour will be seen. Do not cut the corner but keep at least 300m from the coast.

Approach by night
Due to the present lack of full navigational lights, night approach and entrance are not advised.

Anchorage in the approach
Anchor 200m to W of the entrance in 3m sand and weed in the Mouillage de Tarente.

Entrance by day
Approach the entrance with care on a SW course between a line of small red and green buoys whilst sounding and enter between the jetty heads.

Berths
Secure stern-to any vacant berth; visitors' berths are usually along the Jetée Sud Ouest.

Moorings
There are a few moorings, some of which may be vacant.

Formalities
Report to the *bureau du port* on arrival (☎ 94 26 39 8). Open 0800–1200 and 1400–1730.

Facilities
Slips There is a small slip in the NE corner of the harbour.
Crane There is one of 3.2 tonnes on the S side of the harbour.
Fuel This may be obtained from a garage near Les Lecques.
Water There is a tap at the S side of the harbour.
Provisions From a small general stores in the village.
Garbage There are some rubbish bins to S of the harbour.
Chandlery Available from the yard.
Repairs A local shipwright can carry out minor repairs, and there is also an engineer.
Post office At St-Cyr 2M away.
Hotels One ★★, one ★ and one other.
Restaurants One restaurant and two café/bars.
Yacht club The Société Nautique du Port de la Madrague (SNM) (☎ 94 26 27 58) has an office to S of the harbour.
Information Syndicat d'Initiative to NW of the harbour (☎ 94 26 13 46).
Visits The Musée de Tauroentum at an old Roman settlement should be visited.

Baie des Nations, looking NE

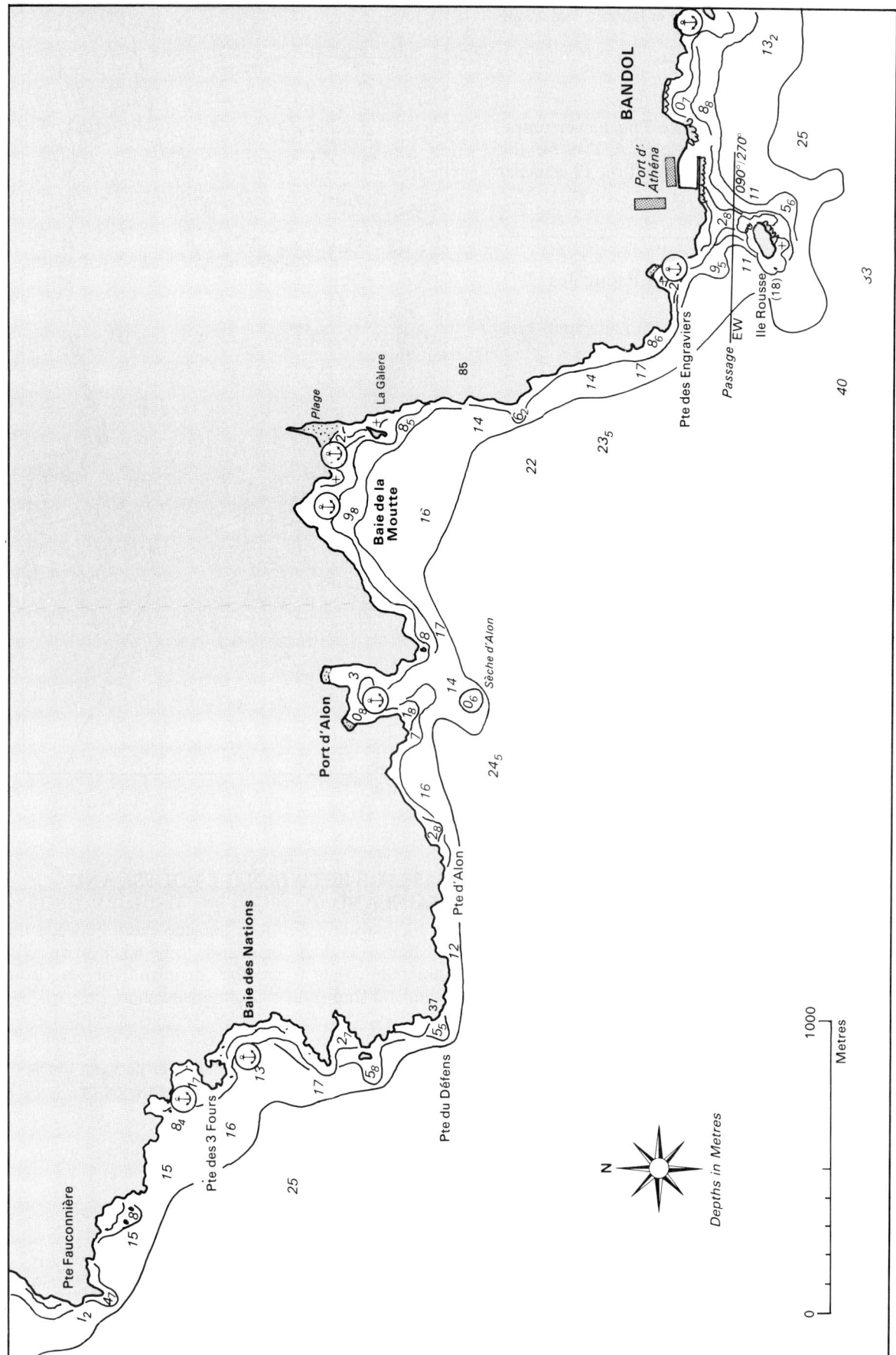

Anchorages W of Port de Bandol

Beaches There is a small beach to N of harbour and a long
  sandy beach half a mile further N.
Communications There is a bus service.

History

The site has been occupied since Phoenician times.
There was a famous naval battle in AD 49 off the
harbour when Julius Caesar destroyed the Phoenician
fleet.

⌕ **First and second bays to N of Pointe des
3-Fours**

Two small bays open to S–SW–W for use with care
due to rocks near the coast.

⌕ **Baie des Nations**

Similar to the anchorage near Pointe des 3-Fours,
but twice as wide and with road and houses ashore.

Pointe du Défens (Cap d'Alon)

A white-cliffed promontory, wood-covered with some
houses. Steep-to and not very prominent.

⌕ **Port d'Alon**

An excellent anchorage open to S, but pay attention
in calm weather to the Sèche d'Alon (0·6m covered),
located 300m to S of the entrance. In any swell the
seas break over it and it is easily seen. Ashore is a
café/restaurant, a large car park under very tall pine
trees and a road to the main road. The two sandy
beaches are crowded in the season.

⌕ **Baie de la Moutte**

A wide bay anchorage open S–SW. There are a
number of rocks off the E side of the bay. Anchor off
sandy beach or in NW corner with care. Houses and
road ashore.

⌕ **Baie des Engraviers**

A small bay with an exposed rock in NW corner and
a sandy beach open to S–SW. Houses and road
ashore.

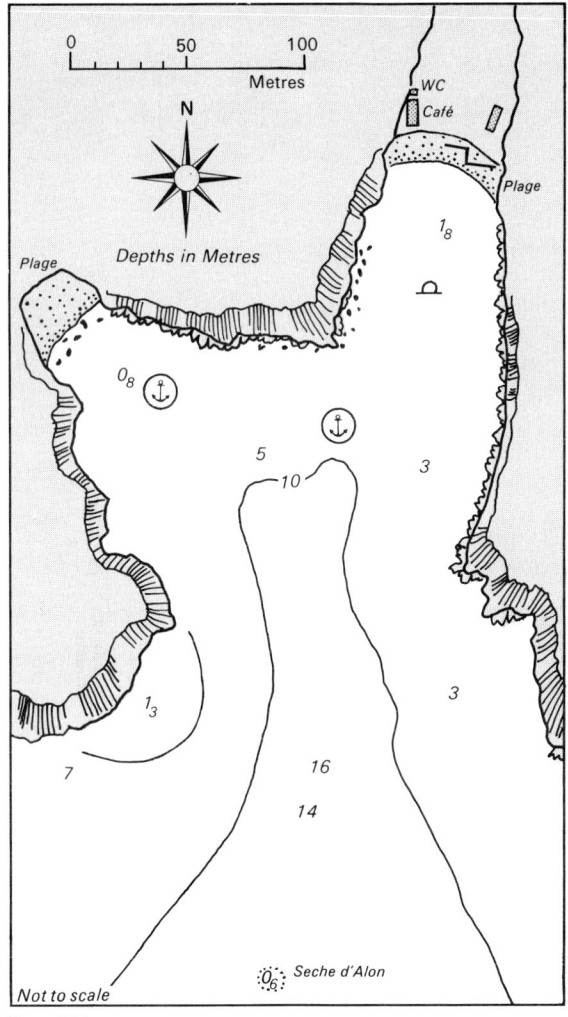

Port d'Alon

PASSAGE BETWEEN ILE ROUSSE AND
MAINLAND

A 100m wide 2.8m deep passage exists between the
Ile Rousse and the mainland, to be taken in an E/W
direction 70m from the mainland or ¼ from
mainland shore and ¾ from inland shore.

Port d'Athena

A private harbour in front of a large ugly block of
apartments, to be used only in an emergency.

Point du Défens, looking NW

Cap Bec de l'Aigle   *Port d'Athéna entrance*

Passage Ile Rousse and mainland

Port d'Athéna

Passage inshore of Ile Rousse, looking E

Entrance

Port d'Athéna (Private harbour), looking NW

Le Creux de Bandol, looking N

Port d'Athena looking N

⌘ **Creux de Bandol**

A well-sheltered anchorage, but shallow at the sides and head, where there is a beach which is crowded in the summer. There are a line of houses ashore and a road. Two jetties on E side of the bay. Open to SW and to some extent to both S and W.

PASSAGE BETWEEN ILE DE BENDOR AND THE MAINLAND

A passage about 200m wide with a minimum depth of 1·8m exists between Ile de Bendor and the mainland. It should be taken in a WNW/ESE direction, slightly closer to Ile de Bendor than to the mainland. The Pointe des Engraviers and La Fourmigue form good transit marks. This passage should not be attempted in heavy weather.

Ile Rousse   *Cap Bec l'Aigle*

Passage inside Ile de Bendor, looking W

Fourmigue beacon tower

Passage between Ile Bendor and mainland, looking E

83 PORT DE BENDOR
83150 Bandol, Var

Position 43°07'·7N 5°45'·2E
Minimum depth in the entrance 3·8m (12ft)
in the harbour 3 to 1m (10 to 3ft)
Width of the entrance 20m
Maximum length overall 13m (43ft)
Population 200
Rating 1–3–4

General

This very small but most attractive harbour, which has been constructed with taste and has the appearance of a film set, is privately owned by M. Paul Ricard. The approach and entrance require care and in strong winds and swell from SE to NW are dangerous. There is little space for manoeuvre inside and facilities are limited. During daylight there is a constant stream of tourist *vedettes* (ferries) from Bandol.

Data

Charts Admiralty 2164
French 5325, 6610
Spanish 49
Navicarte 504

Currents In strong NW winds E-going currents of up to 1 knot flow past this harbour entrance.

Magnetic variation 1°34'W (1994) decreasing by about 6' each year.

Speed limit 3 knots.

Lights
Jetée Est head Oc.R.4s5m7M White tower, red top
Jetée Ouest head Fl(2)G.6s3m5M Green column
Jetée Ouest spur F.G

Beacons La Fourmigue beacon tower, black with red band, 2 black balls topmark, marks a rocky shoal off the harbour.

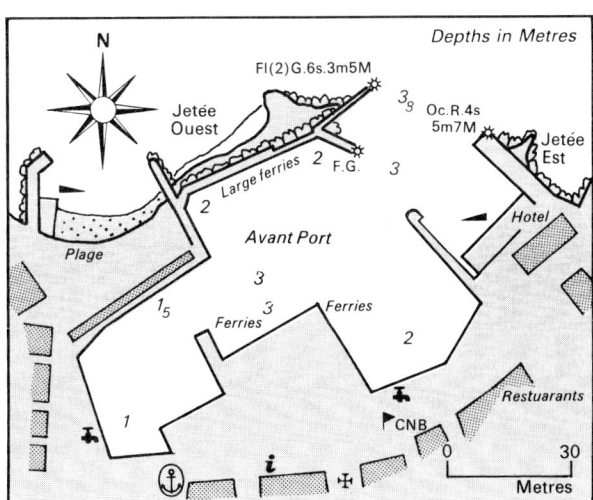

Port de Bendor

Warning

Care is needed if using the passage between Ile de Bendor and the mainland, also the passage between the island and La Fourmigue beacon.

Approach by day

From W Cross the wide Baie de la Ciotat and pass the yellow cliffs of Pointe du Défens (Cap d'Alon). Keep S of the small bare Ile Rousse of reddish rocks and Ile de Bendor also of a red colour which has hotels and other buildings. Round Ile de Bendor at 100m leaving it to port with La Fourmigue black with red band beacon tower, 2 black balls topmark, to starboard. Follow the island coast round at 100m and do not cut the corner; when the harbour lies to SW turn onto this course and approach with caution. Shallow-draught craft can pass to N of the island in good conditions with caution.

From E Leave the W cardinal beacon tower, YBY with ✗ topmark, at Pointe de la Cride to starboard and cross the Baie de Bandol on a NNW course towards La Fourmigue beacon tower, black with red bands, 2 black balls topmark. Leave the tower 100m to starboard and Ile de Bendor 100m to port and follow the island round but do not cut the corner until the harbour is SW then turn onto this course.

Approach by night

Using the major lights:
Ile du Grand-Rouveau Oc(2)W.6s15M in the E approach
Port de Bandol Jetée Sud Head Oc(4)WR.12s13/10M
La Cassidaigne Fl(2)W.6s8M from the W
Navigate to a position 100m S of Bandol Jetée Sud head then turn to SW course and approach the harbour.

Anchorage in the approach

Anchor 100m S of Bandol Jetée Sud head in 5m sand. Show anchor shape or light.

Entrance

By day The entrance lies to the E of two large and prominent buildings, approach it sounding on a SW course and enter between the two jetty heads keeping a sharp lookout for *vedettes* (ferries) leaving or entering at speed.

By night Approach the Oc.R.4s light on 220° and enter between Oc.R.4s and Fl(2)G.6s lights, leave a F.G to starboard.

Berths

Berth alongside on NW side of the harbour clear of *vedettes* (ferries).

Formalities

Report to the *bureau du port* (☎ 94 29 44 34) on arrival.

Miscellaneous

Dogs and other animals are not allowed on the island.

Charges

There are harbour charges.

Facilities

Slips There is a slip in the NE corner of the harbour.
Fuel From a pump on quay at W side of the harbour.
Water There are several points on the quay.
Electricity A few 220v AC points on quays.
Garbage Containers for rubbish on the quayside.

Port de Bendor looking W

Port de Bendor. Approach looking SW

Entrance

Port de Bendor. Entrance looking SW

Repairs Minor repairs are possible at a small shipyard.

Hotels Two **** and two * hotels.

Restaurants There are three restaurants, a café and a snack bar.

Yacht club The Club Nautique de Bendor (CNB) has a fine clubhouse with bar, lounge, showers and WCs, and a dormitory. It also has excellent facilities for dinghies (☎ 94 29 52 91).

Lifeboat A small inflatable lifeboat is stationed here.

Information office An information office is located on the quay at the SE side of the harbour.

Visits There are a museum and a wine exhibition to see, and pleasant short walks around the island.

Beaches There are a number of small rocky bays and a small sandy beach just to W of the harbour.

Communications There are frequent *vedette* (ferry) services to the mainland at Bandol. First and last *vedettes* in summer depart Bendor 0645/1340 and Bandol 0700/1400.

84 PORT DE BANDOL
83150 Var

Position 43°07'·9N 5°45'·5E

Minimum depth in the entrance 5m (18ft)
in the harbour 2·8 to 0·5m (9 to 2ft)

Width of the entrance 40m

Number of yacht berths 1350

Maximum length overall 30m (98ft)

Population 7143

Rating 2–2–2

General

An old natural fishing harbour that has been improved by the construction of breakwaters and has been developed as a major yachting harbour by the addition of pontoons. The facilities for yachtsmen are good and the town and area are attractive. Approach and entrance are easy but strong winds from S quarters can make the approach difficult. Ferries to Ile de Bendor create considerable wash in the harbour due to their high speed. In season the pleasant town is a popular tourist centre.

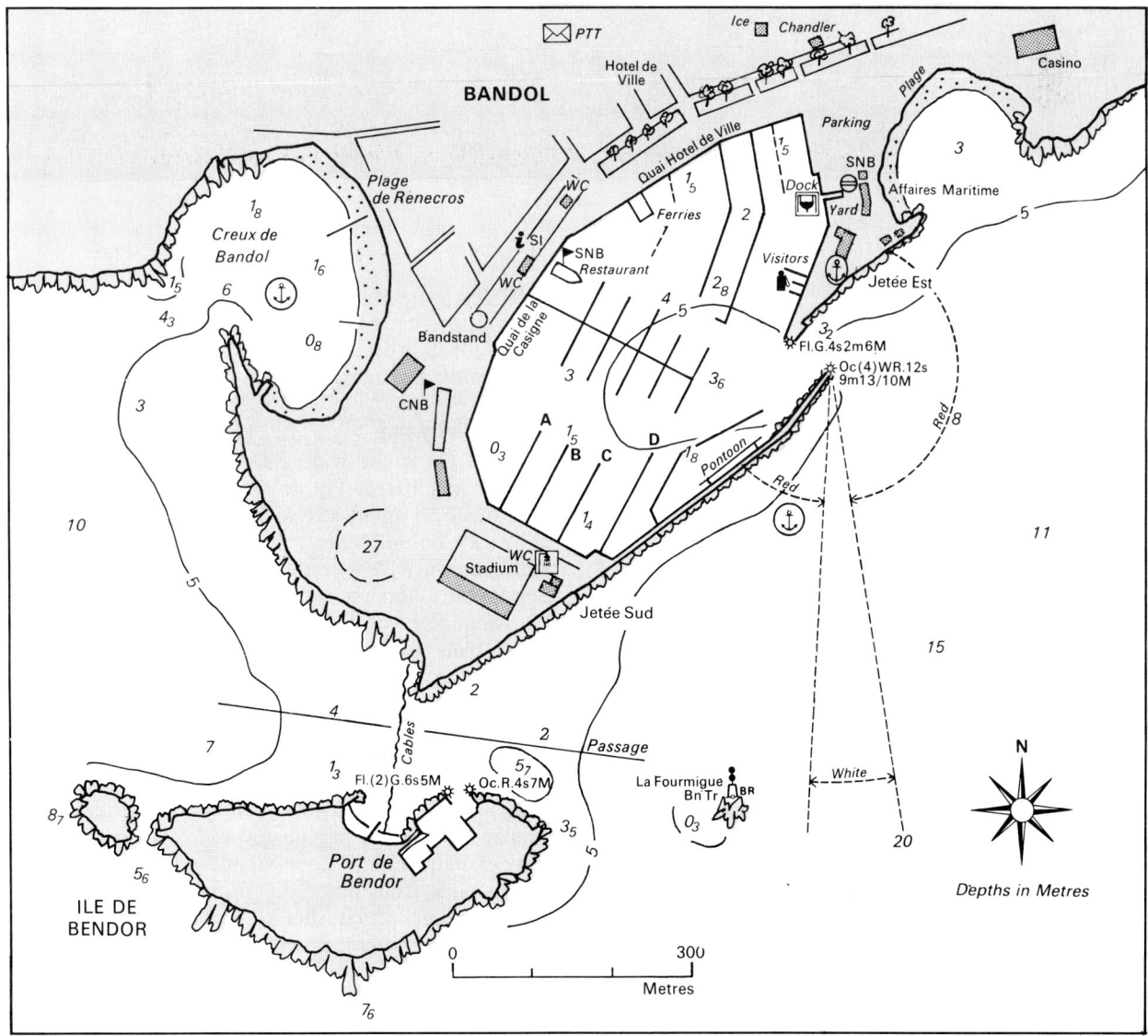

Port de Bandol

Port de Bendor and Bandol, looking N

Data

Charts Admiralty 2164
French 5325, 6610
Spanish 490
Navicarte 504

Port radio VHF Ch 9 and 16.

Currents During the NW *mistral* there is a SE-going current of 1 knot across the mouth of the Baie de Bandol.

Magnetic variation 1°34′W (1994) decreasing by about 6′ each year.

Weather forecasts Posted each day outside the *bureau du port*. Recorded forecasts (☎ 36 68 08 03 and 36 68 08 08).

Speed limit 3 knots.

Lights

Jetée Sud head Oc(4)WR.12s9m13/10M White pylon, red top 003°-R-351°-W-003°
Jetée Est head Fl.G.4s2m6M Green post

Beacon La Fourmigue beacon tower, black with red bands and 2 black balls topmark, marks the E edge of a rocky shoal patch some 60m long.

Warning

La Fourmigue beacon is unlit and is dangerous because it is in the line of approach but it should be seen against the lights of the town.

Approach by day

From W Cross the wide Baie de la Ciotat and pass the yellow cliffs of Pointe du Défens (Cap d'Alon). Ile Rousse, a small red rocky island and the larger red rocky Ile de Bendor, the latter with several large buildings on it, are easily recognised. Round Ile de Bendor at 100m onto a NE course and leaving La Fourmigue beacon tower, black with red bands and 2 black balls topmark, 100m to port approach the entrance on a N course.

From E Pass ½M to SW of the W cardinal, YBY with Ⅹ topmark, beacon tower marking the Sèches des Magnons and proceed on a N course leaving Pointe de la Cride, a low rocky promontory with a similar W cardinal beacon tower to starboard. Long rows of flats behind the town and a large viaduct are conspicuous from this direction as is La Fourmigue beacon tower which should be left 100m to port. Approach the entrance on a N course.

La Fourmigue beacon tower   Entrance

Port de Bandol. Approach looking N

Bureau de Port

Port de Bandol. Approach looking N

Bureau de Port

Port de Bandol. Entrance looking NW

Approach by night

Use the main lights:

Banc de la Cassidaigne Fl(2)W.6s8M

La Ciotat môle head Oc(2)R.6s13M to the W of the port

Ile du Grand-Rouveau Oc(2)W.6s15M to the S

Navigate to a position in the white sector (351°-003°) of Jetée Sud head light (Oc(4)WR.12s) and approach this light keeping a good lookout for La Fourmigue beacon tower (unlit) which must be left 100m to port.

Anchorage in the approach

Anchor 200m to SSW of the head of Jetée Sud in 5m sand and weed. This anchorage is subject to wash from the *vedettes* (ferries) during daylight hours.

Entrance

By day Approach the head of Jetée Sud and round it at 20m onto a NW course keeping a good lookout for *vedettes* (ferries) leaving at speed. Next round the head of Jetée Est at 20m leaving it to starboard.

By night Approach Oc(4)WR.12s in the W sector (351°-003°) and when 50m away divert and round this light at 20m, leaving it to port. Enter on a NW course leaving Fl.G.4s to starboard. Care is needed to distinguish the navigational lights against a background of town lights.

Berths

Berth alongside first pontoon inside Jetée Est near the *bureau du port*. Report to the *bureau du port* for allocation of a berth on a pontoon.

Formalities

Report to the *bureau du port* (☎ 94 29 42 64 or 94 29 59 84 *Fax* 93 29 93 20)) near the head of the Jetée Est. Customs (☎ 94 32 45 56) are to N of *bureau du port*. Open 0800–1900.

Charges

There are harbour charges.

Facilities

Slips There are three slips.

Hards A hard standing to N of *bureau du port*.

Cranes There is a crane on the E side of the harbour (2.5 tonnes). There is also a 30-tonne travel-lift near the crane.

Fuel Diesel and petrol from pumps next to the arrival berth beside the *bureau du port*. 0800–1200 and 1300–1800 every day in season. Thursday only in winter.

Water There are points on the pontoons and quays.

Electricity 220v AC and 380v AC points on the pontoons and some 380v AC.

Provisions Many shops of all kinds near the harbour.

Ice Obtainable from a shop in Avenue de la Gare.

Garbage Rubbish containers on pontoons and quays.

Chandlery There are four chandlers in the town.

Repairs Major repairs can be carried out by the shipyard located on the W side of the harbour. There are a number of engineers and electricians, and a sailmaker.

Laundrette There is one in the town.

Post office At the NW side of the town.

Hotels One ★★★★, seven ★★★, nine ★★, fifteen ★ hotels.

Restaurants There are over 24 restaurants and 42 café/bars which include two Michelin Guide ★★★.

Yacht club The Société Nautique de Bandol (SNB) has a floating clubhouse on an old barge on the W side of the harbour with bar, lounges and showers (☎ 94 29 42 26).

Information office The Syndicat d'Initiative (☎ 94 29 41 35) has an office in a small building on the NW side of the harbour.

Visits The Ile de Bendor, which is most attractive, should be visited. There is also a zoo and tropical garden some 4½M away.

Beaches There is a sandy beach behind and to W of the town, and another at the NE side of the Baie de Bandol.

Communications There are both rail and bus services.

Future development

Minor improvements planned.

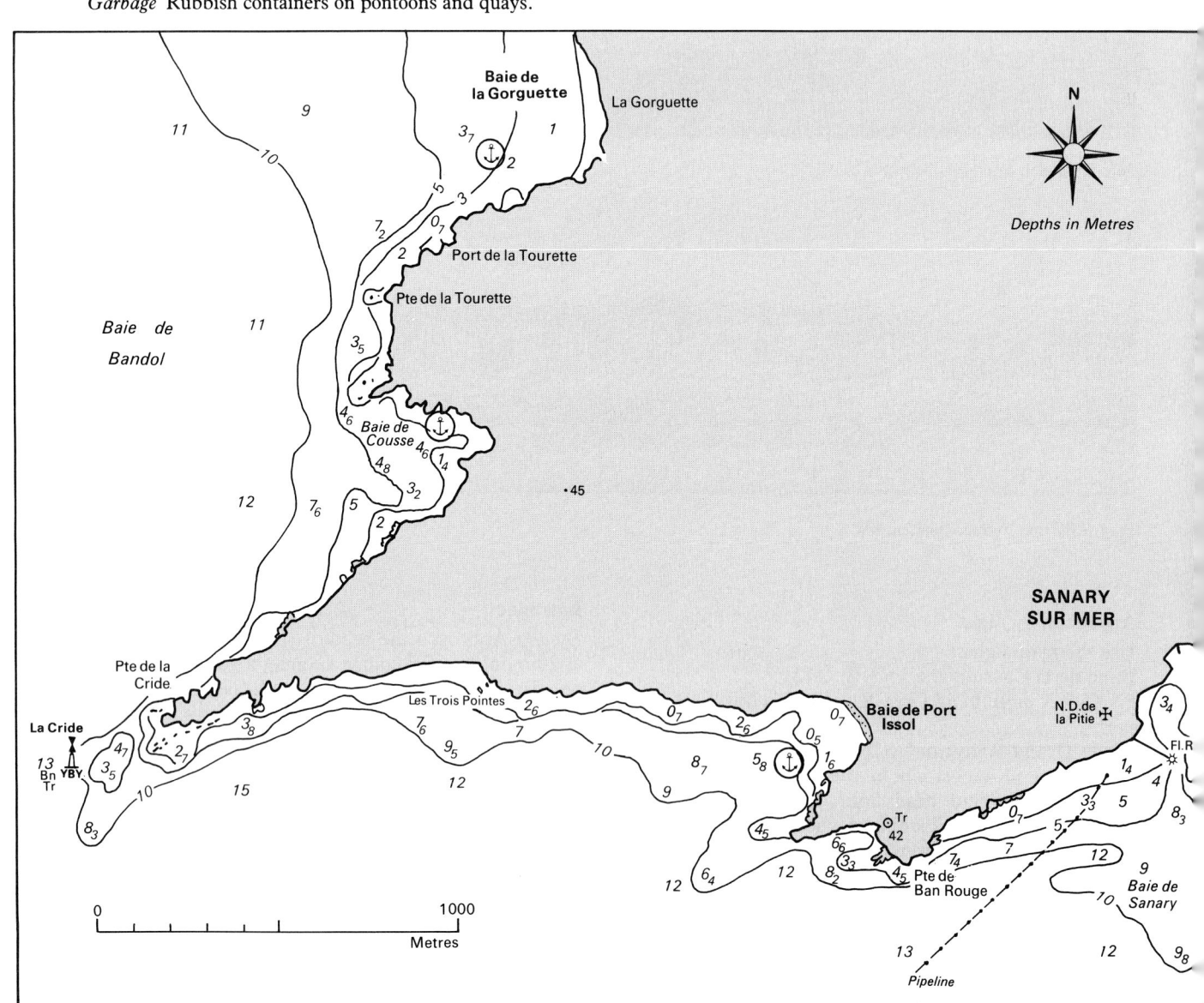

Anchorages between Bandol and Sanary

Pointe de la Tourette

Baie de la Gorguette, looking N

Pointe de la Tourette

Baie de Cousse, looking NE

⚓ **Anchorage Baie de la Gorguette**

Anchorage in a wide sandy bay with good beach, shallow near the shore and open to SW–W and also to strong winds from NW. Road and houses ashore. Small private harbour for dinghies etc.

Port de la Tourette

Owned by a restaurant on the headland just to N of Pointe de la Tourette, only suitable for small craft and dinghies.

⚓ **Baie de Cousse**

Medium-sized bay with rocky sides and small sandy beach at its head. Road and houses ashore. Open to SW–W and also to strong winds from NW.

Pointe de la Cride

A low thin rocky point with outlying rocks extending 100m to S and a 3·5m rocky patch 250m to SW marked by a W cardinal beacon tower, YBY with ⍊ topmark. (In need of paint (1986)).

⚓ **Port-Issol**

A shallow bay surrounded by rocky cliffs with houses and a road ashore, open to S–SW–W and certainly not a port. Sandy beach.

Pointe de la Cride, looking NW

Port Issol, looking N

Port Issol, looking N

85 PORT DE SANARY-SUR-MER
83110 Var

Position 43°07'·0N 5°48'·2E
Minimum depth   in the entrance 4m (14·5ft)
                        in the harbour 4 to 0·5m (14·5 to 2ft)
Width of the entrance 50m
Number of yacht berths 550
Maximum length overall 12m (39ft)
Population 15,000
Rating 2–3–2

General
A small, semi-artificial fishing harbour that has been developed into a yachting harbour by the establishment of a series of pontoons and the improvement of breakwaters. Good facilities for yachtsmen now exist and there is a pleasant small town with adequate shops. Care is necessary in the approach and entrance which could be dangerous in strong S–SW winds, and swell from SE to SW can also make the conditions inside the harbour very uncomfortable.

Data
Charts   Admiralty 2164
            French 6610
            Spanish 49
            Navicarte 504

Magnetic variation 1°34'W (1994) decreasing by about 6' each year.

Weather forecasts Posted daily at *bureau du port*. Recorded forecast (☎ 36 68 08 83).

Speed limit 3 knots.

Lights
Môle Ouest head Fl.R.4s9m10M White tower, red top. Obscured when more than 069°

Buoys A small green pillar buoy with ▲ topmark is established on the E side of the entrance to mark a sand spit.

Warnings
The area to the E of the green pillar buoy is very shallow with dangerous breakers in any swell. A half-submerged broken spur exists just N of head of Môle Ouest.

Approach by day
From W Cross the wide Baie de Bandol and round the W cardinal beacon[1] off Pointe de la Cride. Pointe de la Cride is very prominent and is low and rocky. Then round the higher Pointe de Ban-Rouge which has an inconspicuous ruined tower on top. The

Baie de Sanary looking E

Port de Sanary-sur-Mer. Entrance looking N

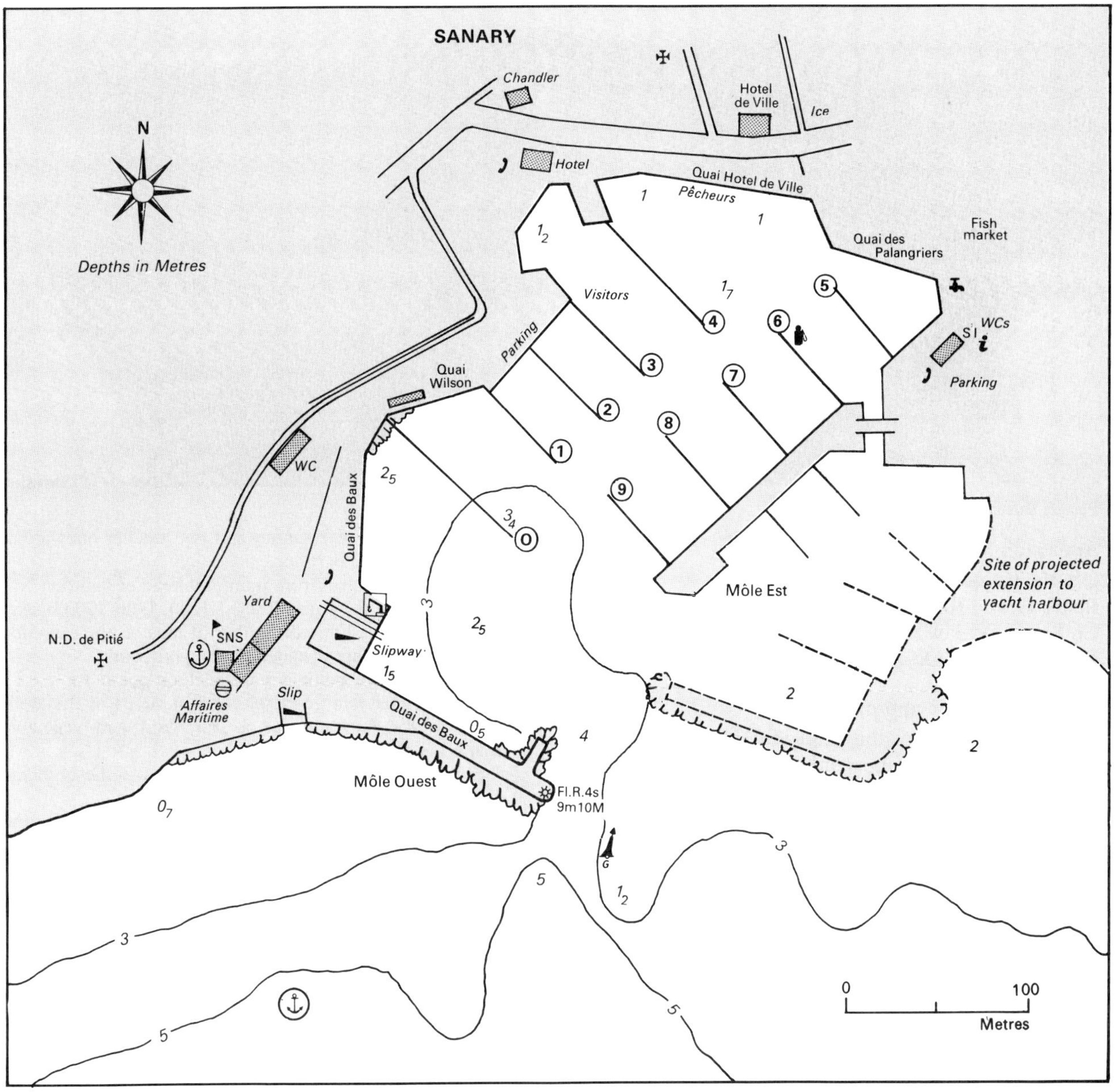

SANARY

Chandler

Hotel
de Ville

Ice

N

Depths in Metres

Hotel

Quai Hotel de Ville

Pêcheurs

1

1

1_2

Fish
market

Quai des
Palangriers

Visitors

1_7

⑤

④

⑥

S1   WCs

Quai
Wilson

Parking

③

⑦

Parking

WC

②

2_5

⑧

①

Quai des Baux

⑨

3_4

Ⓞ

Site of projected
extension to
yacht harbour

3

2_5

Môle Est

N.D. de Pitié

Yard

SNS

1_5

Slipway

0_5

2

Affaires
Maritime

Slip

Quai des Baux

4

2

Môle Ouest

Fl.R.4s
9m10M

0_7

G

3

5

1_2

3

0   100

Metres

3

5

5

Port de Sanary

Entrance

Port Sanary-sur-Mer. Approach looking NW

houses of Sanary and those lining the bay will then be conspicuous as will the light tower on the Môle Ouest in the closer approach.

From E Round the conspicuous small island Ile du Grand Rouveau which has a lighthouse with a square tower at its summit, passing outside the Sèches des Magnons W cardinal, YBY with Ⅹ topmark, beacon

tower . If there is any sea running keep half a mile to S and SW of this beacon. Approach the harbour on a NNE course from which the houses of the town will show up well, as will the tower on Pointe du Ban-Rouge.

[1] In need of paint (1991)
[2] In need of paint and has no topmarks (1991)

Port de Sanary-sur-Mer, looking NE

Approach by night
Use the major lights:
Ile du Grand Rouveau Oc(2)W.6s15M
Le Brusc Oc(3)WR.12s9/6M
Port de Bandol Oc(4)WR.12s13/10M

Anchorage in the approach
Anchor 150m SW of the head of Môle Ouest in 5m sand and weed in fair weather only. Hoist anchor shape or light.

Entrance
By day Approach the head of Môle Ouest with care on a N course and round it at 15m leaving it to port and a small green pillar buoy to starboard. Enter on a NW course.

By night Approach Fl.R.4s on a N course and round it at 15m leaving it to port onto a NW course.

Berths
Secure stern-to No. 3 pontoon on NW side of harbour and report to the *bureau du port* for allocation of a berth.

Formalities
Report to the *bureau du port* on arrival (☎ 94 74 20 95) open in summer 0730–1200 and 1400–1900, in winter 0800–1200 and 1400–1800. The office is in the SW corner of the harbour next door to the customs office (☎ 94 74 20 95).

Charges
There are harbour charges. A stay of up to 6 hours is free.

Facilities
Slips There is a slip in the SW corner of the harbour.
Slipways There are two slipways in the SW corner of the harbour for craft of 20m length and 4m beam, 2·9m draught, 130 tonnes maximum.

Cranes One crane of 7 tonnes and two smaller ones are at SW corner of the harbour.
Fuel Diesel and petrol from pumps at head of pontoon No. 6 at SE side of the harbour 0800–1200, 1400–1700 hours.
Water There are a limited number of taps on the quayside but many more are installed on the pontoons.
Electricity 220v AC points are installed on pontoons.
Provisions There is a good selection of shops in the town close to the harbour and a fish, fruit and vegetable market is alongside.
Ice From M. Cavert in Place Cavert 100m to the N of the harbour.
Chandlery From two shops in the town and also from the shipyard.
Repairs There is a major shipyard which can carry out most repairs to hulls and engines. There are also independent engineers and electricians.
Laundrette There is one in the town.
Post office At the back of the town to the NW of the harbour.
Hotels One ★★★, seven ★★, five ★ and nine others.
Restaurants There are 42 restaurants and many café/bars.
Yacht club The Société Nautique de Sanary (SNS) has a clubhouse at the SW corner of the harbour. There are showers, a lounge and an office (☎ 94 74 16 39).
Showers Six showers and nine WCs.
Information office The Syndicat d'Initiative has an office on the quayside at the NE corner of the harbour.
Lifeboat An inflatable lifeboat is kept here.
Visits The Chapelle de Notre-Dame de Pitié, built in 1560, is interesting, and it commands a fine view. Exotic Garden and Zoo are worth a visit (0800–1200).
Beaches There are fine sandy beaches to the NE of the harbour.
Communications There are bus and rail services.

Future development
The existing Môle Est is being extended and a green light is to be established at its head. Plans exist for an extension of the harbour to the E of the existing port which will have 380 berths.

History
Detailed history from the Syndicat d'Initiative. Various artifacts have been found which show that this area was used by Ligurians and Romans around 600 BC.

Pointe Nègre, looking N

Port de Sauviou

A small private harbour with restaurant, N of Pointe Nègre. Only suitable for dinghies.

---

86 PORT DE LA COUDOURIERE (SIX-FOURS-LA-PLAGE)
83140 Var

Position 43°05'·7N 5°48'·7E
Minimum depth in the entrance 3m (10ft)
           in the harbour 2 to 0·5m (6·6 to 2ft)
Width of the entrance 50m
Number of yacht berths 447
Maximum length overall 8·4m (28ft)
Population (Six-Fours-la-Plage) 25,577
Rating 4–3–4

General

A small artificial harbour in a sheltered bay, originally built for a tile factory which has now been built over. The harbour is used by small yachts and some fishing boats and can be entered with care and good shelter is obtained except from winds from SW to W. Facilities are limited at this harbour, the nearest town being Six-Fours-la-Plage some 2M away. Six lines of buoys have been laid in the harbour for yachts. The harbour is very crowded and a berth may not always be available.

Data

Charts Admiralty 2164
       French 5325, 6610
       Spanish 49
       Navicarte 504

Magnetic variation 1°34'W (1994) decreasing by about 6' each year.

Weather forecasts Posted at the *bureau du port* (☎ 36 08 08 08 and 36 68 08 83).

Speed limit 3 knots.

Port Radio VHF Ch 9

Lights
Jetée Ouest head Fl(3)R.12s7m6M Red metal post

Warnings

Rocks extend some distance from the foot of the breakwater and quays. Four T-shaped rocky breakwaters lie to S of the harbour along the coast. This harbour is difficult to enter when a NW *mistral* is blowing.

Approach by day

From W Pass the Pointe de la Cride, a low rocky promontory with a W cardinal, YBY with ⟆ topmark, beacon tower[1], and cross the Baie de Sanary on an ESE course towards the dark rocky headland of Pointe Nègre which should be left 300m to port. The low rocky breakwaters will not be seen until the closer approach. The tile factory is no longer visible, having been replaced by a housing estate.

From E Round the small rocky Ile du Grand Rouveau with its conspicuous square-towered lighthouse and pass outside the Sèches des Magnons W cardinal, YBY with ⟆ topmark, beacon tower[2], then on a NE course pass to N of La Casserlane N cardinal, BY with ⟑ topmark, beacon tower[1]. The harbour breakwaters will not be seen until the closer approach.

Port de la Coudourière

Port de la Coudurière, looking NW

Approach by night
Use the lights:
Ile du Grand Rouveau Oc(2)W.6s15M
Le Brusc Oc(3)WR.12s9/6M
Port de Bandol Oc(4)WR.12s13/10M

Anchorage in the approach
Anchor 150m S of head of Jetée Ouest in 4m sand.

Entrance
By day Approach the head of Jetée Ouest on an E course and round it at 20m leaving it to port, thence onto a NE course.

By night Approach Fl(3)R.12s on an E course, round it at 20m onto a NE course leaving it to port.

¹ In need of paint (1992)
² In need of paint and has no topmarks (1992)

Berths
Berth alongside the quay on the inner side of Jetée Ouest near its head and report to the *bureau du port*.

Moorings
Buoyed moorings exist in the middle of the harbour and visitors are usually allocated one of these.

Prohibited anchorages
Anchoring outside the harbour is prohibited in an area W and NW of the entrance and inside the harbour.

Formalities
Bureau du port (☎ 94 25 90 09 and 94 34 80 34) at NW corner of the harbour. The hours of opening are very varied, see notice outside office.

Facilities
Hard On N side of the harbour.
Cranes One small 2·5-tonne crane in the N corner of the harbour and a 4-tonne mobile crane.
Water Available from taps on quays.
Electricity 220v AC points on quays.
Repairs Minor repairs by local shipwright and engineers, also a sailmaker.

Chandlery Two chandlers nearby.
Yacht club Association des Pêcheurs Plaisanciers de la Coudourière (APPC) (☎ 94 25 47 03). Clubhouse on N corner of harbour.

---

87 PORT DU BRUSC
83140 Var

Position 43°04'·6N 5°48'·2E
Minimum depth in the entrance 2m (6·6ft)
in the harbour 1·5 to 0·5m (5 to 2ft)
Width of the entrance 40m
Population 1000
Rating 4–3–4

General
An old harbour that has silted up and is now only used by shallow-draught craft and *vedettes* (ferries) to Ile des Embiez. Care is needed in the approach and entrance as shallow sand banks exist around the harbour. In W and NW winds approach can be dangerous and it is very uncomfortable inside the harbour. Facilities are very limited. The area is attractive and comparatively undeveloped.

Data
Charts Admiralty 2164
French 5325, 6610
Spanish 49
Navicarte 504

Magnetic variation 1°34'W (1994) decreasing by about 6' each year.

Speed limit 3 knots.

Lights
Jetée head Oc(3)WR.12s10m9/6M Red pylon 156°-W-166°-R-156°
Brise-lames NE end Iso.G.4s6m6M Green pylon

Buoys There is a small red can buoy, red can topmark, on the port side of the N entrance.

Beacons A small red post with can topmark, and another painted green with ▲ topmark, mark the S entrance.

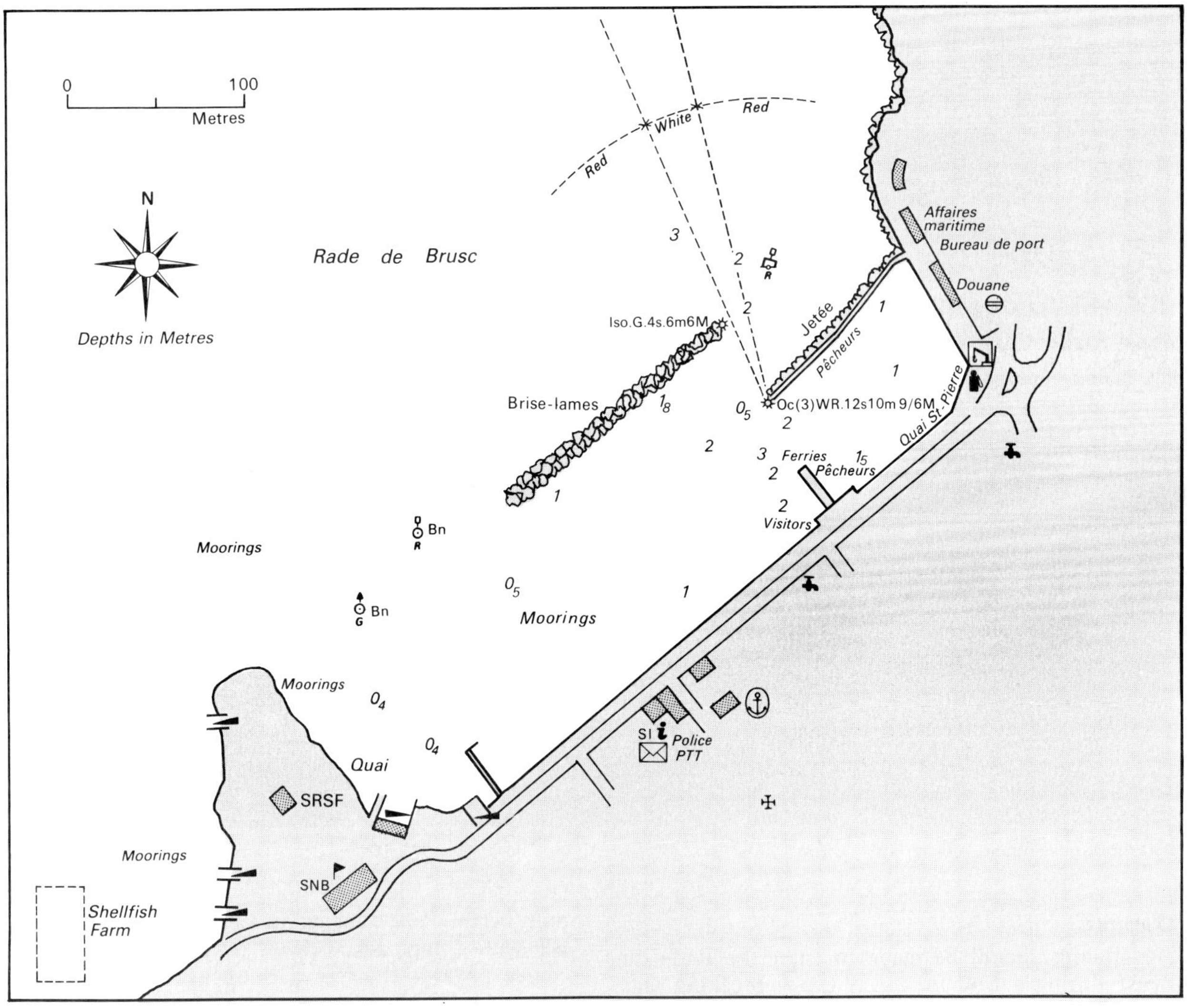

0   100
Metres

N

Depths in Metres

Rade de Brusc

Iso.G.4s.6m6M

Brise-lames

Moorings

Bn
R

Bn
G

Moorings

Moorings

Quai

SRSF

Moorings

*Shellfish
Farm*

SNB

Red

White

Red

3

2

2

D
R

Jetée

Pêcheurs

1

1

0₅

Oc(3)WR.12s10m 9/6M

2

2

3 *Ferries* 1₅

2 *Pêcheurs*

2

Visitors

1

1₈

2

0₅

Moorings

0₄

0₄

S I

Police
PTT

*Affaires
maritime*
Bureau de port

Douane

Quai St. Pierre

Port du Brusc

Entrance   *Ile du Grand Rouveau*

Port du Brusc looking W

Entrance

Port du Brusc. Approach looking SE

323

Entrance

Port du Brusc. Entrance looking E

Port du Brusc. Entrance looking SW

Warning

No attempt should be made to enter the Rade du Brusc during a NW *mistral* as heavy breaking seas occur all over the area. Careful sounding is necessary during the approach and inside the harbour. The pontoon in the NE part of the harbour may not be used by yachts.

Approach by day

From W Having passed Pointe de la Cride, a low-lying rocky promontory with an off-lying W cardinal, YBY with ↘ topmark, beacon tower[1], proceed on a SW course towards the Rade du Brusc leaving the conspicuous Ile du Grand Rouveau with its square-towered lighthouse and the Ile des Embiez with a conspicuous water tower on its summit, some half a mile to starboard. The houses around the harbour are not conspicuous, being low-lying, and the rocky harbour jetty and breakwater will not be seen until the closer approach. The N entrance is near the light towers and should be approached on a SE course.

From E Round the Ile des Embiez and Ile du Grand Rouveau, leaving the Sèches des Magnons W cardinal, YBY with ↘ topmark, beacon[2] to starboard; in rough weather this beacon should be given a half

mile berth. Pass outside La Casserlane N cardinal, BY with ↕ topmark, beacon tower, then on a NE course towards the low dark rocky coast until the harbour is SE, then turn to this course and approach.

Approach by night

Due to shallows a night approach and entrance is not recommended without a a previous visit by day. Approach and enter on a course between 156° and 166° in the white sector of Oc(3)WR.12s.

Anchorage in the approach

Anchor about ¼M to NE of the entrance in 10m sand, mud and weed.

Entrance by day

Approach on a SE course and leave a small red can buoy, red can topmark, to port, then head for the entrance which lies between the head of the jetty to port and the NE end of the detached breakwater to starboard. The S entrance which is very shallow is marked by two posts, one painted red with can topmark, the other green with cone topmark, enter between them.

Berths

Visitors' berths are on the quay on the SW side of the small jetty that is used by the *vedettes* (ferries), secure stern-to quay with anchor ahead this should have a trip-line.

[1]In need of paint (1991)
[2]In need of paint and has no topmark (1991)

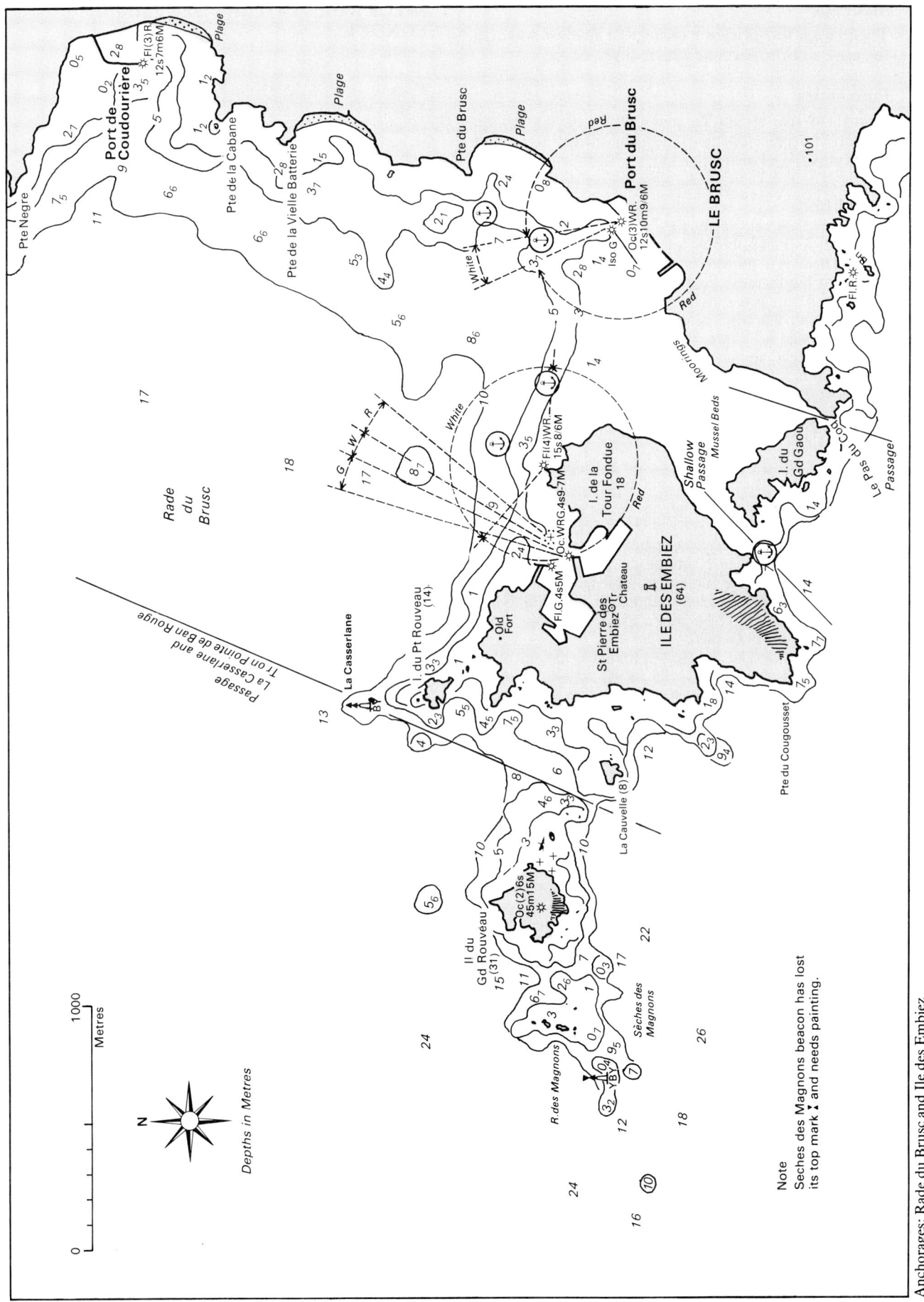

Anchorages: Rade du Brusc and Ile des Embiez

Moorings

There are a few private moorings in shallow water in the centre of the harbour which might be free.

Formalities

Report to the *bureau du port* (☎ 94 25 03 96) on arrival; it is located near the post office. A second office at NE end of the harbour.

Facilities

Slips There are two small slips in the SW corner of the harbour for boats drawing less than 0·4m.

Crane There is a 6-tonne crane in the NE corner of the harbour but there is a depth of only 1m to 1·5m nearby.

Fuel Diesel and petrol from pumps in the NE corner of the harbour but only 1m water is available alongside (☎ 94 25 04 40).

Water A single tap on quay, also available from local restaurants.

Provisions A limited number of shops can provide everyday requirements.

Garbage A very few rubbish containers around the harbour.

Repairs There is an engineer in the village, and a sailmaker.

Post office On the quayside near the centre of the quay.

Hotels Two in village.

Restaurants Nine in village and some café/bars.

Yacht club The Société Nautique du Brusc (SNB) has a clubhouse to S of the harbour with lounge, showers, etc. (☎ 94 25 13 55). Société des Regattes de Six Fours (SRSF) has a small clubhouse to S of the harbour. Open 0930–1200 and 1430–1800.

Information office The Syndicat d'Initiative has an office near the post office.

Visits The nearby islands may be visited by means of a ferryboat.

Beaches Sandy beach to N of the harbour. Dredging may also be carried out.

Future development

Plans exist to construct more breakwaters and pontoons for yachts and to move the *quai* out 10m, providing 300 more yacht berths.

History

Though this harbour and anchorage have been used for hundreds of years very little remains to record the fact.

⚓ Rade du Brusc

A wide bay, shallow at S side open to NW–N and affected by strong W winds. Anchor to suit draught and wind direction in sand with weed. Beach at E side. Houses with road also along E side.

88 PORT DE ST-PIERRE-DES EMBIEZ FONDUE

83140 Var

Position 43°04'·8N 5°47'·3E
Minimum depth in the entrance 3m (10ft)
in the harbour 3 to 1m (10 to 3ft)
Width of the entrance 45m
Number of yacht berths 650
Maximum length overall 35m (115ft)
Population 200
Rating 1–2–2

General

A most attractive artificial yacht harbour recently constructed as part of a development scheme to turn Ile des Embiez into a high-class recreational area. The approach and entrance require some care and would not be possible during a strong NW *mistral*. There is good shelter inside and there are excellent facilities for yachtsmen.

Data

Charts Admiralty 2164
French 5325, 6610
Spanish 49
Navicarte 504

Magnetic variation 1°34'W (1994) decreasing by about 6' each year.

Weather forecast Posted once a day at the *bureau du port*. Recorded forecast (☎ 36 68 08 83).

Speed limit 3 knots in the harbour and 5 knots 300m from the shore.

Port radio VHF Ch 9.

Lights

Quai des Cargos head Iso.W.4s Strip light

Jetée Nord Fl.G.4s5m5M Green metal latticework tower

Quai des Cargos sector lights 200° Oc.WRG.4s3m9-7M 198°·5-G-207°-W-213°-R-221·5°

Ile de la Tour-Fondue N Point Fl(4)WR.15s5m8/6M Small concrete tower, red top 132°-W-275°-R-132°

Port des Jeunes entrance E side Iso.R.4s4M Grey pedestal

Ile du Grand Rouveau Oc(2)W.6s45m15M White square tower, black top Obscured by Iles des Embiez 255°-317°

Buoys The approach channel to the harbour is marked by red can buoys with red can topmarks to port and green conical buoys with cone topmarks to starboard. Several small starboard-hand green conical buoys with cone topmarks are situated on the N side of the island to mark outlying dangers, and some small red buoys mark shallows to port near the entrance.

Beacons A N cardinal, BY with ↕ topmark, beacon tower[1], La Casserlane, marks the NNW extremity of the island.

Warnings

In NW *mistral* conditions the approach and entrance to this harbour could be dangerous and should not be attempted. There are offshore fishing nets in the

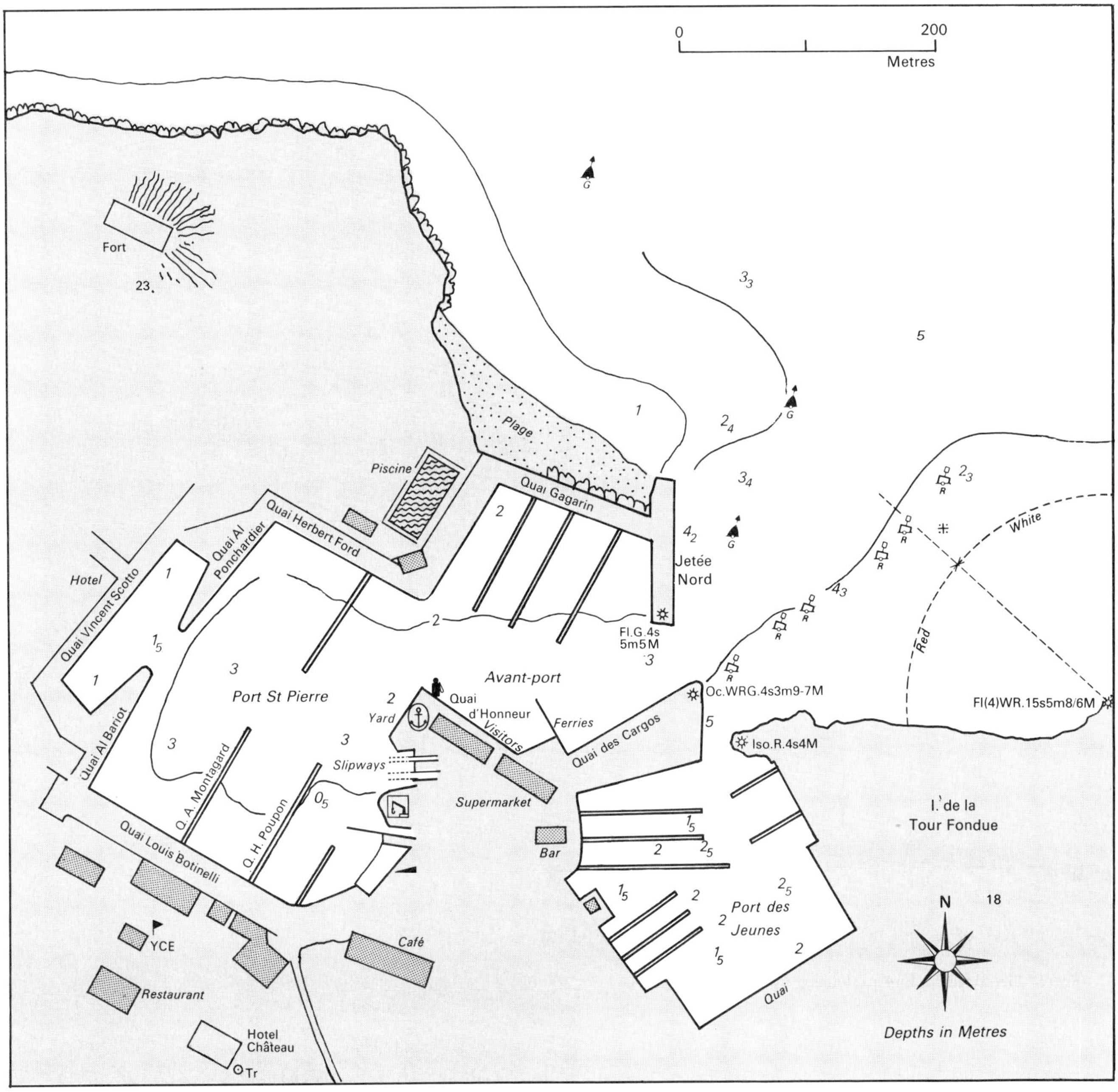

0   200
Metres

G

3₃

5

1

Fort

23.

Plage

2₄

G

3₄

Piscine

Quai Gagarin

2

4₂

Jetée
Nord

2₃
R

White

R

⌗

Hotel

Quai Vincent Scotto

Quai Al Ponchardier

Quai Herbert Ford

1

4₃
R

1₅

2

Red

1

3

Port St Pierre

Avant-port

Fl.G.4s
5m5M
3

R

Quai Al Bariot

Q.A. Montagard

2

Yard

Quai
d'Honneur

R

Oc.WRG.4s3m9-7M

3

Visitors

Ferries

5

Fl(4)WR.15s5m8/6M

3

Slipways

0₅

Supermarket

Quai des Cargos

Iso.R.4s4M

Quai Louis Botinelli

Q.H. Poupon

Bar

1₅

2

2₅

l. de la
Tour Fondue

YCE

1₅

2

2₅

Restaurant

Café

2

Port des
Jeunes

2

Hotel
Château

1₅

2

N   18

Tr

Quai

Depths in Metres

Port de St-Pierre-des-Embiez

Port de St-Pierre-des-Embiez lighthouse on N point of Ile de la Tour Fondue with entrance in background looking W

Beacon tower　　　　　　　　*Ile du Grande-Rouveau*

Port St-Pierre, Ile des Embiez, showing line of approach

Entrance　　*Château and tower*

Port St-Pierre, Ile des Embiez, looking SW

Port St-Pierre, Ile des Embiez, looking N

Bureau de Port

Port St Pierre, Ile des Embiez, looking W–NW

shallower water. There are very shallow waters outside the dredged and buoyed entrance channel.

Approach by day

From W Cross the wide Baies de Sanary and de Bandol which are separated by a low rocky promontory, Pointe de la Cride, with an offlying W cardinal, YBY with ⚑ topmark, beacon tower. On a SE course approach a N cardinal, BY with ⚑ topmark, beacon, La Casserlane, leave this to starboard and follow the NE coast of Ile des Embiez, which can be identified by a large *château* with a tower and a water tower on its summit, at 300m until the harbour entrance and the *château* lie SSW (206°) turn and approach between two green and six red buoys.

From E Round the unmistakable Cap Sicié, a rocky promontory sloping back at an angle of 45° surmounted by a conspicuous TV tower, keeping at least half a mile off the coast as the seas here can be rough even in good conditions. Round Ile des Embiez, topped by a concrete water tower and a *château* with a stone tower, also around the Ile du Grand Rouveau which has a large square lighthouse at its summit. Keep outside Sèches des Magnons shoals, SW of Grand Rouveau which are marked by a W cardinal, YBY with ⚑ topmark, beacon tower[2]. This should be passed at a distance of not less than half a mile in bad weather. Next round La Casserlane N cardinal, BY with ⚑ topmark, beacon tower, and follow the coast at 300m on an ESE course until the *château* and harbour bear 206°, then turn and approach between two green and six red buoys.

Inshore passage There is a passage between Ile des Embiez and Ile du Grand Rouveau which can be taken in good weather and good visibility. See page 129.

Approach by night

Use the major lights:
Ile du Grand Rouveau Oc(2)W.6s15M
Le Brusc Oc(3)WR.12s9/6M
Port de Bandol Oc(4)WR.12s13/10M

Anchorage in the approach

Anchor ¼M to NE of the entrance in 10m sand and weed.

Entrance

By day Enter on 200° leaving a series of small red can buoys with red can topmarks to port and a series of small green conical buoys with green cone topmarks to starboard. Enter between the heads of Jetée Nord and Quai des Cargos.

By night Navigate to a position near the centre of the Rade du Brusc and continue until the harbour lies S. Identify the sectored light of the Quai des Cargos

[2] In need of paint and has no topmarks (1991)

(Oc.WRG.4s) and approach in the W sector. In the close approach keep between a series of green and red buoys.

Berths

Berths are stern-to quays or pontoons, with bow-to mooring buoys. On arrival secure alongside the Quai d'Honneur just inside the entrance.

Miscellaneous

Dogs and other animals are not allowed on the island.

Formalities

On arrival report to the *bureau du port* (☎ 94 94 95 41, 94 94 95 45 and 94 34 07 51. *Fax* 94 74 92 96) which is located on the Quai d'Honneur and is open 24 hours.

Charges

There are harbour charges but a visit of up to 6 hours is free.

Facilities

Slip There is a slip on the SE side of the harbour.
Slipways There is a 75-tonne slipway at the E side of the harbour for yachts up to 23m length, 7m beam and 3m draught.
Crane There is one 15-tonne crane at the E side of the harbour.
Fuel Diesel and petrol from pumps at the NW end of Quai d'Honneur. Open summer 0830–1930 and winter 0845–1200 and 1330–1730 (☎ 94 74 92 55).
Water There are many water points on the quays and pontoons.
Electricity Many points for electricity on the quays and pontoons, 110v and 220v AC.
Provisions A limited selection of food is available from a supermarket near the *bureau du port*.
Ice There is an ice-making machine in the basement of the yacht club outside the shower rooms. Ice is also available from the supermarket.
Garbage Many rubbish containers on the quays and pontoons.
Chandlery Available at the supermarket, the shipyard and a shop.
Repairs A shipyard can undertake most repairs to hull and engines. There is also a sailmaker and an electrician who can undertake repairs to electronic equipment.
Hotels There are three hotels of a simple nature on the island.
Restaurants There are four restaurant/snack bars.
Yacht club The Yacht Club des Embiez (YCE) has a fine clubhouse to S of the harbour with bar, lounge and shower (☎ 94 34 10 63).
Showers 20, and 17 WCs, around the harbour.
Information From the *bureau du port* (☎ 94 34 12 28).
Visits L'Observatoire de la Mer which is run by M. Alain Bombard is worth a visit. The views from the Château de Subron and from the water tower also recommended.
Beaches There are a number of small pebbly beaches around the island. There is also a superb swimming pool with showers to the N of the harbour.
Communications There are frequent *vedette* (ferry) services to the mainland at Port du Brusc.

Future development

The small Port des Jeunes has been developed and an enlargement is expected. Other hotels are to be built and extra facilities to be provided.

History

The history of the Ile des Embiez is connected with that of Le Brusc as it forms the natural defensive position of the latter anchorage. The Château de Subron on the island was built as a fort in the Middle Ages and later converted into a dwelling house, of its many visitors perhaps the most famous was Pope Gregory XI, the last of the Avignon Popes, who spent three days storm-bound on the island.

Beacon tower Sèche des Magnons, looking N (topmark ⚊ missing)

PASSAGE BETWEEN ILE DU GRAND ROUVEAU AND ILE DES EMBIEZ

A passage 100m wide and 3.3m deep exists between these two islands. It should be taken in a 021°/201° direction, using La Casserlane N cardinal, BY with ⚊ topmark, beacon tower as a reference mark. In very clear conditions a tower on Pointe de Ban-Rouge (42m) may be used as the rear mark of a transit with La Casserlane but this tower is very very difficult to see. A SE-going current of over 2 knots is sometimes experienced. Round La Casserlane beacon at 50m leaving it to starboard.

La Casserlane   Tower on Pointe du Ban-Rouge

Passage W of Ile des Embiez

Tower on Pointe du Ban-Rouge   La Casserlane beacon tower

Passage between Ile des Embiez and Ile de Grand Rouveau, looking N

PASSAGES EITHER SIDE OF ILE DU GRAND-GAOU

Very shallow passages of 1m or less exist on either side of this island which are only suitable for dinghies in fair weather and should be used with caution.

Ile des Embiez. Lights on N side of Ile de la Tour Fondue (occasional), looking W

[1] In need of paint (1986)

Passage between Ile des Embiez an Ile du Grand-Gaou, looking N

Point du Cougousset

Anchorage between Ile des Embiez and Ile du Grand-Gaou, looking NW

Tower   *Water tower*

Ile des Embiez, looking W

Lighthouse on Ile du Grand Rouveau, looking NE

⚓ **NE of Pointe du Cougousset (E of Ile des Embiez)**

A fair-weather anchorage in the small bay formed between the Ile des Embiez and Ile du Grand-Gaou. The shores are rocky with a small beach on the W side. Open to E–SE–S–SW.

⚓ **Anchorages between Ile des Embiez and Cap Sicié**

A number of small anchorages exist on the 3½M stretch of coast between the Ile des Embiez and Cap Sicié. Many of these anchorages are encumbered with rocks and are dangerous. They should only be used in calm settled weather with considerable caution. Clear water and a forward lookout is vital.

The use of French chart No 6610 is advised because this shows many of the dangers. These anchorages should not be used by night, unless an anchor watch is kept.

Cap Sicié

A conspicuous and prominent high headland which slopes down to the sea. Les Deux-Frères, twin rocks 20m high, lie ½M to ENE and a 4·5m rocky shallow patch lies 300m to SE of this headland.

Les deux Frères

Cap Siciè, looking NE

Cap Sicié, looking NW

Cap Sicié looking W

332

Appendix

1. GLOSSARY

A complete glossary is obviously impossible in a book of this nature but the following may be found to be of use:

French English

abri, abrité – shelter, sheltered
accastillage – ship chandlery
aigu, -uë – pointed, sharp
aiguille – needle
algue – seaweed
amer – landmark, beacon
amont – upstream, landward
anse – bay, cove
appontement – landing stage
argile – clay
arrière-port – inner port
asséchant – drying
aval – downstream, seaward
azur – blue

baie – bay
bal, balise – beacon
banc – bank
barre – bar
bas, -se – low
basse – shoal
bassin – basin, dock
batterie – battery
blanc, -che – white
bleu, -e – blue
bois – woods
bouche – mouth of a river
boue – mud
bouée – buoy
brisant, brisants – shoal, breakers
brise-lames – breakwater
bureau du port – harbour office
butte – knoll, mound

câble aérien – overhead cable
calanque – cove, inlet
cale – ramp, slip, hard
canal – canal, channel
canot de sauvetage – lifeboat
cap – cape, headland
capitainerie – harbourmaster's office
carburant – fuel, petrol
carénage – scrubbing berth
carré, -e – square
carrière – quarry
champ-de-tir – firing range
chantier – dockyard
château – castle, mansion
chaussée – bank, causeway
chenal – channel
clocher – steeple, belfry
col – neck, mountain pass

French English

colline – hill
conduite – pipeline
corps mort – mooring
côte – coast
courant – current, stream
couvent – convent
crête – ridge, crest
crique – creek
crochet scellé – ringbolt
croix – cross

darse – basin
débarcadère – wharf, landing place
détroit – strait, narrow
déversoir – weir
digue – mole, breakwater
douane – customs
draguer – to dredge
droit – right
dur, -e – hard

eau – water
écluse – lock (of a canal basin)
écueil – rock, reef
église – church
enceinte militaire – military area
épave – wreck
épi – short mole, spur
est – east
estuaire – estuary
étier – navigable creek

falaise – cliff
feu – light
fleuve – river, stream
forêt – forest
fosse – ditch, a deep

galets – shingle
gare – station
gauche – left
golfe – gulf
goulet – inlet
grand, -e – great
gravier – gravel
grève – sandy beach
gris, -e – grey
gros, se – coarse, large
grue – crane
guérite – watch-tower, turret
guet – watch-house

French English

halage – towing
hampe – pole beacon
haut, -e – high, tall
haut-fond – a shoal
havre – harbour
huître – oyster
hutte – hut, cottage

île – island, isle
îlot – islet
interdire – to forbid
interdit – forbidden

jaune – yellow
jetée – jetty

lac – lake
large – broad, wide

maison – house
marais – swamp, marsh
marée – tide
mât – mast
mécanicien – mechanic
mer – sea
méridional, -e – southern
milieu – middle
môle – mole, pier
mont, montagne – mount, mountain
morte-eau – neap tide
mouillage – anchorage
moulin – mill
mur – wall
musoir – mole or pierhead

neuf, -ve – new
nez – nose, promontory
noir, -e – black
nord – north
nouveau, -el, -elle – new

occidental, -e – western
oriental, -e – eastern
ouest – west

parcage, parking – car park
passe – passage, pass
pertuis – opening or strait
petit, -e – small
phare – lighthouse
pic – peak
pierre – stone
pieux – stakes, piles
pignon – gable
pin – pine or fir tree
piscine – bathing pool

French English

plage – shore, beach
plaine – plain
plat, -e – flat, level
plongeoir – diving stage
pointe – point
pompage – pumping station
pont – bridge, deck
pont dormant – fixed bridge
pont mobile – moving bridge
pont tournant – swing-bridge
port – port, harbour
presqu'île – peninsula
prise d'eau – water point
projeté – intended
pylône – pylon

quai – quay, wharf

rade – road, roadstead
récif – reef
redoute – redoubt, fort
réservé – reserved
rivière – river
roche – rock
rocher – rock, generally above water
rond, -e – round
rouge – red
roux, rousse – reddish
ruisseau – rivulet

sable – sand
sablon – fine sand
saline – salt water lagoon/salt works
septentrional, -e – northern
sommet – summit
sud – south

terre-plein – levelled ground, platform
tertre – hillock, knoll
tête – head
torchère – flare
torrent – stream, torrent
tour – tower
tourelle – small tower, turret
travaux projetés – works in progress
traverse – shallow ridge or bar

vagues – waves
val – narrow valley
vallée – valley
vasière – mudbank, mudflat
vedette – ferry

French English
vert, -e – green
vieil, vieille, vieux – old,
    ancient
village – village
ville – town
vive-eau – spring tide
voilier – sailmaker

Note Many of these titles
are preceded by *marchand,
agent, bureau, chez,* etc.

In the town

FrenchEnglish
banque – bank
bibliothèque – library
bijouterie – jeweller
blanchisserie – laundry
boucherie – butcher
*bureau de poste, la poste,
    PTT* – post office

charcuterie – butcher
    cooked meats)
*chemin de fer (SNCF,
SNRP)* – railway
coiffeur – hairdresser
cordonnier – shoemaker
crémerie – dairy

drapier – draper
droguerie – chemist

épicerie – grocer

fruits et légumes –
    greengrocer

gare – railway station
gendarmerie – police station

hôtel de ville – town hall

agencie immobilière – estate
    agent

journaux – newspaper

laverie – laundrette
librairie – bookshop

magasin – shop
mairie – town hall
marché – market
meubles – furniture

papetier – stationer
pâtisserie – cake shop

Syndicat d'Initiative (SI) –
    information office

tabac – tobacconist (also
    sells stamps)
tailleur – tailor
taxi – taxi

vins – wine shop

II. Conversion tables

1 inch = 2.54 centimetres (roughly 4in = 10cm)
1 centimetre = 0.394 inches
1 foot = 0.305 metres (roughly 3ft = 1m)
1 metre = 3.281 feet
1 pound = 0.454 kilograms (roughly 10lbs = 4.5kg)
1 kilogram = 2.205 pounds
1 mile = 1.609 kilometres (roughly 10 miles = 16 km)
1 kilometre = 0.621 miles
1 nautical mile = 1.1515 miles
1 mile = 0.8684 nautical miles
1 acre = 0.405 hectares (roughly 10 acres = 4 hectares)
1 hectare = 2.471 acres
1 gallon = 4.546 litres (roughly 1 gallon = 4.5 litres)
1 litre = 0.220 gallons

Temperature scale

$t°F$ to $t°C$ is $5/9$ ($t°F - 32$) = $t°C$
$t°C$ to $t°F$ is $9/5$ ($t°C + 32$) = $t°F$

So:

70°F = 21·1°C	20°C = 68°F
80°F = 26·7°C	30°C = 86°F
90°F = 32·2°C	40°C = 104°F

metres–feet

m	ft/m	ft
0·3	1	3·3
0·6	2	6·6
0·9	3	9·8
1·2	4	13·1
1·5	5	16·4
1·8	6	19·7
2·1	7	23·0
2·4	8	26·2
2·7	9	29·5
3·0	10	32·8
6·1	20	65·6
9·1	30	98·4
12·2	40	131·2
15·2	50	164·0
30·5	100	328·1

centimetres–inches

cm	in/cm	in
2·5	1	0·4
5·1	2	0·8
7·6	3	1·2
10·2	4	1·6
12·7	5	2·0
15·2	6	2·4
17·8	7	2·8
20·3	8	3·1
22·9	9	3·5
25·4	10	3·9
50·8	20	7·9
76·2	30	11·8
101·6	40	15·7
127·0	50	19·7
254·0	100	39·4

metres–fathoms–feet

m	fathoms	ft
0·9	0·5	3
1·8	1	6
3·7	2	12
5·5	3	18
7·3	4	24
9·1	5	30
11·0	6	36
12·8	7	42
14·6	8	48
16·5	9	54
18·3	10	60
36·6	20	120
54·9	30	180
73·2	40	240
91·4	50	300

kilometres–statute miles

km	M/km	M
1·6	1	0·6
3·2	2	1·2
4·8	3	1·9
6·4	4	2·5
8·0	5	3·1
9·7	6	3·7
11·3	7	4·3
12·9	8	5·0
14·5	9	5·6
16·1	10	6·2
32·2	20	12·4
48·3	30	18·6
64·4	40	24·9
80·5	50	31·1
120·7	75	46·6
160·9	100	62·1
402·3	250	155·3
804·7	500	310·7
1609·3	1000	621·4

kilograms–pounds

kg	lb/kg	lb
0·5	1	2·2
0·9	2	4·4
1·4	3	6·6
1·8	4	8·8
2·3	5	11·0
2·7	6	13·2
3·2	7	15·4
3·6	8	17·6
4·1	9	19·8
4·5	10	22·0
9·1	20	44·1
13·6	30	66·1
18·1	40	88·2
22·7	50	110·2
34·0	75	165·3
45·4	100	220·5
113·4	250	551·2
226·8	500	1102·3
453·6	1000	2204·6

litres–gallons

l	gal/l	gal
4·5	1	0·2
9·1	2	0·4
13·6	3	0·7
18·2	4	0·9
22·7	5	1·1
27·3	6	1·3
31·8	7	1·5
36·4	8	1·8
40·9	9	2·0
45·5	10	2·2
90·9	20	4·4
136·4	30	6·6
181·8	40	8·8
227·3	50	11·0
341·0	75	16·5
454·6	100	22·0
1136·5	250	55·0
2273·0	500	110·0
4546·1	1000	220·0

Index